Clinician's Guide to Neuropsychological Assessment

Second Edition

Clinician's Guide to Neuropsychological Assessment

Second Edition

Edited by

Rodney D. Vanderploeg
James A. Haley Veterans Hospital, Tampa, Florida
University of South Florida

LAWRENCE ERLBAUM ASSOCIATES, PUBLISHERS
2000   Mahwah, New Jersey   London

Lawrence Erlbaum Associates, Inc., Publishers
10 Industrial Avenue
Mahwah, NJ 07430

Cover design by Kathryn Houghtaling Lacey

Library of Congress Cataloging-in-Publication Data

Clinician's guide to neuropsychological assessment/ edited by
Rodney D. Vanderploeg. — 2nd ed.
        p. cm.
Includes bibliographical references and index.
ISBN 0-8058-3655-1 (cloth : alk. paper) —
ISBN 0-8058-2834-6 (pbk.: alk. paper)
1. Neuropsychological tests. 2. Clinical neuropsychology.
I. Vanderploeg, Rodney D.
[DNLM: 1. Neuropsychology—methods. 2. Cognition
Disorders—diagnosis. 3. Interview, Psychological.
4. Neuropsychological Tests. 5. Personality Assessment.
WL 103.5 C6415 1999]
  RC386.6N48G85   1999
  616.8'0475—dc21
  DNLM/DLC
  for Library of Congress   99-31882
                                                 CIP

Books published by Lawrence Erlbaum Associates are printed on
acid-free paper, and their bindings are chosen for strength and dura-
bility.

Printed in the United States of America
10 9 8 7 6 5 4 3 2 1

Dedicated in loving memory to my parents,
Jim and Carolyn Vanderploeg,
teachers who instilled in me
the joys of learning and teaching.

Contents

Preface to the Second Edition

Since completion of the first edition of *Clinician's Guide to Neuropsychological Assessment*, neuropsychology has continued to experience growth and development as a profession. Neuropsychology is a highly respected and frequently utilized clinical service and has expanded its involvement in forensic, rehabilitation, medicine, and psychiatric settings. Developments in clinical practice have resulted in portions of the first edition becoming somewhat outdated, and some major areas of clinical practice were underrepresented in the first edition. Chapter revisions and the addition of new chapters have attempted to rectify these shortcomings. Furthermore, developments in cognitive neuropsychology have resulted in models of normal and disturbed cognitive functioning that are invaluable in understanding and interpreting clinical findings. An additional chapter on interpretation explicates many of these models and demonstrates how they can guide clinical interpretive practice.

Neuropsychological assessment is a complicated endeavor. Part I of the second edition of *Clinician's Guide to Neuropsychological Assessment* has been expanded considerably. It attempts to walk the reader step by step through the fundamental elements of the evaluation process. Chapter 1 provides an in-depth discussion of issues involved in the history gathering, interview, and test administration process. As with all of the chapters in Part I, practical clinical suggestions and assessment strategies are provided. Chapter 2 is an updated and expanded discussion of premorbid estimation approaches, and provides recommendations for estimating premorbid levels of cognitive ability for both adults and children. Chapter 3 carefully details principles of neuropsychological interpretation, while Chapter 4 provides a process for interpretation based on cognitive–anatomical models of neuropsychological functioning. Chapter 5 covers the important topic of personality and psychological evaluation as it relates to neuropsychological assessment. Chapter 6 explores application issues relevant to different clinical contexts: diagnostic, rehabilitation, forensic, and feedback to patients and families. Finally, Chapter 7 provides a model for writing neuropsychological reports, and contains examples of comprehensive and brief reports.

Part II of this text has been expanded significantly from the first edition, and covers special issues, settings, and populations in neuropsychological evaluations. Chapter 8 is devoted to an overview and discussion of psychometric issues in neuropsychology. Chapters 9 and 10 explicate issues relevant to forensic and rehabilitation settings, respectively. Both provide recommendations for more effective and useful evaluations in these settings. Chapters 11 and 12 address special problems unique to pediatric and geriatric neuropsychological assessment.

Part III deals with approaches and methodologies in neuropsychology. Chapter 13 covers flexible approaches to assessment, while Chapter 14 discusses a psychometrically oriented fixed battery approach. These two approaches capture current clinical practice. However, as both chapter authors note, most neuropsychologists utilize aspects of both approaches in their clinical practice. Finally, the book ends with a chapter on computerized scoring and interpretation programs that can assist neuropsychological assessment.

The second edition of *Clinician's Guide to Neuropsychological Assessment* remains a unique text focusing on the practice of neuropsychology. It is intended to serve as a graduate level textbook for courses in neuropsychological assessment. With its focus on clinical practice, this volume also is designed to serve as a handbook for interns and professionals who engage in the practice or teaching of neuropsychological assessment across clinical settings. However, no text can be all things to all readers. This volume does not cover the academic and research background in basic neuroanatomy, neurological, medical, and psychiatric diseases, or the myriad of neuropsychological tests that are available. In addition, coverage of functional neuroanatomy is somewhat limited. Because cognizance of these topics is essential to competent neuropsychological practice, either prior knowledge or companion texts covering them would be necessary. In addition, coverage of assessment issues for special populations such as children, geriatrics, rehabilitation, and forensics is limited to an overview chapter for each area. Other neuropsychology texts are devoted exclusively to these clinical populations and the interested reader will need to refer to them for more in-depth information.

An edited work such as this increases the difficulty in appropriately acknowledging all those who contributed to its successful completion. I would like to convey my gratitude and appreciation to the chapter authors for their thoughtful and articulate contributions to this volume. I am grateful also to Susan Milmoe, Ph.D., Kate Graetzer, Kathryn Scornavacca, and Lawrence Erlbaum Associates for their encouragement, support, and deadline extensions. On behalf of myself and the other authors, I would like to express our gratitude to our families who have endured late evenings of work with patience, support, and understanding. Finally, we owe a debt of gratitude to our colleagues, patients, and students who have contributed in various ways to the formulation of the ideas conveyed in this text.

—*Rodney D. Vanderploeg*

Fundamental Elements
of the Assessment Process

CHAPTER ONE

Interview and Testing:
The Data Collection Phase
of Neuropsychological Evaluations

Rodney D. Vanderploeg
James A. Haley Veterans Hospital, Tampa, Florida,
and College of Medicine, University of South Florida

Neuropsychology is the study of brain–behavior relationships and the impact of brain injury or disease on the cognitive, sensorimotor, emotional, and general adaptive capacities of the individual. Its application is primarily carried out in clinical settings in the provision of diagnostic and treatment services. Diagnostic evaluations attempt either to identify the nature or extent of potential injury to the brain when injury is uncertain (e.g., mild head trauma, early dementia, or toxic exposure), or to delineate the behavioral sequelae of brain injury when pathology is known (e.g., stroke, neoplasms, severe head trauma, or advanced dementia).

Since 1970, the clinical assessment of brain–behavior relationships has advanced from the use of single tests of "organicity" to a complex, multifaceted process. Alternative approaches to assessment have been developed. One approach is to utilize carefully constructed, well-validated batteries. Another is to adapt each examination to the specific questions and clinical needs of individual clients. Other approaches lie on a continuum between these. Regardless of the structure of the evaluation, the process neither begins nor ends with testing, (i.e., the administration, scoring, and comparison of test results with cutoff scores or normative data). The competent neuropsychologist interprets evaluation findings and integrates them with historical data, unique aspects of individual performance, and the life situation of each client. The neuropsychological assessment process has multiple stages. The first stage of that process is the gathering of meaningful and interpretable data and is the focus of this chapter.

Multiple issues require the attention of the neuropsychologist within this initial phase. For the purposes of presentation and discussion these have been broken into four general areas: (a) neuropsychological testing versus assessment; (b) clarification of the evaluation and referral questions; (c) the interview, case history, and behavioral observations; and (d) issues of neuropsychological test selection, administration, and session structure. Of course, during the actual evaluation, the neuropsychologist carries out many of these simultaneously, and makes adjustments in approach and methodology as dictated by each client's unique needs. This chapter identifies assessment principles that can help guide the clinical neuropsychologist. However, competent practice requires the thoughtful consideration of how these assessment issues differentially impact each case. There is no "cookbook" approach.

TESTING VERSUS ASSESSMENT

A *psychological test* is a sample of behavior obtained under controlled conditions (Maloney & Ward, 1976; Anastasi, 1988). It involves the measurement of differences between individuals, or within the same individual across time, utilizing objective, standardized, and quantified data collection procedures. In and of itself, testing is not capable of answering questions and requires minimal clinical expertise other than the correct administration and scoring of test instruments. Testing is a tool that may be utilized during a neuropsychological assessment as one source of information. However, a proper evaluation ultimately rests on much more than test results.

Psychological assessment differs from testing in purpose, goals, and methodologies (Maloney & Ward, 1976; Matarazzo, 1990). Psychological assessment, or, in this case, neuropsychological assessment, involves a *process* of solving problems or answering questions. In conducting a neuropsychological assessment, the clinician must first be able to define and clarify the question(s) that need to be answered to meet particular clinical needs. Formulation of the examination questions (and later interpretation of the obtained data; see Chapters 3 and 4) is based in part on knowledge of a variety of content areas. Lezak (1995) suggested that mastery of four areas is essential: (a) clinical psychological practice, (b) psychometrics, (c) neuroanatomy and functional neuroanatomy, and (d) neuropathologies and their behavioral effects. A fifth essential knowledge area is a theoretical understanding of how the four content areas just listed interrelate and interact. This latter knowledge area might best be viewed as an overarching model or knowledge of brain–behavior relationships that is applicable across clinical settings and diagnoses.

Once the evaluation questions of interest have been clarified, the neuropsychologist must determine what information needs to be collected and how best to obtain it. Testing would be only one of several evaluation methods that might be utilized. Other methods include the case history, the clinical interview, the mental status examination, behavioral observations, and information from other people who are involved with the client (spouse, children, friends, employer, and other professionals such as nursing staff). If testing is to be conducted, issues of test selection must be competently addressed. Structuring the testing session, administration procedures, and scoring and clerical issues are also important factors in the overall competent completion of the data collection phase of the evaluation process.

Within classical test theory, *reliability* refers to the consistency of test scores, whereas *validity* is the extent to which tests assess what they were designed to measure. Apart from factors unique to the test instruments themselves, both reliability and validity can be adversely impacted by population-specific variables (Sattler, 1988). These include factors such as test-taking skill, guessing, misleading or misunderstood instructions, illness, daydreaming, motivation, anxiety, performance speed, examiner–examinee rapport, physical handicaps, and distractibility. Although psychometric issues are addressed in greater detail in chapter 8, it is important to be cognizant of data-collection variables that can adversely impact the reliability and validity of data and how to address these issues in the assessment process.

THE NATURE AND PURPOSE OF THE EVALUATION: CLARIFYING THE EVALUATION QUESTION(S)

Neuropsychological evaluations traditionally have been undertaken for three reasons: diagnosis, client care, and research (Lezak, 1995). Given the nature of the current text, assessments for research purposes are not discussed. Regarding clinical assessments, I strongly believe that a neuropsychological evaluation should not be undertaken unless it is likely to make a relevant difference in a client's treatment, quality of life, vocational or educational plans, placement/disposition planning, or client/family education or counseling. Helping in the diagnostic process at times certainly falls within this pragmatic framework. Often a correct diagnosis is essential in educating clients, their families, and their treatment staff about prognosis, and in helping to develop a treatment plan. The one exception to this rule would be performing an evaluation for professional training purposes, as long as the client is willing and realizes the potential benefits or lack of benefits that might occur. Table 1.1 lists a variety of common and potentially important reasons for conducting an evaluation.

Requests for evaluation arise from a variety of sources: medical professionals, psychologists or other mental health professionals, various rehabilitation treatment staff, attorneys, clients, and clients' families. In practice, all too often the relevant clinical questions for the evaluation are unclear, both to the referring professional and to the neuropsychologist. The referral source may be

TABLE 1.1
Potentially Useful Reasons for Conducting a Neuropsychological Evaluation

1. Diagnosis
   a. Identifying the presence of a neurological condition
   b. Discriminating between behaviorally similar neurological diagnoses
   c. Discriminating between neurologic and psychiatric diagnoses
   d. Identifying possible neuroanatomic correlates of signs and symptoms
2. Descriptive assessment of cognitive/emotional/psychological strengths and weaknesses
   a. Baseline or pretreatment evaluation
   b. Posttreatment or follow-up evaluations
3. Treatment planning
   a. Rehabilitation treatment planning
   b. Vocational planning
   c. Educational planning
4. Discharge/placement planning
5. Disability/personal injury determination
6. Competency evaluation
7. Other forensic issues (e.g., diminished capacity)
8. Research
9. Training of others

aware that this client appears different from those with whom the source typically works. For example, in a psychiatric setting, the client may exhibit atypical psychiatric symptoms, and "organicity" is suspected. Or, there may simply be a history of an incident that suggests the possibility that a brain injury may have occurred. In medical settings, staff may wonder if the client's subjective complaints can be objectively verified, or whether symptom patterns can be identified that suggest a particular diagnostic condition. Alternatively, family members may observe some difficulty with memory and suspect dementia. Yet in each case the relevant clinical questions remain somewhat unclear.

The training axiom of clarifying the referral question(s) with the referral source in practice may not be as easy as it sounds. Apart from the obvious problems of the time and energy this requires and the potential unavailability of the referring professional, referral sources may be unclear in their own minds about exactly what they want or need to know. In fact, their clinical questions may change, based in part on the results of the neuropsychological evaluation, yet follow-up evaluation is impractical. Therefore, these additional consultative questions need to be anticipated and addressed at the time of the evaluation, if at all possible.

How then does the neuropsychologist clarify the evaluation question(s)? This, as with the entire evaluation, is a process that will vary across cases and settings. If actual referral questions are asked, a starting point is provided. If not, the referral information furnished likely provides clues. At times it is indeed practical and helpful to talk with the referring professional or with other staff members who work with the client. It is also frequently useful to ask the client and/or the client's family members about their understanding of why the evaluation was requested and what questions or concerns they have. The history and clinical interview may suggest questions that appear relevant and potentially important. Finally, the observations and results obtained during the evaluation will likely raise questions in the examiner's mind, the answers to which the referring professional and client may also find useful. By imagining what it is you would want and need to know if you were responsible for the client's care (or if you were the client), it is possible to develop meaningful evaluation questions and begin to structure a useful evaluation. The neuropsychologist should answer not only the referral questions that were asked, but also those that should have been asked.

For example, a typical referral might be: "Please evaluate this 57-year-old male with complaints of memory problems for the past six months. Client also appears depressed." This referral suggests the following series of questions:

- Does this man have an amnestic disorder, or is he demented, depressed, or some combination of these conditions?
- Regardless of the underlying diagnosis, does this man have impaired cognitive abilities?
- If cognitively impaired, what is the likely etiology: prior stroke, anoxia, Alzheimer's disease, Pick's disease, multi-infarct dementia, psychiatric disorder, or other?
- If demented/impaired, what is the severity of the dementia/impairment?
- If demented, what other cognitive problems exist in addition to memory problems?
- Even if organically impaired, is there a functional component to any identified cognitive difficulties (e.g., depressed and anxious because of a realization of his difficulties)?
- If cognitively impaired, what is the interaction between his personality/psychological characteristics and his impaired cognitive functioning?
- If demented/impaired, what are the implications of the evaluation results for everyday life: ability to work, manage personal finances, live independently, and so on?
- Is this man still competent?
- What recommendations can be offered to help him manage or cope with his cognitive problems?
- What is the prognosis?
- What treatment or life planning recommendations can be offered?
- What education needs to be provided to his family and what recommendations can be offered to them?

INTERVIEW, CASE HISTORY, AND BEHAVIORAL OBSERVATIONS

The Clinical Interview

The clinical interview and behavioral observations occur prior to any test-based assessment. These preliminary, less formal aspects of assessment yield an essential database and qualitative information that may drastically alter the interpretation of subsequent formal test data (Lezak, 1995; Luria, 1980). In fact, they result in the determination of whether it is even possible to pursue formal testing.

For example, a referral is received to rule out dementia on an elderly psychiatric inpatient who is confused, disoriented, has a variable level of arousal, and appears to be hallucinating during the initial interview. Based on this information, it is likely that this client is either delirious, psychotic, or both. The client is not capable of concentrating on or cooperating with standardized testing. Therefore, formal neuropsychological testing is not likely to provide any meaningful data about the nature and extent of any possible underlying dementia. In this case, testing should be rescheduled for after the acute psychosis or delirium has cleared.

The clinical interview is part of the process by which a case history is developed and integrated with presenting complaints and behavioral observations. This information then can be used to help generate hypotheses about the etiologic bases for symptomatology. Such hypotheses, in turn, serve to guide the ongoing interview and the overall evaluation plan. Although such a hypothesis testing approach is an excellent interview strategy, it is important for the clinician to be aware of "confirmatory bias"—that is, the tendency to seek and value evidence in support of a working hypothesis while ignoring or minimizing contradictory evidence (Greenwald, Pratkanis, Leippe, & Baumgardner, 1986). An example is a neuropsychologist who suspects memory problems and consistently probes for subjective complaints and examples, while failing to recognize evidence of intact memory processes. A client's rich descriptive examples of memory problems are seen as confirmatory, when alternatively they can be viewed as evidence of *intact recall* of some phenomena that the client is interpreting as memory dysfunction. If the neuropsychologist focuses on evidence consistent with working hypotheses and minimizes contradictory data, then hypotheses will always be confirmed, whether correct or not. The corrective measure to confirmatory bias is to systematically list both confirmatory and disconfirmatory information and to consider alternative explanations for observed behaviors.

For clients who have difficulty providing important background information (e.g., demented elderly or children), an interview with family or friends is often critical. In other cases, clients, from their perspective, may be able to provide a reliable history but lack insight into or awareness of problems that are quite apparent to others who know or live with them.

Maloney and Ward (1976) suggested one way to proceed with the interview. They recommended beginning with minimal structure and becoming progressively more structured to clarify details and inconsistencies. An examiner would begin with an open-ended question regarding the presenting complaints or clients' understanding of why they are being evaluated and what they hope to gain from the results. By starting with open-ended questions, the examiner not only obtains the client's perspective but also can begin to evaluate the client's speech, language, thought processes, affective behavior, and ability to identify and structure his or her presentation of relevant information. This is one of the few unstructured times during a neuropsychological evaluation and affords an opportunity to observe how clients handle ambiguity. Subsequent interventions or comments by the examiner are generally designed to have a facilitative effect on the client's self-report. Questions at this stage continue to be rather open-ended: "Can you tell me more about that?" or "What else did you notice?"

Gradually, more specific questions are introduced to help clarify aspects of the client's self-report. As clients report various symptoms, the onset and course should be noted. Typically this will be followed up later in the interview with detailed medical, psychiatric, substance use, educational, vocational, and family histories. It is important to clarify clients' report of their symptoms. At times their subjective label does not correspond to objective findings, yet represents a significant clinical concern. For example, clients commonly report memory problems, when the underlying deficit is in attentional rather than memory processes. By asking for specific examples, rather than descriptive labels, the exact deficit usually can be identified.

Typically, contradictions in a client's self-report are noted by the examiner. These can be pointed out to the client (a process often called "confrontation") to see how the client explains or accounts for such inconsistencies. Discrepancies commonly arise between what clients may report and what is known from the medical record or reports of others. Alternatively, there may be inconsistencies in the information provided by the client. Two other types of inconsistencies may occur: between the content of what clients say and the affect they display, or between different desires or affective states (e.g., feeling disabled at the same time that they do not want to be perceived as disabled). These latter two types of contradictions may be more important in general mental health settings during psychological and personality evaluation, but also may be important considerations during neuropsychological evaluations.

Toward the end of the clinical interview, the examiner may ask direct questions about other factors not previously covered. These might include basic demographic information, and elements of the case history that have not been covered but that the examiner believes may be relevant to the overall evaluation. When clarifying aspects of the history, it may be important to ask the same

TABLE 1.2
Areas to Explore in Neuropsychological Assessment History Taking

1. Presenting problems and concerns (symptom onset and course)
2. Basic demographic information
   a. Age
   b. Gender
   c. Handedness and family history of handedness
3. Developmental history
   a. Congenital abnormalities
   b. Pregnancy and delivery history including complications and problems
   c. Developmental disorders
      1) ADD (with or without hyperactivity)
      2) Developmental learning problems
      3) Childhood illnesses with sustained high fevers
4. Educational history and achievement performance
   a. Average grades obtained
   b. Best and worst subjects
   c. Failed courses or grades
   d. Placement in special education classes
   e. Learning disabilities
   f. Emotional, social, and peer adjustment
   g. Factors that may affect academic performance
      1) Cultural background
      2) Parental interest in education and parental educational levels
      3) Interest in education versus sports versus peer relationships
      4) Drug or alcohol usage
5. Vocational history
   a. Performance and stability
   b. Reasons for job terminations
6. Psychiatric history and current symptoms/problems
   a. Past and present symptoms and diagnoses
   b. Past and present treatment (medication and/or electroconvulsive therapy [ECT])
7. Substance abuse history and current usage
8. Medical history
   a. High fevers
   b. Head injuries
   c. Loss of consciousness
   d. Seizures
   e. Cerebral vascular accidents
   f. Infectious processes (AIDS, encephalitis, meningitis)
   g. Cardiovascular problems
   h. Anoxia/hypoxia
   i. Pulmonary problems
   j. Arthritis
   k. Injuries affecting the extremities
   l. Peripheral neuropathies
   m. Other sensory or motor problems
   n. Cancer
9. Current medication

(continued)

TABLE 1.2 *(continued)*

10. Current general medical and health status
11. Current functioning in day-to-day living
12. How a typical day is spent
13. Hobbies and interests (avocational activities)
14. Legal history and current problems, pending or anticipated legal suits
15. Current life situation (factors that might suggest possibility of secondary gain or malingering)
16. Family history
    a. Academic and vocational achievement
    b. Medical/neurologic
        1) Alzheimer's disease
        2) Huntington's disease
        3) Parkinson's disease
        4) Vascular disease (cardiac and cerebral)
        5) "Senility"
        6) Cancer/tumors
    c. Psychiatric
        1) Depression
        2) Anxiety disorders
        3) Psychotic conditions
        4) Substance abuse

question in a variety of ways. The context of the question can result in different answers. For example, clients may deny having had problems in school, but admit to placement in special classes, failed courses, repetitions of academic grade levels, or school suspensions.

The Case History

The client's report of symptomatology and the problems identified in the referral provide the rationale and serve as the starting point for gathering a more detailed case history. Neurologists commonly teach their residents that the history and clinical exam provide approximately 90% of the information necessary to make a correct diagnosis. Similarly, a careful history will inform the neuropsychologist about the nature and general severity of cognitive and emotional problems, as well as the likely underlying diagnostic condition(s). For both the neurologist and neuropsychologist, additional tests (medical procedures or neuropsychological tests, respectively) can be used to confirm or disconfirm clinical questions developed as a result of the interview and case history. The important historical issue is whether a history of cognitive, affective, or behavioral symptoms can be identified and tracked that suggests particular neurologic, medical, or psychiatric conditions.

Table 1.2 lists significant content areas to explore in history gathering, whereas Table 1.3 covers important issues that the history can help address. These content areas may suggest particular diagnostic conditions or may reveal factors that

TABLE 1.3
Issues That the History Can Help Address

1. Premorbid functioning
   a. General level of ability
   b. Patterns of cognitive strengths and weaknesses
   c. Personality and psychological characteristics or problems
2. Preexisting conditions that may account for or interact with current findings
   a. Developmental problems
   b. Learning disabilities
   c. Attention deficit disorder (ADD) or attention deficit hyperactivity disorder (ADHD)
   d. Psychiatric conditions
   e. Prior CNS injuries or neurological conditions
   f. Current or past medical problems (current medication)
3. Motivational considerations
   a. Family / marital / social issues of secondary gain
   b. Pending legal or disability concerns
   c. Financial gain
   d. Malingering
   e. Problems with authority or with being evaluated
4. Current life-style factors that may influence test performance
   a. Alcohol abuse
   b. Substance abuse
   c. Eating disorder
5. Onset of current problems
6. Course of current symptoms and problems
   a. Worsening
   b. Stable
   c. Improving
7. Family history of similar problems and their presumed etiology

could influence the performance on and interpretation of formal test data. Space does not permit covering these issues in detail. However, the following examples provide some indication of the importance and potential use of historical information in the assessment process.

Sometimes careful questioning will reveal that prior intellectual or neuropsychological testing has been conducted. If this was prior to the development of the current symptomatology such data would be invaluable for premorbid comparative purposes; if conducted postonset, it would help in evaluating the course of a client's problems. When no prior test data are available, academic achievement and vocational history, in conjunction with basic demographic information, may prove useful in estimating premorbid levels of functioning.

Careful questioning will reveal premorbid patterns of cognitive strengths and weaknesses. Certain occupations may have been selected because of innate patterns of cognitive abilities. In addition, once embarked upon, occupational endeavors may differentially enhance particular skills and abilities and consequently affect performance on related tests. One might hypothesize, for example, that artists, designers, and mechanics would perform better on visuospatial tasks because of the visuospatial constructional and psychomotor activities entailed in their work. Similarly, an avid tennis player may show unusual patterns of performance on psychomotor measures, such as an average level of performance on nondominant hand motor tasks (e.g., grip strength), with dominant hand performances at the 90th percentile.

A careful history may reveal a repetitive pattern of cognitive symptoms and complaints that emerge and resolve concomitantly with psychiatric conditions that referring clinicians have interpreted as evidence of brain damage. Alternatively, a positive family history of dementia may never have been diagnosed, yet may be revealed by a careful family medical history. Such information would be very useful in dementia evaluations, particularly in cases where subjective complaints are present and test performance is in the average range, but the individual premorbidly would be expected to have high average range abilities. In such a case the history, in conjunction with a somewhat lower level of achievement than expected, would lead one to the consideration of a possible mild dementia.

This is not to say that all points outlined in Table 1.2 must be explored fully in every assessment. Clinical interviews and history taking will be shortened and tailored to the presenting complaints and referral question(s). However, failure to obtain relevant historical data results in a lack of information that may be essential in test selection and subsequent interpretation.

Obtaining the Case History. There are several ways in which a case history may be obtained. One way is as part of the initial clinical interview, as discussed earlier. If this approach is used, examiners will typically develop some type of guide or outline to ensure that they cover all potentially important aspects of the history. The outline contained in Table 1.2 could be used. A second, but not mutually exclusive, approach is to utilize symptom checklists and history questionnaires. Several such questionnaires are commercially available for use. These include the Neuropsychological Questionnaires developed by Melendez (1978); one form is available for children, another for adults. Schinka (1983) developed the Neuropsychological Status Examination, which consists of two parts. One part is the Neuropsychological Symptom Checklist, a 93-item form that may be completed either by the client, someone who knows the client well, or the examiner in an interview format. The second part is the Neuropsychological Status Examination. It may be used as a guide for structuring and planning the evaluation, as a recording form during the clinical interview, and as an outline for drafting the final report.

It is important to note that these instruments are not tests with normative data available. Rather, they are means of collecting potentially valuable historical and background information that must be evaluated and interpreted by the examiner, and integrated with the rest of the evaluation data (clinical interview, behavioral observations, and test results). Typically the skilled examiner will quickly review completed forms or questionnaires with the client (or a family member), and will obtain more details and clarifying information about items that appear relevant to the evaluation questions and issues.

The Cognitive Behavior Rating Scale (CBRS; Williams, 1987) is a similar symptom questionnaire that was developed to be completed by a family member or close friend of individuals undergoing dementia evaluations. It is mentioned separately here because the items are grouped into nine subscales that can be plotted out on a profile sheet with T-scores and percentile norms available for comparison with nondemented elderly. In this sense the CBRS is more akin to formal psychometric tests than to the other history gathering forms already described.

Use and Review of the Medical Records.   Reviewing the medical records is often the first thing a neuropsychologist does after receiving a consultation referral. The medical record provides an important source of historical information, as well as details of current symptoms, their onset and course, and recent and ongoing evaluative workups and treatments. It will frequently help clarify why a client has been referred, the questions and issues that should be addressed in the evaluation, and what historical data need to be explored further in the interview and history.

Mastering a thorough yet expeditious review of medical records takes practice, familiarity with their layout (which varies from facility to facility), and awareness of what information is potentially available in them. Phay, Gainer, and Goldstein (1986) suggested developing a systematic plan of search and standard format for recording pertinent information. The neuropsychologist will be interested both in various medical diagnostic procedures that are being undertaken, and in other information about suspected diagnostic conditions (e.g., clinical findings, symptom history, and history of past neurologic conditions). Note should be made of the presence of a variety of medical conditions that have been shown to have an adverse impact on aspects of cognition. These would include not only those with known central nervous system (CNS) involvement, such as acquired immune deficiency syndrome (AIDS), epilepsy, multiple sclerosis, and cerebral vascular disease, but also conditions such as hypertension, diabetes, chronic obstructive pulmonary disease (COPD), systemic lupus erythematosus, thyroid disease, and metabolic and nutritional disorders. There is increasing evidence that these latter conditions have an adverse effect on brain function and cognitive status (e.g., Denburg, Carotte, & Denburg, 1987; Skenazy & Bigler, 1984; Tarter, Van Thiel, & Edwards, 1988; Vanderploeg, Goldman, & Kleinman, 1987).

A typical record review might begin with a careful consideration of the admitting history and examination (and discharge summary if already completed), followed by a review of various medical and diagnostic workups that have been undertaken. The consult section of a medical record will contain the evaluations of other professionals who were consulted by the primary physician. Depending on the setting, there might be reports from various medical specialists, clinical psychologists, social workers, speech therapists, occupational therapists, and physical therapists. For the neuropsychologist the diagnostic procedures of interest include the computed tomography (CT) and magnetic resonance imagery (MRI) scans, positron emission tomography (PET) or single-photon emission computed tomography (SPECT) scans, electroencephalography (EEG), event-related potentials (ERPs), cerebral spinal tap results, and other laboratory data, particularly tests that would determine the presence of infectious processes, metabolic disturbances, or nutritional abnormalities. Occasionally there will be data from previous psychological examinations as well. Finally, a review of the "Progress Notes" will often provide information about a client's day-to-day functioning and problems noted by direct caretakers that have not been described elsewhere in the record.

Behavioral Observations

Behavioral observations are a critical, although often minimized, part of any neuropsychological examination. They encompass two parts of the examination process, the interview and formal testing. Behavioral observations allow the examiner to assess variables or behaviors that may:

- Directly influence overall test performance (e.g., motivation, attention, agitation).
- Indicate specific limitations that would influence test selection or interpretation (e.g., sensory or motor handicaps).
- Be pathognomonic of neurological problems themselves (e.g., confusion, perseveration, paraphasic substitutions).
- Point to underlying variables that might explain deficiencies in test performance (e.g., unilateral visual neglect).
- Illustrate personality strengths or deficits that could impact on rehabilitation efforts.
- Suggest alternative, psychological explanations for the data (e.g., anxiety, depression, thought disorders, or malingering).

Naturalistic observation provide an invaluable adjunct to other data collection techniques. For example, during a forensic evaluation of a client with severe memory complaints and very impaired performance on memory testing, observations of intact ability to independently arrive at the appointment on time, follow oral directions to a nearby restaurant for lunch, and return on time in the afternoon certainly call into question the apparent memory difficulties. Similarly, rehabilitation nursing staff may report excellent functional day-to-day independent living skills in a head-injured client who has severe difficulty on formal testing. In this latter case the client may well have developed compensatory strategies that cannot be utilized in formal test situations.

TABLE 1.4

Mental Status Examination

1. Appearance
   a. Clothing (neat/messy, casual/formal, clean/dirty, appropriate/inappropriate)
   b. Personal hygiene (clean/dirty; body odor; grooming)
   c. Physical handicaps (presence or absence)
   d. Unusual features
2. Level of consciousness or arousal
   a. Alert/attentive (distractibility)
   b. Lethargic (sleepy but arousable)
   c. Obtunded (clouding of consciousness, reduced alertness)
3. Orientation
   a. Person (awareness of who they are and what the examiner's role is)
   b. Place (awareness of present physical location and location of their home)
   c. Time (awareness of current year, month, date, day, time of day)
   d. Situation (awareness of what is transpiring [i.e., the evaluation] and why they are being evaluated)
4. Language
   a. Spontaneous speech (rate, fluency, articulation/dysarthria, paraphasias)
   b. Elicited (expressive) language
      1. Speech (confrontation naming)
      2. Writing (spontaneous and to dictation)
      3. Reading aloud
   c. Language comprehension
      1. Oral speech (conversational speech and commands)
      2. Reading comprehension
   d. Repetition
   e. Right-hemisphere contributions (expressive and receptive prosody)
5. Learning and memory
   a. New learning (acquisition, free recall, recognition)
   b. Recent (recent life events)
   c. Remote (past historical information)
6. Intellectual functioning (abstraction, reasoning, problem solving, arithmetic abilities)
7. Psychomotor abilities
   a. Ambulation (limp, weakness, speed, agility, balance, gait)
   b. Motor activity (fidgety, restless, slow, lethargic, tics)
   c. Facial expression(s)
8. Interpersonal
   a. Cooperative
   b. Friendly, unfriendly, or overly friendly
   c. Establishes eye contact
   d. Anxious
   e. Suspicious
   f. Submissive versus dominant
   g. Dependent versus aggressive
9. Mood, affect, and emotional state (angry, irritable, happy, anxious, afraid, suspicious, depressed/sad, apathetic)
   a. Mood: Predominant emotion observed
   b. Affect: Range of emotions displayed in facial expression or voice tone and content
   c. Appropriateness: Appropriate to situational context and/or content of interview
10. Perceptual processes: accurate perception of the world, distractibility, presence of hallucinations (visual, auditory, tactile, olfactory, gustatory)

Continued

TABLE 1.4 *(continued)*

11. Thought content
    a. Focus of thoughts and concerns
    b. Presence of delusional material
    c. Obsessive thoughts or ideas
    d. Report of compulsive actions
    e. Fears or phobias
    f. Sense of unreality or depersonalization
12. Thought process
    a. Organization (organized and sensible progression, or rambling)
    b. Productivity (minimal material presented, normal amount, or excessive)
    c. Flow (fluid, stopping or blocking, loss of train of thought)
    d. Focus (flight of ideas, loosing of associations, circumstantial, tangential)
13. Insight: recognition of present status and problems, psychological mindedness, self-awareness
14. Judgment
    a. Level of decision-making abilities (current and historical)
    b. Nature of problem-solving approach: rational, impulsive, methodical, responsible/
      irresponsible

Some observations appear pathognomonic of underlying neurological problems: a differential arm or leg size suggestive of atrophy, or confusion in response to an apparently straightforward question suggestive of dementia. However, such observations may well have other nonneurologically based explanations, such as previous broken limbs or a psychiatric disorder, respectively. Therefore, unusual observations should always be noted, but interpreted in the overall context of history, environmental situation, and test performance. Certainly, any time a behavioral observation is noted that is abnormal or unusual, alternative explanations should be explored in the history before arriving at the conclusion of brain impairment.

A mental status examination (MSE) "checklist" may or may not be conducted as part of the ongoing interview. However, using the content areas of the MSE is a useful way of organizing behavioral observations. Table 1.4 covers MSE content areas and the ranges of behaviors relevant to each. Of equal importance are observations about clients' test-taking manner and variables that might influence performance. For instance, physical problems may interfere with individuals' ability to take certain tests. Psychological states such as anxiety, depression, or psychosis may have similar adverse affects.

Summary

Clinical interviewing, history gathering, and observation of behavior can and should be a dynamic and interactive process. Observing unusual or unexpected behaviors should lead to questions about why this might be so. Many observations that suggest the possibility of brain damage or impairment have unrelated yet easily ascertained causes. One should never fail to ask about observations, problems, or deficits that appear to have an obvious brain-injury-related explanation. All too often the obvious is not the truth. Failure to utilize observations, follow-up questions, and the history to explore alternative explanations periodically will result in an incorrect "finding" of brain impairment. The opposite is also true. Some observations appear to have obvious non-brain-injury-related explanations (e.g., questionable memory problems in a moderately depressed and anxious 50-year-old man), yet be indicative of neurological problems (beginning stage of Alzheimer's disease). In these cases, a careful history and tracing of symptom onset and development will help clarify the clinical picture.

NEUROPSYCHOLOGICAL TESTING

Test Selection

Different Approaches to Testing. There are several neuropsychological schools of thought with somewhat differing approaches to the neuropsychological assessment process. Differences arise along two continuums: "fixed" versus "flexible" battery approaches to data collection, and "quantitative/normative-based" versus "qualitative/process-based" approaches to data interpretation. The traditional Halstead–Reitan would be an example of a fixed-battery, quantitative/normative approach. On the other end of both continuums would be clinicians utilizing a clinically oriented process approach, a flexible battery with qualitative/process analyses of the results. In a recent survey of randomly selected neuropsychologists (Butler, Retzlaff, & Vanderploeg, 1991), 34% of the respondents described their theoretical orientation as eclectic; many of these also checked other orientations. Thirty-one percent affirmed a hypothesis-testing approach, 25% a process approach, and 20% a Halstead–Reitan approach. In reality, most neuropsychologists combine some fixed set of tests with a flexible use of additional measures, and integrate quantitative and qualitative information during test interpretation. Regardless of whether one takes a battery or nonbattery approach to assessment, some decisions must be made regarding what tests to administer.

Selecting Tests. A wide variety of cognitive and intellectual abilities is typically assessed during a *comprehensive* neuropsychological evaluation. Included are measures of sensory-perceptual input, the two major central processing systems (verbal/language and nonverbal/visuospatial), executive organization and planning, and response output (motor abilities). Interacting with these processing networks would be memory systems, while underlying them all are attention, concentration, arousal, and motivation. Although this list of cognitive functions might be organized or labeled differently by various neuropsychological schools of thought, these behaviors are commonly assessed during neuropsychological evaluations. Frequently, aspects of psychological functioning (psychopathology, behavioral adjustment, and interpersonal issues) also are assessed in a neuropsychological evaluation. Whether selecting a standard battery, choosing a unique set of tests for a particular assessment, or combining these two approaches, various issues are important to consider:

1. Selected measures should cover all relevant behavioral domains of interest, both for that client's particular referral question(s) and for the potential neurologic, medical, and/or psychiatric conditions suspected. The use of general screening measures for organicity fails to take into account the variety and complexity of possible brain-related behavioral patterns.

2. Both lower level (domain specific) abilities and higher level, more general, diffuse, or interactive cognitive functions should be covered. The former includes basic sensory-perceptual and psychomotor abilities, whereas the latter involves not only higher order language and visuospatial abilities, but also complex cross-modal reasoning, problem solving, and abstraction.

3. Use tests with good normative data for your client. As an example, the Peabody Picture Vocabulary Test-Revised (Dunn & Dunn, 1981) is an excellent measure of receptive vocabulary for certain populations, but no normative data are available for individuals over 40 years of age.

4. Use tests with an appropriate level of difficulty for the client under study. Tests that are too easy or too hard for a client result in ceiling or floor effects, reducing possible performance variability, and consequently reducing reliability. Even within adult tests, some measures may be too easy for highly intelligent individuals, whereas others may be too difficult for those of borderline or lower intellectual functioning.

5. Use test measures that have established validity for the assessment of the cognitive ability and associated anatomical functioning that you plan to evaluate. That is, use tests with validated patterns of brain–behavior relationships. A related axiom is that tests of brain damage are always measures of some aspect of cognitive ability, but measures of cognitive abilities are not necessarily tests of brain integrity.

For example, the right temporal lobe has been reported as important in the processing of musical patterns or rhythmic sequences. Thus, tests with similar processing requirements would logically be assumed to reflect the integrity of these brain regions. Some clinicians assume that the Seashore Rhythm test reflects right temporal functioning, and clinical guides suggest this interpretation (Jarvis & Barth, 1984; Golden, Osmon, Moses, & Berg, 1981). However, empirical studies consistently fail to support this interpretation of impaired performance. Instead, the Seashore Rhythm test appears to be a sensitive but nonspecific measure of brain impairment, possibly because of its high attentional requirements (Milner, 1962; Reitan & Wolfson, 1989; Sherer, Parson, Nixon, & Adams, 1991).

6. Many neuropsychologists advocate using several measures within each cognitive domain (e.g., several memory measures) to look for convergence or divergence of findings. This can provide a stronger base for claims of impaired or intact abilities. However, when selecting additional measures, one should be cautious about the use of tests that are highly correlated with each other. This results in redundancy of measurement and limited utility for purposes of clarification. Ideally, multiple measures within a cognitive domain would have relatively low correlations with each other, but strong positive correlations with the criterion ability. This increases the likelihood that convergent findings are related to the actual ability rather than being an artifact.

Standardization Issues

Standardized Administration

Standardized testing consists of uniform administration and scoring procedures. Those procedures are described by test developers for the purpose of ensuring that all administrations of a test are comparable (Anastasi, 1988). Standardized procedures typically include specific phrases used to instruct examinees, specific directions regarding test material and time limits allowed, and explicit scoring criteria for item responses. Calibration procedures for test instruments are standardized as well. Under standard conditions, results can be compared across administrations, across examiners, and with the test normative database. However, following test manual standardized procedures carefully does not ensure that other factors will not influence test performance. Anastasi (1988) reviewed various factors that have been shown to influence test performance: testing environment, examiner–examinee rapport, oral presentation style and rate, similarity or familiarity between the personal characteristics of examiner and examinee, supportive or encouraging gestures and comments, and test-taking anxiety.

During neuropsychological testing, standardized conditions are generally designed to help examinees attain their maximal level of performance. Thus, in the ideal testing situation, standard conditions are also optimal conditions for the client under study (Lezak, 1995). However, during many neuropsychological evaluations, those conditions necessary to help clients engage the task effectively differ substantially from standard conditions. This raises the question of what is important to achieve for standardization: the actual physical conditions, instructions, and procedures, or alternatively, the testing conditions that ensure adequate understanding of what is expected from the examinee and arrangement of environmental variables to allow subjects to work efficiently. Williams (1965, p. xvii) wrote: "The same words do not necessarily mean the same thing to different people and it is the meaning of the instructions that should be the same for all people rather than the wording." The same rule could be applied to other test taking variables. Examiners should strive to achieve standardized conditions in this broader sense.

Variation of test administration procedures may be necessary in working with brain-injured subjects in order to meet this broader definition of standard conditions. Instructions may need to be repeated or amplified to ensure adequate understanding. Some subjects will need to be reminded periodically of what exactly they are to do, even within tests or subtests. The development and maintenance of necessary rapport may also entail more support, encouragement, or reassurance than is discussed in the standardization procedures.

"Testing the limits" during a process-oriented, qualitative assessment often will violate even broadly defined standardization, yet be essential to obtain certain clinically useful information. For example, on memory testing some clients report back very little on story recall measures. This may reflect a number of things: impaired memory encoding and storage, memory retrieval problems, concern over making possible errors, amotivation, or resistance to the examiner or to testing. To determine the cause for such apparent memory difficulties, the examiner could follow a sequence of encouragement, memory cues, and then multiple-choice responses to test the limits of a client's abilities. If clients are able to perform significantly better with only encouragement, amotivation or fear of making errors would be suggested as the cause of the initial poor performance. Accepting and scoring these responses likely would fit within broadly defined standardization. Providing cues or multiple choice responses would violate standardization, yet if recall improved would suggest that the difficulties were secondary to memory retrieval problems rather than encoding and storage. In addition, cueing of immediate recall would invalidate standardization for delayed recall later. Such procedural variations and testing of the limits, although potentially clinically advantageous, adversely affect the applicability of established test norms collected under standardized administration.

In some circumstances, testing the limits can be completed after the standardized administration is completed. The WAIS–R as a Neuropsychological Test Instrument (Kaplan, Fein, Morris, & Delis, 1991) provides examples of this process. At times it is possible to answer questions regarding reasons for failures by administering other similar measures which help fractionate cognitive processes into component parts. These latter approaches preserve standardization and the use of the normative data.

Unclear Aspects of Standardization Procedures. The Wechsler intelligence scales are some of the most carefully standardized instruments available. However, even here certain aspects of administration are not described in detail, and variations can result in substantial differences in performance for certain types of brain injured clients. The WAIS–III manual (Wechsler, 1997a) provides much

more explicit instructions on placement of the stimulus material than did the
WAIS–R (Wechsler, 1981). The stimulus booklet is to be placed "approximately
7 inches from the edge of the table closest to the examinee. If the examinee is
right-handed , the model should be placed a little to the left of a line perpen-
dicular to his or her body; conversely, it should be place to the right, if the examinee is left-handed." However, the drawing in the manual demonstrating the
placement of the stimulus material shows it directly midline. Therefore, it is unclear exactly what "a little to the left" or "right" means. However, for subjects
with neglect the current midline placement is far preferable to the uncertain
placement on the WAIS–R.

Many individuals with brain injury require substantially longer to process information than normal. Even nonaphasic clients may fail to fully process and
comprehend long complicated sentences if they are spoken at a normal conver-
sational rate. This will adversely affect understanding of many test instructions
as well as potentially hamper performance on a variety of test measures. For example, the WAIS–III Arithmetic subtest (Wechsler, 1997a) contains many long
and complicated questions. No instructions are provided as to how to present
these orally to subjects. However, processing and comprehension can be improved substantially if the questions are read somewhat more slowly, but even
more importantly, if pauses are placed following clauses. The following question is an example similar to item 10. When read with pauses (as indicated)
many subjects who would otherwise get the item wrong instead will be able to
correctly answer the question: "If you buy six (pause) 3-cent stamps (pause) and
give the clerk 50 cents, (pause) how much change should you get back?" This
helps isolate calculation ability, by decreasing the language comprehension and
attentional demands of the task.

Instructions for the WAIS–III Digit Span subtest indicate that the presentation rate should be one per second and the pitch of the presenter's voice should
drop on the last digit of each trial. However, other administration factors that
can influence performance are not addressed. For example, the monotone of
the trial-to-trial presentation can be broken up with variations in voice volume,
by side comments, or by asking "Ready?" before some of the trials. These variations will tend to help subjects who have problems with sustained attention,
whose immediate memory span is normal when fully alert.

Tests other than the WAIS–III are even more unclear regarding aspects of administration. Presentation rate and pauses can certainly influence performance
on story recall measures such as the Wechsler Memory Scale–III (WMS–III:
Wechsler, 1997b) Logical Memory subtest. However, the WMS–III manual provides no standardized presentation format other than that the stories should
be "read," and is silent on the permissibility or advisability of varying rate or
pauses. A final example is seen in the wide variability among examiners on
when, what, and how much help to provide during testing. Test manuals are
often not clear on these issues.

Deemphasis of Aspects of Standardization.   Standardized administration and scoring assume that standard procedures were learned by examiners at some point in time. However, with the phenomenon of "examiner drift," even after having learned standard procedures, examiners slowly and unwittingly modify aspects of administration and scoring as time goes by. This phenomenon tends to be ignored in clinical practice. In addition, clinicians sometimes make personal decisions about procedural issues out of convenience or individual preference. Unfortunately, the effects that such changes have on test performance are generally unknown, but at the very least call into question the applicability of the standardization sample as a comparison group.

In working with psychology interns, I have noticed that many fail to use a stopwatch during administration of various WAIS–III subtests (e.g., Arithmetic or Picture Completion) despite the manual's instructions to do so. Many brain-injured clients have significantly delayed responses. However, without a stopwatch, examiners cannot be certain whether a subject's response came within the time allowed. Although the untimed response data are certainly clinically important in knowing about basic neuropsychological abilities, only the carefully timed performance can be scored and compared to the norms.

Variations in "Standard" Administration Procedures.   In working with and talking to colleagues trained in various neuropsychology laboratories across the country, it is clear that there are many administration variations in standard practice. For example, on the finger tapping test, does the examiner alternate hands between trials or attain five (three, or some other number) dominant hand trials before proceeding to the nondominant hand? Reitan's (1979) instructions were to obtain five trials within a 5-point range with the dominant hand, before proceeding to the nondominant hand. How much time is structured into rest breaks between tapping trials, if breaks are employed? Does one use only the finger tapper devices available from Reitan, or tappers available from other sources? (The tappers available from Dr. Reitan have been modified themselves over the years.) On other tasks, how much and how quickly does the examiner provide help when clients have difficulty (e.g., on the Category Test, Wisconsin Card Sorting Test, or Trail Making Test)? Do examiners follow Reitan's instructions (1979) of working through the first three to five circles on the Trail Making Test with the client, both on the sample and on the actual test? Exactly how does an examiner deal with errors during testing on Trail Making or other tests? (In a multicenter cooperative study a few years ago, initially no two centers administered the Trail Making Test the same way.) Manuals themselves vary in administration instructions from one established neuropsychology laboratory to another.

Such variability in "accepted practice" suggests that procedural variations result in little or no difference in test performance; however, this is not always the case (Leckliter, Forster, Klonoff, & Knights, 1992).

Administration Recommendations. The administration variations observed in clinical practice raise the issues of the clarity of instructions in test manuals and of how rigidly examiners follow and should follow such instructions. On the one hand, carefully following the test manual is essential in standardized testing to assure applicability of test norms. On the other hand, if the purpose of administering a test is to assess a particular aspect of brain–behavior relationships, then it would be critical to make sure that the subject completely understood the task to be done and assure that other behaviors (e.g., motivation, arousal, impaired comprehension, etc.) did not interfere with the brain behavior of interest. In these latter cases, variations in instructions, level of help provided, and mode of client response may be necessary to answer the clinical question of interest.

The discussion at the beginning of this chapter about the difference between assessment and testing can serve as a general guide to test administration procedures and variations. The needs of the overall assessment are what are important, because testing is only a tool in the assessment process. Within that framework, a number of more specific principles can help guide the clinician when procedural questions arise:

Principle 1. Follow standardized procedures as outlined in test manuals as carefully as possible. However, some subjects have limitations that prevent them from following the specific conditions as outlined in test manuals. In that case, principle 2 applies.

Principle 2. The testing conditions necessary to have each individual examinee meet the standardized testing conditions is what is important, rather than the actual instructional wording or procedures. Thus, at times the examiner should amplify or repeat instructions to make sure that examinees understand exactly what they are to do. Pauses or slowed rate of instructional presentation can be used to achieve adequate comprehension of instructional set. At other times, alternative response modalities need to be provided (such as pointing), if examinees cannot engage in the standard response (e.g., spoken response). An example of this is on the WAIS–III Picture Completion subtest, where any method of indicating the missing element is acceptable; it does not have to be verbally stated.

Principle 3. Minimize environmental factors extraneous to the brain–behavior relationship under study so that they do not interfere with an examinee's performance. Minimize distractions such as extraneous noises or clutter within the testing environment.

Principle 4. Make sure the examinee is alert and aroused sufficiently to engage in the brain behavior under study. Of course, the exception to this rule would be if arousal is the behavior under study. An adequate level of arousal can be optimized by judicious use of rest breaks or varying environmental factors such as type of tasks or examiner voice volume and inflection.

Principle 5. Present all perceptual and visuospatial tasks at examinees' midline. Although this does not compensate for neglect or field cuts, it allows for a consistent presentation orientation across clients and conditions. If, as the examiner, you suspect that a presentation off midline might enhance or impair performance, complete that after the standard administration as part of testing the limits.

Principle 6. On all timed tasks, carefully time each response with a stopwatch and record the time of the examinee's answer. The performance can then be scored both in the standardized timed fashion and alternatively in an untimed "testing the limits" fashion. Both sets of information can be useful data for interpretation.

Principle 7. Provide only enough help and encouragement to maintain the examinee's behavioral performance in the task under investigation. If clients begin to respond randomly, they are not engaged in the task and no information can be gleaned about their ability or disability in that area. Sufficient help must be provided to make sure they are attempting to perform the task, without providing more help than necessary and inadvertently and artificially enhancing their performance.

Principle 8. Periodically review the test manuals to minimize "examiner drift."

Principle 9. Remember that neuropsychological evaluations are an assessment process, not just testing. In that process the assessment is directed by clinical questions. If there are conflicts between what must be done for the assessment versus the requirements of test administration, assessment needs should take precedence.

Additional Administration Concerns

Various Published Norms Collected with Different Administration Procedures. A search of the literature reveals that different published norms for the same clinical test do not follow the same administration procedures. Given the variability in "standard administration practice" for common neuropsychological tests, this finding should not be surprising. A prime example is the finger tapping test, where some norms were collected following Reitan's (1979) instructions of five dominant hand trials within five taps of each other before proceeding to the nondominant hand. Other published norms follow somewhat different procedures (e.g., Spreen & Gaddes, 1969). There is some indication that these procedural variations do affect performance (Leckliter, Forster, Klonoff, & Knights, 1992). Given this variability, it is important for clinicians to be familiar with the norms they use in terms of how they were collected and their applicability to administration variations or unique client populations.

Use and/or Calibration of Test Instruments. Recently I was called to consult on a case in which some preliminary neuropsychological testing had already been completed. The finger-tapping test had been administered, but the performance was quite slow bilaterally, and dropped off precipitously after the third trial in each hand. There was no other evidence of brain dysfunction. I decided to readminister the test. Upon securing the finger tapper that had been used, I discovered that it was miscalibrated. The angle of the tapping lever was about 10 degrees, rather than the normal approximately 25 degrees. For the counter to click over to the next number at the 10 degree angle the lever had to hit the wooden support platform. Readjusting the tapper and readministering the test with 30-sec rests periods between trials 1, 2, and 3 and between 4 and 5, and a 60-sec rest after trial 3, resulted in a perfectly normal performance.

Grip strength is another commonly used motor test. Reitan (1979) discussed the importance of calibrating the dynamometer to clients' hand size, but provided little information as to how to do this other than providing a range ("3 [small hand] and 5 [large hand]," p. 69) and suggesting adjustment so that it "feels comfortable for the individual subject" (p. 69). Thus, neuropsychometricians and doctoral level clinicians may be completely unaware of or inattentive to instrument calibration during test administration, even for instruments they frequently use. As with other aspects of administration, the principle underlying calibration procedures is adaptability across clients so that the behavior of interest is relatively isolated from extraneous but potentially interfering factors.

Variations or Alterations of Common Tests. Commonly used neuropsychological tests themselves have been altered for various reasons. Examples of this are the alternative or shortened forms of the Category Test (Calsyn, O'Leary, & Chaney, 1980; DeFilippis, & McCampbell, 1979; Gregory, Paul, & Morrison, 1979; Russell & Levy, 1987; Wetzel & Boll, 1987) or modifications of the Wisconsin Card Sorting Test (Axelrod, Henry, & Woodard, 1992; Berg, 1948; Heaton, Chelune, Talley, Kay, & Curtiss, 1993; Nelson, 1976; Teuber, Battersby, & Bender, 1951) that have been proposed. In many cases, new norms are not provided; rather, the user is given a formula to convert the shortened or alternative test results to adjusted scores thought to be comparable to the original test. The few studies of alternative form comparability that have been done suggest that the effects of these various changes and the applicability of the original test norms are unknown, and that new problems with reliability and validity are introduced (Taylor, Goldman, Leavitt, & Kleinman, 1984; Vanderploeg & Logan, 1989). Specifically, shortened forms of the Category test are likely to misclassify focal right-hemisphere-damaged persons as normal (Taylor et al., 1984).

The Testing Session

In Muriel Lezak's (1995) text *Neuropsychological Assessment,* chapter 5, entitled "The Neuropsychological Examination: Procedures," provided an excellent discussion of the clinical issues important during the data collection phase of a neuropsychological evaluation. Lezak addressed the special problems of brain-damaged persons and the nuances of working with them. Here we briefly review some of these issues, focusing on how the testing session can be managed to obtain the most reliable and valid assessment possible of individuals' brain-related behavioral capabilities.

Obtaining a Client's Maximal Performance

Neuropsychological assessment differs somewhat from other types of psychological assessment in that a goal of testing typically is to obtain the client's best possible performance (Heaton & Heaton, 1981). In order to evaluate whether or not brain dysfunction is responsible for an impaired performance, all other possible etiologies must be eliminated, controlled, or at least considered. Thus, it becomes the responsibility of the examiner to help the client attain his or her maximal level of performance, keeping in mind issues of standardization. To do so requires cognizance of possible sources of interference with test performance, and modification of instructions or procedures when necessary. Failure to do so, or at least failure to note that other factors interfered with test performance, becomes a source of possible interpretation error. Two areas are discussed as essential in obtaining clients' maximal performance: (a) the "assessment relationship" and (b) sensitivity to clients' individual differences.

The Examiner–Client Relationship. Establishing an effective working relationship with the client is crucial to a successful testing session. This is commonly referred to as *developing rapport*. There is little point to engaging in testing if clients refuse to actively participate. If after an explanation of the nature, purpose, and importance of the testing clients decline to cooperate, their decision should be respected. If the neuropsychologist proceeds with the evaluation under those conditions the results will be of questionable validity and the capabilities of the client will remain obscure.

Our expectation of clients to work hard and do their best can be conveyed to them directly and their on-task efforts reinforced. Throughout the evaluation, every effort ought to be made to treat the client with honesty, courtesy, and dignity, in the manner in which we would want to be treated if the roles were reversed. Under ideal conditions the assessment is a mutual endeavor in which examiner and examinee are working cooperatively on the task of trying to better understand the behavior, cognitive strengths and problems, and coping abilities of the examinee.

If we expect clients to give an honest effort on the various tasks we ask of them, then they are entitled to honesty from us during the examination process. Lezak (1995) offered several practical suggestions in this regard. Do not "invite" a client to take a particular test as a way of introduction, if in fact you really are not offering the client a choice. Do not use the first person plural when asking the client to do something ("Now let's try a few drawings"). Such phrasing is patronizing, demonstrates a lack of respect for clients, and can only interfere with a good assessment relationship. Lezak (1995) also expressed a personal distaste for the use of expressions such as "I would like you to . . ." or "I want you to . . ." when presenting test instructions. In addition to a matter of taste, such expressions are likely to prove particularly problematic with clients who have issues with authority (e.g., clients with a diagnosis of antisocial personality disorder) or clients who have just "had enough" with trying to meet the wishes of medical staff when they, the clients, are the ones who are feeling poorly. Such test instruction phrasing is common in many standard test administration procedures (see, e.g., the instructions of the Wechsler Memory Scale–III [Wechsler, 1997b] or the Memory Assessment Scale [Williams, 1991]). Unfortunately, it is likely to arouse an internal response of "I couldn't care less what you want," precipitate an antagonistic examination session, and result in either unconscious or conscious decrements in test performance. Substituting phrases such as "Listen carefully, when we are finished tell it back to me as best you can" or "This next task is to see how well you can . . ." is both clinically advantageous and a relatively easy modification.

Emphasizing the importance of the client–examiner relationship, Lezak (1995) also wrote about the necessity of preparing the client for the assessment. She delineated seven topics that should be covered if the examiner wants to be assured of full cooperation and best effort: (a) the purpose of the examination, (b) the nature of the examination, (c) how the results will be used, (d) the nature and extent of confidentiality, (e) if and when feedback will be provided about the results, (f) an explanation of the testing procedures and the role of the client, and (g) how the client feels about the testing. Some of these points are considered so important that they have been written into the latest American Psychological Association's Ethical Principles of Psychologists and Code of Conduct (American Psychological Association, 1992). Assessment within the context of a defined professional relationship and the structuring of that relationship are outlined in the ethics code. Structuring the professional relationship should include discussion of fees, anticipated length of contact(s), and informed consent regarding nature, course, and potential benefits or lack thereof. Feedback to the client of the results also is addressed as a specific ethical point. Although clinicians may pay some attention to these issues, unfortunately all too often these points are not addressed fully and satisfactorily.

Sensitivity to Client's Individual Differences.   Performance on neuropsychological tests can be affected by a multitude of variables, including many of the items discussed above in the context of the case history (see Table 1.2). Table 1.5 enumerates others. In order to obtain a client's maximal performance the examiner must be aware of individual-specific potential problems that may interfere with test performance.

A number of demographic attributes fall within the realm of subject-moder-

TABLE 1.5
Factors That Can Affect Test Performance

1. Demographic	b. Past injuries
a. Age	c. Carpal tunnel syndrome
b. Gender	5. Attention and distractibility
c. Education	6. Sensitivity to fatigue
d. Handedness	7. Frustration tolerance
e. Socioeconomic status	8. Psychiatric/psychological/personality
2. Situational	a. Depression
a. Motivation	b. Psychosis
b. Secondary gain	c. Antisocial/authority problems
c. Malingering	d. Somatization disorders
3. Sensory/perceptual	e. Anxiety disorders
a. Hearing loss	f. Alcohol or substance abuse
b. Visual acuity	9. Medical or health status
c. Field cuts and/or neglect	10. Brain injury
d. Peripheral neuropathies	a. Intrasubject variance
4. Peripheral psychomotor functioning	b. Intragroup variance
a. Arthritis	

ator variables, characteristics that make a group of individuals different in performance in a predictable fashion from the population at large (Anastasi, 1988). Unfortunately, in brain-impaired persons the effects of such moderator variables may be exaggerated, but in an unpredictable fashion. Age, gender, level of education, cultural background, socioeconomic status, motivation, and attention are those most frequently discussed in this context (see, e.g., Anastasi, 1988; Hynd & Semrud-Clikeman, 1990). Additional variables that are less predictable, yet areas of equal concern, are issues of motivation, secondary gain, and malingering. Medical conditions and problems can also adversely affect performance on a variety of neuropsychological test measures and be incorrectly interpreted as reflecting brain damage. It is essential to be aware of subject-specific factors that make an individual's performance noncomparable with the general normative database, to use adjusted norms if available, and to modify one's interpretation regardless. In the present context of the data collection phase of the evaluation, awareness of these variables is essential in making sure that information about them is collected and that their adverse affect on test performance is noted, if and when it occurs.

Brain dysfunction itself can be a moderator variable potentially resulting in unreliable test results. This may seem like a strange statement, but the variability commonly seen within and/or across tasks, within and/or across testing sessions, or unique to certain environmental conditions is certainly a different behavior than that of the brain-unimpaired normative comparison group. Test performance may be different in the morning than in the afternoon, or early in a session as opposed to later. Astute behavioral observations regarding fatigue, environmental distractions, internal distractions, or other factors allow the examiner to help the client compensate for such effects if possible, or at least to note their adverse effects as they occur. This avoids later possible misinterpretation of the results.

Hearing and vision problems can adversely affect performance on numerous tests, with such impaired test performance revealing nothing about brain dysfunction. A careful examiner can easily adjust for many sensory problems by making sure that clients utilize their glasses and hearing aids, or compensate by enunciating clearly and speaking louder and more slowly. Compensating for high-frequency hearing loss (a common problem in elderly males) can sometimes be accomplished by these same procedures.

Similarly, impaired attention and concentration (whether secondary to mood disorders or brain injury) can impair performance on many neuropsychological measures. The careful examiner can learn to modify some administration procedures to compensate for attentional problems, if the purpose for utilizing a particular test is for some reason other than the assessment of attentional resources. Compensation might be accomplished through encouragement, reassurance, careful use of breaks, specific instructions, and reticular activating system arousing techniques (e.g., varying types of tasks, or even voice volume and rate, to avoid attentional habituation).

The knowledgeable clinician will be cognizant of variables possibly confounding test performance, help clients compensate for them if possible, and note them for later interpretive descriptive richness. Failure to carefully assess and control for these factors increases assessment error.

Allowing Deficits to Emerge

It is also the examiner's responsibility to provide every opportunity for clients to demonstrate their deficits. This aspect of proper evaluation has received less discussion than has "maximizing performance," yet is equally important and just as much a source of possible assessment error.

Appropriate selection of tests is an area where examiners may or may not provide an opportunity for clients to demonstrate their problems. If measures sensitive to clients' deficits are not utilized, behavioral impairments may never be seen. The more knowledgeable and experienced the neuropsychologist is, the more likely it is that potential problem areas will be recognized, and the more likely it is that appropriate tests will be utilized (Walsh, 1992).

Clients' compensatory strategies can minimize performance on some measures and mask underlying deficits. One concrete example of this is on drawings of a Greek cross. Most individuals begin their drawing of the cross at the top and proceed clockwise. Thus, individuals with right-hemisphere damage must complete their drawing and connect up with their starting point by working in their impaired hemispatial field. A number of right-hemisphere-impaired clients begin their cross drawings at the top, work counterclockwise, and by following

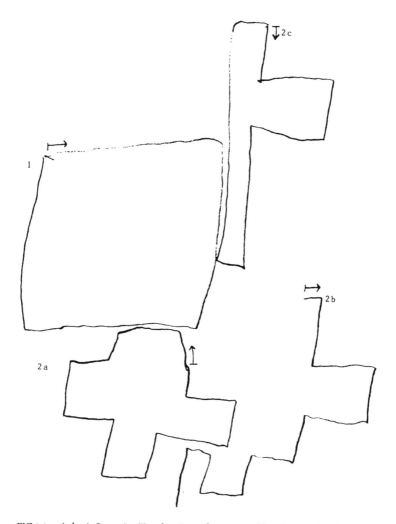

FIG 1.1.   Aphasia Screening Test drawings of a 70-year-old male, 5 weeks after suffering a right frontal-parietal stroke. The square was drawing adequately from copy first,
followed by three attempts to copy a Greek cross (2a, 2b, 2c). After the patient's initial
cross drawing (2a) he was asked to draw it again moving his pencil in a clockwise
rather than counterclockwise direction.

this approach produce adequate figures. When subsequently asking them to re-
draw the cross by starting at the top and proceeding clockwise, severely distorted crosses are drawn (Fig. 1.1). Multiple clinical examples could be provided
where a slight variation in usual procedures resulted in very significant clinical
information being revealed, or where the selection of certain test instruments
was essential to help identify a particular problem.

Another area where deficits may be missed is frontal-lobe dysfunction. Many of the problems associated with frontal dysfunction manifest themselves best in unstructured and novel situations. However, neuropsychological testing tends to be very structured and rapidly becomes less than novel. Therefore, the clinical interview, the "assessment relationship" itself, break periods from "formal assessment," and information from significant others becomes essential in the evaluation of aspects of frontal lobe functioning—for example, response inhibition, behavioral self-monitoring and self-correcting, maintenance of appropriate interpersonal behaviors, appreciation and appropriate expression of humor and wit, ability to form an "abstract attitude," and cognitive and behavioral flexibility. The examiner must not only create an environment where such deficits may freely emerge, but also be trained to correctly recognize and record them when they do. Furthermore, on tests relatively sensitive to such problems (e.g., Halstead Category Test, Wisconsin Card Sorting Test, Trail Making Test part B, visuospatial mazes), a well-structured and supportive examiner may provide external cues and structure too readily in anticipation of problems or errors. In so doing, the opportunity for the client to engage in perseverative, concrete, or "stimulus-bound" behaviors is thwarted.

Structuring the Testing Session

Issues important to structuring the testing session include introducing the testing, pacing and the use of breaks, ordering of the tests administered, and using single versus multiple sessions.

Introducing the Testing. Normally, the clinical interview, as discussed earlier, will precede formal testing. During the interview the examiner will typically introduce the examinee to the nature and purpose of the evaluation. This should also include information regarding the length of time the evaluation is likely to take, if and when breaks will occur, and how meals will be handled, if the evaluation will span a mealtime. Clients should be informed that the actual tests will be of varying levels of difficulty, that no one is expected to do well on everything, but that they should attempt to do their best on all measures to make the evaluation as useful as possible.

Since clinical interviews frequently move from more open-ended questions to structured questioning and history gathering, the subsequent move into actual testing can be accomplished smoothly. By starting with simpler measures such as orientation questions or brief attentional measures (e.g., Information and Orientation from the WMS–III or Digit Span), the examinee may not even note a shift from the direct questions of the case history. Performance on these simple measures will help the examiner evaluate to what extent basic attentional and motivational resources are likely to impact more difficult measures. In addition, the examiner can develop a sense of how easily the client understands and follows instructions, and how quickly the client works.

Pacing and the Use of Breaks.   Examiners should be thoroughly familiar with the various tests so that they can work smoothly and easily with clients, observe any unusual behaviors, and quickly record responses and observations. The pacing of testing should be dictated by the client's ability and comfort level rather than by the examiner's preference. That is, the pacing should never interfere with a client's ability to give his or her best performance. It should proceed quickly enough so that clients do not have idle time, but slowly enough so that they do not feel harried. Examiners' fiddling with test material or excessive time between tasks will lengthen the overall evaluation time and increase the likelihood that client fatigue will become a confounding factor.

Brief breaks from testing should be given when client fatigue appears to be adversely affecting performance. It is usually a good idea to take a 5- to 10-min rest break about every 90 min, whether or not the client appears to need it. This will help maintain alertness. Clients tend to be appreciative of an examiner's consideration of their emotional states and needs, but excessive attentiveness can be experienced as patronizing, interfere with rapport, and disrupt the assessment. A guiding principle is to pace the examination and use breaks so as to help clients do their best.

Ordering of the Tests.   There are several approaches to test administration ordering. One approach is to select and use tests to answer an ongoing series of clinical questions. The initial question would be whether the client can engage in formal testing. As noted earlier, beginning with a few easier tasks will help answer that question. Subsequent clinical questions might concern the client's competence in various cognitive ability domains. Thus, a sequence of tests might move systematically through the cognitive domains of interest: attention, basic sensory-perceptual abilities, psychomotor capability, working memory capacity, language competence, visuospatial competence, learning and memory abilities, and executive abilities. Once having established ability to participate reliably in testing, some neuropsychologists will utilize sensitive "screening" measures within the various domains, and only attempt to "flesh out" abilities within a domain if performance on the sensitive measure(s) appears impaired.

Neuropsychologists utilizing a consistent set of tests should vary the difficulty level so that clients can have a success experience after doing poorly on some measure. Also, although it may be tempting to save the most difficult measures for the end of the evaluation, this would result in the client having to take them when most fatigued. In addition, the client may leave the evaluation with a feeling of failure or inadequacy.

Single Versus Multiple Testing Sessions.   Many neuropsychologists and clients prefer to complete the evaluation in one session and schedule a follow-up session for feedback. As long as clients are able to sustain their attention, motivation, and energy level to complete the evaluation in one session, this approach is quite effective. However, many of the more impaired clients cannot tolerate more than 30 to 90 min of evaluation at a stretch. For these clients, testing must be broken into several sessions. In addition, with forensic evaluations where motivation or malingering may be an issue, the use of multiple sessions can be quite revealing. Significant discrepancies in performance between sessions (and within sessions), particularly if the pattern of difficulties does not fit any known neurological condition, certainly raise the possibility of factors other than brain impairment as accounting for the test findings. Clients who are malingering are likely to have difficulty maintaining a consistently poor level of performance across repeated sessions.

Scoring and Clerical Errors

Scoring or clerical errors are very common. Greene (1980), for example, reported that approximately 30% of hand-scored Minnesota Multiphasic Personality Inventory (MMPI) protocols have some errors. On the MMPI, scoring is simply counting the number of items affirmed on each scale and transferring that total onto a profile sheet. Scoring on the WAIS–III and various neuropsychological test measures is much more complicated and at times involves subjective judgments.

One example of a neuropsychological scoring error was provided by a psychology intern several years ago. This intern indicated that the geropsychologist with whom she was working carefully determined age-adjusted WAIS–R scaled scores on his elderly clients. However, he then proceeded to sum these age-adjusted scaled scores and look up those summary scores in the age-appropriate IQ tables to determine IQ scores. Thus, he was effectively adjusting twice for the client's age. He had apparently been following that practice for several years. Whether this was a case of "examiner drift" or of having learned incorrect scoring procedures initially is uncertain, but this clinician was a doctoral-level psychologist who was specializing in geropsychology.

Little research exists regarding scoring problems with general neuropsychological tests; however, there is some research with the WAIS–R. Ryan, Prifitera, and Powers (1983) compared the scoring of 19 doctoral-level psychologists and 20 psychology graduate students on two WAIS–R protocols. Both experienced examiners and novices made a great many scoring errors. Generally, errors resulted in higher IQ scores than should have been obtained, but this was not always the case. Verbal IQ scores varied as much as 18 points among examiners and Performance IQs up to 17 points. Experienced clinicians did no better than the graduate students, and considerably worse on Performance scales (10- to 17-point ranges for Ph.D. holders versus 4-point ranges for graduate students). Common error types included incorrectly scoring individual items, adding raw scores across subtests, and converting scaled scores to IQ scores. Other common WAIS–R/WAIS–III scoring errors include failure to give credit for initial unadministered items on subtests such as Information and Arithmetic (this is also a common error on the Wide Range Achievement Test–Revised [WRAT–R]), incorrectly looking up scores from tables, or in converting scaled scores to percentage scores for the actual test report. Timed tests can also be problematic unless time limits are strictly followed.

One legitimate area for potential scoring disagreement comes in scoring various Vocabulary, Similarities, or Comprehension items on Wechsler intelligence measures. Although scoring guidelines and sample responses are provided in the manual, clients not uncommonly provide answers that are not covered in the examples. The manual encourages clinicians to clarify ambiguous responses with questions such as "Tell me a little more" or "Explain what you mean." It also indicates that if multiple acceptable responses are provided, the clinician should score the best response. However, if multiple responses are provided and some of them would be 0-point responses, the examiner should ask, "Which one is it?" Despite these helpful suggestions, some subjects will give questionable responses and the clinician must make a judgment about what value to assign.

Although there are times when minor scoring or clerical errors result in little difference in scores or in interpretation of test findings, a grave disservice may result when they do. Realizing how common scoring errors are, a rule of thumb would be to always cross-check test scores and certainly to cross-check scores that do not seem to fit with the clinical picture, past history, or with the rest of the test data. In addition, neuropsychologists should be knowledgeable of where errors are likely to occur and be particularly attentive in those areas.

CHAPTER SUMMARY

Neuropsychological assessment is a complex clinical activity. This chapter has addressed issues relevant to the data collection phase of the assessment process. It was argued that the neuropsychological evaluation is a process that neither begins nor ends with testing. Instead, it begins before the client is ever seen, with an attempt to clarify and define the nature and purpose of each evaluation. The interview, case history, and behavioral observations were discussed as being as important in gathering information, as formal neuropsychological testing. Methods and approaches to the interview process and case history development were reviewed.

Once a decision has been made to pursue formal testing, the neuropsychologist must carefully select which tests to utilize to evaluate the relevant cognitive domains of interest and identify possible areas of brain impairment. Important in test selection is the use of well-normed and validated measures of an appropriate level of difficulty for the client under study. Issues in standardized testing were discussed at some length. It was suggested that what is important for standardized testing is the creation of the conditions that were present for the standardization sample, rather than an inflexible application of the standardized testing conditions. A number of administration principles were offered to help guide the clinician in this area. Issues related to structuring the testing session were reviewed. Important in this regard is helping clients attain their maximal performance, although still allowing opportunities for them to demonstrate their problems and deficits. It was suggested that the pace of the session, the use of breaks, and order of test administration should all be dictated by the client's ability and comfort level, rather than by the examiner's preference. Finally, it was seen that problems related to the actual scoring of test results are quite common and can substantially impact possible interpretation of the evaluation findings.

Subsequent chapters cover the interpretation and application phases of the evaluation process. However, a necessary prerequisite for these stages of the evaluation is some kind of determination of a comparison standard for the individual being evaluated. Estimating premorbid level of functioning is therefore covered in the next chapter.

REFERENCES

American Psychological Association. (1992). Ethical principles of psychologists and code of conduct. *American Psychologist, 47,* 1597–1611.

Anastasi, A. (1988). *Psychological testing* (6th ed.). New York: Macmillan.

Axelrod, B. N., Henry, R. R., & Woodard, J. L. (1992). Analysis of an abbreviated form of the Wisconsin card sorting test. *The Clinical Neuropsychologist, 6,* 27–31.

Berg, E. A. (1948). A simple objective test for measuring flexibility in thinking. *Journal of General Psychology, 39,* 15–22.

Butler, M., Retzlaff, P., & Vanderploeg, R. (1991). Neuropsychological test usage. *Professional Psychology: Research and Practice, 22,* 510–512.

Calsyn, D. A., O'Leary, M. R., & Chaney, E. F. (1980). Shortening the Category Test. *Journal of Consulting and Clinical Psychology, 48,* 788–789.

DeFilippis, N.A., & McCampbell, E. (1979). *The Booklet Category Test.* Odessa, FL: Psychological Assessment Resources.

Denburg, S. D., Carotte, R. M., & Denburg, J. A. (1987). Cognitive impairment in systemic lupus erythematosus: A neuropsychological study of individual and group deficits. *Journal of Clinical and Experimental Neuropsychology, 9,* 323–339.

Dunn, L. M., & Dunn, L. M. (1981). *Peabody Picture Vocabulary Test–Revised manual.* Circle Pines, MN: American Guidance Service.

Golden, C. J., Osmon, D. C., Moses, J. A., Jr., & Berg, R. A. (1981). *Interpretation of the Halstead–Reitan neuropsychological test battery: A casebook approach.* New York: Grune & Stratton.

Greene, R. L. (1980). *The MMPI: An interpretive manual.* New York: Grune and Stratton.

Greenwald, A. G., Pratkanis, A. R., Leippe, M. R., & Baumgardner, M. H. (1986). Under what conditions does theory obstruct research progress? *Psychological Review, 93,* 216–229.

Gregory, R. J., Paul, J. J., & Morrison, M. W. (1979). A short form of the Category Test for adults. *Journal of Clinical Psychology, 35,* 795–798.

Heaton, R. K., Chelune, G. J., Talley, J. L., Kay, G. G., & Curtiss, G. (1993). *Wisconsin Card Sorting Test Manual: Revised and expanded.* Odessa, FL: Psychological Assessment Resources.

Heaton, S. R., & Heaton, R. K. (1981). Testing the impaired patient. In S. B. Filskov & T. J. Boll (Eds.), *Handbook of clinical neuropsychology* (pp. 526–544). New York: John Wiley and Sons.

Hynd, G. W., & Semrud-Clikeman, M. (1990). Neuropsychological assessment. In A. S. Kaufman (Ed.), *Assessing adolescent and adult intelligence* (pp. 638–695). Boston: Allyn and Bacon.

Jarvis, P. E., & Barth, J. T. (1984). *Halstead–Reitan test battery: An interpretive guide.* Odessa, FL: Psychological Assessment Resources.

Kaplan, E., Fein, D., Morris, R., & Delis, D. C. (1991). *WAIS–R as a neuropsychological instrument.* San Antonio, TX: The Psychological Corporation.

Leckliter, I. N., Forster, A. A., Klonoff, H., & Knights, R. M. (1992). A review of reference group data from normal children for the Halstead–Reitan neuropsychological test battery for older children. *The Clinical Neuropsychologist, 6,* 201–229.

Lezak, M.D. (1995). *Neuropsychological assessment* (3rd ed.). New York: Oxford University Press.

Luria, A. R. (1980). *Higher cortical functions in man* (2nd ed., B. Haigh, Trans.). New York: Basic Books.

Maloney, M. P., & Ward, M. P. (1976). *Psychological assessment: A conceptual approach.* New York: Oxford University Press.

Matarazzo, J. D., (1990). Psychological assessment versus psychological testing. *American Psychologist, 45,* 999–1017.

Melendez, F. (1978). *Revised manual for the adult neuropsychological questionnaire.* Odessa, FL: Psychological Assessment Resources.

Milner, B. (1962). Laterality effects in audition. In V. B. Mountcastle (Ed.), *Interhemispheric relations and cerebral dominance* (pp. 177–195). Baltimore, MD: Johns Hopkins University Press.

Nelson, H. E. (1976). A modified card sorting test sensitive to frontal lobe defects. *Cortex, 12,* 313–324.

Phay, A., Gainer, C., & Goldstein, G. (1986). Clinical interviewing of the patient and history in neuropsychological assessment. In T. Incagnoli, G. Goldstein, & C. J. Golden (Eds.), *Clinical application of neuropsychological test batteries* (pp. 45–73). New York: Plenum Press.

Reitan, R. M. (1979). *Manual for administration of neuropsychological test batteries for adults and children.* Tucson, AZ: Reitan Neuropsychology Laboratories.

Reitan, R. M., & Wolfson, D. (1985). *The Halstead–Reitan neuropsychological test battery: Theory and clinical interpretation.* Tucson, AZ: Neuropsychology Press.

Reitan, R. M., & Wolfson, D. (1989). The Seashore rhythm test and brain functions. *The Clinical Neuropsychologist, 3,* 70–78.

Russell, E. W., & Levy, M. (1987). Revision of the Halstead category test. *Journal of Consulting and Clinical Psychology, 55,* 898–901.

Ryan, J. J., Prifitera, A., & Powers, L. (1983). Scoring reliability on the WAIS–R. *Journal of Consulting and Clinical Psychology, 51,* 149–150.

Sattler, J. M. (1988). *Assessment of children* (3rd ed.). San Diego, CA: Jerome M. Sattler.

Schinka, J. A. (1983). *Neuropsychological status examination manual.* Odessa, FL: Psychological Assessment Resources.

Sherer, M., Parson, O. A., Nixon, S. J., & Adams, R. L. (1991). Clinical validity of the speech-sounds perception test and the Seashore rhythm test. *Journal of Clinical and Experimental Neuropsychology, 13,* 741–751.

Skenazy, J., & Bigler, E. (1984). Neuropsychological findings in diabetes mellitus. *Journal of Clinical Psychology, 40,* 246-258.

Spreen, O., & Gaddes, W. H. (1969). Developmental norms for 15 neuropsychological tests age 6 to 15. *Cortex, 5,* 170–191.

Tarter, R. E., Van Thiel, D. H., & Edwards, K. (1988). *Medical neuropsychology: The impact of disease on behavior.* New York: Plenum Press.

Taylor, J. M., Goldman, H., Leavitt, J., & Kleinman, K. M. (1984). Limitations of the brief form of the Halstead category test. *Journal of Clinical Neuropsychology, 6,* 341–344.

Teuber, H.-L., Battersby, W. S., & Bender, M. B. (1951). Performance of complex visual tasks after cerebral lesions. *Journal of Nervous and Mental Disease, 114,* 413–429.

Vanderploeg, R. D., Goldman, H., & Kleinman, K. M. (1987). Relationship between systolic and diastolic blood pressure and cognitive functioning in hypertensive subjects: An extension of previous findings. *Archives of Clinical Neuropsychology, 2,* 101–109.

Vanderploeg, R. D., & Logan, S. G. (1989). Comparison of the Halstead category test and the revised category test: Comment on Russell and Levy. *Journal of Consulting and Clinical Psychology, 57,* 315–316.

Walsh, K. (1992). Some gnomes worth knowing. *The Clinical Neuropsychologist, 6,* 119–133.

Wechsler, D. (1981). *WAIS–R manual.* New York: Psychological Corporation.

Wechsler, D. (1997a). *WAIS–III: Administration and scoring manual.* New York: Psychological Corporation.

Wechsler, D. (1997b). *WMS–III: Administration and scoring manual,* San Antonio, TX: Psychological Corporation.

Wetzel, L., & Boll, T. J. (1987). *Short category test, booklet format.* Los Angeles: Western Psychological Services.

Williams, J. M. (1987). *Cognitive behavior rating scales manual: Research edition.* Odessa, FL: Psychological Assessment Resources.

Williams, J. M. (1991). *Memory assessment scales professional manual,* Odessa, FL: Psychological Assessment Resources.

Williams, M. (1965). *Brain damage and the mind.* Baltimore, MD: Penguin Books.

CHAPTER TWO

Estimating Premorbid Level of Functioning

John A. Schinka
Rodney D. Vanderploeg
*James A. Haley Veterans' Hospital, Tampa, Florida,
and College of Medicine, University of South Florida*

A significant portion of the practice of clinical neuropsychology is assessing for possible changes in cognition attributable to central nervous system insult or disease. As in any endeavor attempting to measure change, the accuracy of the assessment of change is a function of the reliability of both the baseline (premorbid) and postdisease/injury (postmorbid or current) measures. Clinically, neuropsychologists have little difficulty in selecting measures of current cognitive function that have been well constructed and produce scores of known reliability under standardized conditions. Unfortunately, because almost no patients have a premorbid history of cognitive evaluation using these same measures, neuropsychologists are forced to estimate premorbid levels of cognitive ability, an endeavor that in itself is characterized by factors that contribute to error. In this chapter, we attempt to accomplish several goals: a discussion of the primary issues that influence the accuracy of premorbid prediction of cognitive ability, examination of common methods of obtaining premorbid estimates, and recommendations for a strategy of determining premorbid level of cognitive ability in clinical situations. We do not attempt, nor would it be possible in the space available, to review the entire literature on premorbid prediction. A recent article by Franzen, Burgess, and Smith-Seemiller (1997) is an excellent starting point for such a review.

THE STRUCTURE OF COGNITIVE ABILITY: INTRAINDIVIDUAL VARIABILITY

In a monumental piece of work, Carroll (1993) reanalyzed 460 data sets of performance on a wide variety of cognitive tasks. His findings supported a hierarchical theory of higher order abilities, specifically that there was abundant evidence to support a factor of general intelligence (stratum III, commonly called g) that permeates to some degree all cognitive tasks. At a lower order of analysis (called stratum II), Carroll found strong support for eight broad ability factors. These include many factors that are familiar to neuropsychologists (e.g., fluid intelligence, crystallized intelligence, general memory ability, cognitive speed). At the lowest level of analysis (stratum I) are more specific abilities such as associative memory, learning ability, and free recall (all subcomponents of the general learning and memory stratum II factor).

Carroll's work provides a model for discussion of a major problem with current methods of prediction of premorbid cognitive ability. In practice, estimation methods reflect the assumption that there is a single estimate (in practice, this is usually estimated premorbid Wechsler Adult Intelligence Scale FSIQ; WAIS–R [Wechsler, 1981] or WAIS–III [Wechsler, 1997]) that best represents an individual's cognitive abilities. Thus, it is commonly the case that the prediction statement is akin to "the patient's premorbid level of cognitive ability is calculated to have been in the Average range." Such statements are essentially a comment on g, or general intelligence. In neuropsychological assessment, however, our interests lie not only in determining decline in g, but also in assessing decline in cognitive domains (e.g., language, visuospatial ability, memory, executive functions) and specific abilities (e.g., language comprehension, language expression, visual recognition, short-term auditory memory). Thus, our interests are in all three stratums, not just in g. Current approaches to premorbid estimation generally ignore intraindividual scatter, or varying levels of ability, across and within the domains in which we are interested because they focus primarily on Full Scale IQ (FSIQ)—an approximate measure of g (Carroll, 1993). To use predictors of g as estimates of both specific stratum I abilities and general stratum II cognitive domains will inevitably result in incorrect estimates. Stratum II domains are differentially related to g (i.e., they do not correlate perfectly), and the stratum I abilities are differentially related to both g and the stratum II domains (i.e., they have unique sources of variance).

This easily can be seen by examining the standardization data for the WAIS–R. In reference to Carroll's hierarchical model, the WAIS–R Verbal subtests appear to reflect primarily the stratum II factor of crystallized intelligence, while the Performance subtests reflect primarily the fluid intelligence and broad visual perception factors. Given the stratum II domains represented, we might expect significant variability in performance across measures of these domains. In fact, Matarazzo and Herman (1984) showed that almost 18% of the standardization sample had an absolute Verbal IQ–Performance IQ (VIQ–PIQ) difference of 15 points or greater. Because individual subtests reflect differential influence of g and the stratum II domains, we would also expect substantial scatter among the battery of subtests. Matarazzo, Daniel, Prifitera, and Herman (1988) showed that over 18% of the standardization sample had two subtests that differed by

TABLE 2.1
Percentage of Cases at or Above Each Level of Scatter
in the WAIS–R Standardization Sample, by Full Scale IQ

Scatter (range)	Full Scale IQ					
	−79	80–89	90–109	110–119	120+	All
17	0.0%	0.0%	0.0%	0.0%	0.0%	0.0%
16	0.0	0.0	0.2	0.0	0.0	0.1
15	0.0	0.0	0.5	0.3	0.0	0.3
14	0.0	0.0	0.8	0.3	0.0	0.4
13	0.0	0.0	1.5	1.0	1.1	1.0
12	0.0	0.3	2.4	2.6	4.5	2.1
11	0.6	1.0	4.1	6.1	9.0	4.1
10	0.6	3.3	7.8	13.5	20.3	8.6
9	3.0	8.9	18.6	25.3	32.8	18.1
8	7.3	19.5	34.1	40.1	49.7	31.9
7	17.6	31.8	53.1	57.7	67.2	48.7
6	29.7	56.6	73.9	77.6	87.0	69.1
5	60.6	79.1	89.7	91.3	93.8	86.1
4	84.8	93.4	98.3	98.7	99.4	96.5
3	98.2	99.3	99.7	100.0	100.0	99.6
2	100.0	99.7	100.0	100.0	100.0	99.9
1	100.0	100.0	100.0	100.0	100.0	100.0
0	100.0	100.0	100.0	100.0	100.0	100.0
Standard deviation	1.57	1.78	2.02	2.07	2.08	2.08
Median scatter	5	6	7	7	7	6

Note. Data from Matarazzo, Daniel, Prifitera, and Herman (1988, Table 4). Data and table from the Wechsler Adult Intelligence Scale–Revised. Copyright 1988, 1981, 1955 by The Psychological Corporation. Reprinted by permission. All rights reserved. Scatter measured by the range of scaled scores across the 11 subtests.

three or more standard deviations (scatter ranges of nine scale scores or more). This percentage increased to almost 33% in individuals with Full Scale IQ scores of 120 or greater. Table 2.1 shows the pattern of subtest scatter at different levels of intellectual ability for the WAIS–R standardization sample. As expected, with decreased overall range (i.e., lower Full Scale IQ scores), the range of subtest scatter decreases. However, even in a population with Full Scale IQ scores of less than 80, 30% have subtest scatter ranges of two standard deviations or greater. Even within domains, substantial scatter can be expected among abilities. Approximately 18% of the standardization sample had scatter equal to or greater than two standard deviations (i.e., 6 scaled score units) within the Verbal subtests. A similar percentage had scatter of 6 or greater on Performance subtests. Consistent with the model just outlined, Verbal subtest scatter is essentially independent of Performance subtest scatter (Matarazzo et al., 1988).

Note that the pattern of scatter among subtests can take different forms. For

TABLE 2.2

Number of WAIS-R Subtest Scores Significantly Deviating (±3 Points)
From a Persons's Own Mean Required for Abnormality at Several Frequencies
of Occurrence in the Normal Population, by Full Scale IQ

Frequency of Occurrence	Full Scale IQ																	
	79			80–89			90–109			110–119			120+			Total Sample		
	V	P	FS	V	P	FS	V	P	FS	V	P	FS	V	P	FS	V	P	FS
<10%	2	3	4	2	3	4	3	4	4	3	4	5	3	4	6	3	4	4
<05%	3	4	5	3	4	5	4	4	5	4	4	6	4	4	7	4	4	5
<02%	4	4	6	4	4	6	4	5	6	5	5	7	5	5	7	4	5	6
<01%	5	5	7	5	5	7	5	5	7	5	5	8	5	5	8	5	5	7
Sample size	165			301			930			305			179			1880		

Note. Values in this table have been smoothed. (Data and table are from McLean, J. E., Kaufman, A. S., Reynolds, C. R. (1989). Base rates for WAIS–R subtest scatter as a guide for clinical and neuropsychological assessment. *Journal of Clinical Psychology, 45,* 919–926. Reprinted by permission of the copyright holder, Clinical Psychology Publishing Company, Inc., Brandon, VT 05733).

example, one pattern could consist of a single subtest "outlier," with all other subtests having similar subtest scaled scores. Alternatively, there could be substantial variability across the profile of subtest scaled scores. The latter possibility is more likely the situation in most cases. The subtest intercorrelation matrices reported in the WAIS–R manual support the second possibility. For some age groups the intercorrelation matrix contains as many as six values of 0.30 or less (9% or less shared variance). The lowest correlation is only .19 (less than 4% common variance).

McClean, Kaufman, and Reynolds (1989) examined the number of WAIS-R subtests that differed by 3 or more points from a person's mean scaled score. In individuals with Full Scale IQ scores of 120 or greater, as many as 6 of the 11 subtests met this criteria in 10% of the sample. An average of 4 subtests met this criteria in over 10% of the entire standardization sample. Table 2.2 presents data for the number of deviant subtests (3 points or more) from a person's mean subtest scaled score for the entire standardization sample and across different levels of intelligence. As can be seen, WAIS–R subtest scatter is quite common in a non-brain-injured population. Fluctuation across other measures of brain–behavior functions is less well documented, but is likely to be as or more variable. One study did report that the larger the number of neuropsychological measures, the greater the range of obtained scores (Mortensen, Gade, & Reinisch, 1991).

In summary, we believe that it is important to develop premorbid estimates of individual cognitive domains (stratum II), rather than an overall estimate of *g*.

Because most neuropsychologists incorporate at least portions of the WAIS–R Verbal and Performance subtests in their evaluations, in practice this will at least mean estimating Verbal and Performance IQs independently. At this time the prediction of ability levels in other domains has not been explored to any meaningful degree, and we are aware of only a single study (Williams, 1997) extending to other domains. Williams (1997) attempted to estimate memory ability from demographic variables. He discovered that demographic variables predicted scores on the Memory Assessment Scales (Williams, 1992) at a low level (accounting for 8 to 20% variance in different memory indices), in contrast to the findings in the prediction of WAIS–R IQ scores (24% to 38% variance; Barona, Reynolds, & Chastain, 1984).

METHODS OF ESTIMATING
ADULT PREMORBID COGNITIVE ABILITY

There are a number of taxonomies of methods of estimation of premorbid cognitive function (e.g., Smith-Seemiller, Franzen, Burgess, & Prieto, 1997; Vanderploeg, 1994). Regardless of the taxonomy, it is apparent that the methods vary in complexity and statistical sophistication, often sharing common shortcomings. We now discuss and critique eight methods.

Prior Standardized Test Data

The ideal situation in clinical neuropsychological practice would be to have available for comparative purposes the results of a standardized multidimensional intelligence test (e.g., WISC–R, WISC–III, WAIS–R) completed at some point prior to the onset not only of the suspected neurological disorder, but also of common disorders of late adulthood such as hypertension. Although such intelligence test results are rarely available, in the United States results of some form of standardized aptitude or achievement testing frequently can be obtained. Nationally standardized assessment is completed within the educational system at a variety of points in time, beginning in the elementary grades (e.g., the Stanford Achievement Tests) and extending through the college and postgraduate levels (e.g., Scholastic Aptitude Test, Graduate Record Exam). Because many of these standardized aptitude tests address multiple domains of cognitive function, they can provide the clinician with more specific estimates across different cognitive domains. Thus standardized tests with measures of verbal, mathematical/quantitative, and logical/analytic abilities permit more detailed comparisons with results from the neuropsychological evaluation. Finally, military entrance exams (ASVAB) may be another source of information regarding premorbid cognitive functioning.

Use of prior test data can have several shortcomings, however. A practical, but frequent, difficulty is that obtaining results of prior standardized tests can be time-consuming and can delay substantially the completion of the neuropsychological consultation report. For this reason, such data are typically obtained only in forensic cases—few hospital-based consultation practices are likely to attempt to obtain such information for the routine consultation case, in which turnaround for the completed report is likely to be measured in days.

Another significant problem is that the reference normative group for standardized tests administered in the educational system becomes progressively stratified. Standardized tests completed during elementary and secondary school (not including college admission tests) likely reflect the population at large (similar to the normative reference group for Wechsler's intelligence scales), although it should be noted that exceptions to such tests (e.g., exempting children on school lunch programs) are becoming more common. However, fewer individuals take more advanced measures, such as college aptitude tests. The normative base therefore becomes smaller and generally consists of those individuals with higher levels of ability. For example, obtaining an overall score at the 50th percentile on the GRE is likely to be roughly equivalent to a percentile score of 85 on aptitude tests completed in high school (e.g., on the SAT).

History of Educational and Occupational Achievement

In the absence of standardized test results, other aspects of a patient's history can be used to provide estimates of premorbid level(s) of functioning. Because of the relatively high correlations of educational and occupational achievement with intelligence (correlation with WAIS–R Full Scale IQ = .53 and .36, respectively; Barona et al., 1984), these variables are frequently used to estimate premorbid ability levels. Unfortunately, there are few published guidelines for using these achievement variables as estimates. Equivalent IQs for individual occupations and levels of education have been provided by Matarazzo (1972, Table 7.3, p. 178). However, these estimates may no longer be reliable, given changes in the educational system that minimize standards for completion of high school education and admission into colleges and universities. More recent estimates of IQ equivalents for levels of education and general occupational groups (e.g., skilled laborer), based on the WAIS–R standardization sample, have been provided by Reynolds, Chastain, Kaufman, and McLean (1987). These estimates are provided in Table 2.3.

There are three problems in using these education and occupation estimates for premorbid IQ. The first is that there is substantial variability of IQ equivalents for any given occupation or educational level. Application of a band of error equal to ±SD to any estimate of FSIQ generally produces a range of 24–30 IQ points. Thus, other historical information will generally be required to refine the estimate for a given individual. For example, grade-point averages and class ranking might help to reduce the range of the premorbid estimate. A second

TABLE 2.3

Means and Standard Deviations on Verbal, Performance, and Full Scale IQs
for the WAIS–R Standardization Sample, by Demographic Variable

Variable	N	VIQ (SD)	PIQ (SD)	FSIQ (SD)
Gender				
Male	940	100.9 (15.1)	100.5 (15.2)	100.9 (15.3)
Female	940	98.7 (14.7)	99.1 (15.1)	98.7 (14.9)
Race				
White	1664	101.2 (14.5)	101.3 (14.7)	101.4 (14.7)
Black	192	87.9 (13.1)	87.3 (13.7)	86.9 (13.0)
Others	24	94.2 (13.1)	96.5 (13.8)	94.0 (12.9)
Region				
Northeast	464	101.7 (14.8)	101.4 (14.9)	101.6 (15.0)
North Central	497	98.6 (14.3)	100.0 (14.4)	99.0 (14.2)
South	576	98.6 (15.7)	97.1 (16.1)	98.0 (16.3)
West	343	101.0 (14.3)	101.9 (14.2)	101.5 (14.3)
Residence				
Urban	1421	100.4 (15.0)	100.0 (15.2)	100.3 (15.2)
Rural	459	98.0 (14.4)	99.2 (15.1)	98.4 (14.8)
Education				
1 (0–7 years)	133	82.2 (13.6)	84.5 (15.0)	82.5 (14.3)
2 (8 years)	158	90.2 (11.0)	93.0 (14.4)	90.8 (12.0)
3 (9–11 years)	472	96.1 (13.8)	97.7 (14.9)	96.4 (14.2)
4 (12 years [H.S. grad.])	652	100.1 (12.1)	100.2 (13.5)	100.0 (12.5)
5 (13–15 years)	251	107.7 (10.9)	105.4 (12.0)	107.3 (11.1)
6 (16+ years [College grad.])	214	115.7 (11.6)	111.0 (12.9)	115.2 (12.2)
Occupation				
1 Professional and technical	206	111.3 (12.8)	108.2 (13.8)	111.0 (13.4)
2 Managerial, clerical, sales	409	104.3 (12.3)	103.3 (13.1)	104.1 (12.6)
3 Skilled workers	213	98.4 (11.9)	101.2 (13.6)	99.5 (12.6)
4 Semiskilled workers	404	92.7 (13.6)	94.5 (15.3)	93.1 (14.2)
5 Unskilled workers	68	88.9 (15.3)	90.8 (15.4)	89.1 (15.2)
6 Not in labor force	580	99.2 (15.5)	98.5 (15.3)	98.9 (15.6)

Note. Values have been rounded off to one decimal point. Reprinted from *Journal of School Psychology, 25*, Reynolds, Chastain, Kaufman, & McLean, Demographic characteristics and IQ among adults: Analysis of the WAIS–R standardization sample as a function of the stratification variables, 323–342, Copyright (1987), with permission from Pergamon Press Ltd, Headington Hill Hall, Oxford OX3 0BW, UK.

problem is more substantial and reflects the fact that intellectual capability is a necessary, but not sufficient, condition for educational and occupational success. Both socioeconomic and personality factors can limit the utilization of intellectual capability. Peer pressure against academic achievement, lack of family support to achieve, and lack of funds to obtain higher education are common reasons for failure to achieve. Personality disorder, adjustment disorder, and simple refusal to endorse traditional paths of cultural success are also factors that affect socioeconomic achievement. In these cases, use of educational and occupational achievement to estimate premorbid intellectual function is likely to produce underestimates. A final problem is that IQ scores for different education levels vary by age. For older individuals, academic achievement was accomplished at a time when educational standards were more rigorous, and advanced education was not seen as a requirement for most forms of employment. Promotion through grades in elementary and high school was based on performance, with little concern about the social consequences of school failure. As a result, older individuals of a given level of academic achievement have higher IQs than younger individuals. In the WAIS–R standardization sample at all levels of education from 8 to 16 years, individuals in the 55–64 year age range have FSIQ scores that are approximately 5 points higher than individuals in the 35–44 year age range. Similar findings do not hold, however, for occupation.

Best Performance Method

Lezak (1983, 1995) proposed that the highest level of cognitive ability that a client has demonstrated, either on current (postmorbid) evaluation or in the past, should be used as the estimate of premorbid cognitive ability. This method examines current test scores, behavioral observations, reports from family or friends, previous test scores, prior academic or vocational achievement, and/or other historical information, with the highest performance serving to produce the estimate. The best performance method will invariably predict a higher level of premorbid functioning than other methods, and more often than not will estimate too high a level of premorbid functioning. It is easy to see why this would be true for non-brain-impaired subjects, given the performance scatter identified in the WAIS–R standardization sample. As an example, this method would suggest that the highest WAIS–R subtest score and the mean score across all 11 subtests should be about the same. This is obviously rarely the case. However, given that in neurologically impaired subjects all areas of cognitive ability may be somewhat impaired from premorbid levels (Russell, 1972), it could be that the remaining highest performance would best represent premorbid ability level. This possibility was investigated in a study by Mortensen et al. (1991). The results indicated that the best performance method leads to a gross overestimation of functioning (15 to 30 IQ points) for both neurologically normal subjects and patients with diffuse cerebral atrophy.

Traditional "Hold" Measures

The hold approach relies on measures that are considered to be relatively resistant to neurological impairment. For example, certain WAIS subtests have been posited to be relatively resistant to the effects of aging and/or brain impairment (Wechsler, 1958). Scores on these subtests (Vocabulary, Information,

Picture Completion, and Object Assembly) have therefore been used by some clinicians as the best estimate of premorbid functioning abilities, if they are substantially higher than scores on other subtests. Other approaches use performance on WAIS/WAIS–R Vocabulary (Yates, 1956), the average of Vocabulary and Picture Completion, or the highest of Vocabulary and Picture Completion, if one is substantially lower (McFie, 1975), as the best estimate of premorbid functioning.

The problems with the hold approach are obvious. Many types of brain damage significantly affect scores on hold measures. Left-hemisphere damage, with or without aphasia, will certainly impact verbal hold measures (Swiercinsky & Warnock, 1977). In fact, brain impairment can adversely affect performance on all of the Wechsler subtests (Russell, 1972). An additional problem is that hold approaches that employ only one or two measures (e.g., vocabulary) fail to account for the normal variability in cognitive ability in healthy individuals. Thus, if vocabulary were the weakest of premorbid abilities, a Vocabulary subtest score that did in fact hold would produce an underestimate of overall premorbid ability. Given these problems, it is not surprising that researchers have concluded that hold approaches are simplistic, inaccurate, and not supported by the literature (Klesges & Troster, 1987; Klesges, Wilkening, & Golden, 1981; Larrabee, Largen, & Levin, 1985).

Current Reading Measures: An Alternative Hold Approach

A substantial amount of research effort has been focused on the use of reading tests as predictors of premorbid cognitive function. Fortunately, this literature has been thoroughly reviewed by Franzen et al. (1997), and we provide an overview on the three most commonly researched instruments and the issues involved in their use.

Nelson and colleagues (Nelson & McKenna, 1975; Nelson & O'Connell, 1978) noted that scores on a reading test were less influenced than vocabulary performance following brain damage, and subsequently developed the National Adult Reading Test (NART; Nelson, 1982). The NART is composed of 50 "irregular" words that cannot be pronounced through the use of common phonetic rules (e.g., *yacht* or *naive*). The use of irregular words capitalizes on patients' premorbid familiarity with the words and has been found to be a more reliable indicator of premorbid ability than the reading of "regular" words (Hart, Smith, & Swash, 1986; Nelson & O'Connell, 1978). Use of NART scores to estimate WAIS IQ scores was initially found to produce standard errors of estimate of 7.6, 9.4, and 7.6 IQ points for VIQ, PIQ, and FSIQ, respectively in a British sample. The NART has subsequently been cross-validated and its psychometric properties were evaluated and found acceptable (Crawford, Parker, Stewart, Besson, & DeLacey, 1989). Crawford et al. (1989) then combined the original and cross-validation samples and reported refined regression equations to predict IQ scores.

The critical issue in the use of the NART is whether it is immune to the effects of brain damage. A series of studies have reported NART performance to be relatively resistant to cortical atrophy (Nelson & O'Connell, 1978), dementia of the Alzheimer's type (DAT; Nebes, Martin, & Horn, 1984; O'Carroll, Baikie, & Whittick, 1987; O'Carroll & Gilleard, 1986), a variety of other organic conditions (alcoholic dementia, multi-infarct dementia, and closed-head injury; Crawford, Besson, & Parker, 1988), depression (Crawford, Besson, Parker, Sutherland, & Keen, 1987), and schizophrenia, at least in outpatients (Crawford et al., 1992). However, results have not all been positive. Several studies have reported discrepancies between demented and control subjects on NART predicted IQ scores (Hart et al., 1986; Stebbins, Wilson, Gilley, Bernard, & Fox, 1990), particularly in moderately to severely demented subjects (Stebbins, Wilson, Gilley, Bernard, & Fox, 1990), suggesting that NART scores are influenced by dementia. Even in those with only mild dementia, the NART appears to underestimate IQ if there are accompanying language deficits (Stebbins, Gilley, Wilson, Bernard, & Fox, 1990).

Crawford and colleagues (Crawford, Stewart, Parker, Besson, & Cochrane, 1989) have combined performance on the NART with various demographic measures, reasoning that (a) unique variance to the two sets of measures might better relate to intellectual ability and thus together account for more IQ score variance, and (b) demographic variables may mediate the relationship between NART and IQ. Demographic variables included in the study were age, gender, education, and occupation (called *social class* in their study). With the exception of education, each demographic variable added significantly in stepwise regression equations for WAIS FSIQ, VIQ, and PIQ. Education was not included in final regression equations, which may be a problem. Cross-validation and construct validity studies have also been performed (Crawford, Nelson, Blackmore, Cochrane, & Allan, 1990; Crawford, Cochrane, Besson, Parker, & Stewart, 1990). These combined NART/demographic regression equations account for significantly more variance than either set of variables independently (combined = 73% FSIQ variance; NART alone = 66%; demographic alone = 50%), and the standard errors of measurement for these equations are slightly lower than those from the NART alone.

Unfortunately, the development, validation, and examination of the psychometric properties of the NART have been primarily based on British samples. Because of differences in spelling and pronunciation between British and American forms of English, the use of the NART with American samples is questionable.

Schwartz and Saffran (1987) developed a revision of the NART, which they call the AMNART (American version of the NART). They replaced 23 words from the British NART that were unfamiliar to American readers and standardized it on 109 normal adults ages 40–89 years. WAIS regression equations utilizing AMNART error scores and level of education were developed (Schwartz &

Saffran, 1987). A later validation study using discrepancies between predicted WAIS VIQ scores based on the AMNART and a prorated WAIS VIQ based on current performance on Information, Similarities, and Vocabulary scores showed acceptable sensitivity (.83) and specificity (.81) in differentiating demented from nondemented subjects (Grober, Sliwinski, Schwartz, & Saffran, 1989). Scores on the AMNART and years of education have subsequently been used to generate a WAIS–R VIQ regression equation, of which the utility was then evaluated in dementia determination (Grober & Sliwinski, 1991). AMNART/education-predicted premorbid WAIS–R VIQ scores did not differ between demented and nondemented subjects, whereas prorated WAIS–R VIQ scores did. In addition, AMNART estimated premorbid IQ appeared to be relatively unaffected by the presence of a mild language disturbance (Grober & Sliwinski, 1991). The addition of the demographic variable of education may account for the AMNART/education WAIS–R VIQ regression equation being less sensitive to mild language impairment than is the NART (Stebbins, Gilley, Wilson, Bernard, & Fox, 1990).

Blair and Spreen (1989) developed a third version of the NART (NART-R, also called the NAART, North American Adult Reading Test). They expanded and revised the NART word list for North American pronunciations (61 total items), and standardized it on a mixed Canadian and U.S. sample (N = 66). WAIS–R IQ prediction equations were developed. Although demographic variables were included in this study, they did not account for a significant amount of the variance beyond the use of NART–R error scores alone and were not included in the final prediction equations (failing to cross-validate the work of Crawford and his colleagues on the increased effectiveness of the combined NART–demographic equations). Standard errors of estimate were 6.56, 10.67, and 7.73 for WAIS–R VIQ, PIQ, and FSIQ, respectively, roughly comparable to the original NART.

As we noted earlier, support for more traditional hold measures such as various subtests from the WAIS–R (Information, Vocabulary, Picture Completion, and Object Assembly) is unimpressive because these subtests can be adversely affected by various types of brain injury. However, research is more encouraging regarding the use of reading of irregular words as a predictor of premorbid intellectual ability. In its various forms the NART has shown promise for premorbid intelligence estimation of WAIS/WAIS–R VIQ and FSIQ. It is a less effective predictor of PIQ. Although the NART may do an adequate job of estimating premorbid levels of language-based abilities, it is not reasonable to assume that it should predict performance on nonverbal measures. Consistent with this is the finding that the NART accounts for approximately twice the WAIS Verbal IQ variance (60%) compared to Performance IQ variance (32%) (Nelson, 1982). The discrepancy for the NART–R is even greater, 69% of WAIS–R VIQ variance but only 16% for PIQ (Blair & Spreen, 1989).

Including demographic variables in NART IQ predictor regression equations significantly increases the amount of WAIS IQ score variance explained. However, this has not been the case for the NART–R. The AMNART regression equation for WAIS–R VIQ includes only the demographic variable of education. In future studies with larger samples it may be that including additional demographic variables with the AMNART or NART–R will increase their predictive power and accuracy. The inclusion of demographic variables in AMNART or NART–R IQ regression equations should make them more resistant to the effects of neurological impairment. However, all hold approaches to premorbid estimation will invariably be affected by some types of brain damage. In the case of the NART, a dominant-hemisphere injury resulting in even a mild alexia will negate its utility.

At this time WAIS–R regression equations (at least VIQ) are available for the NART–R and the AMNART, and only these measures are appropriate for use with patients in North America.

Regression Methods Using Demographic Data

Regression equations using demographic information to predict premorbid cognitive function are appealing because they eliminate the subjectivity inherent in purely clinical approaches. In addition, they can account for the multivariate nature of relationships among variables whereas a clinician-based tabular approach cannot. Based on data from the standardization samples, such regression equations have been developed to predict IQ scores for both the WAIS (Wilson, Rosenbaum, Brown, Rourke, & Whitman, 1978) and the WAIS–R (Barona et al., 1984). Table 2.4 contains the WAIS–R demographically based regression equations.

Cross-validation studies of the WAIS (Wilson et al., 1978) and WAIS–R (Barona et al., 1984) regression formulas have been mixed. Typically, examination of group data shows that these regression equations do an adequate job of predicting mean IQ scores. However, at the individual level the equations predict IQ scores outside of the actual IQ range of subjects (e.g., High Average range) more than half the time. As might be expected, the equations perform best when actual ability falls within the Average range, while tending to underestimate high IQ scores and overestimate low IQ scores. The distribution of predicted FSIQ scores using the regression formula for the WAIS ranges from about 55 to 150; however, the FSIQ range using the formula for the WAIS–R is much more restricted, running from 69 to 120.

Studies of the WAIS regression formulas using patients referred for evaluation who were judged to either be recovered head trauma cases (Bolter, Gouvier, Veneklasen, & Long, 1982; Gouvier, Bolter, Veneklasen, & Long, 1983) or pseudoneurologic (Klesges, Fisher, Vasey, & Pheley, 1985) have been disappointing. These studies reported either low correlations between obtained WAIS IQ scores and predicted scores, or marginal levels of correct classification (defined as correct if within one standard error of measurement). Summarizing across

TABLE 2.4
Demographically Based Regression Formulas
for Estimating Wechsler IQ Scores

Estimated IQ Score	Formula
WAIS–R VIQ	54.23 + 0.49 (age) + 1.92 (sex) + 4.24 (race) + 5.25 (educ.) + 1.89 (occup.) + 1.24 (U-R resid.) $SE_e = 11.79$; $R^2 = .38$
WAIS–R PIQ	61.58 + 0.31 (age) + 1.09 (sex) + 4.95 (race) + 3.75 (educ.) + 1.54 (occup.) + 0.82 (region) $SE_e = 13.23$; $R^2 = .24$
WAIS–R FSIQ	54.96 + 0.47 (age) + 1.76 (sex) + 4.71 (race) + 5.02 (educ.) + 1.89 (occup.) + 0.59 (region) $SE_e = 12.14$; $R^2 = .36$

Sex:	Female = 1, male = 2
Race:	Black = 1, other ethnicity = 2, White = 3
Educ:	0–7 years = 1, 8 = 2, 9–11 = 3, 12 = 4, 13–15 = 5, 16+ = 6
Age:	16–17 years = 1, 18–19 = 2, 20–24 = 3, 25–34 = 4, 35–44 = 5, 45–54 = 6, 55–64 = 7, 65–69 = 8, 70–74 = 9
Region:	Southern = 1, North Central = 2, Western = 3, Northeastern = 4
Residence:	Rural = 1, urban = 2
Occupation:	Farm laborers, farm foremen, and laborers (unskilled) = 1
	Operatives, service workers, farmers, and farm managers (semiskilled) = 2
	Not in labor force = 3
	Craftsmen and foremen (skilled workers) = 4
	Managers, officials, proprietors, clerical, and sales workers = 5
	Professional and technical = 6

Note. SE_e = Standard Error of Estimate. Formulas and Standard Errors of Estimate (SE_e) from Barona, Reynolds, & Chastain (1984) for the WAIS–R. Reprinted with permission.

these studies, Klesges and Troster (1987) concluded that the classification power of these WAIS regression formulas was "rarely beyond chance levels" (p. 6). However, as Crawford (1989) pointed out, these studies are methodologically flawed. In particular, the utilization of clinical samples in these cross-validation attempts is problematic. At least at some point in time subjects were seen as clinically impaired; whether or not they had fully recovered at the time of the study is certainly debatable. In clinical samples, correlations between predicted and obtained scores should be lower than in nonclinical populations, and predicted scores would be expected to exceed obtained scores. Both were the case in these studies.

Two general approaches have been utilized to examine the predictive accuracy of WAIS/WAIS–R regression equations. One approach is to determine what proportion of predicted scores fall within one standard error of estimate (SE_e) of the actual scores of subjects (Bolter et al., 1982; Eppinger, Craig, Adams, & Parsons, 1987; Gouvier et al., 1983). Because SE_e values are standard deviations, predicted scores should fall outside plus or minus one SE_e of the actual scores only 32% of the time, regardless of the IQ level of the score. A second approach is to investigate what proportion of the predicted scores falls within the same IQ range (e.g., Borderline, Low Average, Average, High Average) as the actual scores (Sweet, Moberg, & Tovian, 1990). The second approach is clinically more meaningful, but is also a more stringent criterion. Standard errors of estimate are about 10 IQ points for the WAIS and 12 points for the WAIS–R regression equations, thus allowing a possible acceptable range of 20–24 points. (These are large "acceptable ranges" and may be too large to be clinically useful.) On the other hand, outside of the Average range, which does have a spread of 20 IQ points, IQ ranges consist of a spread of only 10 points.

Goldstein, Gary, and Levin (1986) investigated the accuracy of the WAIS regression equations for estimating premorbid intelligence in 69 neurologically normal adults. They reported that linear relationships did exist between predicted and actual IQ scores for all three scales, Verbal, Performance, and Full Scale. In addition, statistical analysis did not find a significant difference between predicted and actual IQ scores. However, the slopes of their three regression lines were significantly different from 1.0, indicating that some predicted scores were overestimates and others underestimates of the actual values. By examining their scatter plots of the data it is possible to analyze the percent of predicted scores that fell within one SE_e or within the same IQ range as actual scores. The results of these analysis are disappointing. The Wilson et al. (1978) regression formulas correctly classified subjects within the obtained WAIS IQ range less than half the time: 48%, 46%, and 49% for VIQ, PIQ, and FSIQ, respectively. As would be expected, the percentages of predicted scores within one SE_e of actual scores were higher, 66%, 66%, and 64% for VIQ, PIQ, and FSIQ, respectively.

A more recent study using 77 neurologically normal psychiatric subjects evaluated with the WAIS–R obtained similar results (Sweet et al., 1990). Eight IQ points were subtracted from the WAIS regression predicted scores to correct for the use of the WAIS–R rather than the WAIS (see Karzmark, Heaton, Grant, & Matthews, 1985). The percentages of corrected WAIS-predicted IQ scores that fell within the same IQ range as the obtained WAIS–R scores were only 32%, 40%, and 40% for VIQ, PIQ, and FSIQ, respectively. The WAIS–R regression equations (Barona et al., 1984) were similarly ineffective in correctly classifying subjects within the obtained WAIS–R IQ range: 35%, 40%, and 39% for VIQ, PIQ, and FSIQ, respectively. In addition, the WAIS–R formulas never predicted scores outside of low average, average, or high average ranges, although both uncorrected and corrected WAIS formulas did. This is not surprising in that the possible predictive range of the WAIS–R formulas is only 69 to 120 (Barona et al., 1984). Sweet et al. (1990) concluded that "neither formula does better than a judgment of intellectual classification formed on base rates alone" (p. 43).

There have been two additional studies that reported more favorable results, one regarding the WAIS regression equations (Karzmark et al., 1985), and the other for the WAIS–R (Eppinger et al., 1987). However, some of the findings in both studies were statistical anomalies; therefore, the results should be viewed with caution. Karzmark et al. (1985) reported a high, 70% predictive accuracy (predicted IQ score within a generous ±10 points of actual score) for the WAIS FSIQ regression equation in a sample of subjects with no history of neurological risk factors. In addition, they reported finding "a progressive shift from under-estimation of FSIQ at the lower levels of predicted FSIQ to over-estimation at the higher levels" (p. 416). They also found predictive accuracy to be worse for scores within the average range (67%) than for above average scores (72–77%). These findings run counter to what is expected with regression analyses. Regression analyses by their very nature will regress extreme scores toward the mean, not away from the mean as was reported. In fact, as would be expected, the predicted FSIQ mean of the sample (110.9) was regressed from the actual group mean (112.8) toward the population mean of 100. In addition, with regression analyses predictive accuracy should be best within the average range, not in the high average to very superior range as found.

Eppinger et al. (1987) reported similarly high levels of predictive accuracy for the WAIS–R regression equations in a neurologically normal sample: 75%, 71%, and 69% for VIQ, PIQ, and FSIQ, respectively. In this case accuracy was defined as predicted IQ scores within one SE_e of actual scores (±12–13 IQ points). What makes the results of this study anomalous is that the regression equations accounted for more variance in this cross-validation sample than in the original Barona et al. (1984) study. Cross-validation studies almost always result in a drop in the amount of variance accounted for by the original formulas, not an increase. Thus, the sample in this study may be nonrepresentative of the population, and the favorable findings may not be generalizable.

In conclusion, by base rates, always predicting an average level of premorbid functioning would result in a correct IQ range prediction 50% of the time. The challenge is to correctly predict premorbid functioning outside of the average range. Regression equations have not been particularly useful in this regard, as repeated studies have found (for WAIS: Bolter et al., 1982; Goldstein et al., 1986; Gouvier et al., 1983; Klesges et al., 1985; for WAIS and WAIS–R: Sweet et al., 1990). Although these WAIS/WAIS–R regression formulas appear to be generally reliable for groups of patients (Eppinger et al., 1987; Goldstein et al., 1986; Karzmark et al., 1985), there is no assurance that they will be accurate for individual cases. Unfortunately, it is the individual case, not the group, that faces the practicing clinical neuropsychologist. In the clinical situation, regression formulas at best provide a general range as to expected level of functioning, but they cannot be relied on for an accurate estimate in the individual case.

Regression Methods Using Both
Demographic and Current Ability Measures

Recently some investigators have developed regression equations to predict WAIS–R IQ scores employing both demographic information and ability scores as predictors variables. To date the ability scores examined have included different forms of the NART (Crawford, Nelson, Blackmore, Cochran, & Allan, 1990; Grober & Sliwinski, 1991; Schwartz & Saffran, 1987) and WAIS–R subtests (Krull, Scott, & Sherer, 1995; Vanderploeg & Schinka, 1995). A study by Vanderploeg and Schinka (1995) is representative of this approach to premorbid prediction. WAIS–R Verbal subtests were better predictors of Verbal IQ scores, whereas Performance subtests better predicted Performance IQ. Verbal subtests were superior to Performance subtests in prediction of Full Scale IQ.

Vanderploeg and Schinka used individuals from the WAIS–R standardization sample (Wechsler, 1981) to develop regression formulas that used predictors including age, education, occupation, race, and a WAIS–R subtest scaled score. Given the finding that any WAIS–R subtest may be impaired following brain injury, no subtest was determined a priori to be a hold measure. Instead, separate regression formulas were developed, each combining 1 of the 11 WAIS–R subtests with demographic variables, to predict IQ scores. Vanderploeg and Schinka reasoned that the availability of these formulas allows the clinician to determine which subtest(s) are likely to be the best hold measure(s) in any particular case. A number of these equations doubled the amount of IQ variance accounted for compared to the demographic variable equations of Barona et al. (1984). Similarly, the equations generally accounted for more variance in actual IQ than the previously developed NART/demographic WAIS IQ regression equations (Crawford et al., 1990) or the AMNART/education WAIS–R VIQ regression equation (Grober & Sliwinski, 1991).

For most of the regression equations, 50% or more of the standardization sample obtained predicted scores within a ±6–7 point range of their actual IQ scores. Regression to the mean was not a significant problem; potential ranges extended from lows of 60 to highs of 146. As expected, WAISR Verbal subtests were better predictors of Verbal IQ scores, whereas Performance subtests better predicted Performance IQ. Verbal subtests were superior to Performance subtests in prediction of Full Scale IQ. Two traditional WAIS hold measures (Information and Vocabulary), when included with demographic variables, provided the best predictors of Verbal and Full Scale IQ. Block Design, Picture Completion, and Object Assembly, when included with demographic variables, provided the best predictors of Performance IQ. Although Block Design is generally not a good hold measure following brain injury, Picture Completion can be (Kaufman, 1990; McFie, 1969). In discussing their results within the perspective of research on the effects of brain damage on WAIS/WAIS–R performance, the authors concluded that the WAIS–R Picture Completion subtest is likely to be the best hold measure following left-hemisphere injury, whereas Comprehension, Information, and Vocabulary may all be relatively good hold measures following right-hemisphere impairment.

In a subsequent two-part study (Vanderploeg, Schinka, & Axelrod, 1996), FSIQ, VIQ, and PIQ scores were predicted using the highest score from all 11

Vanderploeg and Schinka (1995) regression equations (termed the BEST-11 approach) and from the three most robust of the regression equations (i.e., those based on Information, Vocabulary, and Picture Completion; termed the BEST-3 approach). These results were compared to estimates based solely on demographic information (Barona et al., 1984). First, these methods were evaluated in the WAIS–R standardization sample. The BEST methods were more highly correlated with actual WAIS–R IQ than were the Barona et al. (1984) estimates. Within this normal population, the BEST-11 approach resulted in overestimates of approximately 9 points, while the BEST-3 approach averaged 5 points over actual performance. The second part of the study applied the BEST-3 and Barona et al. (1984) estimation techniques to samples of neurologic patients and matched normal controls. Correlations between actual and estimated IQ scores were significantly higher for the BEST-3 method than for the Barona et al. (1984) method in both control (BEST-3: FSIQ $r = .86$, VIQ $r = .85$, PIQ $r = .82$; Barona: FSIQ $r = .61$, VIQ $r = .61$, PIQ $r = .54$) and brain-injured samples (BEST-3: FSIQ $r = .74$, VIQ $r = .81$, PIQ $r = .50$; Barona: FSIQ $r = .46$, VIQ $r = .47$, PIQ $r = .33$). More importantly, discrepancies between BEST-3 predicted IQ scores and actual IQ scores were superior at predicting group membership (normal vs. brain-damaged), than were discrepancies between Barona et al. (1984) predicted IQ scores and actual IQ scores. These results support the use of premorbid estimation techniques that use current WAIS–R subtest performance in conjunction with demographic information (BEST-3). In addition, the BEST-3 accounted for more variance in prediction of FSIQ, VIQ, and PIQ than previous studies have found for the NART–R/AMNART (with or without demographic information included). Table 2.5 contains the coding system necessary to calculate the BEST-3 IQ scores, and Table 2.6 contains the equations.

Independently, Krull et al. (1995) developed a regression equation to predict premorbid FSIQ that was based on WAIS–R Vocabulary and Picture Completion subtest performance plus demographic information. Their approach differed from that originally proposed by Vanderploeg and Schinka in that they used a different coding system for demographic variables, employed subtest raw scores rather than scaled scores, and included two WAIS–R subtests within the same regression equation. Their method has come to be known as the Oklahoma Premorbid Intelligence Estimate (OPIE). In a recent study, Axelrod, Vanderploeg, and Schinka (1999) found that BEST-3 and OPIE methods were comparable.

Population-Specific Normative Tables

An alternative to generating estimates of premorbid functioning for one or more domains of ability is using subpopulation specific norms. Thus, if a patient was a 38-year-old male with 14 years of education, his performance might be compared to a normative group of other 35- to 40-year-old males with 13 to 15 years of education. The diagnostic decision of whether or not a decline in cognitive functioning has occurred would depend on whether this patient showed a level of performance that fell significantly below the typical performance of this demographically similar group. Significantly below typical might be defined by the clinician as at less than the 5th percentile for this demographically matched group. Vanderploeg, Axelrod, Sherer, Scott, and Adams (1997) showed that

TABLE 2.5
Predictor Variable Codes for the WAIS–R BEST-3
Premorbid Predictor Equations

Sex:	Male = 1, female = 2
Race:	White = 1, other ethnicity = 0
Age:	16–17 years = 1, 18–19 = 2, 20–24 = 3, 25–34 = 4, 35–44 = 5, 45–54 = 6, 55–64 = 7, 65–69 = 8, 70–74 = 9
Education:	0–7 years = 1, 8 = 2, 9–11 = 3, 12 = 4, 13–15 = 5, 16+ = 6
Occupation:	Unemployed = 1
	Farm laborers, farm foremen, and laborers (unskilled) = 2
	Operatives, service workers, farmers, and farm managers (semiskilled) = 3
	Craftsmen and foremen (skilled workers) = 4
	Managers, officials, proprietors, clerical, and sales workers = 5
	Professional and technical = 6
SES:	Sum of education code and occupation code[a]
	(If unemployed, SES = 2 × Education)[b]

[a]Example for SES code: For a craftsman (coded 4 on Occupation) with 10 years of Education (coded 3), SES = 4 + 3 = 7.

[b]Example: For an unemployed individual with 14 years of education (coded 5), SES = 2 × 5 = 10.

TABLE 2.6
Regression Equations for the BEST-3 Approach

Regression Equation	SE_e	R^2
WAIS–R FSIQ = 3.55(Information) + 1.00(SES) + 58.70	9.10	.64
WAIS–R FSIQ = 3.78(Vocabulary) + 0.70(SES) + 59.09	8.64	.68
WAIS–R FSIQ = 2.94(Picture Completion) + 2.13(SES) + 1.62(AGE) + 49.41	9.57	.60
WAIS–R VIQ = 3.71(Information) + 1.01(SES) + 57.11	7.97	.72
WAIS–R VIQ = 3.96(Vocabulary) + 0.70(SES) + 57.49	7.35	.76
WAIS–R VIQ = 2.66(SES) + 2.10(Picture Completion) + 1.40(AGE) + 53.79	10.53	.50
WAIS–R PIQ = 2.55(Information) + 6.69(RACE) + 0.77(SES) + 64.05	11.82	.39
WAIS–R PIQ = 2.99(Vocabulary) + 5.84(RACE) + 66.84	11.72	.40
WAIS–R PIQ = 3.51(Picture Completion) + 1.54(AGE) + 0.93(SES) + 4.65(RACE) + 49.97	9.31	.62

Note. Based on the WAIS–R standardization sample of 1880 adults. SE_e = Standard Error of Estimate. WAIS–R subtest scaled scores (not age-adjusted scaled scores) are used in the equations. The BEST-3 IQ score would be the predicted score from any one of the three equations above that resulted in the highest score, for FSIQ, VIQ, or PIQ, respectively. Data from the standardization data of the Wechsler Adult Intelligence Scale–Revised. Copyright © 1981 by The Psychological Corporation. Used by permission. All rights reserved.

using such demographically matched norms significantly improved diagnostic accuracy compared to using general population normative data.

Several researchers have provided normative data, based on demographic characteristics, that allow comparisons of a patient's current performance with that of normal peers. For example, Williams (1992) provided normative tables for the Memory Assessment Scales based on gender, age, and education. Similar norms have been provided by Heaton, Grant, and Matthews (1991) for the Halstead–Reitan battery. Such tables are attractive in that they allow a comparison with a sample of normals sharing certain demographic features, and thereby increase certain diagnostic decisions (e.g., brain impairment vs. no impairment).

The use of demographically specific normative tables in premorbid estimation does have shortcomings, however. They are typically based, at most, on the three variables of age, gender, and education. The failure to include other demographic characteristics, such as occupation, that correlate substantially with cognitive ability limits the predictive power of this approach. In addition, this approach results in the clinician being able to describe the patient relative to a narrow demographically matched group, which may not be useful as describing the patient compared to the general normal adult population. For example, stating that Mr. M's performance on visuospatial measures is at the 5th percentile compared to other 45-year-old individuals with college degrees is not as useful for vocational rehabilitation planning purposes as stating that his performance is at the 20th percentile compared to the general normal adult population. It is for this reason that Williams (1992) provides both demographically specific norms and general adult norms for the Memory Assessment Scales. In some demographic groups for some cognitive domains the two comparisons may be quite similar, whereas for other domains the comparisons would be quite different. We view these limitations as factors that significantly limit the utility of this approach to dealing with the premorbid comparisons.

RECOMMENDATIONS FOR PREDICTING PREMORBID FUNCTIONING IN ADULTS

Before providing specific recommendations about premorbid estimation procedures, we feel it is critical to discuss briefly issues related to clinical judgment. It is well known that the use of statistical or actuarial formulas, and not unassisted clinical judgment, provides the highest rates of diagnostic accuracy in a variety of tasks (Grove & Meehl, 1996). Demonstrations of the failure of clinicians to employ predictor information accurately in neuropsychology are not difficult to find. For example, Kareken and Williams (1994) had clinical neuropsychologists estimate the IQs of cases using the demographic variables employed by Barona et al. (1984) to develop their prediction equations. They found that the clinicians greatly overemphasized education in making predictions and underestimated the error in prediction substantially. Kareken (1997) reviewed this literature from the perspective of neuropsychology and listed several factors that can contribute to inaccuracy in clinical prediction. We briefly discuss two of the factors identified by Kareken that we believe are particularly robust, and that actually represent two extremes in the prediction process. The first factor is overrepresenting the size of the relationship between a predictor variable and the dependent variable. The Kareken and Williams (1994) study provided an excellent example of this problem—their clinicians believed that the correlation between education and WAIS–R VIQ was .85 (the actual value is .56), and their predictions revealed an r of .83 between education and VIQ. Overrepresentation of a predictor-dependent variable relationship can thus lead to heavy reliance on a single predictor. At the other extreme, however, is the problem of reliance on multiple predictors, some of which may not contribute to accuracy. Thus, clinicians run the risk of losing accuracy when they incorporate too many variables in their predictions. For example, it may be tempting to consider a patient's national region of origin (e.g., the South), in addition to education and occupation, to refine further an estimated IQ. Region of origin, however, has been shown to have only a negligible relationship to IQ (Vanderploeg & Schinka, 1995), and its inclusion in clinical estimation would likely contribute only to error.

Are there situations in which clinical judgment should be used in estimating premorbid cognitive status? We believe clinical judgment can play an important role in the *application* of statistical/actuarial methods in premorbid estimation, primarily in determining the exceptions to straightforward application of the formulas. To illustrate, we cite a recent example from our own practices. The case involved estimation for a 45-year-old White male who sustained a head injury in a motor vehicle accident several months prior to evaluation. He had completed 11 years of education in the public school system and had been employed as an appliance repairman for the past 20 years. Application of the Barona et al. (1984) formula suggests an estimated WAIS–R FSIQ of 99. Information from a detailed clinical interview, however, revealed information suggesting that the formula might be an underestimate. This individual had been an A to B+ student when his father died, forcing him to leave school to help support his family. For several years he worked in unskilled factory jobs until a family friend hired him as an apprentice in appliance repair. He learned these skills easily and made a reasonable living thereafter, marrying young and supporting a family with several children. In addition to meeting the demands of his job and family, he had developed a strong interest in personal computers and was responsible for establishing and maintaining the computer services of his large church, including software for full bookkeeping system, membership maintenance, newsletter production, and so on. He was also responsible for training and supervising staff. He saw this activity, performed on evenings and weekends, as an avocation and an opportunity to contribute to his church. In addition, his

WAIS–R performance on the current evaluation revealed Vocabulary and Picture Completion scaled scores of 12, although his Information scaled score was 9. Given the details of this individual's admittedly unusual history, the Barona et al. formula would appear to underestimate substantially the individual's premorbid level. We assumed that this individual would have completed a four-year college education, if he had had the opportunity to do so, and that his volunteer work at church was equivalent to that of an office manager. Using those adjusted demographic values in the Barona equation resulted in a predicted FSIQ of 116. Using the BEST-3 approach with the adjusted demographic values resulted in a predicted FSIQ of 118. Thus we adjusted our estimate of his premorbid FSIQ from 99 to being within the range of 115 to 120.

Algorithm for Estimating Premorbid Level of Cognitive Ability

Based on our review of the extant literature, we have developed an algorithm for selecting a method to estimate premorbid level(s) of functioning. Use of the algorithm is straightforward; instructions are provided at each step.

1. Use the results from an individually administered battery of cognitive tests administered prior to any suspected neurological impairment (e.g., WAIS–R). Use the 90% confidence interval to develop a "window of expected performance" for the neuropsychological evaluation. Go to step 6 to determine if modifications to the estimated window of performance should be considered. If these data are not available, go to step 2.

2. Use the results from prior tests or batteries of academic aptitude or achievement, whether administered individually or in a group format. Use percentile scores to provide an estimated window of performance for the neuropsychological evaluation. Go to step 6 to determine if modifications to the estimated window of performance should be considered. If these data are not available, go to step 3.

3. If the WAIS–R is being used in the neuropsychological evaluation, use the BEST-3 method (Vanderploeg et al., 1996) to calculate separately VIQ and PIQ. These formulas, and the method for determining VIQ and PIQ, are provided in Tables 2.5 and 2.6. Go to step 6 to determine if modifications to the estimated window of performance should be considered. If these data are not available, go to step 4.

However, there is a caveat to step 3. In normal individuals the BEST-3 approach is known to overestimate IQ by 5 to 6 points. In addition, research has shown that there is recovery of function over time following cerebral insults. Therefore, the BEST-3 may overestimate premorbid functioning in several cases: (a) individuals suspected of having a brain injury but who in fact do not, (b) individuals with minor or mild brain injuries, and (c) individuals with mild to moderate brain injuries who are a year or more postinsult. In these cases it may be prudent to proceed to step 4, or at least to cross-check the results of step 3 by comparison with steps 4 and/or 5.

4. If the WAIS–R is not being used in the neuropsychological evaluation, use the AMNART to estimate VIQ and the Barona et al. formula (1984) to estimate PIQ. Go to step 6 to determine if modifications to the estimated window of performance should be considered. If these data are not available, go to step 5.

5. If the AMNART is not being used in the neuropsychological evaluation, estimate both VIQ and PIQ using the Barona et al. (1984) formulas. Go to step 6 to determine if modifications to the estimated window of performance should be considered.

6. Examine details of clinical history to determine if there are strong reasons to adjust the estimated window of performance. Pay particular attention to cases in which there are indications that the individual has not been able to achieve in the educational and occupational arena because of limited opportunity. Table 2.3 provides data of WAIS–R IQ equivalents for levels of academic and occupational achievement that can be used as reference points, or adjusted demographic values can be used to recalculate regression formulas.

WAIS–III Caveat

During the development of this chapter, the Wechsler Adult Intelligence Scale–III (WAIS–III; Wechsler, 1997) was released. Although the release of the battery was accompanied by a technical manual providing substantial information on the battery's psychometric characteristics, data (e.g., IQ equivalents for levels of education and general occupational groups) or equations for estimating premorbid WAIS–III IQ scores were not provided. However, some data are presented that provide cross-estimation of WAIS–R and WAIS–III IQ scores. Thus, it is possible to use the Barona et al. (1984) approach to premorbid estimation. These WAIS–R IQ estimates would then have to be translated to WAIS–III IQ scores by reference to the *WAIS–III WMS-III Technical Manual* (Psychological Corporation, 1997, Table 4.2, p. 80). But, as we have discussed, the Barona et al. approach is a relatively ineffective premorbid prediction strategy, although better than none.

We believe that estimation research with previous editions of the WAIS battery indicates that regression approaches that combined demographic and current ability measures are the best candidates for premorbid prediction accuracy. To date, the BEST-3 and OPIE approaches account for more variance in IQ scores than any other premorbid prediction approach and result in the highest prediction accuracy of impairment versus no impairment. Given these findings, predictor variables of WAIS–III performance that have the highest likelihood of a substantial contribution to accurate prediction include demographic characteristics (especially education, occupation, and age), select WAIS–III subtests

(Information, Vocabulary, and Picture Completion are the best candidates), and performance on a reading test such as the AMNART. In the meantime, until the development of such regression equations, WAIS–III users are left with alternatives that are less than ideal.

METHODS OF ESTIMATING PREMORBID COGNITIVE ABILITY IN CHILDREN

Approaches to premorbid estimation in children have received far less research attention than has been the case for adults. Estimation of premorbid function in children has encompassed only two of the methods used with adults: regression methods using demographic data, and regression methods using both demographic variables and current ability measures.

Reynolds and Gutkin (1979) used demographic variables from the Wechsler Intelligence Scale for Children–Revised (WISC–R, Wechsler, 1974) standardization data to develop regression equations to predict children's premorbid IQ scores. A stepwise regression procedure using the demographic variables of father's occupational status and child's gender, ethnicity, urban versus rural residence, and geographic region resulted in three equations with multiple correlations of .44, .44, and .37 with FSIQ, VIQ, and PIQ, respectively. These correlations are substantially lower than those reported by Barona et al. (1984), using the same methodology to predict WAIS–R IQ scores. This is not a surprising finding because regression estimates of children's IQ scores cannot take advantage of the two variables that correlate most highly with IQ—education and occupation.

Vanderploeg, Schinka, Baum, Tremont, and Mittenberg (1998) subsequently conducted a series of regression analyses to predict Wechsler Intelligence Scale for Children–Third Edition IQ scores (WISC–III, Wechsler, 1991), using data from the WISC–III standardization sample. Following Reynolds and Gutkin (1979) and Barona et al. (1984), they first used demographic variables including parental education, parental occupation, and ethnicity in stepwise multiple regression analyses to determine demographic-based premorbid prediction equations. Predicted IQ scores correlated with FSIQ, VIQ, and PIQ at .53, .52, and .45, respectively. These were somewhat higher than the correlations found by Reynolds and Gutkin (1979) for the WISC–R.

Following Vanderploeg and Schinka (1995) and Vanderploeg et al. (1996), Vanderploeg et al. (1998) then conducted a second study to examine the predictive power of combining demographic variables and current ability measures in the regression analyses. The 10 standard subtests individually served as measures of present ability, whereas ethnicity and parental education served as the demographic predictors. These equations doubled or tripled the amount of variance accounted for by demographic variables alone.

The pure demographic prediction approach was then compared with two of the individual formulas (Vocabulary plus demographics and Picture Completion plus demographics) and with a BEST-2 approach (the highest predicted score from the two FSIQ, VIQ, and PIQ regression-based equations from the initial study that included either Vocabulary or Picture Completion) in a clinical sample of brain-injured children and a matched control sample. The pure demographic-based approach was equally effective as the BEST-2 approach, both of which were significantly more effective than using the Vocabulary plus demographics or Picture Completion plus demographics individual formulas. (These equations are presented in Table 2.7.) The comparability of the BEST-2 and demographic approaches was a somewhat unexpected finding, because in adults an approach combining demographic with current ability in a best performance fashion was more effective than a pure demographic approach (i.e., the BEST-3 approach described by Vanderploeg et al., 1996).

TABLE 2.7
Regression Equations Predicting WISC–III IQ Scores

Equations	SE_e	R^2
Demographic-based		
FSIQ = 5.44(Mean Educ.) + 2.80(White/nonwhite) − 9.01(Black/nonblack) + 81.68	12.56	.28
VIQ = 5.71(Mean Educ.) + 4.64(White/nonwhite) − 5.04(Black/nonblack) + 79.06	12.79	.27
PIQ = 4.18(Mean Educ.) + 0.26(White/nonwhite) − 11.85(Black/nonblack) + 88.09	13.35	.20
Current ability plus Demographic-based		
FSIQ = 3.46(Vocabl) + 2.25(White/nonwhite) − 4.39(Black/nonblack) + 64.78	8.74	.65
FSIQ = 2.58(P Compl) + 3.75(Mean Educ.) + 2.50(White/nonwhite)		
− 3.45(Black/nonblack) + 60.81	9.96	.55
VIQ = 3.91(Vocabl) + 3.49(White/nonwhite) − 0.11(Black/nonblack) + 58.97	7.42	.76
VIQ = 1.84(P Compl) + 4.50(Mean Educ.) + 4.43(White/nonwhite)		
− 1.09(Black/nonblack) + 64.20	11.57	.40
PIQ = 2.36(Vocabl) + 0.45(White/nonwhite) − 8.40(Black/nonblack) + 77.64	11.99	.35
PIQ = 2.97(P Compl) + 2.23(Mean Educ.) − 0.09(White/nonwhite)		
− 5.45(Black/nonblack) + 64.07	10.02	.55

Note. Based on a subset of the WISC–III standardization sample composed of 2,123 children and adolescents. SE_e = Standard Error of Estimate. Data from the standardization data of the Wechsler Intelligence Scale for Children–3rd edition. Copyright © 1991 by The Psychological Corporation. Used by permission. All rights reserved.
Ethnicity: White/nonwhite: White = 1, nonwhite = 0; Black/nonblack: Black = 1, nonblack = 0. Parental education: 0–8 years = 1, 9–11 = 2, 12 (or GED) = 3, 13–15 = 4, 16+ = 5. Ethnicity is composed of two variables: White/nonwhite and Black/nonblack. The study in which the regression equations were developed had ethnic information for only three categories: White, Black, and Hispanic. Therefore, the regression equations should not be used with other ethnic groups (Hispanics would be uniquely identified with codes of 0 on both White/nonwhite and Black/nonblack).
Mean parental education equals the mean of the education code from both parents; if information for only one parent is available, that becomes the mean parental education code to use in the regression equations.

Vanderploeg et al. (1998) questioned why the BEST-2 method wasn't more effective than the demographic approach, given the superiority of the BEST-3 method over a method based solely on demographic variables in a study with adults (Vanderploeg et al., 1996). They proposed three possible reasons, all of which point to methodological issues that are likely to be important in any study of premorbid estimation in children. First, they noted that the utility of current ability measures as predictors of premorbid functioning rests on their resilience to the effects of brain injury; that is, they should be stable, crystallized abilities. Although subtests such as Vocabulary and Picture Completion are stable, crystallized measures in adults, they may not be so in children, despite the fact that children do acquire competence in developing a lexicon and in visual perceptual skills. Second, regardless of the stability of existing vocabulary and visual perceptual competence, these abilities are undergoing relatively rapid development in children. In their study, however, the mean interval between injury and testing was only 6.6 days. Thus it seems unlikely that in this period of time a brain-injured subject would fall behind an age-matched peer in ongoing development of vocabulary or visual perceptual abilities. Third, given the recent nature of the brain injuries, it is possible that acute factors other than the severity of the actual brain damage may have adversely affected current performance on Vocabulary and Picture Completion. This could have served to undermine their effectiveness as premorbid predictors in the BEST-2 approach. Vanderploeg et al. concluded that given the finding that the purely demographic-based approach was just as effective as the more complicated BEST-2 approach, it may be a better choice for premorbid estimation in children. Furthermore, because of the ongoing cognitive development of children, if a current ability measure (e.g., a WISC–III subtest) is sampled more than 8 to 12 months following a presumed cerebral insult, a child also may have fallen developmentally behind his or her peer age group. Thus, utility of the subtest–demographic formulas and BEST-2 approach may be limited if used many months after recovery from the acute effects of any presumed cerebral insult. This limitation would not apply to the purely demographic-based formulas.

In predicting premorbid cognitive ability, we recommend calculating both the purely demographic and the BEST-2 predicted scores for FSIQ, VIQ, and PIQ. These scores would provide a baseline window of expected premorbid functioning that might be adjusted as described earlier under step 6 of adult premorbid recommendations.

Remember that if a current ability approach such as the BEST-2 predicts a higher score than a purely demographic approach in a patient who clearly sustained some type of injury to the brain, the higher score is likely a better premorbid estimate. Brain injury would not increase current functioning, so higher predicted scores based in part on hold or current ability measures would be a better premorbid estimate than a lower score based simply on demographic data. This would be true for both child and adult premorbid prediction.

REFERENCES

Axelrod, B. N., Vanderploeg, R. D., and Schinka, J. A. (1999). Comparing methods for estimating premorbid intellectual functioning. *Archives of Clinical Neuropsychology, 14*, 341–346.

Barona, A., Reynolds, C. R., & Chastain, R. (1984). A demographically based index of premorbid intelligence for the WAIS–R. *Journal of Consulting and Clinical Psychology, 52*, 885–887.

Blair, J. R., & Spreen, O. (1989). Predicting premorbid IQ: A revision of the National Adult Reading Test. *Clinical Neuropsychologist, 3*, 129–136.

Bolter, J., Gouvier, W., Veneklasen, J., & Long, C. (1982). Using demographic information to predict IQ: A test of clinical validity with head trauma patients. *Clinical Neuropsychology, 4*, 171–174.

Carroll, J. B. (1993). *Human cognitive abilities.* Cambridge: Cambridge University Press.

Crawford, J. R. (1989). Estimation of premorbid intelligence: A review of recent developments. In J. R. Crawford & D. M. Parker (Eds.)., *Developments in clinical and experimental neuropsychology* (pp. 55–74). New York: Plenum Press.

Crawford, J. R., Besson, J. A. O., Bremner, M., Ebmeier, K. P., Cochrane, R. H. B., & Kirkwood, K. (1992). Estimation of premorbid intelligence in schizophrenia. *British Journal of Psychiatry, 161*, 69–74.

Crawford, J. R., Besson, J. A. O., & Parker, D. M. (1988). Estimation of premorbid intelligence in organic conditions. *British Journal of Psychiatry, 153*, 178–181.

Crawford, J. R., Besson, J. A. O., Parker, D. M., Sutherland, K. M., & Keen, P. L. (1987). Estimation of premorbid intellectual status in depression. *British Journal of Clinical Psychology, 26*, 313–314.

Crawford, J. R., Cochrane, R. H. B., Besson, J. A. O., Parker, D. M., & Stewart, L. E. (1990). Premorbid IQ estimates obtained by combining the NART and demographic variables: construct validity. *Personality and Individual Differences, 11*, 209–210.

Crawford, J. R., Nelson, H. E., Blackmore, L., Cochrane, R. H. B., & Allan, K. M. (1990). Estimating premorbid intelligence by combining the NART and demographic variables: An examination of the NART standardisation sample and supplementary equations. *Personality and Individual Differences, 11*, 1153–1157.

Crawford, J. R., Parker, D. M., Stewart, L. E., Besson, J. A. O., & DeLacey, G. (1989). Prediction of WAIS IQ with the national adult reading test: Cross-validation and extension. *British Journal of Clinical Psychology, 28*, 267–273.

Crawford, J. R., Stewart, L. E., Parker, D. M., Besson, J. A. O., & Cochrane, R. H. B. (1989). Estimation of premorbid intelligence: combining psychometric and demographic approaches improves predictive accuracy. *Personality and Individual Differences, 10*, 793–796.

Eppinger, M. G., Craig, P. L., Adams, R. L., & Parsons, O. A. (1987). The WAIS–R index for estimating premorbid intelligence: Cross-validation and clinical utility. *Journal of Consulting and Clinical Psychology, 55*, 86–90.

Franzen,, M.D., Burgess, E. J., & Smith-Seemiller, L. (1997). Methods of estimating premorbid functioning. *Archives of Clinical Neuropsychology, 12*, 711–738.

Goldstein, F. C., Gary, H. E., Jr., & Levin, H. S. (1986). Assessment of the accuracy of regression equations proposed for estimating premorbid intellectual functioning on the Wechsler Adult Intelligence Scale. *Journal of Clinical and Experimental Neuropsychology, 8*, 405–412.

Gouvier, W., Bolter, J., Veneklasen, J., & Long, C. (1983). Premorbid verbal and performance IQ from demographic data: Further findings with head trauma patients. *Clinical Neuropsychology, 5*, 119–121.

Grober, E., & Sliwinski, M. (1991). Development and validation of a model for estimating premorbid verbal intelligence in the elderly. *Journal of Clinical and Experimental Neuropsychology, 13*, 933–949.

Grober, E., Sliwinski, M., Schwartz, M., & Saffran, E. (1989). *The American version of the NART for predicting premorbid intelligence.* Unpublished manuscript.

Grove, W. H., & Meehl, P. E. (1996). Comparative efficiency of informal (subjective, impressionistic) and formal (mechanical, algorithmic) prediction procedures: The clinical–statistical controversy. *Psychology, Public Policy, and Law, 2,* 293–323.

Hart, S., Smith, C. M., & Swash, M. (1986). Assessing intellectual deterioration. *British Journal of Clinical Psychology, 25,* 119–124.

Heaton, R. K., Grant, I., & Matthews, C. B. (1991). *Comprehensive norms for an expanded Halstead–Reitan Battery.* Odessa, FL: Psychological Assessment Resources.

Kareken, D. A. (1997). Judgment pitfalls in estimating premorbid intellectual function. *Archives of Clinical Neuropsychology, 12,* 701–710.

Kareken, D. A., & Williams, J. M. (1994). Human judgment and estimation of premorbid intellectual function. *Psychological Assessment, 6,* 83–91.

Karzmark, P., Heaton, R. K., Grant, I., & Matthews, C. G. (1985). Use of demographic variables to predict Full Scale IQ: A replication and extension. *Journal of Clinical and Experimental Neuropsychology, 7,* 412–420.

Kaufman, A. S. (1990). *Assessing adolescent and adult intelligence.* Boston: Allyn and Bacon.

Klesges, R. C., Fisher, L., Vasey, M., & Pheley, A. (1985). Predicting adult premorbid functioning levels: Another look. *International Journal of Clinical Neuropsychology, 7,* 1–3.

Klesges, R. C., & Troster, A. I. (1987). A review of premorbid indices of intellectual and neuropsychological functioning: What have we learned in the past five years? *The International Journal of Clinical Neuropsychology, 9,* 1–11.

Klesges, R. C., Wilkening, G. N., & Golden, C. J. (1981). Premorbid indices of intelligence: A review. *Clinical neuropsychology, 3,* 32–39.

Krull, K. R., Scott, J. G., & Scherer, M. (1995). Estimation of premorbid intelligence from combined performance and demographic variables. *The Clinical Neuropsychologist, 9,* 83–88.

Larrabee, G. J., Largen, J. W., & Levin, H. S. (1985). Sensitivity of age-decline resistant (hold) WAIS subtests to Alzheimer's disease. *Journal of Clinical and Experimental Neuropsychology, 7,* 497–504.

Lezak, M. D. (1983). *Neuropsychological assessment* (2nd ed.). New York: Oxford University Press.

Lezak, M.D. (1995). *Neuropsychological assessment* (3rd ed.). New York: Oxford University Press.

Matarazzo, J. D. (1972). *Wechsler's measurement and appraisal of adult intelligence* (5th ed., rev.). New York: Oxford University Press.

Matarazzo, J. D., Daniel, M. H., Prifitera, A., & Herman, D. O. (1988). Inter-subtest scatter in the WAIS–R standardization sample. *Journal of Clinical Psychology, 44,* 940–950.

Matarazzo, J. D., & Herman, D. O. (1984). Base rate data for the WAIS–R: Test–retest stability and VIQ–PIQ differences. *Journal of Clinical Neuropsychology, 6,* 351–366.

McFie, J. (1969). The diagnostic significance of disorders of higher nervous activity. Syndromes related to frontal, temporal, parietal, and occipital lesions. In P. J. Vinkin & G. W. Bruyn (Eds.), *Handbook of clinical neurology* (Vol. 4, pp. 1–12). New York: Wiley.

McFie, J. (1975). *Assessment of organic intellectual impairment.* New York: Academic Press.

McLean, J. E., Kaufman, A. S., & Reynolds, C. R. (1989). Base rates for WAIS–R subtest scatter as a guide for clinical and neuropsychological assessment. *Journal of Clinical Psychology, 45,* 919–926.

Mortensen, E. L., Gade, A., & Reinisch, J. M. (1991). A critical note on Lezak's "best performance method" in clinical neuropsychology. *Journal of Clinical and Experimental Neuropsychology, 13,* 361–371.

Nebes, R. D., Martin, D. C., & Horn, L.C. (1984). Sparing of semantic memory in Alzheimer's disease. *Journal of Abnormal Psychology, 93,* 321–330.

Nelson, H. E. (1982). *National adult reading test (NART): Test manual.* Windsor: NFER-Nelson.

Nelson, H. E., & McKenna, P. (1975). The use of current reading ability in the assessment of dementia. *British Journal of Social and Clinical Psychology, 14,* 259–267.

Nelson, H. E., & O'Connell, A. (1978). Dementia: The estimation of premorbid intelligence levels using the new adult reading test. *Cortex, 14,* 234–244.

O'Carroll, R. E., Baikie, E. M., & Whittick, J. E. (1987). Does the National Adult Reading Test hold in dementia? *British Journal of Clinical Psychology, 26,* 315–316.

O'Carroll, R. E., & Gilleard, C. J. (1986). Estimation of premorbid intelligence in dementia. *British Journal of Clinical Psychology, 25*, 157–158.

Psychological Corporation. (1997). *WAIS–III WMS–III technical manual*. San Antonio, TX: Psychological Corporation.

Reynolds, C. R., Chastain, R. L., Kaufman, A. S., & McLean, J. E. (1987). Demographic characteristics and IQ among adults: Analysis of the WAIS–R standardization sample as a function of the stratification variables. *Journal of School Psychology, 25*, 323–342.

Reynolds, C. R., & Gutkin, T. B. (1979). Predicting the premorbid intellectual status of children using demographic data. *Clinical Neuropsychology, 1*, 36–38.

Russell, E. (1972). WAIS factor analysis with brain damaged subjects using criterion measures. *Journal of Consulting and Clinical Psychology, 39*, 133–139.

Schwartz, M., & Saffran, E. (1987). *The American-NART: Replication and extension of the British findings on the persistence of word pronunciation skills in patients with dementia*. Unpublished manuscript.

Smith-Seemiller, L., Franzen, M.D., Burgess, E. J., & Prieto, L. (1997). Neuropsychologists practice patterns in assessing premorbid intelligence. *Archives of Clinical Neuropsychology, 12*, 739–744.

Stebbins, G. T., Gilley, D. W., Wilson, R. S., Bernard, B. A., & Fox, J. H. (1990). Effects of language disturbances on premorbid estimates of IQ in mild dementia. *The Clinical Neuropsychologist, 4*, 64–68.

Stebbins, G. T., Wilson, R. S., Gilley, D. W., Bernard, B. A., & Fox, J. H. (1990). Use of the National Adult Reading Test to estimate premorbid IQ in dementia. *The Clinical Neuropsychologist, 4*, 18–24.

Sweet, J. J., Moberg, P. J., & Tovian, S. M. (1990). Evaluation of Wechsler Adult Intelligence Scale–Revised premorbid IQ formulas in clinical populations. *Psychological Assessment, 2*, 41–44.

Swiercinsky, D. P., & Warnock, J. K. (1977). Comparison of the neuropsychological key and discriminant analysis approaches in predicting cerebral damage and localization. *Journal of Consulting and Clinical Psychology, 45*, 808–814.

Vanderploeg, R. D. (1994). Estimating premorbid level of functioning. In R. D. Vanderploeg (Ed.), *Clinician's guide to neuropsychological assessment* (pp. 43–68). Hillsdale, NJ: Lawrence Erlbaum Associates.

Vanderploeg, R. D., Axelrod, B. N., Sherer, M. Scott, J., & Adams, R. L. (1997). The importance of demographic adjustments on neuropsychological test performance. *The Clinical Neuropsychologist, 11*, 210–217.

Vanderploeg, R. D., & Schinka, J. A. (1995). Predicting WAIS–R IQ premorbid ability: Combining subtest performance and demographic variable predictors. *Archives of Clinical Neuropsychology, 10*, 225–239.

Vanderploeg, R. D., Schinka, J. A., & Axelrod, B. N. (1996). Estimation of WAIS–R premorbid intelligence: Current ability and demographic data used in a best-performance fashion. *Psychological Assessment, 80*, 404–411.

Vanderploeg, R.D., Schinka, J.A., Baum, K.M., Tremont, G., & Mittenberg, W. (1998). WISC–III premorbid prediction strategies: demographic and best performance approaches. *Psychological Assessment, 10*, 277–284.

Wechsler, D. (1958). *The measurement and appraisal of adult intelligence* (4th ed.). Baltimore, MD: Williams & Wilkins.

Wechsler, D. (1974). *Manual for the Wechsler Intelligence Scale for Children–Revised (WISC–R)*. San Antonio, TX: Psychological Corporation.

Wechsler, D. (1981). *Manual for the Wechsler Adult Intelligence Scale–Revised (WAIS–R)*. New York: Psychological Corporation.

Wechsler, D. (1991). *Wechsler Intelligence Scale for Children–Third Edition (WISC–III) manual*. San Antonio, TX: Psychological Corporation.

Wechsler, D. (1997). *Wechsler Adult Intelligence Scale–Third edition (WAIS–III) administration and scoring manual*. San Antonio, TX: Psychological Corporation.

Williams, J. M. (1992). *Memory assessment scales*. Odessa, FL: Psychological Assessment Resources.

Williams, J. M. (1997). The prediction of premorbid memory ability. *Archives of Clinical Neuropsychology, 12,* 745–756.

Wilson, R. S., Rosenbaum, G., Brown, G., Rourke, D., & Whitman, D. (1978). An index of premorbid intelligence. *Journal of Consulting and Clinical Psychology, 46,* 1554–1555.

Yates, A. (1956). The use of vocabulary in the measurement of intelligence deterioration: A review. *Journal of Mental Science, 102,* 409–440.

CHAPTER THREE

Principles of Neuropsychological Interpretation

Cynthia R. Cimino

University of South Florida

Interpretation of neuropsychological data is the process by which significance and meaning are derived from the information obtained during the evaluation process. In this regard, what comes to mind most readily is the interpretation of test scores obtained during assessment. Test scores in and of themselves have little meaning in isolation. However, when compared to some normative standard, test scores provide much information regarding how the individual performs relative to similarly aged peers, the extent to which that score deviates from the "norm" or average score, and the degree to which that score is likely to reflect spared or impaired abilities.

Although interpretation of test scores is a significant element of the assessment process, it is only one aspect of neuropsychological interpretation. In fact, it is not the case that interpretation occurs only after neuropsychological testing is complete. Neuropsychological interpretation represents a multistage process. This process begins with analysis of the information obtained from records, interview, and behavioral observations and continues on through the selection of test instruments, quantitative and qualitative assessment of performance, and comparisons across as well as within cognitive domains. In essence, neuropsychological interpretation is involved in the assessment enterprise from start to finish.

A very important aspect of the interpretation process involves the integration of information and data from multiple sources including history, behavioral observations, interview, and test results. Neuropsychological interpretation in-

TABLE 3.1
Conceptualization and Interpretation

1. Importance of a conceptual model of brain/behavior relationships.
2. Influence of subject-specific variables.
3. Determining when a difference is a true and meaningful difference.
4. Effects of the interaction of different cognitive domains.
5. Consistency/inconsistency across and within cognitive domains.
6. Distinguishing neurologic, psychiatric, and test-taking conditions that may overlap.
7. Avoiding erroneous assumptions and inferences.

volves continual checks as these additional sources of information are obtained. These data sources, whether they be test scores, elements of the history, information obtained through interview of the patient, or significant other or observations of the patient's test or extratest behaviors, are continually evaluated with respect to each other. They are reviewed and re-reviewed to adequately integrate these various sources of information, with the end result of this integration being the identification of recognizable and consistent patterns of performance. In sum, interpretation involves much more than assigning meaning to test scores. It is the process by which all sources of information about the patient are evaluated and then integrated to form the most coherent clinical picture of that particular individual.

In approaching this topic, it is worth emphasizing the position presented by Walsh (1992) in his address to the First INS-ASSBI Pacific Rim Conference, in which he stated that "clinical neuropsychology is not about test data and the application of statistical rules alone but about a much underused process called thinking." In keeping with this spirit, this chapter is organized around several different domains, which are intended to influence how one "thinks" about various aspects of neuropsychological interpretation; it does not provide a cookbook or step-by-step approach to neuropsychological interpretation. These domains may serve as guides in helping to develop the kinds of thought processes that are of prime importance in neuropsychological interpretation and also may serve as useful means of helping to avoid common errors of interpretation that arise in evaluation of neuropsychological data. These seven domains are identified in Table 3.1.

IMPORTANCE OF A CONCEPTUAL MODEL
OF BRAIN–BEHAVIOR RELATIONSHIPS

The first of these areas is a conceptual model of brain–behavior relationships. In neuropsychological assessment, this represents one of the most basic and fundamental aspects of the interpretive process, yet is all too often overlooked. The extent to which interpretation of data can progress in a systematic, organized,

TABLE 3.2
Foundations of a Conceptual Model
of Brain/Behavior Relationships

1. Neuroanatomy.
2. Neuropathologic conditions and their sequelae.
3. Clinical psychology and psychopathology.
4. Psychometric properties and principles.

and veridical fashion is dependent on an overarching conceptual model of brain–behavior relationships. This approach provides the necessary foundation for making neuropsychological sense out of the data and is one of the key elements in minimizing or avoiding errors in interpretation. Lezak (1995) identified four domains of knowledge essential in neuropsychological assessment (see Table 3.2). These domains form the building blocks for developing a conceptual model of brain-behavior relationships. More importantly, a conceptual model of brain–behavior relationships is built on a working knowledge of the manner and extent to which these different domains *interact*.

Building Blocks of a Conceptual Model Neuroanatomy

Neuroanatomy. Knowledge of functional neuroanatomy is a key building block in the development of a conceptual model of brain–behavior relationships. The significance of neuroanatomy in the interpretation process is recognized to varying degrees by different schools of thought. It is often the knowledge domain that presents the greatest hurdle to students and practitioners of neuropsychology. At first glance, it is often unclear to many how neuroanatomy can have direct and significant relevance to neuropsychological assessment. However, as one continues to observe the performance of patients with varying etiologies and accumulates a repertoire of experience, it becomes apparent that this source of knowledge is key to stretching the limits of thinking about cases and the capacity to work through interpretive dilemmas that present confusing or conflicting information.

Research in neuroanatomy and neuropsychology has revealed much about the organization and behavioral significance of cortical and subcortical regions. Group as well as single-case studies in lesioned patients have provided much information about associations between anatomical structures and psychological processes. Nevertheless, the brain is not composed of discrete and isolated anatomic loci each associated with a particular function or psychological process. Rather, the brain represents a complex and integrated network composed of many functional anatomic systems (Luria, 1980). Within this framework, one must consider not only the presumed psychological functions associated with a particular region but also the afferent and efferent connections of that region.

Norman Geschwind's seminal paper in 1965 highlighted this emphasis on a functional systems approach. Furthermore, he suggested that deficits also may arise as a result of white matter damage resulting in disconnection of two separate anatomic regions.

An example of the extent to which a functional systems approach can influence conceptualization in neuropsychology is evident in recent work in the visual system in humans and other animals. Several investigators have identified distinct behaviors associated with two functional visual systems: one termed the *superior visual route*, coursing from occipital lobe through parietal regions, and one an *inferior visual route*, traversing from occipital regions through temporal zones (Levin, Warach, Farah, 1985; Mishkin, Ungerleider, & Macko, 1983; Ungerleider & Mishkin, 1982). Evidence has accumulated to suggest that damage to the superior route is likely to involve spatial aspects of visual processing— what investigators have referred to as the "where" system. In contrast, damage to the inferior route is likely to involve aspects of object processing in the visual domain—a system investigators have referred to as the "what" system. Armed with this knowledge, one is in a better position to anticipate the kinds of processing deficits with which a patient is likely to present. Similarly, such knowledge helps to organize thinking about several seemingly distinct and varied disorders of higher order visual processing. Using this organizing framework, it is apparent that visual processing disorders that involve some aspects of spatial processing, such as optic ataxia, simultanagnosia, or other visuospatial disorders, are more likely to be present when damage to the superior route is involved. On the other hand, disorders that involve object processing in the visual domain, such as prosopagnosia, object agnosia, and some alexias, are more likely to involve damage to the inferior route already described.

Neuropathologic Conditions and Their Sequelae. Knowledge of neuropathologic conditions and their sequelae is a fundamental base of knowledge that has particular relevance to interpretation in neuropsychological assessment. Disorders of the central nervous system may have very diverse effects on behavior and test performance, yet specific patterns of performance have been identified for different conditions. In addition, acute and/or progressive disorders will present with focal deficits related to particular anatomic areas of dysfunction, as well as diffuse effects due to edema, disturbed biochemical homeostasis, or disruptions of vascular perfusion. For example, stroke may result in diffuse effects such as general slowing in motor and cognitive responses as well as specific effects associated with the region of damage or its associated connections (Lezak, 1995). In head-injured populations, effects of impact may influence the integrity of tissue not only at the site of impact but also at regions well beyond that of the presumed site of impact (Levin, Benton, & Grossman, 1982). Several sources are now available that provide specific case examples of various disorders highlighting distinctive features and patterns of performance (Orsini, Van Gorp, & Boone,

1988; Walsh, 1991). A working knowledge of anatomical systems and pathological processes involved in various disorders is one key element to predicting and identifying patterns of behavioral dysfunction. Similarly, knowing potential patterns of test performance associated with various disorders allows one to recognize inconsistencies as they arise.

Clinical Psychology and Psychopathology. Knowledge of clinical psychology and psychopathology is a fundamental aspect in development of a conceptual model of brain–behavior relationships. By its very nature, neuropsychology represents a multidisciplinary approach and a need to draw from various domains of knowledge. A firm base in understanding the symptoms, course, and treatment of various psychiatric disorders as well as the extent to which such disorders may influence test performance is important. On the other side of the coin, various neurological disorders may present with psychiatric symptoms such as alterations in mood, affect, and other psychological features that may influence performance. Severe anxiety and/or depression may influence performance on some tasks but not others. Neuropsychological measures that emphasize aspects of attention and memory are most likely to be affected relative to tasks where these components are kept to a minimum. An awareness and knowledge of such factors that can influence task performance and the types of neuropsychological measures most susceptible to such factors can be very useful tools in neuropsychological interpretation.

Psychometric Properties and Principles. Lastly, a foundation in the domain of test theory and psychometric principles is at the very heart of test interpretation. At a concrete level, this entails appropriate usage of normative data. Several neuropsychological tests have associated with them different administration procedures; the examiner must be careful to select the appropriate set of norms based on the procedure used in testing. In a similar vein, the composition of the normative group should be comparable to the patient. This has become a very relevant issue as the segment of the population in the upper decades has continued and will continue to steadily increase, whereas available norms may not contain the growing segment of 70-, 80-, and even 90-year-old adults referred for evaluation. Age effects vary considerably across different neuropsychological tests and it is not reasonable to assume that norms derived from a sample of 60-year-olds are applicable to 70- or 80-year-olds. A working knowledge of psychometric properties including the reliability and validity of various neuropsychological tests is also important. This information has become more readily available in several books (Benton, Hamsher, Varney, & Spreen, 1983; Franzen, 1989; Lezak, 1995; Spreen & Strauss, 1991) and journal articles published within the area of neuropsychology.

The difficulty level of neuropsychological measures is also a consideration when interpreting test performance. In testing patients where only mild difficulties in a particular cognitive domain are anticipated, a range of performance in the standardization sample is desirable. Depending on the patient's estimated level of ability, one test may result in normal performance only because the difficulty level of the task was too easy. For example, naming performance on the Western Aphasia Battery (Kertesz, 1982) may not reveal deficits in naming ability, whereas performance on a more difficult measure with greater variability in the performance of the normative sample, such as the Boston Naming Test (Kaplan, Goodglass, & Weintraub, 1978), may well be able to detect such mild deficits. If evaluation of naming ability were restricted to data from the Western Aphasia Battery, one might erroneously conclude that naming abilities were intact when, in fact, mild naming deficits are present.

Developing a conceptual model of brain–behavior relationships involves the capacity to integrate information from several knowledge domains. Such integration is not achieved over a short time span, and it is something that certainly requires a significant degree of persistence and effort. As new findings are revealed and information is acquired, this model will grow and change with the experiences of the individual. With the development of training guidelines for neuropsychology recommended by the INS-Division 40 Task Force on Education, Accreditation and Credentialing (1987), it is apparent that the importance of a conceptual model of brain–behavior relationships in neuropsychology has become more widely recognized. Neuropsychology represents a unique domain within psychology that calls upon a truly multidisciplinary approach to the process of assessment.

Utility of a Conceptual Model

A more fundamental question that arises when considering a conceptual model of brain–behavior relationships is, In what practical way is having a conceptual knowledge of brain–behavior relationships important? That is, in concrete terms, how can it serve as a useful guide to neuropsychological interpretation? Some of these issues have already been addressed to some extent by the material already presented, but this is an issue that warrants additional attention. Table 3.3 identifies six potential ways in which such knowledge can facilitate the inter-

TABLE 3.3

Utility of a Conceptual Model of Brain/Behavior Relationships

1. Sets some reasonable expectation of performance.
2. Anticipates deficits associated with neurobehavioral disorder.
3. Recognizes performance that is inconsistent with a neurobehavioral disorder.
4. Recognizes neighborhood signs.
5. Recognizes low-base-rate conditions.
6. Aids qualitative interpretations of test performance.

pretive process and help avoid errors in interpretation. Each of these is now considered in turn.

Expectations of Performance. Having a conceptual model of brain–behavior relationships allows the examiner to set some reasonable expectation of the level of performance. It sets a window of expectation within which one can continually compare history, test performance, and other observations. For example, in head-injured populations knowledge of the relationships between length of coma, posttraumatic amnesia, and other variables allows one to set some reasonable expectation of performance based on prior research in the area and allows a determination of the extent to which the patient's observed performance matches the expected level of performance (Levin et al., 1982). If emergency medical records indicate that the patient suffered no loss of consciousness and no discernible evidence of posttraumatic amnesia, yet memory performance is falling three standard deviations below the mean, this represents a very discrepant picture from what is known about such relationships and should alert the examiner to consider other potential causes for such test performance.

Anticipation of Deficits. A conceptual model provides the examiner with the capacity to anticipate deficits associated with various neurobehavioral disorders or known anatomic lesions. At the very start, it allows the examiner to anticipate deficits and generate hypotheses about potential test performance. For some clinicians, it may serve as a means of guiding the assessment and selection of test instruments. If there is some information available on the patient's history, presentation, and presumed diagnosis, one can develop predictions of specific test performance that can be tested in the evaluation process and interpreted. This is perhaps one of the most useful aspects for individuals who are in the beginning stages of conducting neuropsychological assessment. When approaching the assessment, it is always useful to have a frame of reference from which to proceed. Knowing which functions are likely to be involved and in need of more thorough evaluation, and coming to the evaluation prepared with such knowledge, is an excellent point of departure.

Recognition of Inconsistent Performance. In addition to anticipating potential deficits, a conceptual model of brain–behavior relationships aids the examiner in recognizing performance that is inconsistent with a neurobehavioral disorder. If one is well acquainted with the prototypic features associated with a particular disorder, then one is in a very good position to recognize when aspects of performance are inconsistent with that disorder. For example, knowledge that Alzheimer's disease affects predominantly association and not primary motor and sensory cortices until more advanced stages of the disease might lead the examiner to question a presumed diagnosis of primary degenerative dementia of the Alzheimer's type in a patient who demonstrates asymmetries in performance on motor tasks. Involvement of primary motor systems is not a typical feature in the early stages of Alzheimer's disease (Cummings & Benson, 1992), and it is the examiner's task to determine the extent to which this finding of asymmetric performance on motor tasks makes sense in the overall clinical context. It is possible that such deficits could represent merely the results of an old peripheral injury. In contrast, these deficits many, in fact, represent the residua of motor deficits following some cerebral insult. In either case, it behooves the examiner to recognize findings that may be inconsistent with a presumed diagnosis and to attempt to integrate these findings into a more coherent conceptualization of the patient.

Recognition of Neighborhood Signs. Weintraub and Mesulam (1985) suggested that recognition of neighborhood signs may be a useful means of localizing a lesion within a particular anatomic network. Recognition of neighborhood signs, however, is dependent upon a working knowledge of brain–behavior relationships. The example they provided assesses the utility of neighborhood signs in the neglect syndrome. Disorders like neglect can be caused by damage in a number of different cortical and subcortical regions and these interconnected regions together form an anatomic network of attention (Heilman, Watson, & Valenstein, 1993; Mesulam, 1985). At the outset, knowledge of such a functional system would alert the examiner to the potential for occurrence of inattention to stimuli on one side of space. In addition, consideration of the occurrence of neighborhood signs such as visual field loss or motor signs would help localize the lesion within this system. If the lesion is cortically based, then presence of visual field loss would likely place the extent of the lesion more posterior, while presence of motor signs would place the lesion more anterior. Recognition of neighborhood signs would, in effect, allow the examiner to make inferences about where in this functional system damage is likely to have occurred. Furthermore, it may help one hypothesize what additional cognitive processes associated with this system or interacting systems are likely to be impaired.

Recognition of Low-Base-Rate Conditions. Knowledge of brain–behavior relationships may allow consideration of a low-base-rate diagnosis in a patient when a higher base rate diagnosis has been proposed. Often in inpatient or even outpatient settings, the examiner is provided with some diagnostic information on the patient in the form of medical history, neurological exam, or even prior neuropsychological testing. Although it is helpful to use this information as a working hypothesis when approaching the assessment and interpretation of neuropsychological data, it is important that the examiner not remain completely wedded to the presumed diagnosis at the exclusion of paying close attention to what the neuropsychological data are revealing. The following case illustrates this point.

A 56-year-old woman presented with profound memory disturbance and mild to moderate "frontal" or executive/self-regulatory difficulties. Nevertheless, she was average to above average in all other domains of function, including attention, language, visuoconstructional, visuospatial, and visuoperceptual abilities. Although she did not meet formal criteria, the working hypothesis was that this patient was perhaps in the very early stages of a primary degenerative dementia. It is not unusual for such patients to present initially and for some extended period of time with predominantly memory deficits. However, it is also possible that other low-probability events could account for her problems. Her test findings and the knowledge that some memory structures such as the dorsal medial nucleus of the thalamus (Butters & Stuss, 1989; Squire, 1987) have significant projections to the frontal lobe (Alexander & Fuster, 1973) allowed us to entertain the possibility of an alternate although low-base-rate condition. The patient demonstrated a profound memory disturbance within the context of only mild executive/self-regulatory difficulties. Given this pattern of performance, it was likely that her performance was most consistent with an amnestic syndrome presenting with executive/self-regulatory deficits. Damage to medial thalamic nuclei such as the dorsal medial nucleus of the thalamus can result in a profound amnestic disturbance as well as executive/self-regulatory difficulties due to strong projections from this nucleus to prefrontal cortex (Butters & Stuss, 1989; Graff-Radford, Damasio, Yamada, Eslinger & Damasio, 1985; Speedie & Heilman, 1982, 1983; Squire & Moore, 1979). The patient was given magnetic resonance imagery (MRI) and bilateral medial thalamic lesions were found. No motor or sensory symptoms were demonstrated because of the location of the lesion, so there were no apparent tip-offs that this was a vascular event. In addition, there was no report from family members to give a historical account of whether memory changes were evident in an acute fashion or progressive over time. Given this woman's age and general clinical presentation, a likely or high-base-rate disorder would have been a progressive degenerative dementia. Nevertheless, the patient did not present with any semblance of language disorder (not even mild naming problems) or visuoconstructional deficits, which are more typical in an Alzheimer's picture. In this case, the inferential process was guided by the data and not the likely probability of a diagnosis that had been previously considered.

This case is useful in illustrating how knowledge of neuroanatomy can have some very significant and powerful practical implications. In this particular case, it allowed for the recognition of neuropsychological data that were not necessarily inconsistent with the initial presumed diagnosis but not the most consistent. In addition, it widened the range of possibilities that could be entertained to account for the pattern of test findings. Lastly, the conceptualization of the case had some very practical implications for the patient and her family. The progressive course of a patient with a presumed degenerative dementia compared to that of a patient with medial thalamic lesions where the deficits may potentially improve and then stabilize had very different implications for the patient and her family's lives. In this regard, the courses of the two disorders would have significantly different impacts on the patient and her family and would have resulted in very different sorts of interventions.

Aids Qualitative Interpretations of Neuropsychological Data. Lastly, a conceptual knowledge of brain behavior relationships assists qualitative interpretations of test performance. Edith Kaplan (1983, 1989) has been the pioneer in qualitative aspects of neuropsychological test interpretation. She has emphasized that knowledge of brain–behavior relationships is an essential component of anticipating deficits, making inferences about the nature of a patient's approach to a task, and analyzing error types. That a patient fails a particular item or task is no more important than *how* that patient fails the item or task. Neuropsychological interpretation should consider not only the quantitative aspects of the patient's performance but also the qualitative aspects of the patient's performance. Different approaches to neuropsychological assessment have traditionally been classified along the continuum of quantitative versus qualitative approaches. Today, it is fair to say that those who engage in neuropsychological assessment with any regularity are likely to consider, at least at some level, both aspects of task performance. A strong conceptual knowledge of brain–behavior relationships is a key element in the richness, complexity, and accuracy of qualitative interpretations. Qualitative analysis of test performance also may help to discern the extent to which motivation and effort are evident in the patient's performance. So at the most fundamental level, such an analysis helps to make determinations about the validity of neuropsychological data.

At a more complex level, process analysis involves close attention to the manner in which the patient attempts and/or completes test items. For example, does the patient's approach to drawing a figure or canceling lines proceed in a typical left-to-right fashion or does the patient proceed with most tasks in a less typical right-to-left fashion? Similarly, Kaplan and others (Goodglass & Kaplan, 1979; Kaplan, 1989; Milberg, Hebben, & Kaplan, 1986) delineated some aspects of performance on the Block Design subtest that may be useful in discerning the potential anatomic basis of qualitative differences in performance. For example, these authors emphasized the relative importance of whether the overall configuration of the design is preserved in the patient's block construction. They indicated that a violation of the two by two or three by three configuration on items is more likely to occur following right-hemisphere damage, whereas an error of internal detail with a relative preservation of the overall configuration of the item is more likely to be observed following left-hemisphere damage. These and other types of qualitative observations of performance may serve as useful means of identifying common strategies used across various tasks, identifying involvement of anatomic systems, and identifying potential strengths and weaknesses that can be used to guide rehabilitative and/or compensatory strategies.

INFLUENCE OF SUBJECT-SPECIFIC VARIABLES

When interpreting neuropsychological data, it is important to consider a number of subject specific variables that may influence performance. A listing of some of the more common subject factors that are likely to influence performance is given in Table 3.4. These can, for heuristic purposes, be divided into demographic/historic factors, state factors, and psychiatric/psychological/personality factors.

Demographic/Historic Factors

Age, gender, and education are factors particularly relevant to procedures that use standard cutoff scores, such as some of the Halstead–Reitan Battery tests. Although the use of an absolute standard cutoff score is still a common practice in clinical neuropsychology, the validity of this approach is questionable. Various abilities and associated neuropsychological measures are influenced to greater and lesser degrees by the effects of age (Heaton, Grant, & Matthews, 1986; Leckliter & Matarazzo, 1989). Using a single cutoff score that does not

TABLE 3.4
Influence of Subject-Specific Factors

Demographic/historic factors
1. Age
2. Sex
3. Handedness
4. Education (LD)
5. Occupation
6. Socioeconomic status
7. Premorbid cognitive/intellectual abilities
8. Native language/culture
9. Medical history

State factors
1. Poor attention
2. Fatigue
3. Poor motivation
4. Secondary gain
5. Malingering

Psychiatric/psychological/personality factors
1. Depression
2. Anxiety
3. Psychosis
4. Alcohol/drug abuse
5. Antisocial disorder
6. Somatization disorder

take into account the marked changes in performance associated with age can result in significant errors of interpretation. Recently, several authors have provided new normative data that adjusts for the influence of subject specific variables such as age, education, and/or gender on such tasks (Heaton, Grant, & Matthews, 1991; Russell & Starkey, 1993).

The influence of age on test performance underscores the importance of using age-corrected scaled scores on the Wechsler Adult Intelligence Scale–Revised (WAIS–R; Wechsler, 1981) when making subtest comparisons. This point is often overlooked when making statements about the pattern of performance across various subtests and the possible interpretive implications for other neuropsychological data. When making comparisons of this type, age-corrected scaled scores must be used. For example, significant age effects are readily apparent on subtests such as Digit Symbol. If regular scaled scores are used, these scaled scores are derived from the 25- to 34-year-old reference group. If the patient is 60 years old, then the patient's regular scaled score would represent their performance relative to that of 24- to 34-year-olds. Using this as the comparative standard, one might erroneously interpret the patient's performance as impaired. For purposes of assessment, the most appropriate comparison is that of similarly aged peers. In this case, the examiner must calculate the patient's age-corrected scaled score, which utilizes the appropriate comparison to individuals aged 55–64 years of age.

Handedness is another factor to consider in neuropsychological interpretation. The most common method of determining handedness is to ask the patients their preferred hand for writing. However, on further inquiry it is often the case, particularly with left-handed individuals and often with some right-handed individuals, that there are some activities for which they have a contralateral preference. Additional questioning of hand preferences or the use of a formal handedness inventory may be useful in more clearly defining the nature and extent of hand preference (Annett, 1967; Briggs & Nebes, 1975). One obvious domain that this factor will influence is interpretation of data from motor tasks. The typical right-hand superiority on tasks such as tapping and grip strength will be reversed for those left-hand-dominant individuals. Another domain for which handedness can influence the interpretation of neuropsychological data is that of language processing. While the majority of left handers are left-hemisphere dominant for language, this is not the case for a subgroup of these individuals (Branch, Milner, & Rasmussen, 1964). Attention to this fact may help clarify results that don't conform to the typical pattern of test findings.

Factors such as educational level and the presence or absence of a learning disability are important to consider. Several neuropsychological measures are highly correlated with education. Although many neuropsychological measures provide normative comparisons for different age ranges, the availability of normative data for various educational levels often is lacking. The examiner should be acquainted with new sources of normative data as they become available and pay close attention to those tasks that may be particularly sensitive to education effects. Information from the interview about educational history, potential difficulty with subject material, or presence of a learning disability can be invaluable in accounting for neuropsychological performance. In addition, this information can be an important component in avoiding potential errors of interpretation by avoiding the erroneous assumption that the behavior was initially within normal limits.

Various occupations can result in uneven performance across tasks, which may be accounted for by a special, developed ability. A more difficult determination may involve the interpretation of average or even low average abilities in an individual of superior talent in a particular domain. This may present one of the most difficult interpretive scenarios, but again must be approached in a systematic fashion by considering information from history, interview, test results, and observation. Socioeconomic status in combination with many of the factors listed in Table 3.4, such as education and occupation, may be useful in providing estimates of premorbid abilities that are critical to the interpretive process. This is discussed in greater detail in chapter 2.

Lezak (1988) suggested that aggregate measures of behavior such as IQ scores fail to provide the specific type of information necessary to characterize the neuropsychological status of a patient. She emphasized that summary scores, such as the IQ, may provide misleading summaries of disparate abilities that do not fully capture the various spared and impaired abilities of the patient. This is a valid criticism of the use of IQ scores in general in the practice of neuropsychology. However, global estimates of the cognitive/intellectual ability of an individual may have some utility in comparing premorbid to current performance, particularly when those levels fall at the extremes. For example, an individual whose premorbid Full Scale IQ score was estimated to be 85 is predicted to perform quite differently on neuropsychological measures than an individual whose Full Scale IQ score was estimated to be 145. We can use this information to construct a window within which performance on neuropsychological measures is likely to fall. In addition, we know that many individuals whose estimated intelligence falls well below average usually perform well below average or in impaired ranges on neuropsychological measures (Lezak, 1995). Again, having information about global estimates of cognitive ability can be useful in some instances, especially when those estimates tend to fall at the extreme ends of the continuum.

Factors such as native language and culture may alert the examiner to the need to consider alternative interpretations of neuropsychological data. The patient's fluency in English, relative ease of communication, and years of experience within a culture are important factors that should be taken into account. Obviously, native language and culture should be considered at the outset during interview and administration of neuropsychological measures. However, these factors become an important part of the interpretation of the data as well.

Native language and culture may significantly influence performance on measures that place significant demands on language processing or familiarity with items specific to a culture.

A careful consideration of medical history is of prime importance in the process of interpreting neuropsychological data. A variety of systemic diseases can have significant and even profound effects on neuropsychological functioning and must be carefully considered in the interpretive process. In addition, certain systemic disorders such as heart disease are strongly associated with cerebral vascular disease and may result in cognitive impairment (Barclay, Weiss, Mattis, Bond, & Blass, 1988; Todnem & Vik-Mo, 1986). Other medical disorders, such as poorly controlled diabetes, endocrine disorders, metabolic disorders, and liver or kidney disease, are just a few of the diseases that can result in diffuse effects on cerebral function (Tarter, Van Thiel, & Edwards, 1988). In addition, a careful consideration of medical history may help to make better sense out of asymmetric performance on motor tasks that is due to peripheral damage to the limb itself, rather than erroneously attributing it to central involvement.

Lastly, medication effects cannot be overlooked and must be carefully considered. Many prescription medications can have adverse effects on neuropsychological function. These effects are often most noticeable on tasks that require sustained attention and concentration and on measures of memory function. Medication containing anticholinergic agents may have significant effects in these domains (Drachman & Leavitt, 1974). One population that is particularly sensitive to these effects is the elderly, making diagnostic determinations in this group more difficult. Consideration of the types of medication and the potential influence on cognitive function is important to keep in mind when interpreting neuropsychological data.

State Factors

Of all subject-specific factors, state factors are perhaps some of the most important factors in determining whether the information obtained is valid and interpretable. Unless it is clear that a patient is able and/or willing to maintain some acceptable level of motivation and effort, the information garnered from neuropsychological evaluation may be questionable at best. Performance that is characterized by lack of motivation and effort may render neuropsychological data uninterpretable; nevertheless, these observations in and of themselves may provide valuable information about the qualitative aspects of the patient's performance. These factors may be of particular importance when dealing with issues of potential feigned performance, secondary gain, or malingering.

State factors such as excessive fatigue and poor attention may significantly influence performance on neuropsychological measures. Unlike those mentioned earlier, fatigue and attentional influences may not necessarily render neuropsychological data invalid or uninterpretable, but such factors will decidedly influence the interpretation of performance on neuropsychological measures. Assuming that the patient is demonstrating adequate motivation and effort, performance that is impaired due to marked attentional deficits or undue fatigue may be valid to the extent that such performance represents the functional level at which that patient is capable of performing. The nature of these influences on neuropsychological interpretation is addressed to a greater extent in subsequent sections.

Psychiatric/Psychological/Personality Factors

Psychiatric, psychological, and personality factors are important domains to consider in interpreting neuropsychological data. Personality and other psychiatric disturbance may present with alterations in many of the state factors noted earlier, such as attention, concentration, motivation, and effort, which can significantly influence performance. In fact, many of these symptoms are listed as criterion for diagnosis in various disorders within DSM–IV (American Psychiatric Association, 1994). Psychotic disturbance may manifest itself in deficits in attention, concentration, bizarre thinking, and use of language. Similarly, anxiety and affective disorders may significantly influence domains of attention and memory, and the pattern of performance within those domains must be carefully assessed in order to derive an accurate interpretation. The problem of affective disturbance in the elderly presents a particular problem for interpretation of neuropsychological data. These and other issues are addressed in greater detail in the section that deals with distinguishing neurologic, psychiatric, and test-taking conditions that may overlap.

DETERMINING WHEN A DIFFERENCE IS A TRUE AND MEANINGFUL DIFFERENCE

In determining when test scores reflect a true and meaningful difference, three types of determinations can be made. These include single-score, multiple-score, and change in performance determinations. Single-score determinations ask: Is a single score significantly different from normal? Multiple-score determinations ask: Are two scores significantly different from each other? Change in performance determinations ask: Has the score on a particular neuropsychological measure changed over time?

Single-Score Determinations

When asking whether a single score on a neuropsychological measure differs from "normal," it must be determined whether normal represents average performance as defined by population-specific norms or whether normal represents what is expected performance for any given individual. For individuals of extremely high premorbid abilities, average performance as defined by population-specific norms may not be what is expected performance for that individual. Performance that is within the low average or even average range may represent performance within "normal" limits for most individuals, yet for someone of extremely high premorbid abilities that may not represent normal performance for that individual and certainly not what is expected performance. Such cases require special consideration when interpreting test scores.

It is usually the case, however, that for most individuals single-score determinations can be made with respect to average performance as defined by population specific norms. Nevertheless, some judgment may be required in determining when a particular score falls outside of the normal range. Although normative data may be provided, on some neuropsychological measures there is not a clear, explicit indication of how far from the average of the normative sample a score must be to be considered a significant deviation from the norm and reflect a neuropsychological impairment. As a general rule of thumb, a score that falls two standard deviations from the average for the appropriate comparison group very likely reflects an impaired score on that test (assuming premorbid performance was within normal limits.) However, scores that fall between one and two standard deviations below the average and, in particular, those that fall between one and a half and two standard deviations below the average (borderline range) may require more careful consideration in interpretation. Foremost among these considerations is the estimated premorbid level of the patient.

Another approach to single-score determinations is the use of standard cutoff scores. Cutoff scores compare an individual's performance against some previously determined cutoff for that test, usually without regard to factors such as age or education. In contrast, population-specific norms provide norms for different age and sometimes education groups, using a standard deviation criterion for impairment. In one study of tests using standard cutoff scores, the percentage of test scores for normal subjects falling into the impaired range was 15–80% for different tests of the Halstead–Reitan Battery (Bornstein, 1986). These findings underscore the importance of utilizing either correction factors or population-specific norms that take into account age and education.

The influence of factors such as age and education on neuropsychological measures is becoming more widely recognized, and the use of population-specific norms or adjustments for such factors is highly recommended. Population-specific norms are an improvement over standard cutoff scores. Nevertheless, it is still the case that many neuropsychological measures have norms available for different age groups, yet do not account for other important variables such as education or gender.

Multiple-Score Determinations

When making multiple-score determinations there is the problem of a lack of a common metric across tasks. Lezak (1995) suggested the use of standard score conversions. The application of z or T score conversions may be beneficial in determining the extent to which a patient's scores on distinct measures deviate from the average performance level. Although this may be one of the best available solutions to this dilemma, the amount of intertest differences may vary secondary to difficulty level of test instruments rather than neuropsychological competence. In addition, samples from which normative data are derived differ in their composition. With these caveats in mind, converting multiple scores to a common metric allows for an examination of which scores fall into the normal range and which fall outside of the normal range of function. In this way, the examiner is able to discern a pattern of spared and impaired functions. This type of profile analysis is a common approach to the interpretation of neuropsychological data.

Another approach (Kaufman, 1990) to determining differences between scores is reflected in procedures used with the Wechsler Adult Intelligence Scale (WAIS–R; Wechsler, 1981). In this approach, test scores may be significantly different from each other in two distinct ways. The difference between two scores may be significant at a statistical level. That is, the difference between scores may be a true and reliable difference, rather than representing merely a difference in fluctuations in error of measurement on the two tests. Second, the difference between scores may be significant or meaningful to the extent that such a difference occurs relatively infrequently in the population. The first represents determination of a significant statistical difference between the two scores and the second represents determination of a meaningful difference between the two scores (a difference that occurs infrequently in the population). Obviously, for two scores to be meaningfully different they must also be significantly different from each other at a statistical level.

Some information on these differences is available for measures of Verbal IQ (VIQ) and Performance IQ (PIQ) differences on the WAIS–R and can be used for illustrative purposes. A difference of 12 points between VIQ and PIQ is considered to be statistically significant, yet this difference occurs in approximately 28% of the normal population, a relatively frequent occurrence (Matarazzo & Herman, 1985). Therefore, although this difference may represent a statistically significant difference, it may not represent a clinically significant difference.

Furthermore, VIQ/PIQ differences vary considerably with respect to overall level of IQ, and this must be carefully considered when interpreting such differences (Matarazzo & Herman, 1985). As IQ increases one is more likely to find a larger VIQ/PIQ difference. For example, a difference of 12 points between VIQ and PIQ occurs in approximately 9.1% of individuals with IQs of 79 or below. Yet this same difference of 12 points between VIQ and PIQ occurs for nearly 37.9% of individuals with IQs of 120 and above. This finding underscores the relative importance of considering level of IQ when making interpretations of VIQ/PIQ differences. Kaufman (1990) constructed useful tables from the data of Matarazzo & Herman (1985), which can aid in this process.

Unfortunately, comparable data for the majority of neuropsychological measures is not available. The Wechsler Memory Scale–Revised (WMS–R; Wechsler, 1987) does provide information on the amount necessary for a difference between various memory indices to be considered statistically significant. However, there is no information on the extent to which such differences are observed in the normative sample.

Change in Score Determinations

When assessing recovery, the question becomes, when is a change a true change from the original score obtained on a particular measure? That is, when does a change represent practice effects versus true recovery? Most neuropsychological measures do not contain estimates of anticipated gains in scores associated with practice effects, making such inferences difficult. In addition, some measures are more prone to the effects of practice than others. There is some information available on the influence of practice effects on the WAIS–R that can be of potential usefulness. Kaufman (1990) constructed a helpful table from data of Matarazzo and Herman (1984) that provides information on degree of unusualness associated with particular gains and losses in VIQ, PIQ, and Full Scale IQ (FSIQ). In this regard, it is noteworthy that practice effects and subsequent gains in PIQ are substantially larger than gains in VIQ. A gain of 15 points in FSIQ was a relatively infrequent occurrence observed in only 5% of subjects. In this particular circumstance, the examiner is better able to conclude that such a gain is likely to represent a change from initial testing or recovery. In this same sample, a gain of 12 points in VIQ was observed in only 5% of subjects. However, a gain of 23 points in PIQ was needed to correspond to the same infrequent occurrence of 5% in this same sample of subjects. These findings emphasize the relative importance of taking into account different influences of practice in changes on VIQ and PIQ measures. These data may be of use when determining whether gains on these various scales represent meaningful gains in intellectual functioning over time.

In addition to potential gains in function, in certain cases it may be important to determine when the patient's performance represents a worsening in function. As a general rule of thumb, losses in IQ points at a second test administration are infrequent. Based on Matarazzo and Herman's data, a loss of five points on VIQ, PIQ, or FSIQ at second test administration was a relatively unusual occurrence demonstrated in only 5% of their sample. When losses in these measures are observed on second test administration, this should alert the examiner to the possibility of worsening of function. Kaufman (1990) provided tables, based on Matarazzo and Herman's data, that list the observed frequency of losses in the various IQ measures from initial test to retest.

Unfortunately, specific information on anticipated gains on repeat administrations of neuropsychological measures is lacking. Such data would provide valuable information in determining the extent to which significant improvement or deterioration are present. This may have important implications in treatment settings for determining whether recovery has taken place. In addition, this information is likely to have implications in forensic determinations.

EFFECTS OF THE INTERACTION OF DIFFERENT COGNITIVE DOMAINS

The law of parsimony and Occam's razor are as apt for inferences about clinical neuropsychological data as they are for inferences about research data. In this regard, it is important to try and identify the most elementary disturbance that can account for failure on a complex task. When reviewing neuropsychological data, it is important to keep in mind that deficits across tasks that appear to be quite different in nature could possibly be attributed to a single underlying difficulty. In evaluating performance on any task, it is important to consider the extent to which performance on that task represents the influence of other cognitive domains. Most neuropsychological measures cannot be considered "pure" measures in the sense that only a single ability is measured. When interpreting performance on a particular neuropsychological test, it is important to keep in mind the component features of that task and the abilities necessary to complete it. On a typical task of naming ability, a patient is shown a picture of an object and asked to name it. What are some of the abilities required in completion of this task? At the most fundamental level, the patient must have an adequate degree of arousal and attention to comply with the task demands. In addition, the patient must be able to comprehend task instructions. The patient also will need to be able to adequately perceive the stimulus material, so primary visual processing must be intact. At a more complex level of visuoperceptual processing, the patient must be able to recognize the specific object. In addition, the patient must be capable of searching and retrieving the correct name for the item from their lexicon. Lastly, the patient must be able to adequately output the response in the form of a verbal utterance. Based on this example, it can be seen that when interpreting the results of neuropsychological measures, the examiner must remain ever vigilant to the complex nature of tests. There are at least four important points to keep in mind when determining whether the basis for impaired performance on a task is due to the interaction of different cognitive domains. These points are identified in Table 3.5.

TABLE 3.5
Effects of the Interaction of Different Cognitive Domains

---
1. Diffuse versus Specific Effects.
2. Influence of lower order abilities on higher order abilities.
3. Primary versus secondary effects.

Diffuse Versus Specific Effects

General cognitive slowing is an example of one diffuse effect of a brain injury that can influence task performance. Response slowing often accompanies brain damage, and its effects on test performance must be evaluated separately from the actual loss of information processing abilities in any specific cognitive domain. Lezak (1995) emphasized the importance of determining whether the patient fails an item because the patient is (a) unable to provide the correct response or (b) able to provide the correct response but only beyond the specified time limits. On the WAIS–R Block Design subtest, for example, both types of responses would constitute a failure on the standard administration of the subtest. Nevertheless, the types of inferences that one can make about the patient's visuoconstructional abilities may be markedly different. Several authors have suggested that when using the WAIS–R a timed as well as untimed PIQ should be derived in an attempt to separate out (a) the effects of a specific deficit on performance and (b) the effects of general slowing on performance. The inferences that can be derived from performance of a patient who is unable to achieve even a partially correct solution given ample time and the performance of a patient who is capable of producing correct reproductions on the Block Design subtest but only beyond the time limit specified are quite different. In the first case, we might infer that the patient's visuoconstructional abilities as assessed by Block Design are disrupted due to the patient's inability to approximate the correct response even when imposed time limits are minimized. In the second case, we might infer that the patient's visuoconstructional abilities as assessed by the Block Design subtest appear to be available to the patient but likely influenced by significant slowing of responses. More recently, Kaplan, Fein, Morris, and Delis (1991) have devised a modified version of the WAIS–R called the WAIS–R as a Neuropsychological Instrument (WAIS–R NI). The manual and accompanying materials allow for modifications in test procedures similar to the example just given. In addition, they suggest other modifications that create opportunities for observing aspects of task performance not available with standard administration.

Lower Order versus Higher Order Deficits

The ability to perform higher order, complex cognitive tasks is based on the integrity of more basic functions. At the very least, the patient must possess an adequate level of arousal in order to sustain performance on any given task. Fluctuating levels of arousal and/or marked waxing and waning of attention when the patient is performing a complex cognitive task such as constructing a copy of the Rey Osterrieth Figure (Osterrieth, 1944; Rey, 1941) would make it erroneous to infer that a patient's poor performance reflects a marked visuoconstructional disorder. In this case, it is the inadequate levels of arousal and attention that have incapacitated the patient's performance. Interpreting performance on higher order tasks in patients with significant difficulties in arousal and attention must proceed with caution. In patients with extreme difficulties, interpretation is particularly problematic. In these cases, poor performance on higher order tasks may not be interpretable in terms of the usual interpretation for such tasks. For example, on a task of simple arithmetic word problems, patients may fail not because of deficits in arithmetic abilities but because they are unable to adequately attend to the items and retain them in memory long enough to complete the task. Although it is correct to conclude that performance on the arithmetic task was impaired, this performance should not be interpreted in terms of poor arithmetic abilities but in terms of the influence of a lower order ability, such as attention, which has resulted in poor performance on a higher order task, the arithmetic task.

Several tasks of writing ability involve the presentation of a standard picture to the patient. The patient's task is to write what he or she sees going on in the picture. In administering such tasks, the primary interest is in obtaining writing samples from the patient under standard conditions. However, if patients have a basic defect in visual scanning and produce an impoverished output or incomplete description because they are unable to appreciate or incorporate various aspects of the picture into a complete whole, performance could be erroneously interpreted as impoverished written language when, in fact, performance was due to difficulties in adequately scanning the picture at the outset. In a similar vein, difficulties associated with hemispatial neglect in which the patient may fail to orient, report, or respond to stimuli contralateral to their lesion could potentially influence performance on a seemingly disparate higher order ability such as receptive vocabulary. Some tasks that assess receptive vocabulary, such as the Peabody Picture Vocabulary Test–Revised (PPVT–R; Dunn & Dunn, 1981), utilize a pictorial multiple-choice format in which the patient must point to the item that correctly portrays a word presented. A patient with left-sided neglect following a right-hemisphere lesion may fail to orient to response alternatives presented on the left side of space (Heilman et al., 1993). In assessing the patient's responses on such tasks, the examiner should remain vigilant to where in space a patient's errors tended to occur. Similarly, more recent investigations have identified that patients sustaining bilateral damage to parietal regions are likely to demonstrate neglect and inattention for lower parts of space, whereas patients with bilateral temporal lesions may show the opposite pattern, neglect of upper parts of space (Rapcsak, Cimino, & Heilman, 1988; Shelton, Bowers, & Heilman, 1990). Therefore, allocation of attention in space may play a role in patients' patterns of performance on the PPVT–R or other measures.

Primary Versus Secondary Effects

In attempting to discern the basis for impaired performance on any task, a useful starting point is to determine whether deficits are in the ability or abilities that are assumed to underlie that task or are due to other deficits not assumed to be primary determinants of task performance. That is, a distinction is made between deficits that are primary in nature and deficits that are secondary in nature. A primary deficit in visuoconstructional abilities refers to the fact that failure on such tasks is most likely accounted for by true deficits in visuoconstructional ability that cannot be accounted for by difficulties in any other cognitive domain. A secondary deficit would reflect the situation where poor performance on a task such as visuoconstructional ability is secondarily influenced by a deficit in some other domain of function (either higher order or lower order). In one of the examples given earlier, we might indicate that poor performance on visuoconstructional tasks was secondarily influenced by marked deficits in arousal and attention.

The Hooper Visual Organizational Test (Hooper, 1958) is a complex test of visuoperceptual and visuosynthetic processing that requires the patient to recognize pictures of objects that have been cut up and rearranged. The purpose of administering this task is to assess abilities of visuoperceptual and visuosynthetic abilities. However, if a patient is unable to produce the name of the object, this failure may be due to significant anomia and not to problems in visuoperceptual/visuosynthetic ability per se. Many items on the Hooper are relatively high-frequency items, which minimizes, to some extent, the influence of naming difficulties. However, it is still the case that naming deficits can influence performance on this task, particularly when those deficits are pronounced. To investigate this possibility, the examiner should consider the patient's performance on more formal measures of naming ability or examine other data for naming failures. In this case, one would infer that performance on this visuoperceptual/visuosynthetic task was secondarily influenced by naming difficulties and that it did not present evidence of a primary disturbance in visuoperceptual/visuosynthetic abilities unless there was evidence to suggest otherwise.

On measures of memory function, it is essential to determine whether deficits in other processing domains can fully account for performance on various memory measures. For example, memory assessment usually includes the evaluation of both verbal and nonverbal memory functions. The Wechsler Memory Scale–Revised (WMS–R; Wechsler, 1987) is one such measure. Two subtests, Logical Memory and Visual Reproduction, require the immediate recall of short stories and line drawings, respectively. In addition, subjects are again asked to reproduce these same items following a 30-min delay. If a patient presents with significant language difficulties, it may be difficult to interpret performance on verbal memory measures apart from language disturbance. Similarly, for patients with significant visuoperceptual difficulties, it may be difficult to infer performance on nonverbal aspects of memory independently of the visuoperceptual deficits. Obviously, the magnitude of the deficits in language or visuoperceptual abilities is an important factor to consider.

One aspect of task performance that can be of some benefit in interpreting these findings is to examine how performance in the immediate recall condition compares to performance in the delayed recall condition. Patients may have difficulty encoding the information as reflected by poor performance in the immediate memory condition but retain nearly all of that information over time as reflected by performance in the delayed recall condition. If so, the primary deficit is likely in perception, secondarily resulting in impaired memory performance. It is difficult to argue for the existence of material specific memory deficit in this situation where specific verbal or visuoperceptual processing deficits appear to set a limit in terms of the amount of information that initially enters the system at immediate recall although very little loss of this same information over time is observed. A second possibility is that performance in the delayed recall condition is significantly worse than performance in the immediate recall condition. The latter scenario does demonstrate loss of information over time. In this case, the examiner may be better able to interpret performance in terms of material specific memory failure. These types of determinations require a significant degree of thought on the part of the examiner.

EVALUATING THE CONSISTENCY OF NEUROPSYCHOLOGICAL DATA

The extent to which neuropsychological data are consistent is at the very heart of the integrative aspects of neuropsychological interpretation. In evaluating consistency of neuropsychological data one must consider the extent to which test data are consistent both within a cognitive domain and across various cognitive domains. This evaluation of consistency involves not only determinations of whether the neuropsychological test data are consistent but also the extent to which test data are consistent with other neuropsychological data such as history and behavioral observations of test and extratest behavior. In determining the consistency of neuropsychological data, at least six different aspects should be considered. These are listed in Table 3.6.

TABLE 3.6

Evaluating the Consistency of Neuropsychological Data

1. Comparisons across multiple measures within a cognitive domain.
2. Determining whether deficits are primary or secondary in nature.
3. Comparison of level and pattern of performance with expectations.
4. Consistency of test behavior and extratest behavior.
5. Easier tasks performed at poorer levels than more difficult tasks.
6. Poorer than chance performance.

Comparisons Across Multiple Measures
Within a Cognitive Domain

Examining the consistency of performance within a cognitive domain is one aspect of integrating results during the interpretation of overall neuropsychological performance. In this regard, several authors have suggested the need for administration of multiple measures within a cognitive domain to better assess the consistency of performance (Larrabee, 1990; Weintraub & Mesulam, 1985). This redundancy of information is an excellent means of evaluating the extent to which the patient's performance is consistent across tests assumed to be measuring the same function. To the extent that results are consistent within a cognitive domain, the examiner is in a stronger position to interpret the results as reflecting spared or impaired function. That is, if all tasks within the language domain are intact, the examiner is better able to infer that such results reflect spared language abilities. Similarly, if all tests of memory are impaired, the examiner is again better able to infer that these results are consistent with the interpretation of impaired memory function.

However, more often than not, the examiner is in the position of interpreting neuropsychological data within a cognitive domain that do not, at least on the surface, appear consistent. In such cases, the examiner must carefully consider task demands that are inherent in the neuropsychological measures. The issues already discussed related to interactions between cognitive domains are essential in determining whether or not findings are internally consistent

For example, within the memory domain a patient may be within normal limits on measures of verbal memory function but impaired on nonverbal memory measures. In this case, we would expect that performance should be consistent across various verbal memory measures, assuming that these tasks do not differ on some significant dimension that could otherwise account for the difference in performance. Similarly, we would expect that performance should be consistent across various nonverbal memory measures, again assuming that these tasks do not differ on some significant dimension that could otherwise account for the difference in performance. As another example, the patient may show poor performance on tasks utilizing free recall, yet perform much better on recognition memory measures, a pattern found in Huntington's disease patients (Butters, Wolfe, Martone, Granholm, & Cermak, 1985). Although these results represent seemingly discrepant findings within the memory domain, they may well be consistent within the context of certain neurobehavioral disorders and their clinical presentation.

In a similar vein, the examiner must reconsider the assumption that various measures within a cognitive domain are tapping the same function. Consideration of the mode of input (visual, auditory, verbal, nonverbal, etc.) as well as the mode of output (verbal response, pointing response, graphomotor response, etc.) helps make sense out of seemingly discrepant findings. Although tasks may be grouped together under various domains, they often differ greatly with respect to task requirements and even specific aspects of the domain in question. For example, while language function may be considered to be a single domain of function, within that domain are disparate abilities including fluency, comprehension, naming, repetition, reading, writing, spelling, and so on, which may be spared or impaired to greater or lesser degrees. In examining data for consistency, it is important to consider all aspects of task requirements and processing demands. Analysis of consistency within a domain is an important step in deriving accurate and veridical interpretations of neuropsychological data. This is particularly important in forensic neuropsychology and in cases in which malingering or feigned performance is suspected.

Determining Whether Deficits
Are Primary or Secondary in Nature

Determining whether deficits are primary or secondary in nature may be involved in evaluating the consistency of neuropsychological data. If within a particular cognitive domain results do not appear consistent, then the examiner may question whether deficits observed in performance on a particular task are primary or secondary in nature. In addressing this issue, it may be helpful to make comparisons across various cognitive domains to determine whether evidence to support the secondary influence on a particular task is present. Let's suppose that a patient is able to perform higher order visual processing tasks that require the subject to actually reproduce the item such as in the copy phases of the Benton Visual Retention Test (Benton, 1974) or the Rey Osterrieth Complex Figure (Osterrieth, 1944; Rey, 1941). Let's also assume that the patient is able to perform well on visuoperceptual and visuospatial tasks in which the patient must recognize the correct response by pointing to the correct response alternative, such as in the Benton Facial Recognition Task (Benton & Van Allen, 1968) and Benton Line Orientation Task (Benton, Hannay, & Varney, 1975). However, this same patient performs poorly on the Hooper Visual Organization Test (Hooper, 1958) and Gollin Figures (Gollin, 1960), in which the patient must indicate the correct response by naming the item. In this case, we may suspect that poor performance on these latter tasks may be secondarily influenced by poor naming abilities. To assess this possible interpretation, we must look at data across cognitive domains. More specifically, we would look to performance in the language domain, particularly on tasks of naming ability, to ascertain whether naming deficits are also present on these tasks. Looking both within a cognitive domain and across cognitive domains can be very helpful in resolving apparent inconsistencies in neuropsychological data to arrive at more parsimonious and veridical interpretations of performance.

Similarly, consideration of the influence of fatigue on task performance may be necessary when interpreting the consistency of results and the extent to which deficits are of a primary or secondary nature. If the neuropsychological evaluation is especially long, undue fatigue may interfere with the patient's ability to complete the task at hand. If optimal conditions for assessment are desirable, this may not yield the patient's maximal performance. On the other hand, it may be the case that specific deficits emerge only when the system is stressed, as with fatigue, and such information could potentially be very useful in terms of its impact on the patient's daily functioning. Alternatively, the influence of fatigue could represent nonspecific effects on task performance. To disentangle potential specific effects of fatigue on a particular cognitive domain versus nonspecific effects of fatigue on performance in general, we would need to look at the pattern of performance across the testing session and across various cognitive domains. If fatigue effects were general and nonspecific, we would expect to find poorer performance as the testing session progressed on tasks administered most recently, irrespective of the cognitive domain. In contrast, if fatigue was influential in eliciting specific effects in a particular cognitive domain, then again we would expect these deficits to arise toward the end of the testing session, but only on those tasks within that particular cognitive domain.

Comparison of Level and Pattern of Performance with Expectations

Consistency between a patient's level and pattern of performance, as assessed by neuropsychological measures, and examiner expectations of the level and pattern of performance of the patient is an important aspect of the interpretation process. Expectations may relate to the level of performance relative to some estimate of premorbid abilities. Similarly, expectations may relate to the pattern of performance known to be associated with various neurobehavioral, psychiatric, or other medical disorders. Comparing obtained data with expected premorbid functioning is essential to the determination of impairment, whereas comparison with specific medical disorders helps delineate the etiological condition. A caveat to this aspect of the interpretation process is to remain vigilant to the tendency to disregard data that are inconsistent with expectations, that is, the tendency toward confirmatory bias.

The extent to which an examiner can generate expectations of test performance and anticipate the potential level and pattern of performance is highly dependent upon the knowledge base and experience of the examiner. In addition, the extent to which the examiner can formulate useful expectations for any particular patient is determined by the information available at the time of the assessment in the form of background information, prior testing, medical history, and current clinical presentation. Knowledge of patterns of deficits associated with various neurobehavioral disorders is also essential. In cases where there is the potential for litigation or secondary gain such as compensation, then the extent to which the level and pattern of performance are consistent with expectations becomes potentially even more important to the interpretive endeavor.

Consistency of Test Behavior and Extratest Behavior

Evaluating the consistency of test behaviors with extratest behaviors represents an important level of analysis. If there is a question about the patient's ability to maintain adequate attention and sustained concentration on the task at hand during assessment, this may be evident in observations of the patient's extratest behavior as well. For example, the patient may fail to attend to the examiner appropriately, show significant delays in responses to questions, or lose the train of thought in conversation. Similarly, if memory difficulties are present, the patient is likely to manifest these deficits in extratest behaviors by being unable to recall the name of the examiner or prior physicians, repeating the same statements or questions without being aware of doing so, demonstrating difficulty in following the thread of interview by forgetting the question, and so on. Severe impairment memory measures, yet accurate recall in vivid detail of the events of that morning's test session, events that occurred at home during the past week, and otherwise good recall of information without the benefit of cueing, is a highly discrepant pattern. Attempts to resolve such discrepancies are an essential aspect of neuropsychological interpretation.

Easier Tasks Performed at Poorer Levels Than More Difficult Tasks

Observing whether easier tasks are performed at poorer levels than more difficult tasks is also an important element in assessing the consistency of neuropsychological data. Performance of higher order or more difficult tasks is predicated on the integrity of lower order or more basic abilities. Thus, performance on easier tasks should be equal to or better than performance on more difficult tasks. We would not expect performance on more difficult tasks to exceed that of impaired performance on easier tasks. For example, on the Trail Making Test (Reitan & Wolfson, 1985), typically a patient would not be expected to perform more poorly on Trails A than Trails B. Normal performance on Trails B is predicated on the ability to successfully complete Trails A. Trails A consists of 25 circles, numbered from 1 to 25, distributed randomly on a sheet of paper. Patients are required to sequentially connect circles with a pencil. Trails B is similar except that the circles are numbered from 1 to 13 and lettered from A to L. Again patients are required to connect the circles, proceeding in an ascending sequence, but now alternating between numbers and letters. In addition to similar visual scanning requirements, Trails B requires mental flexibility and the ability to integrate number and alphabetic sequences. Normal performance on Trails B in the context of impaired performance on Trails A represents an unusual performance, inconsistent with typical patterns of performance on these measures.

Similarly, on the Stroop task (Stroop, 1935), we would not expect performance on the noninterference condition (reading of simple color words [blue, green, red] or naming the color of ink patches) to be in the impaired range while performance on the interference condition (e.g., saying the color of the green ink in which the "color word" RED was printed) fell within the normal range. This pattern of performance does not make sense in terms of what is know about cognitive requirements in these two conditions. Similarly, on memory measures, we would not expect that recognition memory performance would be significantly worse than performance in a free-recall condition. A recognition memory task is typically easier than free recall, and most individuals' performance improves somewhat under test conditions utilizing recognition. The opposite pattern of performance, in which recognition memory is significantly worse than free recall, should raise questions about the consistency of the patient's performance.

Poorer Than Chance Performance

Observations of poorer than chance performance are of greatest concern in cases where the validity of neuropsychological data is in question. In fact, examination of chance versus worse than chance performance has been suggested as a method for assessing symptom exaggeration, that is, Symptom Validity testing (Binder & Pankratz, 1987; Hiscock & Hiscock, 1989). For example, Symptom Validity testing of memory is based on the assumption that if impairment is actually present, then on a task in which the patient must make a yes–no decision, the patient with true memory difficulties should perform no worse than chance. In this case, the patient would be expected to provide the correct response on about 50% of trials. However, performance that is significantly below chance would be a rare phenomenon in such patients and when present would suggest some knowledge of the distinction between correct and incorrect responses.

In addition to observing inconsistencies across neuropsychological data, the use of Symptom Validity testing may prove to be of benefit in cases where feigned performance is suspected. It must be emphasized that distinguishing between conditions in which a patient deliberately or consciously attempts to feign performance and conditions in which nonconscious feigning is present may be very difficult. Although conscious versus nonconscious etiologies for worse than chance performance have very different implications in terms of treatment planning, compensation and legal proceedings, both represent findings inconsistent with an organic-based memory disorder. However, it also may be the case that deliberate attempts to alter performance may coexist with real neuropsychological deficits. In such cases, accurate estimates of a patient's performance may be difficult if not impossible to establish.

DISTINGUISHING NEUROLOGIC, PSYCHIATRIC, AND TEST-TAKING CONDITIONS THAT MAY OVERLAP

As part of the conceptualization and interpretation of neuropsychological data, the examiner is often in the position of attempting to distinguishing between several different conditions that might account for the patient's overall presentation. For example, hallucinations, delusions, paranoia, and other psychotic features can be observed in neurologic as well as psychiatric disorders. Delusions following neurologic insult are most likely to occur following focal right-hemisphere damage superimposed on diffuse atrophy (Levine & Grek, 1984). One content-specific delusional belief, termed *Capgras syndrome,* is the delusional belief that well-known individuals, such as family members, have identical doubles or imposters. This phenomenon can be observed following focal neurologic damage but to the novice may appear to be more consistent with a psychiatric disturbance such as schizophrenia than with a neurologic disorder (Malloy, Cimino, & Westlake, 1992). Various neurologic disorders also overlap in clinical presentation and neuropsychological test performance patterns. Earlier, a patient was described with an amnestic disorder and accompanying mild executive problems following bilateral thalamic infarcts, and the patient had initially been thought to have Alzheimer's disease. These are just two examples of the many types of overlapping conditions of which the examiner must remain aware in distinguishing between neurologic, psychiatric, and test-taking conditions.

In evaluating neuropsychological test data, the examiner must keep in mind that a particular performance may be arrived at in any number of different ways and for a variety of reasons. That a patient's performance on a neuropsychological measure falls in the impaired range does not necessarily mean that such a performance reflects "brain impairment." Interpretation of poor performance will examine the extent to which poor performance may be attributable to some degree of neurologic involvement versus psychiatric, personality factors, or test-taking conditions such as conscious or nonconscious feigned performance. Distinguishing among these various disorders requires close scrutiny of all available data through a systematic and careful consideration of factors identified in Table 3.7.

TABLE 3.7
Distinguishing Neurologic, Psychiatric, and Test-Taking Conditions

1. History.
2. Test-taking behavior.
3. Extratest behavior.
4. Knowledge of cognitive changes associated with different disorders.

History

In attempting to discern various conditions that might account for neuro-psychological data, consideration of history is often crucial. In cases where there is some evidence of psychiatric disturbance together with poor performance on some neuropsychological measures, the history may clarify the interpretation of performance. A case in which there is history of prior psychiatric disturbance including hospitalizations or treatments may be interpreted somewhat differently than a case in which presentation of psychiatric symptoms is of new and recent onset. Similarly, the distinction between dementia and pseudodementia may be aided by history, although this remains one of the most difficult differentiations to make. In cases where there is no formal psychiatric history available, some indication from the interview of recurring bouts of depression might suggest a long-standing problem in this domain. In cases where depression occurs in the context of poor performance on neuropsychological measures, consideration of whether the onset of cognitive difficulties was slow and insidious, as in the case of most progressive degenerative dementias, or relatively abrupt and coincident with a worsening of depressive symptomatology may be useful information in attempting to discern these two conditions (Caine, 1986; Lezak, 1995). Similarly, interviews with family and significant others may provide useful information on behavior patterns including preoccupation with bodily concerns, dependent traits, poor relationships with others, or a tendency to withdraw that may suggest that such traits represent either relatively enduring patterns of behavior or manifestations of undiagnosed psychiatric disturbance.

In addition, many disorders are known to have some genetic component, and family medical history may be useful in differential diagnosis. Family history may be an important variable to consider when disorders are entertained such as Alzheimer's disease, Huntington's disease, schizophrenia, affective disorder, and many others. In addition, in cases where conscious feigned performance is suspected, a history of multiple litigations or antisocial behavior may raise the question of potential secondary gain as accounting for performance on neuro-psychological measures.

Test-Taking Behavior

Consideration of the test-taking behavior of the individual may be of benefit in distinguishing between etiological conditions or when feigned performance is suspected. In working on items, does the patient appear to be exerting adequate effort and motivation? Lack of concern for repeated failures on tasks in the context of good awareness of such performance may lead one to question the occurrence of feigned performance. The patient's tendency to consistently hesitate before responding may also alert the examiner to attempts to modify output prior to responding. In cases where depression is suspected the examiner should be alert to self-deprecating statements and excessive self-monitoring of perform-ance. A tendency to give up easily or become increasingly frustrated with fail-ures may be consistent with test-taking behaviors observed in depression. Some authors (Post, 1975; Wells, 1979) have identified the occurrence of "I don't know" responses as a potential indicator in performance of depressed patients relative to dementia patients; however, this does not appear to be supported empirically (O'Boyle & Amadeo, 1989; Young, Manley, & Alexopoulos, 1985). Nevertheless, depressed patients are observed to have more conservative response criteria rel-ative to patients with dementia (Corwin et al., 1990).

Extratest Behaviors

In addition to careful observation of test-taking behaviors, a consideration of ex-tratest behaviors may prove to be of benefit. Incidental observations of behavior provide useful information about a patient's consistency of performance be-tween cognitive abilities as assessed by neuropsychological assessment and cog-nitive abilities as demonstrated by the individual's behavior in the environment. Recently, a patient was tested who performed beyond two standard deviations below performance of similarly aged peers on nearly all memory measures pre-sented to her. Nevertheless, during a break in testing she was able to wind her way through the many halls of a medical clinic to find a smoking area and subse-quently return at the designated time to the testing room without any apparent difficulty. In addition, she was able to execute these behaviors despite the fact that this was her first visit to clinic. In patients with severe memory difficulties, such good recall of locations in space in an unfamiliar environment would be difficult without additional cues and reminders. This observation together with other in-formation about the pattern of her test performance raised questions about the validity of her performance on neuropsychological measures.

Knowledge of Cognitive Changes
Associated with Different Disorders

Lastly, knowledge of cognitive changes associated with different disorders is per-haps the most important domain that can assist the examiner in differentiating neurologic, psychiatric, and test-taking conditions that may overlap. Knowledge of various patterns of performance associated with different neurologic and psychiatric disorders allows the examiner to recognize patterns of performance that are most consistent with a disorder as well as recognize aspects of perform-ance that may be inconsistent with a disorder. For example, in differentiating de-mentia and depression, several aspects of performance may help in distinguish-ing the relative contribution of depression to performance on neuropsychologi-cal measures. Pseudodementia or the dementia associated with depression is likely to share many features in common with subcortical dementias (King &

Caine, 1990). Cortical signs such as apraxia and aphasia are not likely to be observed in depression but are very likely to be present in a cortical dementia. Similarly, the memory disturbance associated with depression may result in characteristically different patterns of performance than the memory disturbance associated with dementia. In depression, memory disturbance is often secondary to attention and concentration difficulties inherent in the disorder. This results in poor initial registration of information but relatively little loss of this same information over time. Assessing the rate of forgetting of information by comparing immediate recall to subsequent delayed recall is one potentially useful aspect of memory performance in helping to differentiate depression from dementia (Hart, Kwentus, Taylor, & Harkins, 1987). Memory performance of depressed patients is also characterized by poor performance on tasks that require significant effort. Weingartner (1986) reported that when attempts are made to increase the inherent organization and structure of information presented at learning, depressed patients' performance improves. This may be reflected in impaired free recall of material in the context of relatively preserved recognition memory, which represents a less effortful test condition (Kaszniak, Poon, & Riege, 1986). Some qualitative features of performance suggest that depressed patients may show poorer recall of neutral or positive material relative to material with a negative theme, so-called *mood-congruent effects* (Blaney, 1986; Singer & Salovey, 1988). Self-report measures suggest that depressed patients tend to underestimate their memory performance, whereas demented patients are more likely to overestimate the capabilities of their memory performance (O'Boyle, Amadeo, & Self, 1990; O'Hara, Hinrichs, Kohout, Wallace, & Lemke, 1986). In differentiating such cases, the relative importance of serial testing of both cognitive abilities and affect / mood changes is perhaps one of the most useful means of distinguishing between these two disorders. However, it must be kept in mind that dementia and depression are not mutually exclusive. Many patients may present with depression in the early phase of dementia, and following them over time with serial testing may be the only successful means of determining whether a true dementia is present.

AVOIDING ERRONEOUS ASSUMPTIONS
AND INFERENCES

In the process of interpreting neuropsychological data, we often make certain assumptions about the individual's test performance. If these assumptions go unchecked, interpretation of the data may not represent an accurate reflection of the patient's neuropsychological status. Similarly, interpretation of test data can proceed from certain inferences about test performance that may be neither logical nor accurate. Table 3.8 lists several of these erroneous assumptions and

TABLE 3.8
Avoiding Erroneous Assumptions and Inferences

1. Performance was normal in the past.
2. Face validity as true validity.
3. Impaired performance on test X necessarily implies damage to region Y.
4. Overinterpretation and underinterpretation of neuropsychological data.

inferences that may occur in the context of interpretation. When interpreting neuropsychological data, it is important to question whether the assumptions made about a patient's performance are in fact met. Similarly, it may be useful to consider whether the interpretation of a patient's neuropsychological data involves inferences that may threaten the validity of that interpretation.

Performance Was Normal in the Past

A common assumption in the interpretation of neuropsychological data is that the patient's performance was normal in the past. Although this may be the case in the majority of patients evaluated, this assumption should never go unchecked. Assuming that performance was normal in the past, when in fact performance has always been significantly below the average range, may lead to the erroneous interpretation that this represents a change in performance from baseline. One common situation in which this assumption may be violated is in the presence of a learning disability. Poor performance in domains such as reading, spelling, or arithmetic may be erroneously interpreted as reflecting a change from baseline performance if these difficulties have been long-standing in nature. A more thorough investigation of history and consideration of this information when interpreting neuropsychological data would avoid this error.

Similarly, performance on motor tasks that strongly suggests an abnormal pattern of asymmetric performance should be considered within the context of this assumption. Such patterns of performance may alert us to the potential of unilateral brain impairment. However, factors other than central nervous system involvement may result in asymmetries on motor tasks. A history of peripheral nerve damage could account for such a pattern of performance. A careful consideration of history or direct inquiry of the patient would avoid an error in interpretation. In a case where performance for both hands falls within normal limits but an unusually large split is observed, it may be tempting to assume that this pattern represents a change from baseline performance. This assumption, however, might be incorrect in an athlete with overdeveloped abilities in one limb. Again in this case, attention to aspects of the patient's history or direct questioning may help to make better sense out of seemingly abnormal performance.

Face Validity as True Validity

A common error of interpretation involves the mistaken assumption that face validity of a neuropsychological measure is in fact a true type of validity. *Validity of a test* is defined as "the degree to which the test actually measures what it purports to measure" (Anastasi, 1988, p. 28). This can be established through a variety of different methods such as determining the extent to which the test predicts performance on some criterion measure, correlations with other tests known to measure a particular ability, use of factor analysis, and a variety of other means. In contrast, *face validity* refers to what the test appears to be measuring. That is, does the test look like or appear to be a test of memory, arithmetic abilities, visuoconstructional abilities, or naming abilities? In fact, face validity is not a true validity in the psychometric sense of the word. As examiners, we must not be persuaded to believe, because a test looks like it is measuring a certain cognitive ability or because the name of the test or its instruction manual refer to one particular cognitive ability, that this particular test measures *only* that ability. Similarly, as Walsh (1992, p. 127) indicated, we must not "be seduced into taking poor performance on a test to mean that the function said by the test makers to be measured by the test has been affected." It may be the case that an impaired score on that test can be achieved for a variety of reasons. Again, by maintaining an awareness of the complexity of neuropsychological measures and the many component processes involved in the completion of that measure, the examiner is in a better position to avoid this erroneous assumption.

Impaired Performance on Test X
Necessarily Implies Damage to Region Y

It is often the case that in the process of interpreting neuropsychological data, errors of inference arise that lead to incorrect interpretations of the patient's performance. One common error of inference is that if damage to a specific brain region is associated with poor performance on a particular task, then poor performance on that test implies dysfunction of that region in all subjects (Miller, 1983). To illustrate the effects of such an inference, Weintraub and Mesulam (1985) provided the example of memory deficits associated with left and right temporal lobe damage. They suggested that because several studies have shown that patients with left temporal damage are likely to develop a material specific verbal memory deficit, clinicians have a tendency to infer that the presence of a verbal memory deficit always implies the presence of left temporal lobe lesions. This inference is incorrect. We now know that left- or right-sided lesions to subcortical structures such as the dorsal medial nucleus of the thalamus may also result in material specific verbal and nonverbal memory deficits, respectively (Speedie & Heilman, 1982, 1983). Larrabee (1990) provided another example of this erroneous inference in diagnostic decisions regarding the presence or absence of "brain damage." In this instance, the examiner may erroneously assume that because brain-impaired patients fail on neuropsychological measures, then any patient who fails on a neuropsychological measure must have brain impairment. This type of mistaken inference can lead to gross misinterpretations of neuropsychological data that neglect consideration of the fact that patients may fail on neuropsychological measures for many reasons other than brain impairment.

Overinterpretation and Underinterpretation of Neuropsychological Data

Errors of overinterpretation and errors of underinterpretation are based on two misleading and erroneous inferences. Errors of overinterpretation may be due to the mistaken inference that an impaired score equals brain impairment. This inference is very similar to that just described in which the examiner infers that because brain-impaired patients fail on neuropsychological measures, then any patient who fails a neuropsychological measure must have brain impairment. Errors of underinterpretation reflect an erroneous inference that is the converse of that one—that is, no impaired score is equal to no brain impairment. Walsh (1992) noted, "We should bear in mind Teuber's dictum 'absence of evidence is not evidence of absence.'" Cases in which neurologic impairment exists in the context of normal performance on neuropsychological measures are some of the most difficult diagnostic determinations in neuropsychology. In general, there are two scenarios in which this may be the case. The first involves cases in which the individual possesses superior premorbid abilities or talents. The second involves cases of isolated frontal-lobe pathology.

In cases of superior premorbid abilities or talents, an average level of performance in a particular cognitive domain may represent a significant decline in performance from that individual's premorbid status. However, detection of such a decline may be difficult using standard neuropsychological measures. A careful consideration of premorbid estimates of ability would be very helpful in determining the extent to which the current level of performance matches that of expected performance. Use of recent normative data that include individuals of higher educational levels or intellectual levels as part of the normative sample also would be of benefit. Some recently developed neuropsychological screening measures, such as the Assessment of Cognitive Skills (ACS), have been geared toward detection of age-inappropriate cognitive changes in individuals with a presumed high premorbid level of ability as well as in individuals with premorbid abilities estimated to be in the average range (Cimino, Behner, Cattarn, & Tantleft, 1991; Weintraub et al., 1991). Availability of measures with higher ceilings on performance and appropriate normative comparisons may help to address this difficult diagnostic determination.

Cases in which isolated frontal-lobe pathology is present may present as significant diagnostic dilemmas. Several authors (Lezak, 1995; Walsh, 1987, 1991) have commented on the relative insensitivity of intellectual measures in capturing the variety of adaptive behavior deficits observed in frontal-lobe pathology. A patient may evidence gross deficits in everyday instances of judgment, planning, and decision making that render that patient virtually incapable of functioning effectively or independently in his or her environment. Nevertheless, that patient may score average or even well above average on measures of intellectual functioning such as the WAIS–R (Wechsler, 1981). An even more striking example of the insensitivity of standard clinical measures to the disruptive effects of frontal pathology is the case EVR, reported by Eslinger and Damasio (1985): EVR underwent bilateral ablation of ventromedial frontal cortices for the treatment of meningioma. In addition to scoring in the superior range on measures of intellectual ability, this patient demonstrated no deficits in memory, language, visuoperceptual, or visuospatial abilities. Of even greater significance, is the fact that this patient performed normally on tasks assumed to measure so-called "frontal" or executive / self-regulatory abilities. EVR's performance on the Wisconsin Card Sorting Test, the Category Test, verbal fluency, cognitive estimations (Shallice & Evans, 1978), and judgments of recency and frequency (Milner & Petrides, 1984) were all within normal limits. Nevertheless, this patient exhibited marked adaptive behavior deficits that made it impossible for him to maintain employment and function effectively in his environment, due to marked difficulties in planning, decision making, and social behavior.

This case underscores the potential insensitivity of neuropsychological measures in assessing adaptive behaviors that determine the extent to which a patient is able to function competently and independently in his or her environment. This case also underscores the relative importance of considering *all* available data in the interpretation of a patient's performance. Test scores represent only one, albeit important, element in the conceptualization and interpretation of neuropsychological data. Integration of information from the patient's history, data from interview of the patient, family, or significant others, observations of the patient's test and extratest behaviors, and consideration of test performance is necessary to allow for consistent and veridical interpretations of the patient's current neuropsychological status.

SUMMARY

This chapter highlights various fundamental principles involved in neuropsychological interpretation. The chapter is not intended to provide a step-by-step or cookbook approach to interpretation. Rather, this chapter is meant to serve as a guide in developing the kinds of thought processes necessary in careful consideration and interpretation of neuropsychological data. Neuropsychological interpretation is viewed as a multistaged process that involves integration of data from multiple sources, only one of which is test scores. The examiner must consider all available data in the form of history, interview, behavioral observations, and test scores. Furthermore, these sources of information must be checked against each other for evidence of consistencies as well as potential inconsistencies in arriving at veridical interpretations of the patient's current neuropsychological status and likely etiological conditions.

An invaluable tool in approaching the interpretation process is that of a conceptual model of brain–behavior relationships. A conceptual model of brain–behavior relationships involves a working knowledge of how neuroanatomy, neuropathologic conditions and their sequelae, clinical psychology / psychopathology, and psychometric properties and principles interact. From this foundation, the examiner is better able to anticipate potential patterns of behavior as well as recognize consistencies and inconsistencies when they arise, recognize unusual presentations of neurobehavioral disorders, and provide accurate and rich accounts of the qualitative aspects of the patient's performance. Attention to subject-specific variables that may influence neuropsychological data is also discussed with special consideration of how these factors may influence interpretation. Similarly, the importance of recognizing that neuropsychological measures represent complex and often multifactorial tasks and that such tasks may be failed for a variety of reasons is emphasized. This notion is of prime importance in recognizing that cognitive domains may interact and that poor performance on a task may represent either true primary deficits in a particular cognitive domain or secondary effects produced by deficits in a seemingly unrelated cognitive domain. Evaluation of consistencies as well as inconsistencies in neuropsychological data is important in the interpretation process. This evaluation and knowledge of the patterns of performance in various neurobehavioral and / or psychiatric disorders are important elements in distinguishing between neurologic, psychiatric, and test-taking conditions that may overlap. Lastly, some common erroneous assumptions and inferences of interpretation were considered in this chapter.

REFERENCES

Alexander, G. E., & Fuster, J. M. (1973). Effects of cooling prefrontal cortex on cell firing in the nucleus medialis dorsalis. *Brain Research, 61*, 93–105.

American Psychiatric Association. (1994). *Diagnostic and statistical manual of mental disorders* (4th ed.). Washington, DC: Author.

Anastasi, A. (1988). *Psychological testing* (6th ed.). New York: Macmillan.

Annett, M. (1967). The binomial distribution of right, mixed and left handedness. *Quarterly Journal of Experimental Psychology, 61*, 303–321.

Barclay, L. L., Weiss, E. M., Mattis, S., Bond, O., & Blass, J. P. (1988). Unrecognized cognitive impairment in cardiac rehabilitation patients. *Journal of the American Geriatrics Society, 36*, 22–28.

Benton, A. L. (1974). *Visual retention test*. New York: Psychological Corporation.

Benton, A. L., Hamsher, K. de S., Varney, N. R., & Spreen, O. (1983). *Contributions to neuropsychological assessment.* New York: Oxford University Press.

Benton, A. L., Hannay, H. J., & Varney, N. (1975). Visual perception of line direction in patients with unilateral brain disease. *Neurology, 25,* 907–910.

Benton, A. L., & Van Allen, M. (1968). Impairment in facial recognition in patients with cerebral disease. *Cortex, 4,* 344–358.

Binder, L. M., & Pankratz, L. (1987). Neuropsychological evidence of a factitious memory complaint. *Journal of Clinical and Experimental Neuropsychology, 9,* 167–171.

Blaney, P. H. (1986). Affect and memory: A review. *Psychological Bulletin, 99,* 229–246.

Bornstein, R. A. (1986). Classification rates obtained with "standard" cut-off scores on selected neuropsychological measures. *Journal of Clinical and Experimental Neuropsychology, 8,* 413–420.

Branch, C., Milner, B., & Rasmussen, T. (1964). Intracarotid sodium amytal for the lateralization of cerebral speech dominance. *Journal of Neurosurgery, 21,* 345–399.

Briggs, G. G., & Nebes, R. D. (1975). Patterns of hand preference in a student population. *Cortex, 11,* 230–238.

Butters, N., & Stuss, D. (1989). Diencephalic amnesia. In F. Boller and J. Grafman (Eds.), *Handbook of neuropsychology* (Vol. 3, pp. 107–148). Amsterdam: Elsevier.

Butters, N., Wolfe, J., Martone, M., Granholm, E., & Cermak, L. S. (1985). Memory disorders associated with Huntington's disease: Verbal recall, verbal recognition and procedural memory. *Neuropsychologia, 6,* 729–744.

Caine, E. D. (1986). The neuropsychology of depression: The pseudodementia syndrome. In I. Grant & K. M. Adams (Eds.), *Neuropsychological assessment of neuropsychiatric disorders* (pp. 221–243). New York: Oxford University Press.

Cimino, C. R., Behner, G., Cattarin, J., & Tantleff, S. (1991). Concurrent validity of the Assessment of Cognitive Skills (ACS). *Journal of Clinical and Experimental Neuropsychology, 13,* 106.

Corwin, J., & Peselow, E. D., Feenan, K., Rotrosen, J., & Fieve, R. (1990). Disorders of decision in affective disease: An effect of B-adrenergic dysfunction? *Biological Psychiatry, 27,* 813–833.

Cummings, J. J., & Benson, D. F. (1992). *Dementia: A clinical approach* (2nd ed.). Boston: Butterworth-Heinemann.

Drachman, D. A., & Leavitt, J. (1974). Human memory and the cholingeric system. *Archives of Neurology, 30,* 113–121.

Dunn, L. M., & Dunn, L. M. (1981). *Peabody Picture Vocabulary Test–Revised, manual.* Circle Pine, MN: American Guidance Service.

Eslinger, P. J., & Damasio, A. R. (1985). Severe disturbance of higher cognition after frontal lobe ablation: Patient EVR. *Neurology, 35,* 1731–1741.

Franzen, M. D. (1989). *Reliability and validity in neuropsychological assessment.* New York: Plenum Press.

Geschwind, N. (1965). Disconnexion syndromes in animals and man. *Brain, 88,* 237–294.

Gollin, E. S. (1960). Developmental studies of visual recognition of incomplete objects. *Perceptual and Motor Skills, 11,* 289–298.

Goodglass, H., & Kaplan, E. (1979). Assessment of cognitive deficit in the brain-injured patient. In M. S. Gazzaniga (Ed.), *Handbook of behavioral neurobiology* (vol. 2, pp. 2–33). New York: Plenum.

Graff-Radford, N., Damasio, H., Yamada, T., Eslinger, P. J., & Damasio, A. R. (1985). Nonhaemorrhagic thalamic infarction. *Brain, 108,* 485–516.

Hart, R. P., Kwentus, J. A., Taylor, J. R., & Harkins, S. W. (1987). Rate of forgetting in dementia and depression. *Journal of Consulting and Clinical Psychology, 55,* 101–105.

Heaton, R. K., Grant, I., & Matthews, C. G. (1986). Differences in neuropsychological test performance associated with age, education, and sex. In I. Grant & K. M. Adams (Eds.), *Neuropsychological assessment of neuropsychiatric disorders* (pp. 100–120). New York: Oxford University Press.

Heaton, R. K., Grant, I., & Matthews, C. G. (1991). *Comprehensive norms for an expanded Halstead-Reitan battery: Demographic corrections, research findings, and clinical applications.* Odessa, FL: Psychological Assessment Resources.

Heilman, K. M., Watson, R. T., & Valenstein, E. (1993). Neglect and related disorders. In K. M. Heilman & E. Valenstein (Eds.), *Clinical neuropsychology* (3rd ed., pp. 279–336). New York: Oxford University Press.

Hiscock, M., & Hiscock, C. K. (1989). Refining the forced-choice method for the detection of malingering. *Journal of Clinical and Experimental Neuropsychology, 11,* 967–974.

Hooper, H. E. (1958). *The Hooper Visual Organization Test manual.* Los Angeles: Western Psychological Services.

INS-Division 40 Task Force on Education, Accreditation and Credentialing. (1987). Guidelines for doctoral training programs in clinical neuropsychology. *The Clinical Neuropsychologist, 1,* 29–34.

Kaplan, E. (1983). Process and achievement revisited. In S. Wapner & B. Kaplan (Eds.), *Toward a holistic developmental psychology* (pp. 143–156). Hillsdale, NJ: Lawrence Erlbaum Associates.

Kaplan, E. (1989). A process approach to neuropsychological assessment. In T. Boll & B. K. Bryant (Eds.), *Clinical neuropsychology and brain function: Research, measurement, and practice* (pp. 127–167). Washington, DC: American Psychological Association.

Kaplan, E. F., Goodglass, H., & Weintraub, S. (1978). *The Boston naming test.* Philadelphia: Lea and Febiger.

Kaplan, E., Fein, D., Morris, R., & Delis, D.C. (1991). *WAIS–R as a neuropsychological instrument.* San Antonio, TX: Psychological Corporation.

Kaszniak, A. W., Poon, L. W., & Riege, W. (1986). Assessing memory deficits: An information-processing approach. In L. W. Poon (Ed.), *Handbook of clinical memory assessment in older adults* (pp. 168–188). Washington, DC: American Psychological Association.

Kaufman, A. S. (1990). *Assessing adolescent and adult intelligence.* Boston: Allyn and Bacon, Inc.

Kertesz, A. (1982). *The Western Aphasia Battery test manual.* New York: Grune & Stratton, Inc.

King, D. A., & Caine, E. D. (1990). Depression. In J. L. Cummings (Ed.), *Subcortical dementia* (pp. 218–230). New York: Oxford University Press.

Larrabee, G. J. (1990). Cautions in the use of neuropsychological evaluation in legal settings. *Neuropsychology, 4,* 239–247.

Leckliter, I. N., & Matarazzo, J. D. (1989). The influence of age, education, IQ, gender and alcohol abuse on Halstead–Reitan Neuropsychological Test Battery performance. *Journal of Clinical Psychology, 45,* 484–511.

Levin, H. S., Benton, A. L., & Grossman, R. G. (1982). *Neurobehavioral consequences of closed head injury.* New York: Oxford University Press.

Levine, D., Warach, J., & Farah, M. (1985). Two visual systems in mental imagery: Dissociations of "what" and "where" in imagery disorders due to bilateral posterior cerebral lesions. *Neurology, 35,* 1010–1018.

Levine, D. N., & Grek, A. (1984). The anatomical basis of delusions after right cerebral infarction. *Neurology, 34,* 577–582.

Lezak, M. D. (1988). IQ: RIP. *Journal of Clinical and Experimental Neuropsychology, 10,* 351–361.

Lezak, M.D. (1995). *Neuropsychological assessment* (3rd ed.). New York: Oxford University Press.

Luria, A. R. (1980). *Higher cortical functions in man* (2nd ed.). New York: Basic Books.

Malloy, P., Cimino, C., & Westlake, R. (1992). Differential diagnosis of primary and secondary Capgras delusions. *Neuropsychiatry, Neuropsychology and Behavioral Neurology, 5,* 83–96.

Matarazzo, J. D., & Herman, D. O. (1984). Base rate data for the WAIS–R: Test–retest stability and VIQ–PIQ differences. *Journal of Clinical Neuropsychology, 6,* 351–366.

Matarazzo, J. D., & Herman, D. O. (1985). Clinical uses of the WAIS–R: Base rates of differences between VIQ and PIQ in the WAIS–R standardization sample. In B. B. Wolman (Ed.), *Handbook of intelligence* (pp. 899–932). New York: Wiley.

Mesulam, M. M. (1985). A cortical network for directed attention and unilateral neglect. *Annals of Neurology, 10,* 309–325.

Milberg, W. P., Hebben, N., & Kaplan, E. (1986). The Boston process approach to neuropsychological assessment. In I. Grant & K. M. Adams (Eds.), *Neuropsychological assessment of neuropsychiatric disorders* (pp. 65–86). New York: Oxford University Press.

Miller, E. (1983). A note on the interpretation of data derived from neuropsychological tests. *Cortex, 19*, 131–132.

Milner, B., & Petrides, M. (1984). Behavioral effects of frontal-lobe lesions in man. *Trends in Neurosciences, 7*, 403–407.

Mishkin, M., Ungerleider, L., & Macko, K. (1983). Object vision and spatial vision: Two cortical pathways. *Trends in Neuroscience*, October, 414–417.

O'Boyle, M., & Amadeo, M. (1989). Don't know responses in elderly demented and depressed patients. *Journal of geriatric psychiatry and neurology, 2*, 83–86.

O'Boyle, M., Amadeo, M., & Self, D. (1990). Cognitive complaints in elderly depressed and pseudodemented patients. *Psychology and Aging, 5*, 467–468.

O'Hara, M. W., Hinrichs, J. V., Kohout, F. J., Wallace, R. B., & Lemke, J. H. (1986). Memory complaint and memory performance in the depressed elderly. *Psychology and Aging, 1*, 208–214.

Orsini, D. L., Van Gorp, W. G., & Boone, K. B. (1988). *The neuropsychology casebook*. New York: Springer-Verlag.

Osterrieth, P. A. (1944). Le test de copie d'une figure complexe. *Archives de Psychologie, 30*, 206–356.

Post, F. (1975). Dementia, depression and pseudodementia. In D. F. Benson & D. Blumer (Eds.), *Psychiatric aspects of neurologic disease* (pp. 99–120). New York: Grune & Stratton.

Rapcsak, S. Z., Cimino, C. R., & Heilman, K. M. (1988). Altitudinal neglect. *Neurology, 38*, 277–281.

Reitan, R. M., & Wolfson, D. (1985). *The Halstead–Reitan Neuropsychological Test Battery*. Tucson: Neuropsychology Press.

Rey, A. (1941). L'examen psychologique dans les cas d'encephalopathie traumatique. *Archives de Psychologie, 28*, 286–340.

Russell, E. W., & Starkey, R. I. (1993). *Halstead Russell Neuropsychological Evaluation System (HRNES)* [Manual and computer program]. Los Angeles: Western Psychological Services.

Shallice, T., & Evans, M. E. (1978). The involvement of the frontal lobes in cognitive estimation. *Cortex, 14*, 294–303.

Shelton, P. A., Bowers, D., & Heilman, K. M. (1990). Peripersonal and vertical neglect. *Brain, 113*, 191–205.

Singer, J., & Salovey, P. (1988). Mood and memory: Evaluating the network theory of affect. *Clinical Psychology Review, 8*, 211–251.

Speedie, L., & Heilman, K. M. (1982). Amnestic disturbance following infarction of the left dorsomedial nucleus of the thalamus. *Neuropsychologia, 20*, 597–604.

Speedie, L., & Heilman, K. M. (1983). Anterograde memory deficits for visuospatial material after infarction of the right thalamus. *Archives of Neurology, 40*, 183–186.

Spreen, O., & Strauss, E. (1991). *A compendium of neuropsychological tests: Administration, norms, and commentary*. New York: Oxford University Press.

Squire, L. R. (1987). *Memory and brain*. New York: Oxford University Press.

Squire, L. R., & Moore, R. Y. (1979). Dorsal thalamic lesions in a noted case of chronic memory dysfunction. *Annals of Neurology, 6*, 503–506.

Stroop, J. R. (1935). Studies of interference in serial verbal reactions. *Journal of Experimental Psychology, 18*, 643–662.

Tarter, R. E., Van Thiel, D. H., & Edwards, K. (1988). *Medical neuropsychology: The impact of disease on behavior*. New York: Plenum Press.

Todnem, K., & Vik-Mo, H. (1986). Cerebral ischemic attacks as complication of heart disease: The value of echocardiography. *Acta Neurologica Scandinavica, 74*, 323–327.

Ungerleider, L. G., & Mishkin, M. (1982). Two cortical visual systems. In D. J. Ingle, M. H. Goodale, & R. J. W. Mansfield (Eds.), *The analysis of visual behavior* (pp. 549–585). Cambridge, MA: MIT Press.

Walsh, K. W. (1987). *Neuropsychology: A clinical approach*. Melbourne: Churchill Livingstone.

Walsh, K. W. (1991). *Understanding brain damage* (2nd ed.). Melbourne: Churchill Livingstone.

Walsh, K. (1992). Some gnomes worth knowing. *The Clinical Neuropsychologist, 6*, 119–133.

Wechsler, D. (1981). *Wechsler Adult Intelligence Scale–Revised*. New York: Psychological Corporation.

Wechsler, D. (1987). *The Wechsler Memory Scale–Revised*. San Antonio, TX: Psychological Corporation.

Weingartner, H. (1986). Automatic and effort-demanding cognitive processes in depression. In L. Poon (Ed.), *Handbook of clinical memory assessment in older adults* (pp. 218–227). Washington, DC: American Psychological Association.

Weintraub, S., & Mesulam, M. M. (1985). Mental state assessment of young and elderly adults in behavioral neurology. In M. M. Mesulam (Ed.), *Principles of behavioral neurology* (pp. 71–122). Philadelphia: F. A. Davis.

Weintraub, S., Powell, D. H., Caflin, R., Funkenstein, H. H., Kaplan, E. F., Whitla, D. K., Horgan, P.A., Porte, H. S., Ware, J., Whipple, B. S., & Bernstein, F. B. (1991). The "Assessment of Cognitive Skills" (ACS): Mental status screening. *Journal of Clinical and Experimental Neuropsychology, 13*, 106.

Wells, C. E. (1979). Pseudodementia. *American Journal of Psychiatry, 136*, 895–900.

Young, R. C., Manley, M. W., & Alexopoulos, G. S. (1985). "I don't know" responses in elderly depressives and in dementia. *Journal of the American Geriatrics Society, 33*, 253–257.

CHAPTER FOUR

The Interpretation Process

Rodney D. Vanderploeg

*James A. Haley Veterans Hospital, Tampa, Florida,
and College of Medicine, University of South Florida*

As noted in the previous chapter, in the interpretation process the neuropsychologist must consider multiple sources of data, verify them against each other for consistency and patterns, and integrate them into a cogent description of the individual client. Figure 4.1 presents a visual model of how this might be accomplished. Neuropsychological data can be loosely grouped into four domains: (a) observed and reported behavior (behavioral observations, reports of others, medical records, and the case history), (b) neuropsychometric and psychometric test data, (c) possible etiologic conditions and their known symptom patterns (neurologic, medical, and mental health disorders), and (d) functional neuroanatomical knowledge (injury to particular brain regions typically resulting in specific cognitive or behavioral disturbances).

The interpretation process involves examining data within each of these four domains for internal consistency and then considering the implications of findings within that domain for the other three (i.e., external consistency, represented by the arrows within the diagram). That is, for any individual patient, if the available information within one domain is assumed to be reliable and valid, predictable findings should be present in the other three domains. The neuropsychologist sifts through the data, sequentially starting within a different domain of data and examining data within the other three domains for consistent findings. This results in each source of data being internally verified, externally verified, and repetitively cross-checked for consistency. This data analysis and interpretation process continues either until a neuropsychologically consistent

The Neuropsychological Interpretation Process:
Evaluating Consistency Among Data Domains

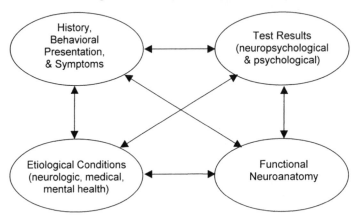

FIG. 4.1.   The neuropsychological interpretation process involves gathering data
in the four domains represented by the ovals. Data are then examined within each
of the four domains for internal consistency. Finally, the implications of data
within each domain are sequentially considered for the other three (i.e., external
consistency, represented by the arrows within the diagram).

pattern emerges or until the neuropsychologist determines that no matter how
much time is spent in this process a consistent pattern will never be detected. Because human behavior is not always consistent and data are not always fully reliable, a consistent pattern will not always be found. In either case, the neuropsychologist describes what consistent patterns are found, reports discrepancies, and offers the best interpretive conclusions and/or diagnostic impressions.

In this interpretive model, the first two domains, observed/reported behavior and test data, both deal with the individual's historic and current behavioral
presentation. These two domains can be subdivided into various cognitive and
behavioral ability areas (sensory-perceptual, psychomotor, attention, memory,
language, visuospatial, executive, and psychological), each of which would need
to be considered for internal and external consistency.

The other two domains, etiological conditions and functional neuroanatomy,
are both sources of knowledge that the competent neuropsychologist possesses
or obtains. In each evaluation, for the various etiologic conditions that are either
known or hypothesized to be present, the neuropsychologist should be familiar
with: (a) the common symptom patterns, (b) the onset, course, and recovery
patterns, (c) the neuropsychological literature about these conditions, (d) the
anatomic correlates, and (e) the common complications. This type of etiological information is not presented in this book. However, numerous volumes exist
that contain such information (e.g., Grant & Adams, 1996; Reitan & Wolfson,

1992; Reynolds & Fletcher-Janzen, 1997; Tarter, Van Thiel, & Edwards, 1988; etc.). Equipped with this knowledge, the neuropsychologist can examine the case history, test data, neuroanatomic imaging results, and other information for consistency with expected patterns. Similarly, knowledge of functional neuro-anatomy allows the neuropsychologist to determine whether symptoms, problems, test scores, and possible etiologic conditions are consistent with the available neuroimaging results.

A case example may be useful to demonstrate this process:

A 55-year-old male is referred from a neurology service. He had been in a good state of health, working and functioning independently up until about a month earlier. At that time he began noticing difficulty with reading, writing, and performing some previously easy and overlearned mechanical tasks, such as starting his lawn mower. As the symptoms worsened he presented to the hospital where an MRI (magnetic resonance imaging scan) was performed. It revealed a focal lesion in the left parietal region in the area of the angular gyrus. A rapidly growing tumor was suspected.

Neuropsychological testing revealed mild naming difficulties, alexia, agraphia, acalculia, finger agnosia, and left–right confusion. He also had difficulty on geometric drawings and block design constructions (see Fig. 4.9). The nature of his difficulty on constructional tasks was that of right-sided inattention and difficulty dealing with the details or inner features of the visuospatial material. He had very mild right-sided weakness and mild difficulty with tactile sensory perceptions, but only on formal testing. Mild verbal memory impairment was present as well.

Interpretively, the recent onset and rapid worsening of his clinical symptoms are consistent with a recent neurologic event that is getting progressively worse over a relatively short period of time. This case history, together with the neuroimaging findings, assisted the neurologist in arriving at a diagnosis of a rapidly growing tumor. The pattern of neuropsychological test results is quite focal in nature. From a functional anatomic perspective, test results (naming difficulties, alexia, agraphia, acalculia, finger agnosia, left–right confusion, and right-sided inattention) were suggestive of a left parietal lesion, posterior to but with a mild adverse effect on the sensory strip (mild right-sided weakness and mild tactile sensory problems). Behaviorally these findings were quite disabling, although in superficial conversation this gentleman appeared grossly intact. Neuroimaging results revealed the angular gyrus focal tumor with surrounding edema due to the acute and rapidly growing nature of the tumor. The left parietal neuroanatomic imaging results are entirely consistent with the clinical presentation, symptoms, and test results. He was considered to have alexia and Gerstmann's syndrome secondary to his left parietal tumor. Data within each of the four domains are internally consistent, and consistent with findings from the other three domains.

This example demonstrates the process of interpretation by highlighting the different domains of information available to the neuropsychologist (see Fig. 4.1) and showing how data across domains can be examined for consistency. However, the example does not provide an interpretive strategy or sequence of steps to follow. A model that outlines the typical steps involved in neuropsychological interpretation is presented next.

INTERPRETIVE SEQUENCE

Typical neuropsychological interpretive steps and issues to consider at each step are outlined in Fig. 4.2. As can be seen, the interpretive process is a complicated endeavor with multiple questions to address. The boxes in the right-hand column of Fig. 4.2 represent a sequence of clinical questions that need to be considered and hopefully answered in the interpretive process. The numbers in the boxes correspond to the outline in the left-hand column of the figure. For each interpretive stage or clinical question, data from all four domains outlined in Fig. 4.1 are considered.

The first step in this interpretive sequence is the estimation of premorbid level of functioning. Although patterns of cognitive strengths and weaknesses can be described without this step, any interpretive statement of "deficits" due to some etiologic factor requires an individual-specific comparison standard against which deficits are described. Chapter 2 in this volume is devoted to a discussion of premorbid estimation.

Steps 2–5 involve a quantitative and qualitative analysis of the data. The process outlined in Fig. 4.1 is used in this interpretive sequence. Test scores are examined relative to normative data and relative to each other to identify patterns of performance that are consistent with different possible pathological etiologies, regions of anatomic dysfunction, and cognitive models of brain functioning. Step 2 is validity assessment. As with any type of psychological assessment, a determination of the validity of the data is essential. Are interview reports, behavioral observations, and test scores an accurate and valid reflection of the client's true brain–behavior capabilities? If not, what is compromising performance and validity, and is it compromised to the point where further evaluation and interpretation of the data cannot be accomplished? Chapter 9 in this volume discusses validity assessment issues and approaches in much more detail.

Neuropsychological assessment is typically deficit oriented. That is, what neuropsychological problems exist? Therefore, in Fig. 4.2 a consideration of deficits (step 3) precedes a consideration of strengths (step 4). However, in reality both occur simultaneously. For both deficits and strengths, data interpretation considers types and patterns of strengths and weaknesses, level of performance, nature of errors, and problem-solving/compensatory strategies. If deficits are identified, step 5 involves a consideration of the status of those deficits. This evaluation typically proceeds along two dimensions, the history of the deficits (recent/acute versus chronic) and their future (resolving, progressive, or static).

Steps 6 and 7 are the diagnostic portion of the interpretation sequence. One aspect of diagnosis is the determination of the pathologic cause of the clinical

Interpretive Sequence

1. To determine if a problem or deficit is present, some comparison standard (premorbid functioning level) must be determined for each client
2. Validity of the data
3–5. Data evaluation:
   a. quantitative level of performance
   b. qualitative nature of performance
   c. relationships between lower-order functions and complex cognitive processes
   d. consistency with history and behavioral observations
   e. consistency with: cognitive ability patterns, anatomic lesions/circuits, causative pathological conditions (diagnoses)
   f. most parsimonious explanation for findings
   g. basis of lowered performance(s): normal variation, previously acquired deficit, recently acquired deficit
   h. nature and status of any deficits: acute vs chronic, progressive vs static
6–7. Diagnostic implications:
   a. etiology: neurologic disease, medical condition, mental health factors, emotional and affective factors, secondary gain, malingering, etc.
   b. anatomic considerations: diffuse, lateralized, localized, disrupted circuits, etc.
8. Treatment and management suggestions, and prognosis (recovery or decline) with and without the recommendations being implemented
9. Implications of the findings for the person's everyday life:
   a. ability to live independently
   b. ability to work or go to school
   c. adjustment issues for the client and the family

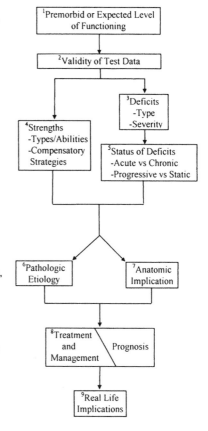

FIG. 4.2.   The interpretive sequence is a complicated endeavor involving multiple steps. The boxes in the right-hand column represent a sequence of clinical issues that needs to be considered and hopefully answered in the interpretive process. The numbers in the boxes correspond to the outline in the left-hand column of the figure. The outline helps explain the steps and issues to consider in each stage of the interpretive process.

presentation (step 6). In neuropsychological assessment, etiologic conditions include neurologic disease, medical conditions (e.g., delirium secondary to systemic infection), mental health conditions (*DSM–IV* axis I and II conditions), other emotional and affective factors, unconscious secondary gain, and malingering. Historically, neuropsychologists also have been asked to help determine anatomic diagnostic issues (step 7). That is, where within the central nervous system or within the brain is the lesion responsible for symptoms and problems? With the advent of more advanced neuroimaging technologies this aspect of diagnostic evaluation is less important. However, as described earlier in relationship to Fig. 4.1, considering anatomic implications of the history, current behavior, test scores, and suspected pathologic conditions aids the neuropsychologist in the interpretive process and provides a further cross-check of interpretive conclusions. Therefore, whether or not possible anatomic implications are described within the final neuropsychological report, they are considered by most neuropsychologists during the interpretation process. This typically takes place as part of steps 3 and 4, and begins with a consideration of whether the findings are consistent with impairment lateralized to the left or right hemisphere or reflect bilateral/diffuse involvement. The next anatomic consideration is localization. Are test results consistent with an anatomic lesion localized to a particular lobe, cortical or subcortical structure(s), or specific anatomic functional system(s) or integrated network(s)?

Step 8 of the interpretive sequence is treatment or management recommendations and consideration of prognosis. These two issues go hand-in-hand because prognosis is likely to differ depending on whether recommendations are implemented. This stage is dependent on accurate interpretation and integration of data in the preceding stages. For example, if the reported pathologic etiology is incorrect, the recommended treatment may be ineffective and prognostic statements inaccurate. Depending on the nature of the evaluation, recommendations and prognosis may not be needed. For example, in differential diagnostic evaluations for dementia, the referring neurologist may simply want to know if evidence for dementia exists, and if so what type of dementia is most likely involved (Alzheimer's disease, vascular dementia, Pick's disease, etc.). However, many referring professionals, clients, and families do desire recommendations and prognostic statements to help them make future treatment, placement, and life planning decisions.

The final stage of interpretation is a consideration of the real-life implications for the individual client in his or her unique life circumstance (step 9). This is the most difficult stage because it is the most removed from the data, and therefore many neuropsychologists omit it. Data are typically collected in a laboratory-like setting (a highly structured office setting), and the neuropsychologist must predict how the individual client will perform in multiple and often very different settings. It also requires consideration of adaptive factors that may not be assessable during the evaluation (e.g., familiarity with everyday tasks and routines; the availability of assistance from family, friends, and colleagues; etc.). Chapters 5 and 10 discuss issues related to this stage of interpretation in much more detail.

In summary, the interpretive sequence is difficult and complicated. Although evaluation of formal test results plays an important role, it is subordinate to the interpretive process of inductive and deductive reasoning, which in turn is dependent on the consistency of the data with various causal models: (a) pathological conditions (diagnoses) and (b) anatomic lesions. In addition, the internal consistency of the client's test performance (i.e., cognitive ability patterns) and the consistency of formal test data with the patient's history and observed behavior are crucial aspects of the interpretive process. Finally, the role of emotional and affective parameters is an essential consideration in the interpretation process, as discussed in earlier chapters.

This interpretation sequence requires some type of methodology for analyzing neuropsychological data, determining if deficits are present, and if so the patterns, severity, and cause(s) of performance difficulties. In current neuropsychological practice there are two general interpretive methods for analyzing data, quantitative and qualitative. These are discussed next.

APPROACHES TO NEUROPSYCHOLOGICAL DATA ANALYSIS

Reitan (1964) was one of the first neuropsychologists to describe a method for analyzing data, and outlined four methods of interpretive inference: (a) level of test performance, (b) differential patterns of ability on test scores, (c) comparison of measures assessing the two sides of the body (e.g., finger tapping speed; grip strength; and tactile, auditory, or visual sensory perception), and (d) pathognomonic signs of brain dysfunction. The first three methods rely on test scores or a *quantitative approach,* whereas the fourth reflects a neurologic syndrome method or a more *qualitative approach.* These two general approaches continue to reflect interpretive methods used today. Neuropsychologists may differ on how much they rely on one approach versus the other, but virtually all neuropsychologists use both quantitative and qualitative interpretive methods.

Each interpretive approach has its strengths and limitations. Quantitative performance on tests can be influenced by many variables other than brain injury (as described in earlier chapters). Therefore, poor performance on formal neuropsychological tests does not necessarily mean that there has been a disruption in the underlying brain–behavior ability. For example, poor performance on language measures does not mean than an individual has impaired basic language abilities (i.e., an aphasia, alexia, agraphia, ideomotor apraxia, etc.). In contrast, many neurologic syndromes or pathognomonic findings cannot occur in the absence of brain damage. For example, visual field cuts, aphasia, alexia, agraphia, unilateral visual neglect, ideomotor apraxia, visual agnosia, and other findings do not occur without some central nervous system damage. However, such syndrome description does not help quantify the severity of the deficit. Therefore, both quantitative and qualitative approaches are essential in interpreting findings and fully describing the brain–behavior capabilities of an individual.

Quantitative Methods

Many neuropsychological tests are firmly rooted in a strong psychometric tradition. Frequency distributions of scores, patterns of scores in both normal and brain-injured populations, and normative reference data result from this psychometric tradition. The hallmark of the quantitative approach is the interpretation of tests based primarily on the formal test scores, their level of performance relative to normative data, and their patterns or profiles of performance. This approach readily lends itself to objective analysis, scientific scrutiny, statistical validation, and research protocols. It also provides a ready avenue for exchanging data or information among professionals who are familiar with the meaning of the test scores.

However, it has been understood for some time that individuals who differ on certain demographic or "attribute" variables will vary in performance on neuropsychological tasks (e.g., slower motor performance in older individuals). The main demographic variables thought to exert influences on neuropsychological tests are chronological age, years of education, and gender. These variables were studied by Heaton, Grant, and Matthews (1986) and developed into comprehensive norms for common neuropsychological tests (Heaton, Grant, & Matthews, 1991). *A Compendium of Neuropsychological Tests: Administration, Norms, and Commentary* (Spreen & Strauss, 1998), and *Halstead Russell Neuropsychological Evaluation System* (Russell & Starkey, 1993) provide two additional collective references for normative data beyond those published by the authors of individual tests.

Demographically specific normative data have greatly assisted the interpretation of neuropsychological tests scores. However, Reitan and Wolfson (1995) argued that the relationship between demographic variables and neuropsychological performance differs in brain-damaged and non-brain-damaged groups. Given this, they advocate extreme caution in using "adjusted" normative data in clinical neuropsychological evaluations. In contrast, Vanderploeg, Axelrod, Scherer, Scott, and Adams (1997) presented empirical data countering Reitan and Wolfson's assertions regarding the inadvisability of using demographically adjusted scores. Vanderploeg et al. demonstrated that the use of demographically adjusted scores resulted in significantly greater diagnostic accuracy and group discrimination.

Potential problems with the quantitative approach concern individual differences. First, similar scores may have very different meanings, depending on the client's original baseline. It is difficult to know if a score reflects a deterioration or a lower innate level of functioning. Thus, premorbid estimation, as discussed in chapter 2, is an essential initial step in a quantitative approach to neuropsychological interpretation. Second, there is often considerable overlap in scores obtained by "normative reference groups" and "brain-damaged" populations. Third, scores may be "impaired" for reasons other than neuropathology.

Fourth, the reporting of composite test scores (e.g., Full Scale IQ, Memory Quotient, or even Verbal IQ and Verbal Memory Index) tends to mask significant variations that might differentiate individual clients who may obtain the same overall score (Lezak, 1988). Fifth, focusing on test scores alone may reveal very little about the basic underlying functional disturbance in the brain.

Qualitative Methods

The qualitative approach is concerned with identifying how patients comprehend and attempt to solve tasks. Underlying this approach is the observation that all neuropsychological tests, no matter how simple they might appear, are multidimensional tasks. As a result, performance can be impaired for a variety of reasons. Knowing the level of performance is secondary to trying to discover the underlying reason for any difficulty. Through a careful analysis of the strategies employed by the client and attention to the types of errors made, the clinician arrives at a better understanding of the fundamental cognitive disturbance(s) of the individual client and of the functioning of the brain itself. Neurological symptoms, syndromes, and pathognomonic signs play an important role in qualitative interpretation strategies.

As with the quantitative approach, there are advantages and disadvantages to focusing on qualitative features of the data. Defining deficits in behavioral terms rather than in terms of "test performance" typically results in a better understanding of the underlying deficits in cognition, perception, or other behavior. This makes it easier to discuss the results in terms of functional behaviors that may be more informative to the referral source and to generalize the findings to everyday life. For example, in reference to the Block Design subtest, it is much easier to predict potential problems in daily living if one has an understanding of the client's unilateral spatial attention, visuospatial analysis abilities, planning ability, and self-monitoring skills, than simply knowing a score on "a measure of two-dimensional construction of geometric patterns."

Over the past 10 years the discoveries and advancements in cognitive neuropsychology have resulted in additional qualitative, model-based interpretive strategies for clinical neuropsychological practice. Cognitive neuropsychology attempts to develop models of normal cognitive functioning, which then can be used to determine whether clinical data suggest intact or impaired functions within these models. If these cognitive models are correct, then neurological diseases should result in systematic breakdowns in one or more components of the model. As an example, models delineating subtypes of aphasic disorders can be viewed as cognitive language models that assist the neuropsychologist in evaluating and describing important aspects of linguistic abilities, as well as integrating any positive findings with possible causative anatomic dysfunction.

Potential disadvantages of an exclusive reliance on a qualitative approach are the converse of some of the advantages of the quantitative approach, such as lack of normative and descriptive statistics and a paucity of research validating this approach to neuropsychological interpretation. Another disadvantage is the qualitative approach's strong reliance on the subjective expertise and clinical judgment of the examiner, who must be able to identify the major factors that might contribute to a poor test performance in each case.

Because of their different advantages, quantitative and qualitative approaches to test interpretation nicely complement each other. In practice, neuropsychologists meld elements of both in their interpretation and reports, thereby accruing the benefits of each.

CONCEPTUAL MODELS OF COGNITION AND BRAIN FUNCTIONING: AIDS IN INTERPRETATION

In interpretive steps 3–7 in the model presented in Fig. 4.2, multiple processes and ability domains are examined at each step. Quantitatively and qualitatively, levels and patterns of performance are examined within and across each domain of cognitive functioning, and domains of cognitive abilities are integrated with anatomic regions or circuits and with pathological factors. To assist in this interpretive endeavor, cognitive–anatomic models for these various domains are presented in the remainder of this chapter. First, an overall model of cognitive processing is presented. This is followed by models of attention, memory, language, visual cognitive abilities, and executive functions. Given space limitations, sensory-perceptual and psychomotor models are not presented. The presented models are viewed as clinically helpful, but not as definitive. They are models I use in clinical practice and reflect my understanding of the relevant literature. However, they do not represent an exhaustive review of the literature; nor do they attempt to capture all known aspects of the different cognitive ability domains and associated neuroanatomy. They are presented to assist the reader in the interpretation process.

A Model of Cognitive Processing

An overall model of cognitive processing that integrates various cognitive abilities with brain functioning helps neuropsychologists begin to conceptualize (a) deficits and residual strengths, (b) where breakdowns occur in cognitive processing, and (c) what brain regions might be involved. Figure 4.3 presents one such model. The bell-shaped curve represents ongoing information processing from simple sensory input, through perceptual analyses and identification, to linguistic and visual spatial analysis, to abstraction, reasoning, and problem solving. Responses to this processing are the final output of the system and begin on top of the right-hand side of the curve with additional problem solving, to conceptual planning, premotor sequencing activities, complex motor organization,

Conceptual Model of Cognitive Processing

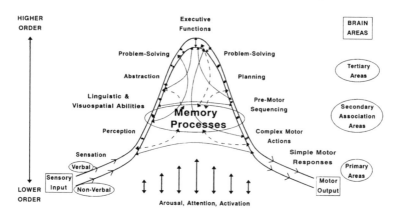

FIG. 4.3.   Conceptual model of cognitive processing, attempting to integrate information processing within and across cognitive stages and abilities, with the brain regions responsible for processing.

and end in observable motoric responses. The curve is composed of two parallel lines, one representing left-hemisphere linguistic processing and the other right-hemisphere nonlinguistic processing. Of course this is an oversimplification, because multiple parallel processes can occur simultaneously even within a hemisphere (e.g., left-hemisphere processing of auditory, visual, and tactile information about a stimulus using linguistic processes and concepts). Connections between these parallel lines represent white matter connections via the corpus callosum. The bell-shaped parallel lines correspond to gray matter cortical structures, and the bidirectional arrows within the bell-curve represent white matter pathways—feedback loops and connections between cortical structures. Some pathways go from sensory-perceptual functions to motor responses, bypassing higher order processing altogether. Reflexive responses would be one example of this.

Disruptions or lesions involving the gray cortical structures or lesions of major white matter pathways (e.g., the arcuate fasciculus connecting Wernicke's area with Broca's area for coordination of speech in ongoing communication) would result in gross impairment of specific cognitive abilities. In contrast, diffuse subcortical white matter disease, such as that seen with multiple sclerosis or subcortical white matter ischemic disease, would not result in losses of specific abilities. Instead, processing speed and efficiency would be compromised, the fidelity of information transfer would be affected, and transfer and retrieval of information would be somewhat sporadic.

In this model, memory processes are seen as interacting with perceptual input. Object identification cannot occur unless the sensory-perceptual system has access to previously acquired percepts, and new percepts cannot be stored in memory without input from sensory-perceptual processes. Similarly, motor skills are acquired through interactions between procedural memory systems and motor activities, and complex motor activities are guided by input from motor (procedural) memory systems. Abstraction, reasoning, and problem solving require input from semantic and episodic memory stores (the bidirectional dashed arrows within the diagram), and output from these cognitive operations results in the acquisition of new conceptual memories (semantic memory system).

Lower portions of the curve correspond with lower order or simpler cognitive abilities, whereas higher portions of the curve represent increasingly complex activities. Identified on the right-hand side of the figure are brain regions thought to be responsible for cognitive activities at that level of processing. Thus, simple sensory processing is the responsibility of primary sensory areas in the temporal, occipital, and parietal cortices, whereas basic motor responses would be the purview of the primary motor cortex (motor strip) in the frontal lobes. Secondary association areas would be responsible for perceptual analysis and synthesis, object recognition, and the beginnings of linguistic and non-linguistic analysis on the input end of the curve (left side), whereas preparation for simple and complex motor actions would be the responsibility of the secondary association areas (premotor regions) in the frontal lobes. Two bilateral tertiary association areas exist, one in the posterior parietal cortices in zones of overlap between occipital, temporal, and parietal regions, and the other in the dorsolateral frontal prefrontal cortex. The posterior region is responsible for the integration of heteromodal sensory-perceptual information into *percepts* with some *conceptual* analysis. It then forwards this information to the prefrontal tertiary association cortices for further abstraction, problem solving, and response planning. Together, and in interaction with each other and with episodic and semantic memory stores, these tertiary association regions are responsible for activities that neuropsychologists typically refer to as *conceptual* and *executive*.

Underlying the processing dimension (the bell-shaped curve) resides the arousal and activation component of the attention system. Arousal and activation are seen as having a greater influence on middle portions of the curve (mid- to higher level cognitive abilities) than the two sides (input and output lower order cognitive abilities). Thus, the arousal/activation arrows are larger in the middle portions of the figure. For example, it takes a greater level of activation and arousal to engage in effective complex reasoning than it does to perceive the color of an object or to move ones hand.

An overarching model of cognitive abilities and brain functioning such as that presented in Fig. 4.3 assists the neuropsychologist in beginning to evaluate the nature of symptoms, problems, or poor test scores; identify the specific abilities that may be compromised; and explore the causes for abnormal performances. Interpretive questions that the model helps to address are: Where is the breakdown in cognitive functioning that is responsible for this abnormal response? What areas of the brain might be impaired? In addition to such a general model of cognitive processing, cognitive–anatomic models for specific cognitive domains also aid the neuropsychologist in the interpretative endeavor. Models of these domains are presented in the remainder of this chapter.

Attention

Attention is now recognized as being a multidimensional construct, and numerous models of attention have been proposed (e.g., Baddeley, 1986; Heilman, Watson, & Valenstein, 1985, 1993, 1994; Mesulam, 1990; Mirsky, Anthony, Duncan, Ahearn, & Kellam, 1991; Posner & Rafal, 1986; Sohlberg & Mateer, 1989). Researchers have attempted to delineate the different components of attention. For example, although Baddeley did not discuss his model in this framework, his working memory model can be thought of as a model for an *encoding and capacity* component to attention. In contrast, Heilman (and colleagues) and Mesulam understood attention as a large-scale integrated network. Mesulam outlined four nodular components: (a) a reticular activating system arousal component, (b) a parietally based sensory-perceptual component, (c) a frontally controlled exploratory component, and (d) a cingulate gyrus mediated valuing (stimulus significance) component. Posner and Rafal broke attention down into three components: arousal, vigilance, and selective attention; Sohlberg and Mateer provided a clinically oriented model that breaks attention down into five components: focused attention, sustained attention, selective attention, alternating attention, and divided attention. More recently, Mirsky et al. (1991) proposed a four-component model, (a) focus-execute, (b) sustain, (c) shift, and (d) encode, and attempted to link these processes to brain regions in an integrated network model similar to that of Heilman et al. (1985, 1993, 1994) and Mesulam (1990).

There is a great deal of overlap among these models, but six basic factors appear to encompass the components described by the different researchers: arousal; capacity; selection or an attentional focus; direction/movement/control of the attentional capacity system; sustaining an attentional focus (i.e., vigilance); and valuing or appraising of stimuli.

Baddeley's (1986) working memory model (see Fig. 4.4) can been seen providing the centerpiece of the attentional system's capacity, which in turn is influenced by processes of arousal, valuing, and selection and direction of attentional focus. Vigilance or sustaining attention can be viewed as a product of the selection and direction of attentional focus based on stimulus value and under appropriate levels of arousal across time. Regardless of exactly how these processes are labeled, it is important to consider these different attentional processes as part of a neuropsychological evaluation. Understanding relationships among the various cognitive operations and underlying anatomical structure(s) is at the heart of examining brain–behavior relationships.

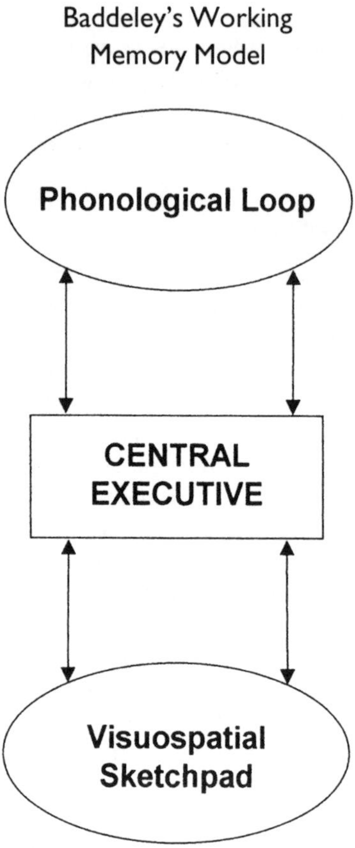

Baddeley's Working
Memory Model

FIG. 4.4.   Baddeley's (1986) working memory model.
The two ovals represent the two working memory capacity slave systems that are under the direction and
control of the central executive. Information is stored
for brief periods of time in the phonological loop or
visuospatial sketchpad, as long as the central executive determines the information is relevant. The central executive also makes decisions about what information in working memory should be stored in long-
term memory (LTM). Similarly, relevant information
within LTM may be retrieved under the direction of
the central executive into the working memory system for online processing.

Baddeley's working memory model is composed of three components: the
phonological loop, the *visuospatial sketchpad,* and the *central executive.* The phonological loop and visuospatial sketchpad are "slave" systems under the control of
the central executive. They hold information, either auditory–verbal or visuospatial in nature, within a working memory space or within a limited capacity
attentional system. Baddeley does not rule out that other slave systems for stimulus material of different types may exist as well, and additional visual–verbal,
visuoperceptual, and spatial systems have been considered (Baddeley, 1992; Mc-
Carthy & Warrington, 1990). The central executive's role is to keep the contents
of the slave systems organized, and to decide what to do with the contents of
the slave systems (maintain the contents active for additional processing, direct
the contents into long term memory storage, or discard the contents by redi-
recting slave system resources).

At this point the models of Mesulam (1981, 1990) and Heilman et al. (1985,
1993, 1994) are seen as clinically useful in integrating other components of atten-

tion and tying them to brain regions. First, in most individuals the right hemisphere is dominant for controlling the distribution of attentional resources, although both hemispheres have significant roles in the direction of attention to the contralateral side of extrapersonal space. The inferior parietal cortex is seen as an attentional access point for sensory-perceptual representation of stimuli and their spatial location. Parietal lobes can be viewed as engaging in an automatic "approach behavior" (Denny-Brown, 1958); stimulus information is attended to unless there is some activity resulting in a disengagement of that attentional focus. Lateralized parietal injuries result in a failure to disengage an attentional focus from an ipsilateral stimulus (Posner, Peterson, Fox, & Raichle, 1988), resulting in inattention to stimuli on the contralateral side of extrapersonal space. What does that mean? It means, for example, that an individual with a right parietal lesion attends to stimuli on the right side of his or her world (attended to by the intact left hemisphere), and neglects stimuli on the left side of space. Presumably this neglect is secondary to an inability of the damaged right hemisphere to attend to left-sided stimuli (the spatial attentional domain of the right parietal lobe), and thus it fails to provide competition to right-sided stimuli to which the left parietal cortex is attending. Without such competition, the left parietal cortex is unable to disengage its attentional focus. This results in the clinical finding of extinction on bilateral simultaneous sensory stimulation tasks. When an client with a right-sided parietal lesion is presented with two identical simultaneous stimuli (either visual, auditory, or tactile), one on the right and the other on the left, the client will fail to *perceive* the left-sided stimulus (or *extinguish* it), even though he or she is capable of perceiving it when it is presented alone. This is a simple example of how Mesulam's sensory-perceptual input or receptive component of attention might manifest itself in the clinical setting.

The dorsolateral frontal cortex is seen as an access point for attentional exploration. Posner pointed out that this is a two stage process: the movement of an attentional focus and then the engagement or reengagement of an attentional focus. In Mesulam's model the movement of attention is a presumed frontal-basal ganglia function, with injury resulting in disruption in exploration or movement. Right-sided lesions would result in difficulty moving the attentional focus toward the left, whereas left-sided frontal lesions would result in problems moving attention toward the right. The common clinical symptom of distractibility can be seen as a failure to engage attention, because the attentional focus keeps moving from one stimulus to another in an ever-changing stimulus world. The engagement of attention is seen as the responsibility of the dorsolateral frontal cortex. Mesulam's frontal exploratory and control of the movement of an attentional focus likely reflect in part the same process as Baddeley's frontally mediated central executive.

The engagement of a particular stimulus, in Mesulam's model, would be under the influence of cingulate cortex (part of the limbic system), whose responsibility would be to evaluate the significance of stimuli. If stimuli have sufficient importance, then the frontal lobes would be responsible for engaging them within an attentional focus. In the model under discussion, vigilance (or sustaining attention) would result from the cooperative interaction among parietal, frontal, and cingulate structures such that the focus of attention remains on the stimulus of most importance. Finally, this entire process would be influenced by arousal, an attentional component modulated by the reticular activating system. It is difficult to engage attention, keep information active within the attentional focus, and evaluate stimulus significance if an individual is under- or overaroused.

Such an integrated model of attention assists the neuropsychologist in determining what aspects of attention may be impaired. Tasks such as Digit Span, Visual Memory Span, or Corsi Blocks assist in the assessment of verbal and visual capacity. Digit Span backward relative to digits forward helps evaluate the integrity of the central executive component of Baddeley's working memory model. If digits forward is average but digits backward impaired, the ability of the phonological loop must be intact. The most likely neuropsychological reason for such a poor backward span would be the inability of the central executive to control, manipulate, and keep organized the contents of the phonological loop under the processing demands of having to reverse the number sequence. Problems with visual, auditory, or tactile extinction would suggest parietal dysfunction in the hemisphere contralateral to the suppressed or extinguished stimulus. Similarly, left-sided neglect would suggest significant right parietal dysfunction. Problems with visual search tasks such as letter or number cancelation tests and the Trail Making test would suggest frontally mediated attentional exploration difficulties. Similarly, problems with distractibility would suggest possible frontal dysfunction. By considering the different components in the attention model, the neuropsychologist is better able to determine where the breakdown in attentional processes occurred, the likely brain structures involved, and where the client is most likely to have attentional difficulties outside of the assessment session.

Memory

Memory complaints are the most frequent client complaints in clinical neuropsychology. That is in part because clients are referring to functional memory, defined as the ability to learn, retain, and recall information and access it at the required time and place. Thus, functional memory reflects many processes in addition to those that neuropsychologists would consider memory. Figure 4.5 outlines some of the processes that might affect "functional memory" performance. In this figure, functional memory is seen as the final outcome of multiple interacting cognitive processes, with deficits in any one of them resulting in complaints of memory difficulties.

Memory as a Process

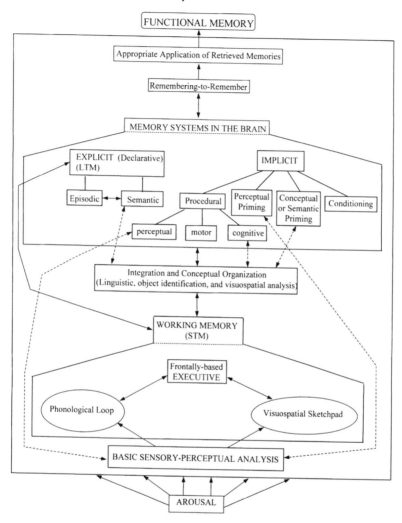

FIG. 4.5. Functional memory model outlining numerous memory and nonmemory processes that come into play during day-to-day memory behavior. In this model information is processed by sensory-perceptual and working memory systems, conceptually processed either linguistically or non-linguistically, and integrated into various long-term memory (LTM) systems. Once information has been stored in LTM, successful application will require remembering to search for and retrieve information and appropriately apply it in the correct functional contexts. Solid arrows represent information being sent from one cognitive system to another. Dashed arrows represent different cognitive processes that presumably share similar anatomically based functional systems. For example, posterior parietal-temporal structures both process linguistic information and are the repository for semantic LTM stores. These same brain regions likely also are involved in successful semantic priming, an implicit memory function.

In contrast to the idea of functional memory, neuropsychologists divide memory systems into short-term and long-term, episodic versus semantic, procedural versus declarative, and implicit versus explicit. In addition, they use terms such as encoding, consolidation, retention, and retrieval to reflect different stages of learning and recall. Although all these concepts are briefly described in this chapter, it is with episodic memory that neuropsychologists typically are concerned. They assess episodic memory with measures of new learning that often involve free recall, cued recall, and recognition recall formats to assess what was learned and retained across short and longer delays (typically immediate recall and up to 30 min delay).

Short-Term Versus Long-Term Memory. Short-term memory (STM) lasts less than a minute unless it is lengthened by rehearsal, and it is a limited-capacity system. In many models STM is a stage that information must pass through to enter long-term memory (LTM) storage, and it is into STM that long-term memories are retrieved (e.g., Atkinson & Shiffrin, 1968). Because STM has a limited capacity, information within STM must be transferred to LTM as new information replaces it. STM is sometimes referred to as working memory, and Baddeley's working memory model (Fig. 4.4) is one STM model. In contrast, LTM provides a relatively permanent record of what has been stored in it. Access to LTM can occur almost as soon as information enters one's attention.

When clinicians and patients use terms such as *short-term, recent, long-term,* or *remote* memory, they may or may not be referring to the same processes as neuropsychologists. A common example of a subjective report of STM difficulties is, "Doc, I got problems with my short-term memory. I walk into another room and forget what I went to get." In fact, this most likely is an STM or working memory problem. The process of walking into the other room was distracting and interfered with the ability of the working memory system to keep the relevant information "online" and available. Being distracted also resulted in the information not being encoded effectively in LTM stores, and therefore not being retrievable easily. However, often LTM retrieval cues (going back where one started) can help one "remember" (i.e., retrieve) why one went to the other room. However, clients also commonly report STM problems when they actually mean difficulties with recent memory. For example, someone with mild Alzheimer's disease may report, "My long-term memory is good, but my short-term memory is horrible." From a neuropsychological perspective, recent memory is recently acquired long-term memories. Such complaints reflect difficulty in the acquisition or storage of new (i.e., recent) long-term memories, but the intact storage and access to familiar, overlearned long-term memories from the more remote past (years ago or even childhood memories).

Also confusing the issue of STM versus LTM are memory tests of immediate and delayed recall. Clinicians may refer to good immediate recall of a short story as "good STM," with poorer delayed recall of the same short story as evidence of "impaired LTM." However, from a neuropsychological perspective, both immediate and delayed recall of short stories are assessing the LTM system. Immediate recall is assessing acquisition (encoding and storage) of new information into LTM storage, whereas delayed recall is assessing retention of that information within LTM across time and the ability to successfully retrieve it. The concepts of encoding, consolidation, storage, retention, and retrieval are discussed in more detail later.

All further discussion of memory terminology in this section refers to LTM systems or models—episodic, semantic, procedural, declarative, implicit, and explicit.

Episodic Versus Semantic Memory.   Tulving (1972) made a distinction between episodic and semantic memory within LTM store. Episodic memory consists of those autobiographical memories to which the personal time and place context remain attached. Discrete episodes or events in time are examples of episodic memory, for example, a memory for one's first puppy received on a 10th birthday in the backyard on a sunny afternoon. Semantic memories are more conceptual in nature; the contextual elements of the memory have been lost. The ability to describe what a puppy is and to indicate to what species of animal it belongs would be examples of semantic memory. The concept of "species" is another example of a semantic memory. Clinical neuropsychologists assess semantic memory with naming tasks or Wechsler Vocabulary and Similarities subtests. However, they generally do not describe the results as reflecting intact or impaired semantic memory. This could be because semantic memory is only rarely impacted by neuropathology. The major exception to this rule is moderate to severe Alzheimer's disease, where a degradation of the semantic memory system occurs and results in word-finding problems and impaired semantic associations.

Procedural Versus Declarative Memory.   This distinction was based on the observation that otherwise amnestic individuals could demonstrate normal learning on some types of motor and perceptual tasks (Cohen & Squire, 1980; Squire, 1987). Thus, procedural memory was defined as knowledge of procedures or operations, or was seen as consisting of developed skills or habits. Procedural memory is rule based and involves knowing how to do something. This stands in contrast to declarative memory, which is data based; it is knowing information that can be stated or declared. Both episodic and semantic memory, described earlier, are examples of declarative memory. The skills of riding a bicycle or juggling would be examples of procedural memory. In the clinical setting, neuropsychologists typically assess declarative memory but do not assess procedural memory. However, it is procedural skills that can assist a brain-damaged individual to compensate for various declarative, episodic memory deficits. For example, the habit of using a schedule, daily log, or memory notebook can help an individual compensate for episodic memory difficulties. Similarly, overlearned cognitive skills, such as a particular problem-solving approach (e.g., outlining problems and possible responses), would be procedural operations that might be useful in compensating for other cognitive deficits.

Implicit Versus Explicit Memory.   Explicit memory is familiar to most of us. It has to do with conscious recollection or recognition of past events or knowledge. Thus, episodic, semantic, and declarative memories, as described earlier, would all be explicit memories. Implicit memory does not require conscious recollection or knowledge. Intact *procedural* memory for juggling in an amnestic individual who denies ever having learned to juggle would be one example of implicit memory. Other examples include instances of *priming*, where prior exposure to a set of stimuli results in a higher probability of those stimuli being reported at a later time, even if the individual has no conscious memory for the original stimuli. For example, if a list of words is presented, even if items are not consciously recallable, the original words are more likely to be reported on a later free association task than are other associated but nonlist words. Finally, classical and operant *conditioning* results in behavior change that often is outside the conscious awareness of an individual. The portion of Fig. 4.5 labeled "Memory Systems in the Brain" shows how these different subdivisions of memory relate to and dissociate from each other.

Incidental memory is sometimes confused with implicit memory; however, these concepts are not the same. Material acquired incidentally is information of an episodic nature within explicit LTM store. Incidental memory refers to information someone acquires simply from working with material or being exposed to a task during which the person is not trying to learn the information but rather simply to work with it in some fashion. An example of this would be the Wechsler Similarities subtest. The task is to report how two items are conceptually similar. However, a measure of incidental learning could be obtained if after completing the task a clinician provided the first word of each pair and asked the client to recall the second word of the pair. The client was never asked to learn the word pairs, but now is being asked to consciously recall (explicit memory) information that may have been incidentally learned. Incidental memory has been reported to be useful in dementia versus pseudodementia evaluations (Hart, Kwentus, Wade, & Hamer, 1987). With depression-related pseudodementia the level of effort and focused concentration required for good performance on most memory tasks may result in a somewhat impaired performance, similar to mild dementia. However, information acquired incidentally does not require that same concentration and effort, and consequently is more intact with pseudodementia, but impaired with neurologically based dementias such as Alzheimer's disease.

Encoding, Consolidation, Retention, and Retrieval.   These terms are used to refer to acquisition and use of new information. They are typically used to describe learning and memory of an explicit episodic nature. Although defined somewhat differently by various researchers and theoreticians, the following definitions are generally accepted. *Encoding* entails processing stimulus information and transforming it into a perceptual or conceptual format that may eventually be stored in LTM. Primary and secondary posterior association cortices (in occipital, temporal, and parietal lobes) would be responsible for such sensory-perceptual and conceptual analyses. Encoding can be thought of as a process outside of and preceding LTM. *Consolidation* is the process of strengthening and solidifying information in LTM storage, such that when complete a relatively permanent record has been stored. Squire and Zola-Morgan (Squire & Zola-Morgan, 1991; Zola-Morgan & Squire, 1990) demonstrated that this process is dependent on the hippocampus and takes place over the course of days and weeks (and perhaps longer, given the periods of retrograde amnesia seen in some cases of bilateral hippocampal damage). Once information has been consolidated and stored in LTM, the process of *forgetting* is seen as occurring through decay. That is, if memories are not reactivated, recalled, or strengthened through associations with new similar memory material, they will gradually decay due to disuse. *Retention* is the opposite of forgetting; it is the saving of information in LTM across time. *Retrieval* is the process of activating or recalling information that has been previously stored in LTM. In assessing learning and memory, neuropsychologists use both *free recall* and *recognition* recall procedures. Free recall requires clients to actively search LTM stores and retrieve information if it has been previously consolidated and stored. Recognition assessment provides the information along with memory foils, and asks clients to indicate which material was previously presented. Recognition memory places fewer demands on memory retrieval. However, for both free recall and recognition testing, success requires that information was previously consolidated and stored.

Recent positron emission tomography research suggests that there are two components to successful retrieval: (a) a prefrontally mediated memory searching process (retrieval attempt), and (b) successful reactivation of memory information from posterior cortical LTM stores (retrieval success; Kapur, Craik, Jones, Brown, Houle, & Tulving, 1995). Medial temporal activity is associated with retrieval success, rather than retrieval attempt, likely reflecting a role in reactivation of previously stored information (Nyberg, McIntosh, Houle, Nilsson, & Tulving, 1996). The prefrontally mediated memory search can be thought of as one function of the central executive component in Baddeley's working memory model. That is, the working memory system's central executive initiates a search of LTM and an attempt to retrieve information into active working memory systems where it can be consciously available. This frontally mediated memory retrieval attempt may be somewhat lateralized: (a) right prefrontal for episodic information, and (b) left prefrontal for semantic information (Buckner et al., 1995; Tulving, Kapur, Craik, Moscovitch, & Houle, 1994). In addition, the left prefrontal region, along with the retrosplenial area of the cingulate cortex, appears to play a role in encoding of new episodic information (Fletcher, Frith, Grasby, Shallice, Frackowiak, & Dolan, 1995; Tulving et al., 1994). As with the general model of information processing presented in Fig. 4.3, understanding the concepts of encoding, consolidation, retention, and retrieval, and their functional neuroanatomical correlates, assists the neuropsychologist in determining why an individual may be having difficulty on various memory tasks.

Memory Assessment in Clinical Neuropsychology

Typically it is tasks involving new learning of an episodic nature that are administered in clinical neuropsychology. These may include story or visual design recall measures, list learning tasks, or verbal and visual paired-associate learning tasks. Often there is an immediate recall and a 20- to 30-min delayed recall and/ or recognition portion. Free recall is used to assess the ability to consolidate, store, and freely retrieve the contents of LTM, whereas cued recall or recognition memory testing is used to assess whether problems with retrieval exist. That is, has information been stored in LTM that cannot be freely recalled, but that can be retrieved with externally supplied memory retrieval cues? Information reported on immediate recall procedures is partly retrieved from STM stores (i.e., working memory) and partly from LTM stores. On delayed recall performance, all retrieved information is from LTM store. However, on both immediate and delayed recall procedures, the working memory system's central executive likely is involved in the retrieval attempt (see Fig. 4.6).

The prememory processing that is necessary to encode information into a format accessible to LTM stores must be intact in all new learning of an episodic nature. Thus, problems with language processing would adversely affect any measure of verbal learning, whereas difficulties with visual perceptual or visuospatial processing would adversely affect visual memory measures.

Figure 4.6 is one conceptual model that integrates Baddeley's working memory model with an explicit/declarative LTM model. Together with the functional memory model of Fig. 4.5, it may be useful in understanding the memory difficulties presented by clients.

Language

Most individuals are left-hemisphere dominant for language. Although certain aspects of effective communication are dependent on right-hemisphere functioning (e.g., melody or prosody in speech), the left hemisphere in most individuals is responsible for the language subcomponents of phonetics, lexical information, semantics, syntax and grammar, language comprehension, speech fluency, articulation, naming, reading, and writing. In addition, arithmetic abilities and ideomotor praxis are commonly discussed in the context of language abilities and can be thought of as language-related functions. These concepts are

Learning, Memory, and Forgetting

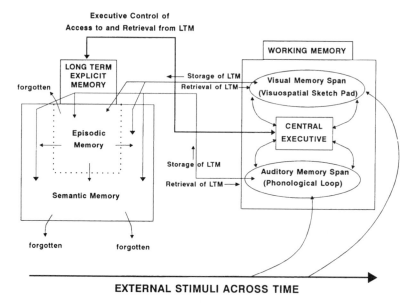

FIG. 4.6.   Learning model that integrates Baddeley's working memory model with an explicit long-term memroy (LTM) model. Stimulus information enters working memory stores (phonological loop or visuospatial sketchpad) and may or may not proceed to episodic LTM stores depending upon the central executive. Information in LTM stores (either episodic or semantic) may be retrieved to working memory for online processing, where it may be integrated with new information and form new episodic memories or modify existing semantic concepts. Information can be lost from both episodic and semantic LTM stores through disuse and decay. This memory model is a sequential model in which information proceeds from working memory into LTM. Other models view information as simultaneously entering STM and LTM systems.

briefly discussed here and a model for naming, writing, and pantomiming is presented that integrates these cognitive subcomponents of language. The anatomical structures necessary for language processing are then discussed and classical aphasic syndromes are elucidated using the language anatomic model of Mesulam (1990).

Cognitive Components of Language Abilities

Phonetics.   Phonetics has to do with speech sounds—their production, combination, and transformation into written language. The translation or conversions of *phonemes* (the simplest units of speech sounds) to *graphemes* (the corresponding written representation) and vice versa is one important aspect of phonetics. Analysis and synthesis of phoneme sequences into neural word representations is another. The end product of the phonetic analysis accesses lexical systems.

Lexicon.   Currently, cognitive language psychologists and speech pathologists recognize multiple lexicons within the language system (Ellis & Young, 1988; Patterson & Shewell, 1987; Rothi, Ochipa, & Heilman, 1997), all of which represent long-term memory stores. There are both input and output lexicons. The neural representations of auditory and visual sensory-perceptual analysis access either the phonologic or orthographic input lexicons where memory of high-frequency or familiar spoken or written words is stored (see Fig. 4.7).

Model for Naming, Writing, and Pantomiming

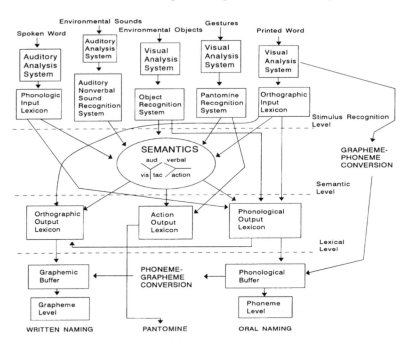

FIG. 4.7.   Model of naming, reading, writing, and praxis and their relationships with sensory-perceptual processing systems, object recognition systems, and semantics. The semantic system is essentially equivalent to semantic memory; it is seen as having dissociable stores for auditory, visual, tactile, verbal, action, and potentially other concepts. This language model has obvious overlaps with visual object recognition, which if impaired would result in agnosia. This model also shows two routes to word recognition—a grapheme–phoneme conversion (sounding out) approach and a whole-word recognition (orthographic input lexicon) approach. Reading, writing, naming, and pantomiming can be performed with and without meaning, depending on whether or not the semantic system has been successfully accessed. This model is adapted and expanded from Ellis and Young (1988), Patterson and Shewell (1987), and Rothi, Ochipa, and Heilman (1997).

These input lexicons allow for rapid word recognition. Auditory and written lexical decision tasks (i.e., Is this a word or not?) are dependent on the stimuli having been stored in these input lexicons. Output lexicons are the long-term memory stores of high-frequency or familiar spoken word articulatory sequences or orthographic word representations that allow for rapid and easy speaking or writing. Input and output, auditory and visual lexicons are independent of each other, as demonstrated by multiple dissociations in abilities following discrete brain lesions. There is increasing evidence of similar input lexicons corresponding to nonverbal sound recognition (horn blowing vs. dog barking vs. telephone ringing), visual object recognition, and gesture or pantomime recognition (i.e., a wave good-bye, a salute, an obscene gesture, etc.). Similarly, a corresponding action or gesture output lexicon is believed to exist that allows easy completion of familiar gestures (Rothi et al., 1997). Deficits in the gesture or action output lexicon would result in ideomotor apraxia, whereas deficits in the pantomime recognition lexicon would result in an inability to recognize common gestures.

Semantics. The semantic system is the long-term memory store of conceptual information or meaning. For an individual to comprehend the meaning of the neural output from the input lexical systems, the semantic system must be accessed. Thus, *language comprehension* is dependent on correct access to an intact semantic system. Case reports have shown dissociations among different semantic categories, resulting in the hypothesis that semantic information is likely stored within specific categories such as auditory, visual, tactile, verbal, nonverbal, gesture, and so forth (Farah, Hammond, Mehta, & Ratcliff, 1989; Farah & McClelland, 1991). Divisions within semantic memory have been reported for living versus nonliving things, and vocational-specific terms/concepts versus general conceptual information (Bunn, Tyler, & Moss, 1998; Hart & Gordon, 1992; Hillis & Caramazza, 1991; Laiacona, Barbarotto, & Capitani, 1993; Sheridan & Humphreys, 1993; Warrington & McCarthy, 1987).

Syntax and Grammar. Syntax and grammar are the rules of spoken and written language. They likely are acquired through implicit learning of a procedural nature (as discussed earlier under Memory). Frontal lesions and aphasias secondary to frontal lesions (Broca's and transcortical motor aphasias) result in difficulty with production of grammatically intact speech and with writing, as well as problems with comprehension of syntactically dependent spoken and written language (e.g., "Before you point to the door, point to the ceiling," or "Pick up the pencil, but not the paper").

Speech Fluency. *Fluency* refers primarily to the average number of words uttered in a breath unit. Fluent speech is characterized by four or more words in a breath unit. However, in considering whether or not an aphasia is fluent versus nonfluent, several other aspects of language are considered:

1. Normal speech is characterized by a balance between high-information words (content, substantive) and functor words (grammatical words such as prepositions, conjunctions, articles, and pronouns). Nonfluent aphasias typically have an overall high number of substantive or content words, whereas fluent aphasias have an abnormally high ratio of functor words.

2. Difficulty with syntax is more characteristic of nonfluent aphasias.

3. A high number of paraphasias is more characteristic of fluent aphasias and less characteristic of nonfluent aphasias. *Paraphasias* are phonemic ("skoon" for "spoon"), semantic ("knife" for "spoon"), or neologistic ("soom" for "spoon") word-sound substitutions in speech.

4. Fluent speech typically remains melodically or prosodically intact, whereas nonfluent speech is often aprosodic.

5. Fluent speech is normally produced easily, precisely, and articulately. Nonfluent speech is effortful, often distorted, and poorly articulated.

Articulation refers to the praxis of speech. *Dysarthria* is a disorder of articulation in which speech is effortful, and speech sounds are distorted, slurred, or occasionally missing.

Ideomotor Apraxia. Ideomotor apraxia is the inability to produce skilled meaningful motor movements. Typically, assessment of ideomotor apraxia is done by asking individuals to perform various actions to command, such as "show me how to salute" or "show me how you would use a key." In theory, there is an input "action" or "pantomime" lexicon in which is stored the neural representations of what these actions would look like, as well as a gesture output lexicon in which are stored kinetic engrams of the motor sequences necessary to complete the gesture (Rothi et al., 1997).

A Model for Naming, Writing, and Pantomiming

Using the concepts just described, Fig. 4.7 shows how environmental stimuli are processed by sensory-perceptual systems and subsequently access input lexicons allowing perceptual recognition of familiar speech sound, nonspeech sounds (telephone ringing, dog barking, door bell, etc.), visual objects, gestures, or written words. At that point the semantic system can be accessed for meaning or bypassed. When it is bypassed, auditory stimuli can be repeated, gestures can be mimicked, written words can be copied, and at times written words can be read aloud, all of which are done without understanding the meaning of the material.

The model also shows two routes to reading. The first is the whole word recognition or sight reading approach, where familiar, high-frequency words are recognized on sight by accessing the orthographic input lexicon. The second approach to reading is the grapheme-to-phoneme conversion approach, or sounding words out. If this system is impaired, individuals have difficulty reading regular words (e.g., "bone" or "horse"). In contrast, irregular words, such as "yacht" or "naive," must be stored in the orthographic input lexicon in order to be read correctly.

When specific problems are present in naming, writing, or pantomiming, this model can help identify which sensory-perceptual or language processes are impaired. This model also can be used to develop specific tasks that would assess different language processes and/or the integrity of connections between these different cognitive processes.

Nodular Components in Mesulam's (1990) Neoclassical Model for Language

Wernicke's Area. Located in the posterior portion of the left superior temporal gyrus, Wernicke's area is seen as the semantic-lexical pole of the language network. Mesulam viewed it as a nodal point for accessing a distributed neuronal network that contains information about sound–word–meaning relationships. Other regions in temporal, parietal, and occipital cortices would be responsible for chunking auditory sequences of oral language or visual graphemic sequences of written language into neural word representations. These neural word representations then activate semantic associations. The semantic associations can be thought of as part of semantic memory, as discussed earlier. This semantic memory is seen as similarly distributed in a network manner in posterior parietal-temporal regions. Once sound–word–meaning (or visual–word–meaning) relationships have been integrated and processed by Wernicke's area, this information would then proceed to Broca's area.

Damage to Wernicke's area results in a multimodal language disturbance that affects spoken and written language. Speech is fluent, articulate, melodically intact, but very paraphasic. Language comprehension is severely impaired, as is the ability to repeat heard speech. Table 4.1 outlines the features of Wernicke's aphasia, along with the other classic aphasic syndromes.

Broca's Area. Located in the frontal operculum, just anterior to the portion of the motor strip corresponding to the face, mouth, and tongue, Broca's area is seen as the syntactic-articulatory pole of the language system. Mesulam viewed it as nodal point for transforming the neural word representations received from Wernicke's area into corresponding articulatory sequences. In addition to sequencing phonemes into words, Mesulam hypothesized that Broca's area is responsible for sequencing words into sentences in a syntactically and grammatically correct manner. In addition to receiving input from Wernicke's area, Broca's area also accesses supplementary motor cortex and prefrontal regions, and directs language motor actions through corticobulbar tracts.

Damage to Broca's area results in a nonfluent, effortful, dysarthric, agrammatic, and somewhat paraphasic speech. In addition, Broca's aphasia results in

TABLE 4.1
Classic Aphasia Syndromes

Aphasia Type	Fluency	Auditory Comprehension	Repetition	Naming	Reading Comprehension	Writing
Broca's	Nonfluent, effortful	Grossly intact	Impaired	Impaired	Grossly intact	Dysmorphic, dysgrammatic
Wernicke's	Fluent, paraphasic	Impaired	Impaired	Impaired	Impaired	Well formed, paragraphic
Global	Nonfluent or mute	Impaired	Impaired	Impaired	Impaired	Impaired
Conduction	Fluent, hesitant	Intact	Impaired	Impaired, variable	Intact	Impaired, variable
Transcortical motor	Nonfluent, akinetic mute	Intact	Intact	Impaired, variable	Intact	Impaired, variable
Transcortical sensory	Fluent, paraphasic	Impaired	Intact	Impaired	Impaired	Well formed, paragraphic
Transcortical mixed	Nonfluent, akinetic mute	Impaired	Intact, echolalic	Impaired	Impaired	Impaired
Anomic	Fluent, circumlocutious	Intact	Intact	Impaired	Intact, variable	Intact, variable

Note. To a certain degree, language comprehension and expression are impaired in all aphasias. Therefore, the performance patterns in the table refer to "relative" levels of performance or performance "profiles," rather than completely intact or completely impaired levels of ability.

difficulty with comprehension of syntactically dependent language. Basic language comprehension for content words (semantic memory) is intact.

Other Cortical Regions in Language. The *supplementary motor cortex* is thought to play a role in initiation and planning of speech output. Damage to this area can result in a transcortical motor aphasia that is very similar to Broca's aphasia except that repetition is intact. Individuals with transcortical motor aphasia have particular difficulty with speech initiation, to the point where, in severe cases, speech is virtually absent ("akinetic mutism") except for echoing back what they hear. *Prefrontal cortex* is believed to play a major role in retrieval of words from superordinate categories. Lesions to this area result in particular difficulty with tasks such as Controlled Oral Word Association ("Tell me as many words that you can think of that begin with the letter __" [e.g., F, A, S]) or Animal Naming ("Tell me as many different animals as you can think of"). *Heteromodal parietal association cortex* is seen as playing a crucial role in linking words to meaning, possibly because it has a major role in the distributed semantic memory network. Damage to this region can result in a transcortical sensory aphasia, which is similar to Wernicke's aphasia except that repetition is intact. Figure 4.8 shows diagramatically the relationships among these various brain regions, language functions, and aphasia subtypes, whereas Table 4.1 shows the language characteristics of the various aphasia syndromes.

Integrated models of linguistic components (Fig. 4.7), anatomic features (Fig. 4.8), and aphasic subtypes (Table 4.1) assist the neuropsychologist in determining what aspects of language might be impaired and possible associated areas of anatomic dysfunction. These models provide a framework that allows the neuropsychologist to evaluate test data for internal and external consistency with cognitive subcomponents and related functional neuroanatomy.

Visual Cognitive Abilities

This section is entitled "visual cognitive abilities" to include visual perceptual functions, visuospatial abilities, and the related clinical behaviors of visuoconstructional and visuopraxic skills. Historically these various abilities have been grouped together under the rubric "visual spatial functions," but, there are separate cognitive–anatomic systems responsible for different visual cognitive skills that interact with each other and with language and motor systems to produce the behaviors neuropsychologists assess and observe. Figure 4.7, presented earlier, shows how visual perception is an initial component of an object identification system, which can result in the behaviors of either orally naming or writing the name of a visual stimulus. Similarly, Fig. 4.7 reveals that for the meaning of a perceived object to be appreciated, the semantic system must be accessed. The lack of access to meaning results in an *associative visual agnosia*—no association between the intact visual percept and the semantic meaning of the object, re-

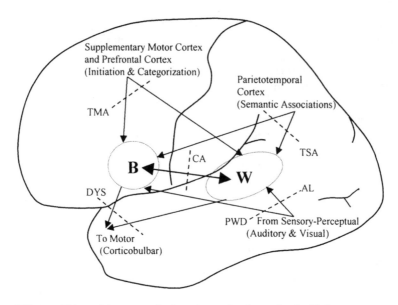

FIG. 4.8.   This model represents brain regions and pathways involved in language processing. It is adapted from Mesulam (1990). Arrows represent connections between or projections from one anatomic region to another. Dashed lines represent lesions disrupting a pathway that results in various language disorders. AL, alexia. B, Broca's area; damage to this region results in Broca's aphasia. CA, conduction aphasia. DYS, dysarthria. PWD, pure word deafness. TMA, transcortical motor aphasia. TSA, transcortical sensory aphasia. W, Wernicke's area; damage to this region results in Wernicke's aphasia.

sulting in the patient having no knowledge of what they are seeing. The semantic system itself is part of a previously acquired declarative long-term memory store (Figs. 4.5 and 4.6). Thus, it is impossible to completely separate cognitive abilities. Instead, different cognitive systems and anatomic regions interact and cooperate with each other to result in the functional behaviors we clinically observe or test.

Lateralized Hemispheric Contributions

It was not that long ago that, just as the left hemisphere was viewed as the language-dominant hemisphere, the right hemisphere was seen as dominant for visual spatial abilities. However, there is increasing recognition that both hemispheres play important roles in visual cognitive abilities. For example, Heimburger and Reitan (1961) reported that constructional dyspraxia (e.g., difficulty drawing simple geometric designs) is associated with left-hemisphere lesions 17% of the time, although it has a higher association with right-hemisphere dysfunction (48%). Similarly, on the Benton Facial Recognition Test, a complex and difficult visual perceptual task, individuals with a left-hemisphere posterior lesion severe enough to result in aphasia fail it 44% of the time, whereas individuals with similar right posterior hemisphere lesions fail it 53% of the time (Benton, Sivan, Hamsher, Varney, & Spreen, 1994). When visual tasks are primarily spatial in nature—for example, the Judgment of Line Orientation—the discrepancy widens, with right-hemisphere lesions resulting in more impairment (failure following right lesions = 46%, failure following left lesions = 10%; Benton et al., 1994). Figure 4.9 shows performance samples of two individuals with lateralized brain injury on the WAIS–R Block Design and the Rey–Osterrieth Complex Figure copy. The quantitative score on Block Design is slightly worse for the individual with a left angular gyrus tumor (age-adjusted scaled score = 5), than for the individual with focal right hemisphere damage from a head injury (age-adjusted scaled score = 6). Their respective quantitative scores on the Rey–Osterrieth Complex Figure copy are similarly impaired (left damage = 12.5/36 points, <1%; right damage = 10/36 points, <1%, Meyers & Meyers, 1995). However, the nature of their impaired performance is quite different, as described later in the Clinical Example section.

What then are the roles of the right and left hemisphere in visual cognitive abilities? Studies by Delis, Kiefner, and Fridlund (1988) and others (Heilman et al., 1985, 1993, 1994; Kinchla & Wolfe, 1979; Martin, 1979; Navon, 1977) suggest two hemispheric differences having to do with the hierarchical nature of the stimulus material and with hemispatial priority.

Hierarchical Analysis. Delis, Robertson, and Efron (1986) employed hierarchical stimuli composed of a higher level (larger) shape or letter constructed of numerous lower level shapes or letters (e.g., an H made up of many smaller x's, or a triangle composed of many small squares). Right-hemisphere-damaged patients were selectively impaired in recognizing forms at the higher structural level, whereas left-hemisphere-damaged patients were selectively impaired on recognizing lower level forms. Similar distinctive deficits were identified in a later study that involved unilateral brain-damaged subjects drawing this same type of stimuli from copy or memory (Delis et al., 1988). These findings were consistent regardless of the verbal versus nonverbal nature of the stimuli. Taken together with other studies (e.g., Martin, 1979; Robertson & Delis, 1986; Sergent, 1982), these findings suggest that the left hemisphere plays a select role in processing lower level aspects (smaller details) of visual stimuli, whereas the right hemisphere has a select role in processing the higher level features (more holistic, gestalt, or contour) of complex visual stimuli.

Hemispatial Attention. Hemispatial inattention has already been discussed in the context of attentional abilities. Unilateral brain damage impairs attention to and processing of visual stimuli presented in the contralateral hemispace (defined by the vertical body axis; Benton, Levin, & Van Allen, 1974; Heilman,

142

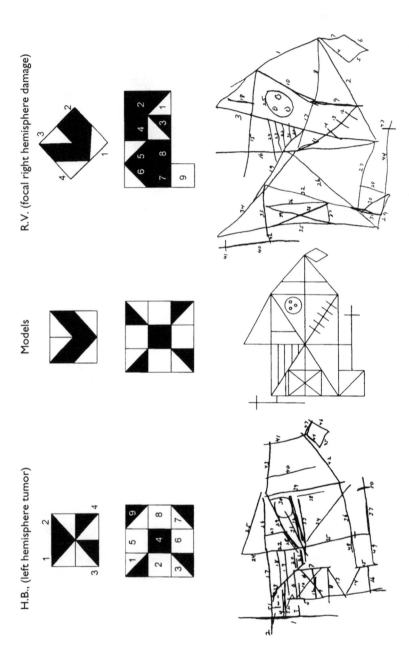

FIG. 4.9. WAIS–R Block Design and Rey–Osterrieth Complex Figure Copy drawings from two patients with lateralized lesions. The left column is H.B.'s performance, an individual with a focal tumor in the left parietal lobe. The middle column shows the models that patients were attempting to produce. The right column is R.V.'s performance, an individual with focal right hemisphere damage. Numbers on the Block Design figures show the order in which blocks were placed during constructions. Numbers on the Rey–Osterrieth Complex Figure show the order in which lines were drawn.

Watson, & Valenstein, 1985, 1993, 1994; Heilman & Valenstein, 1979). Patients will fail to attend to or will neglect stimuli on the side contralateral to their brain damage (e.g., right-hemisphere-damaged patients neglecting the left side of their spatial world).

Clinical Example. An examination of Fig. 4.9 helps highlight these differences in hierarchical analysis and hemispatial attention. Patient H.B. had a focal lesion in the left angular gyrus region. On Block Design he maintained the 2×2 and 3×3 matrix or contour of the designs (higher level feature), but had difficulty with the orientation of individual blocks (lower level feature). He also tended to have more errors on the right side of his block designs. On his drawing of the Rey–Osterrieth complex figure he had relative inattention to the right side of the stimulus. He failed to draw the point of the triangle on the right. In addition, the order in which he completed his drawing revealed that all right-sided portions of the design were drawn last (all higher numbered lines on the right). Drawing of individual lines and smaller details was more problematic. For example, although he correctly drew the circle on the upper right side of the design (relative higher level feature), he failed to draw the three smaller circles within it (lower level feature).

In contrast, patient R.V., with right-hemisphere damage, had opposite findings. He spatially rotated or failed to maintain the 3×3 matrix or outer contour of the Block Designs (higher level feature). On his initial Rey–Osterrieth complex figure drawing (not shown), he showed severe left-sided neglect (the vertical midline and all left-side portions of the figure were omitted). However, within the right side of the figure, all lower level details were correctly drawn. On his drawing 2 months later (shown in Fig. 4.9), left-sided hemispatial inattention remained (left side of the figure drawn last), as did significant difficulties with spatial integration. He clearly perceived individual visual elements (lower level features), but had severe difficulty integrating them into a coherent spatial framework (higher level feature). Thus, the pattern of findings identified by Delis and others with more experimental tasks can also be seen on commonly used clinical neuropsychological tests.

Object Identification Versus Spatial Integration

Ungerleider and Miskin (1982; Ungerleider, 1985) showed that there are two independent and distinct anatomical pathways, one leading from occipital to the inferior temporal lobes responsible for object recognition and the other leading from the occipital regions to the parietal lobes subserving spatial aspects of vision.

Object Identification. Within the occipital region itself there are multiple cortical areas responsible for different aspects of visual analysis (Ratcliff, 1987). Different groups of neurons respond to different properties of the visual stimulus (e.g., color, orientation of lines or angles, movement, etc.). More anterior within the occipital-inferior temporal pathway, neurons respond to increasingly complex shapes. Visual information appears to be processed sequentially along this pathway with ever broader "windows" on the visual world, both in size or extent, as well as in complexity of stimulus features. Cells respond to progressively more of a visual stimulus's physical properties, including size, shape, color, and texture, until the final visual analysis product is a completely synthesized physical representation of the stimulus. For this perceptual representation to be conceptually recognized, semantic memory stores would need to be accessed (refer back to Fig. 4.7). Lesions within the occipital striate cortex would result in a visual field cut or cortical blindness in a portion of the visual field. Somewhat more anterior lesions around the occipital-temporal junction would result in difficulty processing or integrating the various stimulus elements of the visual object. Impairment of the object recognition system would result in difficulty on visual perceptual tasks such as perceptual matching (e.g., Visual Form Discrimination or Facial Recognition; Benton et al., 1994), identifying missing visual details (e.g., Wechsler Picture Completion), figure–ground discrimination, difficulty recognizing degraded visual stimuli, and, in the most severe cases, visual agnosias.

An *apperceptive visual agnosia* results from a breakdown in the ability to synthesize perceived individual physical elements into an integrated whole. Individuals with apperceptive visual agnosia may be able to recognize some features of the visual stimulus without being able to appreciate the whole object. This results in their drawings of objects being fragmented, but containing recognizable elements. In addition, they cannot match identical objects presented in differing perspectives.

Lesions somewhat more anterior within the inferior temporal lobe may result in an *associative visual agnosia*. Individuals with associative visual agnosia can perceive whole visual stimuli, copy or draw them, and match the same or similar objects. However, they cannot name them, or recognize their name, identity, or function. They can correctly name or recognize an object after tactile or auditory presentation (e.g., not recognize a telephone until it rings). Referring back to Fig. 4.7, the underlying cognitive problem would be a disconnection between an intact visual perceptual/analysis system and semantic memory. Thus, the intact percept cannot access meaning within semantic memory store.

Typically, visual agnosia does not result without bilateral damage to occipital-temporal regions or other multifocal or diffuse lesions that include these regions. However, visual agnosia has been reported following right hemisphere lesions to this area (for review see Jankowiak & Albert, 1994). The specific roles of left- versus right-hemisphere processing within occipital-inferior temporal pathways has not been explicated. However, given the lateralized contributions to hierarchical analysis, visual fields, and hemispatial processing described earlier, these features might be hypothesized to play differential roles within lateralized object identification pathways.

Spatial Integration.   Spatial analysis and integration is an area of overlap between directed attention, as discussed earlier (Heilman, Watson, & Valenstein, 1985, 1993, 1994; Mesulam, 1981, 1990), and visual spatial abilities. The same individuals who have parietal lesions resulting in either overt neglect or relative hemispatial inattention also exhibit problems on spatial judgment and visual spatial constructional tasks. Individuals with parietal lesions have difficulty appreciating spatial relationships (Benton & Tranel, 1993). As discussed earlier, in most individuals the right hemisphere is dominant for controlling the distribution of attentional resources, although both hemispheres have significant roles in the direction of attention to the contralateral side of extrapersonal space. Similarly, the right hemisphere, particularly the right parietal lobe, has a major role in spatial analysis and spatial relationships (Benton & Tranel, 1993). However, Mehta and colleagues suggested that the dominant role of the right parietal lobe in visuospatial processing is restricted to tasks that make relatively pure spatial demands, such as the matching of angles. On other tasks, such as judgment of line orientation and shape rotations, the left hemisphere also has important contributions (Mehta & Newcombe, 1991; Mehta, Newcombe, & Damasio, 1987). In addition, the drawings of H.B. (Fig. 4.9) clearly show that focal left parietal lesions can impair spatial integration. Finally, spatial difficulties are typically supramodal in nature, affecting spatial analysis and judgment on visual, auditory (e.g., sound localization), and tactile tasks (e.g., localization of the different shapes on the Tactual Performance Test). This suggests that there may be a common spatial system across sensory-perceptual modalities (Ratcliff, 1987).

Executive Abilities

The frontal lobes are the most complex and least understood brain region, and executive functions are the most poorly profiled cognitive ability. Although the terms *executive abilities* and *frontal abilities* are often used interchangeably, they are not synonymous. Frontal abilities include aspects of cognitive functioning that are not executive (e.g., motor functions, language expression, olfaction, certain aspects of memory, eye–hand coordination). Similarly, executive dysfunction can occur with dysfunction outside of the frontal lobes (Kolb & Wishaw, 1996; Mendez, Adams, & Lewandowski, 1989; Mesulam, 1990; Wolfe et al., 1990). Executive abilities refer to a wide variety of behavioral functions that include sustained anticipation, goal selection, planning, problem solving, abstract reasoning, organization, initiation, self-monitoring, error detection, error correction, control functions, generative behavior, creativity, perseverance, self-awareness, and self-reflection. Whether these are distinct or overlapping abilities and what their exact neuroanatomic correlates are remain uncertain.

A Model of Executive Functioning.   To date there is no cognitive-neuroanatomic model that incorporates all these proposed executive abilities. However,

Stuss and Benson (1986) described a model of executive functions that includes three interacting component processes—control, drive, and sequencing. In their model, a frontally mediated executive system is responsible for providing conscious direction and control of posterior/basal brain functional systems, such as sensation/perception, memory, language, and visuospatial abilities. The posterior/basal cognitive abilities are seen as integrated and fixed functional systems (as described in the models outlined earlier) that perform efficiently in routine, overlearned situations. However, in novel, complex, or nonroutine situations, conscious direction is required by the executive system to facilitate effective utilization and application. Executive abilities are required when a new activity is being learned and are active when control is required. Two frontally mediated effector functional systems are hypothesized, *drive* and *sequencing*. These provide the drive and motivation necessary for posterior/basal systems to function effectively, and the capacity to sequence and integrate information from the posterior/basal systems, as well as sequence behavioral responses. The *executive control* system monitors and controls this interactive process. This latter system would be similar to what Baddeley referred to as the central executive in his working memory model (Baddeley, 1986; see earlier description and Figs. 4.4 and 4.6). Self-awareness, consciousness, and self-reflectiveness are seen as the behavioral consequence of integrated executive control, utilizing posterior/basal systems in a goal-directed manner through frontally mediated drive and sequencing functions. Self-awareness would be the highest psychological attribute of the frontal lobes. Figure 4.10 diagramatically outlines this model. The neuroanatomic structures corresponding to these various executive abilities are not well established. However, there is some evidence that different frontal regions are associated with distinct abilities.

Functional Neuroanatomic Considerations. The most dramatic manifestations of frontal-lobe dysfunction follow bilateral involvement. In contrast, deficits associated with unilateral lesions are often subtle and elusive (Mesulam, 1986). Because lesions rarely confine themselves to isolated frontal regions, the functional anatomic discussion that follows is still a matter of some controversy.

From a functional standpoint the frontal lobe is traditionally divided into motor, premotor, prefrontal, and limbic regions. Although there is not much difficulty defining the posterior boundary of the frontal lobes, because it coincides with the central sulcus, other separations are less clear. Transition from motor to premotor areas generally corresponds to the change from area 4 to area 6 (see Fig. 4.11). Regions anterior to areas 6 and 44 are generally seen as corresponding to prefrontal cortex. On the medial surface, the cingulate gyrus and areas 24 and 26 are generally regarded as frontal paralimbic regions. Prefrontal regions are often further subdivided into dorsolateral (areas 9, 10, 45, and 46), orbital frontal (areas 11, 12 and 47), and medial (medial portion of area 6, and areas 8 and 9).

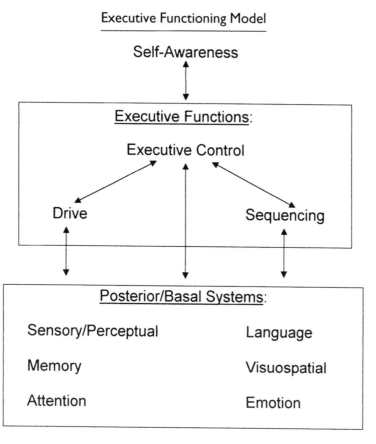

FIG. 4.10.   Stuss and Benson's (1986) executive functioning model.

The dorsolateral prefrontal cortex has been implicated in impaired perform-ance on most of the neuropsychological "frontal" measures such as the Wiscon-sin Card Sorting Test, Halstead Category Test, Trail Making Test, Stroop Test, and Fluency measures (verbal, left hemisphere; figural, right hemisphere). This has resulted in this region being associated with mental flexibility, reasoning, problem solving, cognitive planning, abstraction, and short-term or working memory (Kertesz, 1994). It is this region that is generally believed to be associ-ated with Baddeley's central executive. Thus, in terms of Stuss and Benson's ex-ecutive functioning model (1986), the executive control function would be asso-ciated with this dorsolateral region. However, the dorsolateral frontal cortex, particularly as its boundaries merge with the supplemental motor cortex (area 6 on Fig. 4.11), also has been associated with sequencing abilities, particularly sequencing of complex motor behavior (Kolb & Milner, 1981; Roland, Larsen,

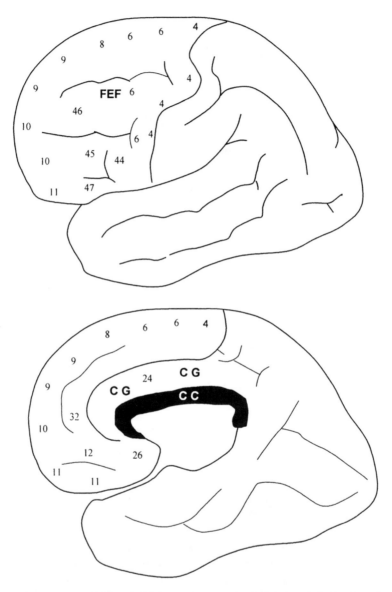

FIG. 4.11. Frontal lobe neuroanatomy. The upper figure shows the lateral surface of the left hemisphere. The lower figure shows the medial surface of the right hemisphere. The numbers represent different Brodmann areas. CC, corpus callosum. CG, cingulate gyrus. FEF, frontal eye fields.

Lassen, & Skinhoj, 1980). This suggests that dorsolateral frontal cortex also is responsible, at least in part, for the sequencing function in Stuss and Benson's executive model.

Dorsomedial left-hemisphere lesions to the premotor and supplemental motor area (area 6) have been associated with transcortical motor aphasia (TMA), a prominent feature of which is akinetic mutism (that is, no initiation of speech). Similarly, problems with generative behavior, such as poor performance on fluency measures, have been implicated with lesions in this medial region. Personality changes also have been associated with medial lesions, resulting in a general slowness to respond, a behavioral apathy, and aspontaneity that has been call pseudodepression (Blumer & Benson, 1975) or a disorder of drive (Walsh, 1987). Therefore, this region may correspond to the drive component of Stuss and Benson's executive function model.

Lesions confined to orbital frontal regions (areas 11 and 12) typically result in minimal or no performance decrements of neuropsychological measures of executive ability. Cognition is intact, behavior is not slowed, but dramatic personality changes occur, particularly following bilateral damage. These individuals are described as immature, emotionally labile, facetious, disinhibited, inattentive, irresponsible, and profane. They have been described as pseudopsychopathic (Blumer & Benson, 1975) or as having a disorder of behavioral control (Walsh, 1987). Similarly, orbitofrontal and anterior cingulate lesions in monkeys result in marked alternations of emotional responses to stimuli (Mesulam, 1986). Monkeys lose their ability to modulate the intensity of an affective response commensurate with the significance of an environmental situation. As a result, social interactions are significantly disturbed (King & Steklis, 1976). Thus, in both human and nonhuman primates orbital frontal or anterior cingulate lesions result in a clear dyscontrol syndrome. However, this dyscontrol is primarily related to emotional and social behavior; these individuals do not necessarily perform poorly on measures of cognitive control, such as mental flexibility (WCST, Trail Making Test) or screening out of irrelevant interference (e.g., Stroop). Thus, at least some aspect of Stuss and Benson's (1986) frontal control component must be related to orbital frontal regions, in addition to the dorsolateral contributions described earlier.

Frontal Roles in Memory: Implications for Understanding Executive Functions. Frontal lesions generally do not result in recent or remote memory difficulties or problems with new episodic memory. However, there are a number of difficulties on some memory tasks following frontal lesions (for review see Kertesz, 1994). These include: (a) impaired working memory, (b) an enhanced proactive interference effect (previous material interfering with learning of new material), (c) impaired retrieval, (d) forgetting to remember (also called "frontal amnesia"), and (e) difficulty with contextual aspects of memory (memory for temporal order of stimulus material, recency judgments, and memory for the source of material). The first two problems are consistent with control difficulties, either in keeping information active and organized in working memory or in screening out irrelevant stimulus material. The next two problems appear to reflect difficulty with initiation, specifically of a memory retrieval search. The last problem, difficulty with contextual elements of memory, suggests difficulty with sequencing, that is, keeping information correctly categorized or sequenced relative to time, place, and other information. Thus, the memory difficulties associated with frontal pathology can be grouped in a manner consistent with Stuss and Benson's model of executive functioning: control, drive (initiation), and sequencing. With these as examples of executive difficulties affecting another cognitive domain, one can see how executive difficulties might also adversely affect performance on language functioning, visuospatial abilities, complex motor skills, or other abilities. In all cases problems have been reported that suggest difficulty with either control, initiation / drive, and organization / sequencing, all of which can be seen collectively as a monitoring and direction system for controlling complex goal directed behavior.

SUMMARY

The previous chapter highlighted the principles involved in neuropsychological interpretation and discussed the importance and utility of conceptual models of brain functioning. Models provide a means of organizing and conceptualizing information, and consequently aiding in the interpretation process. This chapter presented and discussed a series of models.

First a model of the overall interpretation process was presented, followed by a model describing the typical steps undertaken by neuropsychologists in the interpretation endeavor. Clinical questions and issues to consider at each stage of interpretation were discussed. The majority of the chapter then was devoted to cognitive-anatomic models of brain–behavior relationships. This proceeded from an overall model of cognitive functioning, to specific models of attention, memory, language, visual cognitive, and executive abilities. In each case, models delineated the subcomponents of each cognitive ability and provided their neuroanatomic correlates. Areas of interaction between different cognitive ability domains were discussed in an attempt to show how different cognitive systems and anatomic regions interact and cooperate with each other to result in the functional behaviors we clinically observe or test. These models provide a framework that allows the neuropsychologist to evaluate test data for internal and external consistency with cognitive subcomponents and related functional neuroanatomy. When the neuropsychological data (history, behavioral observations, test performance, medical conditions, and neuroimaging information) are fully interpreted and conceptualized, a rich description of a client's cognitive abilities and deficits, together with causal factors, can be provided. This conceptualization and description serves as the foundation for treatment considerations, prognostic statements, and a discussion of the real life implications of the findings. This application aspect of neuropsychological assessment is the focus of chapter 6.

REFERENCES

Atkinson, R. C., & Shiffrin, R. M. (1968). Human memory: A proposed system and its control processes. In K. W. Spence & J. T. Spence (Eds.), *The psychology of learning and motivation: Advances in research and theory* (Vol. II, pp. 89–195). New York: Academic Press.

Baddeley, A. (1986). *Working memory.* Oxford: Clarendon Press.

Baddeley, A. (1992). Is working memory working? The fifteenth Bartlet lecture. *Quarterly Journal of Experimental Psychology, 44A,* 1–31.

Benton, A. L., Levin, H. S., & Van Allen, M. W. (1974). Geographical orientation in patients with unilateral cerebral disease. *Neuropsychologia, 12,* 183–191.

Benton, A. L., Sivan, A. B., Hamsher, K. de S., Varney, N. R., & Spreen, O. (1994). *Contributions to neuropsychological assessment: A clinical manual* (2nd ed.). New York: Oxford University Press.

Benton, A. L., & Tranel, D. (1993). Visuoperceptive, visuospatial, and visuoconstructive disorders. In K. E. Heilman & E. Valenstein (Eds.), *Clinical neuropsychology* (3rd ed., pp. 165–213). New York: Oxford University Press.

Blumer, D., & Benson, D. F. (1975). Personality changes with frontal and temporal lobe lesions. In D. F. Benson & D. Blumer (Eds.), *Psychiatric aspects of neurological disease* (pp. 151–170). New York: Grune and Stratton.

Buckner, R. L., Petersen, S. E., Ojemann, J. G., Miezin, F. M., Squire, L. R., & Raichle, M. E. (1995). Functional anatomical studies of explicit and implicit memory retrieval tasks. *Journal of Neuroscience, 15,* 12–29.

Bunn, E. M., Tyler, L. K., & Moss, H. E. (1998). Category-specific semantic deficits: The role of familiarity and property reexamined. *Neuropsychology, 12,* 367–379.

Cohen, N. J., & Squires, L. R. (1980). Preserved learning and retention of pattern-analyzing skill in amnesia: Dissociation of knowing how and knowing that. *Science, 210,* 207–210.

Delis, D. C., Kiefner, M. G., & Fridlund, A. J. (1988). Visuospatial dysfunction following unilateral brain damage: Dissociations in hierarchical and hemispatial analysis. *Journal of Clinical and Experimental Neuropsychology, 10,* 421–431.

Delis, D. C., Robertson, L. C., & Efron, R. (1986). Hemispheric specialization of memory for visual hierarchical stimuli. *Neuropsychologia, 24,* 205–214.

Denny-Brown, D. (1958). The nature of apraxia. *Journal of Nervous and Mental Disorders, 126,* 9–33.

Ellis, A. W., & Young, A. W. (1988). *Human cognitive neuropsychology.* London: Lawrence Erlbaum Associates.

Farah, M. J., Hammond, K. M., Mehta, Z., & Ratcliff, G. (1989). Category-specificity and modality specificity in semantic memory. *Neuropsychologia, 27,* 193–200.

Farah, M. J., & McClelland, J. L. (1991). A computational model of semantic memory impairement: Modality specificity and emergent category specificity. *Journal of Experimental Psychology: General, 120,* 339–357.

Fletcher, P. C., Frith, C. D., Grasby, P. M., Shallice, T., Frackowiak, R. S., & Dolan, R. J. (1995). Brain systems for encoding and retrieval of auditory-verbal memory: An in vivo study in humans. *Brain, 118,* 401–416.

Grant, I., & Adams, K. M. (Eds.). (1996). *Neuropsychological assessment of neuropsychiatric disorders* (2nd ed.). New York: Oxford.

Hart, J., & Gordon, B. (1992). Neural subsystems for object knowledge. *Nature, 359,* 60–64.

Hart, R. P., Kwentus, J. A., Wade, J. B., & Hamer, R. M. (1987). Digit symbol performance in mild dementia and depression. *Journal of Consulting and Clinical Psychology, 55,* 236–238.

Heaton, R. K., Grant, I., & Matthews, C. G. (1986). Differences in neuropsychological test performance associated with age, education and sex. In I. Grant & K. M. Adams (Eds.), *Neuropsychological assessment of neuropsychiatric disorders* (pp. 100–120.) New York: Oxford.

Heaton, R. K., Grant, I., & Matthews, C. G. (1991). *Comprehensive norms for an expanded Halstead-Reitan Battery: Demographic corrections, research findings, and clinical applications.* Odessa, FL: Psychological Assessment Resources.

Heilman, K. M., Watson, R. T., & Valenstein, E. (1985). Neglect and related disorders. In K. E. Heilman & E. Valenstein (Eds.), *Clinical neuropsychology* (2nd ed., pp. 243–293). New York: Oxford University Press.

Heilman, K. M., Watson, R. T., & Valenstein, E. (1993). Neglect and related disorders. In K. E. Heilman & E. Valenstein (Eds.), *Clinical neuropsychology* (3rd ed., pp. 279–336). New York: Oxford University Press.

Heilman, K. M., Watson, R. T., & Valenstein, E. (1994). Localization of lesions in neglect and related disorders. In A. Kertesz (Ed.), *Localization and neuroimaging in neuropsychology* (pp. 495–524). New York: Academic Press.

Heilman, K. M., & Valenstein, E. (1979). Mechanisms underlying hemispatial neglect. *Annals of Neurology. 5,* 166–170.

Heimburger, R. F., & Reitan, R. M. (1961). Easily administered written test for lateralizing brain lesions. *Journal of Neurosurgery, 18,* 301–312.

Hillis, A. E., & Caramazza, A. (1991). Category-specific naming and comprehension impairment: A double dissociation. *Brain, 114,* 2081–2094.

Jankowiak, J. & Albert, M. L. (1994). Lesion localization in visual agnosia. In A. Kertesz (Ed.), *Localization and neuroimaging in neuropsychology* (pp. 429–471). New York: Academic Press.

Kapur, S., Craik, F. I., Jones, C., Brown, G. M., Houle, S., & Tulving, E. (1995). Functional role of the prefrontal cortex in retrieval of memories: A PET study. *Neuroreport, 6,* 1880–1884.

Kertesz, A. (1994). Frontal lesions and function. In A. Kertesz (Ed.), *Localization and neuroimaging in neuropsychology* (pp. 567–598). New York: Academic Press.

Kinchla, R. A., & Wolfe, J. M. (1979). The order of visual processing: Top-down, bottom-up, or middle out. *Perception and Psychophysics, 25,* 225–231.

King, A., & Steklis, H. D. (1976). A neural substrate for affiliative behavior in nonhuman primates. *Brain Behavior Evolution, 13,* 216–238.

Kolb, B., & Milner, B. (1981). Performance of complex arm and facial movements after focal brain lesions. *Neuropsychologia, 19,* 505–514.

Kolb, B., & Wishaw, I. Q. (1996). *Fundamentals of human neuropsychology.* New York: W. H. Freeman.

Laiacona, M., Barbarotto, R., & Capitani, E. (1993). Perceptual and associative knowledge in category specific impairment of semantic memory: A study of two cases. *Cortex, 29,* 727–740.

Lezak, M. D. (1988). IQ: RIP. *Journal of Clinical and Experimental Neuropsychology, 10,* 351–361.

Martin, M. (1979). Hemispheric specialization for local and global processing. *Neuropsychologia, 17,* 33–40.

McCarthy, R. A., & Warrington, E. K. (1990). *Cognitive neuropsychology.* New York: Academic Press.

Mehta, A., & Newcombe, F. (1991). A role for the left hemisphere in spatial processing. *Cortex, 27,* 153–167.

Mehta, Z., Newcombe, F., & Damasio, H. (1987). A left hemisphere contribution to visuospatial processing. *Cortex, 23,* 447–462.

Mendez, M. F., Adams, N. L., & Lewandowski, K. S. (1989). Neurobehavioral changes associated with caudate lesions. *Neurology, 39,* 349–354.

Mesulam, M.-M. (1981). A cortical network for directed attentioin and unilateral neglect. *Annals of Neurology, 10,* 309–325.

Mesulam, M.-M. (1986). Frontal cortex and behavior. *Annals of Neurology, 19,* 320–325.

Mesulam, M.-M. (1990). Large-scale neurocognitive networks and distributed processing for attention, language, and memory. *Annals of Neurology, 28,* 597–613.

Meyers, J. E., & Meyers, K. R. (1995). *Rey Complex Figure Test and Recognition Trial: Professional manual.* Odessa, FL: Psychological Assessment Resources.

Mirsky, A. F., Anthony, B. J., Duncan, C. C., Ahearn, M. B., & Kellam, S. G. (1991). Analysis of the elements of attention: A neuropsychological approach. *Neuropsychology Review, 2,* 109–145.

Navon, D. (1977). Forest before trees: The precedence of global features in visual processing. *Cognitive Psychology, 9,* 353–383.

Nyberg, L., McIntosh, A. R., Houle, S., Nilsson, L. G., & Tulving, E. (1996). Activation of medial temporal structures during episodic memory retrieval. *Nature, 380,* 715–717.

Patterson, K., & Shewell, C. (1987). Speak and spell: Dissociation and word-class effects. In M. Coltheart, G. Sartori, & R. Job (Eds.), *The cognitive neuropsychology of language* (pp. 273–294). London: Lawrence Erlbaum Associates.

Posner, M. I., Peterson, S. E., Fox, P. T., & Raichle, M. E. (1988). Localization of cognitive operations in the human brain. *Science, 240,* 1627–1630.

Posner, M. I., & Rafal, R. D. (1986). Cognitive theories of attention and the rehabilitation of attentional deficits. In M. J. Meier, A. L. Benton, & L. Diller (Eds.), *Neuropsychological Rehabilitation* (pp. 182–201). New York: Guilford Press.

Ratcliff, G. (1987). Perception and complex visual processes. In M. J. Meier, A. L. Benton, & L. Diller (Eds.), *Neuropsychological rehabilitation* (pp. 242–259). New York: Guilford Press.

Reitan, R. M. (1964). Psychological deficits resulting from cerebral lesions in men. In J. M. Warren & K. Akert (Eds.), *The frontal granular cortex and behavior* (pp. 295–312). New York: McGraw-Hill.

Reitan, R. M., & Wolfson, D. (1992). *Neuroanatomy and neuropathology: A clinical guide for neuropsychologists.* Tucson, AZ: Neuropsychology Press.

Reitan, R. M., & Wolfson, D. (1995). Influence of age and education on neuropsychological test results. *The Clinical Neuropsychologist, 9,* 151–158.

Reynold, C. R., & Fletcher-Janzen, E. (1997). *Handbook of clinical child neuropsychology.* New York: Plenum Press.

Robertson. L. C., & Delis, D. C. (1986). "Part-whole" processing in brain damaged patients: Dysfunctions of hierarchical organization. *Neuropsychologia, 24,* 344–352.

Roland, P. E., Larsen, B., Lassen, N. A., & Skinhoj, E. (1980). Supplemental motor area and other cortical areas in organization of voluntary movement in man. *Journal of Neurophysiology, 43,* 118–136.

Rothi, L. J. G., Ochipa, C. & Heilman, K. M. (1997). A cognitive neuropsychological model of limb praxis and apraxia. In L. J. G. Rothi & K. M. Heilman (Eds.), *Apraxia: The neuropsychology of action* (pp. 29–50). Hove, England: Psychology Press.

Russell, E. W., & Starkey, R. I. (1993). *Halstead Russell Neuropsychological Evaluation System (HRNES) manual.* Los Angeles: Western Psychological Services.

Sergent, J. (1982). The cerebral balance of power: Confrontation or cooperation? *Journal of Experimental Psychology: Human perception and Performance, 8,* 253–272.

Sheridan, J., & Humphreys, G. W. (1993). A verbal-semantic category-specific recognition impairment. *Cognitive Neuropsychology, 10,* 143–184.

Sohlberg, M. M., & Mateer, C. A. (1989). *Introduction to cognitive rehabilitation: Theory and practice.* New York: Guilford Press.

Spreen, O., & Strauss, E. (1998). *A compendium of neuropsychological tests: Administration, norms, and commentary* (2nd ed.). New York: Oxford University Press.

Squire, L. R. (1987). *Memory and the brain.* New York: Oxford University Press.

Squire, L. R., & Zola-Morgan, S. M. (1991). The medial temporal lobes memory system. *Science, 253,* 1380–1386.

Stuss, D. T., & Benson, D. F. (1986). *The frontal lobes.* New York: Raven Press.

Tarter, R. E., Van Thiel, D. H., & Edwards, K. (1988). *Medical neuropsychology: The impact of disease on behavior.* New York: Plenum Press.

Tulving, E. (1972). Episodic and semantic memory. In E. Tulving & W. Donaldson (Eds.), *Organization of memory* (pp. 381–403). New York: Academic Press.

Tulving, E., Kapur, S., Craik, F. I., Moscovitch, M., & Houle, S. (1994). Hemispheric encoding/retrieval asymmetry in episodic memory: Positron emission tomography findings. *Proceedings of the National Academy of Sciences of the United States of America, 91,* 2016–2020.

Ungerleider, L. (1985). The corticocortical pathways for object recognition and spatial perception. In C. Chagas, R. Grattas, & C. Gren (Eds.), *Pattern recognition mechanisms.* Vatican City: Pontifical Academy of Sciences.

Ungerleider, L. G., & Mishkin. M. (1982). Two cortical visual systems. In D. J. Ingle, R. J. W. Mansfield, & M. A. Goodale, (Eds.), *Analysis of visual behavior* (pp. 549–586). Cambridge, MA: MIT Press.

Vanderploeg, R. D., Axelrod, B. N., Sherer, M., Scott, J., & Adams, R. L. (1997). The importance of demographic adjustments on neuropsychological test performance. *The Clinical Neuropsychologist, 11,* 210–217.

Walsh, K. W. (1987). *Neuropsychology* (2nd ed.). Edinburgh: Churchill-Livingstone.

Warrington, E. K., & McCarthy, R. (1987). Categories of knowledge: Further fractionation and an attempted integration. *Brain, 110,* 1273–1296.

Wolfe, N., Linn, R., Babikian, V. L., Knoefel, J. E., & Albert, M. L. (1990). Frontal systems impairment following multiple lacunar infarcts. *Archives of Neurology, 47,* 129–132.

Zola-Morgan, S. M., & Squire, L. R. (1990). The primate hippocampal formation: evidence for a time-limited role in memory storage. *Science, 250,* 288–290.

CHAPTER FIVE

Personality Evaluation
in Neuropsychological Assessment

Carlton S. Gass

Department of Veterans Affairs Medical Center, Miami, Florida

The assessment of personality and emotional status is an essential, yet commonly neglected, component of the neuropsychological evaluation. Its importance is underscored by a number of diagnostic and treatment-related considerations that confront neuropsychologists in their daily practice. First, behavioral changes and emotional disturbances are commonly associated with virtually all forms of brain dysfunction. These changes may be caused by a combination of factors, including psychological reactions to functional loss, endogenous alterations in the neural substrate that influences mood and behavior, and environmental changes that gradually unfold as a result of a patient's altered neurobehavioral status. Regardless of the cause, appropriate treatment is contingent on identification of the psychological disturbances by the clinician.

A second consideration involves the fact that psychological conditions present in a manner that often mimic neurological disorders. The symptoms that exemplify this are numerous and wide-ranging, but commonly include complaints of forgetfulness, poor concentration, fatigue, headache, dizziness, sensorimotor abnormalities, and, less often, nonepileptic convulsions. When confronted with such cases, the neuropsychologist who obtains normal cognitive and sensorimotor test findings may, on that basis, conclude that the patient is neurologically intact. However, the symptoms still exist until the proper diagnosis is made and treatment undertaken.

The fact that neurological symptoms sometimes mimic psychological disturbance is a third consideration that warrants the routine evaluation of emotional status. In some cases, misdiagnosis arising from a failure to assess personality leads to improper treatment. Observations can be misinterpreted. For example, the lack of initiation and apathy that sometimes characterize individuals who have frontal-lobe impairment are easily misinterpreted as signs of depression by caretakers and clinicians alike. This behavior often occurs in the absence of depression, and does not respond well to antidepressant medication or other interventions directed at alleviating depression. Other examples include transient ischemic attacks, which are sometimes misinterpreted as symptoms of panic disorder, or epileptic seizures, which can be mistaken for dissociative episodes.

Fourth, emotional disturbances often cause cognitive inefficiency in everyday living, leading to memory complaints and, in many instances, an eventual referral for neuropsychological evaluation. In some cases, psychological factors may impede an individual's performance on neuropsychological tests, although this point has probably been overstated in the clinical lore. Although poor performance on the widely used Halstead–Reitan neuropsychological battery (Reitan & Wolfson, 1993) is rarely attributable to emotional disturbance in cooperative examinees (Gass, 1991a; Heaton, Baade, & Johnson, 1978; Reitan & Wolfson, 1997), anxiety and depression have been associated with lower scores on other popular neuropsychological tests (Burt, Zembar, & Niederehe, 1995; Gass, 1996a; Gass, Ansley, & Boyette, 1994; Kinderman & Brown, 1997). Therefore, the evaluation of emotional status is often necessary for understanding the sources of everyday cognitive inefficiency about which many emotionally disturbed individuals complain, as well as interpreting their deficient performance on certain neuropsychological measures.

Fifth, once identified, many neuropsychology patients who have emotional difficulties can be helped through relatively clear, straightforward methods of intervention such as psychotherapy and psychotropic medication (Prigatano, 1987a). Early problem identification and intervention may be particularly important because problems such as depression interfere with rehabilitative efforts (Parikh, Robinson, & Price, 1988) and hinder progress in the recovery of function (Sinyor et al., 1986). Likewise, premorbid personality characteristics typically influence rehabilitative outcome through their interaction with acquired cognitive, emotional, and behavioral deficits.

Finally, neuropsychological evaluation is often undertaken to assess an individual's neurobehavioral competencies, and these extend well beyond the limits of cognitive and sensorimotor functioning. Issues such as reality testing, stress-coping skill, impulse control, self-awareness, and emotional maturity are all very germane to the competency questions that are typically addressed by neuropsychologists. A prudent assessment necessarily considers cognitive functioning within the broader context of personality-related variables, such as an individual's work capacity, drive, susceptibility to fatigue, responsibility, and ability to get along satisfactorily with other people (Prigatano, Pepping, & Klonoff, 1986). Assessment of emotional functioning is essential in many instances, because even in the presence of intact cognitive abilities psychopathological conditions can produce substantial disability.

SPECIAL CONSIDERATIONS
IN THE NEUROPSYCHOLOGICAL CONTEXT

Examinee Preparation

Many individuals who are referred for a neuropsychological evaluation do not initially understand why their personality and emotional status are being examined. In most cases, their presenting problems involve concentration, memory, or, less often, other cognitive or sensorimotor symptoms. Most do not suspect that they have a potentially diagnosable psychological disturbance that requires a formal investigation. More concerned with their physical and cognitive difficulties, they may be inclined to view these evaluative procedures as both unnecessary and intrusive. It is therefore important for the clinician to invest a few moments preparing the examinee by discussing the purpose of the personality evaluation. In most cases, it is sufficient to inform the patient that this is a routine part of the overall evaluation, and that this information provides a more complete understanding of how she or he is functioning. Without this preparation, there is a greater risk of noncompliance and/or defensiveness.

Neurologically Relevant Content Areas

The optimal methods and tools used in psychological assessment depend, to some degree, on various aspects of one's particular clinical setting. In a traumatic brain injury (TBI) treatment setting, for example, the evaluative methods should be tailored to address the common problems of limited self-reflective insight, poor social awareness, impulsivity, and concreteness (Stuss, Gow, & Hetherington, 1992), in addition to depression, anxiety, emotional lability, irritability, suspiciousness, and aggression. Settings that require making a differential diagnosis between brain dysfunction and a variety of psychological disturbances should employ methods that assist in the diagnosis of the somatoform disorders, because these masquerade as neurological conditions (e.g., psychogenic seizures, sensory loss, or motoric abnormality) in as many as 20 to 25% of the patients seen by neurologists (Schiffer, 1983).

Diverse behavioral disturbances are encountered in neuropsychological settings. Some of these may not be measurable using tools that were designed specifically for psychiatric patients. One solution has been to develop specialized instruments that address personality content areas linked with specific types of brain pathology, such as epilepsy (Bear & Fedio, 1977; Warner, Dodrill, & Batzel, 1989), Alzheimer's disease (Alexopoulos, Abrams, Young, & Shamoian,

1988; Devanand et al., 1992; Sinha et al., 1992), and closed-head injury (Levin et al., 1987). Another approach has been to custom design a test that assesses areas of importance in a heterogeneous neurologically impaired population, including the rarely assessed areas of denial and communication difficulties (Nelson et al., 1989). Finally, well-established omnibus measures such as the Minnesota Multiphasic Personality Inventory–2 (MMPI–2; Butcher, Dahlstrom, Graham, Tellegen, & Kaemmer, 1989) are often used to assess multifaceted aspects of personality and psychopathology in neuropsychological settings.

Estimating Premorbid Personality and Assessing Personality Change

Evaluating the psychological status of the brain-impaired individual is somewhat unique in that the central substrate for personality and emotion (i.e., the brain) is itself dysfunctional; changes in psychological functioning are therefore not unusual. The estimation of premorbid personality characteristics is important for several reasons. First, evidence suggests that premorbid personality traits correlate with features of postinjury emotional behavior and personality (Chatterjee, Strauss, Smyth, & Whitehouse, 1992; Rutter, 1981). A knowledge of premorbid behavior is therefore useful in predicting difficulties in psychological adjustment. For example, preexisting problems involving substance abuse, aggressive behavior, difficulties with authority figures, noncompliance, and poor motivation all have important implications for rehabilitation and aftercare potential (Prigatano, 1987b). Second, knowledge of premorbid functioning provides a partial basis for estimating potential strengths as well as realistic parameters for behavioral improvement during periods of recovery and rehabilitation from head injury, stroke, and other nonprogressive forms of brain dysfunction. Third, premorbid estimation is important because the degree of personality change has a major impact on the patient's new role within the family, as well as the family's ability to make the necessary adaptations (Klonoff & Prigatano, 1987; Lezak, 1978).

Changes in emotional and behavioral functioning are expected with many types of brain dysfunction. This is not surprising when one considers that the physical status of the brain itself is variable following the onset of a neurologic disease process (e.g., degenerative condition or tumor) or with the occurrence of a brain insult (e.g., traumatic injury or stroke). Not only do environmental contingencies change as a result of diminished brain function (e.g., activities such as reading lose their reward value), but behavioral change in the patient may transform the surrounding environment, effectively reorganizing it and forcing it to adapt to his or her limitations. As a result of bidirectional (person–environment) influences, certain patterns of behavior and emotion may show a gradual shift, and psychologically descriptive information may have time-limited validity (Fordyce, Rouche, & Prigatano, 1983; Prigatano, 1987b). For example, an individual with nondominant hemisphere damage may initially display a normal level of social activity, but this may eventually give way to interpersonal withdrawal and avoidance as others react to the patient's inability to appropriately decipher and respond to their facial, gestural, and prosodic (voice tone) expressions of emotion (Etcoff, 1989). Similarly, the recovery of awareness and insight following acute brain injury is commonly associated with a gradual emergence of emotional difficulties (Godfrey, Partridge, Knight, & Bishara, 1993).

Interview and observational data obtained from relatives are often essential for estimating premorbid personality and measuring subsequent changes. Behavior rating scales can be applied retrospectively and endorsed by relatives or peers in order to provide a baseline estimate of an individual's premorbid personality functioning (Nelson et al., 1989). Changes in behavior and emotional functioning often require repeated assessments and necessitate the use of measurement instruments that are reliable, yet sensitive to change. Perhaps the most useful test information is provided by instruments that combine measures of stable trait characteristics with measures of more changeable features. For example, the MMPI–2 provides information on fairly stable characteristics related to shyness and social nonconformity (Scales 0 and 4, respectively), while assessing more changeable features such as depression and anxiety (Scales 2 and 7, respectively).

Limitations in Test-Taking Ability

Some brain-impaired individuals are unable to manage the administrative requirements of self-report and projective tests. Fatigue, confusion, diminished attentiveness and concentration, perseveration, aphasia, deficient reading skill, and visuoperceptual deficits can all interfere with the taking of tests. Unfortunately, patients do not always alert the examiner to these difficulties, and they sometimes "complete" tests in an invalid manner. For example, the examinee may not report losing track of the appropriate item numbers on an answer sheet, or demonstrate hemispatial neglect and complete inattention for one side of visual stimuli (e.g., Rorschach or TAT cards). It is therefore imperative that the clinician consider the patient's cognitive and perceptual limitations, and make every effort to circumvent any adverse effects these deficits may have on the testing process.

Practical steps that can sometimes improve the validity of test administration include:

1. Breaking the testing period into two or three shorter sessions.
2. Use a taped or compact disk (CD) version of a test instead of the written format whenever reading or sustained visual concentration are suspected or known to be problematic.

3. Carefully modify answer sheets by making them simpler, more concrete, and/or larger in print to suit the special needs of the examinee.

4. In the beginning and periodically throughout the duration of the test, make sure that the examinee is properly following the test instructions.

5. Self-report instruments should be completed in a controlled setting where complete privacy is assured and proper assistance is available if needed. Test responses should not reflect the collective opinion of caretakers, family members, or others present at the time of the test administration!

6. Upon completion of a self-report instrument, the answer sheet should be checked carefully for omitted items.

Unfortunately, some patients are too impaired to provide valid test responses, and the clinician must rely solely on information derived from other sources that are subsequently described in this chapter.

Limitations in Self-Awareness and Insight

Damage to the brain sometimes impairs one's self-reflective awareness, insight regarding acquired cognitive and social deficits, and emotional appreciation of biologically based limitations in behavioral competencies. Patients may be completely unaware of their acquired deficits (anosognosia), or they may be aware but indifferent toward them (anosodiaphoria). The nondominant cerebral hemisphere seems to play a prominent role in mediating this awareness, as neurobehavioral complaints are much more common in individuals who have lesions restricted to the dominant hemisphere (Gass & Ballard, 1998). These limitations have led some clinicians to criticize the use of self-report measures with brain-injured individuals. Most clinicians would agree that self-report measures should be supplemented with other evaluative methods, yet it would probably be a mistake to omit self-report as one approach to understanding the patient. Self-report provides, at the very least, data pertaining to the phenomenological perspective of the patient. This is critical information for several reasons. First, the patient's frame of reference largely determines his or her mood and behavior. Second, it is impossible for the clinician to evaluate the patient's degree of insight in the absence of reliable information about the patient's own perspective and self-perception. Once quantified, an individual's reported perspective on self, problems, and feelings can be compared both normatively and ipsatively, the latter by relying on the judgments of individuals who are most familiar with the patient. A comparison of behavior ratings made by the patients versus their significant others is one way to address the issue of insight. Another method involves the use of self-report instruments that have validity scales. These scales can potentially provide evidence of poor insight or denial as reflected in naive defensiveness in responding to test items. Various evaluative methods can be used to address this and other issues related to personality and emotional functioning. A detailed critique of these approaches is presented by Gass and Ansley (1995).

METHODS OF EVALUATING PSYCHOLOGICAL STATUS

Clinical Interview

The clinical interview is an indispensable source of information regarding personality functioning. Unlike psychological tests that are based on a nomothetic approach and provide general descriptions derived from group studies, interview data provide highly detailed idiographic (individual-based) clinical information. This relatively open-ended approach is advantageous in eliciting specific problem areas, the patient's own perspective regarding these difficulties, and other dimensions of psychological functioning that are not revealed through formal testing. In many cases, the interview must include the patient's family or significant others. This is particularly true in situations in which the neurologically compromised examinee lacks insight, is defensive, or is otherwise incapable of providing accurate information regarding his or her own behavior. Brain dysfunction and severe psychopathology are both common causes of poor recollection and confusion in patients who are asked to provide information regarding their current symptoms, medical history, and other relevant background information.

In evaluating brain-impaired individuals, the interview provides information regarding premorbid psychological characteristics that often influence subsequent psychosocial adjustment and, when applicable, involvement in rehabilitation. Interview information also reveals clues regarding factors that cause or maintain symptoms. It has often been said, "history is 90% of the diagnosis." This maxim reflects the fact that the etiology of a patient's presenting symptoms is often suggested by relevant background information obtained in the interview with patients and their significant others. Critical interview data include a comprehensive description of all of the presenting symptoms, and a historical context for each of these problems. The historical context for understanding each of the presenting symptoms includes relevant antecedent or surrounding events that may have precipitated their onset, quantitative and qualitative variations in the natural course of the symptoms and associated environmental influences, and response to any interventions or treatments. For example, the interview might divulge that forgetfulness of recent verbal and visual material emerges in a person immediately following retirement, and coincide with the onset of other apparently reactive depressive symptomatology. The course of this symptom might show substantial fluctuation in conjunction with perceived spousal support and marital harmony. In addition, the situational effects or consequences of a symptom should be explored. In some cases, symptoms develop, persist and even worsen due to the presence of material rewards, interpersonal benefits (e.g., malingering or conversion disorder), or intrinsic motivational factors such as wanting to adopt the role of medical patient (i.e., factitious disorder), both premorbidly and following the onset of brain dysfunction.

Direct Observation

Many observable behaviors of importance are not always identifiable on the basis of formal testing, including disturbances in affective expression, childish or "regressed" behavior, poor temper control, and signs of impaired social perception and sensitivity, such as may be reflected in unusual remarks or inappropriate actions. Personality characteristics that can be observed in the neuropsychological testing context include frustration tolerance, stamina, task persistence, and impulse control. Appropriate concern and accurate insight might be displayed by an examinee in response to failed test performances, whereas similar failures can also reveal impaired insight and self-awareness, apathy and indifference, or, at the other extreme, marked perfectionism manifested in overt self-criticism. Intense dependency needs are sometimes reflected in repeated requests for feedback and reassurance during testing. Style of stress coping may be evident in behavior characterized by withdrawal from difficult tasks, rationalizing failure, demeaning the tests, or displacing anger toward the examiner.

Behavior Rating Scales

Behavior rating scales provide a systematic means of assessing the observations made by people who are quite familiar with the examinee, such as family members. In some cases, observer ratings conflict with the examinee's self-report. This situation warrants careful investigation, because such a discrepancy can result from a patient's impaired self-awareness or, alternatively, from the inability of observers to correctly "read" the patient's outward affect. In all cases, it must be emphasized that neither observation nor self-report is necessarily more valid as a source of assessment data. Nevertheless, individuals who are quite familiar with the patient can often provide ratings of both premorbid and postinjury behavior that are useful for estimating behavior change. This method has been employed using the Neuropsychology Behavior and Affect Profile (NBAP; Nelson et al., 1989), a 106-item scale that measures five content areas: indifference, mania, depression, behavioral inappropriateness, and communication problems. A second application involves repeated measurements to assess and monitor behavioral changes following brain injury, an approach that has been taken using a modified version of the Brief Psychiatric Rating Scale (BPRS; Overall & Gorham, 1962), the Neurobehavioral Rating Scale (NRS; Levin et al., 1987).

Projective Techniques

Projective techniques are sometimes used in the context of neuropsychological evaluation, although there is surprising little literature addressing their application with the brain-injured population. The limited literature that does exist tends to focus exclusively on response characteristics that discriminate brain-damaged from neurologically intact individuals. The major example of this is the identification of "organic signs" in Rorschach responses (see Goldfried, Stricker, & Weiner, 1971, for a review). More recently, with the availability of better procedures for detecting brain dysfunction, this particular application of personality tests is rarely considered except as a matter of historical interest. Unfortunately, the more general application, that is, for clinically descriptive purposes, has received limited attention with respect to neurological patients. Lezak (1995) described a number of general projective test response characteristics that are exhibited by neurologically impaired individuals. These include constriction, stimulus boundedness, structure seeking, response rigidity, fragmentation, simplification, conceptual confusion, spatial disorientation, confabulated responses, and hesitancy and doubt.

Rorschach inkblot techniques, which are generally classified as projective in nature, vary across existing systems. The Comprehensive System (CS; Exner, 1978, 1986), which has the strongest psychometric foundation, assumes that the inkblot is a stimulus to perceptual-cognitive operations that are representative of those involved in processing analogous situations in daily life (Erdberg, 1990). This approach appears to be ideally suited for assessing the manner in which personality functioning is affected by and interacts with cognitive and perceptual impairments. The structural aspect of the CS is made up of empirically sound elements that were included on the basis of demonstrated reliability and validity. These elements constitute a variety of areas of basic importance to understanding personality, including preferred style and efficacy of stress coping, tendency to function logically and objectively versus being influenced by emotional factors, extent and quality of personal self-focus, quality of reality testing, efficacy in perceptually organizing complex stimulus situations, and responsiveness to affective experiences in daily life.

The Thematic Apperception Test (TAT; Murray, 1938) uses storytelling as a medium for assessing a broad range of personality attributes, including psychological needs or concerns, internal conflicts, and other problem areas. As is the case with most projective measures, the task is more likely to yield valid data when the examinee is intact with respect to visuoperceptual and verbal functions. Unfortunately, brain-impaired patients tend to use fewer words, communicate fewer ideas, show fewer consistent themes, and adopt an approach that is overly simplistic and descriptive rather than creative (Lezak, 1995). Damage that compromises the normal functioning of the prefrontal cortex is often manifested in patients who display impaired initiation (requiring prompting), loss of instructional set (requiring redirection), and test responses that are fragmented and disorganized. Nevertheless, important themes are sometimes communicated, particularly by higher functioning patients. In these cases, the TAT may be particularly sensitive to problems related to dependency, social isolation, and poor impulse control (Bellak, 1986). Problems with perseveration, confusion, concreteness, and ideational impoverishment are also revealed in the TAT protocols of many brain-injured individuals.

Sentence completion tests, having a semistructured format, can provide detailed information related to personality functioning, including the quality of adjustment to disability, effectiveness in coping with loss, and self-concept. Because of its relative simplicity, many neurologic patients can complete this task sufficiently to provide potentially useful information. However, as a last resort, the examiner can read the items and record the responses for those patients who are unable to read and/or write.

Figure drawings, which are often used to assess visuospatial and graphomotor skill, may also constitute a medium through which patients express certain aspects of personality or psychological conflict. However, in view of the association between drawing characteristics and intellectual factors—as well as their general sensitivity to damage in the nondominant cerebral hemisphere— the clinician must exercise caution in using detailed aspects of drawings to make inferences regarding personality and psychological functioning.

Self-Report Instruments

Self-report measures continue to be the most widely used type of instrument for assessing personality and psychopathology in neuropsychological cases. Many of these instruments have been validated using psychiatric samples, have relatively strong psychometric properties, and offer an advantage of yielding a substantial amount of information while requiring limited clinician time. Scores on self-report measures often yield treatment implications that are easily discussed with the patient and family members (Butcher, 1990; Gass & Brown, 1992).

Self-report instruments vary widely with respect to their comprehensiveness in describing the many facets of psychological functioning. The Beck Depression Inventory (BDI; Beck, Ward, Mendelsohn, Mock, & Erbaugh, 1961), for example, is widely used to measure symptoms of depression. Although depression is relatively common in neurologic samples, the focus of this 21-item instrument is quite narrow when considered in the broader context of the many other behavioral disturbances associated with known or suspected brain dysfunction. Depression itself is not a uniform phenomenon that can be adequately measured simply in terms of severity. Components of depression may include psychosis, obsessional thinking, somatic preoccupation, agitation, social avoidance, emotional dependency, and a host of other characteristics, none of which are measured by brief depression scales. The same general limitation applies to a myriad of other brief self-report measures (Speilberger, Gorsuch, & Luschene, 1971; Yesavage et al., 1983; Zung, 1965, 1971). Some clinicians attempt to compensate for this inadequacy by imparting clinical meaning to individual item responses, a practice that is psychometrically naive and ignores the inherent unreliability of individual responses.

The Symptom Checklist 90–Revised (SCL–90–R; Derogatis, 1977) is a 90-item inventory that addresses nine primary symptom dimensions, including Somatization, Obsessive-Compulsive, Interpersonal Sensitivity, Depression, Anxiety, Hostility, Phobic Anxiety, Paranoid Ideation, and Psychoticism. The literature pertaining to the SCL–90–R in neuropsychological settings is quite limited. Several studies suggest that potentially misleading scale elevations on the SCL–90–R occur in brain-injured samples as the result of self-reported cognitive and physical symptoms of central nervous system (CNS) damage (Woessner & Caplan, 1995, 1996). For example, eight items were identified by O'Donnell, DeSoto, DeSoto, and Reynolds (1995) to be sensitive to cognitive impairment in a heterogeneous sample of individuals who had brain damage, and five of these are included in the 10-item Obsessive-Compulsive scale.

The Millon Clinical Multiaxial Inventory–III (MCMI–III; Millon, 1994) and its predecessors are sometimes used in the context of neuropsychological evaluations to help clarify the role of longstanding personality patterns as distinct from more transient emotional disturbances that are associated with brain injury. Russell and Russell (1997) described the potential assets of this instrument as a tool to assist the neuropsychologist in differential diagnosis. Although the MCMI has received a substantial amount of attention in the psychiatric research literature, relatively few empirical studies have addressed the application of the MCMI in neuropsychological settings, particularly in relation to individuals who have brain dysfunction.

THE MINNESOTA MULTIPHASIC PERSONALITY INVENTORY–2 (MMPI–2)

The Minnesota Multiphasic Personality Inventory (MMPI–2; Butcher et al., 1989) warrants more thorough discussion because it is by far the most widely used and extensively researched instrument for evaluating the personality characteristics and emotional status of individuals who have known or suspected neurological dysfunction (Lees-Haley, Smith, Williams, & Dunn., 1996). Its frequency of clinical use is matched by the voluminous amount of neuropsychological research involving the MMPI–2. The MMPI–2 and its forerunner (MMPI) have been investigated in hundreds of neuropsychological studies over the past 50 years, far more than any other personality measure. The remainder of this chapter is devoted to the clinical use of the MMPI–2 in neuropsychological assessment.

The MMPI was originally constructed by Starke Hathaway, a clinical psychologist, and J. Charnley McKinley, a neuropsychiatrist, in the late 1930s and early 1940s for the purpose of assisting in the diagnosis of psychiatric disorders in patients who were treated at the University of Minnesota hospitals. Item response frequencies were contrasted between "Minnesota normals," composed primarily of relatives and visitors of patients in the University of Minnesota Hospitals, and clinical subjects who were patients classified into one of several psychodiagnostic groups. Items that statistically discriminated between the normals and a specified psychodiagnostic group were cross-validated and placed on a scale representing that diagnosis. Restandardized in 1989 (Butcher et al., 1989), the MMPI–2 is superior to the MMPI with respect to its accuracy, normative base, and diversity of measures. Reliability and validity issues are discussed in detail by Groth-Marnat (1997).

Administration of the MMPI–2

In most medical settings, patients expect to be asked about their symptoms, previous medical problems, diet, and family history. They do not expect to be asked by the doctor about playing house as a child, stepping on sidewalk cracks, making donations to beggars, fears of mice and spiders, fascination with fire, enjoying gambling, auto racing, growing house plants, and flirting. The relevance of such inquiries, as well as the credibility of the examiner, may be questioned, leading to defensiveness or noncompliance. The clinician can prevent this by preparing the patient prior to administering the MMPI–2. Patients should never be administered the MMPI–2 or other instruments without an adequate explanation of the test's function and the rationale for giving it. A general approach involves introducing the MMPI–2 as a routine part of the examination process designed to measure feelings and attitudes that are important in developing a complete picture of one's general health.

The MMPI–2 may be used with most individuals who are at least 18 years old and have a minimum eighth-grade level of reading comprehension. A wide variety of conditions can preclude a valid administration of the MMPI–2. These include impatience and low frustration tolerance, visual disturbances, confusion, dyslexia, impaired reading comprehension, inattention and distractibility, and florid psychotic symptoms. Nevertheless, patients who have mild or even moderate neuropsychological impairment secondary to brain injury are typically able to produce profiles that are valid in regard to content–response consistency (Mittenberg, Tremont, & Rayls, 1996; Paniak & Miller, 1993). Completion of the MMPI–2 sometimes requires breaking the session into several shorter periods.

The reading requirement poses difficulties for many examinees. *Based on clinical experience with the MMPI–2, the routine use of the audio version is strongly recommended.* Many brain-injured patients who are unable to manage the standard written format can effectively complete the MMPI–2 using this approach. The audio version requires no reading of narrative material, very little visual concentration, and apparently less mental effort on the part of the examinee. In addition, the rate of compliance is better and the time to completion is typically much less. The cassette tape edition produced by National Computer Systems (NCS), which should be replaced soon by a more durable compact disk (CD) version, requires approximately 2 hr.

Scoring the MMPI–2: The Problem of Content Bias

The MMPI–2 can be scored by hand using the templates provided by NCS, or computer scored. Scores on the basic clinical scales are based on items that were assigned to these scales because of their sensitivity to the personality and emotional characteristics of the original psychiatric samples that had well-defined diagnoses but were, by and large, free of any organic brain disorders. Because the authors did not originally intend to use the MMPI–2 outside of the psychiatric setting, there was no attempt to determine whether the item pool would be systematically endorsed in a biased way by nonpsychiatric populations that might share a particular set of characteristics. Within their limited scope of application, content bias was not a concern. However, scoring the MMPI–2 protocols of brain-impaired individuals must be carefully considered, and a correction may be required because these examinees often inflate their scores by reporting bona fide neurological symptoms.

The presence of neurologic symptom content in the MMPI–2 item pool has been recognized ever since its initial acknowledgment by the authors of the inventory (Hathaway & McKinley, 1940),[1] and has posed a vexing problem for many clinicians who attempt to interpret the profiles of individuals who have central nervous system (CNS) impairment. Attempts to either evaluate or systematically control for the influence of neurologic-symptom endorsement by brain-injured patients have been made by relying on expert opinion in selecting items of suspected relevance (Alfano, Finlayson, Stearns, & Neilson, 1990; Alfano, Paniak, & Finlayson, 1993; Baldwin, 1952; Cripe, Maxwell, & Hill, 1995; Derry, Harnadek, McLachlan, & Sontrop, 1997; Gass & Russell, 1991; Marsh, Hirsch, & Leung, 1982; Meyerink, Reitan, & Selz, 1988; Mueller & Girace, 1988). A more reliable approach based on a set of statistical methods (Kendall, Edinger, & Eberly, 1978) was applied by Gass (1991b), who identified MMPI–2 items that were distinctly associated with traumatic brain injury (TBI). The resulting 14 items were highly discriminative in relation to the MMPI–2 normative sample and factorially distinct from a group of items that reflected psychological adjustment following head injury. They appear to resemble some of the cognitive, sensorimotor, and general health concerns commonly associated with TBI. The

---

[1]Hathaway and McKinley identified several clusters of MMPI items reflecting "general neurologic" (19 items), "cranial nerve" (11 items), and "motility and coordination" (6 items).

association of these 14 items with TBI has been replicated in other head-injury samples (Barrett, Putnam, Axelrod, & Rapport, 1998; Gass & Wald, 1997; Edwards, Holmquist, Wanless, Wicks, & Davis, 1998; Jacobucci, Bowman, & Shercliffe, 1997; Netto, 1997; Rayls, Mittenberg, Burns, & Theroux, 1997). Moreover, when asked directly about these 14 MMPI–2 items, brain-injured subjects reported that the items represented specific symptoms of their head injury. Family members who presumably knew the patient quite well concurred with this attribution (Edwards et al., 1998). The 14-item MMPI–2 correction for TBI is included in the NCS MMPI–2 scoring report for personal injury cases, released in 1998.

The recommended use of the MMPI–2 correction factor has generated some controversy, partly because it has been applied inappropriately to malingerers and compensation-seeking victims of mild head trauma who report symptoms, most likely psychogenic in nature, that persist well beyond the normal recovery period. Proper use of the correction is predicated on a presumption of brain damage. In the absence of brain pathology, the correction "corrects" nothing, and most likely results in an underestimate of psychopathology. Validation studies of the correction that rely on the responses of individuals with probable somatoform disorders and/or malingering are not particularly informative (Brulot, Strauss, & Spellacy, 1997). As yet, none of the critics of the correction have marshaled empirical support for their position using bona fide brain-injured patients. A detailed account of the controversy is presented by Gass (1999).

MMPI–2 Correction Factor for Closed-Head Injury

The MMPI–2 correction for closed-head injury (Gass, 1991b) consists of 14 of the 370 items of the abbreviated MMPI–2 that satisfied four successive empirical criteria. First, responses to each of the items sharply distinguished a sample of 75 bona fide head injury patients, none of whom had premorbid psychopathology or drug addiction, from the MMPI–2 normative sample ($p < .001$). Second, every item was endorsed by at least 25% of the head-injury sample. Third, the items were statistically grouped together, comprising a unitary factor as determined by the application of factor analysis (varimax rotation). The results of the orthogonal analysis revealed these items to be factorially independent of a set of psychiatric symptom items that also emerged as a factor. Fourth, the content of the items showed face validity as representing physical and cognitive symptoms and concerns related to brain injury (see Table 5.1). Cross-validation of correction-factor internal consistency was provided by Barrett, Putnam, Axelrod, and Rapport (1998). Using a separate sample of head-injury patients, they reported a Cronbach's alpha coefficient of .80.

The correction factor is only used with brain-injured patients who do not have a preexistent history of psychopathology or drug addiction. Scoring the MMPI–2 profiles of traumatic brain injury patients should be done twice, once in the standard manner and again after eliminating any correction items that were endorsed in

TABLE 5.1
The MMPI–2 Correction Factor for Closed-Head Injury

---

31. I find it hard to keep my mind on a task or job (T).
101. Often I feel as though there were a tight band around my head (T).
106. My speech is the same as always (not faster or slower, no slurring; no hoarseness) (F).
147. I cannot understand what I read as well as I used to (T).
149. The top of my head sometimes feels tender (T).
165. My memory seems to be all right (F).
170. I am afraid of losing my mind (T).
172. I frequently notice that my hand shakes when I try to do something (T).
175. I feel weak all over much of the time (T).
179. I have had no difficulty in walking or keeping my balance (F).
180. There is something wrong with my mind (T).
247. I have numbness in one or more regions of my skin (T).
295. I have never been paralyzed or had any unusual weakness of any of my muscles (F).
325. I have more trouble concentrating than others seem to have (T).

Note. Minnesota Multiphasic Personality Inventory–2. Copyright © by the Regents of the University of Minnesota 1942, 1943 (renewed 1970), 1989, 1991. Reproduced by permission of the publisher. MMPI–2 and Minnesota Multiphasic Personality Inventory–2 are trademarks owned by the University of Minnesota.

the scored direction. This procedure, which is detailed later, provides the clinician with a systematic means of measuring the degree and manner in which neurological symptom endorsement influences the resulting clinical profile. It eliminates the guesswork and inherent unreliability associated with subjective-based methods assumed under the rubric of "clinical judgment." The correction is individualized in its application. Thus, the amount of correction varies, ranging from none to substantial, depending on an individual's responses to the 14 items.

Scoring the Correction Factor. The correction scoring procedure initially requires checking the answer sheet for specific answers to the 14 neurologically related items listed in Table 5.2. If the examinee's answer is in the keyed direction, as indicated later, then 1 point is deducted from the raw score of the clinical scales that are represented on the same line. For example, if item 31 is answered "True," then 1 point is subtracted from the raw score of Scales 2, 3, 4, 7, 8, and 0. Table 5.2 can be used to tally the total number of pathologically endorsed items for each MMPI–2 scale. If the items (column 1) are answered in the keyed direction indicated, then the item number is tallied wherever it appears across the entire row. After following this procedure for each item, the clinician can work columnwise, counting the number of circled items in each column. The sums are recorded at the bottom of Table 5.2 above the corresponding MMPI–2 scale. The numbers located in the bottom row are the values that should be subtracted from the respective raw scores on the basic clinical profile. Once the corrected

TABLE 5.2
MMPI–2 Correction Table for Closed-Head Injury

Item	F	1	2	3	4	7	8	9	0
31 True	—	—	31T	31T	31T	31T	31T	—	31T
101 True	—	101T	—	101T	—	—	—	—	—
106 False	—	—	—	—	—	—	106F	106F	106F
147 True	—	—	147T	—	—	147T	147T	—	—
149 True	—	149T	—	—	—	—	—	—	—
165 False	—	—	165F	—	—	165F	165F	—	—
170 True	—	—	170T	—	—	170T	170T	—	—
172 True	—	—	—	172T	—	—	—	—	—
175 True	—	175T	175T	175T	—	175T	—	—	—
179 False	—	179F	—	179F	—	—	179F	—	—
180 True	180T	—	—	—	—	—	180T	—	—
247 True	—	247T	—	—	—	—	247T	—	—
295 False	—	—	—	—	—	—	295F	—	—
325 True	—	—	—	—	—	325T	325T	—	—
Sum									
	F	1	2	3	4	7	8	9	0

raw scores are determined, they can be plotted on a National Computer System hand-plotting MMPI–2 profile sheet, or the revised T-scores can be determined using Table A-1 in the MMPI–2 manual (Butcher et al., 1989, pp. 54–55).

As a general rule, clinicians are advised to first establish that there is sufficient evidence of cerebral impairment before applying the correction to an MMPI–2 protocol. By implication, the correction is not appropriate for routine application with the majority of individuals who are seeking compensation for persisting symptoms following mild head injury (Brulot et al., 1997; Dunn & Lees-Haley, 1995). In most of these cases, there is reason to suspect that the symptomatic complaints are largely related to psychological factors, motivational pressures, incentives to acquire compensation, and other important aspects of their medicolegal context (Binder, 1997; Gasquoine, 1997; Reitan & Wolfson, 1997; Youngjohn, Burrows, & Erdal, 1995). Correction application in these cases would potentially distort, rather than enhance, the accuracy of profile interpretation.

MMPI–2 Correction Factor for Stroke

Cerebrovascular disease (CVD), or stroke, is another disorder that is frequently evaluated in neuropsychological settings. Strokes occur in the United States with an estimated annual incidence of 500,000 to 700,000 cases. Gass (1992) addressed the problem of stroke-related item content on the MMPI–2 and designed a correction factor specifically for use with individuals who have had a stroke. The 21-item correction for stroke was designed using 110 patients with

CVD and virtually the same statistical procedures as were used previously with closed head-injury patients (Gass, 1991b). Empirical support for the sensitivity of these 21 items was obtained in a recent cross-validation study of 50 stroke patients (Gass, 1996b). The correction items are presented in Table 5.3. The items can be tabulated using Table 5.4 to derive corrected scores on the clinical scales. Although the corrections for use with closed-head injury and stroke share some common items, there are enough differences to indicate that any corrective method should be tailored specifically for particular neurodiagnostic populations rather than for brain-impaired patients in general. Recent evidence suggests that the MMPI–2 correction for stroke is also applicable with patients who have multiple sclerosis (Nelson & Do, 1998).

Interpretive Sequence for the MMPI–2

Detailed guidelines for MMPI–2 interpretation and descriptions of the various scales are presented in Butcher and Williams (1992) and Graham (1993). The fol-

TABLE 5.3
MMPI–2 Correction Factor for Cerebrovascular Disease

10. I am about as able to work as I ever was (F).
31. I find it hard to keep my mind on a task or job (T).
45. I am in just as good physical health as most of my friends (F).
47. I am almost never bothered by pains over the heart or in my chest (F).
53. Parts of my body often have feelings like burning, tingling, crawling, or like "going to sleep" (T).
106. My speech is the same as always (not faster or slower, no slurring; no hoarseness) (F).
141. During the past few years, I have been well most of the time (F).
147. I cannot understand what I read as well as I used to (T).
148. I have never felt better in my life than I do now (F).
152. I do not tire quickly (F).
164. I seldom or never have dizzy spells (F).
168. I have had periods in which I carried on activities without knowing later what I had been doing (T).
172. I frequently notice that my hand shakes when I try to do something (T).
173. I can read a long time without tiring my eyes (F).
175. I feel weak all over much of the time (T).
177. My hands have not become clumsy or awkward (F).
182. I have had attacks in which I could not control my movements or speech but in which I knew what was going on around me (T).
224. I have few or no pains (F).
229. I have had blank spells in which I did not know what was going on around me (T).
247. I have numbness in one or more regions of my skin (T).
249. My eyesight is as good as it has been for years (F).

Note. Minnesota Multiphasic Personality Inventory–2. Copyright © by the Regents of the University of Minnesota 1942, 1943 (renewed 1970), 1989, 1991. Reproduced by permission of the publisher. MMPI–2 and Minnesota Multiphasic Personality Inventory–2 are trademarks owned by the University of Minnesota.

TABLE 5.4
MMPI–2 Correction Table for Cerebrovascular Disease

Item	F	1	2	3	4	7	8	9	0
10 False	—	10F	10F	10F	—	—	—	—	—
31 True	—	—	31T	31T	31T	31T	31T	—	31T
45 False	—	45F	45F	45F	—	—	—	—	—
47 False	—	47F	—	47F	—	—	—	—	—
53 True	—	53T	—	—	—	—	—	—	—
106 False	—	—	—	—	—	—	106F	106F	106F
141 False	—	141F	141F	141F	—	—	—	—	—
147 True	—	—	147T	—	—	147T	147T	—	—
148 False	—	—	148F	148F	—	—	—	—	—
152 False	—	152F	—	152F	—	—	—	—	—
164 False	—	164F	—	164F	—	—	—	—	—
168 True	168T	—	—	—	—	—	168T	168T	—
172 True	—	—	—	172T	—	—	—	—	—
173 False	—	173F	—	173F	—	—	—	—	—
175 True	—	175T	175T	175T	—	175T	—	—	—
177 False	—	—	—	—	—	—	177F	—	—
182 True	—	—	—	—	—	—	182T	182T	—
224 False	—	224F	—	224F	—	—	—	—	—
229 True	—	—	—	—	—	—	229T	229T	—
247 True	—	247T	—	—	—	—	247T	—	—
249 False	—	249F	—	249F	—	—	—	—	—
Sum									
	F	1	2	3	4	7	8	9	0

Note. Minnesota Multiphasic Personality Inventory–2. Copyright © by the Regents of the University of Minnesota 1942, 1943 (renewed 1970), 1989, 1991. Reproduced by permission of the publisher. MMPI–2 and Minnesota Multiphasic Personality Inventory–2 are trademarks owned by the University of Minnesota.

lowing discussion is a brief overview with a particular focus on neuropsychological applications.

MMPI–2 interpretation consists of generating a series of hypotheses about an individual based on empirically derived behavioral correlates of scores and score patterns. These descriptive correlates are based on systematic studies of individuals who, in most cases, had a psychiatric diagnosis and, in many instances, were receiving some form of psychological and/or psychopharmacological treatment. Several interpretive steps are recommended.

1. Analyze the patient's test-taking attitude and protocol validity by examining scores on the validity scales.
2. Estimate the patient's general level of psychological adjustment based on the number of high scores on the clinical scales ($T > 65$).
3. Identify and interpret the code type of the clinical profile. If the examinee has brain damage, first apply an appropriate correction factor as a

means of identifying scores that may be artificially elevated. If the correction alters the code type, interpretation should proceed on a scale-by-scale basis after the correction has been applied.

4. Interpret secondary scale elevations beginning with the scale that has the highest score. Scale interpretations on Scales 2, 3, 4, 6, 8, and 9 can be enhanced by examining the pattern of scores on the Harris–Lingoes subscales. This is especially important in clarifying the meaning of marginally elevated scores (T 60 to 70) on the parent scales.

5. Interpret components of the profile configuration and the relationships between scores on various scales (see Butcher & Williams, 1992).

6. Interpret the content and supplementary scales. These can help clarify the meaning of other scores, as well as add to the information base derived from the basic clinical profile.

7. Examine responses to the critical items. Answers to these MMPI–2 items could potentially indicate problems of critical importance and should be pursued further (Butcher, 1995). For example, it is often important to follow up when a client responds "true" to the item, "Nobody knows it, but I have tried to kill myself."

The Validity Scales

A major advantage of the MMPI–2 over many other assessment instruments is its measurement of test-taking attitude and profile validity. An examinee's test-taking attitude and openness in reporting problems largely influence the outcome on self-report measures of emotional functioning. Therefore, proper interpretation of the MMPI–2 validity scales lays a necessary foundation for accurately understanding the meaning of scores on the clinical and content scales. In addition, scores on these scales have certain personality correlates that can be very important in their own right for understanding the examinee.

Cannot Say (?). The Cannot Say score is the number of unanswered or double-tallied (true and false) items. Most examinees answer every item. As a general rule, the patient who fails to answer items should be queried and, to whatever extent possible, encouraged to reconsider and respond to any items that were not initially answered.

L Scale. The L (Lie) scale consists of 15 items that measure a tendency to answer the MMPI–2 in a way that expresses a naive defensiveness, as well as an unrealistically high degree of moral virtue and self-control over thoughts, emotional impulses, and behavior. High scores (T > 60) on the L scale suggest limited self-awareness and poor emotional insight. Higher scorers who have impaired brain functioning typically overestimate their cognitive abilities and, as a result, make poor decisions, taking on tasks that are beyond their capability to effectively handle. Increasingly higher scores on L are associated with poorer recognition of cognitive limitations, acquired deficits, and, simultaneously, worse neuropsychological test performance. In a mixed neurological sample, scores on the L scale were mildly predictive of the degree of global neuropsychological impairment on the Average Impairment Rating Scale, $r(144) = -.27, p < .005$ (Gass, 1997).

Scores on L have been linked with the extent of cognitive impairment in several studies of brain-injured patients (Dikmen & Reitan, 1974, 1977; Gass & Ansley, 1994). In neurologically intact individuals, T-scores above 60 on scale L are associated with a psychologically based denial and rigid, stereotypic, and ineffective style of coping with stress. High scorers on L tend to be moralistic, rigid, concrete, and unaware of the impact that their behavior has on other people. They are overly optimistic about themselves, and view themselves as "above" any need for psychological intervention. Elevated scores on L are typically associated with lower scores on the clinical profile, particularly on the higher numbered scales (6, 7, 8, and 9).

F Scale.   The F (Infrequency) scale consists of 60 items that were originally designed to measure random responding and unusual or deviant ways of responding to the inventory. In most cases, the F scale measures the degree of openness to disclosing psychological problems, including attempts to exaggerate or feign psychological disturbance. In some cases, high F scores ($T > 80$) are due to content-independent (random) responding, possibly secondary to poor reading comprehension, confusion, difficulty understanding the meaning of items, or noncompliance (see VRIN and TRIN later).

Neuropsychological referrals frequently score above a T-score of 75, particularly if they have a psychiatric history or are referred by a psychiatrist. If a high F-scale score can not be explained on the basis of content-independent responding (i.e., VRIN and TRIN are less than 80 T), the clinician has to try to differentiate between the profile impact of legitimate psychopathology versus exaggeration or malingering. An F scale score that exceeds 80 T or even 100 T is often produced by patients who have serious psychopathology in the absence of marked exaggeration of symptomatology. In these cases, the clinician should make a very careful attempt to determine whether the associated clinical profile, which in most cases has at least several elevated scores, is corroborated by observation and interview data. Extratest information and observation will often help the clinician to determine whether exaggeration played a role in a person's responses on the MMPI–2. Potentially exaggerated results can also be reviewed and discussed with the patient in an effort to gain clarification of the meaning of high scores and individual item responses.

The deliberate faking or exaggeration of symptoms following mild head trauma is a very common problem confronted by neuropsychologists who are involved in personal injury and other compensation-related forensic cases. Malingering occurs in diverse ways. Claimants who consciously feign symptoms of traumatic brain injury in order to gain financial compensation often emphasize cognitive deficits, physical problems, and general health concerns, while minimizing any claims of severe psychopathology or highly unusual psychological symptoms. They do not want to appear "crazy," just brain-damaged. Although some malingerers also try to appear psychologically disabled (and consequently produce high F-scale scores), many do not. Many produce marginally elevated scores on the F scale (Berry et al., 1995; Greiffenstein, Gola, & Baker, 1995) and high scores on Scales 1 and 3 (Larrabee, 1997; Suhr, Tranel, Wefel, & Barrash, 1997).

Moderate elevations on the F scale (*T* 65 to 79) typically reflect open disclosure of multiple problems, and marginal elevations (*T* 60 to 64) on the F scale suggest openness in reporting problems that are relatively circumscribed in nature. A very large percentage of brain-injured patients produce F scores within this range. Victims of bona fide traumatic brain injury who score below 65 *T* very rarely report a substantial number of cognitive complaints (Gass & Freshwater, 1999). In clinical settings, a score below 50 *T* is rather unusual and is likely to be accompanied by other evidence of defensiveness on scales L and/or K.

K Scale. The K (Correction) scale consists of 30 items that measure defensiveness and an attempt to appear psychologically healthy and emotionally well adjusted. When the score on K is high (*T* > 60), the MMPI–2 profile may be invalid due to "faking good." However, individuals with somatoform disorders (conversion, psychogenic pain, somatization, and hypochondriasis) sometimes produce high scores on K in conjunction with elevated scores on scales L, 1, and 3. This shows a willingness to admit to problems specifically of a physical nature while attempting to appear extremely well adjusted. In clinical settings, marginal elevations on K (*T* 55 to 60) suggest mild defensiveness, positive psychological adjustment, or a combination of the two. Low scores on K (below 40 *T*) usually suggest that an individual feels extremely overwhelmed by problems and is feeling vulnerable and defenseless. Scores on the K scale are independent of educational background.

F − K Index. The combination of an elevated score on F and a very low score on the K scale was reported by Gough (1950) to be especially sensitive to symptom exaggeration or claims of nonexistent problems (dissimulation). Cutting scores have been proposed, although optimal scores vary across settings depending on the local base rates for "faking." Recent research has suggested that the F scale in isolation might be equally as effective as F − K in detecting feigning, and that the incremental value derived by including K in an index is minimal (Graham, Watts, & Timbrook, 1991).

Fb Scale. The Fb or F Back scale was developed for the MMPI–2 to detect deviant or random responding to the items that are presented later in the test.

The interpretative guidelines for the Fb scale are the same as those used with the F scale. Very high scores ($T > 100$) can occur in valid protocols and commonly reflect substantial distress and/or psychosis. Contextual considerations are critical to interpretation, because elevated scores may reflect a plea for special assistance in the form of psychological intervention, obtaining disability status, or financial compensation. Brain-impaired persons can report a wide variety of cognitive, sensorimotor, and health-related concerns without substantially elevating the F or Fb scale score.

F(p) Scale. The F(p) scale (Arbisi & Ben-Porath, 1995) consists of 27 items that are rarely endorsed in the keyed direction by psychiatric inpatients or by normal individuals. F(p) primarily measures an attempt to exaggerate or fabricate the presence of psychological symptoms. To the extent that F(p) is elevated above 80 T in a consistent protocol (VRIN and TRIN < 80 T), the clinician should suspect symptom exaggeration, perhaps as a plea for help, or malingering.

Variable Response Inconsistency (VRIN). VRIN consists of 67 pairs of items that have similar or opposite meaning. Each pair is scored 1 point if the two answers to the item pair are inconsistent or contradictory. A score of 13 or greater (80 T or more) suggests invalidity due to content-independent responding. In these cases the protocol is uninterpretable. VRIN should always be checked for evidence of inconsistent responding when the protocol has a high score ($T > 80$) on the F or Fb scales. If VRIN and TRIN are below 80, then it can be concluded that the high score on F or Fb is not due to careless responding.

True Response Inconsistency Scale (TRIN). Examinees sometimes lapse into a mode of repeatedly answering test items with the same response ("True" or "False"), without attending to or giving due consideration to the content of test statements. The TRIN scale is bipolar. High raw scores indicate acquiescence, and the scaled score is designated with a *T*. Low raw scores indicate responding with "False" to items, and the scaled score is designated with an *F*. Scores that exceed 80 T or 80 F suggest protocol invalidity.

Basic Clinical Scales

Scale 1. Hypochondriasis (Hs). This 32-item scale was originally referred to as the Hypochondriasis scale because item selection was based on the responses of a group of neurotic patients who had multiple physical complaints and health-related preoccupations in the absence of any discernible medical condition or abnormal physical findings. When scores on Scale 1 are high ($T > 70$) and prominently elevated in the profile configuration, they often suggest a diagnosis of a somatoform disorder. In the neuropsychological context, elevations on Scale 1 are quite common. Brain-injured individuals commonly score moderately high on Scale 1 (*T* 65 to 75), not because of somatoform symptoms, but because of their frank endorsement of neurologically related items. These include references to diminished general health status (45), paresthesias (53), tiredness and fatigue (152), weakness (175), pain (224), periodic dizzy spells (164), difficulty walking (179), and numbness (247). Although there are exceptions, empirical data suggest that scored responses to neurologically related items such as these account for an average increase of 10 to 15 *T*-score points on Scale 1, with a range of 0 to 30 points (Gass, 1991b, 1992). For this reason, application of the correction factor is recommended.

Approximately 50% of brain-impaired patients score above 65 *T* on Scale 1, although clinical experience suggests that the incidence of somatoform symptoms is substantially less than this. The frequency of high scores on Scale 1 is much higher in litigating head-trauma cases (Youngjohn, Davis, & Wolf, 1997) and personal injury plaintiffs (Lees-Haley, 1997), many of whom lack any objective evidence of structural brain damage. Secondary gain is clearly a critical factor in a large number of compensation-related cases, and elevated scores on Scales 1, 2, and 3 sometimes reflect feigning of physical symptoms and health-related preoccupations. Elevated scores on these scales have been associated with incomplete effort on neuropsychological testing and an atypical *decline* in cognitive test performance on repeated testing following head trauma (Putnam, Kurtz, Fichtenberg, O'Leary, & Adams, 1995). They are also associated with the presence of physical and cognitive complaints well beyond the period within which individuals normally recover from mild head trauma (Putnam et al., 1995).

Scores on Scale 1 (and probably on other scales) do not differentiate between frank malingering and a somatoform disorder. In both cases, scores on Scale 1 are commonly between *T* 70 and 90, although perhaps slightly higher in persons who are suspected of malingering (Suhr et al., 1997). The client's history and other pertinent data, including life-contextual considerations, are likely to contribute far more useful information to the clinician who has to make this differential diagnosis. Also problematic is the fact that conscious and unconscious feigning of somatic symptoms can occur simultaneously, and in conjunction with brain damage. For example, a reaction to brain damage in certain individuals undoubtedly includes intense physical concerns and heightened somatic sensitivities. In these cases, symptoms of hypochondriasis or somatization disorder can contribute substantially to scores on Scale 1, well beyond the direct influence of reporting bona fide symptoms of neurological impairment.

Scale 2. Depression (D).   The 57-item Depression scale assesses common symptoms of depression. Harris and Lingoes (1955, 1968) divided the item content of Scale 2 into five rationally constructed component subscales. *Subjective Depression* (D1, 32 items) has content that refers to subjective feelings of unhappiness, diminished interest, low energy for coping, feelings of inadequacy, and social uneasiness. *Psychomotor Retardation* (D2, 14 items) suggests lack of energy, emotional immobilization, and social avoidance. *Physical Malfunctioning* (D3, 11 items) contains content related to somatic preoccupations, specific physical symptoms, and generally poor health. *Mental Dullness* (D4, 15 items) refers to diminished attention, concentration, and memory, lack of energy, and self-doubt. *Brooding* (D5, 10 items) suggests crying, ruminating, and, in some cases, feelings of hopelessness. Brain damage is linked with higher scores on *Mental Dullness* (D4) and *Physical Malfunctioning* (D3), reflecting cognitive and somatic difficulties (Gass & Lawhorn, 1991; Gass & Russell, 1991; Gass, Russell, & Hamilton, 1990).

Scale 2 is often elevated in brain-injured patients, partly because it contains items that refer distractibility (31), convulsions (142), diminished reading comprehension (147), memory difficulty (165), generalized weakness (175), and problems with walking or balance (179). Acknowledgment of these symptoms increases the *T*-score on Scale 2 by an average of 5 to 10 points, with a range of 0 to 12 points (Gass, 1991b, 1992). An estimated 40% to 50% of brain-impaired patients score above 65 *T* on Scale 2 (Gass, 1997). Scores on Scale 2 that exceed 75 *T* in brain-injured individuals almost invariably reflect depressive symptoms in addition to any neurologic item-related artifact that might exist.

Although depression sometimes has an adverse impact on cognitive test performance, scores on Scale 2 are not usually predictive of neuropsychological test performance. Studies have suggested that Scale 2 scores in neuropsychological referrals are independent of level of performance on measures of attention and memory (Gass, 1996a; Gass & Russell, 1986; Gass et al., 1990), fluency or mazes (Gass, Ansley, & Boyette, 1994), or alternating attention on the Trail Making Test, Part B (Gass & Daniel, 1990).

Scale 3. Hysteria (Hy).   The Hysteria scale is comprised of 60 items that were associated with conversion disorder in the original Minnesota criterion sample. High scorers (*T* > 70) report somatic symptoms, some of which originate in psychological conflict. These complaints may elicit affectionate attention from others or a reduction in stressful responsibilities (e.g., work). Harris and Lingoes (1955, 1968) identified five content domains on Scale 3 that are routinely scored as subscales. *Denial of Social Anxiety* (Hy1, 6 items) suggests ease in social interaction and a resilience to the influence of social mores. *Need for Affection* (Hy2, 12 items) assesses an emotional dependency on others, denial of unacceptable emotion, and a tendency to suppress negative feelings that would jeopardize such relationships. *Lassitude-Malaise* (Hy3, 15 items) has content that refers to generalized weakness, discomfort, and fatigue, as well as unhappiness, sleep disturbance, and poor concentration. *Somatic Complaints* (Hy4, 17 items) consists of multiple symptomatic complaints of a physical nature. *Inhibition of Aggression* (Hy5, 7 items) suggests a denial of hostile impulses and sensitivity to other people's reactions.

Neuropsychological referrals produce high scores on the Lassitude-Malaise and Somatic Complaints subscales far more commonly than on the other Scale

3 subscales, indicating a prominence of physical discomfort, fatigue, and various other physical complaints in this population. These two subscales include several items that are descriptive of neurological symptoms. Not surprisingly, scores on these subscales are usually elevated to some degree by brain-injured patients, even in the absence of hysterical or histrionic personality characteristics (Gass & Lawhorn, 1991).

Although brain-impaired individuals often produce moderately high Scale 3 scores (T 60 to 70) without having symptoms of a somatoform disorder, very high scores on Scale 3 ($T > 75$) usually indicate the presence of somatoform symptomatology, malingering, or a combination of the two. The same generalization applies to Scale 1. For example, scores on both 1 and 3 are typically higher in nonepileptic seizure (NES) disorder than in epilepsy patients, who are more likely to exhibit primary elevations on Scales 2 and 8 (Ansley, Gass, Brown, & Levin, 1995).

Scale 3 scores are clearly increased when CNS symptoms are reported on the MMPI–2 by examinees who show no evidence of conversion hysteria or other somatoform characteristics. As is the case with Scales 1, 2, 7, and 8, the amount of the increase varies widely across individuals and possibly across neurological diagnoses. Neurological conditions that involve focal brain lesions, such as stroke and multiple sclerosis, frequently produce prominent elevations on Scales 1 and 3. Neurologically relevant item content includes references to work capacity (10), distractibility (31), general health (45, 148), pain (47, 224), tiredness and fatigue (152, 173), periodic dizzy spells (164), tremor (172), weakness (175), and vision (249). The T-score on Scale 3 is increased by an average of 5 to 10 points as a result of reporting neurological symptoms, although the potential increase ranges from 0 to 23 points (Gass, 1991b, 1992). About 25% to 30% of brain-injured patients produce T-scores on Scale 3 exceeding 65. This percentage is higher in compensation-seeking samples in which there an incentive for feigning (Youngjohn et al., 1995).

Scale 4. Psychopathic Deviate (Pd).   Psychopathic or antisocial personality disorder characterized the clinical sample used by Hathaway and McKinley to construct the 50-item Psychopathic Deviate scale. The item content of Scale 4 was divided into five subscales by Harris and Lingoes. *Familial Discord* (Pd1, 11 items) refers to an unpleasant family life characterized by inadequate love or emotional support. *Authority Problems* (Pd2, 10 items) measures attitudes and behaviors that indicate a rejection of authority and run-ins with societal limits. *Social Imperturbability* (Pd3, 12 items) assesses self-confidence and comfort in social situations. *Social Alienation* (Pd4, 18 items) refers to feelings of estrangement and rejection by others, most likely resulting from behavior that is self-centered, insensitive, and inconsiderate of other people. *Self-Alienation* (Pd5, 15 items) measures frustration with both oneself as well as the inability to find life interesting or rewarding.

The interpretation of scores on Scale 4 in persons who have CNS impairment is straightforward because the items comprising this scale appear to have little or no neurological content bias. Scale 4 may be sensitive to some of the personality changes that result from brain injury, including a loss of self-control, outbursts of anger, and a diminished concern with other people's needs and interests. In most cases, however, high scores on Scale 4 reflect premorbid personality characteristics and not secondary effects of brain damage. Among the various neurodiagnostic groups, high scores on Scale 4 are most frequently produced by chronic substance abusers and victims of traumatic brain injury (Gass & Russell, 1991).

Scale 5. Masculinity–Femininity (Mf).   The Masculinity–Femininity scale was originally designed to identify problems in sex-role adjustment and particularly ego-dystonic impulses of a homoerotic nature. Mild to moderate elevations on Scale 5 (T 60 to 75) reflect traditional and stereotypic opposite sex gender-related interest patterns. Females who score in this range are likely to have interests and preferences that are stereotypically masculine, such as sports, science, and outdoor activities such as camping or hunting. Males who score in this range lack many of the stereotypically masculine interests and values, and tend to be more "culturally refined," interested perhaps in art, music, and the theatre.

Low scorers (T < 40) on Scale 5 identify with their own traditional sex-role stereotype in terms of interest patterns. This generalization probably applies more to males than females. In fact, many females who possess academic and professional ambition produce low scores on Scale 5. Low-scoring males, on the other hand, generally have traditionally masculine interests and, in the extreme, might be described as "macho." Poorly educated males tend to score slightly lower on Scale 5 in the normative sample. Among Veterans Administration (VA) neuropsychological male referrals, Scale 5 shows a mild positive correlation with educational background (Gass & Lawhorn, 1991).

Scale 6. Paranoia (Pa).   Individuals who had frank paranoid features or a diagnosed paranoid disorder were used as the criterion sample by Hathaway to select the 40 items on the Paranoia scale. High scorers (T > 75) are occasionally psychotic, whereas moderate scorers (T 65 to 75) are usually rigid, hypersensitive, and predisposed to misinterpret and overpersonalize the words and actions of other people. Harris and Lingoes (1955, 1968) identified several components of Scale 6. *Persecutory Ideas* (Pa1, 17 items) measures feelings and perceptions of being mistreated and victimized. *Poignancy* (Pa2, 9 items) refers to feeling highstrung, sensitive, lonely, misunderstood, and distant from others. *Naiveté* (Pa3, 9 items) refers to optimism about people, naive trust in others, and associated feelings of vulnerability to hurt.

Scale 6 contains few, if any, items that refer directly to physical, cognitive, or health-related symptoms of brain dysfunction. No correction is applied to this scale. Studies suggest that most neurologically impaired individuals score within the average range on Scale 6. However, high scores are not uncommon in acute TBI, suggesting suspiciousness, distrust, and a sense of having received a "raw deal" from life. Posttraumatic paranoia is not uncommon, particularly in acute head injury, although it rarely persists over a period of months (Grant & Alves, 1987). High scores occur in 10% to 35% of brain-impaired individuals, though the frequency may be slightly higher in compensation-seeking patients, many of whom feel victimized and angry.

Scale 7. Psychasthenia (Pt).   The 48 items that comprise this scale were intended to measure psychasthenia, which is roughly synonymous with obsessive-compulsive disorder. In psychiatric samples, high scorers ($T > 65$) on Scale 7 are distressed, anxious, and worried, often over an abundance of seemingly minor issues. In TBI patients, Scale 7 scores correlated the highest with cognitive complaint frequency, $r = .64$, $p < .0005$ (Gass & Apple, 1997). Approximately 25% to 50% of brain-impaired individuals score above 65 T on Scale 7. The high frequency is partially due to their endorsement of neurologically related items that refer to distractibility (31), reading problems (147), memory difficulty (165), generalized weakness (175), forgetfulness (308), and concentration difficulty (325). Acknowledgment of these symptoms increases the T-score on Scale 7 by an average of 5 points, though the effect can be as large as 12 points in an individual case (Gass, 1991b). Thus, slightly elevated scores on Scale 7 do not necessarily reflect anxiety and distress in individuals who have bona fide brain injury. Scores that exceed 70 T, however, usually indicate the presence of these symptoms.

Scale 8. Schizophrenia (Sc).   The Schizophrenia scale consists of 78 items that were pooled by Hathaway and McKinley from several groups of items that they had originally hoped would be specific to four subtypes of schizophrenia (paranoid, simple, hebephrenia, and catatonic). The resulting scale was heterogeneous in item composition. For this reason, scores on this scale can be increased by factors that are largely unrelated to schizophrenia (Butcher & Williams, 1992; Graham, 1993), including acquired brain damage. Nevertheless, the presence of a thought disorder and impaired reality testing should be considered in valid profiles when Scale 8 exceeds 75 T, is significantly higher than Scale 7, and when scores on the Bizarre Mentation content scale are also high ($T > 70$).

Six subscales reflect areas of rationally identified content domains on Scale 8 (Harris & Lingoes, 1955, 1968). *Social Alienation* (Sc1, 21 items) refers to feelings of having been mistreated, misunderstood, and unloved. *Emotional Alienation* (Sc2, 11 items) assesses feelings of depression, apathy, fear, and despair. *Lack of Ego Mastery, Cognitive* (Sc3, 10 items) refers to strange thoughts, feelings of unreality, and difficulties with concentration and memory. *Lack of Ego Mastery, Conative* (Sc4, 14 items) refers to life as a strain, excessive worry, and coping with stress by withdrawing into fantasy and daydreaming. *Lack of Ego Mastery, Defec-*

tive Inhibition (Sc5, 11 items) refers to feeling out of control, restless, and hyper-active. *Bizarre Sensory Experiences* (Sc6, 20 items) assesses unusual sensory experiences and physical changes, in addition to hallucinations and bizarre thought content.

In psychiatric settings, high scores on Sc3 and Sc6 suggest a more severe psychotic symptom picture than do high scores on the other subscales. However, the characteristics that are measured by these two subscales are certainly not specific to psychosis or even psychopathology; they often reflect cognitive and sensorimotor complaints that are common in neurologically impaired individuals (Bornstein & Kozora, 1990; Gass, 1991b; Gass & Russell, 1991). Individuals who have CNS impairment and report their neurological symptoms and related concerns on the MMPI–2 typically increase their scores on Scale 8, independent of psychotic symptoms. Items that are commonly endorsed include references to blank spells (229), distractibility (31, 299), speech changes (106), poor concentration (325), reading difficulty (147), memory problems (165), problems walking (179), anosmia (299), tinnitus (255), numbness (247), and paralysis or weakness (177, 295). The endorsement of neurologically related items on the MMPI–2 increases the T-score on Scale 8 by an average of 5 to 10 points, with a potential increase of as many as 20 points (Gass, 1991b, 1992). High scores on Scale 8 occur in about 40% to 50% of brain-impaired patients (Gass, 1997). These percentages contrast sharply with the incidence of psychosis in neurological disorders, generally, and with the estimated 10% frequency of psychosis following brain injury secondary to trauma (Grant & Alves, 1987).

Individuals who feign traumatic brain injury commonly produce mildly to moderately high scores on Scale 8, often because of their endorsement of MMPI–2 items that have content related to cognitive difficulties (Sc3) and physical abnormalities (Sc6). Similar content is expressed by individuals with bona fide brain injury. The interpretation of high scores on Scale 8 should be made in the context of (a) knowledge of the examinee's history, (b) clinical observation, (c) the examinee's test-taking attitude as measured by the validity scales, and (d) the medicolegal context of the evaluation.

Scale 9. Hypomania (Ma).   The 46 items on this scale measure characteristics of hypomania, including heightened energy and overactivity, emotional excitement, and flight of ideas. High scores on Scale 9 are associated with a potentiation of behavioral correlates of high scores on the other clinical scales. For example, a moderately high score on Scale 6, when accompanied by a high score on Scale 9, is more likely to be associated with overt paranoid features. Harris and Lingoes divided this scale into four major content domains and representative subscales. *Amorality* (Ma1, 6 items) measures characteristics of selfishness, dishonesty, and vicarious satisfaction over others' manipulative exploits. *Psychomotor Acceleration* (Ma2, 11 items) assesses an increased rate of speech, thought, and motor activity, and an unusual need for stimulation and excitement. *Imper-*

turbability (Ma3, 8 items) represents a denial of social anxiety and a lack of concern with the feelings, attitudes, and opinions of other people. *Ego Inflation* (Ma4, 9 items) measures an unrealistically optimistic self-evaluation. Most brain-injured patients score within the average range on Scale 9, with approximately 5% to 25% scoring higher than 65 T. The frequency is closer to 25% in acute TBI (Gass, Luis, Rayls, & Mittenberg, 1999).

Scale 0. Social Introversion (Si). The Social Introversion scale consists of 69 items that measure shyness, discomfort in and avoidance of social situations, and self-doubt. High scorers (T > 65) are socially anxious, timid and retiring, lacking in self-confidence, and bothered by their shyness. Low scorers on Scale 0 (T < 40) are gregarious, friendly, energetic, and outgoing. They prefer social interaction and group activities, and seek out competitive situations. Ben-Porath, Hostetler, Butcher, and Graham (1989) devised several subscales for Scale 0 using rational and empirical techniques. *Shyness* (Si1, 14 items) refers to interpersonal discomfort and a lack of sociability. *Social Avoidance* (Si2, 8 items) measures a tendency to socially withdraw and avoid group situations. *Self/Other Alienation* (Si3, 17 items), which uniquely embodies psychopathological features, refers to a negative self-perception and feelings of alienation and estrangement from other people. High scorers report experiencing distrust, disappointment, and social apprehension.

In neuropsychological settings, the interpretation of Scale 0 scores is straightforward. This scale contains very few neurologically related items and, as such, does not require a consideration of content bias or correction. High scores are more likely to be found in psychiatric referrals than in general medical patients.

Clinical Scale Combinations

Regardless of the profile code type, the relative score elevations on several clinical scale pairs can provide additional information regarding an individual's style of coping. In some cases, these score combinations are specific applications of the general principle that (a) Scales 1, 2, 3, 5, 7, and 0 represent tendencies related to self-control or regulation of impulses, and (b) Scales 4, 6, 8, and 9 generally reflect diminished control and acting out behaviors. The present discussion is limited to the 13/31 combination because of its special importance in neuropsychology. For information regarding other scale combinations, see Butcher and Williams (1992).

Conversion V. If Scales 1 and 3 are prominently elevated and at least 10 T-score points higher than Scale 2, this "conversion V" pattern suggests the presence of physical manifestations of psychological conflict combined with an attitude of relative indifference toward the symptoms. This pattern is also common in individuals who sustain mild head trauma and, for many months or even years thereafter, who continue to report a variety of problems (e.g., distractibility, forgetfulness, headache, diffuse pain, dizzy spells, fatigue) that are difficult to explain on the basis of current medical knowledge (Putnam et al., 1995). These individuals are typically pursuing financial compensation for their alleged injury. Many are presumed to have a somatoform disorder, are consciously malingering, or a combination of the two. In the absence of sufficient evidence of actual brain injury, the MMPI–2 correction for closed-head injury (Gass, 1991b) should not be used. The conversion V pattern on the MMPI–2 is also common in individuals with multiple sclerosis and stroke. In these cases, evidence of brain damage is usually unequivocal, and the correction factor for stroke (Gass, 1992) should be applied to help evaluate the effects of neurological symptom reporting. The exception to this guideline occurs if the patient has a premorbid history of psychopathology or chemical dependency.

Content Scales

Fifteen MMPI–2 content scales were developed using a multistep approach that combined rational and empirical analytic procedures (Butcher, Graham, Williams, & Ben-Porath, 1990). These scales provide important information that augments and supplements the data derived from the basic clinical scale profile. Empirical studies (Butcher et al., 1990) indicate that these scales are psychometrically sound with respect to both reliability and validity. Unlike the basic clinical scales, the content scales are composed entirely of test items that have transparent and obvious meaning to the reader. As a result, the content scale profile provides a much clearer and more direct reflection of how the examinee wants his or her problems to be portrayed to the clinician. Defensiveness results in low scores on these scales ($T < 40$). Exaggeration often produces very high scores on many of the scales ($T > 80$). Interpretation of the content scales is always preceded by a preliminary analysis of the MMPI–2 validity scales, including Fb, VRIN, and TRIN.

Component subscales for many of the content scales were designed by Ben-Porath and Sherwood (1993) using a combined rational–empirical strategy. Scoring can be done through NCS either by computer or using hand-scoring templates. The following descriptions of the content scales were provided primarily by Butcher et al. (1990) and Ben-Porath and Sherwood (1993).

Anxiety (ANX, 23 Items).   ANX measures symptoms of anxiety including tension, somatic problems, (e.g., heart pounding and shortness of breath), sleep difficulties, worries, and poor concentration. High scorers fear losing their minds, find life a strain, and have difficulty making decisions. ANX is closely related to Scale 7, with a correlation of .82 in the MMPI–2 standardization sample. Gass (1997) found a frequency of high scores ($T > 65$) on ANX in 25% to 35% of brain-impaired patients. No correction for neurologically related content is needed on ANX.

Fears (FRS, 23 Items). This scale has two major components that were developed into subscales (Ben-Porath & Sherwood, 1993). *Generalized Fearfulness* (FRS1, 12 items) reflects a general pattern of fearfulness in daily living, and a proneness to be nervous and to overidentify danger in one's environment. *Multiple Fears* (FRS2, 10 items) consists of items that reflect phobic reactions to a large number of specific stimuli. The FRS scale does not correlate substantially with any of the other MMPI–2 scales ($r < .40$). High FRS scores are produced by 15% to 40% of brain-injured patients.

FRS is a unique and relatively powerful predictive of performance on some neuropsychological measures, predominantly visuospatial in nature. FRS predicts poorer performance on Design Fluency Test, Mazes, and the Controlled Oral Word Association Test (Gass, Ansley, & Boyette, 1994), and on visual reproduction from memory (Gass, 1996a). Similar results were found by Ross, Putnam, Gass, and Adams (1997). In psychiatric referrals, scores on FRS are inversely related to the global level of neuropsychological test performance (Average Impairment Rating Scale; Russell, Neuringer, & Goldstein, 1970) (Gass, 1997). FRS does not contain any neurological symptom content.

Obsessiveness (OBS, 16 Items). OBS measures worry, indecision, distress, and a tendency to ruminate. OBS is most closely associated with Scale 7, showing a correlation of .78 in the MMPI–2 restandardization sample. Psychiatric referrals who score high on OBS perform more poorly on verbal memory tests (Gass, 1996a). This relationship was not found in a sample of 48 closed-head-injury patients. Elevated scores are found in 20% to 35% of patients who have brain damage. OBS has very few items that commonly represent physical or cognitive symptoms of CNS impairment.

Depression (DEP, 33 Items). DEP has item content that falls into four categories (Ben-Porath & Sherwood, 1993). *Lack of Drive* (D1, 12 items) suggests an inability to get going and get things done. The person is likely to be experiencing a general lack of drive and motivation, perhaps also lacking an interest in important aspects of her or his life. *Dysphoria* (DEP2, 6 items) indicates symptoms of depressed mood and recurrent spells of the "blues" that are rather persisting. *Self-Depreciation* (DEP3, 7 items) represents a negative self-concept, feelings of uselessness, underestimation of one's abilities, lack of self-confidence, helplessness, and, in some cases, worthlessness. *Suicidal Ideation* (DEP4, 5 items) suggests current contemplation of suicide and, in some cases, a history of one or more attempts. An elevated score on this scale is a red flag indicating a need for further assessment of self-destructive potential.

DEP is a good indicator of general distress, worry, and unhappiness in neuropsychological referrals. Unlike Scale 2, the item composition of DEP is relatively free of neurologically related content and, as a result, is often a better measure of depression in individuals with neurological conditions. High DEP scores are produced by 30% to 50% of brain-impaired individuals (Gass, 1997).

Health Concerns (HEA, 36 Items).   HEA has several components. *Gastrointestinal Symptoms* (HEA1, 5 items) consists of items that reflect chest and stomach pain, and general malfunctioning of the digestive system. *Neurological Symptoms* (HEA2, 12 items) consists of items that refer to various symptoms of CNS disease, such as tinnitus, paresthesia, numbness, syncope, dizziness, and ataxia. *General Health Concerns* (HEA3, 6 items) suggests a perception of poor general health. High scorers worry about catching diseases and report vague symptoms of pain and weakness.

Individuals who report symptoms of brain dysfunction typically produce moderately high scores on HEA (*T* 65 to 75), even in the absence of any neurotic preoccupations or somatoform symptoms. About 50% of brain-injured patients produce high scores on HEA, largely due to an endorsement of neurological symptoms. HEA is very similar to Scale 1, showing a correlation of .90 in the normative sample (Butcher et al., 1990). Not surprisingly, very high scorers on HEA exhibit hypochondriacal tendencies and are overly focused on somatic functioning.

Bizarre Mentation (BIZ, 24 Items).   BIZ has two major components. *Psychotic Symptomatology* (BIZ1, 11 items) refers to frankly psychotic symptoms, including delusions, hallucinations, and, more generally, to what has been referred to as "positive" symptoms of schizophrenia. *Schizotypal Characteristics* (BIZ2, 9 items) suggests a variety of peculiar and unusual experiences, including illusions and ideas of reference. In the MMPI–2 standardization sample, the correlation between BIZ and Scale 8 was .64. BIZ is generally more effective than Scale 8 in identifying psychotic symptoms, probably because of its homogeneous item content. Unlike Scale 8, BIZ is unaffected by the endorsement of neurological symptoms. For these reasons, the clinician should rely more heavily on BIZ in making inferences regarding the presence of psychotic features, especially in examinees who have structural brain damage. The estimated incidence of high scores on BIZ in brain-damaged patients is between 20% and 30% (Gass, 1997).

From the standpoint of cognitive testing, BIZ, like FRS, has a potentially important role as a variable in the quality of certain types of neuropsychological test performance. Gass (1996a) observed that higher BIZ scores were associated with worse performance on attentional tasks ($r = -.40$, $p < .01$) in a closed-head injury sample ($n = 48$), and visual retentive memory ($-.38$, $p < .001$) in a sample of 80 neurologically intact subjects who were referred for a neuropsychological evaluation. These findings were replicated in an investigation of head injury patients by Ross et al. (1997).

Anger (ANG, 16 Items).   ANG includes two components. *Explosive Behavior* (ANG1, 7 items) refers to violent, explosive tendencies when angry, such as hitting or smashing objects, throwing a tantrum, engaging in loud argumentation, and fights. *Irritability* (ANG, 7 items) suggests grouchiness, argumentativeness, and impatience. In brain-injured patients, the estimated frequency of high ANG scores is 20% to 25% (Gass, 1997), although this may be higher in substance abusers. ANG does not contain neurologic symptom items.

Cynicism (CYN, 23 Items). This scale assesses *Misanthropic Beliefs* (CYN1, 15 items), including a view that people are purely self-serving, manipulative, and unwilling to help others. It also measures *Interpersonal Suspiciousness* (CYN2, 8 items), reflecting a pervasive distrust toward others. High scores are relatively common in brain-injured patients, with an estimated frequency of 30% to 40% (Gass, 1997).

Antisocial Practices (ASP, 22 Items). This scale has two main components. *Antisocial Attitudes* (ASP1, 16 items) place self-gain and expedience over ethical consideration or the welfare of others. *Antisocial Behavior* (ASP2, 5 items) refers to misconduct during the school years (e.g., suspension), legal conflicts, and theft. Gass (1997) reported an incidence of 20% to 25% high scorers in a mixed neurodiagnostic sample, although the frequency is probably higher in substance abusers with neurologic conditions.

Type A Behavior (TPA, 19 Items). This scale assesses *Impatience* (TPA1, 6 items), a tendency to be irritable and demanding, and *Competitive Drive* (TPA2, 9 items), reflecting an aggressive, hard-driving, achievement orientation and a need to demonstrate dominance and superiority.

Low Self-Esteem (LSE, 24 Items). LSE includes *Self-Doubt* (LSE1, 11 items), which measures feelings of inadequacy, unimportance, and unattractiveness, and *Submissiveness* (LSE2, 6 items), which refers to a self-effacing tendency to defer to other people across a variety of interpersonal situations. High scorers allow other people to take charge, make decisions, win arguments, and generally assume a dominant role. The estimated incidence ranges from 15% to 30% (Gass, 1997).

Social Discomfort (SOD, 24 Items). This scale assesses *Introversion* (SOD1, 16 items), or, more specifically, an avoidance of interpersonal contact and a general preference to keep other people at a distance. *Shyness* (SOD2, 7 items) refers to anxiety and discomfort in social situations. High scores occur with an estimated frequency of 15% to 20% in neurologic patients.

Family Problems (FAM, 25 Items). FAM measures *Family Discord* (FAM1, 12 items), which reflects considerable strife and animosity, and *Family Alienation* (FAM2, 5 items), which refers to a lack of family ties or emotional support. The estimated incidence of high scores on FAM in brain-injured patients is 20% (Gass, 1997).

Work Interference (WRK, 33 Items).   This scale addresses negative attitudes related to work or achievement, as well as personal problems such as low self-confidence, concentration difficulties, obsessional thinking, tension, and indecision. High scores on WRK occur with an estimated frequency of 35% to 40% in neurologic patients (Gass, 1997).

Negative Treatment Indicators (TRT, 26 Items).   This scale measures attitudes and beliefs regarding receiving help and making behavioral changes. *Low Motivation* (TRT1, 11 items) suggests little or no incentive for self-help and skepticism. *Inability to Disclose* (TRT2, 5 items) measures a reluctance to report personal information. High scores on TRT occur with an estimated frequency of 30% to 40% in neurologic patients (Gass, 1997).

Supplementary Scales

In addition to the basic validity, clinical, and content scales, numerous supplementary scales were created for the original MMPI, some of which continue to be particularly useful in MMPI–2 work. These scales are described in detail in Graham (1993) and Butcher and Williams (1992). They have received very limited attention in the neuropsychology literature and therefore are not reviewed here.

Additional Interpretive Considerations for Neurologic Patients

Regardless of the neuropathological diagnosis, it is reasonable to suspect that patients will report their CNS symptoms on the MMPI–2, thereby producing inflated scores on Scales 1, 2, 3, 7, and 8. If an individual has brain damage, special precautions must be taken to reduce interpretive error when there is an absence of appropriate norms or a diagnostic-specific correction factor for the MMPI–2. In these cases, the clinician should exhibit a greater degree of reliance on information derived from the Harris–Lingoes subscales and the content scales. These measures enable one to estimate the extent to which neurological symptom reporting affects scores on several of the clinical scales.

Scale 2 interpretation is sometimes problematic with brain-injured individuals. The standard psychological correlates are less likely to be accurate in describing brain-injured individuals who have normal-range scores on D1 (Subjective Depression), D2 (Psychomotor Retardation), and D5 (Brooding). If Scale 2 is less than 75 T, and high subscale scores are restricted to D3 (Physical Malfunctioning) and D4 (Mental Dullness), one must consider the possibility that self-reported physical and cognitive symptoms of brain damage (not necessarily depression) explain the elevated score. Very high scores on Scale 2 ($T > 75$) are usually indicative of depressive symptoms, regardless of the subscale results. The score on DEP (Depression) is also very helpful in understanding the significance of high scores on Scale 2, because DEP is a more specific measure of depression and contains very few, if any, items that reflect the physical and cognitive effects of brain dysfunction. Depressive symptoms are less likely to exist if DEP is less than 60 T.

In regard to Scale 3, the traditional behavioral correlates are more likely to apply to a brain-injured individual if an elevated score is accompanied by a high score on Hy1 (Denial of Social Anxiety), Hy2 (Need for Affection), or Hy5 (Inhibition of Aggression). If Scale 3 is less than 75 T, and only Hy3 (Lassitude-Malaise) and Hy4 (Somatic Complaints) are elevated, many of the Scale 3 descriptors are probably inaccurate. Very high scores on Scale 3 (T > 75) are likely to be associated with the presence of somatoform symptoms, malingering, or both, regardless of the subscale results. Research has yet to address the potential discriminative value of the Neurological Symptoms component subscale of HEA.

Marginally elevated scores (T 60 to 65) on Scale 7 produced by brain-impaired individuals are less likely to represent the traditionally ascribed behavioral correlates of this scale when scores on ANX, FRS, and OBS are low (T < 60).

Scale 8 elevations in neurologic patients are more likely to reflect the standard behavioral correlates when they are accompanied by high scores on Sc1 (Social Alienation), Sc2 (Emotional Alienation), Sc4 (Lack of Ego Mastery, Conative), or Sc5 (Lack of Ego Mastery, Defective Inhibition). Many Scale 8 behavioral correlates do not apply to brain-injured patients who produce high scores that are limited to Sc3 (Lack of Ego Mastery, Cognitive) and Sc6 (Bizarre Sensory Experiences). In addition, psychotic symptoms are less likely to exist if BIZ is less than 65 T.

RECOMMENDED READING

Butcher, J. N., & Williams, C. L. (1992). *Essentials of MMPI–2 and MMPI–A interpretation.* Minneapolis: University of Minnesota Press.

Gass, C. S. (1999). Assessment of emotional functioning with the MMPI–2. In G. Groth-Marnat (Ed.), *Handbook of neuropsychological assessment* (chap. 14). New York: Wiley.

Gass, C. S., & Ansley, J. (1995). Personality assessment of neurologically impaired patients. In J. N. Butcher (Ed.), *Clinical personality assessment: Practical approaches* (pp. 192–210). New York: Oxford University Press.

Graham, J. R. (1993). *MMPI–2: Assessing personality and psychopathology* (2nd ed.). New York: Oxford University Press.

Reitan, R. M., & Wolfson, D. (1993). *The Halstead–Reitan Neuropsychological Test Battery: Theory and clinical interpretation.* Tucson, AZ: Neuropsychology Press.

Reitan, R. M., & Wolfson, D. (1997). Emotional disturbances and their interaction with neuropsychological deficits. *Neuropsychology Review, 7,* 3–19.

REFERENCES

Alexopoulos, G. S., Abrams, R. C., Young, R. C., & Shamoian, C. A. (1988). Cornell Scale for Depression in Dementia. *Biological Psychiatry, 23,* 271–284.

Alfano, D. P., Finlayson, M. A., Stearns, G. M., & Neilson, P. M. (1990). The MMPI and neurological dysfunction: Profile configuration and analysis. *The Clinical Neuropsychologist, 4,* 69–79.

Alfano, D. P., Paniak, C. E., & Finlayson, A. J. (1993). The MMPI and closed head injury: A neurocorrective approach. *Neuropsychiatry, Neuropsychology, & Behavioral Neurology, 6,* 111–116.

Ansley, J., Gass, C. S., Brown, M. C., & Levin, B. E. (1995). Epileptic and non-epileptic seizure disorder: A comparison of MMPI-2 profile characteristics [Abstract]. *Journal of the International Neuropsychological Society, 1,* 135–136.

Arbisi, P. A., & Ben-Porath, Y. S. (1995). An MMPI-2 infrequent response scale for use with psychopathological populations: The infrequency-psychopathology scale, F(p). *Psychological Assessment, 7,* 424–431.

Baldwin, M. V. (1952). A clinico-experimental investigation into the psychologic aspects of multiple sclerosis. *Journal of Nervous and Mental Disease, 115,* 299–343.

Barrett, P., Putnam, S. H., Axelrod, B. N., & Rapport, L. J. (1998). Some statistical properties of 2 MMPI neurocorrection factors for individuals with closed head injury [Abstract]. *Archives of Clinical Neuropsychology, 13,* 16.

Bear, D. M., & Fedio, P. (1977). Quantitative analysis of interictal behavior in temporal lobe epilepsy. *Archives of Neurology, 34,* 454–467.

Beck, A. T., Ward, C., Mendelsohn, M., Mock, J., & Erbaugh, J. (1961). An inventory for measuring depression. *Archives of General Psychiatry, 4,* 561–571.

Bellak, J. (1986). *The T.A.T., C.A.T., and S.A.T. in clinical use* (4th ed.). Orlando, FL: Grune & Stratton.

Ben-Porath, Y. S., Hostetler, K., Butcher, J. N., & Graham, J. R. (1989). New subscales for the MMPI-2 Social Introversion (Si) Scale. *Psychological Assessment, 1,* 169–174.

Ben-Porath, Y. S., & Sherwood, N. E. (1993). *The MMPI-2 content component scales: Development, psychometric characteristics, and clinical application.* Minneapolis: University of Minnesota Press.

Berry, D. T. R., Wetter, M. W., Baer, R. A., Youngjohn, J. R., Gass, C. S., Lamb, D. G., Franzen, M. D., MacInnes, W. D., & Buchholz, D. (1995). Overreporting of closed-head injury symptoms on the MMPI-2. *Psychological Assessment, 7,* 517–523.

Binder, L. M. (1997). A review of mild head trauma. Part II: Clinical implications. *Journal of Clinical and Experimental Neuropsychology, 19,* 432–457.

Bornstein, R. A., & Kozora, E. (1990). Content bias of the MMPI Sc scale in neurologic patients. *Neuropsychiatry, Neuropsychology, & Behavioral Neurology, 3,* 200–205.

Brulot, M. M., Strauss, E., & Spellacy, F. (1997). Validity of the Minnesota Multiphasic Personality Inventory-2 correction factors for use with patients with suspected head injury. *The Clinical Neuropsychologist, 11,* 391–401.

Burt, D. B., Zembar, M. J., & Niederehe, G. (1995). Depression and memory impairment: A meta-analysis of the association, its pattern, and specificity. *Psychological Bulletin, 117,* 285–305.

Butcher, J. N. (1990). *The MMPI-2 in psychological treatment.* New York: Oxford University Press.

Butcher, J. N. (1995). Item content in the interpretation of the MMPI-2. In J. N. Butcher (Ed.), *Clinical personality assessment: Practical approaches* (pp. 302–316). New York: Oxford University Press.

Butcher, J. N., Dahlstrom, W. G., Graham, J. R., Tellegen, A., & Kaemmer, B. (1989). *MMPI-2 (Minnesota Multiphasic Personality Inventory-2): Manual for administration and scoring.* Minneapolis: University of Minnesota Press.

Butcher, J. N., Graham, J. R., Williams, C. L., & Ben-Porath, Y. S. (1990). *Development and use of the MMPI-2 content scales.* Minneapolis: University of Minnesota Press.

Butcher, J. N., & Williams, C. L. (1992). *Essentials of MMPI-2 and MMPI-A interpretation.* Minneapolis: University of Minnesota Press.

Chatterjee, A., Strauss, M. E., Smyth, K. A., & Whitehouse, P. J. (1992). Personality changes in Alzheimer's disease. *Archives of Neurology, 49,* 486–491.

Cripe, L. I., Maxwell, J. K., & Hill, E. (1995). Multivariate discriminant function analysis of neurologic, pain, and psychiatric patients with the MMPI. *Journal of Clinical Psychology, 51,* 258–268.

Derogatis, L. R. (1977). *SCL–R administration, scoring, and procedures manual.* Baltimore, MD: Clinical Psychometrics Research Unit, Johns Hopkins School of Medicine.

Derry, P. A., Harnadek, M. C., McLachlan, R. S., & Sontrop, J. (1997). Influence of seizure content on interpreting psychopathology on the MMPI–2 in patients with epilepsy. *Journal of Clinical and Experimental Neuropsychology, 19,* 396–404.

Devanand, D. P., Miller, L., Richards, M., Marder, K., Bell, K., Mayuex, R., & Stern, Y. (1992). The Columbia University Scale for Psychopathology in Alzheimer's Disease. *Archives of Neurology, 49,* 371–376.

Dikmen, S., & Reitan, R. M. (1974). Minnesota Multiphasic Personality Inventory correlates of dysphasic language disturbances. *Journal of Abnormal Psychology, 83,* 675–679.

Dikmen, S., & Reitan, R. M. (1977). MMPI correlates of adaptive ability deficits in patients with brain lesions. *Journal of Nervous and Mental Disease, 165,* 247–254.

Dunn, J. T., & Lees-Haley, P. R. (1995). The MMPI–2 correction factor for closed-head injury: A caveat for forensic cases. *Assessment, 2,* 47–51.

Edwards, D. W., Holmquist, L., Wanless, R., Wicks, J., Davis, C. (1998). Comparing three methods of "neuro-correction" for the MMPI–2 [Abstract]. *Journal of the International Neuropsychological Society, 4,* 27–28.

Erdberg, P. (1990). Rorschach assessment. In G. Goldstein & M. Hersen (Eds.), *Handbook of psychological assessment* (2nd ed., pp. 387–402). New York: Pergamon Press.

Etcoff, N. L. (1989). Asymmetries in recognition of emotion. In F. Boller & J. Grafman (Eds.), *Handbook of neuropsychology* (Vol. 3, pp. 363–383). New York: Elsevier.

Exner, J. E. (1978). *The Rorschach: A comprehensive system: Volume 2. Current research and advanced interpretation.* New York: Wiley.

Exner, J. E. (1986). *The Rorschach: A comprehensive system: Volume 1. Basic foundations* (2nd Ed.). New York: Wiley.

Fordyce, D. J., Rouche, J. R., & Prigatano, G. P. (1983) Enhanced emotional reactions in chronic head trauma patients. *Journal of Neurology, Neurosurgery, and Psychiatry, 46,* 620–624.

Gasquoine, P. G. (1997). Postconcussion symptoms. *Neuropsychology Review, 7,* 77–86.

Gass, C. S. (1991a). Emotional variables in neuropsychological test performance. *Journal of Clinical Psychology, 47,* 100–104.

Gass, C. S. (1991b). MMPI–2 interpretation and closed-head injury: A correction factor. *Psychological Assessment, 3,* 27–31.

Gass, C. S. (1992). MMPI–2 interpretation of patients with cerebrovascular disease: A correction factor. *Archives of Clinical Neuropsychology, 7,* 17–27.

Gass, C. S. (1996a). MMPI–2 variables in attention and memory test performance. *Psychological Assessment, 8,* 135–138.

Gass, C. S. (1996b). MMPI–2 interpretation and stroke: Cross-validation of a correction factor. *Journal of Clinical Psychology, 52,* 569–572.

Gass, C. S. (1997, June). *Assessing patients with neurological impairments.* Paper presented at the University of Minnesota MMPI–2 Clinical Workshops & Symposia, Minneapolis, Minnesota, MN.

Gass, C. S. (1999). Assessment of emotional functioning with the MMPI–2. In G. Groth-Marnat (Ed.), *Handbook of neuropsychological assessment* (chap. 14). New York: Wiley.

Gass, C. S., & Ansley, J. (1994). MMPI correlates of poststroke neurobehavioral deficits. *Archives of Clinical Neuropsychology, 9,* 461–469.

Gass, C. S., & Ansley, J. (1995). Personality assessment of neurologically impaired patients. In J. N. Butcher (Ed.), *Clinical personality assessment: Practical approaches* (pp. 192–210). New York: Oxford University Press.

Gass, C. S., Ansley, J., & Boyette, S. (1994). Emotional correlates of fluency test and maze performance. *Journal of Clinical Psychology, 50,* 586–590.

Gass, C. S., & Apple, C. (1997). Cognitive complaints in closed-head injury: Relationship to memory test performance and emotional disturbance. *Journal of Clinical and Experimental Neuropsychology*, *19*, 290–299.

Gass, C. S., & Ballard, S. (1998). Awareness of deficit in patients with unilateral cerebral lesions. *Archives of Clinical Neuropsychology [Abstract]*, *13*, 71.

Gass, C. S., & Brown, M. C. (1992). Neuropsychological test feedback to patients with brain dysfunction. *Psychological Assessment*, *4*, 272–277.

Gass, C. S., & Daniel, S. K. (1990). Emotional impact on Trail Making Test performance. *Psychological Reports*, *67*, 435–438.

Gass, C. S., & Freshwater, S. (1999). MMPI–2 symptom disclosure and cognitive complaints in a closed-head injury sample [Abstract]. *Archives of Clinical Neuropsychology*, *14*, 29–30.

Gass, C. S., & Lawhorn, L. (1991). Psychological adjustment following stroke: An MMPI study. *Psychological Assessment*, *3*, 628–633.

Gass, C. S., Luis, C. A., Rayls, K., & Mittenberg, W. B. (1999). Psychological status and its influences in acute traumatic brain injury: An MMPI–2 study [Abstract]. *Archives of Clinical Neuropsychology*, *14*, 30.

Gass, C. S., & Russell, E. W. (1986). Differential impact of brain damage and depression on memory test performance. *Journal of Consulting & Clinical Psychology*, *54*, 261–263.

Gass, C. S., & Russell, E. W. (1991). MMPI profiles of closed-head trauma patients: Impact of neurologic complaints. *Journal of Clinical Psychology*, *47*, 253–260.

Gass, C. S., Russell, E. W., & Hamilton, R. A. (1990). Accuracy of MMPI-based inferences regarding memory and concentration in closed-head trauma. *Psychological Assessment*, *2*, 175–178.

Gass, C. S., & Wald, H. (1997). MMPI–2 interpretation and closed-head trauma: Cross-validation of a correction factor. *Archives of Clinical Neuropsychology*, *12*, 199–205.

Godfrey, H. P., Partridge, F. M., Knight, R. G., Bishara, S. (1993). Course of insight disorder and emotional dysfunction following closed head injury: A controlled cross-sectional follow-up study. *Journal of Clinical and Experimental Neuropsychology*, *15*, 503–515.

Goldfried, M. R., Stricker, G., & Weiner, I. B. (1971). *Rorschach handbook of clinical and research applications*. Englewood Cliffs, NJ: Prentice Hall.

Gough, H. (1950). The F minus K dissimulation index for the MMPI. *Journal of Consulting Psychology*, *14*, 408–413.

Graham, J. R. (1993). *MMPI–2: Assessing personality and psychopathology* (2nd ed.). New York: Oxford University Press.

Graham, J. R., Watts, D., & Timbrook, R. E. (1991). Detecting fake-good and fake-bad MMPI–2 profiles. *Journal of Personality Assessment*, *57*, 264–277.

Grant, I., & Alves, W. (1987). Psychiatric and psychosocial disturbances in head injury. In H. S. Levin, J. Grafman, & H. M. Eisenberg (Eds.), *Neurobehavioral recovery from head injury* (pp. 232–261). New York: Oxford University Press.

Groth-Marnat, G. (1997). *Handbook of psychological assessment* (3rd ed.). New York: John Wiley & Sons.

Greiffenstein, M. F., Gola, T., & Baker, W. J. (1995). MMPI–2 validity scales versus domain specific measures in detection of factitious traumatic brain injury. *The Clinical Neuropsychologist*, *9*, 230–240.

Harris, R., & Lingoes, J. (1955). *Subscales for the Minnesota Multiphasic Personality Inventory* [Mimeographed materials]. Los Angeles, CA: Langley Porter Clinic.

Harris, R., & Lingoes, J. (1968). *Subscales for the Minnesota Multiphasic Personality Inventory* [Mimeographed materials]. Los Angeles, CA: Langley Porter Clinic.

Hathaway, S. R., & McKinley, J. C. (1940). A multiphasic personality schedule (Minnesota): I. Construction of the schedule. *Journal of Psychology*, *10*, 249–254.

Heaton, R. K., Baade, L. E., & Johnson, K. L. (1978). Neuropsychological test results associated with psychiatric disorders in adults. *Psychological Bulletin*, *85*, 141–162.

Jacobucci, G. D., Bowman, M. L., & Shercliffe, R. J. (1997). A comparison of two strategies for interpreting the MMPI–2 with TBI patients [Abstract]. *Archives of Clinical Neuropsychology*, *13*, 143.

Kendall, P. C., Edinger, J., & Eberly, C. (1978). Taylor's MMPI correction for spinal cord injury: Empirical endorsement. *Journal of Consulting and Clinical Psychology, 46,* 370–371.

Kinderman, S. S., & Brown, G. G. (1997). Depression and memory in the elderly: A meta-analysis. *Journal of Clinical and Experimental Neuropsychology, 19,* 625–642.

Klonoff, P., & Prigatano, G. P. (1987). Reactions of family members and clinical intervention after traumatic brain injury. In M. Ylvisaker & E. Gobble (Eds.), *Community reentry for head-injured adults* (pp. 381–402). Boston: College Hill Press.

Larrabee, G. J. (1997). Somatic malingering on the MMPI / MMPI–2 in litigating subjects [Abstract]. *Archives of Clinical Neuropsychology, 12,* 353–354.

Lees-Haley, P. R. (1997). MMPI–2 base rates for 492 personal injury plaintiffs: Implications and challenges for forensic assessment. *Journal of Clinical Psychology, 53,* 745–755.

Lees-Haley, P. R., Smith, H. H., Williams, C. W., & Dunn, J. T. (1996). Forensic neuropsychological test usage: An empirical survey. *Archives of Clinical Neuropsychology, 11,* 45–52.

Levin, H. S., High, W. M., Goethe, K. E., Sisson, R. A., Overall, J. E., Rhoades, H. M., Eisenberg, H. M., Kalisky, Z., & Gary, H. E. (1987). The Neurobehavioral Rating Scale: Assessment of the behavioral sequelae of head injury by the clinician. *Journal of Neurology, Neurosurgery, and Psychiatry, 50,* 183–193.

Lezak, M. D. (1978). Living with the characterologically altered brain injured patient. *Journal of Clinical Psychiatry, 39,* 592–598.

Lezak, M. D. (1995). *Neuropsychological assessment* (3rd ed.). New York: Oxford University Press.

Marsh, G., Hirsch, S., & Leung, G. (1982). Use and misuse of the MMPI in multiple sclerosis. *Psychological Reports, 51,* 1127–1134.

Meyerink, L. H., Reitan, R. M., & Selz, M. (1988). The validity of the MMPI with multiple sclerosis patients. *Journal of Clinical Psychology, 44,* 764–769.

Millon, T. (1994). *Millon Clinical Multiaxial Inventory–III manual.* Minneapolis, MN: National Computer Systems.

Mittenberg, W., Tremont, G., & Rayls, K. R. (1996). Impact of cognitive function on MMPI–2 validity in neurologically impaired patients. *Assessment, 3,* 157–163.

Mueller, S. R., & Girace, M. (1988). Use and misuse of the MMPI, a reconsideration. *Psychological Reports, 63,* 483–491.

Murray, H. A. (1938). *Explorations in personality.* New York: Oxford University Press.

Nelson, L. D., & Do, T. (1998). Using the MMPI–2 in patients with multiple sclerosis [Abstract]. *Archives of Clinical Neuropsychology, 13,* 92.

Nelson, L. D., Satz, P., Mitrushina, M., Van Gorp, W., Cicchetti, D., Lewis, R., & Van Lancker, D. (1989). Development and validation of the Neuropsychology Behavior and Affect Profile. *Psychological Assessment, 1,* 266–272.

Netto, D. (1997). *Brain injury and the MMPI–2: Neuro-correction for Hispanics.* Unpublished doctoral dissertation, Nova Southeastern University, Fort Lauderdale, FL.

O'Donnell, W. E., DeSoto, C. B., DeSoto, J. L., & Reynolds, D. M. (1995). *Neuropsychological Impairment Scale (NIS): Manual.* Los Angeles, CA: Western Psychological Services.

Overall, J. E., & Gorham, D. R. (1962). The brief psychiatric rating scale. *Psychological Reports, 10,* 799–812.

Paniak, C. E., & Miller, H. B. (1993). Utility of the MMPI–2 validity scales with brain injury survivors [Abstract]. *Archives of Clinical Neuropsychology, 9,* 172.

Parikh, R. M., Robinson, R. G., & Price, T. R. (1988). Disability and rehabilitation after stroke. *Stroke, 19,* 1055.

Prigatano, G. P. (1987a). Personality and psychosocial consequences after head injury. In M. Meier, A. Benton, & L. Diller (Eds.), *Neuropsychological rehabilitation* (pp. 355–378). New York: Plenum Press.

Prigatano, G. P. (1987b). Psychiatric aspects of head injury: Problem areas and suggested guidelines for research. In H. S. Levin, J. Grafman, & H. M. Eisenberg (Eds.), *Neurobehavioral recovery from head injury* (pp. 215–231). New York: Oxford University Press.

Prigatano, G. P., Pepping, M., & Klonoff, P. (1986). Cognitive, personality, and psychosocial factors in the neuropsychological assessment of brain-injured patients. In B. Uzzel & Y. Gross (Eds.), *Clinical neuropsychology of intervention* (pp. 135–166). Boston: Martinus Nijhoff.

Putnam, S. H., Kurtz, J. E., Fichtenberg, N. L., O'Leary, J. F., & Adams, K. M. (1995). MMPI–2 correlates of unexpected cognitive deterioration in traumatic brain injury [Abstract]. *The Clinical Neuropsychologist, 9,* 296.

Rayls, K., Mittenberg, W. B., Burns, W. J., & Theroux, S. (1997). Longitudinal analysis of the MMPI–2 neurocorrection factor in mild head trauma [Abstract]. *Archives of Clinical Neuropsychology, 12,* 390–391.

Reitan, R. M., & Wolfson, D. (1993). *The Halstead–Reitan Neuropsychological Test Battery: Theory and clinical interpretation* (2nd ed.). Tucson, AZ: Neuropsychology Press.

Reitan, R. M., & Wolfson, D. (1997). Emotional disturbances and their interaction with neuropsychological deficits. *Neuropsychology Review, 7,* 3–19.

Ross, S. R., Putnam, S. H., Gass, C. S., & Adams, K. M. (1997, June). *MMPI–2 predictors of cognitive test performance in traumatic brain injury.* Paper presented at the University of Minnesota MMPI–2 Clinical Workshops & Symposia, Minneapolis, MN.

Russell, E. W., Neuringer, C., & Goldstein, G. (1970). *Assessment of brain damage: A neuropsychological key approach.* New York: Wiley Interscience.

Russell, S. K., & Russell, E. W. (1997). Using the MCMI in neuropsychological evaluations. In T. Millon (ed.), *The Millon inventories: Clinical and personality assessment* (pp. 154–172). New York: Guilford Press.

Rutter, M. (1981). Psychological sequelae of brain damage in children. *American Journal of Psychiatry, 138,* 1533–1544.

Schiffer, R. B. (1983). Psychiatric aspects of clinical neurology. *American Journal of Psychiatry, 140,* 205–207.

Sinha, D., Zemlan, F. P., Nelson, S., Beinenfeld, D., Thienhaus, O., Ramaswamy, G., & Hamilton, S. (1992). A new scale for assessing behavioral agitation in dementia. *Psychiatry Research, 41,* 73–88.

Sinyor, P., Jacques, P., Kaloupek, D., Becker, R., Goldenberg, M., & Coopersmith, H. (1986). Post-stroke depression and lesion location: An attempted replication. *Brain, 109,* 537–546.

Speilberger, C. D., Gorsuch, R. L., & Luschene, R. E. (1971). *Manual for the State-Trait Anxiety Inventory.* Palo Alto, CA: Consulting Psychologists Press.

Stuss, D. T., Gow, C. A., & Hetherington, C. R. (1992). "No longer Gage": Frontal lobe dysfunction and emotional changes. *Journal of Consulting and Clinical Psychology, 60,* 349–359.

Suhr, J., Tranel, D., Wefel, J., & Barrash, J. (1997). Memory performance after head injury: Contributions of malingering, litigation status, psychological factors, and medication use. *Journal of Clinical and Experimental Neuropsychology, 19,* 500–514.

Warner, M. H., Dodrill, C. B., & Batzel, L. W. (1989). Economical screening for emotional disturbance in epilepsy: Anticipating MMPI profile elevations by means of the Washington Psychosocial Seizure Inventory. *Journal of Epilepsy, 2,* 83–89.

Woessner, R., & Caplan, B. (1995). Affective disorders following mild to moderate brain injury: Interpretive hazards of the SCL–90–R. *Journal of Head Trauma Rehabilitation, 10,* 78–89.

Woessner, R., & Caplan, B. (1996). Emotional distress following stroke: Interpretive limitations of the SCL–90–R. *Assessment, 3,* 291–306.

Yesavage, J. A., Brink, T. I., Rose, T. L., Lum, O., Huang, V., Adey, M., & Leirer, V. O. (1983). Development and validation of a geriatric depression screening scale: A preliminary report. *Journal of Psychiatric Research, 17,* 37–49.

Youngjohn, J. R., Burrows, L., & Erdal, K. (1995). Brain damage or compensation neurosis? The controversial post-concussive syndrome. *The Clinical Neuropsychologist, 9,* 595–598.

Youngjohn, J. R., Davis, D., & Wolf, I. (1997). Head injury and the MMPI–2: Paradoxical severity effects and the influence of litigation. *Psychological Assessment, 9,* 177–184.

Zung, W. W. (1965). A self-rating depression scale. *Archives of General Psychiatry, 12,* 63–70.

Zung, W. W. (1971). A rating instrument for anxiety disorders. *Psychosomatics, 12,* 371–379.

CHAPTER SIX

Application of Neuropsychological Assessment Results

Bruce Crosson

Department of Clinical and Health Psychology,
University of Florida, Gainesville

The ultimate reason for conducting a neuropsychological assessment is that test results provide useful information to a consumer. For any single evaluation, the consumer may be one or more of the following: the patient, the patient's family, a referring physician, rehabilitation team members, mental health professionals, other health care professionals, attorneys or judges, school or academic personnel, and others. The purpose of a neuropsychological evaluation varies widely from case to case, but might fit under one or more of three general categories: diagnostic, rehabilitative, and forensic. The practical importance of findings depends both on the consumer and on the reasons for conducting the evaluation. The clinical neuropsychologist must take these factors into account in communicating test results.

The utility of an assessment also depends on the characteristics of instruments employed in the testing endeavor. Each test instrument has strengths and weaknesses relative to the referral question and the context in which the assessment is to be applied. In order to evaluate such strengths and weaknesses, it is necessary for the examiner to be intimately familiar with the technical properties of the tests that the examiner administers (e.g., reliability, validity, test norms). These concerns are addressed in professional guidelines for test administration and application (American Psychological Association, 1974, 1987, Principle 8).

This chapter discusses the process of applying neuropsychological findings to various referral questions and contexts. The first section addresses general properties of neuropsychological tests relevant to applications; limitations are specifically addressed. The following three sections address issues in different referral contexts: diagnostic, rehabilitative, and forensic. Finally, issues in delivering evaluation feedback to patients and family members are discussed. In each section, case examples are given to illustrate important points for application. The reader should keep in mind that the practice of neuropsychology is complex in any context, and the contexts in which neuropsychology might be practiced are numerous and diverse. For these reasons, it would be impossible to cover all the issues concerning neuropsychological assessment in a single chapter. Rather, this chapter raises common issues that can, by example, demonstrate how various problems might be addressed.

PROPERTIES OF NEUROPSYCHOLOGICAL TESTS

Test Properties Affecting Applications

Neuropsychological assessment has sprung from two traditions that have a bearing on our ability to apply test findings to various questions: the tradition of the psychological laboratory and the tradition of psychometrics. In keeping with these influences, neuropsychological measures often attempt to isolate a particular ability or skill from other abilities or skills. For example, we consider it desirable that a test of visual-perceptual ability not be strongly related to measures of language abilities and that a measure of language ability not be strongly related to visual spatial abilities. It is further desirable that tests tap universal abilities, not specific skills acquired through an occupation or pastime. For example, the WAIS–III (Wechsler, 1997) purports to measure more universal intellectual abilities applicable to a broad range of activities, not specific skills such as repairing washing machines or teaching accounting. Although the skills and aptitudes that we do measure have some bearing on the ability to perform such occupational activities, the inferences we can make about a person's ability to perform them are much less direct because we do not measure the activities directly.

Another characteristic of most neuropsychological tests is that we attempt to obtain an optimal performance from the patient (Lezak, 1995). Distractions are kept to a minimum, and efforts are made to be certain that instructions are understood. Further, tasks are performed at the initiation of the evaluator, not the patient, and the patient provides very little in the way of either initiative or their own structure (Lezak, 1995). When interpreting results, the neuropsychologist must keep in mind that environments outside the neuropsychology laboratory may be less than optimal in terms of distractions, degree of structure, the amount of independent initiation required, and other dimensions. Yet these are the environments in which patients must live and function. Distractions cannot always be avoided, and degree of structure is not always optimal.

Changes in personality functioning may be essential diagnostic clues and may determine success or failure in rehabilitation endeavors such as return to work. Yet neuropsychological tests typically do not measure some types of personality change (Lezak, 1978). Frontal lobe functions are particularly important for many facets of personality (see Damasio & Anderson, 1993). For example, the orbital frontal lobes are involved in control of impulses and emotions. Mesial frontal structures, including the anterior cingulate area, are involved in initiation and motivation. The dorsolateral frontal lobes are involved in planning and organization. Patients showing multiple personality changes after frontal injury can do well on extended neuropsychological batteries (e.g., Eslinger & Damasio, 1985). The crux of this matter is the structure of neuropsychological evaluation, which minimizes the need for initiation, independent organization, and impulse control. The California Sorting Test (Delis, Kaplan, & Kramer, in press-a; Delis, Squire, Bihrle, & Massman, 1992) has made some headway in addressing initiation and independent conceptualization by measuring the number sorting principles patients can independently generate in card sets that can be sorted by multiple principles. This instrument also allows separation of initiation and conceptual generation from other putative frontal functions; however, the relationship of this measure to personality functioning has not been established. The Delis-Kaplan Executive Function Scale (Delis, Kaplan, & Kramer, in press-b) also may have other measures useful in detecting initiation and independent organization, such as the California 20 Questions Test, which requires patients to generate questions to determine which of 30 items the examiner has picked. Again, the relationship to personality changes has yet to be determined. Thus, most neuropsychological test procedures are not designed to optimize detection of personality changes related to frontal dysfunction.

Prigatano (1986) and Crosson (1987) noted the need to differentiate between sources of personality dysfunction after head injury or frontolimbic damage. Potential sources of such dysfunction include neurological injury, emotional reaction to deficits and circumstances caused by neurological injury, premorbid personality problems or disorders, or some combination of these factors. Proper diagnosis of causative factors can have a profound impact on treatment of these problems. Traditional personality testing may give some hints of dysfunction, but it quite often fails to distinguish between the possible causes. For example, Alfano, Neilson, Paniak, and Finlayson (1992) alluded to such problems in interpretation of the Minnesota Multiphasic Personality Inventory (MMPI).

Reliability and, in particular, validity considerations also will affect test interpretation and, therefore, application of assessment results. Although many neuropsychological tests are designed to measure a specific construct, most of our instruments are multidimensionally complex. In order to perform any test, patients must be able to apprehend information through the sensory modalities, perceive and analyze such information, and produce an output. Even a test as simple as Finger Oscillation, which is designed to measure motor output, requires the patient to understand a set of instructions relative to the apparatus involved. Misunderstanding of task demands can lead to altered performance even on this test.

Often assumptions are made regarding the construct that certain tests measure that are erroneous or only partially correct. Such errors may be proliferated uncritically in the literature by relying more on clinical lore than on hard data to describe what tests measure. Not infrequently, the construct itself has been accepted without adequate examination. One of the best examples of this type of error is the uncritical interpretation of Digit Span from the WAIS–III as a test of attention. This interpretation has been made for nearly 50 years (e.g., Kitzinger & Blumberg, 1951; Rapaport, Gill, & Schafer, 1945) and is seldom challenged. As Posner and Rafal (1986) and Sohlberg and Mateer (1989) noted, however, a unidimensional construct of attention is inadequate to account for varying clinical phenomena. Posner and Rafal broke attention down into three components: arousal, vigilance, and selective attention. Sohlberg and Mateer broke attention down into five components: focused attention, sustained attention, selective attention, alternating attention, and divided attention. As noted in the case example that follows, aspects of attention can be quite impaired even when Digit Span scores seem to indicate that attention is a strength of performance. In addition to the modest attentional demands of Digit Span, it is obvious that this test requires an ability to decode the auditory information at least at some level, an ability to repeat, and an ability to hold information in short-term memory until it is repeated. Numerous examples can be found where construct validity of tests is misunderstood.

In summary, inherent properties of neuropsychological tests affect our ability to derive adequate cognitive and behavioral diagnoses. Inadequate specification of cognitive and behavioral strengths and deficits in turn can hamper our ability to arrive at adequate diagnoses, to make valid rehabilitation recommendations, and/or to advise members of the legal profession regarding the functional limitations of a brain-injured person. The left side of Table 6.1 summarizes the properties of neuropsychological tests already mentioned that raise issues in applications. A case example will illustrate a few of these points.

Case 1 was a woman in her early 20s who was involved in a motor vehicle accident. She had 15 years of education. Acute magnetic resonance (MR) scans demonstrated bilateral contusions in the frontotemporal region, greater on the right side; an intracerebral hemorrhage in the left globus pallidus and posterior limb of the internal capsule; and white matter shearing bilaterally in the centrum semiovale. Significant deficits on neuropsychological testing included bilaterally slowed finger oscillation, several uncorrected errors on the Stroop Test, impairment on all trials of the Tactual Performance Test, and a lowered Performance IQ. Of interest is that among the Verbal Subtests of the WAIS–R (Figure 6.1), the patient scored considerably higher on Digit Span than on other Verbal subtests (i.e., by at least one standard deviation). Assessing this patient's strengths

TABLE 6.1
Properties of Neuropsychological Tests

Properties of Neuropsychological Tests Affecting Application	Application Principles for Neuropsychological Tests That Address Inherent Limitations in Instruments
1. Attempts to isolate test scores from every-day skills limit the ability of tests to predict every-day skills.	1–4. Always conduct an in-depth interview during evaluation. A portion of this interview should be dedicated to addressing problems not typically covered by the neuropsychological tests employed.
2. Creation of a test environment that promotes optimal performance fails to take into account that everyday tasks are performed in a suboptimal environment.	
3. Structured examination sessions may mask deficits in initiation, organization and planning, or impulse control problems (i.e., frontal lobe deficits).	1–4. Make detailed behavioral observations during evaluation, and, where possible, use them to address problems that test scores do not reveal.
4. Tests scores may not be helpful in determining the source of personality disturbances seen in some types of injury.	
5. Neuropsychological tests may be designed to measure a particular construct, but most tests require multiple cognitive skills for completion.	5. Be aware of the complexity of neuropsychological tests and the multiple reasons for poor performance on tests.
6. Constructs used to define some test findings may be inadequately conceptualized and/or outdated.	6. Do not uncritically accept the collective clinical wisdom regarding the constructs that tests measure. Search for patterns among tests that will reveal the nature of an impairment.

was an important part of her rehabilitative neuropsychological evaluation, and, as noted above, this Digit Span score might traditionally be interpreted as a strength in the patient's attention.

However, her participation in various rehabilitation tasks demonstrated that she had significant problems in attention. In fact, this facet of her performance was clearly identified in a functional evaluation done at the same time as the neuropsychological evaluation. One example of her attentional problems was noted on her job trial during rehabilitation. She had to photocopy articles, and she would copy only half of several pages in various articles. Ordinarily, she would not realize that she had made this mistake. It was necessary for her therapist to intervene to help her master this problem.

A problem of further interest became evident by interviewing the patient and by observing her in rehabilitation. The patient was prone to experiencing strong emotional reactions (positive and negative), which were appropriate in type but out of proportion in intensity to the circumstances in which she experienced them. This problem with emotional disinhibition was not evident in

WAIS-R

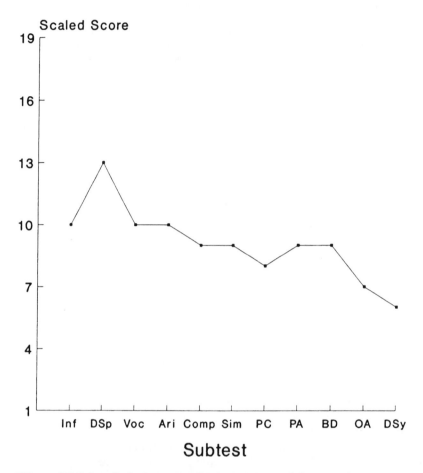

FIG 6.1.   WAIS–R profile for *Case 1*. Note that the Digit Span scaled score is at least one standard deviation higher than any other subtest.

structured neuropsychological evaluation, where she was not likely to experience the strong emotional reactions. Her therapists determined that her attention was particularly vulnerable to disruption at times when she was experiencing an emotional reaction. Thus, her emotional responses also required some attention during rehabilitation.

This case illustrates at least a couple of attributes of neuropsychological tests that must be taken into account in using the evaluation to plan treatment. First, if the traditional interpretation of WAIS–III Digit Span had been used, she would have been judged to have a strength in attentional capacity when, in fact, she had a deficit in this area. Second, her problem with emotions was not evident in the optimized neuropsychological testing environment, nor would the specifics of this problem have been evident on standard personality assessment instruments. The following are a few principles in the application of neuropsychological tests that can help to avoid such problems.

Principles for Application

The right side of Table 6.1 briefly summarizes some principles for the application of neuropsychological tests that are useful in addressing the limitations listed on the left side of the table. The most basic and important principle is to conduct an in-depth interview during any neuropsychological evaluation. Such an interview should cover several important topics: The patient's functioning in every-day activities should be described by the patient, and preferably by an objective relative. Performance in the face of distraction or in other suboptimal circumstances should be explored. The patient's ability to organize and plan should be addressed in interview. Personality deficits such as impulse control problems or difficulties should be noted. In all these areas, changes from premorbid status should be noted. One should not assume that a problem identified during an interview is the result of a neurological injury or illness unless it can be established that the problem arose or was exacerbated concomitantly with the injury or disease.

Some deficits not measured by or not defined by testing can be revealed by careful observation during neuropsychological evaluation. Examples of inappropriate behavior may be seen in patient interactions with the examiner, such as asking inappropriately personal questions or making rude or abrasive remarks. If behaviors like these are frequent, the examiner may attempt a brief intervention. The results of such interventions can provide useful information regarding a patient's ability to respond to cueing and structure. Not infrequently, patients will spontaneously help an examiner manipulate test materials or put them away. Although the absence of such behavior has no diagnostic value, its presence is unusual in patients with adynamic motivational disorders. As a third example, a patient's awareness of deficits can be probed during evaluation. Questioning patients about performance difficulties to see if they recognize impaired performance may test their ability to recognize deficits. There are numerous other ways in which observation can provide useful information.

Mistakes in interpretation and application can be avoided if examiners keep in mind the complexity of neuropsychological instruments. As noted earlier, even in relatively simple tests like Digit Span from the WAIS–III, there are multiple ways of obtaining good or impaired scores. There are at least three ways of addressing the multidimensional nature of test instruments during neuropsychological evaluation: (a) observing the process by which a patient completes or fails a task, (b) supplementing standard administration formats with alternative presentation formats to explore various hypotheses, and (c) analyzing findings between multiple tests to uncover consistencies between them.

Edith Kaplan has been a leader in developing the process approach to neuropsychological assessment, and this approach is epitomized by the WAIS–R as a Neuropsychological Instrument (Kaplan, Fein, Morris, & Delis, 1991). Kaplan used the three principles just listed to help determine the underlying cause for impaired scores on WAIS–R subtests. For example, the process by which a patient completes Block Design is recorded. Errors in the right side of designs or errors in the internal details of designs may indicate dominant-hemisphere dysfunction. Errors in the left side of designs or violating the square configuration of the design may indicate nondominant-hemisphere dysfunction. As another example, if a patient shows a poor performance on the Information subtest, a multiple-choice format can be administered to determine if retrieval deficits play a role in the poor performance.

Consistently poor performance on multiple tests that share an underlying skill can be used to decipher which of the various skills required by a single test contributes to impaired performance. For example, poor performance on Digit Span, the Seashore Rhythm Test, and the Speech Sounds Perception Test could be due to an inability to sustain attention (i.e., a vigilance deficit), although other alternatives might be considered.

A fourth application principle for tests states that the usual way of interpreting a test should not be accepted without examining potential alternative explanations. Searching for patterns among test scores may be helpful in providing alternative explanations for a test score. For example, the Picture Completion subtest of the WAIS–III has typically been interpreted as a measure of attention to visual detail. However, given a standard administration, most patients are inclined to attempt to name the missing part. Thus, patients with language deficits may score poorly on Picture Completion not because they have difficulty finding and recognizing the missing parts but because they have difficulty finding the word (i.e., naming) to express the concept. Similarly, a patient may misname objects represented in line drawings not because the person has an anomia, but because of a problem visually recognizing the picture. Semantic cues have been built into the Boston Naming Test (Kaplan, Goodglass, & Weintraub, 1983) to help tease apart visual recognition from naming errors. In short, mistakes in test interpretation will lead to misapplication of results. The reader may wish to peruse chapters 3 and 4 of this volume for greater detail.

In summary, the properties of neuropsychological instruments, the assessment environment, limitations regarding validity, and interpretive problems all have a bearing on application of assessment results to various referral questions and contexts. Although some problems can be overcome by developing better tests, the inherent limitations of our measurements must also be accepted.

Problems in application of findings can be minimized by careful interviewing to uncover aspects of behavior that testing may not tap, by making careful behavioral observations for the same reason, and by attending to the complexity of individual tests and the patterns between tests. Given this background, we are now prepared to examine how the context of an evaluation affects the application of test results. Three clinical contexts are examined: diagnostic, rehabilitative, and forensic.

DIAGNOSTIC CONTEXT

Importance of Neuropsychological Findings for Diagnosis

It was once common in some locales for neuropsychological interpretations to play a major role in neurological diagnostic workups. Neuropsychological test results were used not only to attempt to localize a brain dysfunction, but even to speculate about the underlying neuropathology. The advent of sophisticated computerized imaging techniques that could be applied to the visualization of structural changes in the brain has greatly reduced the need for neuropsychological evaluations as purely diagnostic instruments. However, a number of important diagnostic applications of neuropsychological assessment continue to be important.

The following are some instances in which neuropsychological evaluation can be useful in making a diagnostic decision:

1. In cases where dementia is suspected and medical colleagues have ruled out toxic, metabolic, structural, and infectious causes of cognitive complaints, it may be important to document the nature and degree of cognitive deficit. Such documentation may be particularly important in the early stages of a dementing process when symptoms are subtle. Neuropsychologists may be called on to distinguish between symptoms likely to be caused by progressive degenerative processes versus affective disturbances or other psychiatric problems.

2. Frequently, neuropsychologists are called upon to assist in diagnosis of psychiatric symptoms. Known or suspected brain disease, injury, or dysfunction can produce symptoms similar to those of psychiatric syndromes such as schizophrenia, mania, depression, or other disorders. Patterns of performance on neuropsychological tests may be useful in distinguishing between these psychiatric syndromes and the impact of brain injury, stroke, toxic and metabolic disturbances, degenerative disorders, and other brain dysfunctions.

3. Persons occasionally experience seemingly minor events that could have implications for neurological functioning, such as a "minor" head injury or brief exposure to toxic matter. Animal models for "minor" head injury (e.g., Povlishock & Coburn, 1989) suggest that microscopic injury to white matter can

occur without grosser structural changes that might be detected by computerized tomography and magnetic resonance scans. This type of damage may account for some of the behavioral changes seen after minor head injury (e.g., see Gentilini, Nichelli, & Schoenhuber, 1989; Gronwall, 1989; Rimel, Giordani, Barth, Boll, & Jane, 1981). In these types of cases, the neuropsychologist may be called on to determine if the "minor" injury or brief toxic exposure has caused cognitive sequelae.

4. Neuropsychological patterns may be useful in conjunction with other medical diagnostic techniques in determining seizure foci. In this diagnostic process, neuropsychological findings will be compared to findings from non-invasive and/or invasive EEG findings, ictal behaviors, neurological examination, structural brain imaging (magnetic resonance or computed tomography), and functional brain imaging (positron emission tomography or single photon emission computed tomography).

In cases such as these, neuropsychological findings both influence the ultimate diagnosis and influence treatment decisions, either by diagnostic implications or by suggesting behavioral management strategies. Thus, diagnostic accuracy is of paramount importance. In the case of a progressive dementia, the family and the patient may want to know a prognosis to assist in making personal, business, or career decisions and to anticipate future needs. On the other hand, prematurely applying a diagnosis of dementia could have a devastating impact on a patient's self-esteem as well as causing disruption in personal and vocational activities. When dementia can be diagnosed, neuropsychological findings may have legal implications regarding competency and guardianship. In the case of psychiatric diagnoses, medication choices and behavioral management can be in part based on information and diagnostic impressions derived from the neuropsychological evaluation. In the case of minor head injury, patients may not understand why their abilities have changed in some areas and how to deal with those changes. A good neuropsychological evaluation can clarify what abilities have changed and suggest methods for dealing with changes. Often, there are also forensic implications for minor head injury. In the case of seizure surgery candidates, neuropsychological findings, along with other diagnostic data, play a role in determining the appropriateness of surgery and the probable focus of dysfunction. Thus, in each case where neuropsychological assessment plays a role in diagnosis, the implications for accuracy are profound.

Potential Problems in Diagnostic Application of Neuropsychological Assessment Results

In many cases where assessment goals are diagnostic, the neuropsychologist is dependent on the pattern of test scores in order to diagnose a dysfunction. For example, the relative performance on verbal versus visual spatial measures can sometimes be used to lateralize dysfunction to the left or right hemisphere. This information might be useful in lateralizing an epileptogenic focus or establishing other types of dysfunction. However, it must be kept in mind that a particular patient might have significant variations in abilities that are unrelated to the diagnostic question. Sometimes, for example, participation in a given occupation might lead to better development of verbal or visual spatial skills. A certain amount of individual variability between test scores should be expected. The critical question in examining a particular patient's pattern of scores is whether one is dealing with a normal degree of variation in abilities or a neuropsychologically meaningful deviation. Schinka and Vanderploeg discuss issues relevant to premorbid functioning in chapter 2 of this volume.

Other premorbid variables may exist that have a direct impact on the interpretation of cognitive test results. For example, Haas, Cope, and Hall (1987) found a surprisingly high percentage of poor premorbid academic performance in their head-injured sample, suggesting that persons with learning disabilities are probably more susceptible to head injury. The cognitive effects of learning disability can be mistaken for those of head injury if a history of premorbid learning disability is not discovered during evaluation. The high incidence of alcohol involvement in traumatic injuries also suggests a greater incidence of alcoholism in head injury samples (Alberts & Binder, 1991). It is known that chronic alcoholism causes memory changes that are related to underlying changes in the brain, even for patients not experiencing amnesic syndromes (see Butters, 1985). Thus, the effects of chronic alcoholism might be mistaken for the effects of head injury or other neurological problems if such a history is not uncovered. Patterns of cultural and language differences can be confused with neurologically mediated cognitive changes as well (Sohlberg & Mateer, 1989). These premorbid variables will have different diagnostic and prognostic implication. They may not merit treatment intervention at all, but when they do, treatment will be different than it would for a bonafide neurological event.

Similarly, the proximal event leading to a neuropsychological referral may not be the only possible reason for cognitive changes. If the neuropsychologist does not obtain a good history of cognitive functioning and probe for other possible causes of cognitive dysfunction, he or she may be misled by the pattern of test scores. For example, an older patient may have been experiencing some decline in functioning prior to a minor head injury that prompted referral. Their spouse may have taken over financial responsibilities several months prior to the injury because the patient was functioning inadequately. Such a circumstance might raise questions about dementia in addition to potential changes related to the head injury.

An additional difficulty for the interpretation of patterns in neuropsychological test results arises when a theoretically probable pattern on which the neuropsychologist might base an inference is not borne out by empirical data. The use of verbal versus visual memory measures to lateralize medial temporal dysfunction in cases of epilepsy is a good example. Early data regarding lateralization of medial temporal lesions on the basis of a verbal–visual dichotomy were encouraging (e.g., Milner, 1970; Jones-Gotman & Milner, 1978). However, more recent data have called into question our ability to adequately detect right medial temporal lobe seizure foci on the basis of conventional visual memory measures, even though the correlation between verbal memory measures and left medial temporal foci is more robust (e.g., Barr et al., 1997; Bauer et al., 1995; Parsons, Kortenkamp, Bauer, Gilmore, & Roper, 1997; Williamson et al., 1993). It is not clear whether the problem is that conventional visual memory measures are inadequate in some way, or whether the concept of right hippocampal involvement in visual memory needs to be revised. While we are waiting for answers to such questions, it is important to stay informed regarding the empirical support for our assumptions.

Another frequent diagnostic problem is differentiating psychiatric or psychological disturbances from brain dysfunction. Commonly this is a difficult task because psychiatric disorders can show some of the same symptoms as acquired brain disorders. For example, patients with schizophrenia can show deficits on tasks thought to measure frontal lobe functioning (e.g., Weinberger, Berman, & Zec, 1986), on right as compared to left hemispatial attention (e.g., Posner, Early, Reiman, Pardo, & Dhawan, 1988), on naming tasks (Barr, Bilder, Goldberg, Kaplan, & Mukherjee, 1989), on speed of processing verbal versus nonverbal information (e.g., Posner et al., 1988), on maintenance of spoken discourse themes (e.g., Hoffman, Stopek, & Andreasen, 1986), on verbal memory span (e.g., Grove & Andreasen, 1985) and verbal working memory (e.g., Condray, Steinhauer, van Kammen, & Kasparek, 1996), and on other functions. In fact, chronic schizophrenics are the psychiatric patients who may be regularly classified as having brain damage on the basis of neuropsychological findings (Heaton & Crowley, 1981). Further, some might argue that dilated ventricles, which can be found particularly in male schizophrenics (see Andreasen et al., 1990), or structural abnormalities in the limbic system and basal ganglia (e.g., Bogerts, Meertz, & Schoenfeldt-Bausch, 1985) mean that schizophrenics have brain dysfunctions. Although this latter statement has a great deal of validity, the question remains of whether neuropsychological tests can be helpful in discriminating schizophrenic patients from patients with other types of brain dysfunction. Proper diagnosis can have treatment implications.

Although other psychiatric patients are less commonly diagnosed as brain injured on neuropsychological tests, psychiatric syndromes other than schizophrenia can produce impaired performance on neuropsychological tests. As an example, patients with depression can have slowed mentation, poor concentration, and memory deficits. Indeed, this pattern of deficits has led some to draw parallels between depressed patients and patients with subcortical dementias (see King & Caine, 1990). Frontal and subcortical dysfunctions can produce symptoms of depression or mania (Robinson, Kubos, Starr, Rao, & Price, 1984;

Starkstein, Robinson, & Price, 1987; Starkstein, Robinson, Berthier, Parikh, & Price, 1988). If not carefully examined, patients with psychogenic amnesia can be mistaken for patients with brain damage. Chapter 3 by Cimino can be consulted for further information regarding distinguishing psychiatric disorder from brain dysfunction.

As noted earlier, neuropsychological tests may not be designed to capture certain aspects of personality functioning which might be relevant to diagnosis. Similarly, these instruments do not tap other aspects of psychological functioning that are particularly important in distinguishing brain dysfunction from psychiatric syndromes. Evidence regarding social and occupational functioning can be important in diagnosing schizophrenia, affective disorders, and certain personality disorders. Sleep disturbance, appetite disturbance or fluctuations in weight, dysphoria, euphoria, suicidal ideation, poor judgment, rapid changes in mood, changes in sexual functioning, and other areas may be relevant to the diagnosis of affective disorder. Evidence of repression or denial can be relevant to diagnosis of dissociative disorders. Yet most of these items are not tested by neuropsychological instruments.

In many of the aspects of neurological dysfunction and psychiatric disorder not covered by neuropsychological tests, it will be necessary to gather information through interview. In doing so, examiners should remember that patients with neurological and psychiatric dysfunction may not be aware of many of their dysfunctions. *Anosognosia* is a term coined by Babinski in 1914 for unawareness of deficits (Heilman, Watson, & Valenstein, 1993). After right-hemisphere injury (e.g., the more acute phase of right-hemisphere stroke), dramatic examples of anosognosia can be seen in patients who may be unaware of a hemiplegia or a hemianopia. However, problems in awareness of deficits also occur after frontal injury (Stuss, 1991) and are common in traumatic brain injury (Prigatano, 1991). The implication concerning interview is that patients with awareness deficits may not be able to give an accurate account of their problems and changes related to brain injury. Patients with neurological dysfunction also may experience psychological denial to avoid the unpleasant implications of their deficits. Such denial also keeps the patient from providing accurate information about deficits during evaluation. For these reasons, it is usually good practice to interview an independent source who is close enough to the patient to give an accurate picture of the patient's difficulties. Most often such a person is a relative, but the neuropsychologist must be aware that some relatives may have difficulties or motivations that limit their ability to give an accurate account of the patient's behavior. For example, after a head injury or stroke, or given a progressive dementia, family members as well as patients may use psychological denial to avoid the intensely unpleasant emotions that recognition of the patient's deficits causes. In these cases, the neuropsychologist will have to be prepared to assess the accuracy of the relative's report.

Not infrequently, neuropsychological results do not clearly answer a referral question or answer the question incompletely. For example, deficits in attention and memory may be seen in a patient for whom the diagnostic issue is differentiating depression from dementia. Depression may be present, but deficits are of a severity or pattern that could indicate other processes in addition to depression. Or perhaps the level or pattern of results could be accounted for by the depression, but the history is suggestive of dementia. As another example, a patient with a mild head injury is demonstrating attentional and memory deficits at a level consistent with a mild head injury, but the patient is also experiencing symptoms of posttraumatic stress disorder, and the anxiety associated with this disorder may affect attention and memory. One mistake that can be made in similar instances is attempting to reach premature closure on a diagnosis.

In some cases, disorders will evolve over time. Dementias such as Alzheimer's disease, Pick's disease, or Binswanger's disease usually show a temporal progression. Severe head injuries may demonstrate improvement months after the injury. Progress may be made over varying intervals in other types of brain damage as well. In the case of differential diagnosis of dementia, families, patients, and referring physicians may make important decisions about careers, finances, legal matters, and social relationships based on the diagnostic label. Considerable damage can be done if the label is applied when there are ambiguities about the diagnosis. Testing across multiple occasions may be needed to achieve an accurate diagnosis. In instances of head injury or other types of brain damage, significant improvement from tests done soon after injury may occur. Significant problems may ensue if attempts are made to predict long-term outcome too soon after injury. Again, important decisions can be made regarding the patient on the basis of inadequate predictions. The issue of improving performance after brain injury or disease is discussed further during the next major section of this chapter.

In summary, pitfalls in the application of neuropsychological findings to diagnostic questions can limit their utility in this endeavor. The cost of making an error in diagnosis frequently can be quite high, especially when the diagnosis is the basis for making critical personal, financial, career, or treatment decisions. For this reason, it is crucial that clinical neuropsychologists be aware of potential problems that might affect the rendering of accurate diagnostic information. Some of these potential problems were mentioned earlier and are summarized on the left side of Table 6.2. However, this list is by no means comprehensive. The reader has probably already realized that different diagnostic circumstances may raise their own unique set of issues. Practitioners must be continually alert for such dilemmas and develop methods for dealing with them.

Case 2 was a young woman in her early 20s. She was in our country studying English in preparation for enrolling in training relevant to her career. She was hit by an automobile while riding her bicycle. She may have been briefly unconscious at the scene of the accident. In the emergency room, she was alert but confused. Computed tomography (CT) scan of the brain was unremarkable;

TABLE 6.2
Pitfalls and Principles for Diagnostic Contexts

Potential Pitfalls in Diagnostic Applications of Neuropsychological Assessments	Principles for Application of Neuropsychological Assessments in Diagnostic Contexts
1. Premorbid patterns of strength and weakness can be mistaken for neuropsychologically meaningful information.	1. Gather as much information as possible about premorbid cognitive strengths and weaknesses.
2. Proximal events prompting referral for neuropsychological assessment may not be the only cause of cognitive dysfunction.	2. Ascertain from history any other potential causes of cognitive dysfunction.
3. Premorbid conditions with specific patterns of cognitive functioning can be mistaken as the product of neurological injury or disease.	3. Inquire about premorbid educational, cultural, legal, and substance abuse history.
4. Empirical findings do not correspond to theoretical/conceptual predictions regarding a test and its diagnostic utility.	4. Be aware of empirical findings with respect to tests and relevant diagnostic issues.
5. Psychiatric illnesses cause cognitive dysfunction, which may be misinterpreted as representing other types of neuropsychological dysfunction.	5. Be aware of patterns of cognitive dysfunction caused by psychiatric illnesses.
6. In addition to not tapping important personality functions, neuropsychological tests do not measure aspects of social and occupational functioning which might be relevant to discriminating psychiatric disorders from other types of brain dysfunction.	6. Obtain a good history of social and occupational functioning.
7. Decreased self-awareness makes patients unable to unable to convey accurate information regarding their deficits during interview.	7. Where possible, check for awareness of changes during interview, and interview relatives when available.
8. Motivations of relatives may limit their ability to give accurate information regarding patients' deficits during interview.	8. When interviewing relatives, assess motivations that might obscure information regarding patient's deficits.
9. Neuropsychological results may leave ambiguities with respect to some diagnostic questions.	9. Do not attempt to reach premature closure when data present ambiguities regarding diagnostic questions.
10. A single battery of neuropsychological tests may not capture elements of progression which are relevant to certain diagnoses.	10. In cases where progression of deficits would be expected for a given diagnosis, but the diagnosis cannot be unambiguously made, recommend reevaluation at an appropriate interval.

she was admitted to the neurosurgery unit for observation. After 3 days, the patient could not remember her name, and she was eventually identified by an acquaintance.

The neuropsychologist was consulted at this time. The patient's limited ability to communicate in English precluded a longer neuropsychological battery. The patient was given the Digit Span, Picture Completion, and Block Design subtests from the WAIS–R. She was also given the Galveston Orientation and Amnesia Test (GOAT; Levin, Benton, & Grossman, 1981), and the stories and figures from the Wechsler Memory Scale–Revised (WMS–R; Wechsler, 1987). The Digit Span scaled score of 8 was slightly below average, and the Picture Completion scaled score of 10 was average. Given the language component to both of these subtests (Picture Completion has a naming requirement), they may have underestimated functioning. The Block Design subtest was performed quite well, yielding a perfect performance with a scaled score of 19! Because others had told her, the patient was able to remember her name and her home country, but she was unable to remember any other personal information such as address and birth date on the GOAT. On the other hand, she was able to name the hospital and was oriented to the various elements of time. Her somewhat limited recall of WMS–R stories may have been related to language phenomena, but it is important to note that she lost no information from immediate (14 of 50 ideas) to delayed (14 of 50 ideas) recall. Further, the patient remembered 38 of 41 details of the WMS–R designs on immediate recall and lost minimal information (36 of 41) at delayed recall. Both of these visual memory scores were at the 86th percentile.

The diagnostic issue was to determine whether the patient was in a state of posttraumatic amnesia or had other, possibly psychological, reasons for her amnesia. It should be remembered that significant traumatic brain injury may exist even in the presence of a normal CT scan (Jennett & Teasdale, 1981). However, there were several reasons to implicate psychological causation. First and probably most important, the patient's retention of information (especially visual) across a delay suggests she was not in a state of posttraumatic amnesia. Patients in posttraumatic amnesia have a rapid rate of forgetting (Levin, High, & Eisenberg, 1988), which causes them to lose most information over even very short intervals (Levin et al., 1981). Second, the normal sequence in recovery of orientation is person, place, and time (Levin, 1989). Although other orders of recovery occur, it is extremely unusual for a patient emerging from posttraumatic amnesia to be oriented to place and time, yet to be disoriented to most aspects of person. Third, Performance subtests of the WAIS–R are likely to be most sensitive to brain dysfunction, especially during the early phases (Mandleberg & Brooks, 1975; Uzzell, Zimmerman, Dolinskas, & Obrist, 1979), and this patient performed quite well on Block Design.

Given these facts, a diagnosis of generalized psychogenic amnesia was suggested, and psychotherapy was initiated. Over the course of the next few days, the patient recovered her personal past. She discussed with her therapist a personal traumatic circumstance that she had discussed with no one previously. Other personal and family stressors that may have been contributory were also uncovered. The patient resumed her normal level of functioning. It is likely that the patient would have eventually recovered her personal history even if a correct diagnosis had not been made. Nonetheless, the therapy initiated with the proper diagnosis did offer her the opportunity to integrate elements of her past into her functioning, making her less vulnerable to future difficulties in functioning. Thus, this case illustrates the importance of knowing detailed information about relevant neuropsychological diagnoses and the alternative psychiatric diagnoses that might be applied to a case.

Principles for Application

Principles for the application of neuropsychological assessments to diagnostic contexts are summarized on the right side of Table 6.2. The principles are indexed by number to the problem on the left side of the table for which they provide a solution. The first is to gather as much information as possible about premorbid strengths and weaknesses. In chapter 2 of this volume, Schinka Vanderploeg discuss estimating premorbid levels of functioning, and such information is invaluable when trying to ascertain if a patient's functioning has deteriorated from premorbid levels. However, premorbid patterns of functioning may also be critical in making diagnostic statements. When a patient has attended college, a person's college major may give some insight into premorbid abilities. High school and college grades, achievement test scores, and college entrance scores may also be indicators of premorbid achievement. Favorite subjects and subjects that patients have found difficult may be valuable pieces of information. Occupation may give information about what skills a patient has had to develop, and level of occupational attainment may be useful in estimating premorbid levels of functioning. Hobbies and interests may be similarly useful. Once some general expectations regarding premorbid abilities have been developed, the neuropsychologist must decide whether test patterns reflect this premorbid functioning or the diagnostic entity in question.

A second recommendation is to gather as complete a history of potential causes of cognitive changes as possible. As noted earlier, obvious recent events prompting referrals are not always the cause of a particular pattern of scores. Other possible causes of cognitive complaints must be ruled out. During interview, the patient's history should be examined for any possible decline in cognitive functioning that may not be obvious from the referral question and recent complaints. A psychiatric history should be taken. Possible past neurological events such as head injury, meningitis, vascular events, or other entities that may affect cognitive performance should be ruled out. History of drug or alcohol abuse, excessive use of caffeine, or other substances that may affect behavior or cognitive performance must be ascertained. As noted earlier, learning disability, attention deficit disorder, and language and cultural differences may all cause patterns of performance that can be mistaken for signs of brain injury by the unwary examiner.

When a neuropsychological test or tests are selected to address a specific conceptual question, such as right temporal seizure localization, the literature regarding the proposed usage should be reviewed. As noted earlier, tests may be imperfect regarding their intended function. In such instances, no good alternatives may be available; nonetheless, the clinician should know the probability of making a mistake and the nature of potential mistakes based on assessment of empirical data. Ideally, when empirical data do not support a logical conceptual framework for a particular test, additional research eventually will provide solutions. Thus, it is necessary to stay current with developments relevant to specific areas of practice.

When neuropsychologists are called on to differentiate the effects of known or suspected brain dysfunction from psychiatric disorder, they must know both the cognitive effects of the brain dysfunction and the cognitive effects of the psychiatric disturbance in question. As noted earlier, psychiatric disorders such as schizophrenia, affective disorder, or dissociative disorders have symptoms that can mimic neuropsychological dysfunction. Works discussing the impact of psychiatric disorder on neuropsychological functioning (e.g., Heaton & Crowley, 1981) can be consulted and monitored for new developments, especially by practitioners who frequently must differentiate the cognitive effects of psychiatric from neurologic disorders. Similarly, the literature concerning various neuropsychological manifestations of brain dysfunctions should be consulted as well. Even very experienced neuropsychologists find it necessary to consult the literature when diagnostic entities they rarely see become an issue for a particular case.

Regarding the differentiation of brain dysfunction and psychiatric disorder, social and occupational functioning often can provide useful diagnostic information. Indeed, in disorders such as schizophrenia, deterioration of social and occupational functioning are among the diagnostic criteria (American Psychiatric Association, 1994). For this reason, a good social and occupational history should be obtained. The neuropsychologist should keep in mind questions such as: Has the patient been able to maintain stable relationships at different points in his or her life? If not, why not? Has the patient ever been arrested or had other significant trouble with the law? Has the patient been able to maintain a stable employment history? What is the longest period the patient has worked in a single job? What are the factors that may have influenced job changes? These are just a few of the questions that should be routinely investigated during interview.

As noted earlier, the information a patient gives regarding cognitive complaints can be affected either by unawareness or by denial of deficits. One must be aware of such possibilities during the interview process. Occasionally, it is possible to check for unawareness or denial by simple questioning. For example, the patient can be asked what significant others say about the patient's functioning. Patients may be aware of a difference in their own and others' opinions even though they are unaware of deficits. If the neuropsychologist suspects certain deficits based on referral or other information, the practioner can probe for recognition of such deficits as an indicator of awareness. Alertness for indications of defensiveness may help in detecting denial.

Of course, relatives should be interviewed when possible. If one suspects that a relative may not be honest in the presence of the patient, then the relative should be interviewed separately. Discrepancies between the relative's and the patient's report can confirm suspicions of unawareness or denial on the patient's part. Nonetheless, neuropsychologists must be alert for motivations on the part of the relative being interviewed that will obscure information about the patient's functioning. Frequently, relatives may be motivated to believe the patient is functioning better than he or she actually may be, but relatives may be motivated to make patients look worse than they are as well. Relatives can be questioned regarding how easy it has been for them to accept changes in the patient's functioning or about what their greatest fears might be. Answers to these and similar questions can help determine if the relative might be denying the nature or severity of deficits. Indications of anxiety when talking about certain subjects or unwillingness to entertain the possibility of change may be among the numerous indicators that relatives may be overestimating functioning. It should be obvious from this discussion that neuropsychologists must be more than technically competent in the administration, scoring, and interpretation of tests; there are numerous diagnostic circumstances when a premium is placed on excellence in clinical interviewing.

As noted earlier, significant damage to patients' lives can occur if the neuropsychological practitioner attempts to reach diagnostic closure in the face of significant ambiguity. Such diagnostic errors can lead to poor decisions regarding career, financial, and other matters. In the face of unresolvable ambiguity, it is best to state the diagnostic dilemma(s) as clearly as possible, highlighting the diagnostic possibilities and the data supporting each possibility. Frequently, the consumer of the diagnostic neuropsychological evaluation is a physician or health care team who has other sources of diagnostic information available. If such persons understand the nature of ambiguities clearly, they may be able (a) to resolve the ambiguity on the basis of other available information, (b) to plan the best strategy for gathering further data to resolve diagnostic questions, or (c) to plot the best course of treatment given the circumstances. Thus, presenting a clear discussion of the possibilities may facilitate diagnosis and treatment, whereas attempts to reach premature closure can cost valuable time and resources when treatment efforts and plans are misdirected.

In cases where a progressive disorder is suspected, such as in Alzheimer's disease, diagnostic ambiguities may be resolved with reevaluation after some period of time. Thus, when the diagnosis is in doubt and progressive disorder is suspected, reevaluation after a specified period of time should be recommended. It is worth noting in this regard that broad-spectrum cognitive and intellectual functions in Alzheimer's disease may remain stable for some period of time (possibly several months) after memory decline has begun (Haxby, Raffaele, Gillette, Schapiro, & Rapoport, 1992). Thus, a single reevaluation may be inadequate for tracking the course of intellectual decline, and multiple reevaluations may be needed before nonmemory disturbances involving language, praxis, and gnosis may be detected and provide strong evidence of an Alzheimer's disease diagnosis.

In summary, it is possible to mistake one diagnostic entity for another on the basis of neuropsychological results. Such mistakes can be minimized if the neuropsychologist uses as many sources of information as are available to derive a diagnostic opinion. Important data include premorbid cognitive, social, and occupational history. In a discussion of patients' deficits during interview, an attempt should be made to estimate awareness of deficits, and a collateral source of information to the patient should be interviewed when possible. Finally, the practitioner should avoid drawing premature conclusions when data do not justify closure and should recommend retesting after a specified time when it is likely to add clarity to the diagnostic picture.

REHABILITATION CONTEXT

Importance of Neuropsychological Findings for Rehabilitation

During the 1980s, clinical neuropsychologists became increasingly involved in the rehabilitation of neurologically impaired patients. This was particularly evident in the rapid proliferation of head-trauma rehabilitation programs. There is only one justification for a clinical neuropsychological evaluation with rehabilitation patients: It must somehow contribute to improving the patient's ability to cope with the patient's ultimate community environment. Such a contribution can be made by (a) defining cognitive dysfunctions which are a target for rehabilitation efforts, (b) measuring progress during rehabilitation and recovery so that goals can be revised if necessary, (c) helping to define realistic goals for community reentry, and (d) defining nonneuropsychological emotional problems that may interfere with rehabilitation.

Potential Problems in Rehabilitation Applications of Neuropsychological Assessment Results

Although the ultimate goals of rehabilitation are functional in nature (i.e., the aims are to increase a person's ability to function in the community), neuropsychological evaluations are conducted with tests that are artificial and microcosmic. The reasons for this type of test structure were discussed earlier and relate to the needs to break cognitive deficits into their simplest components and to establish normative samples that are biased as little as possible by occupations and interests, putting all examinees on "equal footing." These purposes create a paradox in that neuropsychological tests measure various components of cognitive functioning but are isolated from the various functional contexts in which patients must eventually perform on a day-to-day basis. This isolation from functional contexts means that our tests are at best indirect indicators of a person's ability to perform any particular functional activity and at worst misleading in some circumstances. The experienced examiner will recognize the limitations of various neuropsychological instruments in interpreting and integrating results. This discrepancy between the abilities that tests measure and the functional activities patients must routinely perform is central to many of the problems addressed next.

With respect to functional activities, referral sources, rehabilitation team members, family members, and patients may want to know: Is the patient capable of living alone? Can the patient drive? Is the patient capable of managing financial affairs? Is the patient capable of working? If so, in what capacity? How can the family deal with irritability or irrational anger? What remedies are there for memory dysfunction? What can be done about sporadic, seemingly capricious lapses in memory? Answers to such questions affect rehabilitation planning, the patient's quality of life, and the ability to exercise rights and privileges that most of us take for granted. Yet factors other than those we typically measure during evaluation may affect the answers. For example, personality dysfunction has already been mentioned. Or, a person's ability to rely on a premorbid knowledge base for some particular job can on occasion assist in overcoming considerable cognitive deficit.

Some of the problems that are relevant to applications in the rehabilitation settings have been discussed in previous sections. In order to gain an accurate assessment of a patient's various cognitive abilities, neuropsychological testing is conducted in an optimal environment. In particular, examiners go to great lengths to minimize distractions. Yet patients' daily environments are not free from distractions. Thus, the ability of a patient to function in a less than optimal environment is not typically assessed to any great extent.

Concerns of reliability and particularly validity affect the usefulness of a test in a rehabilitation. If the construct validity of an instrument is in doubt, it is likely to be of little value in understanding how cognitive functions have broken down. If the predictive validity has not been established, then the prognostic value of a test is questionable. If a test cannot help to understand how cognition has faltered or what outcomes are likely, it is of no use in rehabilitation.

It is worth mentioning again that neuropsychological tests, for the most part, are not designed to measure personality changes that occur after some forms of brain damage. These changes may have a devastating impact on a patient's ability to function on the job and in the family (Lezak, 1978) and frequently are the most salient reason for rehabilitation and reentry failures. Personality change is particularly common after traumatic brain injury, affecting 60% or more of severely injured patients even when minimal cognitive and motor deficits are present (Jennett, Snoek, Bond, & Brooks, 1981). The propensity for fronto-temporal damage in this type of injury (Jennett & Teasdale, 1981) accounts for much of the personality change. Sohlberg and Mateer (1989) and Lezak (1986) have noted the importance and the difficulty of measuring this type of change. Types of personality change that may occur include irritability, other emotional lability, impulse control problems (disinhibition), decreased initiation and motivation, lack of empathy, loss of ability to take a self-critical attitude, and inability to profit from feedback.

However, emotional changes are caused not only by actual neurological damage; patients also have reactions to their injuries. Depression, denial, and anger are common in patients who are struggling to incorporate significant loss of function into their self-concepts. It is important to distinguish such psychological reactions from neurologically induced personality changes because the treatment implications are different. For persons struggling with self-concept issues, assistance in integrating changes can be offered. Frequently, individual or group psychotherapy can significantly facilitate emotional adjustment (Prigatano, 1986). On the other hand, education and compensation for neurologically induced personality change can be recommended (e.g., Crosson, 1987). Examiners should further realize that not all problems relating to personality may be traceable to neurological substrates or emotional reactions to injury. Patients may carry significant premorbid personality or psychiatric disturbances into the rehabilitation setting. There are indications in the literature that the incidence of preexisting personality or psychiatric dysfunction may be greater in a head-injury population than in the general population (Alberts & Binder, 1991; Levin et al., 1981).

Another problem mentioned briefly earlier is the change in functioning over time. It is particularly likely that the acute effects of brain damage will be mitigated across time. Thus, long-term rehabilitation planning cannot be based on neuropsychological assessments conducted relatively soon after the damage occurred. Attempting to make precise long-term prognostic statements on the basis of acute neuropsychological data frequently can mislead patients, family, and referral sources. Further, when recovery exceeds or fails to meet predictions, patients and family members lose trust in medical, psychological, and rehabilitation professionals. Lezak (1986) estimated that most patients have reached a neuropsychological "plateau" by 2 or 3 years postonset. However, it is the experience of this author that significant changes in cognitive functioning may occur at least as long as 5 years postonset in some head-injured patients if test–retest intervals are long enough. The dilemma for rehabilitation neuropsychologists and their patients is that long-term planning cannot be delayed for years waiting for evidence of plateau.

Lezak (1986) noted another error committed by some examiners. Some clinicians make the mistake of having observation serve test instruments, as opposed to having testing serve the purpose of observation. When too much emphasis is placed on test scores and actuarial approaches, valuable information is lost. Nowhere is this more true than in attempts to evaluate awareness. It has been noted that patients who have an intellectual awareness of their deficits may still be unable to recognize "online" when a deficit is impacting performance (Barco, Crosson, Bolesta, Werts, & Stout, 1991; Crosson et al., 1989). This is termed *emergent awareness*, and this form of awareness is critical to the adequate performance. It can only be assessed during neuropsychological evaluations if the examiner looks beyond test scores and makes a concerted effort to evaluate awareness.

The next step after assessing awareness is to estimate a patient's ability to compensate for deficits. As rehabilitation progresses into its more chronic phase, compensation for lasting deficits becomes increasingly important. The ability to compensate is intimately tied to awareness, because patients who are unaware of how a deficit is impacting them will not think to compensate (Barco et al., 1991; Crosson et al., 1989). The neuropsychologist can use the evaluation as an observational tool to estimate a patient's ability to compensate for deficits. Even so, a complete understanding of how a patient is able to compensate can only be accomplished through extended, intensive rehabilitation.

Issues relevant to the application of neuropsychological tests to rehabilitation are summarized on the left side of Table 6.3. When evaluations are conducted to assist in maximizing daily functions in the community, the neuropsychologist must focus on the practical implications of deficits. In this context, a high premium is placed on construct and predictive validity. Yet, as Lezak (1986) noted, we cannot be satisfied with test scores alone; we must use tests as an observational tool and understand the limitations of our instruments. Indeed, a good neuropsychological evaluation should only be considered a point of departure for rehabilitative treatment planning. Assessment must be an integral part of each treatment session. The results of each treatment task provide new data, which will lead to successive revisions of the original treatment plan as more facets of a patient's cognitive strengths and weaknesses are discovered and the patient improves during rehabilitation. Applications to rehabilitation can be quite complex. The following three case examples illustrate how premorbid learning, awareness deficits, and emotional reactions played a part in rehabilitation. In each case, some type of continuing assessment was an important facet of treatment.

Case 3 was a male in his 40s who was involved in a motor vehicle accident. He taught advanced mathematics as a career. His MR scan demonstrated massive left temporal lobe damage, involving most of the mesial and inferior temporal

TABLE 6.3
Pitfalls and Principles for Rehabilitation Contexts

Potential Pitfalls in Rehabilitation Applications of Neuropsychological Assessment	Principles for the Application of Neuropsychological Assessments in Rehabilitation Contexts
1. Neuropsychological tests generally do not measure the functional activities that are the ultimate target of rehabilitation treatments.	1a. Inquire regarding problems with functional activities during interview, and assess contradictions between this information and test results.
	1b. Be conservative in making predictions about functional activities based on neuropsychological evaluations.
	1c. Refer patients for functional evaluations of activities in question.
2. Test results obtained in an optimal environment must be used to predict performance in less than optimal environments.	2. Inquire regarding environmental factors (e.g., distractions, lack of structure, etc.) that may impact functional performance.
3. In order to facilitate rehabilitation treatment, neuropsychologists must distinguish between emotional reactions to injury, neurologically induced emotional changes, and premorbid personality patterns.	3a. Inquire about premorbid and postinjury emotional and personality difficulties and their context during interview.
	3b. Continue to assess emotional reactions as rehabilitation progresses.
4. Changes in neuropsychological functioning during rehabilitation may make results of previous neuropsychological evaluations obsolete.	4a. During the initial phases of rehabilitation, keep assessments short, deficit specific, and frequent.
	4b. During the more chronic phases of rehabilitation, recommend repeat evaluations if significant changes are likely to occur.
5. Test scores alone will not allow the examiner to assess a patient's ability to be aware of and compensate for deficits.	5. Build into assessments methods for assessing awareness of deficits and ability to compensate for deficits.

lobe. Consistent with this damage, the patient demonstrated decreased performance (0 percentile) on the Visual Naming subtest of the Multilingual Aphasia Examination (MAE; Benton & Hamsher, 1989). Auditory-verbal comprehension (MAE Token Test = 82nd percentile), repetition (MAE Sentence Repetition = 43rd percentile), and word list generation (MAE Controlled Oral Word Association = 74th percentile) were all within normal limits. Although his narrative language included circumlocutions and a few word-finding errors, he generally could be understood at 4 months postinjury. His narrative language was somewhat less impaired than naming performance would lead one to believe. As measured by the California Verbal Learning Test (CVLT; Delis, Kramer, Kaplan, & Ober, 1987), verbal memory was severely impaired: Total learning trials performance, all delayed recall trials, and discriminability for the recognition trial were all 3 to 4 standard deviations below the normative mean. Intrusion errors were a common element of performance. Left-hemisphere dysfunction was also manifested in a lower Verbal than Performance IQ on the WAIS–R (VIQ = 102, PIQ = 111), but above average scores on Vocabulary (scaled score = 12) and Comprehension (scaled score = 11) indicated that language output was less impaired than visual naming.

The patient's neurosurgeon felt that he would make a good adjustment to his injury even without intensive rehabilitation. The patient refused language therapy, and likewise was not interested in more intensive rehabilitation. He planned to return to teaching shortly after his injury. He taught one course with which he was quite familiar, and he prepared a more complex course for the following semester. Because of concerns regarding his possible success, a follow-up schedule was arranged. During these visits, the patient revealed he was successful in his classroom teaching. There was independent confirmation. He occasionally asked for the help of his colleagues in preparing certain aspects of his courses. He also continued other public speaking activities, but he found it more difficult to write about mathematical concepts.

Thus, in spite of language and verbal memory deficits, the patient made a successful reentry into teaching. Even though we recognized his spoken language to be better than his naming score would indicate, we had been pessimistic regarding his ability to succeed. Our prognosis failed to take into account at least two factors: (a) The patient's extensive knowledge about mathematics was largely intact and not tapped by our testing, and (b) the patient's previous teaching experience was extraordinarily useful in providing him with structure and a set of procedures within which he was able to function. In other words, we did not weigh heavily enough in our prognosis how his knowledge of mathematics and teaching experience would be useful during his reentry.

Case 4 was a male in his 30s. At 17 years post closed-head injury, his MR scan showed diffuse atrophic enlargement of the lateral ventricles as well as the upper third ventricle. There was also thinning of the corpus callosum just anterior to the splenium, a defect in the midbrain tegmentum, and areas of increased signal intensity in the periventricular white matter as well as in the centrum semiovale.

His WAIS–R profile demonstrated a significant Verbal–Performance discrepancy (VIQ = 116, PIQ = 98) on the WAIS–R, with the Verbal IQ in the high average range. The patient had severe verbal memory problems as measured by the CVLT (learning trials total and delayed recall trials all 4 standard deviations below normative mean, with recognition trial discriminablility somewhat better) and the Wechsler Memory Scale (Wechsler, 1945) paragraphs. Other problem areas on neuropsychological evaluation included left-hand impairment on the Tactual Performance Test, impaired localization on the Tactual Performance Test, and mildly slowed Finger Tapping with the left hand.

On the surface, the patient looked like an excellent candidate for rehabilitation with excellent verbal skills. However, during rehabilitation, the team discovered that he could not recognize problems when they were happening. The type of awareness for which this patient had a deficit has been termed *emergent awareness* (Crosson et al., 1989). The major means for assessing emergent awareness are through clinical observation (Barco et al., 1991). Relevant to this observation regarding his awareness was the fact that he had failed four professional programs before seeking help. Each time, he was able to perform adequately in the classroom, and it was the practical application experiences that he could not pass. On a job trial as a physical therapy aide, the patient was observed to leave out parts of treatment regimes or to confuse patients when writing unofficial notes. (Of course, he was supervised closely enough that these mistakes did not jeopardize patient care.) The patient was unable to realize that he was making these mistakes, and he had to rely on feedback from his supervisor. Attempts to remediate and compensate for this emergent awareness deficit met with only minimal success. Thus, the emergent awareness deficit had to be considered a permanent deficit. The implication was that he would require close supervision so that someone could catch and inform him of his errors.

For this case, neuropsychological tests did not tap his ability to recognize problem situations when they occurred. This problem was critical for understanding the patient's difficulties in work environments. The best predictor of this deficit on neuropsychological assessment may have been the indicators of right-hemisphere deficit, but the correlation between these indicators and the functional problem is far from a one-to-one correspondence.

Case 5 was a male in his 20s who received a head injury in a fall during an industrial accident. He had a partial right temporal lobectomy to relieve intracranial pressure and remove contused tissue. Acute CT scan also had indicated edema in the left parietal, temporal, and occipital lobes.

Although the patient did not show classical symptoms of aphasia or a recognizable aphasic syndrome, language testing revealed significant deficits: MAE Visual Naming = 2nd percentile; MAE Sentence Repetition = 0 percentile; MAE Token Test < 1st percentile; MAE Controlled Oral Word Association < 1st percentile. His verbal memory as measured by the CVLT was impaired (learning trial total and delayed recall trials 4 to 5 standard deviations below normative mean, with discriminability on recognition trial 2 standard deviations below mean). Verbal memory problems were related, at least to some degree, to his language impairments. His Verbal IQ (79) was in the borderline range of functioning, and his Performance IQ (87) was in the low normal range of functioning. Other impaired performances were seen on the Seashore Rhythm Test, Part B of the Trail Making Test, and the Porteus Maze Test (Porteus, 1959). The patient also had a right homonymous hemianopsia.

During the course of his rehabilitation, it was discovered that the patient was having difficulty controlling his anger, and he was even becoming physically aggressive with his wife. At the same time, it was determined that the patient was depressed. The depression was related to his situation. Although the patient had significant language, verbal intellectual, and verbal memory deficits on testing, it had been determined in therapy that he was able to understand and respond to verbally presented concepts in several instances. Therefore, it was decided to handle the problems in individual as well as group psychotherapy. As his depression lessened with therapy, so did his problems with anger control.

It was important to distinguish anger problems that are related directly to brain injury from those that are related to a reaction to the injury and from those that involve personality structure. Those that are related to the patient's emotional reaction to injury may be amenable to psychotherapy. For those related to neurological injury, it may be best to assume in the chronic phase of recovery that they may be present indefinitely and work on management strategies. Characterological anger problems are sometimes the hardest to treat successfully in brain injury rehabilitation programs.

Principles for Application

These cases are examples of how neuropsychological test results failed to provide a complete understanding of patient functioning relevant to rehabilitation. In case 3, isolation of neuropsychological instruments from functional contexts provided information that led to an underestimation of the patient's abilities. In case 4, the neuropsychological test data suggested that problems in awareness might have been present, but there was no way of confirming this hypothesis on the basis of test scores alone. In case 5, it was necessary to distinguish the source of the patient's anger as well as to understand his functional communication abilities to arrive at an appropriate treatment strategy. In each instance, information other than that from neuropsychological tests was necessary to implement plans that would maximize the patient's functioning. Thus, the diagnostic process and the outcomes in these cases suggest that optimal practice of neuropsychology in a rehabilitation does not end with the completion of an initial evaluation. Optimal practice in a rehabilitation setting involves integration of the neuropsychologist into the treatment team, following the patient over time, and understanding how various causes of emotional difficulties may impact treatment and day-to-day living. As rehabilitation progresses, as the patient becomes more aware of deficits and reacts emotionally, as recovery takes place, as the patient acquires or reacquires skills through rehabilitation, and as limitations become better defined with data gathered during treatment, the neuropsychologist can provide valuable guidance in altering treatment plans and outcome expectations.

Keeping the rehabilitation process in mind, a number of recommendations can make the formal testing and assessment process more effective. The suggestions for rehabilitative applications on the right-hand side of Table 6.3 have been indexed by number to the problems listed on the left-hand side of this table. The first suggestion is to inquire of patients and family members about difficulties in functional activities. For many outpatients, such inquiries will be quite extensive. They should involve what activities the patient performs on a regular basis, any difficulties with such activities, activities the patient has tried to perform but cannot, and the reasons the patient cannot perform those activities. Any difficulties arising in the day-to-day family life can also be useful information.

Because patients do not generally perform functional activities in as ideal an environment as the neuropsychology lab, examiners should inquire regarding environmental factors that impact performance of these activities. For example, what happens when the patient is distracted from an activity? What happens if the patient is not given structure? Does the patient initiate activities on his or her own? Can the patient remember when requested to perform various activities? What compensations have been tried, and which ones have been useful?

Once a picture of functional activities and problems has been established, the examiner can compare this picture to test results. Providing relatives and patients have given a relatively accurate picture of daily functioning (see previous section for problems assessing accuracy of report), any contradictions between what the patient can or cannot do and what might be predicted from test results can provide useful information. In instances where such contradictions exist, the examiner should look for what assets or deficits might have been missed. Do examination results lead to gross underestimation or overestimation of the patient's abilities? And what are the implications of this information for rehabilitation?

Because test results frequently do not correspond with functional abilities in a highly accurate fashion, neuropsychologists should be somewhat conservative in making prognostic statements for rehabilitation. There is a delicate balance between preventing a patient from doing an activity of which the patient might be capable and allowing a patient to participate in an activity at which the person probably will fail. Other factors, including the patient's level of awareness, ability to ultimately compensate for deficits, motivation to participate in the activity, or level of support for the activity in the environment, may affect treatment planning decisions. In some instances where awareness is low and patients insist on performing an activity in which the probability of failure is high, it is better to orchestrate a functional trial and use the results to attempt to change course.

When neuropsychological results and functional reports are in conflict, or when the bearing of neuropsychological findings on functional capacities is not clear, a functional evaluation of the specific activity should be recommended. In many rehabilitation programs today, such functional evaluations are a routine part of rehabilitation. Even the independent neuropsychological practitioner performing an evaluation for rehabilitative reasons may find occasion to make referrals for functional evaluations. For example, driving evaluations can be found in many large rehabilitation centers. Such evaluations may use simulators or even actual driving trials to generate recommendations about a patient's driving status.

Neuropsychologists in a rehabilitation setting should be certain to make adequate inquiry regarding premorbid and postinjury emotional difficulties and changes. Based on knowledge of psychopathology, emotional changes due to neurological injury, and familiarity with reactions to injury, some estimation of the source of emotional problems can be made. Often when trying to differentiate between neurological and reactive causes for emotional difficulties, the circumstances that trigger emotional reactions will give a clue. For example, if a patient tends to have an emotional reaction when confronted by a task the person cannot do, when relatives have to do tasks the patient once did, or when reminded of the discrepancies between premorbid and postinjury abilities, it is likely that the patient is experiencing a reaction to the deficits created by the injury, at least in part. On the other hand, if a patient is more irritable with numerous minor stressors without respect to what such stressors represent to him or her, then the patient may have a neurologically induced change in emotions.

As rehabilitation progresses, the neuropsychologist should continue to assess emotional factors. Sometimes, additional information will clarify a diagnosis. In other instances, as patients become more aware of their deficits, and particularly the functional implications, anger and/or denial will become more evident. In either instance, changes in treatment plans may be justified. In the case of emotional reactions, patients with severe brain injury frequently have substantial insights into their psychological dilemmas and can benefit from psychotherapy (e.g., see Prigatano, 1986).

The likelihood that a patient will make substantial changes can also impact the neuropsychological evaluation. In the early parts of rehabilitation, soon after injury or stroke, patients will be likely to change rapidly. An evaluation conducted today may not present an accurate picture of the patient's abilities in as little as a week. Sohlberg and Mateer (1989) recommended keeping evaluations short, deficit specific, and frequent during this period. Longer, more traditional neuropsychological evaluations may be performed later when they are likely to be useful over several weeks of rehabilitation.

However, even in the more chronic phases of rehabilitation, it may be necessary to repeat more extensive evaluations if the patient is expected to show significant improvement. Improvement may be anticipated as a result of rehabilitation or as a result of continued recovery. In such cases, treatment or community reentry plans may be altered if changes seem to so justify. Thus, neuropsychological tests can quantify underlying cognitive changes. Of course, evaluation results would have to be collated with information about changes in functional activities to increase predictive accuracy.

Finally, in addition to interviewing patients and family to make an estimate of awareness of deficits (see previous section), the neuropsychologist can build into evaluations ways of qualitatively assessing awareness of deficits. This information is particularly useful in rehabilitation because knowledge of awareness deficits can significantly impact rehabilitation. Barco et al. (1991) discussed assessment and treatment of awareness deficits during rehabilitation. The earlier awareness deficits are described, the earlier treatment can begin. In order to assess awareness, examiners can ask patients how well they think they did on various tasks. Observations of attempts to compensate for deficits during evaluation are also informative because such attempts indicate not only some awareness of a problem but also the capacity to compensate.

In summary, the rehabilitation process can be greatly enhanced if the neuropsychologist keeps in mind the likely discrepancies between test performance and functional abilities. Such discrepancies necessitate not only gathering information about functional activities during interview, but also recommendations for functional evaluations. Although emotional factors and awareness will be assessed in the process of rehabilitation, initial neuropsychological evaluations can make a contribution to identifying and specifying such problems early in the rehabilitation process.

FORENSIC CONTEXT

Importance of Neuropsychological Findings for Forensic Questions

There are numerous ways in which a neuropsychologist might become involved in the legal system. Suspected or established brain damage or dysfunction may have a bearing on any number of legal questions. With respect to the criminal arena, competency to stand trial, sanity at the time of an offense, and mitigating circumstances relevant to sentencing are among the most common issues. With respect to civil proceedings, a neuropsychologist may be called on to establish the existence of impairment relative to brain damage or dysfunction in personal injury, worker's compensation, or medical malpractice cases. Neuropsychological functioning might be relevant to cases involving guardianship for person or property as well.

Melton, Petrila, Poythress, and Slobogin (1987) discussed the uneasy alliance between psychology and the legal profession, and they presented some of the reasons why this is the case. In fact, the professional worlds of psychologists and attorneys are frequently quite different regarding basic assumptions. In the legal context, free will is usually presumed as a basic tenet, whereas the science of psychology usually holds human behavior to be determined by any number of influences. Attorneys and psychologists also may differ on what is considered a fact. For the former, a fact, once established, is more or less an all-or-nothing matter, whereas for the latter it is a matter of probabilities with varying degrees of ambiguity. The method of arriving at facts is also different. Attorneys will tend to sharpen conflict as a means of examining disputed issues, but psychologists will tend to look for some convergence of data. Further, psychologists are taught to minimize, prevent, or resolve conflict in order to promote positive interactions. Thus, the assumptions made and methods used by psychologists are often in conflict with the assumptions made by and needs of attorneys.

The complexities for a neuropsychologist functioning within the legal system are so vast that it would be difficult to cover them comprehensively in anything short of an entire volume. Rather, this chapter highlights some of the general issues that a neuropsychologist just beginning forensic activity might wish to consider. For greater detail in forensic psychology and forensic neuropsychology, the reader is referred to some of the volumes dedicated solely to this issue (e.g., Blau, 1984; Doerr & Carlin, 1991; Melton et al., 1987).

Potential Problems in Forensic Applications of Neuropsychological Assessment Results

One of the first problems to be addressed is the pressure in forensic evaluations to derive a definitive opinion regarding the issue in question. As an attorney begins to build a case, it will become obvious that the neuropsychological evaluation could best support the case if a certain outcome were obtained. In criminal cases, the stakes may be quite high. For example, a client's life might hinge on the outcome of an evaluation in a first-degree murder case. Likewise, large sums of money may be at stake in personal injury cases. Subtle, and unfortunately sometimes not so subtle, pressures may be put on the clinician to produce a certain outcome from the evaluation or a certain type of testimony (e.g., see Wedding, 1991). Further, and even more likely, the neuropsychologist may be pressured by the legal needs to give more definitive answers to questions than data justify. For example, the effects of minor head injury are frequently difficult to distinguish from depression or other emotional reactions, and the disposition of the case may hinge on making such a distinction.

A related question is the limits of a neuropsychologist's competence from a legal perspective. The question of competence can be relevant both to the admissibility of a neuropsychologist's testimony and to the way neuropsychologists present themselves and their data to the court. Regarding the issue of admissibility, most jurisdictions in the United States have found neuropsychologists' testimony admissible regarding the presence or absence of brain damage (Richardson & Adams, 1992). However, in some jurisdictions, a neuropsychologist's testimony regarding causal linkage to a particular event, such as a head injury, has been ruled inadmissible. There are not many rulings regarding the admissibility of neuropsychological testimony with respect to prognosis, but Richardson and Adams (1992) suggested that admissibility of testimony regarding prognosis should be expected to parallel admissibility of testimony regarding causal linkage.

Regarding the way neuropsychologists present themselves and their data, they are often asked to answer questions that may relate to the medical status of the patient. For example, it is not unheard of for a neuropsychologist to be asked questions related to neuropathology or neuroanatomy. The nature and range of testimony that a neuropsychologist should give, irrespective of its admissibility, can become an ethical issue. The ability of neuropsychological tests to predict a given functional outcome is as much at issue here as it is in the rehabilitation arena (see earlier discussion). Faust (1991), for example, suggested that neuropsychologists generally should not testify in forensic cases, in part because the validity for neuropsychological tests to make such predictions has not been established.

Issues of diagnostic accuracy in clinical neuropsychology are a matter of some dispute, especially regarding their usefulness in legal proceedings (e.g., see Faust, 1991; Wedding, 1991; vs. Barth, Ryan, & Hawk, 1991; Richardson & Adams, 1992). Although this author advocates caution in applying clinical neuropsychological findings to forensic as well as rehabilitation and diagnostic cases, it should be noted that some of the reasoning suggesting a lack of diagnostic accuracy is based on studies where clinicians were attempting to make actuarial predictions in the absence of data normally available in most clinical contexts, including forensic evaluations. Although it was once popular to perform "blind" interpretations in clinical neuropsychology, no well-trained clinician today will attempt to make diagnostic statements in the absence of face-to-face contact with the patient, including a diagnostic interview. Although some authors justifiably criticize neuropsychological tests for a lack of functional validity, many of the studies they cite regarding the validity of clinical judgments fail to assess clinical judgment the way it is practiced on a day-to-day basis (see Barth et al., 1991).

Nonetheless, one problematic area for the practice of forensic neuropsychology is the issue of malingering (Faust, 1991). Lezak (1995) described a number of methods designed to detect malingering. The Rey 15-Item Test is one popular method that requires patients to remember 15 items across a short delay. In fact, the items are highly related and routinely grouped into obvious sets, reducing the memory demand. Millis and Kler (1995) showed excellent specificity but limited sensitivity for this test, suggesting it is useful primarily for more blatant dissimulation. Symptom validity testing (Binder & Pankratz, 1987; Pankratz, 1979; Pankratz, Fausti, & Peed, 1975) has also gained some popularity. Using this procedure, a large number of trials of some two-alternative forced-choice procedure relevant to presenting complaints is presented. By chance alone, the patient should obtain a score of 50% correct; with a large number of trials, significant deviation below this level are taken as suggestive of malingering. Although this strategy appears promising, a study by White (1992) demonstrated that informed malingerers (college students) score considerably above the 50% correct level on a symptom validity task for memory, although they score below actual amnesics as well as head-injured patients. Analyses indicated that average response time may be the most promising indicator of conscious efforts to manipulate the data in White's study. His data are relatively consistent with similar data from Bickart, Meyer, and Connell (1991). Slick, Hopp, Strauss, Hunter, and Pinch (1994) had somewhat greater success using a similar strategy to detect malingering when easy and difficult trials were mixed during presentation. Another means for detecting malingering is internal inconsistencies among interview and test data. Finally, studies have shown that indices derived from routinely used neuropsychological tests such as the Recognition Memory Test (Warrington, 1984), the Wechsler Adult Intelligence Scale–Revised (Wechsler, 1981), and the Wechsler Memory Scale (Wechsler, 1945, 1987), and the California Verbal Learning Test (Delis et al., 1987) can be used alone or in combination to assist in detecting malingering (Milanovich, Axelrod, & Millis, 1996; Millis, 1994; Millis, Putnam, Adams, & Ricker, 1995). However, the bottom line regarding malingering at this point in time is that it may be difficult to detect in some instances.

Another issue facing neuropsychologists in forensic cases is the adversarial nature of the legal process. Clinicians who are unfamiliar with the process will most certainly find it a foreign method of seeking "truth." Blau (1984) noted that psychologists should be aware that opinions will be subjected to scrutiny regarding the minutest of details by opposing attorneys. In an adversarial system of justice, the job of the latter is to put the expert opinions you offer to the test. For this reason, opposing attorneys are likely to retain their own psychologists or neuropsychologists to examine test reports and depositions for errors, flawed reasoning, or other ways in which the opinions may lack credibility. Thus, neuropsychologists can expect to have their opinions attacked, sometimes in a fairly sophisticated manner.

Finally, attorneys may find neuropsychological procedures and opinions as foreign as psychologists find legal procedures (Melton et al., 1987; Richardson & Adams, 1992). Not only may attorneys be unfamiliar with the strengths of neuropsychological tests, but it probably should be assumed that jurors will know little about these instruments and their utility. If they do not deal with psychologists often, attorneys may be unfamiliar with rulings that impact on the admissibility of evidence in certain jurisdictions. In addition to having little information about tests, some attorneys also will not know how to identify a qualified neuropsychologist. Poor work done by unqualified professionals will ultimately hurt the credibility and effectiveness of the profession in general.

In summary, a few very basic issues concerning forensic neuropsychology have just been discussed and are outlined in Table 6.4. The practical limitations of our instruments often will limit our ability to answer all the questions an attorney might pose. In the adversarial atmosphere of legal proceedings, some pressure may build to answer questions that might not be capable of being answered. However, the neuropsychologist should note that most attorneys are relatively uninformed about neuropsychological techniques and instruments; further making communication difficult.

Case 6 was a 71-year-old male who was tested 2 months after a motor vehicle

TABLE 6.4
Pitfalls and Principles in Forensic Contexts

Potential Pitfalls in Forensic Applications of Neuropsychological Assessments	Principles for Application of Neuropsychological Assessments in Forensic Contexts
1. Neuropsychologists may be placed under indirect or direct pressure to have their data support a particular point of view.	1a. Limit one's role to acting as the attorney's or the court's consultant regarding various aspects of a case related to neuropsychological issues. 1b. Advise attorneys about the strengths and weaknesses of their case on the basis of the neuropsychological data.
2. Neuropsychologists may be pressured to answer questions for which the data do not justify a clear answer.	2. Clarify ambiguities, but do not try to remove them if the data do not so justify.
3. Neuropsychologists' testimony regarding causation of brain dysfunction has been ruled inadmissible in some jurisdictions.	3. Know rulings in the jurisdiction appropriate to the case regarding neuropsychological testimony.
4. During testimony, neuropsychologists may be asked to testify about matters outside their realm of expertise.	4. Do not testify about matters outside a neuropsychologist's realm of expertise.
5. Validity for predicting specific functional outcomes may be limited.	5a. Know the limitations of test instruments relevant to the purpose for which they are being used. 5b. Recommend gathering functional data if necessary.
6. In some instances, the ability of neuropsychological instruments to detect malingering may be limited.	6a. Employ tests for malingering where appropriate. 6b. Do not overstate the validity of neuropsychological procedures in detecting malingering.
7. The adversarial nature of legal proceedings may be foreign to neuropsychologists.	7a. Prepare testimony as if your colleagues were going to scrutinize it. 7b. Understand and accept attorneys' adversarial role in legal proceedings.
8. Attorneys may be unfamiliar with neuropsychological issues relevant to some cases.	8a. Educate attorneys about relevant neuropsychological issues. 8b. Educate attorneys regarding who is qualified to testify as a neuropsychological expert.

accident. Although the referral came directly from his neurologist, the patient had retained an attorney with whom the clinicians were in contact. The patient was a front-seat occupant in an automobile struck from behind; the force of the impact threw the glasses he was wearing into the rear of the car. He claimed to remember the impact of the accident, and he remembered events soon after the accident with no significant gaps in memory otherwise. Thus, the periods of unconsciousness and/or posttraumatic amnesia were minimal if any. Because of headaches and dizziness subsequent to the accident, the patient had an MR scan 3 weeks after the accident, which demonstrated a left parietal subacute subdural hematoma with minimal impingement on the left occipital horn. Complaints at the time of testing included short-term memory problems, difficulty concentrating, and dizziness and nausea when he tilted his head and looked upward. Headaches had decreased since the accident, however.

The patient had a 12th-grade education, was right-handed, and had a stable blue-collar job history. Medical history included disability retirement in his 50s after ulcer surgery. He had prostate and intestinal surgeries 2 years before the evaluation. He was under treatment for cardiac problems. The patient's wife noted that he had some memory problems prior to the accident.

WAIS–R results showed a significant Verbal–Performance discrepancy in favor of Performance IQ (VIQ = 100, PIQ = 120). Although some difference in this direction might be expected given his background, the magnitude was on the high side. On WMS–R stories, the patient's recall was below expectations at immediate recall (28th percentile), but delayed recall performance was more in line with expectations based upon Verbal IQ performance (52nd percentile). His recall of the Complex Figure followed the same pattern (immediate recall = 37th percentile; delayed recall = 75th percentile). However, almost every aspect of performance on the California Verbal Learning Test was significantly below expectations for his age (total learning trials and delayed free recall trials 2 standard deviations below normative mean, with some improvement on cued recall), suggesting he was having difficulty with rote verbal memory. There was an extraordinary number of intrusions in the CVLT performance as well.

Although most of his language scores were within normal limits (MAE Sentence Repetition = 43rd percentile; MAE Token Test = 82nd percentile; MAE Controlled Oral Word Association = 80th percentile; no errors on Reading Sentences and Paragraphs from Boston Diagnostic Aphasia Examination; Goodglass & Kaplan, 1983), his Visual Naming was below expectations (18th percentile). The source of grammatical and punctuation errors in his writing sample was unclear. Visuospatial performances were within the normal range. Motor performance was within normal limits. Although some executive and frontal functions were within normal limits, he was unable to achieve any sorts in 64 cards of the Wisconsin Card Sorting Test (Heaton, Chelune, Talley, Kay, & Curtiss, 1993).

Thus, the patient had evidence for a subtle language disturbance. He did poorly with rote verbal learning. He had difficulty with problem solving, which was below expectations for his age (Spreen & Strauss, 1991), especially given his IQ. Although these findings could be consistent with a head injury and subsequent left parietal subdural hematoma, there were at least a couple of problems that had an impact on the usefulness of such a statement from a legal as well as a diagnostic standpoint. First, the patient's wife had given a history of memory problems before the accident, and a progressive or other process unrelated to the accident was a possibility. Second, there was a probability of some improvement given the short time between the accident and testing. For these reasons, a reevaluation was recommended and performed 9 months later. Unfortunately, the patient's performance appeared to improve in some areas (e.g., Visual Naming) and decline in other areas (e.g., Performance IQ and delayed recall for WMS–R paragraphs and geometric designs). One might have expected some improvement if the head injury and subdural hematoma had been the cause of impairments. On the other hand, one might have expected decline if progressive dementia had been the cause of the original performance deficits. Thus, neither pattern was supported. Neuropsychological assessment, therefore, was not able to clarify the issue of causality, even after repeated assessment. These findings were carefully and clearly stated given the legal implications.

Principles for Application

On the right-hand side of Table 6.4, some general principles for applying neuropsychological assessments to the forensic context are outlined. These principles are indexed by number to the problem on the left-hand side of the table for which the principle provides a solution. Foremost among these applications is getting a proper conceptualization of the job a neuropsychologist must perform in forensic settings. The job is not to tell the attorney what will best strengthen the case if the data do not justify it. If the opposing attorney has competent experts, this will ultimately weaken the case. In the forensic setting, neuropsychologists frequently can conceptualize their role as a consultative one to the attorney and the court. On the basis of the best interpretation of the data, the neuropsychologist can advise the attorney regarding the meaning of the data and its potential impact on the case. If the interpretation substantially weakens the case, the attorney should know why this is so. Of course, this is a collaborative effort, and hopefully the attorney will be willing to discuss the case he or she is building with the psychologist. In general, the "hired gun" philosophy of testifying is to be avoided. When data are distorted to fit the "needs" of a case, every one ultimately loses because the system will be hindered in reaching a reasonable approximation of the facts. If ambiguities exist in the data and a definitive conclusion cannot be reached, explain the nature of the ambiguities clearly.

The neuropsychologist who does not testify frequently may find it difficult to keep up with the changing precedents regarding neuropsychological expert testimony in the appropriate jurisdiction. In such instances, the neuropsychologist might consider asking the attorney with whom the practitioner is working for the relevant rulings. If the attorney seems unaware that such precedents might exist, then the neuropsychologist can inform the attorney that such rulings do exist in some jurisdictions. The neuropsychologist who makes a significant part of a livelihood by testifying frequently should make an attempt to keep up on rulings in relevant jurisdictions that may affect neuropsychological testimony. If an attorney is unaware of the relevant rulings, that person can be informed of them.

Another principle is: Do not testify about matters outside a neuropsychologist's area of expertise. On the surface, this seems relatively straightforward. However, results obtained by other professionals may play a prominent role in reaching a neuropsychological opinion. One state supreme court ruled a doctor might testify regarding the results obtained by another professional if such results were customarily used by the medical profession in arriving at opinions (Rothke, 1992). It is unclear when and where such a ruling might apply to psychologists, but when in doubt, one can consult the attorney with whom one is working.

As noted earlier, some (e.g., Faust, 1991) have suggested that limited evidence regarding the validity of neuropsychological tests in predicting functional outcomes is one factor that should preclude neuropsychologists from acting as expert witnesses. Although the present author wholeheartedly agrees with comments regarding the limitations of test data for predicting specific functional outcomes, the position that neuropsychologists should not act as expert witnesses seems extreme. Most neuropsychological instruments have been developed to measure cognitive status, not functional ability, though there are a few notable exceptions (e.g., Rivermead Behavioural Memory Test; Wilson, Cockburn, & Baddeley, 1991). The validity of many neuropsychological tests for detecting cognitive dysfunction related to brain injury or disease is actually quite good and useful forensically (Barth et al., 1991). Further, in combination with a good history regarding functional activities, neuropsychological tests may indeed be helpful in distinguishing the reasons for functional difficulties in a way that may have functional prognostic significance. This may especially be true for neuropsychologists who have developed some expertise in rehabilitation and are in a position to understand the relationship between their test scores and eventual outcomes. Nonetheless, it is incumbent on the neuropsychologist to acknowledge the limitations of the test scores in predicting functional outcomes. The neuropsychologist should be familiar with limitations of the tests used for particular applications. Specific functional evaluations can be recommended when relevant and available. But it is up to the trier of facts (i.e., the court) to determine the weight given to neuropsychological evidence (Richardson & Adams, 1992).

Richardson and Adams (1992) recommended that the best approach to causation is to use a "historically structured fact-based approach" (p. 306). Such an approach might emphasize functioning before the injury and after the injury, the reports and tests reviewed, the results of tests given by the neuropsychologist, and facts established through other sources. In some jurisdictions, Richardson and Adams recommended avoiding a "medical" or physiological approach to establishing causation. These matters should be discussed with the attorney with whom the neuropsychologist is working prior to testimony.

Regarding malingering, the neuropsychologist can consider employing tests designed to detect malingering when indicated. However, the ability of these tests to detect malingering should not be overstated. Additionally, interview, test, and history data can be examined for internal inconsistencies that might indicate a conscious effort to manipulate test outcomes. Specific interview tactics may be designed to assess whether the patient will exaggerate complaints. For example, the examiner might question a patient about the presence of specific improbable symptoms to ascertain if the patient tends to overendorse pathology.

Given that an opposing attorney might also hire a neuropsychologist to examine test data and statements for veracity, testimony should be prepared as if one's colleagues were going to examine it. Such preparation will lessen the likelihood that it will be discredited.

Regarding the legal process, whether it is criminal or civil, the neuropsychologist must realize it is adversarial in nature. As such, it is a substantially different method of attempting to establish facts than are our methods of inquiry. The validity of the diagnostic opinion will usually not be taken as a given. Questioning of the validity of an opinion should not be taken personally but should be assumed as a part of the procedure.

In the process of preparing a case, attorneys will be better consumers of neuropsychological information if they are well informed about the nature and limitations of the data. Further, several authors (e.g., Richardson & Adams, 1992; Rothke, 1992; Satz, 1988) have suggested that neuropsychologists educate attorneys regarding who is qualified as an expert in neuropsychology. It has been suggested that American Psychological Association Division 40 guidelines (INS-Division 40 Task Force on Education, Accreditation, and Credentialing, 1987) be used as criteria.

In summary, neuropsychological data can be helpful to courts and attorneys in making legal decisions. If neuropsychological information is to be useful, however, it must be presented in a relatively objective manner by a qualified professional. Although not perfect, our data may be among the best available in answering certain types of questions. When appropriate, it is necessary that limitations of neuropsychological findings be clearly stated. In rendering opinions, the experienced neuropsychologist remains mindful of limitations, including ability to detect malingering.

GIVING FEEDBACK TO PATIENTS AND FAMILIES

Importance of Providing Feedback

In order to maximize the usefulness of a neuropsychological evaluation to the patient, it is often desirable to give the patient feedback about performance. Feedback can be used to provide information about cognitive strengths and weaknesses and to enact interventions that will facilitate performance on various functional activities. Indeed, feedback is considered such an integral aspect of psychological evaluation that it has been mandated by the recently revised American Psychological Association ethical standards (Principle 2.09; American Psychological Association, 1992). However, this process should not be undertaken lightly by the clinician. It is the part of a neuropsychological evaluation that may take the most skill and experience.

The difficulty predicting a specific functional outcome from neuropsychological test scores is among the most important limitations. As already mentioned, errors in prognostic statements can have a devastating impact on patients and families, not only in terms of practical decisions but also in terms of patients' self-esteem. A particular patient's level of acceptance may determine how much information about deficits that person is able to process. Although it is desirable that patients be maximally aware of their deficits, too large a single dose of awareness may cause anxiety, resentment, or anger, and paradoxically increase denial.

Generally, brain–behavior relationships are quite complex and not easily understood by lay persons. In addition, behavioral neuroscientists use terminology that is unfamiliar to lay persons or differs from common usage. For example, when neuropsychologists speak of "short-term" memory, they often are referring to the type of memory in which information is held in temporary storage and lasts less than a minute. When a lay person speaks of "short-term" memory, most frequently they are referring to recent as opposed to remote memory. Thus, when giving feedback about testing, the neuropsychologist cannot assume basic knowledge necessary to understand test results, nor can neuropsychologists assume lay persons understand the professional jargon they use for a shorthand among themselves on a daily basis. Many patients and their family members will be somewhat intimidated by psychologists or other health care professionals. If so, they may not ask questions about data they do not understand. Because questions from patients and family members give the neuropsychologist feedback regarding what patients do and do not understand, the lack of such interactive feedback makes it difficult to know what concepts are understood. It almost does not need to be said that neuropsychological information is of no use to patients and families if they do not understand it.

Another potential problem in giving feedback is that neuropsychological assessments are usually deficit oriented. It is by discovering and analyzing deficit patterns that we make diagnostic statements and determine what cognitive problems might underlie specific functional deficits. It is a mistake, however, to focus exclusively or even primarily on deficits when delivering feedback (or when planning rehabilitative treatment). Focusing primarily on deficits may make patients feel devastated, significantly injuring self-esteem and making them more vulnerable to depression. Or, it can have the effect of activating denial in order to protect an understandably fragile self-esteem. In formal rehabilitation efforts or in struggling to make an adjustment to brain dysfunction, some level of self-esteem, as well as some degree of self-awareness, is helpful in accepting changes in functioning and its implications. Therefore, the neuropsychologist must be aware of the potential impact of feedback regarding deficits and consider strengths as well.

A final consideration in giving feedback about assessment results is the other professionals who are working with the patient. At times it is proper for the neuropsychologist to give feedback, whereas at other times it may be better for other health care professionals to give feedback about test results. For example, when neuropsychological assessment is done for diagnostic reasons, it may be only one source of information used to make a diagnosis. A referring neurologist or psychiatrist may be using CT or MR scans, various lab tests, response to medications, consultations from other professionals, their own medical examinations and histories, and other sources of information to assist in making a diagnosis. In such instances, it is important that giving neuropsychological feedback not interfere with the patient care provided by the referring professional or provide premature diagnostic closure. The potential impact of conflicting information must be considered when deciding whether or not to give feedback and when to give it.

Problems arising in giving neuropsychological feedback to patients are summarized on the left-hand side of Table 6.5. The primary challenge of feedback is to make assessment results meaningful and useful to patients. The obstacles to doing so include limitations in predicting functional abilities from neuropsychological tests, the ability of patients and family to accept feedback, limited basic knowledge of patients and family, and a temptation on the part of the neuropsychologist to focus primarily upon deficits. The neuropsychologist should also consider the appropriateness of and timing for giving direct feedback in individual cases.

Case 7 was a woman in her 20s. She was involved in a motor vehicle accident approximately 2.5 years before testing and was self-referred because of increased academic difficulties. She was not unconscious after the accident, by her own recollection. However, she was confused periodically for about a day, and posttraumatic headaches led her to seek medical attention 1 day after the accident. A CT scan at that time was unremarkable. Previously an excellent student, she began to have academic difficulties after the accident. She attributed the academic difficulties to memory problems. By the time she was seen, the "memory" difficulties were better, but she reported she was not back to premorbid levels and was still having some academic difficulty. In particular, she stated that she had to read material twice before she could remember it, a change from premorbid functioning.

The patient had above average intellectual functioning (Verbal IQ = 105, Performance IQ = 117). Memory testing was also above average for both verbal memory (California Verbal Learning Test) and visual memory (Rey–Osterrieth

TABLE 6.5
Pitfalls and Principles for Giving Feedback to Patients and Families

Potential Pitfalls in Giving Patients and Families Feedback About Neuropsychological Assessments	Principles for Giving Feedback About Neuropsychological Assessments to Patients and Family Members
1. Limitations in predicting functional abilities from neuropsychological data may decrease the usefulness of the information for patients and family members.	1. Conduct feedback sessions in an interactive, collaborative fashion in which the functional importance of findings can be further explored with patients and family members.
2. Patients' and family members' level of acceptance of the consequences of neurological impairment may limit their ability to accept feedback.	2. Try to estimate a patient's level of emotional acceptance, and look for signs that the patient may be having trouble with acceptance during feedback.
3. Patients and family members may have a limited knowledge base to aid in the understanding of neuropsychological data.	3a. Check frequently with patients and family members to make certain they are understanding the various concepts being presented.
	3b. Check frequently with patients and family members to ascertain that they have the basic knowledge to comprehend assessment results.
	3c. When basic knowledge is not present, educate the patient and family.
4. A deficit-oriented approach to feedback can have a negative emotional impact on patients and family members.	4. Present balanced feedback, focusing on cognitive strengths as well as deficits.
5. It may not always be appropriate for the neuropsychologist to give extensive feedback to the patient, particularly if the assessment is being used by another health care professional as a part of a more extended diagnostic process.	5. Communicate with referral sources to ascertain the appropriateness of giving feedback to patients.

Complex Figure). Because minor head injury frequently causes attentional problems, tests with attentional components were given (Paced Auditory Serial Addition Test, Stroop Neuropsychological Screening Test, Auditory Consonant Trigrams). Performances on all these tests were within normal limits. On the other hand, the patient had a significantly below normal score on the Boston Naming Test (4 standard deviations below normative mean). Her Spelling score on the Wide Range Achievement Test-Revised (Jastak & Wilkinson, 1984) was below average (25th percentile). When this issue was discussed with the patient's mother after the test score was obtained, she indicated that the patient had been an excellent speller before the accident, but had lost this ability. The patient also admitted that spelling had been a problem since the accident when this score was brought to her attention. Although the patient scored within normal limits on literal (72nd percentile) and inferential (64th percentile) reading comprehension, her ability to read quickly (24th percentile) was more problematic (Stanford Diagnostic Reading Test; Karlsen, Madden, & Gardner, 1974).

Taking all these facets into consideration, it was determined that the patient had a subtle language difficulty. Actually, she was already using a spell-check program on her computer when she wrote papers for school. After consulting with a speech/language pathologist, it was decided that the patient's language difficulty was not severe enough to justify treatment, although there was agreement on the diagnosis. During feedback, the word-finding difficulties were verified; she experienced them on an occasional basis. Some effort was made to differentiate for the patient between memory difficulty, which she thought she had, and the subtle language deficits she demonstrated. Some of the "memory" problems she described were probably related to word retrieval difficulty. It was emphasized that memory might actually be considered a strength. Additional recommendations were made. It was recommended that she try to explain the concept or use an alternative word when she had word-finding difficulty. One of the main issues concerned course load, and it was recommended that she take a reduced course load. Finally, it was suggested that the patient could seek special services at school. The office of student services at her school often worked with students and professors to minimize learning problems.

Prior to testing in this case, the neuropsychologist suspected that the patient would have attention and memory problems, which can occur after minor head injury. When language problems were found instead, further interviewing was done during assessment and feedback to confirm spelling and word-finding problems. Reading problems were consistent with self-report during interview. Because the patient had not recognized the difference between language problems and memory deficit, this difference was explained, and the strength in her memory performance was noted. Recommendations were made on the basis of test findings. This case example illustrates how the feedback session can be used as part of ongoing assessment. The neuropsychologist may need to seek further information after reviewing test findings, either during the evaluation or during the feedback session. This case also demonstrates how the patient's understanding of a problem may need to be corrected or modified to facilitate optimum adjustment to deficits.

Principles for Application

Principles for giving feedback to patients and family members are presented on the right-hand side of Table 6.5. Principles are indexed by number to the problems on the left-hand side of Table 6.5 for which they provide a solution. First, many of the functional limitations of neuropsychological tests can be overcome by conducting feedback sessions in an interactive and collaborative fashion, encouraging the participation of patients and family members. The feedback session should not be considered simply a vehicle for imparting knowledge to the patient and his/her family. It should also be considered an opportunity for gathering further information that will help the neuropsychologist understand the patient and will help the patient and family understand the difficulties present and the strengths that can be used to increase functional capabilities. For example, when discussing a memory problem, the neuropsychologist may ask several questions to ascertain under what circumstances the patient might have noticed the memory problem (if it had not already been covered in interview). The neuropsychologist should also check frequently to make certain the patient and family are understanding the feedback and initiate further elaboration as warranted.

Because the patient's or the family's level of emotional acceptance may affect how well they can integrate feedback, the neuropsychologist should attempt to estimate the level of acceptance. This may be done by noting what the patient does when he or she is having significant difficulty with tasks during evaluation and by noting how the patient reacts to questions about deficits during interview. Probes may also be made during the initial part of the feedback session. Patients can be asked how they felt they did during testing, or it can be noted that some problems were found and ask if it surprises the patient or family member. The neuropsychologist can also watch the patient and family for reactions to specific feedback that may indicate difficulty accepting the feedback. At such points in the feedback session, differences between the neuropsychologist and the patient and family generally should be clarified. The process of clarification potentially can add information about the nature of deficits from a functional standpoint. It may be that differences of opinion can be resolved through clarification. Even if differences cannot be resolved, it is often best if the differences can be clearly stated. In working through this process, it should be remembered that the patient and family are entitled to an opinion, and that opinion may be different than that of the neuropsychologist. Reaching total correspondence of opinion between patient, family, and neuropsychologist is not necessarily the goal of every feedback session. Patients and family may be able to understand the importance of feedback at a later time when its relevance is more immediate or when they are more ready to accept it. Efforts to obtain agreement regarding feedback when patients and family are not ready to accept it may lessen the possibility that they can use the information when circumstances change.

Not infrequently, patients and family will not have some basic piece of information that would help them to understand some deficit or strength clearly. For example, a problem with word finding might not be well differentiated from other types of memory problems by patients. In such instances, the differences between word-finding problems and the ability to acquire new information may have to be emphasized, as in the case example just given. As another example of misunderstanding a deficit, a patient might understand a hemianopia as a difficulty seeing out of one eye. The neuropsychologist should be frequently checking for such misunderstandings during feedback sessions. Patients and family members should be educated regarding such basic facts as necessary and appropriate.

On a different issue, the difficulty that giving deficit-oriented feedback presents can be addressed by giving more balanced feedback that emphasizes both strengths and deficits. Often, emphasizing strengths as well as weaknesses will allow a patient to leave a feedback session feeling that one's self-concept is more intact. Because the probability of denial being invoked is related to the degree of perceived threat to self-esteem, emphasizing strengths will reduce the probability of eliciting denial. If some modicum of hope can be fostered by taking strengths into account, then the patient also may be more ready to participate in rehabilitation. Finally, it should be noted that presenting both strengths and weakness gives a more accurate picture of the patient's functioning than focusing entirely on deficits.

Lastly, it may not always be obvious when a neuropsychologist should give extensive feedback regarding testing and when this should be avoided or delayed. Such a decision may depend partly on the preferences of the referral source, but other factors should be taken into account as well. In some instances, it might be desirable to delay feedback until a more definitive diagnosis is reached. For example, the nature of feedback might change if a patient has a degenerative process versus some more stable or improving condition. Such dilemmas can be most easily resolved by communicating with the referral source and jointly making a decision about giving feedback. In instances where the neuropsychologist works frequently with a single referral source in certain types of cases, it is possible that routine procedures regarding feedback can be developed.

In summary, feedback is most useful to patients and family if it is presented in an interactive and collaborative environment where the functional implications of the data can be further explored. The neuropsychologist can also check to make certain that patients and family understand feedback and have the basic knowledge necessary to understand it. Education and clarification may be necessary. Another principle of feedback is to present strengths as well as weaknesses. Finally, the neuropsychologist will need to check with referral sources about the appropriateness of extensive neuropsychological feedback.

CONCLUSIONS

The potential problems in applications of neuropsychological assessment are numerous. This chapter has attempted to present a few, but there are numerous issues that have been not been addressed. A more complete enumeration and classification of applications problems would take an entire volume; so the current chapter should be considered only a sampling.

The potential issues in any particular assessment will depend on a variety of factors. Among the most important are the referral source to whom assessment findings are addressed and the referral question. This chapter has attempted to show how different contexts for evaluations might lead to modification of clinical practice. In so doing, evaluations were divided into diagnostic, rehabilitative, and forensic. However, knowing the general type of evaluation is usually not enough. For example, questions may differ between inpatient and outpatient rehabilitation programs; stroke rehabilitation versus head injury rehabilitation programs will generate varying types of questions. With each different question come different potential problems. Further, even rehabilitation programs treating identical patient populations may differ significantly if they are structured differently. For example, in some outpatient rehabilitation programs the neuropsychologist may have responsibility for conducting cognitive rehabilitation, and in others, the neuropsychologist may play only a consultative role for this endeavor. Each potential role raises different demands on assessment, and clinical practice will vary to some degree with the different demands.

One factor that is common to all assessment contexts is the important functional aspects of behavior that neuropsychological tests may not measure. Although attempts are being made to develop more ecologically valid measures, it seems unlikely that neuropsychologists will ever opt for completely functional batteries. The attempt to specify how cognition breaks down is an important endeavor, and cannot be determined in the relatively brief behavioral sample of an evaluation if complex functional tasks are used. Perhaps what we must learn is that many specific breakdowns in cognition do not imply a corresponding functional deficit on a one-to-one basis. Yet understanding the breakdown in cognition may have important functional implications once the cognitive evaluation and a functional evaluation are collated. Even then, functional implications may not be entirely understood until treatment is well under way. If this is the case, then neuropsychologists may always have to be aware of the functional limitations of their instruments. We can seek other sources of functional information, including patients' and family members' observations, functional evaluations conducted by other professionals, and frequently most importantly, observations of patients performing various functional activities during treatment.

Unfortunately, no "cookbook" approach to applications issues in neuropsychological assessment will ever be successful. Ultimately, individual clinicians will have to assess the environments in which they practice, the needs of their referral sources, and the needs of their patients and families. From this assessment, potential applications issues can be determined, and means for addressing the problems can be developed. As a clinician's day-to-day practice evolves, new problems will be discovered, and ways of addressing them will be devised. In other words, the good clinician will be constantly alert for problems in the application of neuropsychological assessment results and ways of managing them.

REFERENCES

Alberts, M. S. & Binder, L. M. (1991). Premorbid psychosocial factors that influence cognitive rehabilitation following traumatic brain injury. In J. S. Kreutzer & P. H. Wehman (Eds.), *Cognitive Rehabilitation for Persons with Traumatic Brain Injury* (pp. 95–103). Baltimore, MD: Paul H. Brookes.

Alfano, D. P., Neilson, P. M., Paniak, C. E., and Finlayson, M. A. J. (1992). The MMPI and closed-head injury. *The Clinical Neuropsychologist, 6,* 134–142.

American Psychiatric Association. (1994). *Diagnostic and statistical manual of mental disorders* (4th ed.). Washington, DC: American Psychiatric Association.

American Psychological Association. (1974). *Standards for educational and psychological tests.* Washington, DC: American Psychological Association.

American Psychological Association. (1987). *Casebook on ethical principles of psychologists.* Washington, DC: American Psychological Association.

American Psychological Association. (1992). Ethical principles of psychologists and code of conduct. *American Psychologist, 47,* 1597–1611.

Andreasen, N. C., Ehrhardt, J. C., Swayze, V. W., Alliger, R. J., Yuh, W. T. C., Cohen, B., & Ziebell, S. (1990). Magnetic resonance imaging of the brain in schizophrenia: The pathophysiologic significance of structural abnormalities. *Archives of General Psychiatry, 47,* 35–44.

Barco, P. P., Crosson, B., Bolesta, M. M., Werts, D., & Stout, R. (1991). Training awareness and compensation in postacute head injury rehabilitation. In J. S. Kreutzer & P. H. Wehman (Eds.), *Cognitive rehabilitation for persons with traumatic brain injury* (pp. 129–146). Baltimore, MD: Paul H. Brookes.

Barr, W. B., Bilder, R. M., Goldberg, E., Kaplan, E., & Mukherjee, S. (1989). The neuropsychology of schizophrenic speech. *Journal of Communication Disorders, 22,* 327–349.

Barr, W. B., Chelune, G. J., Hermann, B. P., Loring, D. W., Perrine, K., Strauss, E., Trenerry, M. R., & Westerveld, M. (1997). The use of figural reproduction tests as measures of nonverbal memory in epilepsy surgery candidates. *Journal of the International Neuropsychological Society, 3,* 435–443.

Barth, J. T., Ryan, T. V., & Hawk, G. L. (1991). Forensic neuropsychology: A reply to the method skeptics. *Neuropsychology Review, 2,* 251–266.

Bauer, R. M., Briere, J., Crosson, B., Gilmore, R., Fennell, E. B., & Roper, S. (1995). Neuropsychological functioning before and after unilateral temporal lobectomy for intractable epilepsy. *Journal of the International Neuropsychological Society, 1,* 362.

Benton, A. L., & Hamsher, K. de S. (1989). *Multilingual aphasia examination* (2nd ed.). Iowa City, IA: AJA Associates, Inc.

Bickart, W. T., Meyer, R. G., & Connell, D. K. (1991). The symptom validity technique as a measure of feigned short-term memory deficit. *American Journal of Forensic Psychology, 9*(2), 3–11.

Binder, L. M. & Pankratz, L. (1987). Neuropsychological evidence of a factitious memory complaint. *Journal of Clinical and Experimental Neuropsychology, 9,* 167–171.

Blau, T. H. (1984). *The psychologist as expert witness.* New York: John Wiley & Sons.

Bogerts, B., Meertz, E., & Schonfeldt-Bausch, R. (1985). Basal ganglia and limbic system pathology in schizophrenia: A morphometric study. *Archives of General Psychiatry, 42,* 784–791.

Butters, N. (1985). Alcoholic Korsakoff's syndrome: Some issues concerning etiology, neuropathology, and cognitive deficits. *Journal of Clinical and Experimental Neuropsychology, 7,* 181–210.

Condray, R., Steinhauer, S. R., van Kammen, D. P., & Kasparek, A. (1996). Working memory capacity predicts language comprehension in schizophrenic patients. *Schizophrenia Research, 20,* 1–13.

Crosson, B. (1987). Treatment of interpersonal deficits for head-trauma patients in inpatient rehabilitation settings. *The Clinical Neuropsychologist, 1,* 335–352.

Crosson, B., Barco, P. P., Velozo, C. A., Bolesta, M. M., Cooper, P. V., Werts, D., & Brobeck, T. C. (1989). Awareness and compensation in post-acute head injury rehabilitation. *Journal of Head Trauma Rehabilitation, 4*(3), 46–54.

Damasio, A. R., & Anderson, S. W. (1993). The frontal lobes. In K. M. Heilman & E. Valenstein (Eds.), *Clinical neuropsychology* (pp. 409–460). New York: Oxford University Press.

Delis, D. C., Kaplan, E., & Kramer, J. H. (in press-a). *California Sorting Test.* San Antonio, TX: Psychological Corporation.

Delis, D. C., Kaplan, E., & Kramer, J. H. (in press-b). *Delis-Kaplan Executive Function Scale.* San Antonio, TX: Psychological Corporation.

Delis, D. C., Kramer, J. H., Kaplan, E., & Ober, B. A. (1987). *California Verbal Learning Test.* San Antonio, TX: Psychological Corporation.

Delis, D. C., Squire, L. R., Bihrle, A., & Massman, P. (1992). Componential analysis of problem-solving ability: Performance of patients with frontal lobe damage and amnesic patients on a new sorting test. *Neuropsychologia, 30,* 683–697.

Doerr, H. O., & Carlin, A. S. (Eds.). (1991). *Forensic neuropsychology: Legal and scientific bases.* New York: Guilford Press.

Eslinger, P. J., & Damasio, A. R. (1985). Disturbance of higher cognition after bilateral frontal lobe ablation: Patient EVR. *Neurology, 35,* 1731–1741.

Faust, D. (1991). Forensic neuropsychology: The art of practicing a science that does not yet exist. *Neuropsychology Review, 2,* 205–231.

Gentilini, M., Nichelli, P., & Schoenhuber, R. (1989). Assessment of attention in mild head injury. In H. S. Levin, H. M. Eisenberg, & A. L. Benton (Eds.), *Mild head injury* (pp. 163–175). New York: Oxford University Press.

Goodglass, H., & Kaplan, E. (1983). *Boston diagnostic aphasia examination.* Philadelphia: Lea & Febiger.

Gronwall, D. (1989). Cumulative and persisting effects of concussion on attention and cognition. In H. S. Levin, H. M. Eisenberg, & A. L. Benton (Eds.), *Mild head injury* (pp. 153–162). New York: Oxford University Press.

Grove, W. M., & Andreasen, N. C. (1985). Language and thinking in psychosis: Is there an input abnormality? *Archives of General Psychiatry, 42,* 26–32.

Hass, J. F., Cope, D. N., & Hall, K. (1987). Premorbid prevalence of poor academic performance in severe head injury. *Journal of Neurology, Neurosurgery, and Psychiatry, 50,* 52–56.

Haxby, J. V., Raffaele, K., Gillette, J., Schapiro, M. B., & Rapoport, S. I. (1992). Individual trajectories of cognitive decline in patients of the Alzheimer type. *Journal of Clinical and Experimental Neuropsychology, 14,* 575–592.

Heaton, R. K., Chelune, G. J., Talley, J. L., Kay, G. G., & Curtiss, G. (1993). *Wisconsin Card Sorting Test manual: Revised and expanded.* Odessa, FL: Psychological Assessment Resources.

Heaton, R. K., & Crowley, T. J. (1981). Effects of psychiatric disorders and their somatic treatments on neuropsychological test results. In S. B. Filskov & T. J. Boll (Eds.), *Handbook of clinical neuropsychology* (pp. 481–525). New York: John Wiley & Sons.

Heilman, K. M., Watson, R. T., & Valenstein, E. (1993). Neglect and related disorders. In K. M. Heilman & E. Valenstein (Eds.), *Clinical neuropsychology* (3rd ed., pp. 279–336). New York: Oxford University Press.

Hoffman, R. E., Stopek, S., & Andreasen, N. C. (1986). A comparative study of manic vs schizophrenic speech disorganization. *Archives of General Psychiatry, 43,* 831–838.

INS-Division 40 Task Force on Education, Accreditation, and Credentialing. (1987). Guidelines for doctoral training programs in clinical neuropsychology. *The Clinical Neuropsychologist, 1,* 29–34.

Jastak, S., & Wilkinson, G. S. (1984). *Wide Range Achievement Test–Revised.* Wilmington, DE: Jastak Associates, Inc.

Jennett, B., Snoek, J., Bond, M. R., & Brooks, N. (1981). Disability after severe head injury: Observations on the use of the Glasgow Outcome Scale. *Journal of Neurology, Neurosurgery, and Psychiatry, 44,* 285–293.

Jennett, B., & Teasdale, G. (1981). *Management of head injury.* Philadelphia: F. A. Davis.

Jones-Gotman, M., & Milner, B. (1978). Right temporal-lobe contribution to image-mediated verbal learning. *Neuropsychologia, 16,* 61–71.

Kaplan, E., Fein, D., Morris, R., & Delis, D. C. (1991). *WAIS–R as a Neuropsychological Instrument.* San Antonio, TX: Psychological Corporation.

Kaplan, E., Goodglass, H., & Weintraub, S. (1983). *Boston Naming Test.* Philadelphia: Lea & Febiger.

Karlsen, B., Madden, R., & Gardner, E. F. (1974). *Stanford Reading Test.* New York: Harcourt Brace Jovanovich.

King, D. A., & Caine, E. D. (1990). Depression. In J. L. Cummings (Ed.), *Subcortical dementia* (pp. 218–230). New York: Oxford University Press.

Kitzinger, H., & Blumberg, E. (1951). Supplemental guide for administering and scoring the Wechsler–Bellevue Intelligence Scale (Form 1). *Psychological Monographs, 65*, 1–20.

Levin, H. S. (1989). Memory deficit after closed-head injury. *Journal of Clinical and Experimental Neuropsychology, 12*, 129–153.

Levin, H. S., Benton, A. L., & Grossman, R. G. (1981). *Neurobehavioral consequences of closed head injury.* New York: Oxford University Press.

Levin, H. S., High, W. M., & Eisenberg, H. M. (1988). Learning and forgetting during posttraumatic amnesia in head injured patients. *Journal of Neurology, Neurosurgery, and Psychiatry, 51*, 14–20.

Lezak, M. D. (1978). Living with the characterologically altered brain injured patient. *Journal of Clinical Psychiatry, 39*, 592–598.

Lezak, M. D. (1986). Assessment for rehabilitation planning. In M. J. Meier, A. L. Benton, & L. Diller (Eds.), *Neuropsychological rehabilitation* (pp. 41–58). New York: Guilford Press.

Lezak, M. D. (1995). *Neuropsychological Assessment* (3rd ed.). New York: Oxford University Press.

Mandleberg, I. A., & Brooks, D. N. (1975). Cognitive recovery after severe head injury: Serial testing on the Wechsler Adult Intelligence Scale. *Journal of Neurology, Neurosurgery, and Psychiatry, 38*, 1121–1126.

Melton, G. B., Petrila, J., Poythress, N. G., & Slobogin, C. (1987). *Psychological evaluations for the courts.* New York: Guilford Press.

Milanovich, J. R., Axelrod, B. N., & Millis, S. R. (1996). Validation of the Simulation Index–Revised with a mixed clinical population. *Archives of Clinical Neuropsychology, 11*, 53–59.

Millis, S. R. (1994). The Recognition Memory Test in the detection of malingered and exaggerated memory deficits. *The Clinical Neuropsychologist, 8*, 406–414.

Millis, S. R., & Kler, S. (1995). Limitations of the Rey Fifteen-Item Test in the detection of malingering. *The Clinical Neuropsychologist, 9*, 241–244.

Millis, S. R., Putnam, S. H., Adams, K. M., & Ricker, J. H. (1995). The California Verbal Learning Test in the detection of incomplete effort in neuropsychological evaluation. *Psychological Assessment, 7*, 463–471.

Milner, B. (1970). Memory and the medial temporal regions of the brain. In K. H. Pribram and D. E. Broadbent (Eds.), *Biology of memory* (pp. 29–50). New York: Academic Press.

Pankratz, L. (1979). Symptom validity testing and symptom retraining: Procedures for the assessment and treatment of functional sensory deficits. *Journal of Consulting and Clinical Psychology, 47*, 409–410.

Pankratz, L., Fausti, S. A., & Peed, S. (1975). A forced-choice technique to evaluate deafness in the hysterical or malingering patient. *Journal of Consulting and Clinical Psychology, 43*, 421–422.

Parsons, M., Kortenkamp, S., Bauer, R., Gilmore, R., & Roper, S. (1995). Continuous Visual Memory Test in an epilepsy surgery population: Presurgical discrimination and sensitivity to hippocampal pathology. *Journal of the International Neuropsychological Society, 3*, 9.

Porteus, S. D. (1959). *The maze test and clinical psychology.* Palo, CA: Pacific Books.

Posner, M. I., Early, T. S., Reiman, E. M., Pardo, P. J., & Dhawan, M. (1988). Asymmetries in hemispheric control of attention in schizophrenia. *Archives of General Psychiatry, 45*, 814–821.

Posner, M. I., & Rafal, R. D. (1986). Cognitive theories of attention and the rehabilitation of attentional deficits. In M. J. Meier, A. L. Benton, & L. Diller (Eds.), *Neuropsychological rehabilitation* (pp. 182–201). New York: Guilford Press.

Povlishock, J. T., & Coburn, T. H. (1989). Morphopathological change associated with mild head injury. In H. S. Levin, H. M. Eisenberg, & A. L. Benton (Eds.), *Mild head injury* (pp. 37–53). New York: Oxford University Press.

Prigatano, G. P. (1986). Psychotherapy after brain injury. In G. P. Prigatano (Ed.), *Neuropsychological rehabilitation after brain injury* (pp. 67–95). Baltimore, MD: The Johns Hopkins University Press.

Prigatano, G. P. (1991). Disturbances of self-awareness of deficit after traumatic brain injury. In G. P. Prigatano & D. L. Schacter (Eds.), *Awareness of deficit after brain injury: Clinical and theoretical issues* (pp. 111–126). New York: Oxford University Press.

Rapaport, D., Gill, M., & Schafer, R. (1945). *Diagnostic psychological testing: Vol. 1.* Chicago: Year Book.

Richardson, R. E. L., & Adams, R. L. (1992). Neuropsychologists as expert witnesses: Issues of admissibility. *The Clinical Neuropsychologist, 6,* 295–308.

Rimel, R. W., Girodani, B., Barth, J. T., Boll, T. J., & Jane, J. A. (1981). Disability caused by minor head injury. *Neurosurgery, 9,* 221–228.

Robinson, R. G., Kubos, K. L., Starr, L. B., Rao, K., & Price, T. R. (1984). Mood disorders in stroke patients: Importance of location of lesion. *Brain, 107,* 81–93.

Rothke, S. (1992). Expert testimony by neuropsychologists: Addendum to Schwartz and Satz. *The Clinical Neuropsychologist, 6,* 85–91.

Satz, P. (1988). Neuropsychological testimony: Some emerging concerns. *The Clinical Neuropsychologist, 2,* 89–100.

Slick, D., Hopp, G., Strauss, E., Hunter, M., & Pinch, D. (1994). Detecting dissimulation: Profiles of simulated malingerers, traumatic brain-injury patients, and normal controls on a revised version of Hiscock and Hiscock's forced-choice memory test. *Journal of Clinical and Experimental Neuropsychology, 16,* 472–481.

Spreen, O., & Strauss, E. (1991). *A compendium of neuropsychological tests: Administration, norms, and commentary.* New York: Oxford University Press.

Sohlberg, M. M., & Mateer, C. A. (1989). *Introduction to cognitive rehabilitation: Theory and practice.* New York: Guilford Press.

Starkstein, S. E., Robinson, R. G., Berthier, M. L., Parikh, R. M., & Price, T. R. (1988). Differential mood changes following basal ganglia vs thalamic lesions. *Archives of Neurology, 45,* 725–730.

Starkstein, S. E., Robinson, R. G., & Price, T. R. (1987). Comparison of cortical and subcortical lesions in the production of poststroke mood disorders. *Brain, 110,* 1045–1059.

Stuss, D. T. (1991). Self, awareness, and the frontal lobes: A neuropsychological perspective. In J. Strauss & G. R. Goethals (Eds.), *The self: An interdisciplinary approach* (pp. 255–278). New York: Springer-Verlag.

Uzzell, B. P., Zimmerman, R. A., Dolinskas, C. A., & Obrist, W. D. (1979). Lateralized psychological impairment associated with CT lesions in head injured patients. *Cortex, 15,* 391–401.

Warrington, E. K. (1984). *Recognition Memory Test.* Berkshire, UK: NFER-Nelson.

Wechsler, D. (1945). A standardized memory scale for clinical use. *The Journal of Psychology, 19,* 87–95.

Wechsler, D. (1981). *Wechsler Adult Intelligence Scale–Revised.* San Antonio, TX: Psychological Corporation.

Wechsler, D. (1987). *Wechsler Memory Scale–Revised.* San Antonio, TX: Psychological Corporation.

Wechsler, D. (1997). *Wechsler Memory Scale–III.* San Antonio, TX: Psychological Corporation.

Wedding, D. (1991). Clinical judgment in forensic neuropsychology: A comment on the risks of claiming more than can be delivered. *Neuropsychology Review, 2,* 233–239.

Weinberger, D. R., Berman, K. F., & Zec, R. F. (1986). Physiological dysfunction of dorsolateral prefrontal cortex in schizophrenia: I. Regional cerebral blood flow (rCBF) evidence. *Archives of General Psychiatry, 43,* 114–125.

White, T. (1992). *The use of indirect tests in the evaluation of malingered or exaggerated memory performance.* Unpublished doctoral dissertation, University of Florida.

Williamson, P. D., French, J. A., Thadani, V. M., Kim, J. H., Novelly, R. A., Spencer, S. S., Spencer, D. D., & Mattson, R. H. (1993). Characteristics of medial temporal lobe epilepsy: II. Interictal and ictal scalp electroencephalography, neuropsychological testing, neuroimaging, surgical results, and pathology. *Annals of Neurology, 34,* 781–787.

Wilson, B., Cockburn, J., & Baddeley, A. (1991). *Rivermead Behavioural Memory Test.* Suffolk, England: Thames Valley Test Company.

CHAPTER SEVEN

Neuropsychological Report Writing

Bradley N. Axelrod

Department of Veterans Affairs, Detroit, Michigan

A neuropsychological evaluation is complete only when a written report summarizing the findings is provided to the referral source. This step in the process of an assessment requires as much attention by the clinician as do other aspects of the evaluation. The opinion of most report writers is that the goals of a report are fourfold: (a) describe the patient, (b) record the patient's performance on test materials, (c) communicate the results to a referral source, and (d) make recommendations regarding future care (see Ownby, 1992, for a review of this research). Matthews (1981) stated that a neuropsychological evaluation should translate test data "into a design for action." This sentiment was iterated by Ownby and Wallbrown (1986), who argued that a report should influence the readers' opinions and actions toward the patient, not merely document and promulgate information.

The utility of a neuropsychological assessment easily can be negated by providing written feedback that falls short in any one of a number of areas. The aim of this chapter is to identify the important issues that impact on the clarity and utility of a neuropsychological report. This chapter first presents information on ways to best conceptualize a report, even before the writing begins. Getting to the "heart" of report content, this chapter introduces an expository writing model that has led to greater readability and comprehension by referral agents in general psychological reports. Issues regarding the language, grammar, and other aspects of writing style for reports are next outlined. A description of the major components of a report is presented, with the most common models of data presentation. Finally, the brewing controversy of whether or not to regularly attach a data summary sheet to the report is discussed. The quality of a neuropsychological report will be enhanced by gaining a better grasp of the vital conceptualization, style, content, and format issues.

CONTEXT OF THE EVALUATION

The request for a neuropsychological evaluation typically comes with a specific purpose from a definitive source. In writing a report, the psychologist must keep in mind both of these factors, the reason for the referral and the source of the referral.

Reason for Referral

A neuropsychological evaluation could certainly summarize the data, identify trends in the test results, and offer general recommendations. However, neuropsychological assessments should be "action oriented" to be useful to the referring professional (Anastasi, 1988). Reports that are most appreciated by the reader are those that answer questions asked by the referral source (Affleck & Stider, 1971; Ownby, 1990). Feedback for another professional can be better focused, and therefore more useful, if the evaluation is accomplished for a reason more specific than the ubiquitous "for neuropsych testing." If clear reasons for an evaluation are not provided, the neuropsychologist should contact the referring professional to obtain one.

Reading Audience

The neuropsychological report seeks to provide useful information to the reader, whether that be for the professional who referred the patient, other professionals, the patient, or the patient's family. Prior to writing the report, the training, qualifications, and familiarity with neuropsychology of the referral source need to be considered. A neuropsychologist might write two very different reports (formal, detailed, and lengthy vs. informal, specific, and brief), solely based on the referral sources' familiarity with neuropsychology. Ownby (1992) proposed that the format, model, and type of report might be altered to accommodate a particular reader. Although the content, conclusions, and recommendations of a report should remain the same regardless of the referral source, the comprehension of that information may differ depending on the reader. Therefore, the detail contained in the report and the amount of relevant background information will differ. For example, a neurologist familiar with the neuropsychologist's work might refer a long-time patient with symptoms of mild dementia. The expressed purpose of the evaluation would be to determine whether the patient can remain at home with family members. This report might be presented in the form of a brief letter in which only the specific conclusions and recommendations are stated. On the other hand, the report would be different from a school psychologist's first referral in which a 14-year-old child reportedly experienced a decline in academic performance since a motor vehicle accident 6 months prior. The reason for referral to: "1) evaluate possible cognitive and emotional sequelae and 2) provide recommendation to improve school skills" would require a more in-depth report. This would be particularly important in light of the need for more background information than in the earlier case presented.

The writer of the report must also assume that the referral agent is not the only individual who will read the report. Secondary readers are other individuals who may read the report subsequent to the referral source for which the report was expressly intended. These readers could be medical professional staff, attorneys, case managers, parents/spouses/children of the patient, and even the patients themselves. Although the technical language might be too complex for some of the secondary readers, a report should always provide enough information so an educated lay person will be able to grasp the major ideas, conclusions, and recommendations.

The possibility of a report being read by individuals other than the referring professional may vary depending on the setting from which the referral came. Some settings are more closed and the likelihood of other professionals viewing the report is minimal. Certainly, reports sent to school psychologists and psychotherapists are less liable to be shared with other professionals. However, in a hospital, a neuropsychological evaluation might be read by all members of a treatment team, each of whom may have different levels of understanding of neuropsychology. A report written for a psychiatrist in which depression in an elderly patient was ruled out will likely be read by a treating neurologist a few months later when the patient is then referred for a neurological evaluation. It is the potential variety of professionals and degree of neuropsychological expertise that the writer must consider when preparing a report.

FORMING THE CONTENT OF THE REPORT

Significant findings from the clinical interview, patient history, medical records, behavior during the evaluation, and test performance are to be integrated in the report. It is the purpose of the neuropsychological evaluation to synthesize the available data into an understandable form that responds to the referral question with the most parsimonious explanation. The line of logic from data to conclusions and recommendations needs to be presented clearly to the reader. The writer must keep in mind that the evaluation must be both understandable and persuasive. Without a report first being understood, there is no possibility of it influencing the referral source.

The primary objective of the Expository Process Model (EPM), as defined by Ownby and Wallbrown (1986), is to take the reader of a report from data to recommendations in a clear and understandable manner. The reader wants a comprehensible explanation of how the psychologist reaches conclusions and recommendations based on the data. The EPM model states that reports should be composed of logically sequenced statements that present the data, explain their relationship to an underlying concept, generate conclusions, and lead to specific recommendations. As a result, the conclusions and recommendations made within a report are presented with a clear understanding by the reader.

The EPM proposes three steps in composing a report. First, the writer of a report is responsible to ensure that data are presented in a format that allows the reader to easily understand the theoretical concepts—or middle-level constructs—pointed to by the data. Next, the data are interpreted relative to the construct they represent. Finally, the writer offers conclusions and recommendations that are directly related to the interpretation of the middle-level constructs. Through the use of this step-by-step report writing procedure, readers have rated reports as more credible and more persuasive than reports that did not use the EPM approach (Ownby, 1990).

Using Shared Knowledge to Build a Report

A central key to insure comprehension is by providing information within context (Ownby, 1992). In order for a report to be useful, information needs to be presented in a way such that the writer and the reader are "singing off the same page." Written material needs to begin with a common ground between the writer and the reader (Clark & Haviland, 1977). New material is then added, using the shared material as a foundation on which the new information is added. This process of adding new material to a base of knowledge is referred to as *given–new*. The *new* can only be presented once the reader understands the *given*. By way of example, the use of a pronoun first requires an understanding of who is "he" or "she." In the sentence *Mr. Smith is a 26-year-old accountant who reported completing 16 years of education*, *Mr. Smith* is the given, and the remaining material is new for the reader. Later in the report, information provided previously can be used as a foundation for additional material, as in the following example: "Mr. Smith's [given] performance on the WAIS-R was in the superior range [new]. His [given] achievement test scores fell in the low average range [new]. The discrepancy between performance on these tasks [given] is significant [new]."

The utility of beginning with a shared referent and adding new information applies to both sentences and paragraphs. Paragraphs follow the same logic by adding new information, sentence by sentence, to the foundation information. Linking given–new sentences together can be accomplished with transitions of *equivalence* (e.g., His performance on measures of academic abilities were *com-*

parable to his tested Full Scale IQ), *contrast* (e.g., Verbal IQ fell in the low average range *whereas* Performance IQ was 20 points higher, in the high average range), and *elaboration* (e.g., Memory test performance was impaired not only for immediate recall, *but also* for recall following a delay).

Ownby (1992) suggested three potential sources of error that impede the effective communication of "given" and "new" information. First, the "given" might not actually be common information. Neuropsychology examples would be, *Trail Making Test-B performance was mildly impaired* or *percent conceptual level responding on the WCST was intact relative to demographic peers*. The assumption of the writer is that the reader knows what are the Trail Making Test-B and percent conceptual level responding on the WCST. To the nonneuropsychologist, the use of test names, scoring variables, and numerical results (e.g., MMPI–2 code types) will have little meaning. It is this type of information that is meaningful to the professional, and at the same time is interpreted by the nonprofessional as technical jargon.

The second potential stumbling point in the given–new theory is when the new material is not logically related to the shared referent. This type of error makes for abrupt transitions that the reader cannot easily follow. In the statement *the patient appeared nervous, laughing with the examiner and demonstrating a good sense of humor*, the reader cannot follow the logic going from *anxious* to *sense of humor*. It is the duty of the writer to make these transitions clear, perhaps by stating that with time the patient became more affable or that this behavior is how the patient responds when anxious.

The third way the given–new process is violated is when the new material contradicts previously presented information. Evaluate the contradiction in the following material: *The patient's tapping performance fell in the average range. He scored .3 and .6 standard deviations above demographic means with his right (dominant) and left hands, respectively, implicating left hemisphere involvement.* In the first sentence, the reader is told that the patient's performance is in the average range [given]. However, the second sentence contradicts this "given" information by implying that the left hemisphere is in some way deficient. The reader requires additional information that reconciles the difference between *average range* and *implicating left hemisphere involvement*.

Middle-Level Theoretical Constructs

The report writer must define middle-level theoretical constructs for the reader to establish common referents used in describing the patient's performance. Middle-level theoretical constructs are the link that the reader needs to make the transition from the "given" of the data to the "new" of the conclusions that are reached. This process is as necessary in a report as is providing the data, conclusions, and recommendations. Ownby (1992) referred to these constructs as the "conceptual bridges" that connect the patient data to the conclusions reached within the report. The best way to define a middle-level theoretical construct is by presenting the clinical data as "given" information and the theoretical construct as the "new."

Middle-level constructs include terms that neuropsychologists use regularly when speaking to each other and are the major ideas on which neuropsychological measures are based. It is from these concepts that conclusions and recommendations are made. When speaking to another neuropsychologist, phrases such as *perceptual skills, executive functioning, delayed recall,* and *secondary gain* are all "given." Neuropsychologists know what these expressions mean. On the other hand, nonneuropsychologists usually will not understand the meaning of these words or will have their own definition that differs from that of neuropsychologists. A report that uses these middle-level theoretical constructs without defining them makes the mistake of assuming a "given" when the information is not a shared referent. Instead, the phrases have no meaning to the reader, as they are neuropsychological jargon.

The middle-level theoretical constructs are most often used within a sentence as one describes a task. The following example describes performance on the Wisconsin Card Sorting Test:

> The patient performed in the average range on a decision-making task that required the patient to sort a deck of cards according to a principle that changes without the patient being aware of it. He accurately generated and tested hypotheses, and appropriately changed his strategy when indicated.

Similarly, the following information provides the nonneuropsychologist with an explanation of memory constructs, using common language as the "given."

> The patient demonstrated deficient performance on tasks of memory. He had difficulty generating material that had been presented earlier in the session. Similarly, he was unable to identify items presented earlier from distracter items. When provided with a list of words, he recalled none of the early words in the list and only was able to recall the last few words.

Requirements of the Expository Process Model

The EPM requires the report writer to follow each of the following "rules" (Ownby, 1992):

1. Middle-level constructs must have a shared referent in data presented in the report: The need for defining constructs based on an understandable presentation of test performance is entirely consistent with the discussion previously on establishing middle-level constructs for the reader. The shared referent must be a "given" from which the middle-level construct is defined.

2. Conclusions, which must be supported by the data, are evaluative statements about the middle-level construct: Once the middle-level construct is de-

fined for the reader, the relative quality of that function also needs to be presented. Using the preceding example with regard to performance on memory tasks, the data refer to the patient's difficulty in performing specific tasks. The conclusion reached in the statement is that memory performance was "deficient." In those three sentences, the data, the definition of the middle-level construct, and the conclusion reached by test performance are all presented.

3. Recommendations are derived from the middle-level constructs and conclusions. In addition, the recommendations must be formulated with the referral question in mind: When provided with understandable data, meaningful interpretation of the data, and clear conclusions, the reader should easily follow the logical transition to treatment recommendations.

Incorporating the Expository Process Model

In its most true form, the EPM requires a direct progression from data to middle-level constructs to conclusions to recommendations. The following sentences address the stages required by the EPM to interpret a patient's performance:

> Mr. Jones completed tests of word reading, spelling, and arithmetic calculations, three measures of academic achievement [defining the middle level construct using shared referents]. He performed in the deficient range on the former two tests. In contrast, his performance on the arithmetic measure fell in the average range [evaluative statement about the construct]. In light of his average intellectual abilities, these results suggest the presence of verbal learning disabilities [conclusion]. A referral for remedial assistance in spelling and reading is recommended [recommendation].

In this paragraph about achievement test performance, the naive reader first gains an understanding of the construct to be discussed. The reader then learns the results of the performance, learns the implication of the findings, and finally obtains a specific recommendation based on the data and conclusions. If the middle-level construct were not defined, the reader would not understand the data interpretation and conclusions. Similarly, if the report omitted the conclusion, then the recommendation for remedial assistance would likewise be confusing to the reader.

This example presents the model using a linear format in which each step is followed by the next step. This simplistic form of the model is important for students learning to incorporate the EPM in getting from data presentation to interpretation and recommendations in their reports. Alternatives to the simplified EPM report are accomplished when multiple elements are presented in a single sentence or when the EPM components are in a different order from that already described. Let's rewrite the paragraph on academic testing using a style that combines the components in a less structured manner:

> Mr. Jones performed in the deficient range on tests of reading and spelling, but his arithmetic skills fell in the average range [define the middle-level construct; evalu-

ative statement about the construct]. In light of his average intellectual abilities, these results suggest the presence of verbal learning disabilities in which he would benefit from remedial assistance in spelling and reading [conclusions; recommendation].

In these two sentences, all of the needed EPM components are included. The first sentence defines the construct of academic skills while simultaneously presenting the results. The second sentence presents an evaluative statement about academic skills relative to intellectual skills, which then leads into the conclusion of a verbal learning disability.

A report would be tedious if each test administered in an evaluation was defined, analyzed, interpreted, and generated a specific recommendation. The EPM can be used to create dynamic reports by using more complex sequencing of the components and allowing for multiple data points to feed into a single middle-level construct. A clinician might use the Wechsler Memory Scale–Revised, the Rey Complex Figure Test, and the California Verbal Learning Test, all as measures tapping the constructs of learning and memory.

> Mr. Smith performed in the severely impaired range on multiple tests of new learning, memory storage, immediate recall of the information, and recall after a delay. Specifically, he was unable to benefit from repeated exposure to a list of 16 shopping items. His ability to learn stories that were presented orally and to draw simple geometric designs was also severely impaired.

In a comprehensive neuropsychological evaluation, one would not expect overall conclusions and specific recommendations to be reached before all of the data are presented. In fact, reports can present test results in separate sections or paragraphs to help define the data points that comprise a middle-level construct. Middle-level constructs can be defined within the main body of the report. Conclusions and recommendations reached at the end of the report will follow from the evaluative summary comments reached for each middle-level construct.

The EPM is a powerful model that can adapt to any number of conclusions and recommendations emanating from the data. A finding from a single middle-level construct (e.g., impaired visual spatial processing) could result in multiple possible conclusions (e.g., "the patient's presentation is consistent with cognitive sequelae from his recent right hemisphere stroke superimposed on a history of alcohol abuse") with several recommendations: (a) substance abuse treatment, (b) referral for occupational and physical therapy evaluations, (c) active participation in treatment and discharge decisions. On the other hand, findings across middle-level constructs (e.g., impaired fluid language production, attention, new learning and memory, and executive functioning with intact socialization) can result in a single conclusion (e.g., moderate dementia of the Alzheimer's type) with more than one recommendation [e.g., (a) evaluation for assisted living care need, (b) establish guardian for patient].

Use of the Expository Process Model typically results in reports that are longer than non-EPM reports. However, the final product is more understandable, and therefore more useful, persuasive, and acceptable to referral sources. In addition, the EPM teaches the neophyte neuropsychologist how to best present the results of an evaluation, by requiring an examination of all of the data and the corresponding middle-level constructs. This process requires the writer to conceptualize an entire case before reaching conclusions and offering recommendations. Individuals who would like more detail regarding the implementation of the Expository Process Model are referred to Raymond L. Ownby's book on psychological report writing (1992) in which the process is described in detail and examples are provided.

PRACTICAL REMINDERS WHEN WRITING

The writer must always keep in mind that the purpose of the written evaluation is to communicate specific information in a persuasive manner. Good writing will effectively provide information in an understandable format at a level that is appropriate to the reader. A professional report presents ideas orderly and with parsimony, clarity, and precision (APA, 1994). The following rules of thumb should be considered when preparing a report.

Use Understandable Language

It is always preferred to use vocabulary words that are commonly used, rather than those words that may sound more technical or erudite (Ownby, 1992). However, the reader should be cautioned that "everyday usage" does not imply that informal colloquialisms are acceptable (Sattler, 1988). Using common words eliminates the potential for ambiguity by the reader. Another potential for ambiguity is using approximations (e.g., *a lot of therapy, many prior hospitalizations, somewhat late*) rather than specific numbers. In most instances, a shorter word or a more parsimonious phrase should be used in place of a larger and longer word or phrase. There is no need to include words such as *utilize, in order to,* or *competency* when *use, to,* and *skill* convey the same message.

Avoid "Neuropsychology-Speak"

Many supervisors will speak of the need to avoid technical jargon in a report. Jargon usually refers to information that is specific to a profession, but nonsensical to individuals outside of that specialty. However, for the beginning report writer, it is difficult to discriminate jargon from what might appear parsimonious.

Use Words That Accentuate Precision

Qualifiers and modifiers are often employed to consider more accurately the limitations of neuropsychological test results. Nonetheless, these techniques can also serve either to weaken the persuasiveness of a report or to overzealously interpret the findings of an evaluation. Ownby (1992) noted that too many modifiers give the impression of hedging on the results. He presented the statement "it appears at least somewhat possible that the client may develop a potentially more serious disorder" as clearly weaker than "the client may develop a more serious disorder." The words *probably* or *likely* are best used in discussing the prognosis of a patient based on the test results. In contrast, these words invalidate the credibility of an evaluation if used as in *current intellectual functioning probably falls in the low average range.* It is the test scores and behavioral presentation of which we are most confident; the report should reflect this confidence.

Barnum statements are another source of potential error in report writing. Named after the circus showman, these comments are vague and general, usually applying to most individuals. Keeping information specific to the patient will avoid these useless statements that serve to pad a report, or worse, mislead the reader.

Write Short Sentences

Hollis and Donn (1979) advocate the use of simple grammatical structure in psychological reports. They support the notion of using short words, sentences, and paragraphs to best convey the information of an evaluation. Shorter sentences are usually more understandable and effective in communicating information than are longer sentences that contain multiple phrases. Other psychologists (APA, 1994; Ownby, 1992) express the need for paragraphs to contain sentences of varying length to maintain the readers' interest and comprehension.

Present One Main Idea in a Paragraph

Recalling your early writing lessons, remember that paragraphs should convey a unified thought or idea, supported by multiple sentences. Paragraphs should be composed of sentences that contain closely related information. Paragraphs that contain only one sentence are blunt, whereas paragraphs that are too long make it difficulty for the reader to sustain attention.

Don't Include Irrelevant Material

As stated earlier, the written evaluation identifies patterns and themes to generate conclusions about the patient. Thus, there is no reason to include information that does not contribute to these conclusions. In fact, adding irrelevant material might alter the reader's impression of the patient by raising red flags. For example, a former psychology intern included in a neuropsychological report that the patient "never had any formal legal charges filed against him, nor was he ever investigated by a military tribunal." Rather than providing additional information, these comments added nothing to the report of this law-abiding patient with dementia, other than make the reader wonder if there were any grounds for such disciplinary actions. Sattler (1988) mentioned omitting references to the "absence of behavior," as in a patient "not appearing anxious, not appearing depressed, and not having difficulty understanding instructions." Of course the disclaimer to these examples occurs when these absences have meaning (e.g., a patient previously suicidal now denies suicidal thoughts). This rule of thumb of omitting extraneous information does not apply to the test results section of a report. The neuropsychological report should retain test performance references when test scores fall "within normal limits" or are in the "average range."

Address Ambiguities and Inconsistencies

In the ideal world, a neuropsychological evaluation would generate a single parsimonious explanation for the patient's presentation. Unfortunately, quite often there is no clear-cut etiology or diagnosis that can be derived from the evaluation. This problem is particularly common when multiple contributory factors in the patient's history are present. A patient with a history of poor education, 20 years of alcohol abuse, multiple assault injuries, and a 4-year-old traumatic brain injury with 1-hr loss of consciousness will probably not have a unitary reason that wholly explains the patient's cognitive performance. Although we may appreciate this fact when formulating theories regarding an evaluation, the report should also reflect our difficulty in reaching a specific answer to the referral question. A neuropsychologist must be comfortable in reaching equivocal findings in which a few possibilities enter the differential. Similarly, alternative reasons for a patient's neuropsychological presentation (e.g., medication effects, performance anxiety, poor motivation, sensory deficits) must be evaluated for the reader of the report in light of deficient test performance. Despite the fear this generates in interns, truthfully reporting one's difficulty in generating a single explanation of the test findings is preferred by the referral source to making a "best guess" without presenting the other possibilities. Claiming *uncertainty* is not the same as claiming *ignorance*.

Proofread the Final Report

A common problem, yet an obvious one, is the need to create a report that is grammatically correct and free from spelling errors. Poor grammar not only can make reading a report difficult, but it also diminishes the confidence of the reader in the professionalism and competence of the neuropsychologist. Thus, simple steps such as spell-checking and proofreading are required steps in the report writing process. Unclear writing often results when a report is dictated and later returned for a final edit. Do not underestimate the importance of checking not only the words that you dictated, but the potential errors that occur when a tape is transcribed by someone else.

Example of Poor Professional Style

The following excerpt is used to assist the reader to better understand style errors that occur in reports. Additional examples for improving reports and incorporating the professional style appear in Table 23-1 in Sattler (1988, pp. 740–744). The summary that follows is from a neuropsychological evaluation that I received in my clinical practice, and it accompanied a request for reevaluation. The patient was a 26-year-old male who sustained a mild traumatic brain injury 16 months prior to the evaluation below. The seven sentences here are from the conclusions section of the 31-page report.

> The patient is a pleasant, cooperative 26 year old who possesses an average range of intellectual ability. Intellectual ability is reflective of the impact of damage upon the developing brain. There are specific problem areas of short term and verbal memory as well as an overall impact to attention and concentration skills impacting his ability to focus, sustain attention to task and not become distracted. Problems solving skills, logical analysis and reasoning abilities are well developed and scoring did not present evidence of these abilities due to the impact of speed on these timed measures. He is vulnerable to being distracted by his external and internal environment, highly subject to missing information and thus prone to make assumptions based upon a loss of information and thus erroneous, miscue conversations and communications in general. Everyday functioning has been impacted to the degree that he cannot no longer trust himself or his performance thus initiating a substantial degree of anxiety as well as significant symptomatology of depression. He is functioning primarily with the skills of the ability to utilize logical reasoning, analysis and synthesis to problem solve his way through situations that are confusing to him.

I would certainly hope that initial reactions to this summary paragraph include confusion with the text, annoyance with the writer, and a desire to reread the passage for better understanding. I will not address the content of this report, such as whether a 26-year-old has a "developing brain" or an individual can be "distracted by his . . . internal environment" when not hallucinating. However, compare the original summary with the following rewrite of the same information:

> The patient is a 26-year-old male who was referred for an evaluation of his current cognitive and emotional functioning in light of a traumatic brain injury he suffered 16 months prior to the evaluation. He performed in the average range on

measures of general intellectual functioning and complex problem solving. In contrast, he demonstrated relative difficulty performing tasks of sustained attention and concentration, as well as verbal memory. His affective presentation is significant for symptoms of depression and anxiety. He reports having difficulty effectively communicating with others, as he tends to misread social cues as a result of being distracted and experiencing diminished attentional abilities. He appears to rely on his preserved abilities to cope with his disrupted concentration and memory skills.

REPORT STYLES

The report style that will be used for an evaluation may vary depending on the audience of the report. These formats can be as informal as letters, as brief as a consultation form, or as comprehensive as a narrative report. The type of report used will be dictated by the setting and the intended recipient of the evaluation.

Narrative

The narrative report is the most comprehensive report style, which is also the most formal format for a neuropsychological report. The narrative format gives the writer an opportunity to present the data and conclusions in detail for the reader. This format allows for a complete description of the test results, and therefore a thorough portrayal of the patient's neuropsychological functioning. The conclusions and recommendations reached at the end of a narrative report also can be discussed in detail. This style is most often used for forensic evaluations and for reports that are being sent to a professional that would be interested in a report of this depth.

Another version of the narrative report is best named a *brief narrative report* (Ownby & Wallbrown, 1986). These reports contain most of the information included in a comprehensive narrative report, but substantially reduce the description of the test results. The result is a summary of neuropsychological functioning that presents the data concisely and reaches precise conclusions. The focused nature of this report style is favored among many medical referral sources, as the report briefly discusses the data and relates the conclusions, while devoting more space to treatment recommendations. Ownby (1992) suggested that these reports should average two single-spaced typed pages. He stated, "Voluminous reports, while personally gratifying displays of professional diagnostic skill, are often useless to the persons who receive them."

Letter

A professional, yet less formal, method of presenting test results to a referral source is by way of a letter. This report style is a common method among health care professionals to communicate information between medical clinics. In writing a neuropsychological report in the form of a letter, the recipient will expect to see a reason for the referral, the method of assessment, understandable conclusions, and information as to the referral agent's next role, in terms of treatment or additional diagnostics. The letter format follows a similar structure to the brief narrative report, in that the salient elements of the data are succinctly presented. Most important, the neuropsychologist is clearly responding to a specific question initially asked by the referring agent. As in any report, the conclusions reached by the neuropsychologist explicitly respond to the question asked. Reports written as letters should ideally be kept to less than two typewritten pages.

Consultation/Summary Report/Progress Note

There are some occasions in which a full report is not requested or of interest to the referral source. This demand for brevity is most often observed when a referral request is done internally within a medical setting. A consultation request might be to assist in narrowing the diagnostic differential, or to confirm whether a patient is appropriate for understanding a treatment regimen. In a consultation report, conclusions and recommendations form the body of the report; test data are typically omitted. This is done because the data might be misinterpreted by nonprofessionals (e.g., in a multidisciplinary treatment meeting), the data may not be secure, or expedience overrides breadth and depth. Often a neuropsychologist will later write a full narrative report that will be entered into the patient's medical record.

FORMAT OF THE
NEUROPSYCHOLOGICAL REPORT

The content of a report is better understood by the reader when the material is presented in an organized format. In the same way that an outline is helpful in understanding the content of a lecturer's talk, sections within a report provide the reader with a structure within which the relevant information is presented. The sections of the report assist the reader in differentiating behavioral data, historical data, assessment data, evaluative statements, and recommendations. A secondary benefit to using a structured format is that it compels the neuropsychologist to organize all of the components of the evaluation in a standardized method. As noted by Anastasi (1988), there is no single standard form for a report. However, the most commonly used report sections, as reported by Mendoza (1997), Ownby (1992), and Sattler (1988), are presented here.

Identifying Information

A report needs to establish "given" information for the reader prior to launching into specifics about the patient's history or current presentation. For that reason, identifying information should be clearly presented on the first page. Required are the patient's name, identifying personal information (e.g., social security number, medical record number, insurance case number), and the date of evaluation. Additional data, such as date of birth, age, gender, date of report, name of the examiner, and referral source, are optional, as that information is often included elsewhere in the report.

Reason for Referral

This section clearly outlines the specific reasons for the referral for a neuropsychological evaluation. As discussed earlier, by the time the report is being written, the neuropsychologist should have clarified the reason for the referral and formulated specific clinical questions. Sometimes it is helpful to highlight historical information that provides context for the referral (e.g., "the patient was referred to assess his ability to care for himself in light of his history of multiple strokes, the last of which occurred one month ago").

Tests Administered/Assessment Procedures

A list of all of the measures, interviews, questionnaires, and other materials used in the neuropsychological evaluation is presented here. If measures are to be referred to by their common abbreviations later in the report, this would be the place to provide the abbreviations after the full name of the instrument. Listing the instruments used in the evaluation assists neuropsychologists reading the report by providing a quick reference guide as to what was administered. I have taken to listing the measures grouped by the functional domain assessed rather than alphabetically. On the occasion of a reevaluation, the listing of tests provides a single place where all of the measures can easily be found. Mendoza (1997) noted that the list of tests is more often than not of interest only to other neuropsychologists. Although this is generally the case, there are nonneuropsychologists (e.g., speech pathologists, school psychologists) who are familiar with the names of measures. Furthermore, auto insurance companies, managed care companies, and other third-party payers often require a listing of the specific measures used.

Background Information/Patient History

The material presented in this section provides the framework for why the patient was referred for the assessment. Most of what is contained in this section is information that serves as a backdrop by describing the patient's past symptoms, diagnoses, and treatment; education and social history; ongoing stressors; and current presentation. This information is then integrated with the psychometric data and behavioral observations in reaching the conclusions and recommendations presented later in the clinical report. The review of the patient's background information must emphasize only the relevant historical data. Lengthy and overly detailed background sections only serve to confuse, distract, and frustrate the reader.

First, relevant demographic information is presented, including the patient's age, education, occupation, gender, and ethnicity. This information is often followed by the specific precipitating event that resulted in the need for cognitive evaluation. In the case of a motor vehicle accident, for instance, details regarding what the patient recalls of the accident, pretraumatic and posttraumatic memories, symptoms at the scene, emergency treatment, and subsequent medical, rehabilitation, or mental health treatment are all necessary pieces of information in putting the neuropsychological evaluation in context. If a patient is referred with questionable dementia, background information should include information from the patient's family as to changes in behavior observed, as well as evaluations made by professionals prior to referring the patient.

The current symptom presentation, as reported by the patient, can be included at this point in the background information. In addition to getting independent information from other sources, the subjective report of the patient's most significant problems (e.g., back pain, headaches, difficulty learning new information, tinnitus, etc.) at the time of the evaluation should be summarized in a condensed format.

As is the case in any psychological evaluation, relevant aspects of the patient's developmental history, past medical interventions, medical hospitalizations, and current medical conditions are included. Additionally, the patient's relevant mental health and substance abuse history is detailed. If relevant to the reason for doing the evaluation, the report should cover past inpatient and outpatient mental health treatment, and their perceived effectiveness for the patient. Information regarding prior psychological and neuropsychological evaluations is also summarized in the background section. It may be useful to include a social history pertaining to the patient's relationship history and marital status, vocational record, and account of conflicts with the law, and pertinent family history also should be contained. In some cases, a report of family medical (e.g., Alzheimer's disease, cerebrovascular disease) and psychiatric (e.g., alcohol dependence, major depressive disorder) history is included in this section.

Finally, details about current psychological functioning are important to include in the evaluation. These data are often obtained from questions posed during the clinical interview. Specifically, the report needs to put the test data and historical information in the context of this unique individual's environment. This environment includes aspects such as interpersonal relationships, activities of daily living, daily life and work activities (e.g., grocery shopping, yard work, housework), and mental health factors.

Review of Medical Records

In some cases, a referral for neuropsychological evaluation will arrive with voluminous past medical records. Although this information is usually presented in the section on background information, in some circumstances the medical records will contradict material presented directly from the patient. This is particularly common in forensic evaluations. The differentiation between "patient report" and documentation from objective professionals is better made when the sets of data are presented as distinct sources of information.

Behavioral Observations

In developing and reporting a clinical conceptualization, the neuropsychologist presents historical information in the context of current functioning. *Current functioning* includes (a) test performance and (b) patient behavior during the interview and while carrying out the neuropsychological measures. It is the manner in which the patient performed, spoke, moved, and responded to the environment that is discussed here. An accurate description of the patient's behavior should offer a clear picture for the reader.

Descriptors that do not enhance the reader's understanding of the patient should be avoided (Ownby, 1992). For example, physical descriptions of a patient (e.g., height, weight, hygiene) are not important to discuss unless that information is pertinent to interpretation of the test data. Similarly, statements indicating that the patient "responded appropriately to test material" do not add sufficient additional description of the patient to warrant inclusion in a report (Ownby, 1992). This is especially true because all descriptive information are data and, like test data, should have a direct relationship with a middle-level construct. On the other hand, it may be important to describe level of cooperation, because this has direct implications regarding the validity of the evaluation.

Most neuropsychologists agree on the basic information expected to be seen in this section. With regard to speech, important material is gleaned from an account of the patient's speech quality (e.g., rate, articulation, prosody), speech content (goal directed versus tangential, paraphasic), response style to interview questions, and language comprehension. A patient's response to failed performance or difficult test items may also be of interest. Sensory and motor abilities should be evaluated, as any impairment may impact test performance. Specifically, the patient's manipulation of test materials, hearing of interview and test questions, and visual acuity are sensory-motor areas addressed by clinicians. Clinical reports should explicitly speak to the affective presentation of the patient, such as range of affect, mood, and response to humor or praise. Behavioral displays of confusion, emotional lability, confabulation, disinhibition, and poor insight are of particular importance in a neuropsychological report, as they obviously will impact on the diagnostic impression of the patient (Mendoza, 1997).

The neuropsychologist's overall impression of the reliability and validity of the patient's performance in the evaluation should be addressed in a direct manner (Mendoza, 1997; Sattler, 1988). It is important to keep in mind that a patient's level of attention, motivation, fatigue, psychosis, or orientation might deleteriously impact the ecological utility of the evaluation and/or its reproducibility.

Test Results/Test Interpretation

The heart of the psychometric aspect of the evaluation is presented in this section. Much of the information discussed with regard to the EPM is particularly relevant when providing the reader with the details of test performance and interpretation. This section can be subdivided into sections of specific cognitive and emotional domains (i.e., middle-level theoretical constructs). There are a few different models for outlining test performance for the reader. The structure of the data presentation and the order in which the tests are described are less important than is the clear interpretation that guides the reader from data to conclusions and then to recommendations.

Some neuropsychologists offer a test-by-test model of data presentation. Although this is usually seen in the early stages of one's professional career, some clinicians deliberately adopt this method to ensure that their report includes all measures administered.

Most often neuropsychologists report the test data in terms of the cognitive function that was tested. The common subsections or paragraphs that are often used include intellectual functioning; attention and concentration; verbal processing and language skills; academic skills; visual spatial processing; orientation; new learning and memory; executive functioning/cognitive flexibility; sensory and motor processing; and emotional and personality functioning. There is no mandate that each of these areas needs to be explicitly addressed in a neuropsychological report. In actual practice, there are few clinicians who present separate sections or paragraphs for each of these neuropsychological functions. More often, multiple functions are combined in a sensible manner, such as discussing orientation and memory skills together.

Another style that is used to present the neuropsychological data organizes the findings by psychometric strengths and weaknesses of the patient. This type of report can begin the Test Results section by first providing an overall level of cognitive functioning or impairment. Then the abilities that are significant strengths are reported, followed by those abilities that are significant weaknesses. Most of the measures that fall between the extremes are mentioned only in a cursory manner.

A fourth format for summarizing the data presents test results as they pertain to relevant brain structures. This can be accomplished by presenting data using the distinctions of anterior/posterior, cortical/subcortical, cortical lobes, and lateralization. This model for presenting test results has become less common, especially as the role of neuropsychological evaluations has expanded beyond the question of detecting the etiologic localization of impairment.

Finally, objective test results can be presented in a manner that specifically addresses the referral questions asked. In a manner similar to that used in examining strengths and weaknesses, only test performance results that relate to the referral questions are discussed; other tasks are omitted from the report. The purpose of this type of presentation is to address precisely defined questions. Information that strays from this charge is viewed as extraneous to the reader. This format would not discuss the results by component tests or cognitive domains (i.e., middle-level constructs). This type of results section is typically seen in a forum where brief rather than comprehensive reports are used.

Summary/Conclusions

This section first serves to highlight the salient features of the evaluation. Once the primary features of the protocol are reviewed and integrated, conclusions regarding the meaning of these findings are made. The use of a summary within a report has been criticized (e.g., Sattler, 1988). Sattler (1988) viewed a summary in a report as optional, because it is a recapitulation of what has already appeared in the report and adds nothing but length. Professional colleagues have complained that when a summary statement is included in an evaluation, referral agents merely skip to the summary without reading the remainder of the report. My opinion contrasts with these. I believe that the summary is an important area to emphasize the significant evaluative findings for the middle-level constructs. This information highlights the important objective data, historical information, and behavioral observations that will lead to the overall conclusions regarding the patient. If the summary were not present, then a professional who skips to the end of the report—which will occur anyway—will have no frame of reference as to how the conclusions were reached. Furthermore, neuropsychologists cannot take responsibility for other professionals refusing to read an entire report. Because the evaluation is trying to answer specific questions for a patient, we should attempt to provide written feedback that will offer the best useable outcome.

The final conclusions reached by the neuropsychologist are articulated here, originating from the referral questions. The clinical findings should emanate from the data presented, in keeping with the Expository Process Model. For example:

> The patient presented with deficient new learning, remote memory, and executive functioning skills, in conjunction with intact socialization abilities. His cogni-

tive performance, in light of a reported gradual change in his cognitive status over the past two years, is consistent with the findings of a progressive dementia.

With an ear to the reason why the patient was originally referred, the impressions reached with the evaluation should explicitly respond to those queries. Prognostic appraisals are best provided here following the overall conclusions regarding current functioning. The summary and conclusions presented should assist in making a smooth transition from data interpretation to recommendations.

Diagnostic Impression

Often contained within the Conclusions section, some reports explicitly state the diagnosis of the patient based on the evaluation. The diagnosis presented here can be a full five-axis or just an Axis I diagnosis from the *Diagnostic and Statistical Manual–IV* (*DSM–IV*; American Psychiatric Association, 1994) or the International Classification of Diseases, 9th Edition, Clinical Manifestations (*ICD-9-CM*; Jones, Schmidt, & Aaron, 1996). ICD-9-CM codes are often used when a nonpsychiatric diagnosis is indicated.

Recommendations

Once conclusions are made regarding the referred patient, neuropsychologists may have evaluation or treatment recommendations. In making recommendations, the neuropsychologist must keep in mind the reason why the patient was initially referred. Opinions regarding a patient's ability to participate in treatment decisions or discharge plans and to manage finances might be important to the referral source for the patient's ongoing care. Referrals to other professionals for evaluation or treatment (e.g., neurologist, vocational rehabilitation, speech therapy, audiology, physical therapy, occupational therapy, psychotherapy) are also frequently recommended. Suggestions for reevaluation (e.g., in 12 months if his condition changes, in 6 months to rule out a progressive decline) can be presented if so indicated. There are times when no recommendations are necessary, such as when a patient is referred only for diagnostic purposes (e.g., forensic independent medical examination).

ROUTINE APPENDING OF RAW DATA

Neuropsychologists debate the utility of various measures, the methods in which tests are selected (e.g., battery versus process approaches), and interpretation of results. However, few issues pertaining specifically to report writing had been met with controversy in the field until an opinion paper by Freides was published in 1993. In this paper, Freides proposed that "all quantitative data obtained in the neuropsychological examination be displayed in the report, for example, in an appendix" (p. 234). Subsequent papers by Freides (1995), Matarazzo (1995), and Naugle and McSweeny (1995, 1996) debated this issue. A survey of 81 directors of neuropsychology training programs found 35% in favor of the routine inclusion of raw data, whereas 63% opposed the proposal (Kelland & Pieniadz, 1997).

Arguments Favoring the Proposal

In his initial proposal, Freides (1993) opined that by attaching raw test data to the neuropsychology report, the writer could refer to the data without being required to present the results in the text. He offered that this would result in more efficient use of the report by allowing the author to focus on data interpretation rather than presentation. Another argument in support of releasing raw data is to allow for the comparison of test performance of an individual patient over multiple evaluations, especially when subsequent assessments are performed in other sites. The necessity of obtaining a release of information for the raw data from another professional, and the waiting time to receive them, would be eliminated if the data were already included in the report already at the disposal of the clinician. Immediate access to prior test data not only would help the clinician to evaluate prior patient performance, but the neuropsychologist would also be able to validate the conclusions of the previous evaluation (Matarazzo, 1995).

Responding to concerns that test data should be considered "sensitive material" and therefore restricted, Matarazzo (1995) argued that test scores should not be viewed as more sensitive than the interpretation of the same data. In other words, the information contained in a report draws conclusions and recommendations that are disseminated to others. These conclusions are generated from the raw data in the evaluation. Matarazzo's belief was that the data from which inferences are made are not more sacred and should not be more protected from inspection than the conclusions themselves. Freides (1995) supported this stance and firmly stated, "The possibility that data may be more harmful than judgments regarding their meaning strikes me first as preposterous and secondly as professional-protective" (p. 248).

Three additional benefits were offered pertaining to maintaining the standards of the field of neuropsychology. Specifically, arguments were made that a data summary sheet for neuropsychologists would (a) force all tests to be scored, (b) require that all test data are reviewed prior to reaching conclusions, and (c) prevent a professional from "hiding" data by not reporting them (Freides, 1993, 1995).

Arguments Opposing the Proposal

Naugle and McSweeny (1996) made the argument that refusing to disclose test scores to unqualified professionals—as protection to professional integrity and patient privacy—is quite different from omitting or concealing data. The primary concern raised by opponents of the automatic inclusion of raw data in the clinical report lies in the potential misuse of the data by nonpsychologists (Naugle & McSweeny, 1995, 1996). Although there is no concern regarding the release of the data to other psychologists, there is a fear that sending data to anyone who requests it could violate the ethical principle 2.02(b) (Competence and Appropriate Use of Assessments and Interventions; APA, 1992) that restricts release of data to unqualified individuals. The restriction on releasing raw data to unqualified professionals extends to subpoenas from attorneys. Many neuropsychologists will request that the attorney provide a name of another psychologist to whom the data will be sent.

A secondary consideration in opposing the routine attachment of raw data relates to the possibility that the information can violate a patient's privacy by including sensitive information that is not "germane to the purpose for which the [evaluation was] made" (principle 5.03(a) [Minimizing Intrusion on Privacy]).

The final three points raised in the preceding subsection are otherwise addressed by the Ethical Principles of Psychologists and Code of Conduct (APA, 1992). Any psychologist who would not score all of the measures administered to the patient, review all data prior to reaching conclusions, or consciously omit reporting a finding because it contradicts conclusions already reached is clearly in violation of the APA ethical principles. In particular, principle 2.01(b) (Evaluation, Assessment, or Interventions in Professional Context) states that the conclusions and results "are based on information . . . sufficient to provide appropriate substantiation for their findings." This position is further bolstered by principle 2.02(a) (Competence and Appropriate Use of Assessments and Interventions), which states that assessment techniques are used "appropriately" and "properly." When performing a forensic evaluation, psychologists are bound to "testify truthfully, honestly, and candidly" (principle 7.04(a) [Truthfulness and Candor]). Finally, if the psychologist has failed to score, consider, or report relevant data due to lack of competence in the field, then principle 1.04(a) (Boundaries of Competence) would apply.

Another issue to consider when evaluating the benefit of releasing raw data as a standard within our field falls in the area of "perceived competence." Because much of the language used in neuropsychology has been incorporated into mainstream speech, individuals outside of the area of psychology claim familiarity with our field. There is a misperception of truly understanding the psychology nomenclature among health professionals and lay persons alike. Terms such as *intelligence, depression,* and *dementia* have neuropsychological definitions that are all too often misunderstood by nonpsychologists. Unlike the viewing of laboratory results of viral titers, hard copies of x-ray films, or a histology report of a biopsy, reporting "the patient had an IQ of 90" will be *misunderstood* rather than *not understood*. It is for this additional reason of the perceived competence of nonprofessionals that I believe the release of raw data should not be routine.

One Solution

There is a compromise that can be approached between the two opposing schools of thought. First, rather than appending all raw data to the report, the interpretation of the data could be included in the text of the report. Information regarding the level of impairment (e.g., mild, moderate, severe) or performance relative to peers (e.g., low average, average) needs to be presented to provide justification for the interpretation of the middle-level constructs. Second, when there is concern that raw data may make their way to individuals who are not competent in understanding them, percentile scores could be used instead. Percentile scores are less frequently misinterpreted than are standard scores. Medical professionals understand their meaning and can glean needed information from these data.

SUMMARY

The purpose of this chapter was to highlight important aspects in the preparation and actual writing of a neuropsychological report. Before beginning the report, the writer must have clear understanding of who referred the patient and why the patient was referred. The professional writing style should be clear, concise, nonderogatory, and understandable. The Expository Process Model offers a clear process for guiding the reader from the data, through the middle-level constructs, to conclusions and to recommendations based on the evaluative interpretation of the middle-level constructs. This model was shown to be dynamic when used to establish multiple conclusions and recommendations that cross over the findings of the middle-level constructs. With regard to the format, the customary subject headings used in neuropsychological reports usually seen were presented. Attending to the aspects of report writing presented in this chapter should make for more decisive, understandable, convincing, and persuasive reports.

Two sample reports that use the EPM model follow. The first example is a comprehensive narrative report and the second one is a brief narrative report.

Sample of a Comprehensive Narrative Report

Name: Joseph (Joe) Clark
Examination Dates: June 15,16,19, and 20, 1995
REASON FOR REFERRAL:
   Mr. Joseph Clark is a 31-year-old Black male who was referred for an evaluation of his current cognitive abilities. He reportedly suffered a hemorrhage of an anterior communicating artery aneurysm while doing push-ups on 3-18-95.
BACKGROUND INFORMATION:
   Mr. Clark underwent a right frontotemporal craniotomy (3-21-95) to clip the

aneurysm. This was done at Beaumont Army Medical Center in El Paso, TX. A postoperative angiogram showed severe vasospasm of the anterior communicating artery and the distal internal carotid artery on the right. He subsequently developed postoperative diabetes insipidus, suggesting possible pan hypopituiterism. A postoperative EEG revealed moderately severe generalized dysrhythmic slowing most prominent in the bifrontal temporal region. An MRI scan showed an old hemorrhage in the caudate and internal capsules in both hemispheres.

Mr. Clark was not a good historian, and the following information is based on his self-report. He completed 12 years of school as a C+ student. He had some difficulty with math, failing a high school math course. He reports participating in track and steeple chase. He was unable to tell me when he joined the Army or of what his work assignments consisted. In terms of his complaints, he denied having diabetes; he reported having seizures, with his most recent being in January. This information could not be confirmed in his medical record.

BEHAVIORAL OBSERVATIONS:

Mr. Clark's level of arousal varied substantially from day to day and even within the session. At times he appeared to actually fall asleep, whereas at other times he was alert. His attention also varied widely, from highly distractible, to relatively easy to keep on task, to difficult to get him to initiate responses. His speech was low in volume and difficult to understand. His facial affect was flat and generally nonresponsive. He was able to ambulate, but walked slowly and had to be encouraged to follow along with the examiners due to his initiation difficulties.

ASSESSMENT PROCEDURES:

Clinical Interview, Medical Records Review, partial Wechsler Adult Intelligence Scale–Revised (WAIS–R), partial Wechsler Memory Scale–Revised (WMS–R), California Verbal Learning Test (CVLT), Visual Spatial Learning Test, Boston Naming Test, MAE: Controlled Oral Word Association Test (COWA), BDAE: Animal Naming, Supermarket Item Naming, Rey–Osterrieth Complex Figure Drawing, Trail Making Test, Stroop Color-Word Test, Luria Complex Motor Programs, Wisconsin Card Sorting Test.

TEST RESULTS:

Based on Mr. Clark's educational and vocational background, as well as his performance on portions of the current assessment, his premorbid level of intellectual and cognitive ability is estimated as at least within the mid-average range. Currently, his performance is significantly lower than his estimated premorbid level. All areas of cognitive functioning are adversely affected, and he is seen as having at least a moderately severe degree of impairment. Memory is particularly problematic; he shows a pattern of classic amnesia—generally intact immediate recall, virtually no new learning, and confabulatory responses on memory measures. Details of the present findings are reported below. The percentile scores reported are age adjusted, or age and education adjusted.

Verbal/Language Abilities: Mr. Clark has general initiation problems that are seen in all behaviors including spontaneous speech. His speech was low in volume and difficult to understand. However, no paraphasia or dysarthria was noted. On word list production tasks his scores generally fell around the 1st to 3rd percentile level (moderately to severely impaired). He also had significant difficulty on the Boston Naming test, correctly naming only 16 of the 30 even numbered items (less than the 1st percentile, severely impaired). Neither semantic or phonemic cues helped him recall the names of items. His difficulty on this naming task appears to reflect two factors: (a) a premorbid vocabulary that was likely somewhat low (low average), and (b) difficulty in retrieving previously learned information (long-term and remote memory retrieval problems).

Mr. Clark's performance on the WAIS–R Information subtest also suggests memory retrieval problems. His score fell at the 2nd percentile level (moderately impaired), indicating significant difficulty accessing previously learned information. Arithmetic skills and verbal reasoning concepts of semantic similarities were slightly better (5th percentile, mildly impaired), but still significantly lower than expected mid-average premorbid levels of functioning. His performance on the WAIS–R Digit Span test was unusual. He repeated back only one of three numerals on the first two trials of digits forward, but eventually appeared to understand the nature of the task. He finally was able to repeat 5 numbers forward and 4 backward, but in an inconsistent fashion. This inconsistency is seen as due to at least two factors: (a) a variable level of attention and concentration, and (b) difficulty in initiating responses. However, when he is attentive and "into a task," he is able to show average verbal immediate recall ability.

Visual Cognitive Abilities: His performance on various measures of visuospatial abilities follows a pattern similar to that seen with language measures. His attention and concentration are variable and interfere with his overall level of functioning. When attentive, he is able to demonstrate at least borderline to low average visual perceptual and visuospatial functioning. His overall score on two different measures of visuospatial ability fell around the 10th percentile (low end of low average range). His problem-solving approach to the Block Design subtest of the WAIS–R was somewhat concrete and more trial-and-error, as opposed to a reasoned problem-solving approach. Thus, his difficulty with this task appears to reflect more of a "frontal or executive" problem rather than difficulty with visuospatial analysis.

Orientation: Mr. Clark was disoriented to day, date, and place and obtained a Memory, Orientation, and Amnesia Test (MOAT) score of 48 (mental status severely impaired). He recalled 0 of 3 objects, and cueing and multiple choice did not aid recall.

Memory: Mr. Clark has particular difficulty with learning and memory. On immediate recall of two short stories he was only able to recall an average of only 2.5 out of 25 ideas (less than 1st percentile, severely impaired). He could recall nothing of either story after a 30-min delay (less than 1st percentile, severely impaired). Immediate recall of visual material was somewhat better (26 of 41 details; 12th percentile, low average range), but he recalled nothing after a 30-min delay (less than 1st percentile, severely impaired). On a multiple trial list learning task he never was able to recall more than 3 of 16 items, and showed no increase in performance across trials (i.e., no learning curve). Following both short (a couple minutes) and long delays (20 minutes) he could recall none of the 16 items. His performance is consistently at less than the 1st percentile (severely impaired).

Executive Control, and Information Processing Speed and Flexibility: Mr. Clark's performance was somewhat variable on measures of attention, concentration, cognitive flexibility, and processing speed. As already mentioned, he had a great deal of difficulty on the WAIS–R Digit Span subtest. With extra trials and prompts he was eventually able to repeat 5 numbers forward and 4 backward, but in a very inconsistent fashion. This inconsistency is seen as due to at least two factors: (a) a variable level of attention and concentration, and (b) difficulty in initiating responses. However, when he was attentive and "into the task," he was able to show an average level of basic attention and *immediate* verbal recall ability. This same average level of performance was demonstrated on reading and color naming speed (Stroop Words and Color trials), and he even showed an average level of ability to overcome an interference effect (Stroop Color-Word trial). However, this lack of excessive susceptibility to interference may be due to the fact that he is essentially amnestic and therefore less likely to "build up an interference effect."

In contrast to some relatively good scores on some measures of basic attention, his speed of both cognitive and motor processing was severely slowed (WAIS–R Digit Symbol = 1st percentile, Trails A and B = 1st percentile). On part B of the Trail Making test he made 3 errors, indicating difficulty with "mental tracking" and a tendency to become cognitively confused. This tendency to become cognitively overwhelmed and confused was also seen on the Wisconsin Card Sorting Test. He "happened" on the correct initial sorting principle quickly, but when the correct sorting principle changed he was unable to switch cognitive sets. He continued to sort in a perseverative fashion to the first sorting principle, even though he was receiving continual feedback that this was incorrect and was even prompted by the examiner to consider other ways that cards could be "matched or sorted." His score on the WCST was at less than the 1st percentile (severely impaired).

CONCLUSIONS AND RECOMMENDATIONS:

Mr. Clark is a 31-year-old Black male who suffered a hemorrhage of an anterior communicating artery aneurysm on 3-18-95. He subsequently underwent a right frontotemporal craniotomy (3-21-95) to clip the aneurysm. A follow-up MRI scan showed old hemorrhage in the caudate and internal capsules in both hemispheres. Basic language, visual perceptual, and visuospatial abilities are seen as being generally intact, although performance on tests of these measures is not. The current neuropsychological evaluation shows severe problems in virtually all areas of cognitive ability. Specifically, he demonstrates slowing of motor and cognitive processing speed, poor attention, confusion, impaired learning and memory of new information, and impairment in most executive functions. It is unclear how much recovery Mr. Clark might be expected to have.

With regard to recommendations, compensatory techniques (e.g., memory notebook utilization) and environmental management techniques might prove beneficial to Mr. Clark. Because Mr. Clark is unlikely to be an active participant in treatment decisions and discharge planning, the possibility of guardianship should be raised with his family.

Sample of a Brief Narrative Report

Name: John Smith

Examination Date: 11-30-95

REASON FOR REFERRAL:

Mr. Smith is an 83-year-old, married Caucasian male with 9 years of formal education who was referred from the Primary Care Clinic for a dementia evaluation. He had a history of weight loss, decreased energy, and memory problems. The differential diagnostic referral question was dementia versus a depression-related pseudodementia.

BACKGROUND INFORMATION:

Mr. Smith had been career military (first 4 years in the Navy, followed by 16 years in the Air Force). He retired from the Air Force in 1959, after which he worked as a pipe fitter at different shipyards. He stopped working altogether at the age of 64 when his physical condition prevented him from working further. He has had a pacemaker for about 8 years and a replacement pacemaker for 1 year. He also reports having a left knee replacement. His only reported current medication is Ibuprofen.

BEHAVIORAL OBSERVATIONS:

Mr. Smith was accompanied to the current evaluation by his wife of 55 years. He was alert, cooperative, and generally oriented (off by 1 day of the current date). He admits to problems with forgetfulness, mild word-finding difficulties, and mild problems in keeping his bills straight and paying them (due to organization and forgetfulness problems, not financial difficulties). He also reported being more irritable, frustrated with some of his limitations, and being short-winded. He mood and affect were good, and there was no indication of depressive symptoms. Mrs. Smith reported that her husband has been quite forgetful for at least 4 months. She also reported an episode in July 1995 in which he could not recall how to turn on the air conditioner in their car.

TESTS ADMINISTERED:

Clinical Interview, CERAD Neuropsychology Battery (Consortium to Establish a Register for Alzheimer's Disease), Wechsler Memory Scale–Revised (Logical Memory subtest), MAE: Controlled Oral Word Association Test (COWA), Cued Supermarket Naming Test, WAIS–R Digit Span and Digit Symbol subtests, Trail Making Test.

TEST RESULTS:

Based on Mr. Smith's educational and vocational background, as well as his performance on portions of the current assessment, his premorbid level of intellectual and cognitive ability is estimated as mid to low end of the average range. Currently, he demonstrates significant memory problems, whereas other aspects of cognitive functioning remain within the expected low to mid-average range.

Mr. Smith had a great deal of difficulty learning the 10-item CERAD word list over three trials, and could not recall any of the items after a several-minute delay (severely impaired). Similarly, his memory for narrative material (short stories) was poor on immediate recall (borderline impaired), but severely impaired on delayed recall. He was unable to recall anything about the stories after a 20-min delay. Visual memory was equally impaired (Memory for the CERAD Praxis drawings = 0, severely impaired).

In contrast, Mr. Smith showed only mild difficulty on a naming or word-finding task (Boston Naming Test = 3rd percentile), and average to low average abilities in generating words conforming to different semantic or phonemic rules. Thus, his language abilities are generally intact, with the exception of mild word-finding problems.

Visuospatial functioning is also intact (CERAD Praxis = 23rd percentile, low average). Attention, concentration, and processing speed are also relatively intact and comparable with age- and education-matched peers (scores ranged from the 14th to 63rd percentile, low average to average ranges).

SUMMARY:

Mr. Smith is an 83-year-old man with moderate to severe learning and memory problems, mild word-finding problems, but intact language, visuospatial, attentional, and executive abilities. Mr. Smith does not meet the formal criteria for dementia (because he has memory difficulties that interfere with his daily functioning, but no clear deficits in other cognitive abilities), although he may be in the early stages of Alzheimer's disease. Alternatively, he may present with the rare diagnosis of Isolated Memory Impairment.

RECOMMENDATIONS:

A follow-up evaluation in 6 to 9 months is recommended to assess the potential progressive nature of his deficits.

REFERENCES

Affleck, D., & Stider, F. (1971). Contribution of psychological reports to patient management. *Journal of Consulting and Clinical Psychology, 37*, 177–179.

American Psychiatric Association. (1994). *Diagnostic and statistical manual of mental disorders* (4th ed.). Washington, DC: Author.

American Psychological Association. (1992). Ethical Principles of Psychologists and Code of Conduct. *American Psychologist, 47*, 1597–1611.

American Psychological Association. (1994). *Publication manual of the American Psychological Association* (4th ed.). Washington, DC: Author.

Anastasi, A. (1988). *Psychological testing* (6th ed). New York: Macmillan.

Clark, H. H., & Haviland, S. E. (1977). Comprehension and the given-new contract. In R. O. Freedle (Ed.), *Discourse production and comprehension* (pp. 91–124). Norwood, NJ: Ablex.

Freides, D. (1993). Proposed standard of professional practice: Neuropsychological reports display all quantitative data. *The Clinical Neuropsychologist, 7*, 234–235.

Freides, D. (1995). Interpretations are more benign than data? *The Clinical Neuropsychologist, 9*, 248.

Hollis, J. W., & Donn, P. A. (1979). *Psychological report writing: Theory and practice*. Muncie, IN: Accelerated Development.

Jones, M. K., Schmidt, K. M., & Aaron, W. S. (Eds.). (1996). *ICD-9-CM code book*. Reston, VA: St. Anthony Publishing.

Kelland, D. Z., & Pieniadz, J. (1997). To report or not to report (Quantitative data, that is): A survey of actual practice and training in neuropsychology [Abstract]. *Archives of Clinical Neuropsychology, 12*, 344.

Matarazzo, R. G. (1995). Psychological report standards in neuropsychology. *The Clinical Neuropsychologist, 9*, 249–250.

Matthews, C. G. (1981). Neuropsychology practice in a hospital setting. In S. B. Filskov & T. J. Boll (Eds.), *Handbook of clinical neuropsychology* (pp. 645–685). New York: Wiley-Interscience.

Mendoza, J. E. (1997). Neuropsychological report writing: Format, content and issues. In *Neuro-*

psychology program / resource guide: Including guidelines for training, hiring, credentialing & practice (pp. B1–B13). Milwaukee, WI: National Center for Cost Containment, Department of Veterans Affairs.

Naugle, R. I., & McSweeny, A. J. (1995). On the practice of routinely appending raw data to reports. *The Clinical Neuropsychologist, 9,* 245–247.

Naugle, R. I., & McSweeny, A. J. (1996). More thoughts on the practice of routinely appending raw data to reports: Response to Freides and Matarazzo. *The Clinical Neuropsychologist, 10,* 313–314.

Ownby, R. L. (1990). A study of the expository process model in mental health settings. *Journal of Clinical Psychology, 46,* 366–371.

Ownby, R. L. (1992). *Psychological reports: A guide to report writing in professional psychology* (2nd ed.). Brandon, VT: Clinical Psychology Publishing Company.

Ownby, R. L., & Wallbrown, F. (1986). Improving report writing in school psychology. In T. R. Kratochwill (Ed.), *Advances in school psychology* (Vol. V, pp. 7–49). Hillsdale, NJ: Lawrence Erlbaum Associates.

Sattler, J. M. (1988). *Assessment of children* (3rd ed). San Diego, CA: Sattler.

Special Issues, Settings, and Populations

CHAPTER EIGHT

Neuropsychometric Issues and Problems

Paul D. Retzlaff
University of Northern Colorado, Greeley

Michael Gibertini
Organon, Inc., West Orange, New Jersey

The field of psychometrics is concerned with the study of the adequacy of measures of human behavior. Nearly a century old, the field has grown in complexity and scope to a point at which it represents one of the most developed areas of measurement theory in all of science today. Practically all of its more recent advances have been a consequence of our great need to have accurate and fair appraisals of student and employee ability. Modern psychometrics is, in other words, a product of psychologists' efforts to improve and defend the tests that are now responsible for determining the educational and occupational fates of millions of Americans. Because there are great need, enormous pools of subjects, and large profits at stake, measurement technology has kept pace with the demands of consumers and politicians that tests be defensible against all attacks on their accuracy. Statistical and mathematical models not usually studied by psychology graduate students have been pressed into service for this defense and advancement of what is now a very large testing industry. For better or worse, the sum of the older and newer technologies sets the standard for all related disciplines. The result is that today the practicing psychologist is more likely than not to have inadequate and even obsolete training in test usage and evaluation. Obsolescence of graduate training is a situation no doubt common to all rapidly advancing sciences.

More troubling than the educational deficiencies of practicing psychologists, however, is the extremely uneven quality of data underlying the psychometric clinical instruments. Industry is at work here no less than in the educational or personnel arenas. Publishers of clinical and neuropsychological tests are expanding their libraries greatly. But the data required to meet the highest measurement technology standards typically are not collected. Nevertheless, clinical psychological and neuropsychological tests published today must meet higher standards of accuracy, representativeness, and fairness than ever before. But rarely are sufficient data available or published in test manuals to allow the user to evaluate the test against modern standards. Without high need, enormous subject pools, and huge profits at stake, the data necessary for evaluation according to classical reliability, generalizability, item response, or operating characteristics theories are too expensive to collect.

Neuropsychology has high need in the sense that the consequences of the evaluation are extremely powerful for individual patients. But the number of patients is relatively small, and patients are dispersed among thousands of practitioners who are rarely organized for collaborative data gathering. Profits are also dispersed, so that the individual test builder or publisher has little incentive for putting investment of time and money into modern comprehensive psychometric study of the test. And because the consumer (i.e., the psychologist using the test) won't demand what he or she can't interpret, there is no press for publishers or authors to update established instruments according to the latest advances in measurement technology. Clinical and clinical neuropsychological testing is a mere cottage industry, lagging far behind educational or personnel testing in measurement precision, sophistication, and technology use.

The intent of this chapter is to provide a practical framework for understanding psychometrics as they apply to neuropsychology. Initially, traditional psychometric concepts are reviewed, including reliability, validity, test referencing, and test theories. Second, the specific psychometric challenges that neuropsychologists face are placed in perspective. Third, validity is reexamined through a discussion of operating and sampling distribution characteristics of tests.

Readers interested in the psychometric properties of specific tests are referred to Spreen and Straus (1991) and Franzen (1989). Those who would like an accessible mathematical perspective of psychometrics are encouraged to read Suen (1990). And of course, the classic on psychometrics is Nunnally (1978).

TRADITIONAL PSYCHOMETRICS: CONCEPTS AND APPLICATIONS

Reliability

In using tests to sample and quantify behavior, variations in test performance may occur due to true differences in examinees' behavior or error. The reliability of a test is the estimate of what proportion of variance in performance can be attributed to true differences in behavior. Because many factors can contribute to error, various procedures for estimating reliability have been developed, each of which identifies somewhat different variables as components of error.

Although reliability is probably one of the most central constructs to psychometrics, indeed, the term *reliability* should probably not be used. It is used to connote three differing concepts: internal consistency, stability, and interjudge concordance.

From a behavioral sampling perspective, the most important of these concepts is internal consistency. *Internal consistency* refers to the homogeneity of the test and items within it and is grounded in the problems of error in the sampling of behavior. Classically, a number of different types of internal consistency can be calculated. *Alternative forms* is when two tests built at the same time seeking to assess the same behavioral functions are correlated. The fact of the matter is that at present most test developers only develop one version of a test. Therefore, in practice, rarely will alternative forms be available, although in many clinical situations they should be. The second method of calculating internal consistency is the split-half method. Here, the first half is correlated with the second half of a test, or the sum of odd-numbered items is correlated with the sum of even-numbered items. In essence, this is a more primitive form of the third and final method, which is the Cronbach alpha method (Nunnally, 1978). The Cronbach alpha method of internal consistency estimation relies on the intercorrelations of all items with each other. Indeed, in this way we get around the problem of alternative forms or split-half; the homogeneity of items is judged on the basis of their intercorrelation. As such, under classical theory, all multisampled behavioral tests have a reliability, and the best estimate of that reliability is the Cronbach alpha measure of internal consistency.

Stability is often mistermed test–retest reliability. *Stability* is the performance on a test across time. To determine test–retest stability (reliability), a test is given to a sample twice within a number of weeks or months and the two scores are correlated. This is an appropriate statistic to reflect the generalizability of a patient's score to another point in time, which is often of interest in neuropsychology. As such, it is useful when a clinician is interested in determining if a patient's scores represent a true and significant change in performance across time. Difficulties with this particular method include the fact that stability is not an interchangeable measurement with internal consistency. Therefore, it cannot be used to estimate true score, standard error of measurement, or most standard errors of estimation. This is because differences across time are related to both the internal consistency of a test and true and natural changes in people's scores across time. Additionally, different domains, constructs, and content behave differently in the face of a stability study. There are some constructs, such as certain aspects of intelligence, that are highly stable for 20 or 30 years of a person's life. Other constructs, such as attention, anxiety, or motivation, may be very situationally variable. Therefore, within stability studies, the design of the study must be consistent with the underlying theoretical assumptions of that particular behavioral domain or disorder.

The final type of reliability is *interjudge reliability*. Again here, *reliability* is probably a poor term, and perhaps a better one would be *interjudge concordance*. In essence, one is looking at the degree to which two judges make a similar diagnosis regarding a particular neuropsychological deficit in a single patient. There are fairly specific statistical calculations for this, including the kappa statistic (Cicchetti, 1991). The kappa statistic very importantly deducts from the observed consistency of judgments that which is specific to chance. Indeed, if two judges tend to find 90% of a particular sample as having a particular disorder, at least 81% of the time they will be in agreement simply on the basis of chance. Therefore, the prevalence of a particular disorder or the prevalence of normality within a particular sample highly affects apparently concordant judgments.

Power Versus Speed Tests.   Although the calculation of internal consistency through a Cronbach alpha is the preferred method of reliability estimation, tests that include speed as a component are inappropriate for the use of this technique. Power tests that have no time limit are well served by the Cronbach alpha, but speed tests will have artificially high alphas. In the case of tests where speed is central to the construct, such as the time score on a Trails B, the split half or alternate forms methods of reliability estimation should be used. The alternate forms method is preferable as more items are available, but it is rare in neuropsychology for alternate forms to be available, either due to construction cost or because the entire domain of possible items has already been exhausted. Many neuropsychological tests are timed, yet speed may not play a significant role in the underlying construct. The cost of speeding tests is the inability to properly estimate internal consistency and the loss of important measurement concepts such as the standard error of measurement that depend on proper estimation of reliability.

Test Theories

Test theory is a highly complex and difficult to understand area of psychometrics and psychology. Often, unfortunately, test theory is relegated to mathematical psychologists. Largely, there are two major schools of thought in test theory, and under each there are two subschools. The first school is primarily concerned with the test as a whole. The first such theory is that of classical test theory (Nunnally, 1978). Classical test theory is probably the type of test theory most widely taught in current American graduate schools. The second type concerned with the test as a whole is an extension of classical test theory brought to us by Lee Cronbach, that is, generalizability theory (Cronbach, Gleser, Nanda, & Rajaratnam, 1972). The other major school is concerned more at an item level. First, this includes conventional item analysis, and second, the relatively sophisticated item response theory (Rasch, 1980). For the purposes of this chapter, only the applications of classical test theory are discussed. It should be understood, however, that due to the inherent heterogeneity and complexity of neuropsychological work, classical test theory has serious limitations. Generalizability theory, conventional item analysis, and item-response theory will undoubtedly play major roles in neuropsychological assessment in the decades to come.

Classical Test Theory.   Classical test theory has been with us since the 1920s. In classical theory a particular score for a particular patient is composed of a true score and some amount of error variance. The attempt of classical test theory is to come as close as possible to the "true score." To this end, confidence intervals around obtained scores can be calculated with varying degrees of probability that the true score falls within that interval.

Among the important lessons that can be learned from classical test theory is first that the obtained score is not necessarily the "true score." Indeed, the estimation of the true score is based on the internal consistency of the test. It is calculated by multiplying the reliability times the deviation score of a particular patient. For example, with a test internal consistency of .50 and an obtained *T*-score of 70 (a 20-point deviation), the estimated true score is very different from the 70. When the observed deviation is multiplied by the reliability, an estimated true *T*-score of 60 results (a 10 point drop from the obtained *T*-score). At this point the second intent of classical test theory is to develop confidence limits around that estimated true score. The formula for this "standard error of measurement" is the test's standard deviation multiplied by the square root of one minus the test's reliability. If a neuropsychological test has a reliability of .50, we then have the square root of 1 minus .50, which is .71. Multiplying that by the test's standard deviation (10 points for a *T*-metric) results in a standard error of measurement of 7. Therefore, there is a 68% level of confident that the patient's "true score" is a *T*-score of 60 plus or minus 7 points. So, although a patient on a particular test with a reliability of .50 may have attained a *T*-score of 70, according to classical test theory there is only 68% degree of certainty that the "true score" is between 53 and 67. The importance of this example (showing regressions to the true score and banding of confidence intervals) is to illustrate how imprecise neuropsychological testing can be, and, more generally, how imprecise tests are that are not reliable.

An additional use of true score theory and its confidence intervals is in the determination of the significant differences between two tests for a single patient. Often in the case of learning disabilities it is important to see if a child's ability is different from a child's achievement. Reynolds (1990) does a good job of providing the rationale and various formulas for such differences. A more common example, however, may be from the WAIS–R and the clinical practice of interpreting differences between scale scores. A clinician may be interested in seeing if the Vocabulary score of a patient (viewed as a good premorbid intelligence predictor) is statistically different from Digit Symbol (perhaps seen as a current global functioning indicator). Table 13 of the WAIS–R manual (Wechsler, 1981, p. 35) provides the requisite difference at a 15% level of confidence. In this case, Vocabulary must be 2.02 scale score units above Digit Symbol for the clinician to conclude that there is a good chance that current functioning is significantly below premorbid level.

These levels of significant difference are derived from the internal consistency of each subtest via a calculation of standard error of measurement formulas. As evidence of this, note that the two most internally consistent WAIS–R subscales are Vocabulary at 0.96 and Information at 0.89. These have standard errors of measurement of 0.61 and 0.93, respectively. The two subscales with the lowest internal consistency are Object Assembly at 0.68 and Picture Arrangement at 0.74. These have standard errors of estimate of 1.54 and 1.41, respectively. Using the data as calculated in the manual for a 15% confidence interval, a difference of only 1.60 is required for a significant difference between Vocabulary and Information, whereas a difference of 3.01 is required for the less internally consistent Object Assembly and Picture Arrangement.

Although this is appropriate for determining if two scores are statistically different during one testing session, stability coefficients may be used to calculate the analogous standard error of estimate for comparing a patient's scores on a single test at two different times.

A problem with classical test theory is that the reliability calculation methods allow for only one source of true and one source of error variance within a score. Classical test theory does not deny multiple sources of true and error variance, but can account or control for only one at a time. It is obvious that when tests are complex, there may be multiple sources of true variance (different behaviors, all of which are essential to completing a test). Additionally, error variance may occur due to many factors such as fatigue, malingering, or the traditional error of the sampling of the items of behavior.

It is often tempting in a new field of psychology to presume that it is somehow immune to the psychometric and statistical requirements of other domains of psychology. However, all areas of psychology, including neuropsychology, require internally consistent measures to make highly confident inferences regarding patients' behavior and functioning.

Test Referencing.   Test referencing is briefly discussed as preface to the next major issue, validity. There are three types of tests that can be developed: norm-referenced and two types of criterion-referenced tests.

The norm-referenced test is probably the most typical test within psychology. In it, a person's score is interpreted and inferences are made based on that individual's position in the distribution of all scores—how many standard deviations the scores may be above or below the mean. It is in this context that standard scores such as *T*-scores and *z*-scores, or percentile scores are typically discussed. For some psychological constructs, norm referencing is an important and relevant method of inference, such as constructs such as intelligence. Knowing at what percentile against the norm reference an individual is contributes to our understanding of that individual's intellectual functioning. Norm referencing is also useful in the determination of change within an individual, through the determination of estimated "true score" changes as already discussed.

There are other cases within neuropsychology, however, where norm referencing is clearly inappropriate. For instance, in the case of aphasia, the fact that a person is two standard deviations above or below the mean for nonaphasics on an aphasia test is not a particularly good indication of whether the individual has had a stroke or whether the individual has a receptive or expressive aphasia. In these types of situations, criterion-referenced tests are much more useful. There are two types of criterion-referenced tests: content and prediction (or expectancy).

In content-referenced tests, the measure of performance is the amount of content material that an individual has successfully accomplished. This type of test is probably most common within academic settings, where a professor will construct a test of 50 items based on the lectures and readings for a particular class; students are graded on the percentage of that information that they know. Within neuropsychology, such content referencing is probably highly appropriate for some things such as competency. If patients are unaware of their income, their bills, the status of their bank accounts, and the signatory authority over their bank accounts, it is highly probable that they are not competent for financial purposes. There is no need to reference their performance against a norm, nor do we need to predict an individual's ability and future behavior, because the patient is unable to impress us with an understanding of present fiscal condition. We and the courts recommend that this individual is financially incompetent.

The second type of criterion reference test is predictive or expectancy criterion referencing. Here the reference is the score or performance on, or classification made by, some criterion measure. For example, a neuropsychological test may be referenced to findings on neuroimaging studies (computed tomography [CT] or magnetic resonance imaging [MRI] scans). Thus, a poor performance on some measure of visuospatial ability may be referenced to the probability of finding demonstrable lesions in the right parietal region. The criterion is not one of content, but an external criterion, which, hopefully, properly categorizes individuals into "normals" or "brain impaired."

Validity

Validity is second in importance only to reliability as a psychometric variable. You can have the most reliable test in the world, but if it is not valid, it is of little utility to the clinician. In fact, validity refers to a test's usefulness; *validity* is the degree to which a test fulfills the purposes for which it was intended. There are three traditional types of validity: content validity, construct validity, and predictive (or criterion-related) validity. These obviously often parallel the test referencing approaches just discussed.

Content validity is the most primitive of the validities. With content validity through rational, logical analysis, experts judge the content of a particular test and infer its ability to tap a particular domain. Obviously, different judges may view the content in vastly different ways, and there may be little unanimity of agreement on the validity of a particular test when viewed from a content prospective. Indeed, there is no statistic that can operationalize content validity. Therefore, it should be viewed as the most primitive and minimally necessary form of validity. The unfortunate case within neuropsychology is, however, that many of our tests have no more than content validity. Face validity is often erroneously used interchangeably with content validity. However, face validity technically is not a type of validity at all and refers simply to whether or not a test appears to assess what it was designed to measure, regardless of what expert judges may think.

Construct validity is a far more sophisticated method. Campbell and Fiske (1959) in the late 1950s presented the model of the multitrait, multimethod matrix. The intent of the multitrait, multimethod matrix was to assess a number of underlying domains through a number of different methods. Within neuropsychology, this may take the form of assessing intelligence, language, and executive processes through paper-and-pencil tests and report of significant others. Determination of construct validity is accomplished through examination of a triangular intertest, intermethod correlation matrix in which on the diagonals are the reliabilities of the particular measures. Through an analysis of this intercorrelation matrix, one could determine the degree to which a particular trait or domain held up across different methods, and assess the amount of variance accounted for by differing measurement methods.

This multitrait, multimethod matrix came under fire, however, because it involves a large number of univariate analyses. Currently, factor analysis is commonly viewed as the most appropriate multivariate method of determining the actual underlying dimensions of such a matrix. Indeed, at this point, it is common in neuropsychology to attempt to validate a construct underlying a particular test through factor analysis. The construct validity of a measure is examined by including in a factor analysis a number of "marker" variables of specific abilities. This serves to determine the extent to which abilities such as intelligence, memory, or attention play a role. In more homogeneous tests (high internal consistency), factor analysis often is used to determine how specific a particular test is to a focal domain. With proper sampling, a new memory scale should have high loadings on the same factor as two or three well-known memory scales. It should not necessarily load on intellectual, language, or visuospatial factors. Construct validity is critically necessary within neuropsychology, particularly due to the idiosyncratic construction techniques often used.

The final major type of validity is criterion-related validity, which reflects the relationship between performance on the test and on a criterion measure. There are two types of criterion-related validity: predictive and concurrent. The difference between them is related to the timing of the administrations of the test and the criterion measure. However, for all practical purposes both reflect the predictive relationship between the test and the criterion measure and establish the statistical relationship between them. In neuropsychology the criterion variable may be a known pathological factor. The test may be correlated with known diagnostic groupings, anatomical lesions as evidenced by CT or MRI scans, or other biological variables. Predictive validity within neuropsychology is probably the most important method of determining validity. Although there are a number of different assessment approaches to neuropsychology, including anatomical, cognitive domain, and neurobehavioral syndromes, all have standards of outcome. Therefore, it should be the goal of all neuropsychological tests to withstand criterion-related or predictive validity.

These three types of validity are not mutually exclusive; ideally, a test should stand up to all three. The content of a test should logically be associated with the ability, the disorder, or anatomical considerations. Additionally, the construct validity should be established through formal and sophisticated factor analytic techniques. Finally, and most importantly, these tests should actually predict external behaviors/criteria. Neuropsychological tests that contain content, construct, and predictive validities will prove to be the best tests available.

NEUROPSYCHOMETRICS:
PUTTING THE CLASSICS IN PERSPECTIVE

Every measurement context is composed of two parts: the measurement procedure and the object of measurement. Both components have aspects that influence the final interpretation of the data. Psychometrics is concerned exclusively with aspects of the measurement procedure and leaves alone aspects of the object of measurement. Psychometrics grew up in an environment where aspects of the object of measurement could be readily controlled, categorized, or measured separately (and thereafter "controlled statistically"). Educational, personnel, and, to some extent, personality psychologists have had the ability to isolate that part of their subjects' functioning that they intended to measure. The object of measurement, in other words, brought no serious confounds to the procedures of measurement. Neuropsychologists have no such luck.

The object of measurement for clinical neuropsychologists is the function, not the structure, of a damaged or diseased brain. To infer structural changes from data on function may be a reason for undertaking the measurement procedure, but the reason for testing and the object of testing are not to be confused. The object of measurement in neuropsychological testing is always the same, but the reasons can be many: infer structure changes, aid in treatment planning, chart the course of a disease, educate the patient on his disabilities, and so on. The function of the damaged brain may be decomposed into as many parts as the investigator can imagine, and all are presumably measurable. Each function may be measured by a test that has the same properties of measurement as any other psychological test, namely, adequate reliability and validity. To illustrate, in neuropsychological assessment, intelligence is decomposed into verbal versus nonverbal, and these may be further decomposed into problem solving, reasoning, sequencing abilities, and so on. Memory is decomposed to immediate span, short-term register, and long-term store. These are divided into verbal and visual domains. The decomposition of brain function into smaller units is not a problem because each is merely a target at which the neuropsychologist aims assessment procedures. In fact, the decomposition of brain function into smaller units is a part of the measurement procedure and not, strictly speaking, a part of the object of measurement. Breaking brain functioning down or building it up for measurement purposes is what is meant by developing psychological constructs. The relationship of the construct to the object of measurement can never be more than theoretical, so construct development belongs to the measurement side of our original dichotomy.

Decomposition of the object of measurement into smaller units is part of the measurement procedure and does not interfere with the psychometric purity of the neuropsychological situation. The special problems that neuropsychologists have are not in the realm of psychometrics, per se; they are not related to measurement procedures. Tests are tests, and there is no technical reason why adequate psychometric statistics could not be generated for every neuropsychological procedure from finger tapping to the Wisconsin Card Sort. Adequate statistics do not exist, not because the tests are different, but because the population on which they are used is ill-suited to classical test theory or any other psychometric theory yet devised. Neuropsychologists have trouble not with their measurement procedures but with their object of measurement.

Specifically, the object of measurement in neuropsychology is unstable. In psychometrics, the metaphor of the archer is used to illustrate the concepts of and relationship between reliability and validity. If the archer places all of the arrows in a small radius anywhere on the target, it is said to be reliable. If a tight radius of arrows is placed in the bull's-eye, it is said to be reliable and valid. A neuropsychologist is shooting at a moving target that is moving at an unknown velocity and in unknown directions. The functions of a damaged brain are unstable, and from a strictly technical standpoint, this makes the psychometrics of the measurement procedure unassessable. If the archer hits the bull's-eye with the first arrow and misses the entire target with the second, was the archer unreliable, was the archer–target relationship invalid, did the target move, or was there some combination of these possibilities? Without an external vantage that could separate these possibilities, the question is unanswerable. The neuropsychologist does not have any vantage but what is given in feedback from the test scores. Data from the test procedure are confounded with this unfortunate aspect of the object of measurement, and the two cannot be separated in the usual case. For most neuropsychological tests, the psychometric statistics that are available have been generated with normal populations and are not useful in estimating the reliability, validity, or errors of measurement and estimate of test results in the clinical situation.

Now that the Medusa has been named, it can be made more terrifying by describing its several heads. The problem of instability of the functions of the damaged brain can be divided into two major types. From the perspective of the measurement procedure, these are (a) changing foreground functions and (b) short- and long-term fluctuations in background conditions.

The Foreground

Changing foreground functions refers to the instability of the specific object of measurement. The neuropsychologist seeks to measure the patient's memory, for example. Is the obtained score the same today as what would have been obtained yesterday or what may be obtained tomorrow? From a psychometric standpoint, this a simple question of stability. But for the neuropsychologist, it is also a question about the functional state of the brain and thus part of the object of measurement. Each question is usually answered in terms of the known properties of the other. If both are unknown (the stability of the test and the stability of the function), then, as the mathematicians say, the system is indeterminate. Unfortunately, problems don't end with this indeterminacy. There is also a validity problem caused by the nonunitary nature of the object of measurement. Is memory a single functional unit? In truth, it should be remembered that memory doesn't exist; it is a construct that can be decomposed to simpler constructs. All of these may be changing and at different rates. Which of the many subcomponents of memory is the test measuring: attention, perception, encoding, transfer efficiency, storage, retrieval, and so on?

The changing foreground functions compound three problems for the neuropsychologist: (a) estimation of premorbid status, (b) construction of premorbid profiles, and (c) discernment of interactions among subcomponent processes of cognitive functions.

Issues related to premorbid functioning have been discussed in detail in chapter 2. Discussion included both approaches to estimating premorbid functioning and difficulties in that regard due to variability in premorbid profiles of abilities. However, for the purposes of the present discussion, it is important to emphasize that current ability measures that may be used to estimate premorbid functioning should have demonstrably high reliability (internal consistency) and stability coefficients. There can be no substitute for reliability when trying to estimate the past in the face of a changing present.

Uncoupling Cognitive Subcomponents.   All cognitive behavior involves the co-ordinated execution of many individual component processes. For example, it is current practice to divide memory assessment into verbal and visual domains. The clinician attempts to measure verbal memory independent of visual memory and vice versa. Is this possible? Verbal memory may be assessed by collecting the subject's store of remembered items from a list of verbally presented words after some time interval. If the subject used an intensely image-dependent mnemonic to transfer the words from immediate register to short-term storage, is that purely "verbal memory"? And what about other functions that are necessary for this type of test, such as the ability to maintain attention, the ability to hear, the ability to understand language, the ability to follow instructions, or the ability to speak? Tests of verbal memory assume that these abilities are intact; to the extent that they are not, they influence the test score and detract from the test's reliability (if the collateral ability is changing), its construct validity (if the collateral ability is impaired to the point that the obtained score is very far off from where it would be if the collateral ability were intact), or both. Cognitive functions are interconnected and to some extent hierarchically organized (you can't measure verbal memory in an inattentive or aphasic patient). Reliability suffers in this situation because the test sometimes measures more of the higher order function (e.g., memory), and sometimes more of the lower order function (e.g., attention). Can an archer shoot a single arrow at two targets? A correction that can be made is to arrange the evaluation in a way that assesses the lower order functions first and then uses data from this initial assessment to inform the choice of tests for the higher order evaluation. However, this is a clinical solution and does not address threats to the psychometric properties of the tests due to the interconnection among cognitive abilities.

The Background Conditions

The foreground is the foreground because the tests illuminate the cognitive components that are the focus of concern. But these selected functions are merely part of a vast cognitive landscape that is more like an undifferentiated prairie than the neatly quartered garden the examiner attempts to describe. Any function that is "lifted" out for examination carries with it connections to the whole brain and all its energies and fluctuations. The background that envelopes the artificially defined foreground cannot be ignored. There are many ways of attending to the background effects. For our purposes, four varieties of background effects are described: two short-term fluctuations (fatigue and motivation) and two long-term fluctuations (learning and maturation).

Short-Term Fluctuations.   Cognitive tests require work. Ironically, brain-damaged patients, who may be eventually declared unfit to work, are often required to sit through 4 to 6 hours of intense and often intimidating mental tasks that would fatigue anyone. Fatigue leads to mistakes and mental slowing, which increase the error of the test scores. We may expect less error in the tests given at the beginning of the session and more in those administered at the end of the session. Motivation works in the same way. Interestingly, motivation may increase during the session, owing to rapport-building efforts of the examiner, and then drop off precipitously when fatigue sets in. Aspects of both fatigue and motivation may be functions of the disease state, as well of premorbid personality. This very complicated picture demands that the examiner be constantly aware of the patient's level of arousal and engagement. The point to be made is that the reliability and validity of a test depend on the administration context every bit as much as they do on the actual items of the test. When the context changes, so do the reliability and validity of the test. Neither of these indices is fixed at values given in the manuals; these values are upper bounds at best. And, because background conditions can be so volatile, reliability and validity can change during the course of an evaluation.

Long-Term Fluctuations. Some neuropsychological tests are eminently learnable. Memory tests are obvious examples. Many clinicians have had an opportunity to reassess supposedly amnesic patients 1 and 2 years after the initial assessment, only to be told Wechsler Memory Scale–Revised stories before they are administered. In addition, Amelia Earhart has been getting a lot of press lately, a truly unfortunate development for Information item number 14 of the WAIS–R. The clinician who has opportunity to collect multiple assessments over time can obviate many of the threats to reliability and validity outlined earlier. But multiple testing brings the threat of artifacts due to learning the material and maturation of the individual. These changes may be independent of the disease state that precipitated the original referral and thereby threaten the reliability and validity of the tests. The solution to problems caused by learning is the use of multiple equivalent forms of the test, rarely available in neuropsychological assessment. The solution to problems caused by maturation and historical changes is to include them in the interpretation of the test score. Obviously, the available solutions are not satisfactory.

OPERATING CHARACTERISTICS AND SAMPLING: TOWARD USEFUL VALIDITIES

Operating Characteristics

Having conceptually discussed the traditional concepts of validity, including content, construct, and predictive validity, it becomes apparent that these approaches often do little to help the clinician in the *N* of one clinical situation. As evidenced by the discussion above, patients present changing fore- and backgrounds.

Traditionally, to examine whether or not a test is valid an empirical study is conducted. To that end, 50 normals and 50 patients may be selected and given the test. The problem with this is, however, that rarely are we faced with a clinical situation where we have 50 normals and 50 pathological patients and have to determine whether the groups are different. Indeed, in most clinical settings, we have one patient and must determine whether the patient is normal or brain impaired. As such, many of the validity statistics used in neuropsychology are not ecologically useful.

Such group studies are attempts to model the means and variances and determine whether groups are different. However, a significant t or F statistic at .05 does little to tell us whether or not the individual case in front of us is a patient or a normal. Indeed, an analysis of variance (ANOVA) statistic's probability value may be as small as .00001, and we may feel more confident in the use of that particular test, but have little information to tell us whether or not we are making an accurate diagnosis, inference, or prediction.

Alternatively, with regression approaches, not only is there a test of whether or not the overall R squared is statistically significant, but also the appearance of having more information since the correlation has far more continuity to it. Therefore, a test with having a correlation with the outcome criterion of .76 is viewed as a far better test than one with a correlation of .21. Here again, however, we may be very good at predicting what one group may be vis-à-vis another or one variable vis-à-vis another, but at a loss with our $N = 1$ case.

Within experimental and industrial/organizational psychology, signal detection theory is often used to represent hit rates. Within signal detection theory, true positives are analyzed as well as true negatives, and overall efficiency is gleaned through a d-prime statistic. Within medicine, these concepts are called operating characteristics. Operating characteristics arose largely from laboratory tests in which there is a need to determine whether or not tests are valid. If, for example, there is a blood marker for a cancer and that marker comes back positive, it is necessary to know what the chances are that indeed that patient actually has cancer. And conversely, if that blood test comes back negative, what are the chances that the patient actually does not have the cancer? Obviously in this case, both of those types of validity or hit rates are critically necessary. To tell a patient and physician that the patient has cancer will set that patient along a long road of remediative therapies, and very definitely change that patient's life. Conversely, should the test come back indicating no cancer, a patient would not be afforded the therapies necessary to perhaps save his or her life. An error of that type would result in a premature demise.

Psychology only recently has adopted the concept of operating characteristics. Indeed, relatively few tests use them. However, it is only operating characteristics that can allow a clinician to understand with an individual patient what the probabilities are that a patient has or does not have a disorder, has an anatomical lesion or not, or has a significant decrement in functioning or not. Operating characteristics take into account the prevalence of a disorder and the a priori probability that a patient may or may not have a disorder.

Getting back to the earlier example of 50 normal subjects and 50 clinical patients, what are the chances that a test properly identified the normals and properly identified the pathological subjects? If hit rates are given, other than a t test or an ANOVA, a typical finding may be that the test identified perhaps 30% of the normals and 95% of the patients as having the disorder. Such a finding suggests that the test is good at identifying patients with the disorder but tends to overinclude normals. There may be situations, also, where a test does not identify a great number of normals but then also does not identify most of the patients.

Within the framework of operating characteristics, these two statistics are known as sensitivity and specificity. Sensitivity is the concept of how sensitive a test is to a specific ability, disorder, or anatomical condition. If a person has a disorder, what are the chances the test will pick it up? Table 8.1 is adapted from Table 4.8 in Benton, Hamsher, Varney, and Spreen (1983, p. 41) regarding performance on the Facial Recognition Test. As can be seen, 53% of patients with right posterior lesions are identified by their scores on the facial recognition test. In this particular case, pathological scores are viewed as scores of less than 38. With 19 of the 36 patients properly identified, the test has a sensitivity to the disorder (right posterior lesions) of 0.53. This answers the question, "Knowing that the patient has the disorder, what are the chances that the test will identify it?"

Specificity answers the question of how specific a test is to that disorder alone versus its tendency to identify others who do not have the disorder. In the Facial Recognition Test example, 276 of 286 normals are properly identified. This gives us a specificity of .965. Indeed, only 3.5% of normals are misidentified by the

TABLE 8.1
Operating Characteristics of the
Facial Recognition Test at a Prevalence of .11

| | Pathology | | |
	Present	Absent	Totals
Test			
Positive	19	10	29
Negative	17	276	293
Totals	36	286	322
Prevalence		$36/322 = .11$	
Sensitivity		$19/36 = .53$	
Specificity		$276/286 = .965$	
Positive predictive power		$19/29 = .66$	
Negative predictive power		$276/293 = .94$	
Overall predictive power		$(19+276)/322 = .92$	

test as having the disorder. Specificity answers the question, "Knowing that this patient does not have this disorder, what are the chances that the test will not identify them as having the disorder?"

Although a sensitivity of .53 and a specificity of .965 appear to be very good, one must be cognizant of the fact that the group membership of these individuals was known a priori. The fact is, however, that when a patient is in your office, rarely do you know whether the person is a member of the control or the experimental group. It is the true positives and the true negatives divided by the *other* marginals that identify this information for us. It is positive predictive power and negative predictive power that allow us to understand the $N = 1$ patient in front of us.

Table 8.1 reveals that 29 individuals were identified by the test as having the lesion whereas only 19 actually had the lesion. The ratio of 19 over 29 is the positive predictive power. Positive predictive power answers the question, "Only knowing that this person has a positive test score, what are the chances the person actually has the disorder?" One will notice that the dependent clause within that sentence is far more typical of the clinical situation. We never know whether the person is a control or an experimental group member. All we know is whether the person has a positive result on the test or have a negative result on the test. In the case of Benton's Facial Recognition Test, there is a positive predictive power of .66, which indicates that should a patient of yours have a positive test with this particular prevalence rate, there is a two-thirds chance that the patient indeed has a right posterior lesion.

The flip side of positive predictive power is negative predictive power. One would think that this should be one minus the positive predictive power, and that if you are correct 66% of the time in one direction, you ought to be perhaps wrong 34% of the time in the other direction. This is not actually true because within operating characteristics, varying prevalences are taken into account. Indeed, should a patient score fairly well on Benton's Facial Recognition Test, above or equal to a 38, what we find is that 276 individuals are properly identified out of the 293 who are identified as being "normal." This proportion, .94, is the negative predictive power. In this case what we can say is, "My patient had a good score on the Facial Recognition Test; I am 94% positive that they do not have a right posterior lesion."

Finally, as in the case of other hit rate statistics, overall predictive power is in essence the true positives plus the true negatives over the total number of cases. In this case we have 19 plus 276 over 322, giving us an overall diagnostic efficiency of .92. If this statistic alone were presented, it would appear that this is a very good test. However, one must realize that the positive predictive power is only a moderately strong .66.

What makes operating characteristics more powerful than other psychometric statistics is their ability to adapt to varying prevalences. Again, in group research studies we usually have a .50 prevalence rate because we have 50 in one

TABLE 8.2
Operating Characteristics of the
Facial Recognition Test at a Prevalence of .02

	Pathology		
	Present	Absent	Totals
Test			
Positive	3	11	14
Negative	3	305	308
Totals	6	316	322
Prevalence			6/322 = .02
Sensitivity			3/6 = .50
Specificity			305/316 = .965
Positive Predictive Power			3/14 = .21
Negative Predictive Power			305/308 = .99
Overall Predictive Power			(3 + 305)/322 = .96

group and 50 in the other group. Taking Benton's hit rate statistics as an example, and only varying the number of patients having right posterior lesions, important changes can be seen. Table 8.2 shows the effects of changing the prevalence rate from .11 (as in Table 8.1) down to a .02. In this case, out of the 322 subjects, only 6 have the disorder. Although the original example had 53% positively identified through sensitivity, here this becomes a 0.50 because of rounding. We have 3 patients identified by the test and 3 patients not identified by the test, for a total of 6 patients. Specificity remains the same, with .965 of the 316 being identified as not having the disorder by the test, or 305 of them. This leaves 11 false positives. Here, although sensitivity and specificity remain constant from the prior example, prevalence has dropped from .11 to .02. The dramatic effects of the change of prevalence are primarily seen in positive predictive power. Calculating positive predictive power (3 over 14), we discover that it drops to a .21. If you were a clinician with this scenario, you would only be ⅕ positive that the patient had a right posterior lesion.

Negative predictive power also changes, but because negative predictive power capitalizes on the great preponderance of people who don't have the focal disorder, it does not change as dramatically. This calculation of 305 over 308 shows us a negative predictive power of .99.

Overall predictive power in this example actually rises to 0.96. Again, should only overall predictive power be provided, we would believe that this example showed the test to be a stronger, better, and more valid test than the .92 of the prior example. However, within a clinical setting, positive predictive power is the most critical statistic. And in low-prevalence situations, this statistic drops precipitously.

What should be taken from the foregoing examples are two things. One, operating characteristics are by and large the best statistical mechanism for the representation of the validity of a test in neuropsychology when that validity is a dichotomous decision placing a patient into a group such as disordered, impaired, improved, or significantly changed. Specifically, positive predictive power should and must be calculated for all dichotomous predictions of brain abnormality and specific neurological disease. Second, it should be noted that as prevalence and the base rate of a pathology within a specific clinical practice drop, positive predictive power is forced down. Attempting to predict any low-base-rate behavior is difficult. Operating characteristics are not as useful when a clinician is interested in multifactorial information such as interaction with psychological variables or other continuous variables.

Data and Their Distribution

Classically, we are trained that psychological and neuropsychological behaviors are normally distributed and that if a behavioral sample is not normally distributed we must make it so. Indeed, the normal distribution serves as a model. Unfortunately, the single largest threat to the proper determination of reliabilities, validities, and operating characteristics is poor modeling of our samples. This includes an overreliance on the normal distribution, the lack of true test specific distributions, and poor subject selections for sampling.

Why the normal curve is used is both a behavioral assumption and a matter of statistical convenience. There is a general consensus within the physical, biological, and psychological communities that a great many of their variables are normally distributed. From a statistical perspective, there is the assumption that errors of measurement and errors made in estimating population values are normally distributed.

The strengths of the normal curve model are that it allows us to model our data in such a way as to limitedly interpret individual cases, to compare the means of populations, and, through regression models, to predict with certain degrees of confidence other behavioral data. The weaknesses of the normal distribution, however, are that some phenomena and some behaviors do not fit the normal distribution. An argument is made here that a great many neuropsychological variables (or at least performance on neuropsychological tests) are either heavily skewed or have heavy kurtosis to the point where the normal distribution does a very poor job of modeling them. This is particularly problematic in the $N = 1$ case.

Modeling of Data.   Much behavioral research involves the modeling of means and standard deviations for the purposes of finding differences between groups or for analyzing one variable's effect on another variable. A *t* test using data from brain-damaged individuals and normals compares the two means. Additionally, within regression models the modeling of the means and the standard deviations is a necessary aspect with which to quantify covariance and predict the variable of interest.

Uses of the normal curve include a number of widely popular linear transformations of the sample's test scores. The most basic form of the normal distribution can be viewed as a z-score distribution with a mean of zero and standard deviation of 1. A patient 2 standard deviations below the mean would have a z-score of −2. Transformations of this type also include the T-score, which is probably most popularly found in the MMPI. Here, a linear transformation occurs where the mean is made to be 50 and standard deviations become 10. This is simply done by adding 50 to the z-scores after multiplying the deviations by 10. Further, within the WAIS–R, the mean is 100 and the standard deviations are 15. There are no differences among any of these scores other than arbitrary metric.

It is important to realize that such transformations are done because of an underlying assumption that the construct is normally distributed (and so the data should actually be normally distributed). If the obtained data are not normally distributed, this must be due to sampling error. Therefore, normalizing the data transforms the "biased" sample distribution to the "correct" normal distribution. This, however, is probably rarely the case.

At times within neuropsychology, researchers and clinicians utilized percentile scores to model data. Normalized percentiles are simply a further transformation of a normal distribution; someone two standard deviations above the mean would be assigned a percentile score of 97.5. This approach is deceptive in that actual or "cumulative" percentile scores may differ widely from "normalized" percentile scores. The use of cumulative percentile scores is most appropriate with large samples because the actual data drive the assigned percentiles. The 190th person out of 200 falls at the 95th percentile. It is important when looking at neuropsychological norms and data to determine whether the percentiles are based on the actual population parameters, or whether they are simply "normalized" transformations from means and standard deviations of a sampling distribution that was not normally distributed in the first place. If the latter is the case, the percentile scores will not reflect reality, particularly toward the distribution tails.

Recently with the advent of the MMPI–2, blind use of normal distributions and their assumptions have come under revision. With the MMPI–2, the authors used a uniform T-score. The uniform T-score adjusts for the problem of skewed distributions. What was discovered with the MMPI–1 was that the percentage of scores above a T-score of 70 on each of the 10 scales varied widely. With a normal distribution, exactly 2½% should be above that cut score. In the MMPI–2, uniform T-scores have been used to correct that problem by adjusting in a nonlinear fashion the T-statistics so that exactly 2½% of the population is above 70 on all scales. The problem with this of course is that 2½% of the population does not necessarily have a particular psychopathology, for example, major depression. In some areas it may be greater; in other areas it may be less.

Skewed Distributions.   If with the MMPI we find skewed distributions of data, it is highly likely that within other psychopathologies we will find similar types of distributions. Indeed, this is the case in neuropsychology. There are very few neuropsychological data, whether due to measurement problems or the underlying cognitive domain, that are clearly, normally distributed data. More often, they are skewed and have kurtosis.

Skew refers to how asymmetrical the two sides of the distribution are. For a normal bell-shaped curve, the two sides are perfectly symmetrical. However, within a skewed distribution, one of the two sides goes out in a long tail. In a positively skewed distribution, this extends to the right or in a positive direction. In a negatively skewed distribution, this tail drops well below the mean for some distance and to the left. *Kurtosis* is viewed as a parameter of the flatness or peakness of the distribution. All bells are not created equally. Some are very tall and narrow. This would be a form of high positive kurtosis. Other bells and distributions are relatively flat, and this flatness is negative kurtosis.

Much of the data in the neuropsychological literature are skewed and have kurtosis. In fact, both may exist on the same variable depending upon the population sampled. For example, on Benton's Visual Form Discrimination Test (Benton et al., 1983, p. 60) the normal control group had a highly negatively skewed distribution, with the bulk of subjects attaining near perfect scores of 30–32, but a number of subjects obtaining scores down to 23. Examination of the "brain disease group" reveals a very flat distribution, with patients attaining scores ranging from a perfect score (32) all the way down to scores in the single digits. Here there are no peaks; it is a flat distribution almost rectangular in nature. The same variable in the normal sample is skewed and in the clinical sample has negative kurtosis.

Some domains and/or measurement techniques do not lend themselves to a normal distribution. The Visual Form Discrimination Test does not allow scores above 32. For normals, therefore, we find no right side to the distribution. The modal score of the control group is the maximum score of 32. No one can achieve a 33 or greater. However, one can achieve less. Theoretically, it is possible that some people have a superior ability to discriminate forms that cannot be assessed utilizing this particular instrument.

It is obvious from these examples that the normal distribution does not properly model either the control group or the pathological group. Many researchers simply calculate means and standard deviations and present these in the literature. But in so doing they are implying an underlying normal distribution and lose most of the important information in the original data.

Sitting in your office diagnosing an individual patient requires models that allow that patient to be properly placed along the data's continuum and to determine whether or not the person has an impairment. We need models that more properly model the skew and at times the kurtosis of the distribution. A good example of such a model is the Millon Clinical Multiaxial Inventory (Millon,

1987), a broad-range test of noncognitive psychopathology. The author of this particular test made nonlinear transformations from raw scores to develop what he called a *base rate score*. An arbitrary base rate score of 85 was set for the lower boundary of those individuals manifesting each disorder of interest (e.g., major depression). A base rate score of 30 was used for the mean of a normal sample. To accomplish this, Millon came down from the top of each distribution until the percentage of interest was found. For instance, there may have been 17% with major depression. At that point the author placed the 85 base rate score. In this way, an individual clinician can actually look at an individual patient's score and determine whether or not the patient is within the "normal group" or within the "pathological group." This also forms the basis of the operating characteristics of this test.

The MMPI, on the other hand, indicates that all patients who are above a 70 have a significant score on the 2 scale, which is depression, but this supposes that 2½% of your patients and individuals in the general population have major depression. This is inappropriate. To advance the psychometrics in neuropsychology, the $N = 1$ case must be the object of interest, and that case's position on a skewed tail must be maintained in the data transformation procedure.

Although base rate scores may more clearly delineate the group membership of an individual patient, they must be creatively used to apply to other questions of interest. Neuropsychology is no longer answering the simple question, "Is this patient organic?" Instead, it attempts to answer a series of questions including:

1. Is some unusual or abnormal finding present?
2. If so, does this represent a neurological, or psychological, or other disorder?
3. If it is a neurological disorder, what is its nature?
4. Perhaps, what are its anatomical correlates?
5. How severe is the disorder?
6. What are the prognostic implication of the disorder?
7. What are the functional limitations of the disorder in this particular patient?

Here difference scores between tests or administrations may need to be modeled. Because neuropsychology is not answering only simple dichotomous questions, obviously the data on and between tests must be viewed in many different ways to answer the many different questions. To date, these modeling procedures have not been done.

Sampling Considerations. An advantage of using the normal distribution and the assumptions therein is that relatively small sample sizes of about 30 or so will accurately model the mean and the standard deviation. Errors in the assumption of the mean can be calculated and similar confidence statistics for the standard deviation can be developed. With sample sizes as small as 30, the mean will be fairly stable and, surprisingly, the standard deviation will actually be even more stable. The problem with small sample sizes is dealing with skewed and kurtosed distributions. Attempting to model the lower 5% of a skewed distribution when that portion of the sample consists of those subjects who have a disorder of some sort results in highly unstable findings or models with small sample sizes. For instance, with 30 subjects, only 1 would fall within the lowest 5%. It is impossible to model the tail of a distribution based on one or two subjects. Even increasing the sample size to 100 results in only five subjects falling within the distribution tail of interest. Depending on sampling techniques and the populations being used, performance of this tail of the distribution may vary widely. Small samples result in unstable and unreliable distribution tails. Therefore, neuropsychology must get away from small sample sizes, and must utilize large-scale sampling techniques to begin to understand and accurately predict criterion measures.

It will be important to develop large samples for not only normals on our neuropsychological tests but also for our pathological samples. Obviously, operating characteristics and the accurate differentiation of our patients require samples from both populations. Increasingly, therefore, we should utilize and demand tests that have good norms for both normals and pathological cases. As indicated earlier, very often the shapes of these distributions differ widely and, aside from sophisticated operating characteristics, it is clinically necessary to know where a patient is on each of those distributions.

SUMMARY

Neuropsychology is not immune to psychometric problems. The intent of this chapter was to review some of the psychometric concepts within psychology in general and neuropsychology in particular. Psychometrically, these disciplines differ only in the level of complexity of procedures and patients. The complexities inherent in neuropsychological assessment require greater, not less, understanding of psychometric theory and application.

A number of specific issues and principles were emphasized in this chapter. An understanding of the reliability and validity of tests is essential to appreciating the limits to inferences that can be made from a test performances. In neuropsychology traditional concepts of normal curve performance distributions must be questioned, because at times highly skewed distributions are found. Additionally, it was argued that neuropsychology should not be bound by traditional norm-referenced tests and should move toward the modeling of the tails of sample distributions through operating characteristics. The reader should also understand that there is no way to get around the problem of collecting large samples to build norms so as to be able to appropriately interpret test performances. Without large samples, the tails of the distributions will be poorly modeled. Much hard psychometric work lies ahead for the field of neuropsychological assessment.

REFERENCES

Benton, A. L., Hamsher, K., Varney, N. R., & Spreen, O. (1983). *Contributions to neuropsychological assessment.* New York: Oxford University Press.

Campbell, D. T., & Fiske, D. W. (1959). Convergent and discriminant validation by the multitrait-multimethod matrix. *Psychological Bulletin, 56,* 81–105.

Cicchetti, D. V. (1991). When diagnostic agreement is high, but reliability is low: Some paradoxes occurring in joint independent neuropsychological assessment. In B. P. Rourke, L. Costa, D. V. Cicchetti, K. M. Adams, & K. J. Plasterk (Eds.), *Methodological and biostatistical foundations of clinical neuropsychology* (pp. 417–434). Berwyn, PA: Swets & Zeitlinger.

Cronbach, L. J., Gleser, G. C., Nanda, H., & Rajaratnam, N. (1972). *The dependability of behavioral measurements: Theory of generalizability for scores and profiles.* New York: John Wiley and Sons.

Franzen, M. D. (1989). *Reliability and validity in neuropsychological assessment.* New York: Plenum Press.

Millon, T. (1987). *Manual for the MCMI-II.* Minneapolis, MN: National Computer Systems.

Nunnally, J. C. (1978). *Psychometric theory.* New York: McGraw-Hill.

Rasch, G. (1980). *Probabilistic models for some intelligence and attainment tests.* Chicago: University of Chicago Press.

Reynolds, C. R. (1990). Conceptual and technical problems in learning disability diagnosis. In C. R. Reynolds, & R. W. Kamphaus (Eds.), *Handbook of psychological and educational assessment of children: Intelligence and achievement.* New York: Guilford Press.

Spreen, O., & Straus, E. (1991). *A compendium of neuropsychological tests.* New York: Oxford University Press.

Suen, H. K. (1990). *Test theories.* Hillsdale, NJ: Lawrence Erlbaum Associates.

Wechsler, D. (1981). *Manual for the Wechsler Adult Intelligence Scale–Revised (WAIS–R).* New York: Psychological Corporation.

CHAPTER NINE

Forensic Neuropsychological Assessment

Glenn J. Larrabee
Independent Practice, Sarasota, Florida

Forensic neuropsychology is the application of neuropsychology to civil and criminal legal proceedings. At times, neuropsychological deficits have a direct bearing on legal issues—for example, establishment of damages in a personal injury case. At other times, a person may have impaired neuropsychological test scores, but the impairment alone does not provide the complete answer to the legal issue. Hence, an older person may have dementia, but still possess competency to execute a valid will; a person facing criminal charges may have neuropsychological impairment but be found competent to stand trial.

The lack of a one-to-one correspondence between legal issues and neuropsychological test scores requires a high level of neuropsychological expertise, as well as experience dealing with a variety of civil and criminal issues. Moreover, the value of neuropsychology to the courts is growing, with neuropsychologists being asked to address a wider range of competencies. This expansion into new areas requires a close working relationship between the neuropsychologist and the attorney requesting the expert opinion. By working together, the expert neuropsychologist and the attorney can combine their respective expertise and better provide information to assist the trier of fact.

PROFESSIONAL ISSUES AND RESPONSIBILITIES

Expertise

The field of neuropsychology has grown dramatically over the past 15 years. The recognition of neuropsychology as a specialty area by the American Psychological Association (APA) is a testimony to the growth and specialization of our field. Recently, representative neuropsychologists and major professional organizations, including the National Academy of Neuropsychology, Division 40 of APA, the American Academy of Clinical Neuropsychology, and American Board of Clinical Neuropsychology (ABCN) have developed consensus guidelines for specialty education and training in clinical neuropsychology (Hannay et al., 1998).

At present, the clearest evidence of competence as a neuropsychologist remains as defined in *The Clinical Neuropsychologist* (Division 40, 1989): attainment of the ABCN/ABPP Diploma in Clinical Neuropsychology. Although this diploma is not held as prerequisite to engage in the clinical or forensic practice of neuropsychology, it is the clearest evidence of the type of expertise expected of a neuropsychologist wishing to provide forensic neuropsychology services. Indeed, the new guidelines for specialty education and training list eligibility for board certification by ABCN/ABPP as one of the exit criteria for successful completion of a neuropsychological residency program (Hannay et al., 1998).

Melton, Petrila, Poythress, and Slobogin (1997) provided a detailed review of the definition and role of the expert in legal settings. Rule 702 of the Federal Rules of Evidence allows a witness qualified as an expert by knowledge, skill, experience, training, or education to testify if scientific, technical or other specialized knowledge will assist the trier of fact to understand the evidence or determine a fact in issue.

Melton et al. (1997) also discussed the impact of the Frye rule and Daubert standards in defining expertise. The Frye rule holds that admissible scientific evidence should be conditioned on having been sufficiently established that it is generally accepted in the particular scientific field to which it belongs. As Melton et al. (1997) observed, the standards for scientific evidence changed in 1993 with the Supreme Court's decision in *Daubert v. Merrel Dow Pharmaceuticals*. Consequently, admissibility of evidence is not dependent on general acceptance by the scientific field; rather, acceptability is based on an inference or assertion derived by the scientific method, and the court must decide whether the reasoning and methodology on which expert testimony is based are scientifically valid and can properly be applied to the facts in issue. Criteria for deciding acceptability include the testability of the theoretical basis, error rate of the methods used, and "Frye-like" factors such as approval by peer reviewers and level of acceptance by experts in the field.

Neuropsychologists have encountered challenges regarding their qualifications for identifying the cause of, and prognosis for, conditions of the brain. Richardson and Adams (1992) and Adams and Rankin (1996) discussed these issues and noted that several states now allow neuropsychological testimony as to etiology and prognosis.

Ethical and Practical Issues

Professionally appropriate practice in any area of psychology must adhere to the Ethical Principles of Psychologists and Code of Conduct (APA, 1992). Binder and Thompson (1994) discussed sections of the Ethics Code with direct relevance to neuropsychology. Key sections include Competence, Multiple Relationships, Validity of Test Results and Test Interpretation, Documentation of Assessment Results, Records and Confidentiality, Forensic Activities, Avoiding Harm, Supervision of Subordinates (technicians), and Fees. Binder and Thompson provided 20 recommendations for applying the APA Ethics Code to neuropsychological practice.

As recommended by Binder and Thompson (1994), fee arrangements should be made as early as possible in the professional relationship. Most professional neuropsychological services are provided on an hourly basis. In forensic cases, it is important to have an understanding between the neuropsychologist and referring attorney of what the fees and charges will be before examination is conducted, and before sworn testimony is provided in deposition or at trial. A fairly common practice in forensic neuropsychology is to request a retainer agreement specifying charges, and a prepayment, which is applied toward final charges after provision of services is completed. Accepting a case on "letter of protection," —that is, the psychologist's fee will be paid if litigation is successful—is problematic. With a letter of protection, the psychologist can (and probably will) be portrayed by opposing counsel during testimony as having a vested interest in the outcome of the case.

Increasingly, demands are being made by opposing counsel for video or audio recording of neuropsychological examinations, or for having complete examinations transcribed by a court reporter (McCaffrey, Fisher, Gold, & Lynch, 1996). McCaffrey et al. noted that in many, but not all, state law jurisdictions, there is an underlying assumption that third-party attendance should be permitted, based on the long-standing practice of allowing attorneys to accompany their clients to physical examinations. This practice is inadvisable on two major grounds: (a) The presence of third party observation or recording can affect the validity of test performance and (b) the confidentiality of the test instruments can be compromised if made a part of the public record. McCaffrey et al. (1996) reviewed multiple research investigations demonstrating social facilitation effects on task performance (see their Table 1). McCaffrey et al. also found that social facilitation effects extend to the use of one-way mirrors and videotaping. Binder and Johnson-Greene (1995), using a clever, A–B–A reversal design, demonstrated motivational fluctuation in a patient dependent on whether or not her mother was present in the room. McCaffrey et al. (1996) concluded that, in general, social facilitation effects are negative on complex cognitive tasks, but positive on simpler tasks. Extended to the observation or recording of a neuropsychological evaluation, this could conceivably make deficits appear worse on measures of memory and complex problem-solving tasks, and cause strengths on simpler cognitive tasks to appear to be stronger.

Presently, the court's decision to allow the presence of third-party observers varies state by state, and in some states on a case-by-case basis. The federal courts have ruled specifically against allowing the presence of third-party observers (*Ragge v. MCA/Universal Studios,* 1995).

When presented with a request for third-party observation, the examining neuropsychologist can object to the court, through the retaining attorney. This involves preparing an affidavit with supporting materials. The affidavit prepared by the current author notes the potential effects of third-party observation on test performance, referencing McCaffrey et al. (1996) and Binder and Johnson-Greene (1995), as clearly demonstrating effects of third-party observation on neuropsychological test performance. Both of these articles are included as exhibits. This affidavit also points out that the tests were not standardized in the presence of third-party observers, and consequently, validity can be compromised due to lack of appropriate normative standards for comparison. Also noted are the potential distracting effects of observation, which can be particularly problematic for patients with attentional problems. Lastly, the impact of third-party presence on increasing the adversarial and decreasing the clinical nature of the examination is discussed. The relevant APA ethical principles regarding test security and release of data to parties not trained in test interpretation are cited, with the Ethics Code appended as an exhibit. The affidavit explains that permitting nonpsychologists to possess complete test procedures and raw test data can invalidate use of these procedures on future cases, because the questions and answers will be known ahead of time. This is underscored by Youngjohn's (1995) recent report of confirmed attorney "coaching" of a client prior to neuropsychological examination.

Requests for release of raw test data to attorneys are far more common than requests to observe or record an examination. The current author has been quite successful with contacting the attorney issuing the subpoena for records, explaining the appropriate ethical principles, and offering to immediately send the records to a licensed psychologist of their choice. This approach has been much more successful than "I cannot release the data, because of the APA Ethics Code." The Ethics Code also directs psychologist to attempt to effect a resolution between ethical principles and the demands of the law. The offer to send the data to a licensed psychologist, who also has to abide by the Ethics Code, provides that this other psychologist can analyze the data and maintain test security, but still provides the requesting attorney with the information he needs. In certain instances, the attorney issuing the subpoena may not wish to disclose the identity of the expert. This is handled easily by picking a third licensed psychologist as "middleman," who can then forward the data to the licensed psychologist of the attorney's choice.

SCIENTIFIC APPROACH
TO FORENSIC NEUROPSYCHOLOGY

If symptoms such as dizziness, blurred vision, and concentration and memory impairment only occurred with brain damage, if neuropsychological tests were only failed by brain-damaged persons, and if test data and symptoms predicted behavior perfectly, the practice of neuropsychology would be uncomplicated and error free. Obviously, this is not the case, as neuropsychological "symptoms" can occur for reasons other than neurological dysfunction (Lees-Haley & Brown, 1993), and performance on neuropsychological tests can be poor for reasons other than brain damage (Binder, 1997; Larrabee, 1990). Hence, it is important to take a careful, scientific approach to forensic neuropsychology.

The goals of science are many. Through application of careful, systematic, controlled observations and measurement, the scientist hopes to obtain a better understanding of a phenomenon, make predictions about future events involving that phenomenon, and analyze the phenomenon in relationship to past events that may be causally associated (Badia & Runyon, 1982; Kerlinger, 1973). The successful application of the scientific approach depends on accuracy of measurement and observation, appropriate use of logic, and careful consideration of alternative explanations or hypotheses (Badia & Runyon, 1982; Kerlinger, 1973; Faust, Ziskin, & Hiers, 1991).

Presently, there is a growing problem of overdiagnosis of neuropsychological deficits in legal settings (Faust et al., 1991; Larrabee, 1990; Russell, 1990). Russell (1990) attributed the increased use of neuropsychology in legal settings to the fact that neuropsychologists can easily diagnose brain damage when there is none. The problem of overdiagnosis is the direct result of a failure to analyze cases critically and scientifically. This failure frequently results in inadequate differential diagnosis (Binder, 1997).

Faulty logic commonly leads to diagnostic error. As Miller (1983) noted, the argument "if damage to structure X produces a decline on test T, then any new subject with a poor performance on T must have a lesion at X" is the same as the argument "if a horse is a large animal with four legs, then any newly encountered large animal with four legs is a horse." Larrabee (1990) extended Miller's (1983) example to the diagnostic decision of "brain damage" versus "no brain damage": if brain-damaged patients perform poorly on neuropsychological tests, then any new patient who performs poorly on neuropsychological tests must be brain-damaged. Of course, neuropsychological tests are measures of cognitive abilities, rather than tests of brain damage (Russell, 1990), and performance can be poor for a host of reasons other than brain damage, including poor motivation, limited cooperation or inattentiveness due to fatigue, pain, discomfort, medication, substance abuse, learning disability, and psychiatric diagnosis (Binder, 1997; Larrabee, 1990).

Faust et al. (1991) discussed a variety of sources of judgment error. The base-rate problem is one of the major factors in neuropsychological overdiagnosis. Simply put, *base rate* refers to the frequency with which something occurs; for example, if 5 in 100 persons with mild head trauma (MHT) suffer persisting neuropsychological deficits, the base rate is 5%. Lack of awareness of base rates can lead to the formation of illusory correlations or "seeing" relationships that do not exist.

Faust et al. (1991) discussed the phenomenon of illusory correlation in some detail. The original work on this phenomenon was conducted by the Chapmans (Chapman & Chapman, 1967), who presented clinicians with human figure drawings accompanied by randomly paired symptom statements (e.g. "suspiciousness" would appear in association with accented eyes as frequently as in association with nonaccented eyes). Despite the absence of systematic relationships in the data, clinicians attributed diagnostic "signs" to the relationships they had assumed existed in the first place (e.g., associating accented eyes in human figure drawings with "suspiciousness"), demonstrating both a failure to consider base rates, and a confirmation bias.

Lees-Haley and Brown (1993) provided important base-rate data on the frequency of neuropsychological complaints in two groups of subjects: (a) 50 outpatients from a group family practice clinic and (b) 170 claimant patients filing claims for emotional distress or industrial stress, with no known history of head injury, toxic exposure, seizure disorder, or neuropsychological impairment, and without claim for central nervous system (CNS) injury (non-CNS litigants). Complaints commonly thought of as symptomatic of head trauma and toxic exposure occurred frequently in the medical controls (MC) and non-CNS litigants; for example, 62% of MC and 88% of non-CNS litigants reported headaches; 26% of MC and 78% of non-CNS litigants reported difficulty concentrating; and 38% of MC and 77% of non-CNS litigants reported irritability.

The base-rate data provided by Lees-Haley and Brown (1993) are sobering. These data highlight significant problems with the sensitivity and specificity of common neuropsychological symptom checklists. *Sensitivity* refers to the frequency or rate of occurrence of a finding among patients with the condition in question, whereas *specificity* refers to the frequency of negative test results among patients who do not have illness or condition in question (Baldessarini, Finklestein, & Arana, 1983). Ignoring the baserates of a symptom such as "difficulty concentrating" could lead to a misdiagnosis of brain damage in one of four MC, and three in four non-CNS litigants; in other words, a symptom complaint common in neurological settings (i.e., with high sensitivity) has poor specificity (74% of MC and only 22% of non-CNS litigants are correctly classified as being without neurologic impairment).

As shown by Faust et al. (1991), citing research by Dodrill (1985) and Bornstein (1986), the base rates of neuropsychological test patterns are also important. Hence, Dodrill (1985) found no differences in frequency of altered orientation of drawings of a key in patient versus normal controls. Bornstein (1986) found that normal individuals frequently exceeded the 10% performance advantage for the dominant hand on motor tasks. In discussing WAIS–R VIQ–PIQ discrepancies, Kaufman (1990) noted that a 9-point difference is statistically significant, but 42.4% of normal adults ages 25–74 obtained discrepancies of 9 or more points. A 12-point WAIS–R VIQ–PIQ discrepancy is significant at $p < .01$, but 28.6% of normal people achieve a VIQ–PIQ difference of 12 or more points.

Faust et al. (1991) and Wedding and Faust (1989) discussed various biases in clinical judgment. Wedding and Faust defined *hindsight bias* as the tendency to believe, once the outcome of an event is known, that the outcome could have been more easily predicted than is actually the case. Hence, knowing about an event through clinical history—for example, a blow to the head in an automobile accident—leads clinicians to believe they can predict the event and diagnose neuropsychological deficits consistent with closed-head injury.

Hindsight bias can be closely intertwined with *confirmation bias* or the tendency to seek confirming evidence, at the expense of ignoring disconfirming evidence for one's diagnostic hypothesis. As Wedding and Faust (1989) noted, "What one looks for, one finds" (p. 241). This leads to the tendency to favor one's initial hypotheses, and to subject one's initial hypotheses to preferential analysis. Hence, the clinician may be much more lenient or accepting of information supporting the initial hypothesis, and more critical and less accepting of information contradicting the initial hypothesis, a phenomenon characterized as asymmetric error costs (Trope, Gervey, & Liberman, 1997). Trope et al. also observed that people are more likely to terminate hypothesis testing prematurely, once they receive evidence supporting their desired hypothesis.

Evidence of confirmation bias in clinical decision making is abundant, and directly related to illusory correlation (Chapman & Chapman, 1967). The neuropsychologist engaging in confirmation bias selectively attends only to evidence that supports the hypothesis of brain damage. The current author saw one case where it was questionable that the patient even struck her head (she claimed she did; records did not substantiate this). In either event, she had no loss of consciousness or posttraumatic amnesia, yet was diagnosed as suffering brain damage on the basis of a WMS–R Attention Concentration Index of 75. This psychologist selectively ignored the WMS–R General Memory Index (GM) of 129, which not only contradicted the presence of brain damage but also was highly inconsistent with the patient's WMS–R Attention Concentration (AC) score of 75. It is logically inconsistent that a person with impaired attention, at the 5th percentile, could have memory function at the 97th percentile. Indeed, the 54-point GM minus AC difference score had a probability of malingering beyond .99, in Mittenberg, Azrin, Millsaps, and Heilbronner's (1993) research on malingered head trauma on the WMS–R.

Wedding and Faust (1989) provided a variety of strategies that can be used to reduce confirmation bias, beginning with advising that the clinician know the

TABLE 9.1
Analysis of the Consistency of Neuropsychological Data

1. Are the data consistent within and between neuropsychological domains?
2. Is the neuropsychological profile consistent with the suspected etiologic condition?
3. Are the neuropsychological data consistent with the documented severity of injury?
4. Are the neuropsychological data consistent with the client's behavioral presentation?

literature on human judgment (see Trope et al., 1997, for a concise review of human judgment and decision making). Their recommendation to avoid premature abandonment of useful decision rules is aided by strategies of starting with the most valid information, listing alternative diagnostic options and seeking evidence for each, and systematically listing disconfirmatory information. This last recommendation is particularly important in reducing confirmation bias. As Wedding and Faust observed, neuropsychologists frequently make up lists of test findings that support particular hypotheses. They recommend also listing all data that argue *against* one's hypotheses. In this vein, the present author has found it useful to frame hypothetical questions such as, What kind of brain damage causes poor performance on the Category Test, Auditory Verbal Learning Test, and Finger Tapping, with above average performance on Controlled Oral Word Association, Verbal Selective Reminding, Trail Making B, and the Grooved Pegboard?

Larrabee (1990, 1992, 1997) suggested a four-component consistency analysis in neuropsychological diagnostic decision making (see Table 9.1). The data subjected to the consistency analysis include a detailed and extensive interview, detailed record review, and extensive and redundant neuropsychological testing, with multiple test measures within each of several functional domains, including language, perception, sensorimotor function, attention and information processing, verbal and visual memory function, and intelligence and problem solving.

The clinical interview is conducted prior to testing, and yields information about the subject's recollection of the original injury or traumatic exposure, subsequent symptoms and change in symptoms over time, other health care providers the patient has seen, and the procedures, diagnoses, and treatments they have received. Background interview concerning early development, nuclear family, school experiences, work history, marital history, substance abuse, prior medical history, and prior litigation and criminal history must also be conducted. The data from this interview are validated against medical records, school records, work records and criminal records.

Following collection of the interview data, record review data, and test data, the consistency analysis is conducted. First, the consistency within and between domains should be evaluated. Within domains, a person who performs poorly on Trail Making A should not perform normally on Trail Making B; a person with very poor performance on Finger Tapping should not have normal Grooved Pegboard performance. Between domains, a person with very poor attention should not perform normally on memory tests; a person with borderline scores on intelligence and problem solving should not have superior memory function.

Second, the neuropsychological test score profile should be consistent with established patterns for known disorders such as amnesia and dementia. Hence, amnestics do not perform poorly on WAIS–R Digit Span or Arithmetic; patients with dementia do not usually perform at above-average levels on complex problem-solving tasks such as the Category Test or WAIS–R Block Design. Larrabee (1990) noted a case of misdiagnosis wherein a psychologist diagnosed left-hemisphere brain damage in a patient with a mild head trauma (MHT) who had reduced right-motor functions, lower Verbal IQ relative to Performance IQ, and poor verbal memory. The psychologist did not consider the patient's limited educational attainment, learning disability verified through school records, and the effects of peripheral injury to the right upper extremity (with functional overlay).

The third consistency requirement is that level of neuropsychological test performance should be consistent with the severity of injury. This can be considered as biological or physiological severity "indexing" or "referencing" (Larrabee, 1990, 1997). Dikmen, Machamer, Winn, and Temkin (1995) provided 1-year outcome data for the full spectrum of head trauma severity, ranging from persons who could follow a doctor's commands within 1 hr, to persons who took greater than 1 month to follow a doctor's commands. Hence, a patient who was briefly unconscious at the scene of the accident, who recalls transportation to the hospital, and who has a Glasgow Coma Scale (GCS) of 15 in the emergency room, no focal neurologic signs, and normal computed tomography (CT) scan of the brain, should not perform on neuropsychological tests at a level equivalent to patients who have sustained 2 weeks of coma.

Lastly, test performance should be compared with other aspects of a patient's behavior. A patient who has good memory in the clinical interview, demonstrated by accurate recall of doctors seen, evaluations, and treatments, validated by correlation with record review data, should not demonstrate impaired memory on neuropsychological testing. One case of minor head trauma (MHT) seen by the current author accurately analyzed his current WAIS–R Digit Symbol performance as superior to testing conducted two years earlier, showing evidence of excellent memory, yet performed very poorly on all memory tests administered by the author. Another MHT patient performed on memory tests at a level similar to Alzheimer's disease, and on the second day of examination noted that the clock had been removed from the wall of the examining suite.

The key to this consistency analysis is that everything must make "neuropsychological sense" (Larrabee, 1990; Stuss, 1995). When significant inconsistencies are observed, invalid performance must be considered.

VALIDITY ASSESSMENT

General Validity Considerations

Comprehensive and accurate neuropsychological evaluation must be based on test procedures that are reliable, yielding consistent and stable scores, and valid, yielding true measures of the abilities and traits that we assume we are measuring; in other words, memory tests should yield reliable assessments of memory, and problem-solving tests should yield reliable assessments of problem-solving skills. However, test procedures that have proven reliability and validity may yield scores that are not reliable or valid measures for the individual patient being examined. The preceding section and Table 9.1 provided general guidelines for evaluating the consistency of scores for an individual patient. Inconsistency in scores for a particular patient generally indicates some variation in motivation on the part of the patient, provided that examiner error can be excluded and there is no error arising from the context of the examination (e.g., observer effects via attorney observation and / or recording / transcription can be excluded; cf. Binder & Johnson-Greene, 1995; McCaffrey et al., 1996). As Larrabee (1990) noted, variation in motivation can be outside of the patient's control (e.g., disruptive effects of anxiety, depression, fatigue, and pain on test performance; conversion reaction), or may be under the conscious, intentional control of the patient who is malingering and deliberately performing poorly on neuropsychological tests.

The next section reviews assessment of malingering. As with any diagnostic conclusion, the determination of malingering is associated with issues of sensitivity and specificity, and is dependent on the base rate of occurrence of malingering in forensic settings. Some have estimated this base rate to be low (20% or less; Trueblood & Schmidt, 1993), whereas others have found malingering and performance invalidity base rates to be high (up to 47%, Binder & Kelly, 1996; 70%, Millis, 1992).

Malingering

Malingering is the intentional production of false or grossly exaggerated physical and / or psychological symptoms for external incentives such as obtaining monetary compensation or avoiding criminal prosecution (American Psychiatric Association, *DSM–IV*, 1994; Rogers, 1997). In the course of neuropsychological evaluation, malingering can manifest as (a) false and / or exaggerated reporting of symptoms (Berry et al., 1995), (b) intentionally poor performance on neuropsychological tests (Binder & Pankratz, 1987; Millis & Putnam, 1996), or (c) a combination of symptom exaggeration and intentional performance deficit (see Table 9.2).

TABLE 9.2
Evaluation of Malingering

---

1. Exaggerated symptom reporting.
   a. Exaggeration of psychopathology (MMPI–2 F, Back F, VRIN, TRIN, Infrequency Psycho-pathology Scale).
   b. Exaggerated somatic symptomatology (elevations over T 79 on Scales 1 and 3, plus elevated Lees-Haley Fake Bad scale).
2. Poor motivation and effort on neuropsychological testing.
   a. Poor performance on tasks that are easily performed by nonlitigating persons who have bona fide neurological disorder (Rey 15-Item Test).
   b. Pattern analysis (disproportionate impairment of attention relative to memory, cf. Mittenberg et al., 1993; discriminant function equations differentiating noninjured simulators from bona fide head-injured patients, cf. Mittenberg et al., 1993, 1995, 1996).
   c. Forced-choice symptom validity testing (Portland Digit Recognition Test, Binder & Kelly, 1996; Test of Memory Malingering, cf. Tombaugh, 1996; Warrington Recognition Memory Test, cf. Millis, 1992).

Exaggerated Reporting of Symptoms. The Minnesota Multiphasic Personal-ity Inventory (MMPI)/MMPI–2 (Butcher, Dahlstrom, Graham, Tellegen, & Kaemmer, 1989), is frequently used as an objective measure of personality func-tions in neuropsychological evaluation (Butler, Retzlaff, & Vanderploeg, 1991). A major advantage of the MMPI/MMPI–2 is that it allows an assessment of the validity of a person's response pattern.

Heaton, Smith, Lehman, and Vogt (1978) compared noninjured persons at-tempting to feign the effects of closed-head trauma to nonlitigating persons who had actually sustained closed-head injury (CHI). The MMPI F scale was one of the best discriminators between the two groups.

More recently, Berry and colleagues (Berry et al., 1995) compared the MMPI–2 profiles of four groups of subjects: nonclinical subjects answering under stan-dard instructions, noninjured CHI dissimulators trying to feign impairment, noncompensation-seeking CHI subjects, and compensation-seeking CHI sub-jects. Following Bonferroni correction, the CHI dissimulators had lower K than the other groups, with higher F, Fb, F − K, F(p) (Arbisi & Ben-Porath, 1993), and Ds^2 (Dissimulation scale; Gough, 1954; Berry et al., 1995).

One problem in relying on more traditional MMPI–2 exaggeration-sensitive scales such as F and Fb is that F is more sensitive to exaggeration of severe psy-chopathology and psychosis than it is to exaggeration of somatic and non-psychotic emotional symptomatology. Indeed, there is only one F scale item on either Scale 1 (Hypochondriasis) or Scale 3 (Hysteria), and there are only two F scale items on Scale 2 (Depression; Butcher et al., 1989). Lees-Haley and col-leagues, noting the relative insensitivity of F and F − K to personal injury malin-gering, developed a new scale, the Fake Bad Scale (FBS; Lees-Haley; 1992; Lees-Haley, English, & Glenn, 1991). Lees-Haley et al. (1991) observed that personal injury malingerers presented, paradoxically, with a mixture of fake-good and fake-bad self-reports, directed toward (a) appearing honest, (b) appearing psychologically normal except for the influence of the alleged cause of injury, (c) denying preexisting psychopathology, (d) when preexisting complaints have been documented, minimizing the significance of these complaints, (e) concealing or minimizing antisocial behavior, and (f) attempting to present a degree of injury or disability within perceived limits of plausibility.

Lees-Haley et al. (1991) identified the 43 items comprising the FBS based on unpublished frequency counts of malingerers' MMPI data, and contrasted the FBS score of a group of personal injury malingerers with noninjured persons simulating effects of motor vehicle accident, work stress, and toxic exposure. Lees-Haley (1992) conducted a cross-validation study of spurious posttraumatic stress disorder and established the current cutoffs for exaggerated symptom report on the FBS.

Other research has provided independent support for the FBS. Slick, Hopp, Strauss, and Spellacy (1996) found that the FBS demonstrated more numerous significant correlations with the Victoria Symptom Validity Test (VSVT; a two-alternative forced-choice test of malingering) than did other MMPI–2 validity scales, including the F scale. Millis, Putnam, and Adams (1995) found that the FBS was the most diagnostically efficient MMPI–2 validity scale, for separating MHT with poor motivation from severe CHI patients.

Larrabee (1998) demonstrated the superiority of the FBS to traditional MMPI/MMPI–2 malingering scales in detecting somatic malingering in 12 litigants with no medical or radiological evidence of brain damage but with objective evidence of invalidity on symptom validity tests. All litigants had elevations on Scales 1 and 3 exceeding average values for chronic pain patients, and values reported by noninjured dissimulators in research on malingering, but only 3 of the 12 had elevated F, whereas 11 of the 12 had elevations on FBS. Larrabee suggested that somatic malingering should be considered whenever elevations on Scales 1 and 3 are T 80 or greater, accompanied by a significant elevation on the FBS. Larrabee concluded that two types of malingering can occur on the MMPI: (a) globally exaggerated psychopathology (Berry et al., 1995; Heaton et al., 1978) and (b) specific exaggeration of somatic symptomatology.

Intentionally Poor Performance on Neuropsychological Tests. Also, patients can deliberately perform poorly on neuropsychological tests. This intentionally poor cognitive performance can be relatively independent of the exaggeration of symptomatic complaints detected by the MMPI–2 (Greiffenstein, Gola, & Baker, 1995).

Relatively Simple Tests Performed Well by Neurologically Impaired Patients. Various different strategies have been developed for evaluation of malingering on measures of cognitive performance. One approach is to present a test that has the appearance of measuring a complex cognitive function such as memory, but that is really quite easy for most patients to perform. The best example of this procedure is the Rey 15-Item Test (Lezak, 1995). This procedure, developed by the French psychologist Rey, requires the subject to draw, from memory, 15 items; however the items are easily grouped (e.g., identical numeric sequences of Arabic and Roman numerals; identical alphabet sequences in upper and lower case), so that even patients suffering significant brain dysfunction can perform well. Lezak (1995) noted that Rey originally suggested recall of three rows or less (nine or fewer items) was suggestive of motivational deficit. Lee, Loring, and Martin (1992) compared the performance of temporal-lobe epileptics with memory deficits (TLEs), outpatient neurological disorder patients (OPs), and litigating outpatients (MHTs) on the Rey 15-Item Test. They found that a score of 7 or less was at the fifth percentile for TLE and OP, who did not differ from one another on overall level of 15-item performance. By contrast, the MHT litigants, as a group, performed significantly less well than either the TLEs, or OPs, and 6 of 16 litigants scored 7 or below on the 15-Item Test.

Schretlen, Brandt, Krafft, and Van Gorp (1991) administered the 15-Item Test to normal subjects instructed to feign amnesia or insanity, suspected malingerers, true amnestics, mixed neuropsychiatric patients, persons with moderate to severe traumatic brain injury, patients with mixed dementia, patients with severe mental illness, and normal controls. The suspected malingerers performed at the lowest level. A score of 8 or less had a sensitivity of 43% for detection of suspected fakers (43% of suspected fakers were detected), with a specificity of 73% for all patients (27% of patients were misclassified as fakers). A score of 9 or less increased the sensitivity to 71%, but lowered specificity to 64%. Patients with genuine amnesic disorder and dementia demonstrated very poor performance on the 15-Item Test. Schretlen et al. suggested that in the absence of gross cognitive impairment, demonstrable neurologic disease, or severe psychiatric illness, persons with at least borderline intelligence should not recall fewer than nine items.

Greiffenstein, Baker, and Gola (1996) evaluated several different scoring methods for the 15-Item Test as to their ability to discriminate persons with severe traumatic brain injury from persons with MHT claiming permanent severe disability. Overall, their data supported Lezak's (1995) description of Rey's cutoff score of 9 or less as producing predictive accuracies above base-rate guessing. New scoring methodologies based on spatial aspects (correct within-row reproductions) improved the sensitivity and specificity of the Rey 15-Item Test for detection of malingering. Greiffenstein et al. (1996) reiterated the caveats expressed by Schretlen et al. (1991) regarding interpretation of Rey 15-Item scores produced by patients who have documented evidence of severe cerebral dysfunction.

Pattern Analysis. A second methodology employed in research on malingering is the pattern analysis approach. This approach identifies poor motivation by score patterns atypical for neurological disorder—for example, demonstrating free recall superior to recognition on memory testing. This approach has been applied in research contrasting the performance of noninjured persons attempting to simulate brain damage with the performance of actual brain-injured patients.

Benton and Spreen (1961) demonstrated that simulators performing administration A (10 sec exposure, immediate reproduction) of the Visual Retention Test made more errors of distortion but fewer errors of omission than did actual brain-damaged patients. Gronwall (1977) observed that on the Paced Auditory Serial Addition Test (PASAT), performance typically decreases across the four test trials in concussed patients. Inconsistency with this pattern can demonstrate motivational problems, as Gronwall exemplified by her discussion of a 14-year-old schoolgirl who made as many errors on the fourth (most rapid) PASAT trial as she had made on the first (slowest) trial. When confronted with her inconsistency, she admitted she had not wanted to return to school, and, when advised she had no choice but to return, her PASAT scores normalized.

Heaton et al. (1978) contrasted the neuropsychological test results of 16 volunteer malingerers feigning the presence of neuropsychological impairment with those of 16 cooperative, nonlitigating head-trauma patients. Ten neuropsychologists, reviewing the score patterns "blind" to group membership, had generally poor diagnostic accuracy, ranging from chance to 20% better than chance. By contrast, discriminant function analysis, based on the neuropsychological test results (WAIS and Halstead–Reitan Battery or HRB), correctly classified 100% of subjects, and discriminant function analysis, based on the MMPI, correctly classified 94% of the subjects. On the neuropsychological testing, in comparison to actual head-injured patients, the simulating malingerers had significantly poorer performance on WAIS Digit Span, and HRB Speech Sounds Perception, Finger Tapping, Grip Strength, Finger Agnosia, and Suppressions. By contrast, malingerers outperformed head-injured subjects on the HRB Category Test and the Tactual Performance Test. On the MMPI, simulating malingerers produced higher scores on F, 1, 3, 6, 7, 8, and 0, in comparison to head injured subjects.

Bernard, McGrath, and Houston (1996) contrasted the Wisconsin Card Sorting Test (WCST) performance of noninjured simulating malingerers with groups of patients with either closed-head injury or with mixed CNS pathology other than CHI alone (e.g., fetal alcohol syndrome, developmental delay, and CHI; multiple sclerosis; encephalitis). The simulating malingerers performed more poorly on WCST Categories achieved than did the two brain-injured groups. Moreover, the malingerers showed a lower ratio of categories obtained to perseverative errors than did either brain-injured group. Bernard et al. interpreted their data as supporting the pattern of performance theory of the effects of malingering on neuropsychological tests; that is, persons malingering do more poorly on obvious rather than subtle tasks compared with brain-injured persons.

Similar data, demonstrating poorer performance on easier relative to more difficult motor tasks in patients with poor motivation, have been reported by Greiffenstein, Baker, and Gola (1996). The Grip Strength, Tapping Speed, and Grooved Pegboard performance of patients with moderate to severe CHI who also had neurological evidence of impaired motor function was compared to the motor performance of persons with postconcussion syndrome (PCS) who either had posttraumatic amnesia (PTA) for less than 1 hr or no PTA, claims of three or more persistent cognitive or emotional symptoms for more than 1 year, perceived disability in at least one social role, and normal physical and neurological examinations. Additionally, PCS subjects selected for study had to demonstrate performance on at least one motor skills score that was equal to or poorer than a T-score of 40 utilizing the Heaton, Grant, and Matthews (1991) normative data. Greiffenstein et al. (1996) found the expected upper motor neuron pattern of performance in the moderate to severe CHI patients, with better performance on Grip Strength than on Finger Tapping, with poorest performance on the Grooved Pegboard. By contrast, PCS subjects demonstrated a nonphysiologic pattern, with poorest performance on Grip Strength, with relatively better performance on Tapping and on the Grooved Pegboard. Because objective measures of behavioral pain and emotional distress did not correlate with motor performance, Greiffenstein et al. (1996) concluded that motor skill deficits in PCS were probably functional in nature.

Mittenberg and colleagues (Mittenberg et al., 1993; Mittenberg, Theroux-Fichera, Heilbronner, & Zielinski, 1995; Mittenberg, Rotholc, Russell, & Heilbronner, 1996) reported discriminant function analyses for the WMS–R, WAIS–R, and HRB to discriminate noninjured dissimulators from persons with significant closed-head trauma. Mittenberg et al. (1993) correctly discriminated 91% (cross-validated at 87.2%) of subjects based on a WMS–R discriminant function. Using the WAIS–R, Mittenberg et al. (1995) obtained a 79% hit rate (74% on cross-validation). Mittenberg et al. (1996) correctly classified 88.8% of simulators and head-injured patients using an HRB discriminant function, with 83.8% correctly classified on cross-validation. Their HRB discriminant function also correctly classified subjects in several other published data sets, including the original Heaton et al. (1978) subjects.

Mittenberg et al. (1993, 1995) also studied two rationally derived score relationships: WMS–R General Memory minus Attention/Concentration (note that amnestics do not have poorer attention than memory), and WAIS–R Vocabulary minus Digit Span (note that patients with delirium or dementia of sufficient severity to perform poorly on Digit Span do not have normal word definition skills). WMS–R General Memory minus Attention/Concentration correctly identified 83.3% of subjects, a value nearly as high as that obtained by the full discriminant function (Mittenberg et al., 1993). WAIS–R Vocabulary minus Digit Span correctly identified 71% of subjects, a value nearly as high as that obtained by the full discriminant function (Mittenberg et al., 1995). Actual head-injured persons produced higher WMS–R Attention/Concentration than General Memory, and equivalent scores on WAIS–R Vocabulary and Digit Span (Mittenberg et al., 1993, 1995).

Forced-Choice Symptom Validity Testing. A major advance in the evaluation of malingering has been the application of forced-choice methodology and the binomial theorem to assess intentionally poor performance (Binder, 1990; Binder & Pankratz, 1987; Hiscock & Hiscock, 1989). In a forced-choice task (e.g., identifying whether one has been touched once or twice; identifying which of two 5-digit numbers was presented previously), it is conceivable that someone with severe brain damage could perform at chance level. If someone performs significantly worse than chance, based on application of the normal approximation to the binomial theorem, the assumption can be made that they had to know the correct answer to perform at such an improbably poor level. At extreme levels of probability (.05 or .01), it can be argued that such an improbable performance is tantamount to confession of malingering.

Thus, forced-choice methodology provides an opportunity to directly infer intentionally poor performance, when someone performs significantly below chance. Yet many persons whose behavior is suspicious for malingering do not perform at worse than chance levels on two alternative forced-choice testing. Consequently, Binder and Willis (1991) determined an objective performance cutoff on the Portland Digit Recognition Test (PDRT; a two-alternative forced-choice test for recognition memory of a 5-digit number), based on the worst performance of a nonlitigating sample with documented brain damage (BD). Fifteen percent of a compensation-seeking minor head trauma (MHT) group performed below the worst performance of the BD group for the Easy PDRT items, 20% for the hard items, and 26% for the total score. By contrast, only 15% of MHT performed worse than chance.

Millis (1992) compared the performance of MHT patients seeking compensation for inability to return to work to the performance of nonlitigating moderate and severe head trauma patients on the Warrington Recognition Memory Test (RMT), a two-alternative forced choice test for recognition memory of words and faces. Scores of 28 or below out of 50 on the RMT words had a specificity of 100% (i.e., no moderate to severe patients performed this poorly) and a sensitivity of 70% (i.e., 70% of the MHTs performed at 28 or less). The RMT Faces had a much lower sensitivity, likely due to the fact that it is a much more difficult test than the RMT words (Millis, 1992).

More recently, Binder and Kelly (1996) improved the sensitivity of the PDRT to malingering by raising the cutoff to the bottom 2% of brain-damaged performance. Binder and Kelly first replicated the previous cutoffs originally determined by Binder and Willis (1991), combining the original brain-injured sample with a new sample of 65 patients who had moderate to severe head trauma. None of the combined brain damage sample of 120 scored below the original

PDRT cutoffs of 19/36 easy, 18/36 hard, or 39/72 total. Of 103 patients with MHT, 16% performed below the easy cutoff, 26% below the hard cutoff, and 30% below the total score cutoff. When the cutoff was raised to the bottom 2% of brain-damaged subjects' performance (21 or fewer easy, 19 or fewer hard, and 43 or fewer total), 31% of MHT exceeded the easy cutoff, 47% exceeded the hard cutoff, and 43% exceeded the total score cutoff.

Both the PDRT and Warrington RMT have been used to study the effects of low motivation on standard neuropsychological tests. Binder and Willis (1991) defined minor head trauma (MHT) groups of low and high motivation based on PDRT scores, and contrasted the performance of these groups on a variety of neuropsychological tests. The low-motivation group performed more poorly on Finger Tapping, the Grooved Pegboard, Tactile Sensory measures, and the WAIS–R Full Scale IQ. The low motivation group also had a higher Global Symptom Index on the SCL–90.

Binder, Villanueva, Howieson, and Moore (1993) evaluated the effects of financial incentive on Rey Auditory Verbal Learning Test (AVLT) performance in groups of PDRT-defined high- and low-motivation compensation-seeking MHT, and non-compensation-seeking patients with documented brain dysfunction. The three groups were matched on age, education, and AVLT acquisition. The low-motivation MHT subjects produced significantly lower AVLT recognition scores than the high-motivation MHT and brain dysfunction groups, which did not differ from one another. Only 5% of the brain-damaged group obtained AVLT recognition scores less than 6, whereas 20 of 75 (27%) of the combined MHT group obtained scores less than 6.

Millis, Putnam, Adams, and Ricker (1995) compared the California Verbal Learning Test (CVLT) performance of litigating MHTs with low motivation (defined by below chance Warrington RMT scores) to the CVLT performance of nonlitigating patients with moderate to severe CHI. The poor-motivation MHTs scored significantly lower on CVLT Total Trials, Recognition Discriminability, Recognition Hits, and Long-Delay Cued Recall. The best predictors of group membership were Recognition Discriminability and Long-Delay Cued Recall. Recognition Discriminability, as a single variable, provided excellent discriminability between the low-motivation MHTs and the CHI group, with an overall classification rate of 93%. The Millis et al. (1995) CVLT results are consistent with the Binder et al. (1993) AVLT data demonstrating unreasonably poor recognition memory in persons with motivational deficit.

Tombaugh (1996) published a two-alternative forced-choice task, the Test of Memory Malingering (TOMM; also see Rees, Tombaugh, Gansler, & Moczynski, 1998). The TOMM presents 50 line drawings of common objects, which are then presented with a foil in 50 two-alternative forced-choice trials. Testing is conducted over two acquisition trials and following a brief delay of 15 min. A particular advantage of the TOMM is that patients with bona fide neurological disorders such as aphasia typically perform normally on the task. The TOMM can be scored using objective cutoffs set to maximize specificity (i.e., keep false positive detection of malingering at a minimum), and can be scored using the normal approximation to the binomial, to evaluate for significantly worse than chance performance.

Summary of Malingering Assessment. The preceding review of malingering was not intended to be exhaustive, as this is a rapidly growing area of research in neuropsychology. Indeed, the proliferation of malingering research has closely followed the substantial increase in forensic neuropsychology.

Given the potentially high financial stakes in personal injury settings, and potentially high personal costs in criminal settings, there is significant potential for attorney–client coaching. Youngjohn (1995) reported a case study where this actually occurred and was admitted to by plaintiff's counsel in a Worker's Compensation action. In his paper, Youngjohn noted the existence of a "how-to" manual on preparing mild head trauma patients for examination, published in the legal literature (Taylor, Harp, & Elliott, 1992). The current author also had suspected (but not confirmed) coaching on the PDRT, in a case where the plaintiff performed well enough to be administered the short form of the PDRT (34 of 36 easy, 9 of 9 hard items correct; cf. Binder, 1993), yet performed significantly worse than chance on Warrington RMT Words (15 of 50 correct) and Faces (11 of 50 correct) and on forced-choice examination of items of personal history (eg., birth date), only obtaining 9 of 22 correct.

Ironically, published research on malingering can ultimately lead to ineffectiveness of test procedures. L. M. Binder (personal communication, November 1997) noticed a lower rate of motivationally impaired performance on the PDRT in recent years. On a positive note, once Youngjohn circulated his 1995 paper on attorney coaching in the Scottsdale and Phoenix legal community, his rate of detection of poor motivation increased substantially (J. R. Youngjohn, personal communication, October, 1997).

These observations underscore the importance of developing patterns of clinical test scores that are pathognomonic of poor motivation. The papers by Binder et al. (1993), Binder and Willis (1991), Heaton et al. (1978), Millis et al. (1995), and Mittenberg et al. (1993, 1995, 1996) are important in this regard. As these authors demonstrated, tasks that are perceived as requiring effort or complex mental function, such as attention, memory, and motor function, are those on which patients are most likely to malinger.

In the current author's forensic practice, he utilizes multiple procedures to evaluate for exaggerated symptomatic complaint and for poor effort on neuropsychological testing. Symptom exaggeration is evaluated with the standard MMPI-2 validity scales, Infrequency Psychopathology scale (Arbisi & Ben-Porath, 1995), and Lees-Haley Fake-Bad Scale (Larrabee, 1998; Lees-Haley, 1992). Effort on neuropsychological tests is evaluated with the Rey 15-Item Test, PDRT, TOMM, and Warrington Recognition Memory Test. In forensic cases where a second opinion is being requested, the Mittenberg discriminant functions and pattern analyses (Mittenberg et al., 1993, 1995, 1996) are applied to data obtained by other neuropsychologists. Obviously, a stronger case can be made for malingering if a particular patient performs poorly on motivational tasks on your own examination and also shows definite motivational patterns on the Halstead–Reitan, WAIS–R, and WMS–R data collected on a previous neuropsychological evaluation.

Some have argued that the only way one can be absolutely certain that malingering has occurred is if the client confesses (Brandt, 1988). Obviously, confession is very rare, and the clinician must infer the presence or absence of deliberate symptom exaggeration and deliberately poor test performance. The current author has used the phrase *tantamount to confession* when describing significantly worse than chance performance on forced-choice tasks such as the PDRT, TOMM, or Warrington. When less extreme levels of poor performance occur, he may employ a phrase such as *worse than 100% of persons with bona fide brain damage in the Binder and Willis investigation*. When referring to pattern analysis, the current author has used phrases such as *the 35 point difference between General Memory and Attention/Concentration has a .99 probability of malingering based on Mittenberg et al.'s research*. These descriptive statements help link a particular client's performance to published research on motivation and malingering. Of course, the more abnormal the test patterns, and the more frequent the motivational abnormalities, the more certain one can be about the presence of malingering. As an example, a clinician can be confident of malingering in a client who scores 3 of 15 on the 15-Item Test, 5 of 36 on the hard PDRT, recognizes 3 words on Rey AVLT Recognition, performs at the 1st percentile on Finger Tapping and Grip Strength but at the 80th percentiles on Purdue Pegboard and Grooved Pegboard, has an age-scaled score of 5 on WAIS–R Digit Span, with a 14 on WAIS–R Vocabulary, and produces elevations of 90 on MMPI–2 scales 1 and 3, with a Lees-Haley Fake-Bad Scale of 31.

Finally, once the forensic neuropsychologist has concluded that malingering is present, the practitioner must still address the issue of brain dysfunction. Persons with no other objective evidence for brain dysfunction, such as history of coma and/or abnormal CT scans or electroencephalographs (EEGs), who perform abnormally on multiple neuropsychological tests and significantly worse than chance on the PDRT, typically will produce some scores indicative of normal brain function on sensitive measures such as Trail Making B or the PASAT. Assessing true cognitive abilities becomes more difficult when all neuropsychological tasks are poorly performed in addition to poor performance on motivational tasks. In these situations, a clinician may have to rely on the base rates for outcome in published research (e.g., Dikmen et al., 1994, 1995), as well as on behavioral observations and clinical assessment. As an example, the patient with evidence of malingering and globally impaired neuropsychological scores, who arrives on time, on his own, for the appointment and is an excellent and insightful provider of medical history, who has sustained a blow to the head without loss of consciousness or posttraumatic amnesia, and who has normal CT, magnetic resonance imagery (MRI), and EEG, likely also has normal brain function.

FORENSIC SETTINGS

Personal Injury Damages

The major forensic application of neuropsychology to date has been the determination of personal injury damages caused by accident or medical malpractice. In civil or Worker's Compensation trials for personal injury, there is a much more direct application of the actual neuropsychological test results; in other words, the test scores themselves represent the outcome of injury and effects of injury. The neuropsychologist must still explain the functional consequences of neuropsychological strengths and weaknesses, for example, social and occupational consequences. Within this area of forensic practice, the most frequent cases are those involving closed head injury, although there has been an increasing demand for evaluation of the neuropsychological effects of neurotoxic exposure, and effects of electrical injury.

This section is not intended to be a review of the neuropsychological effects of head trauma, toxins, and electric shock; rather, it highlights some important aspects of each traumatic insult. Basic knowledge of the neuroanatomic, neurobehavioral and medical correlates of a condition, together with an understanding of its course, allows the neuropsychologist to better evaluate the data in individual cases and arrive at empirically based and appropriate diagnostic and prognostic conclusions.

Closed-Head Trauma. The best predictor of outcome following closed-head trauma is the initial injury severity, as documented by initial Glasgow Coma Scale (GCS), and length of posttraumatic amnesia (Dikmen et al., 1995; Levin, Benton, & Grossman, 1982; Levin, Grafman, & Eisenberg, 1987; Wilson, Teasdale, Hadley, Wiedman, & Lang, 1994). Duration of coma / vegetative state correlated at −.47 with independent living status and −.32 with neuropsychological functioning at an average follow-up of 6.2 years post trauma (Putnam & Adams, 1992). Particularly important variables related to outcome of severe closed-head injury, in addition to memory and cognitive changes, are degree of awareness of deficits, and personality changes such as impulsivity and emotional lability (for reviews, see Prigatano, 1985, 1987, 1991).

Dikmen et al. (1994) provided data relative to employment following head trauma for a large cohort of head-injured subjects, contrasted with a non-head-injured trauma control group. Sixty three percent of patients with mild CHI (GCS 13–15) returned to work at 6 months, with 80% back to work at 12 months, and 83% at 2 years. One-year return to work was only slightly higher for non-head-injured orthopedic trauma control patients, approximately 86%. By contrast, 44% of patients with moderate CHI (GCS 9–12) were back to work at 6 months, with 56% back to work at 1 year, and 64% at 2 years. For the severely injured (GCS 8 or less), 13% were back to work at 6 months, with 26% back to work by 1 year, and 37% by 2 years. Within the severe group, time to follow commands was strongly predictive of return to work. Of those who followed commands at between 7 and 13 days, 69% were back to work by 1 year, whereas only 8% of persons who took over 39 days to follow commands were back to work at 2 years. Return to work was also predicted by preinjury demographic variables, such that persons over 50 years of age at the time of injury or who had less than high school education or unstable work history had a lower rate of return to work.

The outlook for a full neuropsychological recovery following a single minor head trauma (MHT) is good. Dikmen et al. (1995) found no significant differences between non-head-injured trauma control subjects and subjects with MHT at 1 year posttrauma. Binder, Rohling, and Larrabee (1997) conducted a meta-analysis of 8 MHT studies with 11 samples including the Dikmen et al. (1995) data, and found overall effect sizes equivalent to one-eighth of a standard deviation (equivalent to 2 WAIS–R IQ or 2 WMS–R General Memory Index points), and two-tenths of a standard deviation for attentional tasks (equivalent to 3 points on WMS–R Attention/Concentration), values smaller than the measurement errors of these indices. These meta-analytic data were subjected to a variety of analyses, to estimate a 5% prevalence of persistent deficits following MHT. Binder et al. (1997) demonstrated that with this small prevalence, the positive predictive value of neuropsychological testing in MHT was less than 50%; in other words, the clinician would be more accurate in concluding that there were no persistent effects of MHT when making interpretations of neuropsychological data. Given these results, Binder (1997) argued for careful differential diagnosis of patients who present with persistent deficits following MHT, as the persistent complaints may be due to factors other than brain damage.

Although variability in outcome certainly occurs in moderate to severe head trauma, initial GCS and time to follow commands are fairly widely accepted measures of estimating initial severity of head trauma. Dikmen et al. (1995) published the largest single data set, covering the full spectrum of head trauma severity. Thus, data on an individual head trauma case can be compared to these data, for the biological or physiological indexing described earlier in this chapter; in other words, the Dikmen et al. data allow the neuropsychologist to "dose" severity of trauma, so that milder cases who followed commands within 1 hr are expected to perform better on neuropsychological testing than more severely injured cases with over 2 weeks of coma. Dose effects can be much more difficult to obtain or estimate in the individual toxic and electric shock case.

Neurotoxic Injury.   Although any head trauma case can be analyzed in relation to standards of initial severity, there is a myriad of substances with potential for toxic effects on the central and peripheral nervous system (Bleecker, 1994; Goetz, 1985; Chang & Slikker; 1995; Hartman, 1995). The mere fact that someone is exposed to a substance with known potential for neurotoxicity does not mean that brain damage has occurred. The occurrence of central and/or peripheral nervous system damage is dependent on the *amount* of the exposure and *duration* of exposure, potentially interacting with many other variables (e.g., route of exposure). Ottoboni (1991) discussed issues of toxicity in a very readable text, appropriately entitled *The Dose Makes the Poison*. Nonetheless, it remains critical that the neuropsychologist attempt to estimate exposure severity in any neuropsychological evaluation of suspected toxic injury, because of the nonneurological effects on both symptomatic complaint and neuropsychological test performance, discussed in earlier sections of this chapter (Binder, 1997; Lees-Haley & Brown, 1993).

Given the complexity of issues in neurotoxic cases, it is advisable that a toxicologist also be involved as a member of the expert team evaluating a particular patient or group of patients. Also, one is better able to obtain exposure severity estimates when seeing a group of persons alleged to have been exposed to a potential neurotoxin, rather than when seeing an individual case. This is because there is a better opportunity to rank the group by exposure severity, and subsequently determine whether neuropsychological test scores correspond to severity ranking. If so, there is a greater likelihood that significant exposure actually occurred.

The author evaluated a series of patients alleged to have suffered central and peripheral nervous system damage at a construction site due to exposure to potentially toxic materials from prior industrial activities at the site. Despite normal medical, radiologic, laboratory, EEG, nerve conduction, and electromyographic studies, these patients had multiple cognitive, somatic, and personality complaints, and demonstrated significant abnormalities on neuropsychological testing. They also demonstrated a high rate of motivational impairment, with two-thirds falling below the cutoff on symptom validity testing. Because none of the medical data provided any basis for determining exposure severity, a crude ranking of the patients by time working on the job site was used as the exposure severity index. The number of significant Spearman rho values obtained between time on the site, symptom complaint, and neuropsychological test performance did not exceed that expected by chance alone. Indeed, one of the significant Spearman rho values demonstrated the opposite of a toxic effect: There was a positive correlation between time on the site and visual memory; in other words, the men on the job site the longest had *better* visual memory.

Various test batteries for assessing neuropsychological effects of toxic exposure are discussed by Hartmann (1995). Sensory-perceptual procedures not typically evaluated in standard neuropsychological batteries, such as odor identification and measures of achromatopsia, can be useful in neurotoxic evaluation (Braun, Daigneault, & Gilbert, 1989; Doty, 1995). Psychological factors, including somatization, can account for continuing complaints following toxic exposure (Bolla & Rignani, 1997), similar to what has been reported for minor head trauma (Putnam & Millis, 1994).

Electrical Injury. Electrical injury can result in neuropsychological deficits, particularly if the charge passes through the head (i.e., there is direct head contact), or if there is significant cardiopulmonary arrest, causing hypoxic injury (Gorman, 1993). Barrash, Kealey, and Janus (1996) described a pattern of verbal learning and memory deficits, and irritability accompanied by assaultive behavior, in a series of patients who suffered high-voltage electrical injury. In their particular series, presence/absence of cardiopulmonary arrest did not appear to be related to presence of neurobehavioral sequelae. Additionally, electrical injury was not associated with reduced performance on visual memory (Benton Visual Retention; Rey Complex Figure), or attention and psychomotor speed (WAIS–R Digit Symbol; Trail Making B). These data led Barrash et al. to consider explanations other than brain damage as possible etiologies (e.g., Post Traumatic Stress Disorder).

At present, there is no standardized, accepted means of grading severity of electrical injury regarding potential for persistent neuropsychological sequelae (Gorman, 1993; Kelley, Pliskin, Meyer, & Lee, 1994). Similar to head trauma and neurotoxic evaluations, careful differential diagnosis is important, including evaluation for somatization and malingering (Gorman, 1993; Kelley et al., 1994).

Civil Competencies

Melton et al. (1997) provided a comprehensive review of psychological evaluations in both civil and criminal jurisdictions. Civil competencies include evaluation to determine the need for guardianship, competency to consent to treatment, competency to consent to research, testamentary capacity, and competency to work.

Guardianship. Obviously, changes in a person's judgment, impulse control, memory, and thinking abilities that can occur following brain damage can bear directly on the person's ability to manage daily affairs. Guardianship—that is, the delegation by the state of authority over an individual's person or estate to protect the interests of incompetent persons—can be general, or restricted to particular types of decisions (Melton et al., 1997). Melton et al. recommended that any clinical evaluation for competency be as thorough as possible in documenting what a person can and cannot do in functional activities; merely rendering a diagnosis or describing the nature of a mental disorder is insufficient. It is also important to assess whether weaknesses in the patient's abilities are reduced or might be reduced or eliminated by assistance from others. Melton et al. observed that when complex estates are not involved, everyday use of money is highly correlated with general success in independent living.

Marson, Sawrie, Stalvey, McInturff, and Harrell (1998) have developed a Financial Capacity Instrument (FCI) for assessment of declining financial capacity in patients with Alzheimer's disease. Marson et al. (1998) found that multiple cognitive factors, including executive function, semantic memory, verbal abstraction, attention, and receptive language, were associated with performance on the FCI. Nevertheless, when evaluating an individual for competency to manage his or her financial affairs, both neuropsychological measures and functional measures such as the FCI should be used.

Competency to Consent to Medical Treatment. Marson and colleagues developed a prototype instrument for assessing the competency of patients with Alzheimer's disease to consent to medical treatment (Marson, Ingram, Cody, & Harrell, 1995), and analyzed the predictive relationship of neuropsychological tests to competency on this prototypic instrument (Marson, Cody, Ingram, & Harrell, 1995). They developed two clinical vignettes describing a hypothetical medical problem (neoplasm or cardiac problem), symptoms, and two treatment alternatives with associated risks and benefits. After reading and listening to a vignette, subjects answered questions designed to test competency under five well-established legal standards:

- LS1, the capacity to evidence a treatment choice (focusing on the presence or absence of a decision, not the quality of the decision).
- LS2, the capacity to make the reasonable treatment choice (emphasizing outcome rather than decision alone; failure to make the decision a reasonable person would make is viewed as incompetent).
- LS3, the capacity to appreciate the emotional and cognitive consequences of treatment choice (emphasizing awareness of the consequences of treatment decision).
- LS4, the capacity to provide rational reasons for choice (capacity to use logical processes to analyze risks and benefits in decision-making).
- LS5, the capacity to understand the treatment situation and choices (requiring memory for words, phrases, ideas, and comprehending the basic nature of information about treatment).

Marson, Ingram, Cody, and Harrell (1995) compared the performance of healthy older adults to that of persons with mild and moderate Alzheimer's disease (AD). The groups did not differ on LS1 and LS2, but control subjects performed significantly better than patients with mild AD on LS4 and LS5, and significantly better than moderate AD on LS3, LS4, and LS5. Persons with mild AD performed better on LS4 and LS5 than those with moderate AD. Hence, dementia severity was correlated with degree of competency to make decisions regarding medical treatments. Over 50% of patients with mild AD and virtually all patients with moderate AD demonstrated compromise in providing rational reasons for treatment choice (LS4). These data support the value of using standardized clinical vignettes to evaluate medical decision making competency, and were interpreted as raising concerns regarding the competency of patients with mild AD to make informed decisions regarding their medical treatment.

In an accompanying article, Marson, Cody, Ingram, and Harrell (1995) analyzed the relationship of performance on a comprehensive battery of neuropsychological tests to performance on LS4: evidence of a rational choice. Measures of word fluency (Controlled Oral Word Association, Benton & Hamsher, 1989; Initiation Perseveration from the Dementia Rating Scale, Mattis, 1988) were the best single predictors of competency in healthy elderly ($R^2 = .33$) and in AD ($R^2 = .36$). Interestingly, measures of memory and verbal reasoning were not strongly associated with performance on LS4.

The work of Marson et al. (Marson, Ingram, Cody, & Harrell, 1995; Marson, Cody, Ingram, & Harrell, 1995) is important in several respects. First, the work demonstrated that an instrument can be developed that is ecologically valid for assessment of competency to make medical treatment decisions. Second, their work demonstrates the critical need for research on neuropsychological correlates of competency. On an a priori basis, one would certainly expect measures of memory and judgment to be strongly associated with competency; however, as Marson, Cody, Ingram, and Harrell (1995) demonstrated, word fluency is the best predictor.

Testamentary Capacity.   Testamentary capacity refers to competency of a person to execute a valid will (Melton et al., 1997; Spar & Garb, 1992). Testamentary capacity generally requires that four conditions be met:

1. The testator (person making the will) must know, at the time of making the will, that he or she is making a will.
2. The testator must know the nature and extent of the "bounty" (estate).
3. Testators must know the "natural objects of their bounty" (natural objects are heirs).
4. They must know the manner in which the will they are making distributes their property (Melton et al., 1997).

Wills may be challenged on the basis of lack of testamentary capacity, as well as on the basis of evidence of undue influence, defined as containing an element of "coercion, compulsion or constraint" (Spar & Garb, 1992). Neuropsychology has a role in assessment of both testamentary capacity and undue influence. One would certainly anticipate that language, memory, and intellectual functions would be directly related to testamentary capacity, and that patients with impulsivity and poor social judgment would be particularly susceptible to undue influences. However, the Marson, Cody, Ingram, and Harrell (1995) research on neuropsychological predictors of medical decision making indicates these assumptions should be tested empirically.

Examination of a patient for testamentary capacity and/or undue influence should involve both a neuropsychological evaluation and a direct questioning of the patient regarding the four conditions of testamentary capacity, with the patient's responses compared to the actual factual data (e.g., extent of assets, names of heirs).

Dementia does not preclude the ability to possess testamentary capacity (Spar & Garb, 1992). It is important, however, to have a relatively contemporaneous neuropsychological evaluation to show that all aspects, neuropsychological and testamentary, have been considered. If the will is not to be executed on the same day as the neuropsychological evaluation and testamentary capacity examination, then the testamentary capacity examination should be repeated on the day the will is executed. The current author also repeats the standardized mental status examination, the Mini Mental State Examination, that was conducted during the original neuropsychological evaluation, to assess global cognitive status at the time of execution of the will.

It is not uncommon to be asked to provide a retrospective evaluation of a decedent's testamentary capacity, because will challenges frequently occur after the testator is deceased. As Spar and Garb (1992) observed, careful review of medical records can be very helpful, to see if the records contain formal diagnoses of mental or physical illnesses that could compromise mental abilities. If this evidence is found, it is critical to scrutinize the records for descriptions of the testator's behavior and for evidence of formal clinical examination of mental status or psychological testing. Depositions of persons not having a vested interest in the will can also provide important information regarding the decedent's capacity at the time the will was executed, as can review of old records regarding bill payment, bank statements, and so on.

The current author has found it helpful to scrutinize medical and nursing home records on patients who suffered dementia and, from the information contained therein, rank the patient on dementia severity scales such as the Global Deterioration Scale (GDS; Reisberg, Ferris, deLeon, & Crook, 1982) and Clinical Dementia Rating (CDR; Hughes, Berg, Danziger, Coben, & Martin, 1982). These scales allow the clinician to rate a particular patient as to severity of decline, using behaviorally anchored points. The behaviorally anchored levels of severity on either the GDS or CDR can then be used to retrospectively address the likelihood that the person did or did not have testamentary capacity. Persons at a GDS of 5 could possibly retain testamentary capacity ("they retain knowledge of many major facts regarding themselves and others; invariably know their spouse's and children's names but may forget their grandchildren"), but this capacity would be lost at GDS stage 6 ("may occasionally forget the name of the spouse upon whom they are entirely dependent for survival; retain some knowledge of their past life, but this is very sketchy"). There is a strong correlation between the GDS and the Mini Mental State Examination (MMSE), $r = -.90$ (Reisberg et al., 1989). Consequently, if descriptions of the patient in the medical records are insufficient to compute a GDS, but the records contain a MMSE score, the GDS can be estimated. MMSE scores less than 10 are produced by patients with GDS of 6 (Reisberg et al., 1989).

Criminal Settings

In criminal settings, motivational factors are more associated with avoidance of punishment than with financial gain as seen in civil settings. Martell (1992) observed that the role of forensic neuropsychology evolved almost exclusively in the realm of the civil law. As Martell noted, the traditional function of clinical psychology in criminal settings has been to address issues of major mental illness and the impact of such illness on the defendant's behavior relative to the requirements of the law. Consequently, the focus has been almost exclusively on psychosis, rather than on potential sequelae of brain dysfunction. Consistent with the prior discussion of dementia and testamentary capacity, criminal responsibility and/or competency is not determined by mere presence of a brain lesion or neuropsychological impairment. Rather, it is the functional consequences of the brain lesion or disease that determine competency and responsibility.

Forensic neuropsychology is increasingly used in determining the competency of a defendant to stand trial, and in determining criminal responsibility (Martell, 1992; Rehkopf & Fisher, 1997). Per *Dusky v. United States,* competence to stand trial requires a two-pronged test (Martell, 1992; Melton et al., 1997):

1. A cognitive prong: Does the defendant, as a result of mental disease or defect, lack the capacity to understand the proceedings against him or her?

2. A cooperation prong: Does the defendant lack the capacity to consult with his attorney and meaningfully assist in his or her own defense?

Related to the cognitive prong are orientation and memory, a capacity to understand the charges, the court principals, the adversarial nature of the courtroom, and the potential pleas and outcomes. Related to the cooperation prong are the defendant's ability to communicate effectively with an attorney, understand an attorney's instructions or advice, make reasoned decisions on that advice, attend to and remember the testimony of witnesses, and inform the attorney of discrepancies or concerns.

Two standards have been applied to regulate insanity determinations: the McNaughten standard, and the American Law Institute (ALI) standards (Martell, 1992; Melton et al., 1997; Rehkopf & Fisher, 1997). The McNaughten standard is a cognitive standard, concerned with the extent to which the defendant did or did not know what he or she was doing (Martell, 1992). The ALI standard includes cognitive, affective/emotional, and volitional factors in that the defendant must lack substantial capacity to either appreciate the wrongfulness of his or her conduct or to conform his or her conduct to the requirements of the law. Forensic neuropsychologists can play an important role in evaluating cognitive, emotional, and volitional factors in assisting the court on sanity determinations.

Martell (1992), Melton et al. (1997), and Rehkopf and Fisher (1997) discussed several other areas of criminal competency in which neuropsychology can play a role. These include competency to waive Miranda rights, competency to confess, competency to make a plea, competency to be sentenced, and competency to be executed.

In addressing issues of criminal competencies and responsibility, the role of the neuropsychologist is to provide the court with the information necessary to decide the issue. The court makes the final determination, not the neuropsychologist. Neuropsychological test data are important to establish the defendant's abilities in language, memory, insight, judgment, reasoning, and impulse control. The examination should also include information specifically relevant to the actual case being considered, as defendants can have brain damage, but maintain competence to stand trial, or be judged as possessing responsibility at the time of offense (i.e., be found to be sane).

Assessment of malingering is as important in criminal as in civil cases; only the motivational sources differ. The malingering assessment procedures discussed in the earlier sections of this chapter are useful in both civil and criminal forensic settings. Malingering of psychosis is more frequent in criminal as apposed to civil settings (Resnick, 1997). The MMPI–2 is very useful in detection of malingered psychosis, as is the Rogers (1992) Structured Interview of Reported Symptoms.

In criminal settings, defendants wishing to malinger incompetency may choose to feign memory impairment, particularly if there is a requirement for them to recall events connected with an offense so that they may assist their attorney in their defense. Denney (1996) described a creative application of forced-choice methodology to address issues of claimed "memory loss" for material relevant to alleged offenses in three criminal cases. Denney performed a careful record review of facts relevant to each of the three cases and then constructed forced-choice questions for data pertinent to each case. Each of the defendants, when examined with these forced-choice tests, performed significantly worse than chance, based on the normal approximation to the binomial. Additionally, Denney administered the three forced-choice tests to 60 normal adults who had no prior knowledge of the events in question, and demonstrated that the sample results for the overall test scores were consistent with what was hypothesized about the binomial distribution, even though the individual item answers varied in probabilities of identification.

PROVIDING NEUROPSYCHOLOGICAL TESTIMONY

Sworn testimony is provided in two contexts: at deposition, and in the courtroom. In civil cases, attorneys frequently conduct depositions for purposes of discovery—in other words, to determine and explore the opinions of the expert on the opposing side. Hence, defense attorneys conduct discovery depositions of doctors who will be providing testimony on behalf of plaintiff at the time of trial, and vice versa. In discovery depositions, it is common that the deposing attorney alone asks questions.

Trial testimony differs. In trial testimony, the retaining attorney begins the questioning, termed direct examination. This begins by establishing the credentials of the expert, including education, training, licensure, board certification, current position, and relevant research publications. Once this qualification process has been completed, the retaining attorney will ask the expert to provide the findings of the examination, opinions, and conclusions. Following conclusion of direct examination, the opposing counsel conducts the cross-examination. On cross-examination, the opposing counsel will attempt to discredit the expert, focusing in particular on potential sources of bias. Also, specific examination findings may be disputed, and conclusions challenged. The retaining counsel may conduct a redirect examination following cross-examination, if he or she feels the need to follow up on issues raised by opposing counsel. If there is a redirect examination, opposing counsel may also choose to do re-cross-examination.

Several sources cover examples of types of questions and effective strategies in providing sworn testimony (Adams & Rankin, 1996; Brodsky, 1991; Doerr & Carlin, 1991; Laing & Fisher, 1997). Above all, the expert is sworn to tell the truth. Federal courts now require that experts provide lists of cases in which they have previously provided sworn testimony. This underscores the need to be consistent in one's forensic work. The expert who does 50% plaintiff and 50% defense, finding deficits when retained by plaintiff and no impairment or malingering for defense, is probably not being consistent or objective. Such an "expert" can be assured that competent opposing counsel will bring this information out in the courtroom, by pointing out inconsistencies with testimony provided on previous cases. On the other hand, the expert who has previously been retained by plaintiff and found malingering or retained by defense and found brain damage will have little problem demonstrating objectivity and lack of bias, even if that expert's forensic case load is not evenly divided between plaintiff and defense.

It is important to understand the adversarial nature of the American jurisprudence system. The ultimate goal of a trial by jury is to establish the truth. This is brought about by an adversarial process with plaintiff opposing defense in civil courts, and defense opposing prosecution in the criminal courts, and the judge, jury, or trier of fact finding the "truth" at some point in between these opposing arguments. The only advocacy position that a forensic expert should adopt is to be an advocate for the facts within that expert's realm of expertise. Also, one must stay within one's area of expertise. It is important to avoid being caught up in the role of "expert," for a skillful attorney can lead a "know-it-all" expert into testifying about matters outside legitimate areas of expertise, then attack the overall credibility of the expert. It does not damage an expert's credibility to say, "That is outside my area of expertise."

If asked to identify a source as "authoritative," one can be sure that opposing counsel will later ask a question related to that source and, if the expert disagrees, call to the jury's attention, "But doctor, you said earlier that this text was authoritative." Indicating that a source is one of many widely read or referenced resources, rather than authoritative, is a response less likely to cause an expert difficulties in later testimony.

The probabilities relied on in forensic neuropsychology differ from the probabilities that psychologists or neuropsychologists rely on in conducting and/or interpreting published research. In the civil courts, a reasonable degree of neuropsychological probability translates to "better than 50%," not ".05 or .01." After a neuropsychologist has expressed his or her expert opinions, within this reasonable degree of probability, opposing counsel may try to get the expert to acknowledge the possibility of alternative conclusions. If the alternative is not likely, it is perfectly appropriate to respond, "I suppose that is possible, but I do not think it is probable."

Lastly, the expert should take care to present material to the court in clear, nontechnical language. It is easier for the jury to understand where a plaintiff's performance places the person in a line of 100 people than it is to understand a percentile. In explaining an improbable forced-choice performance, "99% chance of faking" is better understood than "probability of .01 that this occurred by chance."

CONCLUSIONS

This chapter has reviewed, in broad strokes, the area of forensic neuropsychology. This is a complex and rapidly evolving area that requires both a thorough knowledge of the field of neuropsychology and an ability to evaluate and communicate the relevancy of cognitive deficits to civil and criminal legal issues. As such, forensic neuropsychology reflects the highest level of both the scientific and clinical aspects of neuropsychological practice.

ACKNOWLEDGMENTS

The author gratefully acknowledges the assistance of Susan M. Towers and Kristin Kravitz in the preparation of this chapter.

REFERENCES

Adams, R. L., & Rankin, E. J. (1996). A practical guide to forensic neuropsychological evaluations and testimony. In R. L. Adams, O. A. Parsons, J. L. Culbertson, & S. J. Nixon (Eds.), *Neuropsychology for clinical practice. Etiology, assessment, and treatment of common neurological disorders* (pp. 455–487). Washington, DC: American Psychological Association.

American Psychological Association. (1992). Ethical principles of psychologists and code of conduct. *American Psychologist, 47,* 1597–1611.

American Psychiatric Association. (1994). *Diagnostic and statistical manual of mental disorders* (4th ed.). Washington, DC: Author.

Arbisi, P. A., & Ben-Porath, Y. S. (1995). An MMPI–2 infrequent response scale for use with psychopathological populations: The Infrequency Psychopathology Scale F(p). *Psychological Assessment, 7,* 424–431.

Badia, P., & Runyon, R. P. (1982). *Fundamentals of behavioral research* (2nd ed.). Reading, MA: Addison-Wesley.

Baldessarini, R. J., Finklestein, S., & Arana, G. W. (1983). The predictive power of diagnostic tests and the effect of prevalence of illness. *Archives of General Psychiatry, 40,* 569–573.

Barrash, J., Kealey, G. P., & Janus, T. J. (1996). Neurobehavioral sequelae of high voltage electrical injuries: Comparison with traumatic brain injury. *Applied Neuropsychology, 3,* 75–81.

Benton, A. L., & Hamsher, K. deS. (1989). *Multilingual aphasia examination* (2nd ed.). Iowa City: AJA Associates.

Benton, A. L., & Spreen, O. (1961). Visual memory test: The simulation of mental incompetence. *Archives of General Psychiatry, 4,* 79–83.

Bernard, L. C., McGrath, M. J., & Houston, W. (1996). The differential effects of simulating malingering, closed head injury, and other CNS pathology on the Wisconsin Card Sorting Test: Support for the "Pattern of Performance" hypothesis. *Archives of Clinical Neuropsychology, 11,* 231–245.

Berry, D. T. R., Wetter, M. W., Baer, R. A., Youngjohn, J. R., Gass, C. S., Lamb, D. G., Franzen, M. D., MacInnes, W. D., & Buchholz, D. (1995). Over reporting of closed-head injury symptoms on the MMPI–2. *Psychological Assessment, 7,* 517–523.

Binder, L. M. (1990). Malingering following minor head trauma. *The Clinical Neuropsychologist, 4,* 25–36.

Binder, L. M. (1993). An abbreviated form of the Portland Digit Recognition Test. *The Clinical Neuropsychologist, 7,* 104–107.

Binder, L. M. (1997). A review of mild head trauma. Part II: Clinical implications. *Journal of Clinical and Experimental Neuropsychology, 19,* 432–457.

Binder, L. M., & Johnson-Greene, D. (1995). Observer effects on neuropsychological performance: A case report. *The Clinical Neuropsychologist, 9,* 74–78.

Binder, L. M., & Kelly, M. P. (1996). Portland Digit Recognition Test performance by brain dysfunction patients without financial incentives. *Assessment, 3,* 403–409.

Binder, L. M., & Pankratz, L. M. (1987). Neuropsychological evidence of a factitious memory complaint. *Journal of Clinical and Experimental Neuropsychology, 9,* 167–171.

Binder, L. M., Rohling, M. L., & Larrabee, G. J. (1997). A review of mild head trauma. Part I: Meta-analytic review of neuropsychological studies. *Journal of Clinical and Experimental Neuropsychology, 19,* 421–431.

Binder, L. M., & Thompson, L. L. (1994). The ethics code and neuropsychological assessment practices. *Archives of Clinical Neuropsychology, 10,* 27–46.

Binder, L. M., Villanueva, M. R., Howieson, D., & Moore, R. T. (1993). The Rey AVLT Recognition Memory Task measures motivational impairment after mild head trauma. *Archives of Clinical Neuropsychology, 8,* 137–147.

Binder, L. M., & Willis, S. C. (1991). Assessment of motivation after financially compensable minor head trauma. *Psychological Assessment: A Journal of Consulting and Clinical Psychology, 3,* 175–181.

Bleecker, M. L. (Ed.). (1994). *Occupational neurology and clinical neurotoxicology*. Baltimore, MD: Williams & Wilkins.

Bolla, K., & Rignani, J. (1997). Clinical course of neuropsychological functioning after chronic exposure to organic and inorganic lead. *Archives of Clinical Neuropsychology, 12*, 123–131.

Bornstein, R. A. (1986). Consistency of intermanual differences in normal and unilateral brain lesion patients. *Journal of Consulting and Clinical Psychology, 54*, 719–723.

Brandt, J. (1988). Malingered amnesia. In R. Rogers (Ed.), *Clinical assessment of malingering and deception* (pp. 65–83). New York: Guilford Press.

Braun, C. M. J., Daigneault, S., & Gilbert, B. (1989). Color discrimination testing reveals early print-shop solvent neurotoxicity better than a neuropsychological test battery. *Archives of Clinical Neuropsychology, 4*, 1–13.

Brodsky, S. L. (1991). *Testifying in court. Guidelines and maxims for the expert witness*. Washington, DC: American Psychological Association.

Butcher, J., Dahlstrom, W., Graham, J., Tellegen, A., & Kaemmer, B. (1989). *Manual for administering and scoring the MMPI-2*. Minneapolis: University of Minnesota Press.

Butler, M., Retzlaff, P., & Vanderploeg, R. (1991). Neuropsychological test usage. *Professional Psychology Research and Practice, 22*, 510–512.

Chang, L. W., & Slikker, W. (Eds.). (1995). *Neurotoxicology. Approaches and methods*. San Diego, CA: Academic Press.

Chapman, L. J., & Chapman, J. P. (1967). Genesis of popular but erroneous psychodiagnostic observations. *Journal of Abnormal Psychology, 74*, 271–280.

Denney, R. L. (1996). Symptom validity testing of remote memory in a criminal forensic setting. *Archives of Clinical Neuropsychology, 11*, 589–603.

Dikmen, S. S., Machamer, J. E., Winn, H. R., & Temkin, N. R. (1995). Neuropsychological outcome at 1-year post head injury. *Neuropsychology, 9*, 80–90.

Dikmen, S. S., Temkin, N. R., Machamer, J. E., Holubkov, M. A., Fraser, R. T., & Winn, H. R. (1994). Employment following traumatic head injuries. *Archives of Neurology, 51*, 177–186.

Division 40. (1989). Definition of a clinical neuropsychologist. *The Clinical Neuropsychologist, 3*, 22.

Dodrill, C. B. (1985). Incidence and doubtful significance of non-standard orientations in reproduction of the key from the Aphasia Screening Test. *Perceptual and Motor Skills, 60*, 411–415.

Doerr, H. O., & Carlin, A. S. (Eds.). (1991). *Forensic neuropsychology. Legal and scientific bases*. New York: Guilford Press.

Doty, R. L. (1995). *The Smell Identification Test. Administration manual*. Haddon Heights, NJ: Sensonics, Inc.

Faust, D., Ziskin, J., & Hiers, J. B. (1991). *Brain damage claims: Coping with neuropsychological evidence* (Vol. 1). Los Angeles: Law and Psychology Press.

Goetz, C. G. (1985). *Neurotoxins in clinical practice*. New York: Spectrum.

Gorman, W. F. (1993). *Legal neurology and malingering*. St. Louis, MO: Warren H. Green.

Gough, H. (1954). Some common misperceptions about neuroticism. *Journal of Consulting Psychology, 18*, 287–292.

Greiffenstein, M. F., Baker, W. J., & Gola, T. (1996). Motor dysfunction profiles in traumatic brain injury and post-concussion syndrome. *Journal of the International Neuropsychological Society, 2*, 477–485.

Greiffenstein, M. F., Gola, T., & Baker, W. J. (1995). MMPI-2 validity scales versus domain specific measures in detection of factitious traumatic brain injury. *The Clinical Neuropsychologist, 9*, 230–240.

Greiffenstein, M. F., Gola, T., & Baker, W. J. (1996). Comparison of multiple scoring methods for Rey's malingered amnesia measures. *Archives of Clinical Neuropsychology, 11*, 283–293.

Gronwall, D. M. A. (1977). Paced Auditory Serial-Addition Task: A measure of recovery from concussion. *Perceptual and Motor Skills, 44*, 367–373.

Hannay, H. J., Bieliauskas, L., Crosson, B. A., Hammeke, T.A., Hamsher, K. de S., & Koffler, S. (1998).

Proceedings of the Houston Conference on Specialty Education and Training in Clinical Neuropsychology. *Archives of Clinical Neuropsychology, 13*, 157–250.

Hartman, D. E. (1995). *Neuropsychological toxicology. Identification and assessment of human neurotoxic syndromes* (2nd ed.). New York: Plenum Press.

Heaton, R. K., Grant, I., & Matthews, C. G. (1991). *Comprehensive norms for an expanded Halstead–Reitan neuropsychological test battery.* Odessa, FL: Psychological Assessment Resources.

Heaton, R. K., Smith, H. H., Lehman, A. W., & Vogt, A. T. (1978). Prospects for faking believable deficits on neuropsychological testing. *Journal of Consulting and Clinical Psychology, 46*, 892–900.

Hiscock, M., & Hiscock, C. K. (1989). Refining the forced-choice method for the detection of malingering. *Journal of Clinical and Experimental Neuropsychology, 11*, 967–974.

Hughes, C. P., Berg, L., Danziger, W. L., Coben, L. A., & Martin, R. L. (1982). A new clinical scale for the staging of dementia. *British Journal of Psychiatry, 140*, 566–572.

Kaufman, A. S. (1990). *Assessing adolescent and adult intelligence.* Needham, MA: Allyn and Bacon.

Kelley, K. M., Pliskin, N., Meyer, G., & Lee, R. C. (1994). Neuropsychiatric aspects of electrical injury. The nature of psychiatric disturbance. *Annals of the New York Academy of Sciences, 720*, 213–218.

Kerlinger, F. N. (1973). *Foundations of behavioral research* (2nd ed.). New York: Holt, Rinehart, & Winston.

Laing, L. C., & Fisher, J. M. (1997). Strategies for precluding the use of unscientific neuropsychological evidence in a mild head injury case. In R. J. McCaffrey, A. D. Williams, J. M. Fisher, & L. C. Laing (Eds.), *The practice of forensic neuropsychology: Meeting challenges in the courtroom* (pp. 177–210). New York: Plenum Press.

Larrabee, G. J. (1990). Cautions in the use of neuropsychological evaluation in legal settings. *Neuropsychology, 4*, 239–247.

Larrabee, G. J. (1992). Interpretive strategies for evaluation of neuropsychological data in legal settings. *Forensic Reports, 5*, 257–264.

Larrabee, G. J. (1997). Neuropsychological outcome, post concussion symptoms, and forensic considerations in mild closed head trauma. *Seminars in Clinical Neuropsychiatry, 2*, 196–206

Larrabee, G. J. (1998). Somatic malingering on the MMPI and MMPI–2 in personal injury litigants. *The Clinical Neuropsychologist, 12*, 179–188.

Lee, G. P., Loring, D. W., & Martin, R. C. (1992). Rey's 15 Item Visual Memory Test for the detection of malingering: Normative observations on patients with neurological disorders. *Psychological Assessment, 4*, 43–46.

Lees-Haley, P. R. (1992). Efficacy of MMPI–2 validity scales and MCMI–II modifier scales for detecting spurious PTSD claims: F, F – K, Fake Bad Scale, Ego Strength, Subtle-Obvious subscales, Dis and Deb. *Journal of Clinical Psychology, 48*, 681–688.

Lees-Haley, P. R., & Brown, R. S. (1993). Neuropsychological complaint base rates of 170 personal injury claimants. *Archives of Clinical Neuropsychology, 8*, 203–209.

Lees-Haley, P., English, L. T., & Glenn, W. J. (1991). A fake bad scale on the MMPI–2 for personal injury claimants. *Psychological Reports, 68*, 203–210.

Levin, H. S., Benton, A. L., & Grossman, R. G. (1982). *Neurobehavioral consequences of closed head injury.* New York: Oxford University Press.

Levin, H. S., Grafman, J., & Eisenberg, H. M. (1987). *Neurobehavioral recovery from head injury.* New York: Oxford University Press.

Lezak, M. D. (1995). *Neuropsychological assessment* (3rd ed.). New York: Oxford University Press.

Marson, D. C., Cody, H. A., Ingram, K. K., & Harrell, L. E. (1995). Neuropsychologic predictors of competency in Alzheimer's disease using a rational legal standard. *Archives of Neurology, 52*, 955–959.

Marson, D. C., Ingram, K. K., Cody, H. A., & Harrell, L. E. (1995). Assessing the competency of patients with Alzheimer's disease under different legal standards. A prototype instrument. *Archives of Neurology, 52*, 949–954.

Marson, D., Sawrie, S., Stalvey, B., McInturff, B., & Harrell, L. (1998, February). *Neuropsychological correlates of declining financial capacity in patients with Alzheimer's disease.* Paper presented at the Annual Meeting of the International Neuropsychological Society, Honolulu, HI.

Martell, D. A. (1992). Forensic neuropsychology and the criminal law. *Law and Human Behavior, 16,* 313–336.

Mattis, S. (1988). *Dementia Rating Scale (DRS).* Odessa, FL: Psychological Assessment Resources.

McCaffrey, R. J., Fisher, J. M., Gold, B. A., & Lynch, J. K. (1996). Presence of third parties during neuropsychological evaluations: Who is evaluating whom? *The Clinical Neuropsychologist, 10,* 435–449.

Melton, G. B., Petrila, J., Poythress, N. G., & Slobogin, C. (1997). *Psychological evaluations for the courts. A handbook for mental health professionals* (2nd ed.). New York: Guilford Press.

Miller, E. (1983). A note on the interpretation of data derived from neuropsychological tests. *Cortex, 19,* 131–132.

Millis, S. R. (1992). The Recognition Memory Test in the detection of malingered and exaggerated memory deficits. *The Clinical Neuropsychologist, 6,* 406–414.

Millis, S. R., & Putnam, S. H. (1996). Detection of malingering in post-concussive syndrome. In M. Rizzo & D. Tranel (Eds.), *Head injury and postconcussive syndrome* (pp. 481–498) New York: Churchill Livingstone.

Millis, S. R., Putnam, S. H., & Adams, K. M. (1995, March). *Neuropsychological malingering and the MMPI–2: Old and new indicators.* Paper presented at the 30th Annual Symposium on Recent Developments in the use of the MMPI, MMPI–2, and MMPI–A. St. Petersburg Beach, FL.

Millis, S. R., Putnam, S. H., Adams, K. M., & Ricker, J. H. (1995). The California Verbal Learning Test in the detection of incomplete effort in neuropsychological evaluation. *Psychological Assessment, 7,* 463–471.

Mittenberg, W., Azrin, R., Millsaps, C., & Heilbronner, R. (1993). Identification of malingered head injury on the Wechsler Memory Scale–Revised. *Psychological Assessment, 5,* 34–40.

Mittenberg, W., Rotholc, A., Russell, E., & Heilbronner, R. (1996). Identification of malingered head injury on the Halstead–Reitan Battery. *Archives of Clinical Neuropsychology, 11,* 271–281.

Mittenberg, W., Theroux-Fichera, S., Heilbronner, R., & Zielinski, R. E. (1995). Identification of malingered head injury on the Wechsler Adult Intelligence Scale–Revised. *Professional Psychology: Research and Practice, 26,* 491–498.

Ottoboni, A. M. (1991). *The dose makes the poison. A plain-language guide to toxicology.* New York: Van Nostrand Reinhold.

Prigatano, G. P. (1985). *Neuropsychological rehabilitation after brain injury.* Baltimore, MD: Johns Hopkins University Press.

Prigatano, G. P. (1987). Psychiatric aspects of head injury: Conceptual and methodological problems. In H. S. Levin, J. Grafman, & H. M. Eisenberg (Eds.), *Neurobehavioral recovery from head injury* (pp. 215–231). New York: Oxford University Press.

Prigatano, G. P. (1991). Disturbances of self-awareness of deficit after traumatic brain injury. In G. P. Prigatano & D. L. Schacter (Eds.), *Awareness of deficit after brain injury. Clinical and theoretical issues* (pp. 111–126). New York: Oxford University Press.

Putnam, S. H., & Adams, K. M. (1992). Regression-based prediction of long-term outcome following multi-disciplinary rehabilitation for traumatic brain injury. *The Clinical Neuropsychologist, 6,* 383–405.

Putnam, S. H., & Millis, S. R. (1994). Psychosocial factors in the development and maintenance of chronic somatic and functional symptoms following mild traumatic brain injury. *Advances in Medical Psychotherapy, 7,* 1–22.

Ragge v. MCA/Universal Studios, 165 F.R.D. 605: 1995 U.S. Dist. LEXIS 20669.

Rees, L. M., Tombaugh, T. N., Gansler, D. A., & Moczynski, N. P. (1998). Five validation experiments of the Test of Memory Malingering (TOMM). *Psychological Assessment, 10,* 10–20.

Rehkopf, D. G., & Fisher, J. M. (1997). Neuropsychology in criminal proceedings. In R. J. McCaffrey,

A. D. Williams, J. M. Fisher, & L. C. Laing (Eds.), *The practice of forensic neuropsychology* (pp. 135–151). New York: Plenum Press.

Reisberg, B., Ferris, S. H., deLeon, M. J., & Crook, T. H. (1982). The global deterioration scale for assessment of primary degenerative dementia. *American Journal of Psychiatry, 139,* 1136–1139.

Reisberg, B., Ferris, S. H., Kluger, A., Franssen, E., deLeon, M. J., Mittelman, M., Borenstein, J., Rameshuar, K., & Alba, R. (1989). Symptomatic changes in CNS aging and dementia of the Alzheimer type: Cross-sectional, temporal, and remediable concomitants. In M. Bergener & B. Reisberg (Eds.), *Diagnosis and treatment of senile dementia* (pp. 193–223). New York: Springer-Verlag.

Resnick, P. J. (1997). Malingered psychosis. In R. Rogers (Ed.), *Clinical assessment of malingering and deception* (2nd ed., pp. 47–67). New York: Guilford Press.

Richardson, R. E. L., & Adams, R. L. (1992). Neuropsychologists as expert witnesses: Issues of admissibility. *The Clinical Neuropsychologist, 6,* 295–308.

Rogers, R. (1992). *Structured Interview of Reported Symptoms.* Odessa, FL: Psychological Assessment Resources.

Rogers, R. R. (Ed.). (1997). *Clinical assessment of malingering and deception* (2nd ed.). New York: Guilford Press.

Russell, E. W. (1990, June). *Twenty ways of diagnosing brain damage when there is none.* Paper presented at the meeting of the Florida Psychological Association, St. Petersburg Beach, FL.

Schretlen, D., Brandt, J., Kraft, L., & Van Gorp, W. (1991). Some caveats using the Rey 15-Item Memory Test. *Psychological Assessment, 3,* 667–672.

Slick, D. J., Hopp, G., Strauss, E., & Spellacy, F. J. (1996). Victoria Symptom Validity Test: Efficiency for detecting feigned memory impairment and relationships to neuropsychological tests and MMPI-2 Validity Scales. *Journal of Clinical and Experimental Neuropsychology, 18,* 911–922.

Spar, J. E., & Garb, A. S. (1992). Assessing competency to make a will. *American Journal of Psychiatry, 149,* 169–174.

Stuss, D. T. (1995). A sensible approach to mild traumatic brain injury. *Neurology, 45,* 1251–1252.

Taylor, J. S., Harp, J. H., & Elliott, T. (1992). Preparing the plaintiff in the mild brain injury case. *Trial Diplomacy Journal, 15,* 65–72.

Tombaugh, T. N. (1996). *TOMM. Test of Memory Malingering.* North Tonawanda, NY: Multi-Health Systems.

Trope, Y., Gervey, B., & Liberman, N. (1997). Wishful thinking from a pragmatic hypothesis-testing perspective. In M. S. Myslobodsky (Ed.), *The mythomanias: The nature of deception and self-deception* (pp. 105–131). Mahwah, NJ: Lawrence Erlbaum Associates.

Trueblood, W., & Schmidt, M. (1993). Malingering and other validity considerations in the neuropsychological evaluation of mild head injury. *Journal of Clinical and Experimental Neuropsychology, 15,* 578–590.

Wedding, D., & Faust, D. (1989). Clinical judgement and decision making in neuropsychology. *Archives of Clinical Neuropsychology, 4,* 233–265.

Wilson, J. T., Teasdale, G. M., Hadley, D. M., Wiedman, K. D., & Lang, D. (1994). Post-traumatic amnesia: Still a valuable yardstick. *Journal of Neurology, Neurosurgery, and Psychiatry, 57,* 198–201.

Youngjohn, J. R. (1995). Confirmed attorney coaching prior to neuropsychological evaluation. *Assessment, 2,* 279–283.

CHAPTER TEN

Assessment to Rehabilitation: Communicating Across the Gulf

Michael Pramuka
Defense and Veterans Head Injury Program,
James A. Haley Veterans Hospital, Tampa, Florida

Michael McCue
Center for Applied Neuropsychology, Pittsburgh, Pennsylvania

Neuropsychological assessment has made dramatic advances in recent years. Revisions of standard assessment instruments continue to be published, and journals are filled with data that characterize neuropsychological profiles of various populations. Lacking amid this progress, however, is a format for communicating this information to others so that it can be applied to rehabilitation efforts (Johnstone & Farmer, 1997). In chapter 6 of this text, Bruce Crosson provided an excellent overview of methods to make neuropsychological assessment more relevant to rehabilitation. The goal of this chapter is to provide both a theoretical overview of rehabilitation issues related to neuropsychological assessment, and to offer guidelines to make the assessment process and written reports more useful to rehabilitation practitioners.

Before additional discussion of options for changes, however, it may be useful for the reader to consider how wide the "gulf" might actually be, and what might lie between the shores of assessment and rehabilitation. Neuropsychological assessment has numerous goals, including differential diagnosis, localization of brain dysfunction, prognostic description, eligibility determination for various services, and treatment planning. Although clinicians often integrate the client's history, interview information, and performance on standardized tests to provide diagnostic conclusions or to define eligibility criteria, treatment planning and recommendations are usually contained in a few brief sentences at the end of the report. This is unfortunate for the assessed individual, the potential purchaser of rehabilitation services, and the reputation and perception of neuropsychology. Neuropsychological assessments hold a wealth of data if the clinician is willing to bridge the gap from standardized tests to real-life issues (Johnstone et al., 1996). In other words, there is a gap because neuropsychological evaluations often do not make rehabilitation recommendations a primary goal of the assessment. Rather than presume that clinicians neglect this important role of neuropsychological assessment, this chapter posits instead that well-educated psychologists understand principles of learning theory, behavior modification, and neuropsychology, but have not had the opportunity to apply these principles to rehabilitation issues.

Although this may be the central issue in the "gulf," several others are also worthy of consideration. First, consider who is most likely to actually provide rehabilitation services to an individual after a neuropsychological assessment. In inpatient settings, it is frequently occupational, physical, or speech-language therapists. In outpatient programs, master's-level rehabilitation counselors and "cognitive therapists" from various backgrounds are often employed. In other settings, nurses, social workers, and master's-level mental health workers may be the most frequent provider of services. Few assessing neuropsychologists, however, will actually be the individuals providing treatment for the individual under consideration. There is no guarantee that providers will read the neuropsychological assessment or have the background to make use of the data unless they are written in a manner that is understandable and applicable to treatment endeavors with the client.

A final contributor to the gap between assessment and rehabilitation is an essential difference in perspective. The assessment is conducted and interpreted from the perspective of normative behavior. In contrast, meaningful rehabilitation interventions need to be designed from the perspective of each individual with unique environmental demands and expectations. Although the evaluation perspective may be essential for objective clarification of deficits and diagnostic determination, it distances the end result of the assessment from the client's unique rehabilitation needs.

Several options are available to "bridge the gulf." First, the neuropsychologist can adopt a rehabilitation mindset and modify basic assessment procedures. Second, the clinician can modify how results are presented in the report to make better use of the data as it relates to the client's possible rehabilitation intervention. Finally, the clinician can modify how and with whom results are shared, to ensure that there is continuity of service provision. Each of these options is discussed in detail next.

THE REHABILITATION MINDSET

If the neuropsychological assessment and resulting report are to address rehabilitation issues in addition to diagnostic concerns, then the clinician needs to move beyond comparison of results to normative standards and in addition interpret findings in terms of how clients will be able to meet their unique environmental demands. Psychologists have the academic training to be aware of various psychological factors that contribute to rehabilitation of individuals with cognitive disabilities; however, many do not have experience in applying these principles to rehabilitation. This section provides an overview of some of the most critical issues in the rehabilitation of an individual with cognitive disability so that the clinician is better equipped to evaluate from what type of rehabilitation the client would benefit and to make specific recommendations about those rehabilitation efforts. The factors to be discussed include: (a) functional systems, (b) learning and generalization, (c) environmental demands, (d) the functional interview and functional obstacles, (e) the limited capacities model, and (f) disability adjustment.

Functional Systems

Seminal work in the scientific exploration of how recovery occurs after a brain injury was conducted by Luria (1963). He identified two levels of injury, a permanent loss of a specific portion of a functional system, and a temporary disruption of a system due to "inhibition." After encouraging and facilitating direct recovery of remaining brain systems, Luria viewed the process of restoration of function to be primarily one of "de-inhibition" of remaining systems and development of strategies that may not currently be used for the tasks in question. Luria's focus, then, is not on "treating the deficit," but on identifying, building up, and transferring unimpaired cognitive systems to the skill and task areas previously managed by the impaired system. This process of *compensating* for deficits through recruitment of intact cognitive areas is critical to the development of rehabilitation strategies after brain injury.

Luria's work in rehabilitation stressed the value of evaluating the integrity of "functional systems" that have a behavioral manifestation, such as writing or walking. Deficits typically do not destroy entire functional systems, and some brain insults may have no noticeable impact on many everyday functions. For example, an individual who performs poorly on prose recall tasks and is therefore described as having a deficit in verbal memory may still be able to function in everyday memory tasks that are meaningful and allow for repetition and clarification. Because part of "functional memory" in everyday life is a result of executive abilities, the narrowly defined deficit in verbal memory will not necessarily translate to poor memory functions in the real world. Despite the narrow focus of our typical assessments and reports, the client under observation is not so much "demonstrating deficits" as demonstrating goal-oriented behavior, with fewer parts of the system operating. Individuals do not wait for rehabilitation professionals to educate and train them in compensatory strategies; adaptation and compensation occur spontaneously from the moment of injury and are in operation at the time of assessment.

In trying to understand the mechanism of language change after brain injury,

Luria (1981) described the experimental work of Vygotsky on "inner speech" as a conceptual basis for understanding both motor losses and higher level "executive dysfunction" after brain injury. He suggested that humans guide movement and actions by internal, automatic speech. A disruption of this speech or the reduced automatic generation of this speech may be at the core of some impairment after brain injury. Following from this theory, rehabilitation entails active, explicit modeling of activities guided by speech in a graded manner. The treatment assumption is that over time the individual will again learn to impose automatic, guided, internal speech independently, or at least use external representations of inner speech to accommodate for the lost ability to generate inner speech guidance.

Luria's work, then, offers two concepts regarding how rehabilitation for cognitive problems can work: (a) functional systems may be disrupted, but are rarely destroyed, and can be facilitated by compensation, and (b) cognitive improvement can be guided by recapitulation of developmental cognitive growth through explicit, verbally modeled behavior.

Learning and Generalization

Rehabilitation efforts require an individual to either relearn old habits and tasks, or learn new approaches to meet old goals. In either case, rehabilitation of cognitive disabilities imposes a learning environment for the client. The clinician can expand the contribution of neuropsychological assessment by providing a description of the client's premorbid learning style and by setting the stage for rehabilitation as a cooperative learning venture, rather than as some procedure to be performed by an expert. For example, during the neuropsychological evaluation the clinician can inquire about premorbid experiences with education, level of education attained, attitudes toward school versus on-the-job learning, and knowledge about how job abilities were acquired. Individuals who have enjoyed the education process, continued to educate themselves through reading or leisure classes, or developed a profession will have extensive background in the need to attend to new information and rehearse it through "homework," and an understanding of how new information can be "owned" by them over time. Many other people will be able to describe a different approach in which they depended on hands-on learning, visual demonstration, and rote practice before new information was useful to them. Still others may indicate from attitude and history that learning new information has been difficult for them; they are not likely to find a "didactic-based" approach to rehabilitation to be very palatable. Regardless of the circumstances described, information about premorbid learning will provide essential information about how easy or difficult the client might find rehabilitation and will suggest ways in which the neuropsychologist can present rehabilitation tasks and goals that will be least threatening to the client.

One factor complicating the "new learning" aspect of rehabilitation is the nature of cognitive impairment itself. Deficits in attention, memory, synthesis, and executive functions will reduce learning efficiency, and result in a problem with generalizing from one situation to another. Understanding lack of generalization is critical to the rehabilitation planner, as it suggests that rehabilitation tasks should occur in the most familiar and "real-world" or "in vivo" setting possible to reduce the need for the client to generalize. Baddeley's work (1986) provided conceptual support for in vivo cognitive rehabilitation by pointing to the greater efficacy of retrieving and using new learning when the learning and information retrieval environments are similar. His concept of *encoding specificity* derives from work with normal memory but, when applied to cognitive rehabilitation, implies that training of persons with brain injuries should be "domain specific." In addition, Glisky and Schachter (1986) documented the phenomenon of "hyperspecificity" of learning after brain injury, in which even minor deviations in stimulus presentation or environment confuse the individual and greatly decrease ability to use newly acquired information.

Reviewing the literature on cognitive rehabilitation, Wilson (1988) expressed dismay over the lack of experimental evidence showing any generalization of strategies or improvement from lab training to other environments, and further encouraged development of strategies that are based on the client's environment. Others argued (Abreu & Toglia, 1987; Toglia, 1991) that generalization can occur when the rehabilitation strategies are practiced in multiple environments and when a metacognitive approach is employed.

The role of *metacognition* in cognitive rehabilitation as an overall guiding principle is consistent with Luria's theory, and was developed into a model by Ylvisaker and Szekeres (1989). Essentially, these authors proposed that metacognition consists of two parts: (a) a knowledge base about cognition, and (b) an executive functioning system that regulates higher level thinking such as goal development, planning, self-directing, and problem solving. Ylvisaker and Szekeres remarked on the disabling impact of poor executive functioning after brain injury, even when capacities such as language, memory, and spatial skills are intact. They identified numerous methods of assessing and treating executive dysfunction. Stress is placed on the need to make the individual aware of each subcomponent of cognition under consideration, label it as an important part of normal functioning, and teach individuals to think about their thinking, and how it may differ from before.

Although these authors do not explicitly discuss in vivo cognitive rehabilitation, their model cautions helpers against the often-observed trap of improvement in restricted situations under the guidance of a therapist, with no carryover to the individual's goals or real-life demands. This occurs due to the lack of any metacognitive framework for the individual to utilize in novel situations or due to a lack of awareness of exactly how and why compensations are necessary and how accommodations might facilitate a task. As with premorbid learning

history, the neuropsychologist can build an important bridge to useful rehabilitation goals by discussing ways in which the client will be able to generalize information from the rehabilitation setting to the demands of everyday life and by
recommending and defining rehabilitation goals as an "in vivo" process.

Environmental Demands

The status of the environment vis-à-vis clients' cognitive abilities is as much a
factor in rehabilitation as is their cognitive status. Although the neuropsychological assessment is not designed as a functional evaluation that would clarify
an individual's ability to perform in specific environments, the clinician offering
rehabilitation recommendations can begin to describe how environments challenge individuals with cognitive disabilities, and the relationship between various neuropsychological deficits and functional performance in different environments. The level of cognition needed to perform a practical task may be
extremely variable, depending on the environmental context. Some examples of
the impact of cognitive deficits on everyday real-life performance are provided
in Table 10.1.

The *ecological validity* of tests refers to their ability to provide accurate and reliable information regarding an individual's ability to function in the natural environment. Unfortunately, most traditional psychological and neuropsychological tests were not developed to predict behavior in the natural environment.
Psychological tests measure abstract concepts such as intellectual capacity, episodic memory, or personality, and most neuropsychological tests were developed to detect brain damage. As they are typically conducted, neuropsychological evaluations fail to provide much of the information that is necessary for
effective rehabilitation planning. Evaluations often are effective in identifying
the cognitive problems resulting from brain injury, but typically neuropsychological reports do not describe how these problems might interact with task and
environmental demands to impact the individual's functioning in real life situations (Tupper & Cicerone, 1990). In fact, it is possible that performance on formal neuropsychological tests can be quite misrepresentative of an individual's
actual functional level. An individual may function far above or below levels suggested by neuropsychological test results (Naugle & Chelune, 1990).

To address these problems with ecological validity, the clinician can supplement the assessment battery with incidental observations, self-report and other
report of functioning in everyday life, attention to detail in the client's history,
and awareness of everyday examples of cognitive domains. Some suggestions
for sources of functionally relevant information are offered in Table 10.2.

Information from observations, reports, and history can offer hypotheses
about where clients may break down cognitively. Furthermore, much of this
information can be sought in collaboration with the client. This allows the
neuropsychologist to explore with the client which domains of functioning

TABLE 10.1
Everyday Impact of Cognitive Deficits by Cognitive Domain

Cognitive Domain	Everyday Functional Impact of Deficits
Executive function	Excessive time and distress when grocery shopping
	Chronic tardiness or missed deadlines
	Unable to schedule own time or projects effectively
	Unaware of supervisor's perception of client's performance
	Surprised by and unprepared for problems on the job
	Slow to "catch on" to office procedural changes
Attention	Loses track of current tasks
	Frequently observed to be "off task"
	Unable to sit through a lecture at school
	Difficulty proofreading
	Unable to be productive in busy environment
Communication	Misunderstands telephone messages
	Frequent arguments with family / friends
	Poor or very slow report writing
	Does not catch on to "hints" from others
	Talks too slowly to keep others' attention
	Confuses others when attempting to explain / teach tasks
	Frequently misinterprets supervisor memos
Sensory perceptual	May get lost easily
	Requires repetition / simplification of messages
	Incorrect recording of telephone messages
	Unable to recognize differences between similar work materials
	Problems assembling items from a diagram
Motor skills	Clumsiness or slowness handling equipment
	Frequent accidents / injury on the job
	Messy work due to poor dexterity
	Slow or inaccurate typing, data entry, or handwriting
	Problems with mobility or lifting
Social / emotional	Conflict with coworkers / supervisor
	Unable to "connect" with customers or to deal with complaints
	Problems accepting constructive feedback
	Highly distressed or agitated over everyday work demands
	Perceived as cold or unhelpful by retail customers
	Shares personal life details with clients or coworkers

are most negatively affected by the presenting problem, and to further assess clients' awareness and perceptions of impairment from objective descriptions of everyday functioning. These hypotheses can then be formalized in the recommendations section as a series of prescribed experiences or simulations, or recommendations of additional information that could be gathered to clarify real-world limitations. For example, rather than predict, based on poor test performance, that a client will not be able to succeed at stated goals of earning a college degree, recommendations can be offered suggesting that a noncredit

TABLE 10.2
Obtaining Functionally Relevant Information

Demand Setting	Source of Information
Employment	Job descriptions
	Dictionary of Occupational Titles (DOT)
	Task analyses
	Previous performance evaluations
	Employer/coworker interview
Education	Course syllabi
	School/course catalogs
	Textbooks required of client
	Graded papers
	Teacher/instructor interviews
Independent living evaluations	Independent living/occupational therapy home evaluations
	Informant interviews
	Analyses of social demands

course be taken at a community college as a means of self-evaluating actual academic abilities.

Functional Interview and Functional Obstacles

A useful method for gathering additional information about the conflict between personal abilities and the environment is to augment the traditional clinical interview with a functional interview. A functional interview is an extension of the information-gathering process that starts with collecting specific background information. A primary goal for the neuropsychologist conducting a functional interview should be to determine the individual's view of the problems or obstacles being encountered in his or her daily activities. The nature and cause of perceived problems should be explored, as well as any strategies or accommodations attempted or currently in use.

Relevant information for a functional interview is usually available from multiple sources, including the individual being assessed, various records, past testing, and reports of family and friends. Questions can be phrased either as a deficit/diagnostic issue (poor memory, math learning disability) or as everyday behavior (class failure, too slow on the job). These diverging approaches both provide valuable material for an interview; a comprehensive functional interview will make use of both, as described next.

When deficits, impairments, or diagnoses are under discussion, the neuropsychologist should follow up with questions exploring the daily impact of these factors. The clinician makes no assumptions about what understanding or meaning a diagnosis carries for the individual, and instead explores these issues with the client and family. The role of the deficits are best discussed in terms of the individual's environment and personal goals. In some cases, it may become evident that there is minimal to no impact on everyday life due to a stated deficit, or at least that the individual has no awareness of the ramifications of the deficit. Alternatively, discussion of diagnoses and deficits may elucidate significant connections to performance in everyday life, and thus provide direction for intervention.

The second approach makes use of presenting complaints about life problems to explore possible impairment. Although cognitive status is by definition the area of greatest concern, the functional interview makes no assumptions about the neuropsychological deficit underlying problems in everyday life. Issues in mental health, motivation, living circumstances, interpersonal relationships, financial status, and personal values may all be sources of everyday problems or incorrectly be perceived to be the result of cognitive problems.

By using both strategies, individuals are taken through a careful examination of what they know and believe about the relationship between cognitive status and everyday life competence. Daily life demands and possible obstacles to meeting these demands are explored from several directions, so that the interactions between neuropsychological impairment and environment become clearer for both the individual and the clinician. A brief foray into the details of everyday schedules and personal understanding about cognition provides significant data for generating recommendations that will help the individual match abilities with personal life goals and style.

By considering the information gained in a functional interview, the neuropsychologist can develop a better awareness of the type of environment in which the client is expected to function. This knowledge, used in conjunction with an appreciation of a client's premorbid functioning and learning style, can assist the clinician in identifying functional obstacles that are likely to result in a breakdown in the client's functional performance. These obstacles to succeeding in everyday life activities then provide targets for different types and levels of rehabilitation interventions.

Limited Capacities Model

Borrowing from work with noninjured persons, the limited capacities model (Levine & Sandeen, 1985) assists the neuropsychologist in describing optimal modification for persons after a brain injury. This model assumes that, for any person, there is only a limited capacity available for "thinking," and when a mismatch occurs between cognitive capacity and environmental demands, the client experiences a problem. The destruction of brain tissue results in a reduction in an individual's overall capacity to deal with environmental demands. Information processing is slowed and there is a greater reliance on fewer remaining cognitive strengths. These factors contribute to a relatively permanent decline in capacity for complex cognitive work. The person with a brain injury may not be precluded from engaging in complex cognitive activities such as writing, reading, or planning social events. However, the residual cognitive capacity is stressed, resulting in a "cognitive fatigue" and a reduced capacity to sustain performance to meet ongoing life demands.

The limited capacity model can assist neuropsychologists in suggesting accommodations that are likely to minimize the client from becoming cognitively or emotionally overwhelmed or exhausted when endeavors are attempted that would otherwise extend a person beyond his or her capacity. Specific recommendations might include breaking complex tasks or information into smaller segments, preparatory writing out of sequences for completing problematic tasks, prescribed reductions in number / type of decisions to be made on a daily basis, or training in how to restate verbal information as a means of slowing down incoming information and clarifying main points of conversations.

Disability Adjustment

Finally, success in brain injury rehabilitation is not limited to improvement in cognitive function. The goal of rehabilitation, in fact, is not to improve cognition per se, but rather to improve overall life status. Therefore, the client's emotional status, behavioral presentation, family dynamics, and knowledge of brain dysfunction are all critical factors to evaluate and legitimate targets of rehabilitation in the context of assisting the individual adjust to disability.

Both emotional responses to the acquired disability and preexisting emotional characteristics will impact rehabilitation. Often impaired cognitive functioning and emotional adjustment are intimately related. Successful rehabilitation planning demands that the direction and relationship between these factors be carefully delineated. For example, an individual with memory problems may appear upset and confused. Although this might reflect the severity of memory impairment, the individual's inability to recall details from a previous day may result in anxiety due to the awareness that there is a lack of continuity in everyday events. Alternatively, a long-standing history of obsessive / compulsive decision making may be compounded by slowed information processing, but interpreted as a cognitive deficit in problem solving. In a third case, it may be the interpretation of others that is skewed by attributions: Clients may be described as "splitting" staff or family, when in fact it is poor memory and slow information processing that result in incomplete recall of information. Although the examples will shift with each client, to reduce the gap between assessment and rehabilitation, careful scrutiny and description of emotional status in concert with cognitive status are essential.

As in formulating any treatment, the family constellation and the level of support available to the individual with brain injury will make a difference both in the manifestation of disability and in the opportunities for rehabilitation. For example, a family system in which the client's spouse is content to prepare daily lists, drive the client to the store, and remind the client of weekly appointments may not experience much of a negative consequence of an impaired memory. For many severely impaired individuals, family cooperation is an essential component to developing compensatory strategies, and families will be critical for client follow-through with tasks and exercises. In every neuropsychological assessment, it will be useful to identify who constitutes the functional family and what roles they can or will serve in rehabilitation.

How a person presents behaviorally can be very helpful in making recommendations regarding goals, appropriate rehabilitation and living settings, and specific rehabilitation options. From observations, interview, and family reports, a behavioral presentation can be described by the psychologist and matched to type of treatment setting that makes most sense. Some individuals, by virtue of behavior, will require a locked unit or highly supervised setting due to confusion; others may require a similarly restrictive atmosphere but secondary to psychiatric, rather than cognitive, presentation. Some clients fit well in settings with other people with brain injury, whereas others may be better served in a setting for individuals with developmental disabilities. In any case, recommendations will be most useful if the setting matches the behavioral presentation of the client. Similarly, behavioral problems may far outweigh concerns over impaired cognition, and may be the focal point for intervention because they are too difficult for families and communities to tolerate.

Another useful aspect of appropriate rehabilitation planning is to evaluate clients' understanding of their disability and provide recommendations to assist with personal adjustment to disability. Referrals to local support groups are useful to this end, as are reading or videotaped materials that provide the client and family with a clearer understanding of disability. By having a clear understanding of how these broad psychological factors contribute to rehabilitation efforts, the neuropsychologist can then make more useful recommendations that take into account preexisting personality characteristics, current emotional adjustment, and specific cognitive problems.

A summary of rehabilitation issues and their ensuing rehabilitation strategies is provided in Table 10.3.

An enlightening example of the rehabilitation mindset was provided by Randall Evans (1997) in his article synthesizing measured outcomes of postacute rehabilitation. Looking across numerous settings, rehabilitation consumers, organizational systems, and studies on the effectiveness of rehabilitation programs, Evans developed a matrix of descriptive outcome variables. The outcome areas, although certainly affected by impaired cognition, are based in everyday life functioning. They include productive focus, work/education/life status, community access, living situation, daily living status, safety awareness, and domestic stability. The reader is referred to this excellent synopsis of rehabilitation outcomes for more detail, but two overall lessons stand out for the neuropsychologist attempting to bridge the gap between assessment and rehabilitation: (a) In reha-

TABLE 10.3
Rehabilitation Concepts and Relevant Recommendations

Key Concept	Recommendations and Strategies
Functional systems	Identify and compensate with strengths
Functional obstacle/ environmental issues	Change the environment, not the person. Define the focus of rehabilitation as conflict between cognitive ability and environmental demand on that ability.
Premorbid learning	Match type of rehab strategy to premorbid personal strategies.
Generalization	Rehearsal of functional tasks, naturalistic supports, treatment in most natural setting possible.
Limited capacities model	Simplify tasks, clarify, presequence.
Deficit awareness/ metacognition	Checklists, ways to anticipate and monitor errors, prepared scripts, metacognitive strategies.
Disability adjustment	Prescribe periods of poor functioning, seek realistic feedback from others in support groups and in family/friends, identify personal attributes and contributions, redefine roles.

bilitation, the topics of interest are based in everyday human life, and (b) the criterion measure used by rehabilitation providers and funding sources is return to everyday function. Improvements in cognition, test performance, or affective change per se are not valued as an outcome.

MODIFY THE WRITTEN REPORT

Beyond making changes in the approach to assessment and the conceptualization of useful recommendations, neuropsychological assessments can be linked much more directly to rehabilitation when clinicians modify how treatment is described and presented in the neuropsychological report.

Write Goals at a Person-Specific Level

Often neuropsychological reports couch recommendations in terms of impairment level (type and level of impaired cognitive abilities) or disability status (inability to carry out some specific aspects of functional behavior), suggesting that the writer, the client, and future clinicians should also direct their work to the level and type of impairment. Although these statements may technically be accurate, they are short-sighted and overly narrow in the recommendations they imply. Goals that are described at the personal level of concern, rather than at the impairment level, will resonate much more clearly with the client and family and will open the door to consideration of a variety of mechanisms to address the issue. For example, the memory impairments accompanying Alzheimer's in an older woman may not be amenable to amelioration; nevertheless, the goal remains for her to continue to live independently and provide for herself and husband as long as possible by carrying out her various responsibilities (e.g., shopping, cooking, and socializing). Once this is recognized, recommendations can be described regarding the type and level of assistance that may be needed for planning or safety in completing housekeeping tasks, rather than recommending that others do these activities for her. Similarly, the young man with poor visual-spatial skills and slowed motor responses is not interested in a course of physical and cognitive therapy, but is interested in driving or at least getting out to see friends. Recommendations need to address how he might continue to meet his transportation and socialization needs even if he never gains the cognitive and physical status to resume driving.

In developing goals from a client-based perspective, neuropsychologists have three other important sources of data, beyond basic neuropsychological test data: (a) an understanding of the behavioral consequences associated with the etiological event (i.e., various brain injuries and medical problems), (b) knowledge of different types of therapy indicated given the time frame of the disability, and (c) a consideration of the interplay between premorbid personality and current adaptation factors when considering alternative rehabilitation interventions. By drawing on data from these areas, the clinician can offer recommendations that are individualized to the client's specific situation. Recommendations about rehabilitation of memory, for example, should not be based on scores on a standardized measure of memory, but instead on the everyday problems caused by the memory disorder. Similarly, an understanding of the nature of different medical conditions and their patterns of recovery helps the clinician make important distinctions between an amnestic individual in the first few months after traumatic brain injury versus an amnestic individual several years postonset of Korsakoff's.

In terms of basic style of adaptation before cognitive decline, the psychologist may find that the use of extensive written compensatory strategies is acceptable to a graduate student, but that many other individuals will only be able to effectively use brief checklists based on a simple daily routine. In developing functional goals for individuals, the neuropsychologist serves a valuable role in anticipating and acknowledging the everyday problems that individuals and their families will face. In addition, neuropsychologists may be in the best position to assist clients and families in coming to accept that there are compensatory techniques to assist daily functioning even if complete recovery of cognitive function is not possible.

As an example of less than ideal recommendations, the often cited "memory notebook" recommendation fails to clarify the real-life goals of the individual. Depending on the person's life demands, the real goals behind a memory notebook may be to show up at work on time (prospective memory), to recall what to do after arriving at work (sequencing/initiation of previously learned tasks), to remember the main points of important conversations (semantic encoding), or to organize one's thoughts on paper prior to talking in order to enhance effective communication (executive function). If neuropsychologists invest the time and energy in conveying the real goals of using a compensatory memory strategy for the individual at hand, there will be increased motivation to use the system, and additional strategies may become apparent.

In conjunction with a shift in mindset from simple interpretation of cognitive deficits to one of also describing client strengths and best learning modalities, treatment recommendations will become more obvious if the neuropsychologist develops a client-centered perspective. Once the clinician takes the client's perspective on life activities and goals, and how these have been disrupted by the disability, it will be much easier to identify realistic needs and goals that the client will be motivated to pursue.

Describe and Prescribe Accurately

Neuropsychologists often accurately recommend general treatment approaches, but fail to specify how and by whom the interventions should be carried out, and fail to delineate the justification for the recommended treatments. Recommendations for "an intensive course of outpatient day treatment for brain injury," "cognitive rehabilitation to remediate the above documented cognitive deficits," "psychotherapy to assist with adjustment to disability," or "memory retraining to address the significant impairments observed in both short- and long-term memory" may have specific meaning to the writer, but offer misinformation and ambiguity to clients, rehabilitation case managers, and treatment staff in other rehabilitation centers. In keeping with goals written from the client's perspective, avoid constructing a rehabilitation plan based on existing programmatic needs or rehabilitation disciplines. Recommendations for "occupational therapy 3 to 5 times per week" or for "6 to 12 weeks of daily attendance at our outpatient brain injury program" beg the question as to the legitimate and meaningful client goals to be addressed, and instead meet programmatic needs to maintain census. Furthermore, the services that individual providers from the rehabilitation disciplines and rehabilitation programs are able to offer differ widely across settings. The only way to ensure that the needs of the assessed client will be met is for the neuropsychologist to specify them in detail, and to identify what resources might meet these goals. Johnstone and Farmer (1997) concurred that it is essential for neuropsychologists to educate themselves on the specific activities and types of programs available in various rehabilitation programs through visits and direct contact with staff. Suggestions for doing so are offered in Table 10.4.

Psychologists typically make recommendations for psychotherapy based on a clear understanding of, and usually experience with, the type of therapy recom-

TABLE 10.4
Sources for Community Rehabilitation Resources

Learn about, attend, and keep a list of local support groups by type of disability you assess.

Review phone book listings under rehabilitation and ask for written brochures, contact staff, and a tour.

Contact the local state vocational rehabilitation department to determine which providers it uses and the eligibility criteria for services.

Contact local universities to determine what demonstration projects or research treatment protocols may be ongoing for individuals in various disability groups.

Contact the closest regional office of Veterans Affairs to determine what rehabilitation services it provides, or at least obtain the name of a contact person there.

Call the county and request any listing of United Way or county-based human services; on receipt, call those most relevant and gather information.

Call the county mental health/mental retardation department to determine what services it provides and what the eligibility criteria are by disability type.

---

mended. The psychotherapy literature supports specific types of therapy for certain populations and diagnoses. Similarly, the neuropsychologist will only be able to offer legitimate recommendations to treat different cognitive deficits when he or she has an understanding of various models of cognitive rehabilitation and is familiar with the literature and the options for treatment. A simple synopsis of the continuum of care for individuals with brain injury is presented in Table 10.5, along with suggested criteria for entering that level of treatment.

Neuropsychologists might better focus on accurate and thorough presentation of treatment options if the final section of the report were considered "prescription for treatment" rather than "recommendations," much as a physician would be expected to delineate a variety of options, their pros and cons, and expected outcomes. Neuropsychologists need to consider the availability of the recommended treatment in the community and possible funding sources. If there are no services available or no resources to purchase them, the report should indicate that the recommended interventions are not available and offer alternative recommendations that might meet the client's needs and be carried out by family, friends, community organizations, and so forth. Additionally, the neuropsychological report should make the point that the lack of rehabilitation will significantly impede a meaningful part of the individual's life, such as independence, financial future, or emotional status. This is a great exercise for all clinicians to conduct regardless of client resources—what are the expected ramifications of *not* receiving recommended treatment? If it is difficult to specify any negative impact from a lack of services, the services are obviously not indicated.

Perhaps most importantly, an accurate and well-documented neuropsychological description of an individual's rehabilitation needs will act as a definitive document to establish eligibility for services (diagnosis/etiology) and to justify

TABLE 10.5

Continuum of Care in Rehabilitation: Definitions and Entry Criteria

Setting	Location	Goals/Activities	Entry Criteria
Inpatient acute rehabilitation	Hospital-based	Improve ambulation, basic ADLs, begin deficit awareness, introduce concept of compensation and accommodation, improve attention, memory, and language skills	Recent onset of impairment, out of coma, expectation for ongoing neurologic recovery, medically stable
Outpatient day treatment	Hospital, outpatient clinic, or community building	Increased independence in community activities, understanding of cognitive/physical deficits, ongoing therapy for cognitive, emotional, and physical problems; comes closer to endurance demands of job and school schedules	Able to live with family or alone and arrive at site on time; usually required to be continent and to meet basic ADLs
Transitional living programs	Homes or apartments in community	Incorporates daily activities into everyday home tasks and community activities to replicate the demands of living independently; retrains in completing tasks of real world (cook, clean, shop, pay bills, manage time) while providing support that can be reduced with increased independence	Able to meet personal ADL independently; interest in working toward living independently; most relevant after neurologic recovery is considered complete
Community reentry programs	Home-based therapy or office in community	Assist individual in resuming real-life roles of employee, friend, family member; work through specific details required to succeed at retaining these meaningful roles via compensation, accommodations, and adjustment to disability	Understanding of personal strengths and limitations; able to identify specific goals based on life roles rather than cognitive or neurologic problems
Neurobehavioral treatment programs	Residential facility with locked wards or secured grounds; often rural	Long-term behavioral management and treatment of neurologically based behavioral problems; employs highly structured rules and environment along with medications, usually with gradual decrease in structure over time	Primary problem of unmanageable behavior; unable to live in nursing home or other facility due to behavior; beyond acute recovery (not simple agitation)

Note. ADLs, activities of daily living.

352

future rehabilitation service from funding sources. It is likely that it will be the only document that clearly links norm-referenced psychometric performance, personal functional limitations, client-centered goals, and rehabilitation potential and needs to specific, functionally oriented goals and specific rehabilitation services. Furthermore, the document is powerful in that it is often provided from an impartial consultant who does not stand to benefit from the provision or purchase of the indicated services. For those evaluations done as an initial step in a treatment program (where there is some inherent potential benefit to the clinician if the client follows the recommendations), it is even more important to describe the client's needs and the potential services from the perspective of the client's goals, rather than listing services provided by the program. In this way the assessment can legitimately serve as a rehabilitation planning tool for any future planner or program.

Clarify Recommendations in Report

One of the simplest but most useful mechanism in making results more accessible to readers is to discard the narrative, paragraph style typically used in a summary format. Both for summary conclusions and recommendations, ideas will be more clearly delineated with numbered, brief statements. If the referral questions have been well identified, it will be easy to restate them one at a time, with a brief summary response to each. (Does the client demonstrate a dementia? What can be done to improve the client's problems with memory and planning? Does the client demonstrate cognitive problems related to the client's multiple sclerosis? Is the client able to succeed academically in a challenging college curriculum given his or her learning disability and history of poor academic performance in high school?) Some examples of specific recommendations are summarized in Table 10.6.

TABLE 10.6
Clarity in Rehabilitation Recommendations

Provide detailed, person/environment specific descriptions of problems, how to avoid them, and how to intervene.

Write as if you were the clinician who had to conduct the intervention.

Do not assume programmatic support.

Make specific recommendations for places to pursue recommended therapy; if you don't know it yourself, spend some time familiarizing yourself with local and community resources, seek out resources, or consider developing them yourself.

Just as you would when embarking on a therapeutic contract with a client, consider what funding options are available. Learn what the constraints are on the population and referring sources you typically assess, and incorporate these recommendations into the report.

Address and suggest interventions regarding self-awareness and self-monitoring as two central abilities to be facilitated by neuropsychological rehabilitation, even if central deficits remain in the person.

DISSEMINATE REPORT FINDINGS

Although changing the manner of report dissemination may be the least intellectually challenging or the least "different" from standard practice, it may actually be the most demanding for busy clinicians, especially those in a highly structured institutional environment or those for whom billing and accountability for each service are essential.

For better dissemination of results, the following recommendations are offered. First, and most importantly, provide a brief, typewritten summary to the assessed individual and family or others involved. This can serve as a surrogate "prescription" in the sense of imparting an importance to the results and a specific plan that can be followed. Telephone or even face-to-face verbal discussions of results and recommendations are not sufficient, given the cognitive problems of the clients being assessed. A similar letter or summary to the referring party serves as a nice "thank you" and usually can convey the essential diagnostic and treatment issues within a short paragraph, while skipping the complexities of the complete report. Second, call or speak with the referring party to see if therapy was initiated and if you can be of assistance in clarifying what recommendations were made and how they can be accessed. Third, consult with the treating therapist or cotreating clinician. Too often referred sources repeat assessments to develop their own treatment plan. If you already have a plan in mind, share it! Although it may appear to be presumptuous of one provider to "tell another" what to do, the client and the funding agency paying for assessment and treatment will both benefit greatly.

SUMMARY AND CONCLUSIONS

This brief chapter assumes that standard neuropsychological assessment procedures and reports have tremendous value to offer clients and rehabilitation providers, and that clinicians can bridge the gap from assessment to rehabilitation with some shifts in orientation and report presentation. First, change how you think. Focus on functional systems, not deficits. Educate yourself about rehabilitation resources and the rehabilitation continuum of care. Second, change what you do in written reports. Describe problems and recommendations in detail. Document eligibility for services (diagnosis/etiology) and potential to benefit from rehabilitation services (treatment justification). Answer referral questions directly. Finally, make sure report recommendations are conveyed to future providers. With practice and feedback from clients and referral sources, these changes will quickly close the gap between assessment and rehabilitation, and ultimately make the neuropsychologist a much more integral part of the rehabilitation team.

REFERENCES

Abreu, B. C., & Toglia, J. P. (1987). Cognitive rehabilitation: A model for occupational therapy. *American Journal of Occupational Therapy, 41,* 439–448.

Baddeley, A. D. (1986). *Working memory.* Oxford: Oxford University Press.

Evans, R. (1997). Post-acute neurorehabilitation: roles and responsibilities within a national information system. *Archives of Physical Medicine and Rehabilitation, 78,* 17–25.

Glisky, E. L., & Schacter, D. L. (1986). Remediation of organic memory disorders: Current status and future prospects. *Journal of Head Trauma Rehabilitation, 1,* 54–63.

Johnstone, B., & Farmer, J. E. (1997). Preparing neuropsychologists for the future: The need for additional training guidelines. *Archives of Clinical Neuropsychology, 12,* 523–530.

Johnstone, B., Frank, R. G., Belar, C., Berk, S., Bieliauskas, L. A., Bigler, E. D., Caplan, B., Elliott, T. R., Glueckauf, R. L., Kaplan, R. M., Kreutzer, J. S., Mateer, C. M., Patterson, D., Puente, A. E., Richards, J. S., Rosenthal, M., Sherer, M., Shewchuck, R., Siegel, L. J., & Sweet, J. J. (1996). Psychology in health care: Future directions. *Professional Psychology: Research and Practice, 26,* 341–365.

Levine, F. M., & Sandeen, E. (1985). The limited capacities model. In F. M Levine & E. Sandeen (Eds.), *Conceptualization in psychotherapy* (pp. 43–59). Hillsdale, NJ: Lawrence Erlbaum Associates.

Luria, A. R. (1963). *Restoration of function after brain injury.* New York: Oxford University Press.

Luria, A. R. (1981). *Language and cognition.* Washington, DC: V. H. Winston.

Naugle, R. I., & Chelune, G. J. (1990). Integrating neuropsychological and "real life" data: A neuropsychological model for assessing everyday functioning. In D. E. Tupper & K. D. Cicerone (Eds.), *The neuropsychology of everyday life: Assessment and basic competencies* (pp. 57–74). Boston: Kluwer.

Toglia, J. P. (1991). Generalization of treatment: A multicontext approach to cognitive perceptual impairment in adults with brain injury. *American Journal of Occupational Therapy, 45,* 505–516.

Tupper, D. E., & Cicerone, K. D. (1990). Introduction to the neuropsychology of everyday life. In D. E. Tupper & K. D. Cicerone (Eds.), *The neuropsychology of everyday life: Assessment and basic competencies* (pp. 3–18). Boston: Kluwer.

Wilson, B. (1988). Future directions in rehabilitation of brain injured people. In A. Christensen & B. Uzzell (Eds.), *Neuropsychological rehabilitation* (pp. 69–86). Boston: Kluwer.

Ylvisaker, M., & Szekeres, S. F. (1989). Metacognitive and executive impairments in head-injured children and adults. *Topics in Language Disorders, 9,* 34–49.

CHAPTER ELEVEN

Issues in Child Neuropsychological Assessment

Eileen B. Fennell

Department of Clinical and Health Psychology
University of Florida, Gainesville

Neuropsychological assessment of children and young adolescents imposes certain unique demands on the examiner. Although the question of the impact of a lesion on brain behavior is a central theme in all neuropsychological assessments, the effects of differing types of brain lesions on developing brain systems poses somewhat different challenges to those who assess children and adolescents. Knowledge about the primary or secondary effects of lesions must be applied in the context of brain systems whose functional relationships are still under development (Kolb & Fantie, 1997). Furthermore, the child neuropsychologist must possess a clear understanding of the typical patterns of emergence of intellectual, memory, language, motor, and visuospatial skills in order to appreciate deviations from patterns of normal development. Finally, the child neuropsychologist must have an appreciation of the spectrum of behavioral symptoms and disorders that can be manifestations of childhood psychopathology or family discord (Walker & Roberts, 1992). Thus, the task of the examiner is to integrate knowledge about normal and pathological development in order to better describe and predict the impact of a brain lesion on the developing brain.

This chapter presents an overview of relevant issues in assessing children and young adolescents. In the first section, general issues in child neuropsychological assessment are addressed. After that, a brief overview of types of child assessment and models of influence applied in child or adolescent cases is discussed. Following that overview, the next section presents a broad model of areas to be examined when this age group is assessed. The content of the clinical interview and the essential elements of a comprehensive examination and report are also described. Issues relating to psychometric measurement, test norms, and test revisions form the content of the next section. The chapter concludes with a discussion of current needs and future directions in child neuropsychological assessment.

GENERAL ISSUES IN ASSESSING CHILDREN

Historical Trends

In a recent review, Tramontana and Hooper (1988) characterized child neuropsychology as emerging through four historical stages. The first stage, from the mid-1940s to the mid-1960s, was dominated by the single-test approach, in which single tests were used to diagnose brain damage or organicity. The major intent was to separate brain-damaged children from normal children according to differences in their scores on a particular test such as the Bender Visual Motor Gestalt Test (Koppitz, 1964) or by interpreting patterns of performance on an omnibus measure such as the Wechsler Intelligence Scale for Children (Wechsler, 1960). By the mid-1960s, the second stage of development occurred, in which fixed batteries of tests were administered to brain-damaged children (Ernhart, Graham, Erchman, Marshall, & Thurston, 1963). By the early 1970s, the earliest data on the Reitan battery for collections of children with head injuries as well as other types of brain impairments as well as the scores of same-aged normal children became available (Reitan & Davison, 1974). The third stage began in the late 1970s and early 1980s, when child neuropsychologists began to emphasize the functional effects of various types of childhood disorders, rather than attempting solely to arrive at a decision about the presence or absence of brain disorder (Rourke, 1982). The most recent, fourth, stage involves an emphasis on the ability of individual tests or test batteries to better identify and describe the impact of a brain lesion or brain dysfunction on the demands of everyday functioning. The role of the neuropsychologist has evolved to include prescriptions for interventions at both home and school. These prescriptions are designed to help parents and educators accommodate to the special needs of a child with a developmental disability arising from brain disorder. Specific remediation strategies based on the identification of the child's strengths and weaknesses are offered. A fifth stage in child neuropsychology has now begun to emerge, reflecting advances in pediatric medicine. As a consequence of newer treatment technologies, large numbers of children are surviving previously fatal illnesses directly affecting the central nervous system (e.g., brain tumors) or illnesses whose successful treatment may compromise central nervous system functioning (e.g., childhood leukemias). With the emergence of organ transplantation, child neuropsychologists are increasingly called on to understand the effects of such dramatic interventions on subsequent development as well as to advise physicians, parents, and educators about the special needs of these children. Thus, in addition to the empirical knowledge gained over the past 50 years about common handicapping conditions (e.g.,learning disabilities, attention deficit disorders, autism, head trauma, cerebral palsy, and epilepsy), the child neuropsychologist must be familiar with new evidence about the impact of systemic illnesses and their treatments on survivors of acute and chronic medical disorders of childhood.

Issues in Child Neuropsychological Assessment

In the recent past, a number of excellent textbooks devoted to the field of child neuropsychology have been published (Baron, Fennell, & Voeller, 1995; Hynd & Willis, 1988; Reynolds & Fletcher-Janzen, 1997; Rourke, Bakker, Fisk, & Strange, 1983; Rourke, Fisk, & Strange, 1986; Rutter, 1983; Spreen, Risser, & Edgell, 1995; Spreen, Tupper, Risser, Tuokko, & Edgell, 1984; Tramontana & Hooper, 1988, 1992). In addition, several tests and chapters devoted to specific topics in child neuropsychology are now available (Bernstein & Waber, 1990; Broman & Michel, 1995; Fletcher & Taylor, 1997; Goldman-Rakic, 1994; Pennington, 1991; Rourke, 1995). These publications document the diverse impact of acquired or congenital brain disorders on children's development. A common feature of all this literature is the recognition of three key variables that affect the outcome of brain lesions in children: (a) type of lesion, (b) location of lesion, and (c) age at time of lesion.

Lesion Type.   Type of lesion refers to the underlying pathological processes that have primary effects on the central nervous system. *Lesion* is a general term used to refer to an abnormality of either structure or function within the brain. Table 11.1 provides examples of types of primary lesions that can occur within the central nervous system. In addition to the structural or functional primary lesions, brain functioning can be disrupted as a secondary effect of a systemic disorder involving a different organ system or as a consequence of treatment of a systemic disorder. For example, primary lesions may include disorders of central nervous system development (e.g., spina bifida), tumors (e.g., gliomas), vascular lesions (e.g., malformations, infarcts), infections (e.g., meningitis), injury (e.g., closed-head trauma), paroxysmal disorders (e.g., epilepsy), and hereditary disorders (e.g., Prader–Willi syndrome; Menkes, 1990). Also, there are a number of developmental disorders with a putative basis in primary central nervous system dysfunction including specific learning disabilities (Gaddes & Edgell, 1994; Pennington, 1991) and attention deficit hyperactivity disorder (Barkley, 1990). In addition, there are a number of systemic disorders that exert a secondary effect on the central nervous system. These include cardiac disease (e.g., ventriculo-

TABLE 11.1
Primary Lesions and Medical Disorders
That Can Affect Brain Functioning

I. Primary lesion
   Developmental malformations
   CNS tumors
   Vascular lesions
   Infections
   Paroxysmal disorders
   Hereditary / genetic syndromes
   Demyelinating diseases
   Brain trauma

II. Medical disorders affecting brain functioning
   Cardiac disease
   Pulmonary disease
   Hematological disorders
   Renal failure
   Liver failure
   Endocrine disorders

III. Medical treatments that affect brain functioning
   Chemotherapy
   Irradiation
   Immune suppression

septal defects), hematological disorders (e.g., sickle-cell anemia), chronic renal or liver disease, endocrine dysfunction (e.g., juvenile-onset diabetes), and other multisystem pathologies (e.g., cystic fibrosis). Finally, treatment of systemic disease with irradiation, chemotherapy, or immune suppression can also affect the functions of the central nervous system (Berg & Linton, 1989; Tartar, Van Thiel, & Edwards, 1988). As might be expected from such a diverse picture, the clinical pattern one might expect from examining a child will vary according to the type of lesion. Structural lesions can exert focal or diffuse effects, depending on location and impact on surrounding structures. For example, a brainstem glioma may press against outlets for the cranial nerves, leading to changes in eye movements, and at the same time causing obstructive hydrocephalus, leading to generalized slowing, disorders of attention and learning, and irritability.

In addition to differences in the type of lesion according to its primary, secondary, or tertiary effects on the central nervous system, lesions may also vary in the velocity of their development (Reitan & Davison, 1974). Lesions can be described as static or progressive. A *static* lesion is one that is not evolving. A *progressive* lesion continues to evolve and develop and its effects may progress. An example of a static lesion in children would be a small stroke in the thalamus suffered during the perinatal period, which has resulted in mild spasticity. In contrast, there are a number of progressive lesions in childhood such as exemplified by an enlarging brainstem astrocytic tumor (Menkes, 1990). Another way to describe brain lesions is on the dimension of acuity versus chronicity. Acute lesions typically are recent in onset and can have both generalized and focal effects. Chronic lesions are typically of longer duration, are often static, and, in childhood, can lead to brain reorganization. An example of a chronic lesion is the case description of a 16-year-old who sustained a left middle cerebral artery stroke in the perinatal or neonatal period (Stringer & Fennell, 1987). However, one may not be able to ascertain on the basis of the neuropsychological findings alone whether a lesion is static or progressive or chronic versus acute. Conclusions regarding the velocity of a lesion may not be possible without information from the medical records as to the type of lesion. In general, more than one assessment may be needed in order to chart any change in neuropsychological functioning. Follow-up assessments should include a number of measures that are sensitive to changes in the child's state. Examples of such tests include Trails A and B, Finger Tapping, and Verbal Fluency, as well as selected subtests from the age-appropropriate Wechsler Scales such as Coding or Digit Span. Broadband tests of areas of functioning such as achievement may not respond as rapidly to alterations in the child's functioning arising from an acute or rapidly progressive lesion. Furthermore, accommodations to a slowly progressive lesion can take place over time, and it may emerge only over a longer time of follow-up.

It is essential for the practicing child neuropsychologist to develop greater knowledge of the effects of type of lesion on brain functioning in children. This requires the examiner to remain current on the clinical neuropsychological literature about the behavioral effects of different types of primary or secondary lesions as it becomes available through professional psychological and medical journals and textbooks. Fundamental to an appreciation of the effects of different types of lesions is a current knowledge base about childhood neurological disorders and neurological or neurosurgical treatments (Feinchel, 1988; Fishman & Taylor, 1987; Menkes, 1990).

Location of Lesion. Where a lesion is located is another important brain variable in child neuropsychological assessment. Increasingly, our appreciation of brain–behavior relationships has expanded from a focus on cortical and brainstem structures to the complexities of the subcortical and cerebellar regions (Crosson, 1992; Schmahmann, 1991; Tranel, 1992). Although current medical technology such as computed tomography (CT), magnetic resonance imagery (MRI), positron emission tomography (PET), or single-photon emission computed tomography (SPECT) scans has permitted more precise localization of brain lesions, medical science still relies on the neuropsychologist to describe the dynamic impact of a lesion on behavior. Knowing where a lesion is located allows the neuropsychologist to develop hypotheses regarding the expected effects of a lesion (Fennell & Bauer, 1997). Neuropsychological testing can then determine whether such lesion-related effects are present, as well as whether other problems in higher brain functioning are also evident. Knowing that a child has suffered a subarachnoid bleed due to sickle-cell disease may not, in and of itself, explain why the child is now described as failing in school. Determining that the bleed has lead to significant problems in attention, motivation, fatigu-ability, and memory functioning allows behaviorally based interventions and recommendations to be developed to help that child.

Much of our understanding of regional differences in brain functioning has derived from the study of adult brain lesions (Heilman & Valenstein, 1993; Lezak, 1995). Nevertheless, understanding differences in how the child's brain is affected by a brain lesion should be linked to knowledge about normal brain maturation and cognitive development (Kolb & Fantie, 1997; Schneider & Pres-sley, 1990; Williams, 1983) as well as abnormal brain development (Spreen et al., 1995). For example, the anatomical basis of memory processes (e.g., encoding, retrieval) is in functional networks involving medial temporal, diencephalic, and orbitofrontal brain structures. These structures develop at different rates (Baron et al., 1995) and myelinate at different rates and ages (Yakolev & Lecours, 1967). Not surprisingly, younger children may normally manifest fewer and simpler encoding strategies than do older children whose brain systems are more func-tionally mature (Kail, 1985). And so, for example, to conclude that a 6-year-old child has a deficit in semantic encoding is to describe a normal-for-age behavior, not a neuropsychological deficit (Schneider & Pressley, 1990).

Age at the Time of Lesion. The child's age at the time of acquiring a lesion is a particularly important variable in child neuropsychology (Boll, 1983; Boll & Barth, 1981). Injury to the brain from the many types of lesions described earlier can occur pre-, peri-, or postnatally, during infancy, or throughout the course of early childhood into adolescence. Depending on when the lesion occurred, there may be different effects on the brain systems that are developing or have yet to develop (Hynd & Willis, 1988; Kolb & Fantie, 1997; Spreen et al., 1995). There may be both an acute effect of the injury, such as neuronal death, and more long-term effects on the development of functional connections, such as the growth of aberrant connections (Goldman, Rosvold, & Mishkin, 1970; Stringer & Fennell, 1987).

Two closely related concepts are *critical periods* for development and plastic-ity. The concept of critical period relates to that period of time between the anatomic and functional development of a brain system (Spreen et al., 1995). Critical periods have been identified in prenatal and postnatal development that are affected both by brain lesions and by the lack of stimulation (Kolb & Wishaw, 1990). From a developmental perspective, focal lesions in brain regions prior to their complete anatomic maturation may not produce behavioral defi-cits until a later age, when that anatomic substrate becomes critical to the attainment of some neuropsychological function. For example, the frontal lobes continue to develop and mature well into adolescence and early adulthood (Yak-olev & Lecours, 1967). As a result, a significant injury to the frontal lobes may not produce a behavioral deficit until the child reaches late childhood and early adolescences and fails to develop normal frontal executive behaviors (e.g., self-control, appropriate self-control of "unacceptable" urges).

Plasticity is a related concept and is based on observation of the capacity of the brain to adapt to change. Earlier views (Kennard principle) held that it was better to have a brain lesion early than later in life, based on the apparent ability of the immature brain to develop functions after early lesions. However, more recent views recognize that although some function may be achieved, it may be compromised in some fashion (Goldman & Galkin, 1978). With prenatal and perinatal neurological disorders or genetic syndromes, the child may never have experienced the functioning of a normal brain. Instead, the child's development is marked by adaptation to the maturational changes wrought by these early chronic or progressive lesions. Reitan (1984) suggested that early brain lesions, regardless of lateralization, will have a devastating effect on the child's potential to develop normal abilities. Brain lesions occurring later might result in more selective impairments because some normal maturational processes preceded the injury, allowing for the development of some normal cognitive abilities.

The child neuropsychologist must have a clear view of the emergence of normal functional abilities with which to compare the behavior of a child who has suffered from some type of brain lesion (Gesell & Amatruda, 1974). Absence of this window through which to view behavior may lead to incorrect decisions regarding the presence or absence of behavioral effects of the brain lesion. Further, this implies that the child neuropsychologist must inevitably adopt a longitudinal-developmental approach to assessment. Fletcher and Taylor (1984) articulated one such approach, which views child neuropsychology as requiring knowledge of the manifest behavioral pathology of the child, the biological/neurological substrate underlying the pathology, the limits that these factors impose on the developing behavioral competencies of the child, and the moderating effects of the family system or educational setting. This integrated approach is advocated here as well.

In addition to understanding impact of type of lesion, the location of the lesion, and the timing of the lesion, there are a number of factors, unique to assessment of children, that distinguish child from adult neuropsychological assessment (Baron et al., 1995; Baron & Fennell, in press). When one assesses adults with an acquired neurological disorder, the changes in function that result are often conceptualized in terms of "loss of function" (test deficits). With children, acquired lesions may impact functions that are not yet developed. For example, a 4-year-old boy who has suffered an unilateral left middle cerebral artery stroke during a cardiac catherization may not demonstrate deficits in written language comprehension until he begins to learn how to read. Congenital lesions can result in structural brain changes that may alter both the structure and function of various brain systems (e.g., alterations in the size of the corpus callosum secondary to congenital hydrocephalus). Early acquired brain lesions may alter the trajectory of development of affected brain lesions, may lead to reorganization of the affected brain systems, or may result in atypical brain connectivity (Baron et al., 1995).

Brain development proceeds at different rates in different regions of the brain. As a result, acquired early brain lesions or trauma may have at least three different effects: injury to a fully matured brain system, resulting in loss of function; injury to a developing brain system, resulting in alteration of function; and, injury to those brain systems not yet scheduled to be "online," resulting in either failure to mature or abnormal maturational patterns. As a result, there is variable expression of the impact of a brain injury at different ages (Baron & Fennell, in press). Another related issue is a consequence of this variability: The brain–behavior "rules" that guide inferences about localization of lesions in adult patients cannot be easily applied to children and can only be applied cautiously in adolescents.

Still another factor encountered in child neuropsychological assessment is the remarkable variety of test-taking behaviors that normal children exhibit. Determining whether a particular behavior represents a normal variation in how a child performs versus an atypical behavioral response versus a "pathological" sign requires that the child neuropsychologist have considerable experience and understanding of the patterns of normal and abnormal maturation in children. Normal children acquire skills at different rates, resulting in large standard deviations on many tests. This is particularly the case in the preschool and early-to-middle childhood years, making decisions about atypical versus abnormal performance more difficult (Leckliter, Forster, Klonoff, & Knights, 1992; Spreen & Strauss, 1997). Finally, socioeconomic, cultural, and family factors may also influence the timing and expression of skills acquisition in normally developing children, as well as affecting the child's and family's response to congenital, developmental, or acquired brain dysfunction.

ASSESSMENT APPROACHES IN CHILD NEUROPSYCHOLOGY

As in adult neuropsychology, there are three main assessment approaches in child neuropsychology (Fennell & Bauer, 1997): the fixed battery approach, the flexible battery approach, and the individualized or patient-centered approach (see also chaps. 13 and 14). These approaches are distinguished by the nature of the test battery employed by the examiner.

The *fixed battery approach* involves the administration of the same set of standardized tests to each child seen, regardless of diagnostic question. The battery may vary somewhat according to the age of the child, typically differentiating younger (5–8 years old) from older (9–15 years old) children. These batteries have generally been empirically derived and are based on their ability to separate normal children from groups of children with brain dysfunction, such as the work of Reitan and his coworkers (Reitan & Davison, 1974) or the more recent Nebraska Neuropsychological Children's Battery (Golden, 1989). These batteries were both derived from adult versions of the tests employed with items altered, deleted, or eliminated to make them more age appropriate for children. The emphasis in most fixed batteries is on the quantitative differentiation of patient groups from normal children. As a result, there is little emphasis on such qualitative indices as age-related changes in how a score is achieved (Bernstein & Waber, 1990). Some fixed batteries also include rules for decision making (Selz & Reitan, 1979). A major concern for the examiner who uses a fixed battery is the match between the sample of brain-injured children who were used in the validation or cross-validation studies and the child to whom these interpretive rules will be applied. Typically these batteries will include normative data by age and by gender but not by grade placement (Reitan & Wolfson, 1992a, 1992b).

The *flexible battery approach* typically utilizes a core battery of tests that are administered, along with additional tests that are selected to address specific referral questions (Rourke et al., 1986) or to clarify findings that emerge from the core battery. One such example would be the use of a screening battery followed by the use of a comprehensive language battery in the assessment of language deficits following closed-head injury (Ewings-Cobbs, Levin, Eisenberg, Marshall, & Thurston, 1987). This type of approach allows the examiner to follow both a nomothetic approach (core battery) and an ideographic approach (additional tests) to better describe a particular childhood syndrome. Often the additional tests are derived from clinical evaluations of selected groups of brain-impaired children but may also include more laboratory-based assessment techniques such as dichotic listening, use of computerized continuous performance tasks, or specialized tests of lateralized brain functions. Flexible batteries may sometimes take more time than a fixed battery, and the tests utilized may vary from child to child. As a result, the examiner may have more or less clinical experience with a given subset of tests in the battery.

In the *patient-centered* approach, the examiner selects tests to be employed based on both the referral question and the child's performance on a given task. Unlike the two other approaches described, the emphasis in this examination is on the isolation of the specific neurological mechanism that underlies a particular behavioral disorder (Bernstein & Waber, 1990). Thus, this approach requires that the examiner have a very thorough understanding of the clinical presentation of a variety of specific brain disorders as well as an underlying model of brain functioning against which to match the clinical findings and to infer the brain pathology (Fennell & Bauer, 1997; Tramontana & Hooper, 1988).

Regardless of assessment approach, most child neuropsychologists assess children with a set of tests that tap many areas of brain functioning. Thus, typically, tests of intellectual functioning, memory, language, sensory, motor, and visuospatial functions are included in the examination. What differs is the emphasis placed by the examiner on the match or mismatch between examination results and: (a) the performance of normal children; (b) the performance of children with brain injuries from different etiological causes; (c) the performance of children with similar types and location of lesions; (d) the known behavioral effects of a lesion in a specific functional system; and (e) the changes in test performance that are a function of age at time of lesion and/or time since the lesion occurred. This comparison between the individual case and multiple companion groups is fundamental to the inferential process in child neuropsychology (Fennell & Bauer, 1997).

Once the test battery has been administered, the next critical steps in the evaluation process take place. These steps involve the clinical integration of several additional sources of information beyond the test scores (Baron & Fennell, in press). These sources include:

1. Developmental history of the child.
2. History of the neurological or medical events that gave rise to the current referral question.
3. History of the child's academic and social functioning.
4. History of any adjustment problems experienced as a consequence of the child's neurological or medical problem.
5. Family history of developmental or adjustment difficulties.
6. Psychological, psychiatric, or rehabilitative interventions that may have occurred.

Interpretation of the test data itself must be undertaken in light of cautions against four potential fallacies noted by Taylor and Fletcher (1990) in interpreting child neuropsychological assessment from an "adult assessment" frame of reference. The four fallacies noted by these authors include that:

1. Testing procedures from adult neuropsychology are also differentially sensitive when applied to children.
2. Tests developed on adults are measuring the same or similar abilities in children.
3. The pattern of test deficits or behavioral problems "signals" abnormal brain functions.
4. Test scores serve as a descriptors of brain rather than of behavior.

It is the inferential model, not the test alone, that links test scores to brain behavior (Fennell & Bauer, 1997).

A MODEL FOR NEUROPSYCHOLOGICAL
ASSESSMENT OF CHILDREN

Domains of Assessment

The neuropsychological examination of a child or young adolescent involves assessment of several broad domains of functioning: (a) biological, (b) social-interpersonal, and (c) educational. Each domain should be examined from the framework of past history of development and current problems. Within the biological domain, the examiner seeks to obtain knowledge about prior development, including past medical history, history of the specific complaint, prior medical diagnostic evaluations, and any family history factors that could affect the presenting problem. The child's performance on the neuropsychological examination constitutes the descriptive basis for current problems. Along with scores on the neuropsychological exam, parents of younger children may frequently complete general developmental inventories such as the Childhood Development Inventory (Ireton & Twang, 1992) and the Vineland Adaptive Behavior Scales (Sparrow, Balla, & Cicchetti, 1984).

Similarly, the social-interpersonal domain involves exploration of the prior history of social or behavior problems manifested by the child, history of familial disorders or discord, and the family's response to the child's behavioral problem (Tramontana & Hooper, 1997). With young children, parent-report measures of problem behaviors may be employed, such as the Child Behavior Checklist (Achenbach & Edelrock, 1983). Older children who can read may also complete several self-report measures assessing affective symptoms such as anxiety (Spielberger, 1973) or depression (Kovacs, 1992), as well as indices of self-esteem (Harter, 1983).

Finally, because a major task of childhood is to succeed in school, the educational domain needs to be examined. A careful history of schooling beginning from any preschool experiences should be obtained from the parents. Information to be gathered includes not only academic but also behavioral problems that the child encountered. Prior achievement testing, school changes, placement in any special classes, and history of school adjustment should be carefully gathered during interview. Current placement and any problems in achievement or adjustment are also needed, including teacher reports of problem behaviors (James & Selz, 1997). When achievement data are not available, the child may be given an individualized achievement test to assess for competencies in current grade placement, such as the Woodcock–Johnson Psychoeducational Battery–Revised (Woodcock & Mather, 1989). Although many neuropsychologists prefer to use a briefer achievement screening instrument, such as the Wide-Range Achievement Test–3 (Wilkinson, 1993), these briefer instruments may suboptimally assess reading competence and mathematics ability (Goldman, L'Engle-Stern, & Guerry, 1983).

The intent of the careful examination in each of these three domains is to be able to develop a clear understanding of developmental factors that could affect the current presentation of biological, social, or educational problems of the child. Against this background of developmental history, special behavioral problems that the child exhibits on the neuropsychological examination, in social or interpersonal relationships, or in educational settings may be evaluated. This evaluation requires that child neuropsychologists possess knowledge regarding the developmental effects and outcomes of brain, social, or educational problems. For example, if a child suffered a closed-head injury at age 6 years, the child neuropsychologist must be familiar with the early and late behavioral effects of closed-head injury in order to ascertain whether the current problems of the child are a direct result of the injury (Fennell & Mickle, 1992; Fletcher & Taylor, 1997) or a manifestation of prior behavior problems. However, if this same child comes from a family in which there are two siblings and one parent with a history of learning disability, the decision-making process becomes more complicated without an understanding of the neuropsychology of learning disabilities (Pennington, 1991; Taylor, 1989). Many adolescents who sustain traumatic brain injuries have a history of prior learning disabilities (Levin, Ewing-Cobbs, & Eisenberg, 1995). Similarly, if a child has manifested problems in hyperactivity or inattention but has been medicated for a seizure disorder, the examiner must appreciate the potential effects of epilepsy or adverse side effects of anticonvulsant medication on test performance (Menkes, 1990). Finally, it is rarely the case that children (or adults) undergo a neuropsychological assessment prior to an adverse event. However, if this same child had been given a McCarthy Scale of Children's Abilities (McCarthy, 1972) at age 4 years but is now administered the Wechsler Preschool and Primary Scale of Intelligence–Revised (Wechsler, 1991) in the context of a personal injury lawsuit, the child neuropsychologist must often interpret differences in scores between tests that occurred prior to and subsequent to a brain injury. Appreciation of the comparability between tests requires that the child neuropsychologist remain cognizant of the psychometric characteristics of many childhood measures (Reynolds, 1997).

Elements of a Comprehensive Child Neuropsychological Examination

Table 11.2 presents the essential elements of a comprehensive neuropsychological examination. Prior to beginning the examination, the neuropsychologist should review all records of prior medical treatments or diagnostic procedures undertaken on the child. Often parents have an incomplete understanding of the meaning of these procedures or are unable to recall critical information re-

TABLE 11.2
Essential Elements in a Child
Neuropsychological Examination

1. Clinical Interview
   a. History
      1. Prenatal to present development
      2. Medical illnesses or injuries
      3. School
      4. Psychosocial and emotional functioning
   b. Current problems
      1. Medical
      2. Emotional
      3. Learning and/or behavioral
      4. Interventions
2. Neuropsychological tests
   a. Intelligence
   b. Memory
      1. Verbal
      2. Nonverbal
   c. Learning
      1. Verbal
      2. Nonverbal
   d. Language
      1. Expression
         Oral
         Written
         Fluency
      2. Comprehensive
   e. Motor
      1. Fine motor speed
      2. Manual dexterity
      3. Gross motor
   f. Visuospatial Functions
      1. Analysis
      2. Synthesis
      3. Construction
   g. Frontal Executive
      1. Attention
      2. Speed of responding
      3. Response inhibition
      4. Tracking
      5. Abstraction
3. Achievement
   a. History
   b. Current
4. Social emotional functioning
   a. Child behavioral problems
   b. Family problems

lated to the child's health status. When CT scans or electroencephalographs (EEGs) have been conducted, these should be summarized in the report.

The clinical interview is intended to develop a history of the child and the family from the three perspectives already described: the biological (medical and neurological), the social-interpersonal (psychological and emotional development), and the educational (experiences and competencies). The typical interview may last for an hour or longer, depending on the purpose of the examination. Within the biological domain, the examiner should begin with the mother's pregnancy and delivery and proceed through each year of development to the present date. Early childhood milestones should be examined (language or motor milestones, toilet training, early peer experiences). It is often helpful to ask the parents to compare this child to other siblings with regard to milestones. As noted earlier, careful descriptions of preschool and school history should be obtained. If the child has sustained an acquired lesion (e.g., head trauma, central nervous system [CNS] infection), it is important to obtain detailed description of behavioral changes early and later in time from the date of the acquired injury. Questions of early temperament and adjustment should precede any detailed description of current behavioral problems. Again, it is helpful to obtain comparisons of this child with siblings. It is also helpful to gather information about parenting styles, including discipline methods or conflicts between the parents over child-rearing practices. Finally, the interview should develop a detailed description of current problems experienced by the child at home, at school, and at play. Parental and sibling reactions to these problems should be explored. At the conclusion of the interview, the child neuropsychologist may wish to restate his or her understanding of the purpose of the examination as well as the questions to which the parents hope to obtain answers as a result of the examination.

The types of neuropsychological tests that can be given in the examination are outlined in the next section of Table 11.1. It is not the intent of this chapter to provide detailed descriptions of the measures to be used. Instead, the scope of the examination is presented. The typical examination covering these areas will last about 4 to 4½ hours, depending on the age of the child and the child's difficulty with different task demands. If a child is to be followed with repeated examinations, tests should be selected within each area that have an adequate span across the ages.

Probably the most commonly administered intelligence tests are the Wechsler scales: the Wechsler Primary and Preschool Scale of Intelligence–Revised (WPPSI–R; Wechsler, 1989); the Wechsler Intelligence Scale for Children–III (WISC–III; Wechsler, 1991), and the newest Wechsler Adult Intelligence Scale–III (WAIS–III; Wechsler, 1997). These omnibus intelligence tests consist of a variety of individual subtests, which are broadly grouped into a Verbal Scale and a Performance Scale. Individual subtest raw scores are converted into age-normed scaled scores (WPPSI–R; WISC–III), then summed and converted into a Verbal IQ, Performance IQ, and Full Scale IQ score. Factor-analytic studies of the Wechsler scales suggest that the subtests group into several factors: a verbal comprehension factor, a perceptual organization factor, and a freedom from distractibility factor. However, some controversy exists regarding the clinical viability of these factors in neuropsychological assessment (Kaufman, 1990).

A number of broad-band memory batteries and verbal learning tests normed specifically for children are now available. Knowledge about normal memory development and memory strategies in children is essential in order to meaningful interpret scores from such batteries or tests (Kail, 1985; Schneider & Pressley, 1989). In general, these memory batteries allow for the derivation of both individual subtest scores and more global summated memory indices. For example, among the currently available memory batteries are the Wide Range Assessment of Memory and Learning (WRAML; Sheslow & Adams, 1990), the Children's Memory Scale (CMS; Cohen, 1997), and the Test of Memory and Learning (TOMAL; Reynolds & Bigler, 1994). Each battery assesses elements of immediate, short-term, and delayed memory for verbal and pictorial memory as well as providing tests of verbal and visual learning. In addition, a number of specific tests of verbal learning have also recently been published, such as the California Verbal Learning Test–Children Version (CVLT–C; Delis, Kramer, Kaplan, & Ober, 1994) and the Children's Auditory Verbal Learning Test–2 (CAVLT–2; Talley, 1993).

There are also a number of tests of language competency in children now available, such as the Clinical Evaluation of Language Fundamentals–3 (CELF–3; Semel, Wiig, & Secord, 1993). However, unless the examiner is very familiar with the different types of language and articulation disorders that children can manifest, these language batteries should not be attempted by the examiner. Clinical observation of problems in articulation, grammar, syntax, or fluency should be part of the language evaluation of children and adolescents. Evidence of word-finding problems, circumlocutions, or paraphasic errors in spontaneous speech may lead to screening of confrontation naming abilities, sentence repetition, comprehension of multistep commands, or tests of word generation to target alphabet letters or categories. Specific tests along with normative data for age 6–12 years have been complied in a recent test compendium (Spreen & Strauss, 1997). When questions of language disorder emerge from this initial examination, the child should be referred to a speech pathologist for a more comprehensive speech and language assessment. The speech pathologist may also provide treatment recommendations to address the child's language problems.

Evaluation of the broad domain of visuomotor or visuoperceptual functioning requires familiarity with the normal developmental course of these skills (Williams, 1983). There are a wide variety and large number of tests available that assess either the input (perceptual) side of visual processing of lines, designs, or faces, and the output (visuomotor/visuocontructional) side of these higher brain functions. It is often useful to "take apart" failures on a test of visuocontructional ability, such as design copying, by also giving the child a motor-free, match-to-sample test to help determine whether the errors occurred as a consequence of problems in perceptual analysis and synthesis versus problems in programming the motor output requirements of the task (copying or building a copy of the stimulus). Tests of visuomotor output, such as the Beery Test of Visuomotor Integration–Revised (Beery, 1997), require motor control along with perceptual skills and planning for normal performance. However, certain aspects of each of these contributing skills may be impaired in a child with neurological problems (e.g., perceiving the picture, motor control of pencil, motor programming of output). As a result, interpreting a low score as reflecting problems in "visuomotor integrative abilities" does little to help describe or differentiate the source(s) of the child's apparent difficulties on this task.

Similarly, appreciation of the development of so-called "frontal lobe" behaviors is a prerequisite to interpreting the meaning of any abnormalities noted in test performance. Frontal-lobe behaviors involve both elementary and complex motor functions as well as a variety of so-called "executive functions." The term *executive functions* has been used to describe a variety of higher order behaviors involving sustained, focused, and selective attention, the ability to self-monitor one's own behavior in the face of changing task demands, the ability to shift attention or problem-solving strategies, and the ability to sustain effort (Baron & Fennell, in press). Recent literature on the development of executive functions in children (Denckla, 1996) and on the potential impact of frontal lobe dysfunction on developmental disorders such as attention-deficit hyperactivity disorder (Barkley, 1996) has brought into focus both the normal development of these abilities and the potentially adverse consequences of problems in development that can arise from neurological disorders, acquired or developmental. Increasingly popular are a number of computerized tests of visual vigilance and attention such as the Conners Continuous Performance Tests (Conners, 1994) or auditory continuous performance tests (Keith, 1994). Some limited children's norms are also available for the Wisconsin Card Sorting Test (WCST; Heaton, Chelune, Talley, Kay, & Curtiss, 1993) which has been widely used in adult patients as one index of frontal-lobe functioning (Lezak, 1995).

Once the neuropsychological test scores have been obtained, the examiner may proceed through both a quantitative and qualitative analysis of the test findings. The intent here is to integrate the data into a meaningful picture of the child's functioning. Next, the examiner should begin to relate the current data to any developmental history factors. Following this, the examiner should compare the current picture and history with what is known about child neuropsychological disorders, including the presumptive brain systems or structures involved in the behavior pathology. Next, problems in academic achievement and school adjustment must be integrated, along with any evidence of behavioral or psychiatric pathology. The examiner must attempt to determine whether these problems are directly related to brain pathology, have arisen in reaction to brain pathology, or are a consequence of the family's or child's inability to cope with the direct or indirect effects of the underlying brain disorder. Finally, the child neuropsychologist should write a report that covers both past and present problems, describes the nature of the child's neurobehavioral problems, relates these problems back to the history, and offers recommendations to help the child, the family, or the school adapt to these problems and to enhance the child's ability to meet the demands in the environment in order to continue to develop and grow. Earlier chapters in this book describe these interpretations and report writing issues in more detail. The three primary differences between children and adults have to do with neurodevelopmental, academic, and parent–child issues.

MEASUREMENT ISSUES IN CHILD NEUROPSYCHOLOGICAL ASSESSMENT

Psychometric Issues

Recently, a number of widely used measures of children's intelligence have been updated and revised. These include the Stanford–Binet, the Wechsler Preschool and Primary Scale of Intelligence, and the Wechsler Intelligence Scale for Children (Stanford–Binet IV: Thorndike, Hagen, & Sattler, 1986; WPPSI–R: Wechsler, 1989; WISC–III: Wechsler, 1991). Paralleling changes in test comparability observed when the Wechsler Adult Intelligence Scale was revised in 1981 (Wechsler, 1981), these test revisions have resulted in slightly lower scores compared to earlier versions of these tests. In addition, new subtests have been added or old tests have been substantially revised (Sattler, 1988). The child neuropsychologist should become quite familiar with changes in scores and in content that may result from these revisions, to avoid misinterpretation of the meaning of declines in scores when the new forms are employed. An extended revision of the Bayley Scales is now also be available to those who work with younger children (Bayley, 1993). This newly revised version assesses infants and children up to age 42 months. It maintains the two primary scales (Mental, Motor) along with a Behavior Rating Scale assessing attention, orientation, emotional regulation, and quality of motor activity.

Test Norms

A continuing problem in child neuropsychology is the need for more standardized tests of other cognition functions such as memory, learning, and visuospatial skills. Despite the critical role that such functions play in describing brain development, there is still a relative lack of good measures of verbal and nonverbal memory and learning and of visuospatial analytic or synthetic skills available across the age span from 4 or 5 to 18 years. Often normative data, when available, is provided by grade level (e.g., Benton's Multilingual Aphasic Examination; Benton & Hamsher, 1989) up to the sixth grade only or is provided for discontinuous age groups (e.g., Children's Auditory Verbal Learning Test–2; Talley, 1993) with no adjustment for intellectual level. A further problem relates to the conceptual basis of many available childhood tests. For example, children's measures that simply step down the number of items given to adults, such as the Nebraska Neuropsychological Battery for Children (Golden, 1989), or that use an adult test model of mnemonic strategies (e.g., California Verbal Learning Test for Children; Delis, Kramer, Kaplan, & Ober, 1994) ignore the very real differences in cognitive strategies that occur along the course of development of a particular skill. Similarly, rarely have memory batteries developed for children taken into account the different memory strategies available to children at different ages. There are two excellent texts that extensively describe available research on memory development and the development of memory strategies, which address these issues in great detail from early childhood into the adult years (Kail, 1985; Schneider & Pressley, 1990). In addition, children's tests rarely provide norms that reflect racial or ethnic minorities. Thus, the child neuropsychologist who utilizes such measures should be very familiar with the limitations of these tests in accounting for normal variations in development and in the types of clinical groups on which normative data was derived.

Normative Data in Special Populations

There continues to be a need for more normative data on the test performances of groups of children suffering from a variety of neurological and systemic disorders (Fennell & Bauer, 1997). Examination of recent texts in child neuropsychology suggests that, with the exception of such disorders as learning disabilities and attention deficit-hyperactivity disorder, most data available about the neuropsychological profiles of common childhood neurological and systemic disorders relate to intellectual functioning and school achievement (Menkes, 1990; Hynd & Willis, 1988). However, clinical neuropsychological data on children treated for leukemias (Berg et al., 1983), diabetes (Ryan, 1990), renal disease (Fennell, Fennell, Mings, & Morris, 1988), cardiac disease (Aram, Ekelman, Ben-Schachar, & Lewinsohn,1985), and organ transplantation (Bailey, Wood, Razzouk, Arsdell, & Gundry, 1989) are becoming available. Special texts focusing on traumatic brain injury in childhood are now available, as well as general texts dealing with the neuropsychology of children's medical disorders (Broman & Michel, 1995; Baron et al., 1995). This parallels the growth of the clinical specialty of pediatric psychology (Routh, 1988) as a hospital-based practice area. Increasingly, child neuropsychologists work as part of a team of pediatric psychologists, physicians, nurses, and other health professionals providing diagnostic and treatment services to children and their families, faced with the stresses associated with coping with the effects of chronic medical disorders (including neurological disorders) and their treatments. Neuropsychologists who work with these children not only must be familiar with the specific primary, secondary, or tertiary effects of these illnesses but also must be flexible in their clinical assessment. Modifications in testing procedures to accommodate to the adverse effects of physical illness or its treatment, including fatigue, medication side effects, disruption due to medical procedures, and the limitations of bedside testing. Lengthy testing procedures more typical of outpatient visits may not be possible. As a result, the neuropsychologist may find it necessary to develop a shorter and more focused testing procedure designed to answer more immediate questions related to patient status and management.

Table 11.3 presents an example of an abbreviated battery that can be completed in about 1.5 to 2.0 hrs. At our university, such approaches have been utilized with pediatric patients undergoing bone-marrow transplantation procedures, with patients initiating chemotherapy or irradiation for brain tumors, and with pediatric patients being followed for organ transplantation and AIDS.

TABLE 11.3
Example of an Abbreviated
Child Neuropsychological Assessment Battery

Cognition
    Vocabulary (WISC–III)[a]
    Comprehension (WISC–III)[a]
    Block Design (WISC–III)[a]
    Object Assembly (WISC–III)[a]
Memory
    Digit Span (WISC–III)[a]
    Wide Range Assessment of Memory and Learning (WRAML)[b]
    Story Recall[b]
    Verbal Learning[b]
Motor
    Repetitive and successive finger movements[c]
Constructional
    Beery VMI[d]
Frontal
    Symbol Search (WISC–III)[a]
    Mazes (WISC–III)[a]
    Trail Making Test[e]
    Go No Go
    Verbal Fluency[f]

[a] Wechsler (1991).
[b] Sheslow and Adams (1990).
[c] Denckla (1973).
[d] Beery (1989).
[e] Reitan and Davison (1974).
[f] Benton and Hamsher (1989).

Selection of this modified test battery should be guided by an awareness of the potential brain effects of the disease process or its treatment, as well as the tests' ability to address specific neurobehavioral deficits that may affect treatment decisions (e.g., memory dysfunction) and neurobehavioral syndromes that may reflect adverse treatment effects (e.g., attentional disorder). In responding to questions about potential treatment effects, the child neuropsychologist needs to communicate the limitations of the tests selected and the need for appropriate comprehensive follow-up when this is possible. As the healing child returns to school, it is imperative that a careful, comprehensive assessment be undertaken to allow better description of any potential residual dysfunctions that may impact on the child's ability to function in the classroom.

FUTURE DIRECTIONS IN CHILD NEUROPSYCHOLOGICAL ASSESSMENT

As noted earlier, the next few years should see the continued development of normative data among groups of children suffering from a variety of neurological or systemic disorders. A similar growth of knowledge about the neuropsychology of other childhood disorders is also needed and anticipated. Among these are continued studies of neurodevelopmental disorders such as autism, studies of childhood conduct disorders, psychiatric disorders including childhood schizophrenia and childhood affective disorders, and the neuropsychology of retardation. Much research is still needed in genetic disorders such as Angelmann's and Prader–Willi syndrome. The recent intensive investigation of the neurobehavioral effects of pediatric acquired immune deficiency syndrome (AIDS) is still beset with a number of methodological problems that affect our interpretation of treatment interventions (Fennell, 1993). Ideally, future research will profit from the approaches to subtyping of learning and attention disorders (Barkley, 1990; Satz & Morris, 1981) that have proved helpful in discerning differences between and among subgroups of children affected by these disorders. There is a continued need for longitudinal studies that will provide information on the longterm effects of brain lesion acquired at various ages or present from the earliest stages of brain development. Without such data, the ability of the child neuropsychologist to prescribe for the future needs of the affected child will remain limited. Finally, there is a clear need for research on the effectiveness of cognitive remediation therapies currently available to children (Lyon, Moats, & Flynn, 1988). Linkages between child neuropsychological assessment and treatment planning largely remain empirically rather than theoretically driven (Rourke et al., 1986). Large-scale studies of cognitive remediation treatments in children are, as yet, unavailable, and the limitations of our current assessment approaches need to be remedied. Several recent publications in the rehabilitation of traumatic brain injuries in children (Bigler, Clark, & Farmer, 1997;

Fletcher-Janzen & Kade, 1997) attest to the continued development of methods of intervention as well as measurement of outcomes of treatment in childhood rehabilitation. Although the focus of this recent literature is on traumatic brain injury, the hope is that these methodologies will be extended to other types of neurological disorders in children. Fortunately for the child neuropsychologist, these future needs pose a positive challenge for continued enhancement of our scientific knowledge base and our clinical assessment and intervention skills.

REFERENCES

Achenbach, T. M., & Edelbrock, C. (1983). *Manual for the Child Behavior Checklist.* Burlington, VT: University Associates in Psychiatry.

Aram, D. M., Ekelman, B. L., Ben-Shachar, G., & Lewinsohn, M. W. (1985). Intelligence and hypoxemia in children with congenital heart disease: Fact or artifact? *Journal of the American College of Cardiology, 6,* 889–893.

Bailey, L. L., Wood, M., Razzouk, A., Arsdell, G. V., & Gundry, S. (1989). Heart transplantation during the first 12 years of life. *Archives of Surgery, 124,* 1221–1226.

Barkley, R. A. (1990). *Attention deficit-hyperactivity disorder: A handbook for diagnosis and treatment.* New York: Guilford Press.

Baron, I. S., Fennell, E. B., & Voeller, K. K. S. (1995). *Pediatric neuropsychology in a medical setting.* New York: Oxford University Press.

Baron, I. S., & Fennell, E. B. (in press). Neuropsychological and intellectual assessment of children. In H. I. Kaplan & B. J. Sadock (Eds.), *Comprehensive textbook of psychiatry* (7th Edition). Baltimore, MD: Williams & Wilkins.

Bayley, N. (1993). *The Bayley Scales of Infant Development—Second edition.* San Antonio, TX: Psychological Corporation.

Beery, K. (1997). *Manual for the Development Test of Visual Motor Integration–Revised.* Cleveland, OH: Modern Curriculum Press.

Benton, A. L., & Hamsher, K. de S. (1989). *Multilingual Aphasia Exam: Manual of instructions* (2nd ed.). Odessa, FL: Psychological Assessment Resources.

Berg, R. A., Ch'ien, L. T., Bowman, W. P., Ochs, J., Lancaster, W., Goff, J. R., & Anderson, H. R. (1983). The neuropsychological effects of acute lymphocytic leukemia and its treatment—A three year report: Intellectual functioning and academic achievement. *International Journal of Clinical Neuropsychology, 5,* 9–13.

Berg, R. A., & Linton, J. C. (1989). Neuropsychological sequelae of chronic medical disorders. In C. R. Reynolds & E. Fletcher-Janzen (Eds.), *Handbook of clinical child neuropsychology* (pp. 107–127). New York: Plenum Press.

Bernstein, J. H., & Waber, D. P. (1990). Developmental neuropsychological assessment: The systematic approach. In A. A. Boulton, G. B. Baker, & M. Hiscock (Eds.), *Neuropsychology: Volume 17, Neuromethods* (pp. 311–371). Clifton, NJ: Humana Press.

Bigler, E. D., Clark, E., & Farmer, J. E. (Eds.). (1997). *Childhood traumatic brain injury.* Austin, TX: Pro-Ed.

Boll, T. M. (1983). Neuropsychological assessment of the child: Mythis, current status and future progress. In C. E. Walker & M. C. Roberts (Eds.), *Handbook of clinical child psychology* (pp. 186–208). New York: Wiley.

Boll, T. M., & Barth, J. (1981). Neuropsychology of brain damage in children. In S. Filskov & T. J. Boll (Eds.), *Handbook of clinical neuropsychology* (Vol. 1, pp. 418–452). New York: Wiley.

Broman, S. H., & Michel, M. E. (Eds.) (1995). *Traumatic head injury in children.* New York: Oxford University Press.

Cohen, M. (1997). *Manual for the Children's Memory Scale*. San Antonio, TX: Psychological Corporation.

Conners, C. K. (1994). *Manual for the Conners' Continuous Performance Test*. San Antonio, TX: Psychological Corporation.

Crosson, B. (1992). *Subcortical functions in language and memory*. New York: Guilford Press.

Delis, D. C., Kramer, J. H., Kaplan, E., & Ober, B. A. (1994). *Manual for the California Verbal Learning Test–Children's version*. San Antonio, TX: Psychological Corporation.

Denckla, M. B. (1973). Development in speed of repetitive and successive finger movements in normal children. *Developmental Medicine and Child Neurology, 16*, 729–741.

Denckla, M. B. (1996). A theory and model of executive function: A neuropsychological perspective. In G. R. Lyon & N. A. Krasnegor (Eds.), *Attention: Memory and executive function* (pp. 263–278). Baltimore, MD: Paul H. Brooks.

Ernhart, C. B., Graham, F. K., Eichman, P. L., Marshall, J. M., & Thurston, D. (1963). Brain injury in the preschool child: Some developmental considerations. II. Comparisons of brain-injured and normal children. *Psychological Monographs, 27*(No. 574), 17–33.

Ewings-Cobb, L., Levin, H. S., Eisenberg, P. L., Marshall, J. M., & Thurston, D. (1987). Language functions following closed head injury in children and adolescents. *Journal of Clinical and Experimental Neuropsychology, 2*, 575–592.

Fenichel, G. M. (1988). *Clinical pediatric neurology: A signs and symptoms approach*. Philadelphia: W. B Saunders.

Fennell, E. B. (1993). Methodological approach to the understanding of pediatric HIV infection. *Annals of the New York Academy of Sciences, 693*, 141–150.

Fennell, E. B., & Bauer, R. M. (1997). Models of inference in evaluating brain-behavior relationships in children. In C. R. Reynolds & E. Fletcher-Janzen (Eds.), *Handbook of clinical child neuropsychology* (2nd ed., pp. 204–215). New York: Plenum Press.

Fennell, E. B., Fennell, R. S., Mings, E., & Morris, M. K. (1988). The effects of various modes of therapy for end-stage renal disease on cognitive performance in a pediatric population—A preliminary report. *The International Journal of Pediatric Nephrology, 7*, 107–112.

Fennell, E. B., & Mickle, J. P. (1992). Behavioral effects of head trauma in children and adolescents. In M. Tramontana & S. R. Hooper (Eds.), *Advances in child neuropsychology* (Vol. 1, pp. 24–49). New York: Springer-Verlag.

Fishman, J. M., & Taylor, H. G. (1987). *Pediatric neurology*. New York: Grune & Stratton.

Fletcher, J. M., & Taylor, H. G. (1984). Neuropsychological approaches to children: Towards a developmental neuropsychology. *Journal of Clinical Neuropsychology, 6*, 39–56.

Fletcher, J. M., & Taylor, H. G. (1997). Children with brain injury. In E. J. Mash & L. G. Terdal (Eds.), *Assessment of childhood disorders* (pp. 453–480). New York: Gulford Press.

Fletcher-Janzen, E., & Kade, H. D. (1997). Pediatric brain injury rehabilitation in a neurodevelopmental milieu. In C. R. Reynolds & E. Fletcher-Janzen (Eds.), *Handbook of clinical child neuropsychology* (2nd ed., pp. 452–481). New York: Plenum Press.

Gaddes, W. H., & Edgell, D. (1994). *Learning disabilities and brain function*. New York: Springer-Verlag.

Gesell, A. L., & Amatruda, C. S. (1974). *Developmental diagnosis: The evaluation and management of normal and abnormal neuropsychologic development in infancy and early childhood* (3rd ed.). Hagerstown, MD: Harper & Row.

Golden, C. J. (1989). The Nebraska Neuropsychological Children's Battery. In C. R. Reynolds, & E. Fletcher-Janzen (Eds.), *Handbook of clinical child neuropsychology* (pp. 193–204). New York: Plenum Press.

Goldman, J. R., L'Engle-Stein, C., & Guerry, S. (1983). *Psychological methods of child assessment*. New York: Bruner Mazel.

Goldman, P. S., & Galkin, T. W. (1978). Prenatal removal of frontal association cortex in the fetal rhesus monkey: Anatomical and functional consequences in postnatal life. *Brain Research, 152*, 451–485.

Goldman, P. S., Rosvold, H. E., & Mishkin, M. (1970). Evidence for behavioral impairments follow-ing prefrontal lobectomy in the infant monkey. *Journal of Comparative and Physiological Psychology, 70,* 454–462.

Goldman-Rakic, P. S. (1994). Specification of higher control functions. In S. H. Broman & J. Grap-man (Eds.), *Atypical cognitive deficits in developmental disorders* (pp. 3–17). Hillsdale, NJ: Lawrence Erlbaum Associates.

Harter, S. (1983). *Supplementary description of the Self-Perception Profile for Children. Revision of Perceived Competence Scale for Children.* Unpublished manuscript, University of Denver.

Heaton, R. K., Chelune, G. J., Talley, J. L., Kay, G. G., & Curtiss, G. (1993). *Wisconsin Card Sorting Test manual: Revised and expanded.* Odessa, FL: Psychological Assessment Resources.

Heilman, K., & Valenstein, E. (1993). *Clinical neuropsychology* (3rd ed.). New York: Oxford University Press.

Hynd, G. W., & Willis, W. G. (1988). *Pediatric neuropsychology.* New York: Grune & Stratton.

Ireton, H., & Twang, E. (1992). *Manual for the Minnesota Child Development Inventory.* Minneapolis: University of Minnesota Press.

James, E. M., & Selz, M. (1997). Neuropsychological bases of common learning and behavior prob-lems in children. In C. R. Reynolds & E. Fletcher-Janzen (Eds.), *Handbook of clinical child neuro-psychology* (2nd ed., pp. 157–179). New York: Plenum Press.

Kail, R. (1985). *The development of memory in children* (2nd ed.). San Francisco: W. H. Freeman.

Kaufman, A. S. (1990). *Assessing adolescent and adult intelligence.* Boston: Allyn and Bacon.

Keith, R. W. (1994). *Auditory continuous performance test.* San Antonio, TX: The Psychological Corpo-ration.

Kolb, B., & Fantie, B. (1997). Development of the child's brain and behavior. In C. R. Reynolds & E. Fletcher-Janzen (Eds.), *Handbook of clinical child neuropsychology* (2nd ed., pp. 17–41). New York: Plenum Press.

Kolb, B., & Whishaw, I. Q. (1990). *Fundamentals of human neuropsychology* (3rd ed.). San Francisco: W. H. Freeman.

Koppitz, E. M. (1992). *The Bender Gestalt Test for Young Children.* New York: Grune & Stratton.

Kovacs, M. (1992). *The Childhood Depression Inventory.* North Tonowanda, NY: Multi Health Systems.

Leckliter, I. N., Forster, A. A., Klonoff, H., & Knights, R. M. (1992). A review of reference group data from normal children for the Halstead–Reitan Neuropsychological Test Battery for Older Chil-dren. *The Clinical Neuropsychologist, 6,* 201–229.

Levin, H. S., Ewing-Cobbs, L., & Eisenberg, H. M. (1995). Neurobehavioral outcome of pediatric closed head injury. In S. H. Broman & M. E. Michel (Eds.), *Traumatic head injury in children* (pp. 70–94). New York: Oxford University Press.

Lezak, M. (1995). *Neuropsychological assessment* (3rd ed.). New York: Oxford University Press.

Lyon, G. R., Moats, L., & Flynn, J. M. (1988). From assessment to treatment: Linkage to interven-tions with children. In M. Tramontana & S. R. Hooper (Eds.), *Assessment issues in child neuro-psychology* (pp. 113–144). New York: Plenum Press.

McCarthy, D. (1972). *McCarthy scales of children's abilities.* New York: Psychological Corporation.

Menkes, J. H. (1990). *Textbook of child neurology* (4th ed.). Philadelphia: Lea & Febiger.

Pennington, B. F. (1991). *Diagnosing learning disorders: A neuropsychological framework.* New York: Guilford Press.

Reitan, R. M. (1984). *Aphasia and sensory-perceptual deficits in children.* Tucson, AZ: Neuropsychology Press.

Reitan, R. M., & Davison, I. A. (Eds.). (1974). *Clinical neuropsychology: Current status and applications.* New York: Wiley.

Reitan, R. M., & Wolfson, D. (1992a). *Neuropsychological evaluation of young children.* Tucson, AZ: Neuropsychology Press.

Reitan, R. M., & Wolfson, D. (1992b). *Neuropsychological evaluation of older children.* Tucson, AZ: Neuropsychology Press.

Reynolds, C. R. (1997). Measurement and statistical problems in neuropsychological assessment of children. In C. R. Reynolds & E. Fletcher-Janzen (Eds.), *Handbook of clinical child neuropsychology* (2nd ed., pp. 180–203). New York: Plenum Press.

Reynolds, C. R., & Bigler, E. (1994). *The test of memory and learning.* Austin, TX: Pro-Ed.

Reynolds, C. R., & Fletcher-Janzen, E. (1997). *Handbook of clinical child neuropsychology* (2nd ed.). New York: Plenum Press.

Rourke, B. P. (1982). Central processing deficiencies in children: Toward a developmental neuropsychological model. *Journal of Clinical Neuropsychology, 4,* 1–18.

Rourke, B. P. (1995). *Syndrome of nonverbal learning disabilities: Neurodevelopmental manifestations.* New York: Guilford Press.

Rourke, B. P., Bakker, D. J., Fisk, J. L., & Strange, J. D. (1983). *Child neuropsychology: An introduction to theory, research and practice.* New York: Guilford Press.

Rourke, B. P., Fisk, J. L., & Strange, J. D. (1986). *Neuropsychological assessment of children: A treatment-oriented approach.* New York: Guilford Press.

Routh, D. K. (Ed.). (1988). *Handbook of pediatric psychology.* New York: Plenum Press.

Rutter, M. (Ed.). (1983). *Developmental neuropsychiatry.* New York: Guilford Press.

Ryan, C. (1990). Neuropsychological consequences and correlates of diabetes in childhood. In C. Holmes (Ed.), *Neuropsychological and behavioral aspects of diabetes* (pp. 58–84). New York: Springer-Verlag.

Sattler, J. M. (1988). *Assessment of children's intelligence* (3rd ed.). San Diego: Jerome M. Sattler.

Satz, P., & Morris, R. (1981). Learning disability subtypes: A review. In F. J. Perozzolo & M. Wittrock (Eds.), *Neuropsychological and cognitive processes in reading* (pp. 109–141). New York: Academic Press.

Schmahmann, J. D. (1991). An emerging concept: The cerebellar contribution to higher cortical function. *Archives of Neurology, 48,* 1178–1187.

Schneider, W., & Pressley, M. (1990). *Memory development between 2 to 20 years.* New York: Springer-Verlag.

Selz, M., & Reitan, R. M. (1979). Rules for neuropsychological diagnosis: Classification of brain function in older children. *Journal of Clinical and Consulting Psychology, 47,* 258–264.

Semel, E., Wiig, E., & Secord, W. (1995). *Manual for the clinical evaluation of language fundamentals–3.* San Antonio, TX: Psychological Corporation.

Sheslow, D., & Adams, W. (1990). *Manual for the Wide Range Assessment of Memory and Learning.* Wilmington, DE: Jastak Associates.

Sparrow, S., Balla, L. D. A., & Cicchetti, L. D. V. (1984). *Vineland Adaptive Behavior Scales.* Circle Pines, MN: American Guidance Services.

Spielberger, C. D. (1973). *Manual for the State-Trait Anxiety Scale for Children.* Palo Alto, CA: Consulting Psychologists Press.

Spreen, O., Risser, A. H., & Edgell, D. (1995). *Developmental neuropsychology.* New York: Oxford University Press.

Spreen, O., & Strauss, E. (1997). *A compendium of neuropsychological tests.* New York: Oxford University Press.

Spreen, O., Tupper, D., Risser, A., Tuokko, H., & Edgell, D. (1984). *Human developmental neuropsychology.* New York: Oxford.

Stringer, A. V., & Fennell, E. B. (1987). Hemispheric compensation in a child with left cerebral hypoplasia. *Clinical Neuropsychologist, 1,* 124–138.

Talley, J. L. O. (1995). *Manual for the Children's Auditory Verbal Learning Test–2.* Odessa, FL: Psychological Assessment Resources.

Tartar, R. E., Van Thiel, D. H., & Edwards, K. L. (1988). *Medical neuropsychology.* New York: Plenum Press.

Taylor, H. G. (1989). Neuropsychological testing: Relevance for assessing children's learning disabilities. *Journal of Consulting and Clinical Psychology, 56,* 795–800.

Taylor, H. G., & Fletcher, J. M. (1990). Neuropsychological assessment of children. In G. Goldstein & M. Hersen (Eds.), *Handbook of psychological assessment* (2nd ed., pp. 228–255) New York: Wiley.

Thorndike, R., Hagen, E., & Sattler, J. (1986). *Stanford–Binet Intelligence Scale* (4th ed.). Chicago: Riverside.

Tramontana, M., & Hooper, S. R. (1988). *Assessment issues in child neuropsychology.* New York: Plenum Press.

Tramontana, M. G., & Hooper, S. R. (1992). *Advances in child neuropsychology* (Vol. 1). New York: Springer-Verlag.

Tramontana, M. G., & Hooper, S. R. (1997). Neuropsychology of child psychopathology. In C. R. Reynolds & E. Fletcher-Janzen (Eds.), *Handbook of clinical child neuropsychology* (2nd ed., pp. 120–139). New York: Plenum Press.

Tranel, D. (1992). Functional neuroanatomy: Neuropsychological correlates of cortical and subcortical damage. In S. C. Yudosky & R. E. Hales (Eds.), *American Psychiatric Press textbook of neuropsychiatry* (2nd ed., pp. 57–88). Washington, DC: American Psychiatric Press.

Walker, C. E., & Roberts, M. C. (1992). *Handbook of clinical child psychology* (2nd ed.). New York: Wiley.

Wechsler, D. (1960). *Manual for the Wechsler Intelligence Scale for Children.* New York: Psychological Corporation.

Wechsler, D. (1981). *Manual for the Wechsler Adult Intelligence Scale–Revised.* New York: Psychological Corporation.

Wechsler, D. (1989). *Manual for the Wechsler Preschool and Primary Scale of Intelligence–Revised.* New York: Psychological Corporation.

Wechsler, D. (1991). *Manual for the Wechsler Intelligence Scale for Children–III.* New York: Psychological Corporation.

Wechsler, D. (1997). *Manual for the Wechsler Adult Intelligence Scale–III.* San Antonio, TX: Psychological Corporation.

Wilkinson, G. S. (1993). *Manual for the Wide Range Achievement Test–3.* New York: Psychological Corporation.

Williams, H. G. (1983). *Perceptual and motor development.* Englewood Cliffs, NJ: Prentice Hall.

Woodcock, W., & Mather, N. (1989). *The Woodcock Johnson Psychoeducational Battery–Revised.* Allen, TX: DLM Teaching Resources.

Yakolev, P. I., & Lecours, A. R. (1967). The myelogenetic cycles of regional maturation of the brain. In A. Minkowski (Ed.), *Regional development of the brain* (pp. 3–70). Oxford, England: Blackwell.

CHAPTER TWELVE

Geriatric Neuropsychological Assessment

Deborah C. Koltai
Kathleen A. Welsh-Bohmer
Joseph and Kathleen Bryan Alzheimer's Disease Research Center,
Departments of Psychiatry and Medicine, Duke University Medical Center

Cognitive losses, particularly decline in recent memory functions, are common with age (Blanchard-Fields & Hess, 1996; Craik & Salthouse, 1992). Because similar changes are often the heralding signs of pathological processes, such as Alzheimer's disease (AD), distinguishing the relatively benign changes of aging from the more malignant memory problems of disease is a challenge to today's clinician. However, the tremendous advances in clinical neuropsychology within the last 20 years facilitate the diagnostic process. Based on the neuropsychological definition of AD, the medical diagnosis of AD can now be more reliably rendered based on the presence of "inclusionary" signs evidenced through a distinctive cognitive and behavioral profile (McKhann et al., 1984) rather than based solely on the exclusion of possible medical causes for dementia.

This chapter is divided into three sections outlining the current practice of geriatric neuropsychology with attention to frequently encountered factors and distinctive variables affecting the assessment of cognition in older aged adults. The first two sections deal with the many different uses of neuropsychology in geriatrics and the practical issues involved in geriatric assessment. Like general adult neuropsychology, the examining geriatric neuropsychologist must have a firm grasp of testing variables and an understanding of basic brain–behavior relationships. However, with the rapid changes and discoveries in the cognitive neurosciences, knowledge of brain–behavior relationships alone is not sufficient. Today's geriatric neuropsychologist must also be conversant with a multidisciplinary field encompassing neuropsychology, psychometrics, geriatrics, neurobiology, and genetics. As a consequence, the discussion could not be complete without some consideration of the changing face of geriatric neuropsychology with the advances in the identification of genetic risk factors of AD. The final section of the text deals with recent advances in genetics and the place of this new information in current geriatric neuropsychology practice.

NEUROPSYCHOLOGY IN CLINICAL GERIATRICS

Neuropsychological Assessment in Clinical Diagnosis and Prognosis

There are at least four different applications of neuropsychological testing in geriatrics: diagnostics, estimation of functional status, intervention planning, and research. The most common role continues to be in differential diagnosis of cognitive disorders in aging. Frequently, neuropsychological assessment is requested in cases of suspected early dementia, where symptoms of cognitive loss may be ambiguous or not at all apparent in a clinical interview. The neuropsychological evaluation allows an objective characterization of potential deficits and avoids many sources of error inherent in clinical impressions based on subjective observational methods (Davison, 1974; Katz & Stroud, 1989). Consequently, the neuropsychological evaluation continues to play a key role in diagnostics, despite new advances in neuroimaging (for review see Bigler, 1996) and with the identification of biological markers of disease such as genetic risk factors (Mayeux et al., 1998; Welsh-Bohmer, Gearing, Saunders, Roses, & Mirra, 1997). The neuropsychological evaluation allows documentation of the presence and severity of cognitive compromise regardless of whether there is a biological or structural-imaging correlate. The examination also provides profiles of impairment useful for ruling in or ruling out different disorders (e.g., normal aging vs. AD vs. depressive disorder). Because of its clinical utility, the neuropsychological examination is now recognized as playing a central role in the medical evaluation of Alzheimer's disease and other memory disorders of aging (Cummings & Technology and Therapeutics Assessment Subcommittee, 1996). The diagnostic process is reviewed further in later sections.

Importantly, over the last two decades the practice of contemporary neuropsychology has moved beyond the realm of diagnostics and is important in patient management and rehabilitation (e.g., Prigitano, 1997). The neuropsychological characterization of function permits an objective baseline from which an individual's condition may be tracked over time. If treatments are implemented, such as treatment for depression, or if deterioration in function is reported, the neuropsychological evaluation can be repeated, permitting an objective analysis of change. This function of the assessment is also important in instances where pharmacotherapy or cognitive intervention may be attempted; it provides an objective means for assessing cognitive outcome and quality of life (Albert et al., 1996). The baseline is also critical in capturing decline in function (as would be expected in a progressive condition like AD), improvement (e.g., treated depression), or fluctuations (e.g., untreated depression, diffuse Lewy body disease). This information is then used to enhance diagnostic confidence and guide future decision making, as illustrated in the following case example.

Case 1: The patient was a 73-year-old, right-handed, widowed (× 2 years) White secretary with 12 years of formal schooling. She had been experiencing a memory problem for a number of years, but the problem had become more noticeable and worrisome within the last 2 years since her husband's death. Her children, who accompanied her to the clinical visit, reported that she tended to repeat herself in conversation and that she was having difficulty keeping track of the different cards played in her bridge game. She had given up her bridge group as a result. Despite these problems, she continued to remain active in civic groups and she was driving in her small town without incident. The patient continued to run her household unassisted; this included bill paying and attention to her bank account and investments. She was aware and embarrassed by her memory problems and had sought evaluation through her local doctor, who ascribed the changes as likely due to normal aging and recent life events, but referred her on to the geriatric clinic for additional workup for possible early dementia. Medically the patient had been quite healthy her entire adult life with no acute or chronic conditions. She had a closed-head injury as a child at age 5 with a brief LOC [loss of consciousness] when she fell from the loft of her grandfather's barn; however, there were no developmental delays, academic problems, or reported sequelae from the injury. Recently, she had been experiencing some mood depression and anxiety related to her concern about her memory loss and the death of her husband to whom she had been married for 48 years. She was taking vitamin B_{12}, antioxidants (vitamins C and E), but was on no other prescription or over-the-counter medications. She had a strong family history of Alzheimer's disease. Her mother died of the illness at age 82 and had autopsy verification of AD. Her mother's parents both suffered from memory loss in their later years, and two of the patient's four living siblings were currently affected by probable AD. The patient and her family were concerned that she may be in the early stages of the same disorder and were eager to try any medication or techniques that might improve her abilities.

A neuropsychological evaluation was conducted at the request of the referring geriatrician. This examination assessed a broad range of cognitive abilities amenable to testing, including orientation, mental status, intellect, memory, attention, calculation, abstraction, executive functions, language, constructional praxis, visuospatial judgment, form perception, fine motor speed, fine motor dexterity, and mood and personality. The results are summarized in Table 12.1. Although general mental status screening revealed performance within the normal range, profound deficits were identified on more challenging tests of discrete functions. The most noteworthy difficulty was identified in recent memory function, with rapid forgetting seen after delays as short as 5 min. Also seen were deficits in so-called "frontal executive functions" characterized by difficulties in her case in working memory (e.g., Digit Span Backwards, WMS–R Attention & Concentration), and cognitive flexibly (e.g., Trails Part B). Language was preserved with the exception of a relatively isolated deficiency in semantic fluency. Visuoperception, spatial judgment, and motor coordination were normal. Mild depressive symptoms were observed and self-reported by the patient.

The neuropsychological profile of profound delayed recall deficits and mild deficits in semantic fluency (but not lexical fluency) and aspects of executive functions are classic for early stage AD (see later text and Butters, Delis, & Lucas, 1995, for review). Based on the results, additional diagnostic testing was ordered to rule out treatable causation and to identify the presence of genetic risk factors (i.e., apolipoprotein e4 allele, APOE-ε4, discussed later) for AD. These additional test results indicated an absence of medical causation and revealed a genotype of APOE-ε4/ε3 supporting a diagnosis of early stage AD. However, given the early nature of the disorder, caution was exercised. The diagnosis of "memory disorder —possible early AD" was made with follow-up evaluation scheduled in 12 months in order to track the course, verify progression, and clarify the diagnosis. Because of the patient's insight into her condition and her depressive reaction, clinical intervention was pursued to assist her in adjusting to the diagnosis and its meaning in her life. Her motivation to improve her memory allowed her to benefit from training in the use of auxiliary memory aids and other cognitive strategies to facilitate her recall abilities in her activities of daily living. The weekly intervention sessions, which continued for 8 weeks, were individualized and focused on practical solutions to some of her concerns and on coping and adjustment using a behavioral psychotherapeutic approach.

The case example illustrates the many ways that neuropsychological assessment can be useful in contemporary geriatric practice. First, the examination assisted in clinical diagnosis. As can be appreciated from the case vignette, the clinical history of memory loss was ambiguous. The family history suggested an ominous process, but the diagnostic picture was clouded by the possibility of depression or "anticipatory dementia," the realistic fear that the symptoms may reflect familial disease (Cutler & Hodgson, 1996). Neuropsychological assessment was useful in sorting out these clinical diagnostic issues. The examination allowed the generation of a cognitive profile of impairments and strengths across a broad range of functions and behaviors. The profile generated was characteristic of the early stages of AD (for review see Butters et al., 1995) but was not particularly suggestive of the type of profiles seen in depression or anxiety (see later discussion). Consequently, the effects of two comorbid processes, an early-stage dementia and a superimposed depressive reaction, were effectively disentangled by the neuropsychological evaluation. The examination was additionally useful in defining management approaches and for providing an objective baseline for the tracking of symptom progression. The results of the assessment then informed the ensuing psychotherapeutic intervention by characterizing areas of relative strengths and limitations that would influence choice of approach and the patient's ability to benefit from treatment.

TABLE 12.1
Early-Stage Alzheimer's Disease with Reactive Depression

Orientation/mental status (MMSE)					
Total score	27/30	(low normal)			
Orientation	9/10	(date–low normal)			
Registration	3/3				
Language	8/8				
Memory	1/3	(impaired)			
WORLD backwards	5/5				
Praxis	1/1				

Intellect (WAIS–R; Wechsler, 1981)			**Executive functions**		
VIQ	104	(61% Average)	Wisconsin Card Sort: Categories = 6 (normal)		
PIQ	92	(30% Average)	Trails A 34 sec (0 error)	(normal)	
FSIQ	99	(50% Average)	Trails B 191 sec (1 error) (mild impairment)		
Memory (WMS-R; Wechsler, 1987)			**Visuospatial functions**		
Verbal Index	**80****	**(10% low average)**	Visuospatial Judgment 21 + 4 (57% normal)		
Visual Index	**81****	**(9% low average)**	Form Perception (Faces) 45 + 2 (71% normal)		
Delayed Memory Index	**74****	**(4% borderline)**	Constructional Praxis 10/11	(normal)	
Attn./Conc. Index	**85***	**(16% low average)**	WAIS–R Block Design 8	(average)	
Memory (CERAD WLM; Morris et al., 1989)					
CERAD Trial 1,2,3	5,7,9	(normal)			
CERAD Delay memory	**2****	**(impaired)**			
CERAD Recognition	18/20	(low normal)			
Language			**Motor Functions**		
MAE Naming	52 + 4	(64% average)	Finger Oscillation		
Category Fluency	**10***	**(mild impairment)**	Left T = 50 Right (Dom.) T = 48 (average)		
Lexical Fluency	34 + 6	(average)	Grooved Pegboard		
Repetition	18/18	(normal)	Left T = 42 Right (Dom.) T = 44 (average)		
Token Test	36/36	(normal)			
Mood/personality			**Functional ability**		
Beck Depression Inventory 15* **(mild depression)**			**Clinical Dementia Rating = 0.5**		
Neuropsychiatric Inventory: subclinical depression			**(questionable dementia)**		

Note. Raw scores with appropriate age corrections for age, education, and gender (+) are indicated. Bold print highlights significant findings. Asterisk indicates significant impairment relative to appropriate norms, and double asterisk represents highly significant deviations from normative standards.

Neuropsychology and Estimation of Functional Status and Competency

A common practice in geriatrics is the request for neuropsychological assessment in order to assist clinical decision making in the areas of independent functioning or competency. However, it should be pointed out that the vast majority of neuropsychological tests were developed to detect and differentiate brain illnesses rather than predict function (see Lezak, 1995). Thus, caution must be exercised when results are generalized from tests to predict function. Little has been known until fairly recently about the predictive relationship between neuropsychological test performance and various functional outcomes. Such knowledge is critical because the information from neuropsychological testing is frequently used to predict functions and guide decisions affecting independence and autonomy such as driving capability or need for supervision (e.g., Odenheimer et al., 1994; Rebok, Keyl, Bylsma, Blaustein, & Tune, 1994).

Research in predicting functional outcomes suggests that cognitive performance directly relates to ability to function adequately in everyday life (Baum, Edwards, Yonan, & Storandt, 1996; Diehl, Willis, & Schaie, 1995; Fitz & Teri, 1994; Greiner, Snowdon, & Schmitt, 1996; Nadler, Richardson, Malloy, Marran, & Hostetler Brinson, 1993) and to related variables such as health care utilization and institutionalization (Branch & Jette, 1982; Branch et al., 1988; Rockwood, Stolee, & McDowell, 1996; Willis & Marsiske, 1991). The studies also suggest that neuropsychological testing and functional assessment measure related but not overlapping domains. Information from cognitive testing is complementary to but does not replace other more direct measures of activities of daily living (ADL), including measures of physical function and instrumental activities of daily life (IADL) such as financial management, work performance, and the like. This point is illustrated by analyzing the shared variance between neuropsychological measures and behavioral outcomes. For instance, Nadler and colleagues (1993) examined the relationship between neuropsychological test scores and performance on a standardized behavioral measure of tasks related to daily living (e.g., medication management, cooking) and demonstrated significant shared variance ranging from 27% to 49% on these measures. A good review of the studies examining the relationship between neuropsychological test performance and rated or performance-based measures of independence has recently become available (McCue, 1997).

The recent studies are not without their differences and controversies. The areas of greatest disparity in the literature have arisen when considering issues of degree of shared variance between tests and outcomes, and which of several neurocognitive domains is the most predictive of functional ability (Baum, Edwards, Yonan, & Storandt, 1996; Goldstein, McCue, Rogers, & Nussbaum, 1992; McCue, Rogers, & Goldstein, 1990; Nadler et al., 1993; Richardson, Nadler, & Malloy, 1995). Most of the discrepancies across reports are likely attributable to the methodological differences across studies (choice of functional and neuropsychological measures) as well as sample characteristics. Future studies are needed that involve comprehensive assessments with adequate sampling. The use of statistical modeling may also be a promising avenue for predicting functional decline with cognitive measures (e.g., Lemsky, Smith, Malec, & Ivnik, 1996).

Specific IADLs, such as driving, are gaining more attention as clinicians attempt to promote safety without unnecessarily limiting independence and autonomy. Although preliminary pilot work suggests that cognitive test scores are related to driving performance tests (e.g., Rebok et al., 1994), this area also warrants further study involving comprehensive assessment.

In addition to questions about functional status as it relates to independence, the neuropsychologist may be called on to address issues of competence. Although there are no clear standards at present for the evaluation of competence, some support for the use of neuropsychological data in these situations has emerged. There are some variations in which specific cognitive constructs or test scores best predict competence (e.g., Marson, Cody, Ingram, & Harrell, 1995; Stanley, Stanley, Guido, & Garvin, 1988; Tymchuk, Ouslander, Rahbar, & Fitten, 1988), again underscoring the need for further study. One consistent finding across studies is that although dementia patients may be like controls in their ability to evidence a choice or make a reasonable choice, they differ from controls in their appreciation of choice consequences, ability to provide a rationale for choices, and understanding of the treatment situation and choices (Marson, Ingram, Cody, & Harrell, 1995). Cognitive skills related to frontal lobe integrity are significantly associated with the capacity to formulate rational reasons for a treatment choice (Marson, Cody, Ingram, & Harrell, 1995).

As the relationship between neuropsychological test performance and decision-making ability awaits further clarification, it is important for clinicians to recognize that competency "is not a unitary concept or construct" and that different legal standards may be applied to general versus specific legal competencies (Marson, Schmitt, Ingram, & Harrell, 1994). Competency decisions based on diagnoses such as dementia provide little information about the functional capabilities of the patient (Scogin & Perry, 1986), as the individual may function quite well in some areas while not in others. From both a clinical and a legal standpoint, the patient benefits most when competency is viewed in a broader framework that involves distinguishing between personal (i.e., psychosocial), financial, and medical decision-making capacities. An individual may be competent for some matters, such as social decisions, but not others, such as financial decisions (Baker, 1987; Kloezen, Fitten, & Steinberg, 1988). The use of standardized tests to assess competency is an area of growing interest and shows promise by counteracting bias based on clinical impression alone (Steinberg, Fitten, & Kachuck, 1986). For more discussion, see chapter 9 of this volume.

Neuropsychological Assessment and Intervention Planning

Neuropsychological data are also frequently used to plan for and measure the effects of cognitive interventions. Cognitive training typically involves individuals who have sustained traumatic brain injury (for review see Prigatano, 1997; Sohlberg & Mateer, 1989; Wilson, 1997), but has also been used with normal elders (e.g., Baltes & Willis, 1982; Schaie and Willis, 1986; Yesavage, 1985) and with elderly dementia patients with neurodegenerative illnesses to maximize adjustment and function (e.g., Backman, Josephsson, Herlitz, Stigsdotter, & Viitanen, 1991; Camp, Foss, O'Hanlon, & Stevens, 1996; McKitrick, Camp, & Black, 1992; Quayhagen, Quayhagen, Corbeil, Roth, & Rogers, 1995). Although a comprehensive neuropsychological evaluation is not always necessary when designing a treatment approach, the overall outcome will likely be enhanced if techniques selected capitalize on better preserved abilities to compensate for relative deficits. These neuropsychological data, as well as information relevant to diagnosis, general mental status, insight, goals, and motivation, are used in conjunction with basic principles of brain-behavior relationships to guide the treatment process (Koltai & Branch, in press). Both cognitive and psychotherapeutic interventions are affected by the patient's cognitive and affective status. Consequently, some knowledge of the patient's neuropsychological function is important prior to the initiation of therapy so that this information can be integrated into the treatment plan (Koltai & Branch, in press; Prigatano, 1997).

Neuropsychology and Geriatric Research

The neuropsychological evaluation plays an important role beyond its clinical application by providing the necessary outcome measures for many types of experimental designs in geriatric research. Neuropsychological investigations are aimed at a large number of different clinical topics of aging, such as defining the "cognitive phenotypes of disease" or cultural differences in the expression of illness. Other studies use functional imaging combined with neuropsychological measures to explore basic cognitive science issues of brain organization. Although a full consideration of this topic is beyond the scope of this discussion, good overviews may be found in Poon (1986) and Tuokko and Hadjistavropouolos (1998).

One point worth emphasis is the importance of neuropsychology in multidisciplinary investigations of normal aging, AD, and other neurological disorders. Neuropsychology has contributed significantly to clinical trial research and other multicenter studies, not only by providing objective methods for defining subject groups across centers (e.g., Morris et al., 1989; Welsh-Bohmer & Mohs, 1997) but also by providing reliable and valid measures for determining treatment efficacy (e.g., Claman & Radebaugh, 1991; Mohs et al., 1997). Neuropsychological measures have also found a prominent role in contemporary epidemiological studies of dementia (e.g., Breitner et al., 1995, in press; Ebly, Parhad, Hogan, & Fung, 1994; Evans et al., 1990). The inclusion of neuropsychological measurements in lieu of self-report methods or simple cognitive screens has ensured more accurate estimates of prevalence and incidence of AD and other cognitive disorders of aging (Colsher & Wallace,1991; Herzog & Rodgers, 1992).

THE GERIATRIC ASSESSMENT PROCESS

Planning the Test Battery

Whether a neuropsychological assessment is for clinical purposes or for research, there are a number of constraints, including sensory losses and motor slowing, that must be considered in the evaluation of elderly patients to avoid behavioral confounding. In situations where there are significant auditory acuity deficits, amplification devices can be used if necessary. For visual deficits, enlarged stimuli are now available for many tests. A skilled clinician will typically explore potential troublesome variables during the initial contact with the patient and will then select assessment approaches in accordance. If neuropsychological data are collected by psychometricians, these technical staff members should also be trained to identify potential confounding problems and instructed as to how to make necessary modifications (e.g., use of voice amplification devices) and when to seek guidance from the supervising neuropsychologist.

Fortunately for today's clinician, there are a number of available neuropsychological batteries that have been designed with the special needs of the elderly in mind and appropriate normative data (e.g., Ivnik, Malec, Smith, Tangalos, Petersen, Kokmen, & Kurland, 1992; Welsh et al., 1994). One example is the neuropsychological battery from the Consortium to Establish a Registry for Alzheimer's Disease (CERAD), which uses enlarged print and oral responses to avoid sensory confounding (Morris et al., 1989). It should be cautioned that even with these accommodations, the effects of sensory loss on neuropsychological performance cannot be entirely controlled. It is still important for the clinician to consider the potential role of these confounding factors when interpreting performance so as to avoid incorrectly attributing deficits in test performance to comprehension or mnestic losses (Mattis, 1990).

Another factor to consider when working with elderly patients is the reasonable length of the battery. Geriatric patients, particularly those with cognitive deficits, often fatigue easily, and efforts should be made to conserve time and energy. When testing exceeds 2.5 hr, fatigue effects become a worrisome problem in older patients (Cunningham, Sepkoski, & Opel, 1978). Consequently, the test battery selected by the neuropsychologist to use in these scenarios may have to be modified to be shorter, focused, and include less taxing instruments than might be used with a younger population. The examination might also be structured so that not all sampling of a neurocognitive domain occurs at the same time, thereby minimizing the differential effects of fatigue on functions reserved for later in the examination. As an example, if a patient performs well on all visuospatial tasks except the last one given and decreased effort and inattention were noted here, the reliability of this one outlier could be reasonably questioned.

Finally, rapport is a variable affecting performance and is a factor that cannot be overlooked in the evaluation of the older patient (Lawton & Storandt, 1984). Neuropsychological evaluation may be the geriatric patient's first contact with a professional psychologist, and extra time may be needed to address the purpose of the evaluation and to "normalize" the experience for the patient. For example, it is often helpful to inform patients that some tests will be easy for them to complete, whereas others may prove more difficult, and that this is the normal experience. Taking the time with patients to put testing in such a context serves to reduce the likelihood of emotional distress and results in maximizing performance without invalidating standardization. Any distress that does occur should be addressed immediately with corrective measures including the discontinuation of testing until a more conducive time if necessary. Assessment in an agitated or uncooperative patient is of little use because its reliability will be severely compromised.

Fixed Versus Flexible Assessment Approaches

In constructing the assessment battery, some uniformity is required to assure that all testable areas of cognition are assessed. The areas surveyed must include measures of orientation, intellect, executive functions, memory, expressive and receptive language, visuospatial functions, motor skills, mood and personality, and functional status (Lezak, 1995). The selection of tests from the many available is guided by two principles: (a) the referral question, and (b) the appropriateness of the instruments selected for the patient under evaluation, including the availability of suitable normative information. The referral question may dictate more detailed assessment of one domain (e.g., in-depth language assessment in a case of primary progressive aphasia). The psychometric issues guiding the selection are whether there are appropriate norms for the individual under evaluation, such as norms for patients where English is not the first language. Table 12.1 presented an example of a geriatric assessment. Note that some tests provide information in more than one cognitive domain.

Because of the variation in patient and clinical factors that affect test selection, many clinicians develop standard assessment practices using a "flexible battery" approach to address specific referral questions. This method is more commonly used with geriatric patients because the long, fixed batteries are not feasible and may not include measures ideally suited for the questions asked. Typically, a flexible battery will assess the various domains with measures that have the greatest psychometric documentation for the population in question. The Wechsler Adult Intelligence Scale–Revised (WAIS–R; Wechsler, 1981) or Wechsler Memory Scale–Revised (WMS–R; Wechsler, 1987) and likely their newer revisions (WAIS–III, WMS–III) are frequent choices for assessment of intellect and memory, respectively. However, these tests may be too taxing for a severely demented patient or for a physically frail patient. Other tests may then be selected, such as the neuropsychological battery from the Consortium to Establish a Registry for Alzheimer's Disease (CERAD; Morris et al., 1989), discussed later, with the goal being to obtain an adequate measure of abilities in the most efficient manner.

Whether selecting tests of memory, language, or intellectual function, an effort must be made in every patient situation to avoid ceiling and floor effects that can result from tasks being too easy or too difficult for the patient. To not do so will result in little meaningful information. For instance, a higher functioning elderly patient with very mild impairments may perform at ceiling levels on the word list learning test of the CERAD battery, as it involves learning only 10 words. Many sites utilize this task because of its brevity and utility in dementia evaluations (see Welsh-Bohmer & Mohs, 1997), although caution must be exercised in cases such as the example given. Finally, measures of general mental status, although limited when used exclusively (see discussion to follow), are often retained in assessment batteries as they are descriptively helpful, particularly when defining research samples.

Screening Batteries

A common occurrence in contemporary practice is the use of short batteries or "screening batteries," which can be completed in 30 min or less. The CERAD battery and the Neurobehavioral Cognitive Screening Examination (NCSE; Kiernan, Mueller, Langston, & Van Dyke, 1987) are examples of short batteries. These shortened neuropsychological batteries provide information about the presence of cognitive compromise and give a general estimate of the degree of compromise. They are typically constructed to sample abilities in the cognitive domains likely to show change in the context of neurological dysfunction. Because of their nature, they have limits to their sensitivity and specificity. Screening batteries can miss subtle cognitive compromises or not sample the domains needed to provide differential diagnosis. In addition, screening tests, particularly very brief tests such as mental status tests, may underestimate decline in individuals who had premorbidly superior abilities or higher levels of education, and overestimate impairment in patients with less education (Anthony, LeResche, Niaz, Von Korff, & Folstein, 1982). For example, the Mini Mental Status examination (MMSE; Folstein, Folstein, & McHugh, 1975), one of the most popular mental status screening tools, is heavily affected by age, education, and lifetime principal occupation (Anthony et al., 1982; Launer, Dinkgreve, Jonker, Hooijer, & Lindeboom, 1993; Frisoni, Rozzini, Bianchetti, & Trabucchi, 1993). It is also less sensitive to right-hemisphere dysfunction and mild forms of cerebral dysfunction (Naugle & Kawczak, 1989). Consequently, use of the MMSE alone is likely to result in high false positive rates in low-educated, older individuals and high false negative rates in highly educated, mildly impaired patients.

Knowledge of the various limitations of screening instruments is essential when the clinician is weighing the choice of which to include in their clinical practice. Although requiring more time for administration, the Mattis Dementia Rating Scale (DRS; Mattis, 1988) may be a more clinically desirable instrument in older groups. A number of investigations have revealed favorable psychometric properties (Chase et al., 1984; Coblentz et al., 1973; Gardner, Oliver-Munoz, Fisher, & Empting, 1981; Shay et al., 1991; Smith et al., 1994; Vitaliano et al., 1984). Subscale scores also provide some information about functioning in particular cognitive domains, in addition to overall level of functioning.

Interpretation of Neuropsychological Data

The interpretative process forms the crux of the neuropsychological evaluation and sets the neuropsychologist apart from a technician trained in test administration and from a computer algorithm. The interpretation of test findings is an inferential process that begins with the use of standardized normative information against which individual performance is measured but involves more than simple application of cutting scores. It is the constellation of neuropsychological test results, rather than any single observation, that is considered when determining diagnosis. This topic is considered more fully in chapters 3 and 4.

In the very elderly population, the so-called "old-old," the interpretative process has been traditionally hampered by rather limited normative information in ages older than 74 years. However, the situation has greatly changed in the last decade. Supplementary normative data are now available for individuals up to age 96 years for the most popular tests such as the WAIS–R, WMS–R, and Rey Auditory Verbal Learning Test (Ivnik, Malec, Smith, Tangalos, Petersen, Kokmen, & Kurland, 1992; Ivnik, Malec, Tangalos, Petersen, Kokmen, & Kurland, 1992; Malec et al., 1992; Ryan, Paolo, & Brungardt, 1990). Some other commonly used tests remain without older reference groups, or reference groups that differ significantly from the patient population due to educational, regional, or other demographic factors. The needed data may be forthcoming via epidemiological studies in older populations (Breitner et al., in press). In the absence of this information, many laboratories develop their own normative standards based on studies conducted on control subjects with demographic characteristics similar to that of the patients. Cohort effects must also be considered when using some of the well-normed, but older, test versions. Inadequate normative groups should not absolutely preclude the use of a test. However, the properties and limitations of each instrument should be well known, and interpretation should occur within this framework.

To facilitate the reliable interpretation of acute impairments, as opposed to long-standing low-level functioning (such as developmental learning disability), the neuropsychologist considers the individual's estimated or known level of premorbid functioning (see Lezak, 1995). For more thorough consideration of this topic, refer to chapter 2. Given the tremendous variability between patients, this practice is ideal in principle, but determination of premorbid ability is not easy because testing results earlier in the life span are a rare occurrence (Plassman & Breitner, 1996). Several methods available to clinicians for estimating level of function are based on demographic factors such as the patient's previous academic and occupational achievements (e.g., Barona, Reynolds, & Chastain, 1984), factors that have been found to covary with performance on neuropsychological tests (Ardila & Rosselli, 1989; Heaton, Grant, & Matthews, 1986). Other methods use performance on verbal tests that are thought to be relatively resistant to decline as predictors of premorbid ability (e.g., Shipley Institute of Living Scale, Shipley, 1946; North American Adult Reading Test, Blair & Spreen, 1989). Each of these methods has merit, but some caution is necessary when applied in the elderly. Educational level or occupational background may not reliably predict intelligence in this aged cohort, because historically many individuals stopped schooling from necessity rather than ability, and many who had the potential did not pursue professional careers. In addition, as with age, education does not influence performance in all cognitive domains equally (Heaton et al., 1986). Thus, the clinician needs to be appropriately judicious in the use of these approaches and consider interpretation differences if the estimate is in error. In cases where there is strong potential for error, such as in distinguishing mild AD from normal aging, longitudinal follow-up, preferably 12–18 months apart, may be necessary to allow the needed verification of the progressive or stable nature of the suspected condition (Bowen et al., 1997).

Once the data have been evaluated against normative and premorbid standards, the neuropsychologist then considers the results in light of known brain–behavior profiles and proceeds to generate hypotheses to explain the obtained results. An appreciation of neurobehavioral relationships allows some inferences about potentially impaired neuroanatomical systems (e.g., Tranel, 1992). Knowledge of the frequency or base rates of various dementing disorders is also essential, along with familiarity with the age distributions for various disorders, their associated risk factors, and their typical behavioral presentations (Breitner & Welsh, 1995). When drawing conclusions, the clinician must remain cognizant that there is marked individual variability in normal cognitive abilities, in the presentation of various illnesses, in general brain morphology, and in the effects of brain pathology on behavioral outcomes. Consequently, statements about causation based on neuropsychological data must be made with caution. The validity of the neuropsychological interpretation is, however, greatly enhanced by consideration of available attendant data, particularly history of present symptoms and assessment of functional activities. A number of recent studies indicate that neuropsychological tests tend to be highly sensitive to cognitive losses, but their specificity is low and is improved substantially by consideration of historical information such as change in functional ability (e.g., Gallo & Breitner, 1995). Structural imaging (computerized transaxial tomography [CT] or magnetic resonance imaging [MRI]) and functional brain imaging results may also provide supportive or refuting information as the neuropsychologist begins to develop explanatory models for patterns of deficit detected (Dodrill, 1997).

Finally, the limits of diagnostic evaluation using neuropsychological data should also be known by the neuropsychologist and acknowledged in the interpretation (Dodrill, 1997). Particularly in the area of dementia and aging, there are some illnesses that cannot be clinically differentiated and diagnosis must be confirmed by post-mortem analysis. An example of this is frontotemporal dementia, which can manifest as at least three different clinical syndromes: (a) symmetrical involvement, predominantly of the frontal lobes; (b) asymmetrical involvement of the dominant cerebral hemisphere or temporal lobes, manifesting as progressive aphasia; or, (c) frontal-temporal atrophy involving an amyotrophic form of motor neuron disease (Mann, Neary, & Testa, 1994). Histopathology causation of the frontotemporal dementias is heterogeneous and may include uncommon forms of Alzheimer's disease, Pick's disease (defined by Pick inclusion bodies), or more commonly a frontal dementia of non-AD type characterized by generalized cortical cell loss in the frontal and temporal lobes, pyramidal cell loss in outer cortical layers, microvacuolation, and astrocytosis (Mann et al., 1994). A clinical diagnosis of frontotemporal dementia can be made with confidence based on the clinical features; however, assigning the causation of this syndrome to either a primary idiopathic frontotemporal dementia, Pick's disease, or a frontal variant of AD cannot be done reliably without neuropathological information.

Role of Attendant Data in Neuropsychological Interpretation

An important part of neuropsychological interpretation is the consideration given to supportive data provided by the patient and informants or caregivers who are familiar with the patient, as well as the information gleaned from the patient's medical records. This information serves to support or refute clinical hypotheses and may suggest other explanations for effects to be considered in the differential diagnosis. Both the patient's and the caregiver's perspectives of the types of difficulties experienced are informative in diagnostic evaluations. The information obtained from these various sources provides important historical documentation of the appearance of symptoms from the patient and an outside observer perspective. It also provides valuable information about the functional sequelae of the cognitive compromise, as well as the patient's insight and coping.

Perhaps the most critical piece of attendant data to consider in the evaluation of the elderly is the patient's history of symptoms (Steffens et al., 1996). Establishing the onset of the illness and the general course are critically important variables when attempting to distinguish between disorders such as AD, depression, and multi-infarct dementia (Small et al., 1997). The insidious onset of cognitive compromise and gradual, progressive decline over time typically signals the presence of a neurodegenerative illness. Relatively abrupt onset coinciding with depressed affect or recent loss raises the possibility of a depressive reaction (Breitner & Welsh, 1995), whereas sudden disturbances with no progression or a stepwise deterioration frequently indicate the presence of cerebrovascular dysfunction (Friedland, 1993).

Determining the magnitude of cognitive deficits compared with the reported duration of cognitive compromise can also provide information about how rapidly the dementia is progressing. For example, a patient who presents with a moderately severe dementia who has only a 5-month history of cognitive compromise would be suspected of having a rapidly progressive illness, such as Creutzfeldt–Jakob disease (Brown, Cathala, Castaigne, & Gajdusek, 1986). Patients with relatively isolated memory impairments that remain stable for years before progressing in the manner that is more typical of neurodegenerative diseases may suggest other sources of memory loss, such as hypoperfusion, stroke, or protracted cases of AD (Bowen et al., 1997).

Information regarding past or current medical and psychiatric illnesses and medications is also important because any of these factors can affect neurocognitive performance. For instance, some antidepressant medications have significant anticholinergic side effects that may be contributing to the severity of cognitive compromises (Alexopoulos, 1992). In addition, past and current life stressors that may be influencing affective status and thus cognitive status should be reviewed. Knowledge of the patient's family history of dementia or other psychiatric disturbance can also be helpful in conceptualizing the patient's cognitive impairments, given that familial trends have been observed in a number of dementing illnesses (see Plassman & Breitner, 1996, for review).

Other sources of useful attendant data, sometimes minimized in clinical textbooks, are the observations the neuropsychologist makes of the patient's behavior in testing. Information gained through these observations can be useful both diagnostically and in addressing test validity, as previously described. Evidence of expressive and receptive language deficits in casual conversation, such as the entry interview, provide validation for deficits that might be detected on formal aphasia examination. Likewise, qualitative information from the patient's approach to testing materials, such as the patterns of errors on naming tests or when scanning other visual materials, may provide useful information about the possibility of neglect, attentional disturbances, or complex visual system problems. The patient's affective status in testing may alert to the operation of emotional factors. Finally, the speed and quality of the patient's thought formulation and the patient's overall insight into both the presence and degree of cognitive dysfunction can suggest different sources of brain compromise. Slow and effortful processing may reflect the effects of depression or herald conditions such as Parkinson's disease. Reduced insight may suggest any of a variety of dementias involving frontal structures, but not usually depression (Breitner & Welsh, 1995).

Neuropsychological Differentiation of Dementia

To make reliable diagnoses in today's clinical practice, the geriatric neuro-psychologist needs to remain current on the ever-changing field of geriatric medicine and dementia (e.g., Rabins & Cummings, 1998; Small et al., 1997). The rapid changes in the clinical neurosciences have helped to identify a variety of genes and other biological markers that may be useful in the diagnosis of conditions such as Alzheimer's disease (e.g. Welsh-Bohmer et al., 1997) and some types of familial frontotemporal dementias (e.g. Yamaoka et al., 1996). In the last two decades the area of clinical diagnosis of dementia has advanced considerably, in large part due to the contribution of neuropsychology in the definition of clinical syndromes. AD is a good example of this phenomenon. At one time AD was a diagnosis based on exclusion or "ruling out" other diagnoses; it is now a diagnosis made by consideration of inclusionary criteria and well-described neuropsychological signs (McKhann et al., 1984; Freidland, 1993).

In neuropsychology, one useful approach to the differential diagnosis of dementia has been the application of a popular classification schema of conditions as either "cortical" or "subcortical" according to the profile of impairment associated with specific neuroanatomic involvement (Cummings & Benson, 1992). *Cortical dementias* refer to a profile of cognitive loss typical of the class of illnesses that primarily involve cortical grey structures (e.g., AD, Pick's disease). By contrast, *subcortical dementias* refer to a pattern of cognitive change occurring in illnesses primarily involving damage to the diencephalon, neostriatum, midbrain, and brainstem structures (e.g., Huntington's disease, progressive supranuclear palsy, Parkinson's disease). The dichotomy has been criticized as flawed and reductionistic, with the terms *cortical* and *subcortical* not reflecting the true nature of disease and lacking anatomical validity. However, the terms have been useful, nonetheless, in providing a nomenclature between clinicians, and the dichotomy continues to be used currently.

The neuropsychological profiles of these so-called subcortical and cortical dementias are now well described (for review see Welsh-Bohmer & Ogrocki, 1998). Subcortical disorders are conceptualized as resulting in retrieval deficits despite adequate storage of information, whereas cortical damage is thought to result in difficulties with the encoding and consolidation of new information (Cummings & Benson, 1992). The subcortical dementias are described as including patchy deficits in memory that are facilitated by structural support (e.g., recognition), along with changes in affect and mood regulation, generalized motor slowing, and executive dysfunction. The profile of cortical dementia, typified by AD, is dominated by a profound and relatively complete anterograde memory impairment that benefits little from structural supports or cueing, and that also includes expressive language impairments (anomia, dysfluency), visuospatial disturbances, and apraxia (Butters et al., 1995).

Once the presence of dementia is suspected, assignation of likely cause requires consideration of virtually hundreds of neurological disorders and incorporates multiple sources of medical information, including the results of the neuropsychological evaluation. AD and its variants, such as dementia with Lewy bodies (Cercy & Bylsma, 1997; McKeith, Perry, Fairbairn, Jabeen, & Perry, 1992), represent the largest proportion of dementias, roughly 50–60% in North America and Europe (Breitner et al., in press; Ebly et al., 1994; Evans et al., 1990). Vascular dementias are the second most common organic cause of cognitive decline in the elderly, accounting for 13–20% or more of the cases depending on the age of the sample (Skoog, Nilsson, Palmertz, Andreasson, & Svanborg, 1993; Ebly et al., 1994). Frontotemporal dementias account for 8–10% of the progressive dementias in some series (Gustafson, 1993) and even higher in others (Jackson & Lowe, 1996). Other neurodegenerative dementias, such as Parkinson's disease (PD), are less common (Cercy & Bylsma, 1997, for review). Infections of the central nervous system, metabolic or endocrine system dysfunction, and electrolyte disturbances are also less frequent but have the potential to cause substantial changes in mental status. Table 12.2 presents some common diagnoses with their typical cognitive manifestations and supportive data. This table is not exhaustive, but rather attempts to capture the more frequently observed geriatric illnesses. In addition, variants of these illnesses are commonly observed. This heterogeneity within diagnostic categories should be considered when reviewing diagnostic alternatives. For instance, AD may present with prominent frontal-temporal features or as a visual-spatial variant (e.g., Furey-Kurkjian et al., 1996; Martin et al., 1986). Frequently, longitudinal follow-up will provide clarification of diagnostic considerations, as the pattern of change can often be as helpful as the pattern observed on initial evaluation. For additional information about the clinical diagnosis of the various dementias, the reader is referred to other recent reviews of the topic (Bondi, Salmon, & Kaszniak, 1996; Butters et al., 1995; Welsh-Bohmer & Ogrocki, 1998).

Neuropsychology of Normal Aging

Normal aging of the nervous system is the most common explanation for relatively mild changes in cognitive status occurring after the fifth decade (Albert & Heaton, 1988). The profile of change with normal aging is best conceptualized as a loss of *fluid* abilities, that is, the skills associated with problem solving and novel tasks (Horn, 1982). By contrast, *crystallized* abilities are those skills that are overlearned and tend to be less susceptible to age effects. Neuropsychological investigations reveal time after time that abilities related to tasks measuring more verbal, rehearsed knowledge tend to be more resistant to decline, whereas perceptual-organizational subtests tend to show normal age-related decline. Memory abilities, executive skills, and speed of processing are particularly vulnerable (e.g., Cullum, Butters, Troster, & Salmon, 1990; Erkinjuntii, Laaksonen, Sulkava, Syrjalainen, & Palo, 1986; Salthouse, Fristoe, & Rhee, 1996; Van

TABLE 12.2
Disease-Specific Clinical Descriptions

Alzheimer's disease

Impaired consolidation of new information manifested by rapid forgetting on tests of delayed recall is the hallmark of this disease. Diminished executive skills, confrontation naming, and semantic fluency (category fluency) but relatively preserved lexical fluency (e.g., CFL) are observed. Progression inevitably involves global impairment with pronounced memory and expressive language deficits, executive dysfunction, and visuospatial compromises. Limited insight, tangential thought processing, depression, and bradyphrenia are common.

Frontotemporal dementia

Prominent personality and behavioral changes characterize many of the frontal lobe disorders. Common changes include disinhibition or apathy syndromes, gross impairments in judgement, inappropriate behavior, diminished insight, loss of social awareness and personal awareness, and psychiatric symptoms. Neuropsychological testing reveals disproportionate impairment of executive skills related to frontal lobe integrity (e.g., impaired abstraction, fluency, and cognitive flexibility measured by tests such as Similarities, Verbal Fluency, Wisconsin Card Sort, respectively), within the context of less prominent memory deficits. The condition progresses over a period of approximately 8–10 years, resulting in mutism and vegetative states. May present with frontotemporal features alone, as a primary progressive aphasia, or frontotemporal dementia with motor neuron disease.

Lewy body disease

There is no consensus as to whether this disorder is a unique condition or a variant of AD. Neuropsychological characteristic features are a nonfocal, global impairment, akin to AD, with disproportionate impairments in attention, problem solving, or visuospatial functions. The disorder is uniquely identified by fluctuations in cognitive status along with the Parkinsonian signs, acute confusional states, paranoid delusions, neuroleptic sensitivity, and unexplained falls with orthostatic hypotension. Visual hallucinations are usually prominent early in the disease.

Vascular dementia (MID; multi-infarct dementia)

This is a family of vascular dementias, which include clear-cut MID, and progressive dementias in the context of stroke or hypoperfusion. The neuropsychological profile typically is one that suggests "subcortical" dysfunction, with evidence of inefficient cognitive processing and difficulty retrieving information. Recall is facilitated with structural supports such as retrieval cues (i.e., recognition formats). Fluency is frequently impaired but not naming, a situation in contrast to that of AD where both are typically impaired. Relatively focal impairments in the context of well-preserved skills are common. Some of the variation is easily explained by the pattern of known strokes and their afferent / efferent pathways. Frequently there are also asymmetric motor signs, again depending on the site of lesions.

Parkinson's disease

Executive functions and memory abilities are frequently compromised . Memory impairments are typically characterized by retrieval deficits characteristic of "subcortical" dementias described previously. Motor and gait dysfunction (stiffness, cogwheeling, tremor), bradykinesia, and bradyphrenia are common.

Alcohol dementia

The disorder is characterized by a profound impairment in recent memory (anterograde amnesia) with lesser deficits in retrograde memory. Executive impairments and visuospatial deficits are also common but frequently less impressive than the memory deficit. Qualitatively, the behavioral and cognitive profile is notable for bradyphrenia, confabulation, intrusions, and perseveration. The disorder can be mistaken for AD in the elderly. Diagnosis hinges on the clinical

Continued

TABLE 12.2 *(continued)*

history, and the testing profile noted earlier, with a relative absence of the expressive dysphasia (naming and semantic fluency) common in AD.

Dementia of depression

The neuropsychological profile includes cognitive inefficiency, with significant attentional compromises. The disorder is characterized by impairments on tests requiring effort as opposed to more automatic processing. Frequently this is manifest as executive compromises and retrieval memory deficits. Behaviorally, there is bradyphrenia, psychomotor slowing, and dysphoria.

Creutzfeldt–Jacob disease (CJD)

This uncommon disorder is typically characterized by a rapidly progressive course, ranging from 6 to 12 months. More protracted types are also now described but are even more rare. Initial stages typically involve behavioral complaints, such as vague physical discomfort, changes in sleep and appetite, and forgetfulness. Visual or motor changes may also be observed. Within weeks, a dementia with cortical, pyramidal, and extrapyramidal signs develops. Final stages involve a vegetative akinetic state. The dementia associated with CJD involves multiple cortical features (e.g., aphasia, apraxia, amnesia, agnosia). Clinical variants exist, with at least three types described. Manifestation of these variants parallels the principle structures involved. Diagnosis requires confirmation by characteristic clinical findings (e.g., transient spikes on electroencephalograph, EEG).

Normal-pressure hydrocephalus

A specific triad of symptoms signals the likely presence of hydrocephalus: mental status changes, gait disturbance, and incontinence. Significant variation is observed in symptom severity and with the presence of additional, nonspecific symptoms. The cognitive and behavioral changes associated with hydrocephalus also vary considerably, but typically involve slowed information processing, memory impairment, and apathy.

Progressive supranuclear palsy (PSP)

This extrapyramidal syndrome involves ophthalmic abnormalities (initially loss of volitional downgaze is common), axial rigidity, pseudobulbar palsy, and dementia. Although bradykinesia is common, tremor is atypical. Hypophonia, poor articulation, and mutism are common. Although behavioral changes involving apathy and slowness may be observed early, only mild compromises due to executive dysfunction are usually apparent on neuropsychological evaluation. Later in the course, deficits in memory and executive skills and slowed speed of processing are more prominent.

Huntington's disease

This degenerative disorder involves choreiform movements and dementia. The illness is inherited as an autosomal dominant trait. It is uncommon in the elderly, as the average age of onset is typically between age 35 and 40, with a course duration of approximately 15 years. The classic "subcortical" dementia profile is characteristic, involving slowed information processing, impaired verbal fluency, and poor retrieval. Other cognitive impairments emerge as the illness progresses, with disproportionate executive and mnestic deficits.

Gorp, Satz, & Matrushina, 1990). Measures that use distraction and delayed free recall have been shown to be particularly sensitive to the effects of aging (Craik, 1984), as are some tests of visuoperceptual, visuospatial, and constructional abilities (Howieson, Holm, Kaye, Oken, & Howieson, 1993; Koss et al., 1991).

There has been some suggestion that speed of performance may be the important factor in the effects detected on perceptual-organizational tasks with age, because many of these tasks involve motor responses or reaction times (e.g., Benton & Sivan, 1984). However, the "speed of processing" notion as the unifying explanation for aging effects has been challenged by other lines of evidence that age-related decrements are demonstrated on performance-based tasks even when they are administered in an untimed manner (Klodin, 1975). It appears that many of the differences between studies are largely methodological in origin. Different neuropsychological instruments are used, and there are commonly large differences in subject samples and in the screening criteria employed for defining "normal, healthy elderly" adults (Naugle, Cullum, & Bigler, 1990). Many early studies of aging did not screen subjects for illnesses affecting the central nervous system thoroughly, resulting in conclusions that may be confounded by medical or neurological factors (Albert, 1988). Finally, there is large interindividual variability in performance with age, representing another confounding variable in normal aging research (Levin & Benton, 1973). It appears that some individuals carry more of a cognitive reserve against age-related decline than others, which can only partially be accounted for by differences in education and medical status.

In clinical practice, the dilemma most commonly encountered is distinguishing between the cognitive effects of aging and those of early AD, because both involve similar mnestic and executive skills. In general, a useful rule of thumb is to interpret normal performance based on: (a) a profile of test findings consistent with normal age-related changes as described earlier, (b) an absence of consistent deviations in test scores, particularly in recent recall and working memory functions, suggesting AD, and (c) no significant change in instrumental activities of daily living such as ability to work, manage the home, or function independently, reflected by Clinical Dementia Rating (Hughes, Berg, Danziger, Cohen, & Martin, 1982) scores of 0 (normal) to 0.5 (questionable). Supporting data to bolster the interpretation may include normal imaging studies, particularly functional imaging studies such as positron emission tomography (PET) or single-photon computed tomography (see Welsh-Bohmer & Hoffman, 1996, for review). Even with adherence to these standards and with supportive tests, there can remain some ambiguity. In these instances, longitudinal follow-up conducted 12–18 months later is often essential to document course (progression in symptoms in dementia; stability or improvement in normal aging) and clarify diagnostic suspicions.

Neuropsychology of Depression and Mood Disorders

Essential in the diagnostic process is the identification of treatable causes of cognitive decline. Clarfield (1988) reviewed studies that provided follow-up. Although most dementias are not reversible, a significant proportion, 8%, are reported to resolve partially and another 3% resolve fully if identified and treated. Methodological flaws and inconsistencies have impeded the thorough understanding of dementias resulting from treatable causes (Barry & Mosko-witz, 1988; Nussbaum, 1994). The most common sources of treatable intel-lectual impairment are reported as being depression, drug intoxication, and metabolic or infectious disorders (Albert, 1981; Clarfield, 1988). Some of these conditions have cognitive hallmarks that aid in their identification, as in the case of depression.

Reports of clinical depression in the elderly general population vary consid-erably. In 1984 Myers and colleagues reported an estimated prevalence of major depression and dysthymia in the elderly to be very small in community-dwelling individuals (below 2% and 4% for both men and women at all sites, respec-tively). However, the frequency of symptoms of clinically significant depression has been consistently estimated to be approximately 15% (Blazer, 1994; Koenig & Blazer, 1992). In their review of the literature, Koenig and Blazer (1992) stated that prevalence rates for primary care elderly outpatients are approximately 5% higher than that for community-dwelling elders, that about 40% of elderly med-ical inpatients have some form of depressive syndrome, and that 12% to 16% of institutionalized elders have major depression and 30% to 35% more experience other depressive disorders. Kaszniak (1987) stated that the largest source of mis-diagnosis among elderly patients results from difficulty in distinguishing de-pression from dementia. The frequency of subjective memory complaints in-creases with age and may or may not coexist with actual depression, making the distinction more difficult. Dementia patients also may have a concurrent de-pression. However, a significant amount of research has been conducted investi-gating both the quantitative and qualitative types of errors in performance that these different subgroups make on neuropsychological tests (Jones, Tranel, Ben-ton, & Paulsen, 1992; Kaszniak, 1987; Silberman, Weingartner, Laraia, Byrnes, & Post, 1983). Results of affective screening, in combination with the pattern of deficits revealed during neuropsychological evaluation, can assist in differentiat-ing between dementias resulting from central nervous system compromise and dementia of depression.

In addition to the dementia of depression, affective distress frequently at-tends dementias resulting from other etiologies. The devastating sequelae of the deterioration associated with dementia can be appreciated in many ways. Although changes in cognition are the cardinal sign, changes in affective status are frequently observed. Depression was one of five areas of prime importance identified by a task force convened by the National Alzheimer's Association (Teri et al., 1992), who stated, "Research . . . consistently shows depression to be a pre-valent, persistent, and often devastating problem for patients and caregivers alike" (p. 81). The concept of "excess disability", or treatable factors that may account for greater than warranted functional incapacity, studied by Brody, Kleban, Lawton, and Silverman (1971) has received considerable attention. Esti-mates of the prevalence of depression among elderly individuals with dementia are indeed alarming. In one study, 27% of dementia patients had minor depression and 25% had major depression (Ballard, Bannister, Solis, Oyebode, & Wilcock, 1996). Consistent with this, a recent study found that among AD patients, 28% had dysthymia and another 23% met criteria for major depression (Migliorelli et al., 1995).

Depression tends to predominate in the early rather than later stages of AD or PD with dementia (Soliveri et al., 1994). Dysthymia typically starts after the onset of AD and is more prevalent in the early stages, while major depression typically has an earlier onset and similar prevalence across stages, suggesting that dysthymia may be reactive to the cognitive decline, whereas major depression may be more associated with biological factors (Migliorelli et al., 1995). Although major depression has been found to occur more often in patients with vascular dementia than AD patients (Ballard et al., 1996; Reichman & Coyne, 1995), depressed mood and anhedonia, and depressive symptoms without these features, have a high prevalence (34%–49%) in patients with AD or multi-infarct dementia (MID) (Reichman & Coyne, 1995). Similar frequency and patterns of psychiatric problems have been found among AD and MID patients, with agitation, depression, and apathy being the most frequent symptoms (Cohen et al., 1993). Wagner, Teri, and Orr-Rainey (1995) found that among behavior problems of special care unit demented patients, those related to emotional distress were second only to problems related to memory impairment. These studies highlight the need to identify and treat these factors that lead to excess disability. Successful treatment of depression, even in the context of a neurodegenerative illness, may optimize the use of residual capacities and delay the need for formal care. Although some studies report that depression does not exert a discernible additional affect on cognition or IADL status or predict later cognitive status (Agbayewa, Weir, Tuokko, & Beattie, 1991; Dufouil, Fuhrer, Dartigues, & Alperovitch, 1996; Migliorelli et al., 1995), other studies have revealed more cognitive compromise among depressed patients (Lichtenberg, Ross, Millis, & Manning, 1995; Rovner, Broadhead, Spencer, Carson, & Folstein, 1989; Troster et al., 1995). Fitz and Teri (1994) remarked that although both depression and cognitive status have been related to ADL and IADL abilities in AD patients, the contributions of different variables appear to vary by level of cognitive impairment and which IADL is studied. These authors suggested that the influence of affect on IADL performance may be contingent on the severity of cognitive dysfunction.

CURRENT ADVANCES IN GENETICS AND CONTEMPORARY GERIATRICS

A thorough discussion of contemporary practice in geriatric neuropsychology is not complete without a consideration of the major advances in the identification of genetic markers of AD and other dementias and the implications of these findings for diagnosis and management. Over the last decade, substantial progress has been made toward understanding the role of genetics in various dementias including AD, vascular dementia, and frontal-lobe disorders (see Plassman & Breitner, 1996; Yamaoka et al., 1996). These efforts bring clinicians, researchers, and families alike closer to the development of accurate diagnostic methods and rational treatments.

AD research has been particularly fruitful. In 1993 Strittmatter and colleagues at Duke University Medical Center demonstrated a highly significant relationship between the presence of apolipoprotein E (APOE)-ε4 allele on chromosome 19 and AD. Every person inherits an APOE allele from each parent, of three possible alleles: ε2, ε3, and ε4. Distribution of these alleles is not equal; the APOE ε-3 allele is the most common in European and American Caucasian populations, and there is some evidence for variation in the frequency of the alleles across different ethnic groups (Plassman & Breitner, 1996). Numerous studies have investigated the value of APOE in determining the probable presence of AD with favorable results, as well as its correlates to other biological and cognitive markers (e.g., Saunders et al., 1996; Small et al., 1995; Welsh-Bohmer et al., 1997). The increased frequency of the ε4 allele has been confirmed in a number of late-onset familial and sporadic AD series (e.g., Saunders et al., 1993, 1996; Welsh-Bohmer et al., 1997). Development of AD is not contingent on inheritance of an ε4 allele, although the frequency of the allele is higher in patients with sporadic AD than in the normal elderly population, and its presence results in a decrease in the age of onset of AD for those who are affected (Saunders et al., 1996). However, there is also recent evidence suggesting that the risk associated with the ε4 allele varies by age of onset, and that the ε4 allele exerts its maximal effect among those under age 85 (Blacker et al., 1997; Farrer et al., 1997; Breitner et al., in press).

A number of lines of investigation suggest that genes may be exerting their effects on brain function many years before the onset of obvious symptoms. One study using normal adult twin pairs discordant for the APOE ε4 allele revealed poorer mean neuropsychological performance for the twin carrying the APOE-ε4 allele as compared to the cotwin (Reed et al., 1994). Others reported that the APOE ε4 allele is a strong predictor of clinical progression from mild cognitive impairment to dementia (Petersen et al., 1995) and that the combined use of memory test performance and genetic status (APOE genotype) are perhaps the most instructive when identifying likely incident disease cases in memory impaired populations (Tierney et al., 1996). Combined information showed accuracy of 92.5% in predicting those memory-impaired cases that would progress versus 73.8% accuracy based on genotype information alone. Studies using neuroimaging show similar preclinical effects related to genotype. One investigation using PET imaging demonstrated that the presence of an APOE-ε4 allele is associated with reduced cerebral parietal metabolism and increased asymmetry in nondemented relatives at risk for AD who had mild memory complaints (Small et al., 1995). Another investigation showed reduced temporoparietal metabolism akin to probable AD, in cognitive normal subjects who are homo-zygous for the APOE-ε4 allele (Reiman et al., 1996). Similarly, decreased hippo-campal volume asymmetry has been shown with MRI in nondemented elderly subjects carrying the ApoE-4 allele (Soininen et al., 1995).

It must be emphasized that although substantial progress has been made over the past decade in the genetics of AD, the significance of these factors for the ultimate diagnosis and treatment of AD patients remains undetermined at pres-ent. The genes associated with AD to date account for no more than approxi-mately 50% of cases (Plassman & Breitner, 1996), suggesting that environmen-tal factors or gene–environment interactions may be playing an important role in the other 50% of cases. Currently, it is recognized that APOE genotyping is a useful diagnostic adjunct but is not a biological test for AD. A number of studies in pathologically confirmed samples now indicate a high positive predictive value of the APOE-ε4 allele (94%–100%) in diagnosis of dementia cases (Saun-ders et al., 1996; Welsh-Bohmer et al., 1997; Mayeux et al., 1998). However, it is also very clear that not all individuals homozygous for the ε4 allele develop AD even if they live to very old age (Breitner et al., in press), and a sizeable fraction (35%–38%) of the prevalent cases of AD confirmed at autopsy do not carry an APOE-ε4 allele at all (Mayeux et al., 1998). Consequently, when using APOE genotype information diagnostically the limitations as a disease marker must be kept in mind. The presence of an ε4 allele in a case of memory impairment may confirm clinical suspicions of AD; however, its absence provides no useful diag-nostic information because only two-thirds of the cases of AD carry an allele. The absence of the ε4 allele in the context of dementia defines a subgroup of patients for whom additional evaluation may be indicated, particularly if the presentation is unusual (e.g., Welsh-Bohmer et al., 1997). Genetic testing for prediction in nonsymptomatic individuals is premature and unwarranted at this time (see Post et al., 1997; Roses, 1995). The recent announcement that a gene on chromosome 12 is linked to AD, from researchers at Duke University Med-ical Center and Massachusetts General Hospital (Pericak-Vance et al., 1997), and the linkage of some frontotemporal dementias to the short arm of chromo-some 17 (Yamaoka et al., 1996) mark continued efforts to understand the genet-ics of AD and associated dementias.

CONCLUSIONS

As the elderly population continues to increase, the practice of geriatric neuro-psychology will likely remain an integral part of the assessment and care of the geriatric patient. Valid and effective evaluations require attention to factors that frequently attend this population. Evaluations are enriched when they occur in conjunction with other sources of information, such as historical information, functional change measures, and behavioral observations. The advances in technology including improved neuroimaging methods and the continued progress in neurobiology and clinical genetics hold promise for the future early and reliable detection of AD and other dementias before symptoms are undeniably manifest. These advances hold open the possibility of early intervention at a point in illness when such treatments are most likely to be effective in preventing or minimizing symptoms. However, as has been seen in other diseases, such as Huntington's disease, the technology (such as the reliable identification of causative genes), may predate the availability of effective treatments. Today's clinical neuropsychologist might anticipate this dilemma and focus future research efforts on the efficacy of clinical management approaches, including cognitive training, traditional psychotherapy, and combination of these methods, in maximizing cognitive function, emotional health, and the overall quality of life in early, moderate, and late-stage dementing diseases.

ACKNOWLEDGMENTS

This work was supported in part by grants from the National Institute on Aging (NIA grants AG05128 and AG09997) and private donations to the Joseph and Kathleen Bryan Alzheimer's Disease Research Center.

REFERENCES

Agbayewa, M., Weir, J., Tuokko, H., & Beattie, L. (1991). Depression in dementia: Its impact on functional ability. *Dementia, 2,* 212–217.

Albert, M. (1981). Geriatric neuropsychology. *Journal of Consulting and Clinical Psychology, 49,* 835–850.

Albert, M. (1988). General issues in geriatric neuropsychology. In M. Albert & M. Moss (Eds.), *Geriatric neuropsychology* (pp. 3–10). New York: Guilford Press.

Albert, M., & Heaton, R. (1988). Intelligence testing. In M. Albert & M. Moss (Eds.), *Geriatric neuropsychology* (pp. 13–32). New York: Guilford Press.

Albert, S. M., Del Castillo-Castaneda, C., Sano, M., Jacobs, D. M., Marder, K., Bell, K., Bylsma, F., Lafleche, G., Brandt, J., Albert, M., & Stern, Y. (1996). Quality of life in patients with Alzheimer's disease as reported by patient proxies. *Journal of the American Geriatrics Society, 44,* 1342–1347.

Alexopoulos, G. (1992). Treatment of depression. In C. Salzman (Ed.), *Clinical geriatric psychopharmacology* (pp.137–174). Baltimore, MD: Williams & Wilkins.

Anthony, J., LeResche, L., Niaz, U., Von Korff, M., & Folstein, M. (1982). Limits of the Mini-Mental State as a screening test for dementia and delirium among hospital patients. *Psychological Medicine, 12,* 397–408.

Ardila, A., & Rosselli, M. (1989). Neuropsychological characteristic of normal aging. *Developmental Neuropsychology, 5,* 307–320.

Backman, L., Josephsson, S., Herlitz, A., Stigsdotter, A., & Viitanen, M. (1991). The generalizability of training gains in dementia: Effects of an imagery-based mnemonic on face-name retention duration. *Psychology and Aging, 6,* 489–492.

Baker, F. (1987). Competent for what? *Journal of the National Medical Association, 79,* 715–720.

Ballard, C., Bannister, C., Solis, M., Oyebode, F., & Wilcock, G. (1996). The prevalence, associations and symptoms of depression amongst dementia sufferers. *Journal of Affective Disorders, 36,* 135–144.

Baltes, P., & Willis, S. (1982). Plasticity and enhancement of intellectual functioning in old age: Penn State's Adult Development and Enrichment Project (ADEPT). In F. Craik & S. Trehub (Eds.), *Aging and cognitive processes* (pp. 353–389). New York: Plenum Press.

Barona, A., Reynolds, C., & Chastain, R. (1984). A demographically based index of premorbid intelligence for the WAIS-R. *Journal of Consulting & Clinical Psychology, 52,* 885–887.

Barr, A., Benedict, R., Tune, L., & Brandt, J. (1992). Neuropsychological differentiation of Alzheimer's disease from vascular dementia. *International Journal of Geriatric Psychiatry, 7,* 621–627.

Barry, P., & Moskowitz, M. (1988). The diagnosis of reversible dementia in the elderly: A critical review. *Archives of Internal Medicine, 148,* 1914–1918.

Baum, C., Edwards, D., Yonan, C., & Storandt, M. (1996). The relation of neuropsychological test performance to performance of functional tasks in dementia of the Alzheimer type. *Archives of Clinical Neuropsychology, 11,* 69–75.

Benton, A., & Sivan, A. (1984). Problems and conceptual issues in neuropsychological research in aging and dementia. *Journal of Clinical Neuropsychology, 6,* 57–63.

Bigler, E. (1996). *Human brain function: Assessment and rehabilitation. Neuroimaging II: Clinical applications.* New York: Plenum Press.

Blacker, D., Haines, J., Rodes, L., Terwedow, H., Go, R., Harrell, L., Perry, T., Bassett, S., Chase, M., Albert, M., & Tanzi, R. (1997). ApoE-4 and age at onset of Alzheimer's disease: The NIMH genetics initiative. *Neurology, 48,* 139–147.

Blanchard-Fields, F., & Hess, T. M. (Eds.). (1996). *Perspectives on cognitive change in adulthood and aging.* New York: McGraw Hill.

Blair, J., & Spreen, O. (1989). Predicting premorbid IQ: A revision of the National Adult Reading Test. *The Clinical Neuropsychologist, 3,* 129–136.

Blazer, D. (1994). Is depression more frequent in late life? An honest look at the evidence. *American Journal of Geriatric Psychiatry, 2,* 193–199.

Bondi, M. W., Salmon, D. P., & Kaszniak, A. W. (1996). The neuropsychology of dementia. In I. Grant & K. M. Adams (Eds.), *Neuropsychological assessment of neuropsychiatric disorders* (2nd ed., pp. 164–199). New York: Oxford University Press.

Bowen, J., Teri, L., Kukull, W., McCormick, W., McCurry, S., & Larson, E. (1997). Progression to dementia in patients with isolated memory loss. *The Lancet, 349,* 763–765.

Branch, L., & Jette, A. (1982). A prospective study of long-term care institutionalization among the aged. *American Journal of Public Health, 72,* 1373–1379.

Branch, L., Wetle, T., Scherr, P., Cook, N., Evans, D., Hebert, L., Masland, E., Keough, M., & Taylor, J. (1988). A prospective study of incident comprehensive medical home care use among the elderly. *American Journal of Public Health, 78,* 255–259.

Breitner, J. C. S., & Welsh, K. A. (1995). Diagnosis and management of memory loss and cognitive disorders among elderly persons. *Psychiatric Services, 46,* 29–35.

Breitner, J. C. S., Welsh, K. A., Gau, B. A., McDonald, W. M., Steffens, D. C., Saunders, A. M., Magruder, K. M., Helms, M. J., Plassman, B. L., Folstein, M. F., Brandt, J. Robinette, C. D., & Page, W. F. (1995). Alzheimer's disease in the National Academy of Sciences–National Research Council Registry of Aging Twin Veterans III: Detection of cases, longitudinal results, and observations on twin concordance. *Archives of Neurology, 52,* 763–771.

Breitner, J. C. S., Wyse, B. W., Anthony, J. C., Welsh-Bohmer, K. A., Steffens, D. C., Norton, M. C., Tschanz, J. D., Plassman, B. L., Meyer, M. R., Skoog, I., & Khachaturian, Z. (In press). APOE e4 predicts age when prevalence of Alzheimer's disease increases—then declines. *Neurology.*

Brody, E., Kleban, M., Lawton, M. P., & Silverman, H. (1971). Excess disabilities of mentally impaired aged: Impact of individualized treatment. *The Gerontologist, Summer Part I,* 124–133.

Brown, P., Cathala, F., Castaigne P., & Gajdusek, D. (1986). Creutzfeldt–Jakob disease: Clinical analysis of a consecutive series of 230 neuropathologically verified cases. *Annals of Neurology 20,* 597–602.

Butters, N., Delis, D. C., & Lucas, J. C. (1995). Clinical assessment of memory disorders in amnesia and dementia. *Annual Review of Psychology, 46,* 493–523.

Camp, C., Foss, J., O'Hanlon, A., & Stevens, A. (1996). Memory interventions for persons with dementia. *Applied Cognitive Psychology, 10,* 193–210.

Cercy, S. P., & Bylsma, F. W. (1997). Lewy Bodies and progressive dementia: A critical review and meta-analysis. *Journal of the International Neuropsychological Society, 3,* 179–194.

Chase, T., Foster, N., Gedio, P., Brooks, R., Mansi, L., & Di Chiro, G. (1984). Regional cortical dysfunction in Alzheimer's disease as determined by positron emission tomography. *Annals of Neurology, 15,* 170–174.

Claman, D. L., & Radebaugh, T. S. (1991). Neuropsychological assessment in clinical trials of Alzheimer's disease. *Alzheimer Disease and Associated Disorders, 5,* S49–S56.

Clarfield, A. (1988). The reversible dementias: Do they reverse? *Annals of Internal Medicine, 109,* 476–486.

Coblentz, J., Mattis, S., Zingesser, L., Kasoff, S., Wisniewski, H., & Katzman, R. (1973). Presenile dementia: Clinical aspects and evaluation of cerebrospinal fluid dynamics. *Archives of Neurology, 29,* 299–308.

Cohen, D., Eisdorfer, C., Gorelick P., Paveza, G., Luchins, D., Freels, S., Ashford, J. W., Semla, T., Levy, P., & Hirschman, R. (1993). Psychopathology associated with Alzheimer's disease and related disorders. *Journal of Gerontology, 48,* M255–M260.

Colsher, P. L., & Wallace, R. B. (1991). Epidemiological consideration in studies of cognitive function in the elderly: Methodology and nondementing acquired dysfunction [Review]. *Epidemiologic Reviews, 13,* 1–27.

Craik, F. (1984). Age differences in remembering. In L. Squire & N. Butters (Eds.), *Neuropsychology of memory* (pp. 3–12). New York: Guilford Press.

Craik, F., & Salthouse, T. A. (Eds.). (1992). *The handbook of aging and cognition.* Hillsdale, NJ: Lawrence Erlbaum Associates.

Cullum, C., Butters, N., Troster, A., & Salmon, D. (1990). Normal aging and forgetting rates on the Wechsler Memory Scale–Revised. *Archives of Clinical Neuropsychology, 5,* 23–30.

Cummings, J., & Benson, D. (1992). *Dementia: A clinical approach.* Stoneham, MA: Butterworth-Heinemann.

Cummings, J., and the Technology and Therapeutics Assessment Subcommittee. (1996). Assessment: Neuropsychological testing of adults: Considerations for neurologists. Report of the Therapeutics and Technology Assessment Subcommittee of the American Academy of Neurology. *Neurology, 47,* 592–599.

Cunningham, W., Sepkoski, C., & Opel, M. (1978). Fatigue effects on intelligence test performance in the elderly. *Journal of Gerontology, 33,* 541–545.

Cutler, S. J., & Hodgson, L. G. (1996). Anticipatory dementia: A link between memory appraisals and concerns about developing Alzheimer's disease. *Gerontologist, 36,* 657–664.

Davison, L. (1974). Introduction. In R. Reitan & L. Davison (Eds.), *Clinical neuropsychology: Current status and applications* (pp. 1–18). Washington, DC: V. H. Winston & Sons.

Diehl, M., Willis, S., & Schaie, K. (1995). Everyday problem solving in older adults: Observational assessment and cognitive correlates. *Psychology and Aging, 10,* 478–491.

Dodrill, C. B. (1997). Myths of neuropsychology. *The Clinical Neuropsychologist, 11,* 1–17.

Dufouil, C., Fuhrer, R., Dartigues, J.-F., Alperovitch, A. (1996). Longitudinal analysis of the association between depressive symptomatology and cognitive deterioration. *American Journal of Epidemiology, 144,* 634–641.

Ebly, E. M., Parhad, I. M., Hogan, D. B., & Fung, T. S. (1994). Prevalence and types of dementia in the very old: Results from the Canadian Study of Health and Aging. *Neurology, 44,* 1593–1600.

Erkinjuntii, T., Laaksonen, R., Sulkava, R., Syrjalainen, R., & Palo, J. (1986). Neuropsychological differentiation between normal aging, Alzheimer's disease and vascular dementia. *Acta Neurologica Scandanavia, 74,* 393–403.

Evans, D. A., Scherr, P. A., Cook, N. R., Albert, M. S., Funkenstein, H. H., Smith, L. A., Hebert, L. E., Wetle, T. T., Branch, L. G., Chown, M., Hennekens, C. H., & Taylor, J. O. (1990). Estimated prevalence of Alzheimer's disease in the United States. *Milbank Quarterly, 68,* 267–289.

Farrer, L. A., Cupples, L. A., Haines, J. L., Hyman, B., Kukull, W. A., Mayeux, R., Myers, R. H., Pericak-Vance, M. A., Risch, N.., van Dujin, C. M., for the APOE and Alzheimer Disease Meta Analysis Consortium (1997). *Journal of the American Medical Association, 278,* 1349–1356.

Fitz, A., & Teri, L. (1994). Depression, cognition, and functional ability in patients with Alzheimer's disease. *Journal of the American Geriatrics Society, 42,* 186–191.

Folstein, M., Folstein, S., & McHugh, P. (1975). Mini-Mental State: A practical method for grading the cognitive state of patients for the clinician. *Journal of Psychiatric Research, 12,* 189–198.

Friedland, R. (1993). Alzheimer's disease: Clinical features and differential diagnosis. *Neurology, 43,* S45–S51.

Frisoni, F., Rozzini, R., Bianchetti, A., & Trabucchi, M. (1993). Principal lifetime occupation and MMSE score in elderly persons. *Journal of Gerontology: Social Sciences, 48,* 310–314.

Furey-Kurjian, M., Pietrini, P., Graff-Radford, N., Alexander, G., Freo, U., Szczepanik, J., & Schapiro, M. (1996). Visual variant of Alzheimer disease: Distinctive neuropsychological features. *Neuropsychology, 10,* 294–300.

Gallo, J. J., & Breitner, J. C. S. (1995). Alzheimer's disease in the N.A.S.–N.R.C. Registry of aging twin veterans IV. Performance characteristics of a two stage telephone screening procedure for Alzheimer's dementia. *Psychological Medicine, 25,* 1211–1219.

Gardner, R., Oliver-Munoz, S., Fisher, L., & Empting, L. (1981). Mattis Dementia Rating Scale: Internal reliability study using a diffusely impaired population. *Journal of Clinical Neuropsychology, 3,* 271–275.

Goldstein, G., McCue, M., Rogers, J., & Nussbaum, P. (1992). Diagnostic differences in memory test based predictions of functional capacity in the elderly. *Neuropsychological Rehabilitation, 2,* 307–317.

Greiner, P., Snowdon, D., & Schmitt, F. (1996). The loss of independence in activities of daily living: The role of low normal cognitive function in elderly nuns. *American Journal of Public Health, 86,* 62–66.

Gustafson, I. (1993). Clinical picture of frontal lobe dementia of non-Alzheimer type. *Dementia, 4,* 143–148.

Heaton, R., Grant, I., & Matthews, C. (1986). Differences in neuropsychological test performance associated with age, education, and sex. In I. Grant & K. Adams (Eds.), *Neuropsychological assessment of neuropsychiatric disorders* (pp. 100–120). New York: Oxford University Press.

Herzog, A. R., & Rodgers, W. L. (1992). The use of survey methods in research on older Americans. In R. B. Wallace & R. F. Woolson (Eds.), *The epidemiological study of the elderly* (pp. 60–90). New York: Oxford University Press.

Horn, J. (1982). The theory of fluid and crystallized intelligence in relation to concepts of cognitive psychology and aging in adulthood. In F. Craik, & S. Trehub (Eds.), *Aging and cognitive processes* (pp. 237–278). New York: Plenum Press.

Howieson, D., Holm, L., Kaye, J., Oken, B., & Howieson, J. (1993). Neurologic function in the optimally healthy oldest old: Neuropsychological evaluation. *Neurology, 43,* 1882–1886.

Hughes, C., Berg, L., Danziger, W., Cohen, L., & Martin, R. (1982). A new clinical scale for the staging of dementia. *British Journal of Psychiatry, 140,* 566–572.

Ivnik, R., Malec, J., Tangalos, E., Petersen, R., Kokmen, E., & Kurland, L. (1992). Mayo's older American normative studies: WMS–R norms for ages 56 to 94. *The Clinical Neuropsychologist, 6,* 49–82.

Ivnik, R., Malec, J., Smith, G., Tangalos, E., Petersen, R., Kokmen, E., & Kurland, L. (1992). Mayo's older American normative studies: Updated AVLT norms for ages 56 to 97. *The Clinical Neuropsychologist, 6,* 83–104.

Jackson, M., & Lowe, J. (1996). The new neuropathology of degenerative frontotemporal dementias. *Acta Neuropathologica, 91,* 127–134.

Jones, R., Tranel, D., Benton, A., & Paulsen, J. (1992). Differentiating dementia from "pseudodementia" early in the clinical course: Utility of neuropsychological tests. *Neuropsychology, 6,* 13–21.

Katz, S., & Stroud, M. (1989). Functional assessment in geriatrics: A review of progress and directions. *Journal of the American Geriatrics Society, 37,* 267–271.

Kaszniak, A. (1987). Neuropsychological consultation to geriatricians: Issues in the assessment of memory complaints. *The Clinical Neuropsychologist, 1,* 35–46.

Kiernan, R., Mueller, J., Langston, J., & Van Dyke, C. (1987). The Neurobehavioral Cognitive Status Examination: A brief but differentiated approach to cognitive assessment. *Annals of Internal Medicine, 107,* 481–485.

Klodin, V. (1975). *Verbal facilitation of perceptual-integrative performance in relation to age.* Doctoral dissertation. Washington University, St. Louis, MO.

Kloezen, S., Fitten, L., & Steinberg, A. (1988). Assessment of treatment decision-making capacity in a medically ill patient. *Journal of the American Geriatrics Society, 36,* 1055–1058.

Koenig, H., & Blazer, D. (1992). Epidemiology of geriatric affective disorders. *Clinics in Geriatric Medicine, 8,* 235–251.

Koltai, D., & Branch (in press). Cognitive and affective interventions to maximize abilities and adjustment in dementia. In R. Cacabelos, C. Fernandez, & E. Giacobini (Eds.), *Annals of Psychiatry: Basic and Clinical Neurosciences* (Vol. 7). Barcelona: Prous Science Publisher.

Koss, E., Haxby, J. V., DeCarli,C., Schapiro, M. B., Friedland, R. P., & Rapoport, S. I. (1991). Patterns of performance preservation and loss in healthy aging. *Developmental Neuropsychology, 7,* 99–113.

Launer, L., Dinkgreve, M., Jonker, C., Hooijer, C., & Lindeboom, J. (1993). Are age and education independent correlates of the Mini-Mental State Exam performance of community-dwelling elderly? *Journal of Gerontology: Psychological Sciences, 48,* 271–277.

Lawton, M. P., & Storandt, M. (1984). Clinical and functional approaches to the assessment of older people. In P. McReynolds & G. Chelune (Eds.), *Advances in psychological assessment* (Vol. 6, pp. 236–276). San Francisco: Jossey-Bass.

Lemsky, C., Smith, G., Malec, J., & Ivnik, R. (1996). Identifying risk for functional impairment using cognitive measures: An application of CART modeling. *Neuropsychology, 10,* 368–375.

Levin, H., & Benton, A. (1973). Age and susceptibility to tactile masking effects. *Gerontologia Clinica, 15,* 1–9.

Lezak, M. (1995). *Neuropsychological assessment.* (3rd ed.). New York: Oxford University Press.

Lichtenberg, P., Ross, T., Millis, S., & Manning, C. (1995). The relationship between depression and cognition in older adults: A cross-validation study. *Journal of Gerontology, 50,* P25–P32.

Malec, J., Ivnik, R., Smith, G., Tangalos, E., Petersen, R., Kokmen, E., & Kurland, L. (1992). Mayo's older americans normative studies: Utility of corrections for age and education for the WAIS-R. *The Clinical Neuropsychologist, 6,* 31–47.

Mann, D., Neary, D., & Testa, H. (1994). *Color atlas and text of adult dementias.* London: Mosby-Wolfe.

Marson, D., Cody, H., Ingram, K., & Harrell, L. (1995). Neuropsychologic predictors of competency in Alzheimer's disease using a rational reasons legal standard. *Archives of Neurology, 52,* 955–959.

Marson, D., Ingram, K., Cody, H., & Harrell, L. (1995). Assessing the competency of patients with Alzheimer's disease under different legal standards. *Archives of Neurology, 52,* 949–954.

Marson, D., Schmitt, F., Ingram, K., & Harrell, L. (1994). Determining the competency of Alzheimer patients to consent to treatment and research. *Alzheimer Disease and Associated Disorders, 8,* 5–18.

Martin, A., Brouwers, P., Lalonde, F., Cox, C., Teleska, P., Fedio, P., Foster, N., & Chase, T. (1986). Towards a behavioral typology of Alzheimer's patients. *Journal of Clinical and Experimental Neuropsychology, 8,* 594–610.

Mattis, S. (1988). *Dementia Rating Scale: Professional manual.* Odessa, FL: Psychological Assessment Resources.

Mattis, S. (1990). Neuropsychological assessment of competency in the elderly. *Forensic Reports, 3,* 107–114.

Mayeux, R., Saunders, A. M., Shea, S., Mirra, S., Evans, D., Roses, A. D., Hyman, B. T., Crain, B., Tang, M.-X., & Phelps, C. H., for the Alzheimer's Disease Centers Consortium on Apolipoprotein E and Alzheimer's Disease. (1998). Utility of the Apolipoprotein E genotype in the diagnosis of Alzheimer's disease. *New England Journal of Medicine, 338,* 506–511.

McCue, M. (1997). The relationship between neuropsychology and functional assessment in the elderly. In P. Nussbaum (Ed.), *Handbook of neuropsychology and aging* (pp. 394–408). New York: Plenum Press.

McCue, M., Rogers, J., & Goldstein, G. (1990). Relationships between neuropsychological and functional assessment in elderly neuropsychiatric patients. *Rehabilitation Psychology, 35,* 91–99.

McKeith, I., Perry R., Fairbairn, A., Jabeen, S., & Perry, E. (1992). Operational criteria for senile dementia of the Lewy body type (SDLT). *Psychological Medicine, 22,* 911–922.

McKhann, G., Drachman, D., Folstein, M., Katzman, R., Price, D., & Stadlan, E. (1984). Clinical diagnosis of Alzheimer's disease: Report of the NINCDS–ADRA work group under the auspices of Department of Health and Human Services Task Force on Alzheimer's disease. *Neurology, 34,* 939–944.

McKitrick, L., Camp, C., & Black, F. W. (1992). Prospective memory intervention in Alzheimer's disease. *Journal of Gerontology, 47,* P337–P343.

Migliorelli, R., Teson, A., Sabe, L., Petracchi, M., Leiguarda, R., & Starkstein, S. (1995). Prevalence and correlates of dysthymia and major depression among patients with Alzheimer's disease. *American Journal of Psychiatry, 152,* 37–44.

Mohs, R. C., Knopman, D., Petersen, R. C., Ferris, S. H., Ernesto, C., Grundman, M., Sano, M., Bieliauskas, L., Geldmacher, D., Clark, C., & Thal, L. J. (1997). Development of cognitive instruments for use in clinical trials of antidementia drugs: Additions to the Alzheimer's Disease Assessment Scale that broaden its cope. The Alzheimer's Disease Cooperative Study. *Alzheimer Disease and Associated Disorders, 11,* S13–S21.

Morris, J., Heyman, A., Mohs, R., Hughes, P., Van Belle, G., Fillenbaum, G., Mellits, E., & Clark, C. (1989). The Consortium to Establish a Registry of Alzheimer's Disease (CERAD), I: Clinical and neuropsychological assessment of Alzheimer's disease. *Neurology, 39,* 1159–1165.

Myers, J., Weissman, M., Tischler, G., Holzer, C., Leaf, P., Orvaschel, H., Anthony, J., Boyd, J., Burke, J., Kramer, M., & Stoltzman, R. (1984). Six-month prevalence of psychiatric disorders in three communities. *Archives of General Psychiatry, 41,* 959–970.

Nadler, J., Richardson, E., Malloy, P., Marran, M., & Hostetler Brinson, M. (1993). The ability of the Dementia Rating Scale to predict everyday functioning. *Archives of Clinical Neuropsychology, 8,* 449–460.

Naugle, R., Cullum, C., & Bigler, E. (1990). Evaluation of intellectual and memory function among dementia patients who were intellectually superior. *The Clinical Neuropsychologist, 4,* 355–374.

Naugle, R., & Kawczak, K. (1989). Limitations of the Mini-Mental State Examination. *Cleveland Clinic Journal of Medicine, 56,* 277–281.

Nussbaum, P. (1994). Pseudodementia: A slow death. *Neuropsychology Review, 4,* 71–90.

Odenheimer, G., Beaudet, M., Jette, A., Albert, M., Grande, L., & Minaker, K. (1994). Performance-based driving evaluation of the elderly driver: Safety, reliability, and validity. *Journal of Gerontology: Medical Sciences, 49,* M153–M159.

Pericak-Vance, M. A., Bass, M. P., Yamaoka, L. H., Gaskell, P. C., Scott, W. K., Terwedow, H. A., Menold, M. M., Conneally, P. M., Small, G. W., Vance, J. M., Saunders, A. M., Roses, A. D., & Haines, J. L. (1997). Complete genomic screen in late onset familial Alzheimer's disease. Evidence for a new locus on chromosome 12. *Journal of the American Medical Association, 278,* 1237–1241.

Petersen, R., Smith, G., Ivnik, R., Tangalos, E., Schaid, D., Thibodeau, S., Kokmen, E., Waring, S., & Kurland, L. (1995). Apolipoprotein E status as a predictor of the development of Alzheimer's disease in memory impaired individuals. *Journal of the American Medical Association, 273,* 1274–1278.

Plassman, B., & Breitner, J. (1996). Recent advances in the genetics of Alzheimer's disease and vascular dementia with an emphasis on gene-environment interactions. *Journal of the American Geriatrics Society, 44,* 1242–1250.

Poon, L. W. (1986). *Handbook for clinical memory assessment.* Washington DC: American Psychological Association Press.

Post, S., Whitehouse, P., Binstock, R., Bird, T., Eckert, S., Farrer, L., Fleck, L., Gaines, A., Juengst, E., Karlinsky, H., Miles, S., Murray, T., Quaid, K., Relkin, N., Roses, A., St. George-Hyslop, P., Sacks, G., Steinbock, B., Truschke, E., & Zinn, A. (1997). The clinical introduction of genetic testing for Alzheimer disease: An ethical perspective. *Journal of the American Medical Association, 277,* 832–836.

Prigatano, G. P. (1997). Learning from our successes and failures: Reflections and comments on "Cognitive rehabilitation: How it is and how it might be." *Journal of the International Neuropsychological Society, 3,* 497–499.

Quayhagen, M., Quayhagen, M., Corbeil, R., Roth, P., & Rodgers, J. (1995). A dyadic remediation program for care recipients with dementia. *Nursing Research, 44,* 153–159.

Rabins, P., & Cummings, J. (Eds.). (1998). Alzheimer's disease management: The emerging standard of care. *American Journal of Geriatric Psychiatry, 6* (Suppl. 1), S1–S100.

Rebok, G., Keyl, P., Bylsma, F., Blaustein, M., & Tune, L. (1994). The effects of Alzheimer disease on driving-related abilities. *Alzheimer Disease and Associated Disorders, 8,* 228–240.

Reed, T., Carmelli, D., Swan, G., Breitner, J., Welsh, K., Jarvik, G., Deeb, S., & Auwerx, J. (1994). Lower cognitive performance in normal older adult male twins carrying the apolipoprotein E-4 allele. *Archives of Neurology, 51,* 1189–1192.

Reichman, W., & Coyne, A. (1995). Depressive symptoms in Alzheimer's disease and multi-infarct dementia. *Journal of Geriatric Psychiatry and Neurology, 8,* 96–99.

Reiman, E., Caselli, R., Yun, L., Chen, K., Bandy, D., Minoshima, S., Thibodeau, S., & Osborne, D. (1996). Preclinical evidence of Alzheimer's disease in persons homozygous for the 4 allele for apolipoprotein E. *The New England Journal of Medicine, 334,* 752–758.

Richardson, E., Nadler, J., & Malloy, P. (1995). Neuropsychologic prediction of performance measures of daily living skills in geriatric patients. *Neuropsychology, 9,* 565–572.

Rockwood, K., Stolee, P., & McDowell, I. (1996). Factors associated with institutionalization of older people in Canada: Testing a multi-factorial definition of frailty. *Journal of the American Geriatrics Society, 44,* 578–582.

Roses, A. (1995). Apolipoprotein E genotyping in the differential diagnosis, not prediction, of Alzheimer's disease. *Annals of Neurology, 38,* 6–14.

Rovner, B., Broadhead, J., Spencer, M., Carson, K., & Folstein, M. (1989). Depression and Alzheimer's disease. *American Journal of Psychiatry, 146,* 350–353.

Ryan, J., Paolo, A., & Brungardt, T. (1990). Standardization of the Wechsler Adult Intelligence Scale–Revised for persons 75 years and older. *Psychological Assessment, 2,* 404–411.

Salthouse, T. A., Fristoe, N., & Rhee, S. H. (1996). How localized are age related effects on neuropsychological measures. *Neuropsychology, 10,* 272–285.

Saunders, A., Hulette, C., Welsh-Bohmer, K., Schmechel, D., Crain, G., Burke, J., Alberts, M., Strittmatter, W., Breitner, J., Rosenberg, C., Scott, S., Gaskell, P., Pericak-Vance, M., & Roses, A. (1996). Specificity, sensitivity, and predictive value of apolipoprotein E genotyping for sporadic Alzheimer's disease. *The Lancet, 348,* 90–93.

Saunders, A., Schmader, K., Breitner, J., Benson, M., Brown, W., Goldfarb, L., Goldgaber, D., Manwaring, M., Szymanski, M., McCown, N., Dole, K., Schmechel, D., Strittmatter, W., Pericak-Vance, M., & Roses, A. (1993). Apolipoprotein E 4 allele distributions in late-onset Alzheimer's disease and in other amyloid-forming diseases. *The Lancet, 342,* 710–711.

Schaie, K., & Willis, S. (1986). Can decline in adult intellectual functioning be reversed? *Developmental Psychology, 22,* 223–232.

Scogin, F., & Perry, J. (1986). Guardianship proceedings with older adults: The role of functional assessment and gerontologists. *Law and Psychology Review, 10,* 123–128.

Shay, K., Duke, L., Conboy, T., Harrell, L., Callaway, R., & Folks, D. (1991). The clinical validity of the Mattis Dementia Rating Scale in staging Alzheimer's dementia. *Journal of Geriatric Psychiatry and Neurology, 4,* 18–25.

Shipley, W. (1946). *Institute of Living Scale.* Los Angeles: Western Psychological Services.

Silberman, E., Weingartner, H., Laraia, M., Byrnes, S., & Post, R. Processing of emotional properties of stimuli by depressed and normal subjects. *Journal of Neurological and Mental Disorders, 171,* 10–14.

Skoog, I., Nilsson, L., Palmertz, R., Andreasson, L.-A., & Svanborg, A. (1993). A population based study of dementia in 85 year olds. *New England Journal of Medicine, 328,* 153–158.

Small, G., Mazziotta, J., Collins, M., Baxter, L., Phelps, M., Mandelkern, M., Kaplan, A., La Rue, A., Adamson, C., Chang, L., Guze, B., Corder, E., Saunders, A., Haines, J., Pericak-Vance, M., & Roses, A. (1995). Apolipoprotein E type 4 allele and cerebral glucose metabolism in relatives at risk for familial Alzheimer disease. *Journal of the American Medical Association, 273,* 942–947.

Small, G., Rabins, P., Barry, P., Buckholtz, N., DeKosky, S., Ferris, S., Findel, S., Gwyther, L., Khachaturian, Z., Lebowitz, B., McRae, T., Morris, J., Oakley, F., Schneider, L., Streim, J., Sunderland, T., Teri, L., & Tune, L. (1997). Diagnosis and treatment of Alzheimer's disease and related disorders. Consensus Statement of the American Association for Geriatric Psychiatry, the Alzheimer's Association, and the American Geriatrics Society. *Journal of the American Medical Association, 278,* 1363–1371.

Smith, G., Ivnik, R., Malec, J., Kokmen, E., Tangalos, E., & Petersen R. (1994). Psychometric properties of the Mattis Dementia Rating Scale. *Assessment, 1,* 123–131.

Sohlberg, M., & Mateer, C. (1989). *Introduction to cognitive rehabilitation: Theory and practice.* New York: Guilford Press.

Soininen, H., Partanen, K., Pitkanen, A., Hallikainen, A., Hanninen, T., Helisalmi, S., Mannermaa, A., Ryynanen, M., Koivisto, K., & Riekkinen, P. (1995). Decreased hippocampal volume asymmetry on MRIs in nondemented elderly subjects carrying the apolipoprotein E 4 allele. *Neurology, 45,* 391–392.

Soliveri, P., Zappacosta, M., Austoni, L., Caffarra, P., Scaglioni, A., Testa, D., Palazzini, E., Caraceni, T., & Girotti, F. (1994). Differing patterns of psychiatric impairment in Alzheimer and demented parkinsonian patients. *Italian Journal of Neurological Sciences, 15,* 407–411.

Stanley, B., Stanley, M., Guido, J., & Garvin L. (1988). The functional competency of elderly at risk. *Gerontologist, 28,* 53–58.

Steffens, D. C., Welsh, K. A., Burke, J. R., Helms, M. J., Folstein, M. F., Brandt, J., McDonald, W. M., & Breitner, J. C. S. (1996). Diagnosis of Alzheimer's disease in epidemiological studies by staged review of clinical data. *Neuropsychiatry, Neuropsychology, and Behavioral Neurology, 9,* 107–113.

Steinberg, A., Fitten, L., & Kachuck, N. (1986). Patient participation in treatment decision-making in the nursing home: The issue of competence. *Gerontologist, 26,* 362–366.

Strittmatter, W., Saunders, A., Schmechel, D., Pericak-Vance, M., Enghild, J., Salvesen, G., & Roses, A. (1993). Apolipoprotein E: High-avidity binding to B-amyloid and increased frequency of type 4 allele in late-onset familial Alzheimer disease. *Proceedings of the National Academy of Science, 90,* 1977–1981.

Teri, L., Rabins, P., Whitehouse, P., Berg, L., Reisberg, B., Sunderland, T., Eichelman, B., & Phelps, C. (1992). Management of behavior disturbance in Alzheimer disease: Current knowledge and future directions. *Alzheimer Disease and Associated Disorders, 6,* 77–88.

Tierney, M., Szalai, J., Snow, W., Fisher, M., Tsuda, T., Chi, H., McLachlan, D., & St. George-Hyslop, P. (1996). A prospective study of the clinical utility of ApoE genotype in the prediction of outcome in patients with memory impairment. *Neurology, 46,* 149–154.

Tranel, D. (1992). Functional neuroanatomy: Neuropsychological correlates of cortical and subcortical damage. In S. C. Yudosky & R. E. Hales (Eds.), *American Psychiatric Press Textbook of Neuropsychiatry* (2nd ed., pp. 57–88). Washington, DC: American Psychiatric Press..

Troster, A., Paolo, A., Lyons, K., Glatt, S., Hubble, J., & Koller, W. (1995). The influence of depression on cognition in Parkinson's disease: A pattern of impairment distinguishable from Alzheimer's disease. *Neurology, 45,* 672–676.

Tuokko, H., & Hadjistavropoulos, T. (1998). *An assessment guide to geriatric neuropsychology.* Mahwah, NJ: Lawrence Erlbaum Associates.

Tymchuk, A., Ouslander, J., Rahbar, B., & Fitten, L. (1988). Medical decision-making among elderly people in long term care. *Gerontologist, 28,* 59–63.

Van Gorp, W., Satz, P., & Matrushina, M. (1990). Neuropsychological processes associated with normal aging. *Developmental Neuropsychology, 6,* 279–290.

Vitaliano, P., Breen, A., Russo, J., Albert, M., Vitiello, M., & Prinz, P. (1984). The clinical utility of the Dementia Rating Scale for assessing Alzheimer patients. *Journal of Chronic Disabilities, 37,* 743–753.

Wagner, A., Teri, L., & Orr-Rainey, N. (1995). Behavior problems of residents with dementia in special care units. *Alzheimer Disease & Associated Disorders, 9,* 121–127.

Wechsler, D. (1981). *Wechsler Adult Intelligence Scale–Revised.* New York: Harcourt, Brace, Jovanovich.

Wechsler, D. (1987). *Wechsler Memory Scale–Revised.* New York: Psychological Corporation.

Welsh, K. A., Butters, N., Mohs, R. C., Beekly, D., Edland, S., Fillenbaum, G., & Heyman, A. (1994). The Consortium to Establish a Registry for Alzheimer's Disease (CERAD) Part V. A normative study of the neuropsychological battery. *Neurology, 44,* 609–614.

Welsh-Bohmer, K. A., Gearing, M., Saunders, A.. M., Roses, A. D., & Mirra, S. M (1997). Apolipoprotein E genotypes in a neuropathological series from the Consortium to Establish a Registry for Alzheimer's Disease (CERAD). *Annals of Neurology, 42,* 319–325.

Welsh-Bohmer, K. A., & Hoffman, J. M. (1996). Positron emission tomography neuroimaging in dementia. In E. Bigler (Ed.), *Neuroimaging II: Clinical applications* (pp. 185–222). New York: Plenum Press.

Welsh-Bohmer, K. A., & Mohs, R. C. (1997). Neuropsychological assessment of Alzheimer's disease. *Neurology, 49,* S11–S13.

Welsh-Bohmer, K. A., & Ogrocki, P. K. (1998). Clinical differentiation of memory disorders in neurodegenerative disease. In A. K. Troster (Ed.), *Memory in neurodegenerative disease: Biological, cognitive, and clinical perspectives* (pp. 290–313). New York: Cambridge University Press.

Willis, S., & Marsiske, M. (1991). Life span perspective on practical intelligence. In D. Tupper & K. Cicerone (Eds.), *The neuropsychology of everyday life: Issues in development and rehabilitation* (pp. 183–198). Boston: Kluwer.

Wilson, B. (1997). Cognitive rehabilitation: How it is and how it might be. *Journal of the International Neuropsychological Society, 3,* 487–496.

Yamaoka, L., Welsh-Bohmer, K. A., Hulette, C. M., Gaskell, P. C., Murray, M., Rimmler, J. L., Rosi-Helms, B., Guerra, M., Roses, A. D., Schmechel, D. E., & Pericak-Vance, M. A. (1996). Linkage of frontotemporal dementia to chromosome 17: Clinical and neuropathological characterization of phenotype. *American Journal of Human Genetics, 59,* 1306–1312.

Yesavage, J. (1985). Nonpharmacologic treatments for memory losses with normal aging. *American Journal of Psychiatry, 142,* 600–605.

Approaches
and Methodologies

CHAPTER THIRTEEN

The Flexible Battery Approach to Neuropsychological Assessment

Russell M. Bauer

Department of Clinical and Health Psychology,
University of Florida, Gainesville

Clinical neuropsychology represents an increasingly well-defined and well-respected specialty within the neuroscientific community. The field has enjoyed great success not only in contributing to scientific knowledge about brain–behavior relationships, but also in applying such knowledge through the provision of humane and effective assessment, treatment, and advocacy services for persons with central nervous system (CNS) impairment. Of all these activities, assessment of the behavioral and cognitive effects of brain disease has been by far the most common applied task performed by neuropsychologists (Meier, 1974), and a great number of testing instruments have emerged over the past few decades. These instruments, known as neuropsychological tests, represent formal observation-measurement systems in which behavior is examined under certain specified conditions and evaluated against normative or individual comparison standards (cf. Lezak, 1995).

Despite the fact that most neuropsychologists would agree as to the major purposes of the discipline, there is diversity of opinion about which procedures best achieve the goals of clinical assessment (Kane, 1991). Even when basic psychometric yardsticks such as test reliability and validity are considered, there is a wide range of opinion about the stability or accuracy of neuropsychological measures and about the relative importance of criterion-oriented versus construct validity considerations in test development. Because of this diversity, there are no consensually agreed-on "acid tests" or even empirical criteria (other than basic standards of reliability and validity) for including or excluding particular tests in one's neuropsychological toolbox. The selection of specific neuro-psychological tests thus remains an individual professional decision.

Most modern neuropsychological test procedures derive either from the psychometric tradition within clinical psychology (cf. Russell, 1986) or from the information-processing tradition in cognitive psychology (Neisser, 1967) and experimental neuropsychology (Ellis & Young, 1986; McCarthy & Warrington, 1990). Most contemporary neuropsychologists are sufficiently familiar with these two great traditions to be confronted by literally hundreds of instruments having potential diagnostic utility in the neuropsychological setting. As a result, every practicing neuropsychologist must make fundamental decisions about which tests to use, which cognitive abilities to sample, how to balance breadth and depth, and how to relate behavioral test data to the underlying (physical) neurological substrate.

The issue of test selection can be illustrated by considering the following two case scenarios.

Case 1: A 62-year-old patient is referred from the Inpatient Psychiatry unit with a 9-month history of depression and progressive intellectual decline. Over the past 9 months, she has gradually withdrawn from family and social activities, and has neglected personal finances and self-care. She is hospitalized for evaluation of recent well-formed visual hallucinations of "strangers in her house" and of her belief that her dead husband has sent these individuals to harass her. She has adapted well to the ward milieu, except that she needs prompting to perform even the most simple activities. She has not learned the names of her doctors and seems occasionally disoriented and lost when she attempts to return to her room from the dayroom.

Case 2: A 21-year-old college sophomore is referred for evaluation of the effects of a well-documented closed-head injury in an alcohol-related automobile accident 18 months prior to the evaluation. The accident occurred in the early morning hours when the car the patient was driving crossed the center line on a rural highway and struck an oncoming truck. His best friend, a front-seat passenger in the car, was killed instantly. The patient was comatose at the scene of the accident and has an extensive period of posttraumatic amnesia. Although the parents deny any preinjury problems, academic records indicate that he was a C–D student before his injury, and that he had not yet picked a major field. Current problems include memory impairment, aggression and irritability toward family and friends, and poor academic performance since his return to school 6 months ago. The patient's law firm requests the evaluation. The patient himself seems disinterested in the testing, and generally minimizes or denies having any significant postaccident problems.

The clinical issues faced by these two patients are quite different, and although both consultations may contain only minor variations on the simple request to "please evaluate," the referring professionals are likely to have very different questions in mind when they refer their patients for neuropsychological consultation. Although examination of Case 1 might require a detailed evaluation of intellectual and neuropsychological functioning and may incorporate formal evaluation of psychiatric symptoms, the evaluation of Case 2 might focus more specifically on academic achievement, learning ability, and the capacity for behavioral self-control. The results of neuropsychological assessment may have different treatment relevance in the two cases. Especially in Case 2, specific impairments that exist in memory and attention/concentration might be used to help plan rehabilitation efforts or to design appropriate educational experiences. In contrast, neuropsychological test performance in Case 1 might be used to assist a differential diagnosis between depression and dementia, and repeated testing over time might be used to chart the course of the disease or to assess the effects of an intervening treatment.

It is important to ask whether such differences in purpose or focus will be reflected in the neuropsychological assessment plan. Some clinicians take the point of view that, despite such differences, both referrals require, as a starting point, a comprehensive assessment of neuropsychological skills. For others, the tests selected in response to these two referrals will be quite different and will reflect the different goals of assessment in these two instances. The next chapter describes the *fixed battery approach,* in which the clinician gives the same tests to every patient regardless of the specific referral question. This chapter describes another approach, the *flexible battery* approach, in which the nature of the patient's neuropsychological deficits helps determine the direction the evaluation will take.

Before discussing the distinctive characteristics of the flexible battery approach, it should be noted that *flexibility* as a dimension in neuropsychological assessment refers more directly to a way of thinking about the neuropsychological assessment process than to the specific tests or assessment protocols that are used in the course of case evaluation. As shown later, many flexible battery clinicians do, in fact, utilize a limited "core" battery of neuropsychological tests (Milberg, Hebben, & Kaplan, 1986). However, such a core is used primarily to provide a basis for generating pertinent clinical hypotheses about the patient's neuropsychological status; the subsequent course of the evaluation and the manner in which such tests are used will depend on the strengths and weaknesses of the individual patient, and on the dimensions of performance that are important in describing the patient's problem (Goodglass, 1986).

The flexible battery approach is different, both practically and conceptually, from the fixed battery strategy. Such differences are discussed in the next section, after which an intermediate position between fixed and flexible approaches (the *multiple fixed battery*) is defined. Most flexible battery approaches emanate from a preferred theoretical position regarding (a) the manner in which behavioral impairment reflects underlying brain pathology and (b) the focus and methodology of the neuropsychological examination. Three such positions, the neuropsychological investigative programme of Luria, the European cognitive neuropsychology approach, and the Boston process approach, are highlighted. The specific skills and knowledge required of a flexible battery proponent are then described. Advantages and limitations of the flexible battery approach are then outlined. The chapter concludes with an assertion that both fixed and flexible battery approaches reflect an important part of our heritage and that effective clinical practice typically utilizes elements of both.

DISTINGUISHING FIXED AND FLEXIBLE BATTERIES

Fixed and flexible battery approaches have been distinguished in three ways. Important differences exist in (a) the nature and timing of test-selection decisions, (b) the relative reliance on psychometric versus neurologic concepts in conceptualizing the process and goals of neuropsychological assessment, and (c) the relative emphasis placed on quantitative versus qualitative performance criteria in case formulations and interpretations. Each of these distinctions is briefly discussed next.

Nature and Timing of Test-Selection Decisions

In the fixed battery approach, decisions regarding test selection are made a priori, whereas in the flexible battery approach, decision making occurs "online" in a Markovian (decision-tree-oriented) manner. Implementation of the flexible battery approach involves a process of selection, hypothesis testing, and selective attention to relevant subsets of data (Rourke & Brown, 1986). Data collection is selective in the sense that decisions made early in the assessment focus the specific direction the evaluation will take and thus limit the domains of behavior assessed (Rourke & Brown, 1986). Whether such selectivity clarifies the relevant issues or blinds the examiner to other important possibilities depends largely on whether correct decisions are made early in the process.

The flexible battery clinician views the neuropsychological examination as an "experiment-in-evolution" in that both the methods used and the results obtained change as a function of early data returns. For the most part, flexible batteries represent clinical applications of the classic hypothetico-deductive method, the purpose of which is to uncover meaningful cause–effect relationships between independent and dependent variables. Quantitative and qualitative performance measures comprise the relevant dependent measures. Three sets of independent variables (dimensions of brain function, organismic variables [age, education, preillness abilities, etc.], and task factors) combine interactively to produce the complex behavioral outcomes observed on neuropsychological tests.

One important feature of the hypothetico-deductive method is that possible accounts of a phenomenon (e.g., a test performance) are phrased in the form of experimental hypotheses that can be tested empirically. Attention is gradually focused on those hypotheses that survive experimental disconfirmation (Platt, 1966; Popper, 1959). The virtues of this approach to neuropsychological assessment are apparent when it is considered that most neuropsychological tests impose diverse input, processing, and output demands on the patient. That is, most neuropsychological tests are multifactorial; in addition to the more obvious "face valid" ways of describing neuropsychological tests as measures of memory, language, attention, and so on, a more microgenetic analysis suggests that such tests can be described and classified in terms of input (task), processing (solution), and output (response) requirements.

On the input side, most conventional neuropsychological tests provide stimuli to one sensory-perceptual channel (visual, auditory, tactile), so that hypotheses related to a pattern of deficits across tasks can be evaluated in terms of whether a specific sensory modality is involved. Second, tasks can be grouped in terms of whether they impose the same, or similar, information-processing requirements on subjects. For example, tests can be easily classified in terms of their focus on certain levels of processing (e.g., phonological, orthographic, semantic, etc.; see Craik & Lockhart, 1972) and in terms of their relative demands on data-driven versus conceptually driven processes (Jacoby, 1983). Finally, tasks can be described and classified in terms of the output demands (e.g., verbal, graphomotor, pointing, naming, etc.) imposed on the patient. Although this descriptive analysis of neuropsychological tests is intended to be heuristic, hypothesis disconfirmation is often threatened by the fact that most neuropsychological tests are not "pure" in terms of their input, processing, and output demands. Because of this, most tests can be failed (or passed) for a number of different reasons. Thus, simply knowing a patient's score on such a test may reveal little about why or how such a score was achieved. A flexible process of hypothesis formulation and hypothesis testing is frequently needed to more precisely characterize the nature of the impairment. This is why the flexible battery approach has sometimes been referred to as the "hypothesis-testing" approach (cf. Lezak, 1995).

The fundamentals of the flexible approach can be illustrated by considering a common clinical example. WAIS–R Digit Symbol is one of the most sensitive tests to acquired neurologic damage (Kaplan, Fein, Morris, & Delis, 1991; Lezak, 1995). It is a complex test that requires graphomotor speed, symbol manipulation, short-term memory, visual acuity, and manual dexterity. If Digit Symbol is impaired, a deficit in any or all of these skills might be implicated. Determining the cause of such impairment requires treating these dimensions as independent variables and then performing subsequent testing in which the potential influence of each variable is manipulated and the resulting effects on behaviors are observed. For example, the influence of unfamiliar symbol manipulation can be evaluated by presenting the patient with symbols and requiring the patient to respond with more familiar numbers (this is one basis of the

Symbol Digit Modalities Test; Smith, 1973). If the patient's performance level is improved by this maneuver, then a difficulty with processing of unfamiliar symbols remains as a viable explanation of the defect because its manipulation resulted in task improvement. If not, then other factors remain alive as rival explanations of the deficit in Digit Symbol. Subsequent testing would then attempt to evaluate the potential contribution of all potential factors that survived disconfirmation. In some cases, the examiner must create new tests or modify existing instruments for purposes of more precisely zeroing in on which input, processing, or output dimension is responsible for the patient's deficit. Neuropsychological modifications of existing psychometric tests have been a particularly important contribution of the Boston "process approach" to neuropsychological assessment (Kaplan, 1983, 1990; Kaplan et al., 1991; Milberg et al., 1986).

Reliance on Psychometric Versus Neurologic Concepts

Russell (1986) distinguished between psychometric and behavioral-neurologic approaches to neuropsychology, and the fixed versus flexible battery distinction reflects this dichotomy in a general way. The best historical example of the fixed battery approach, the Halstead–Reitan Neuropsychological Battery (HRNB; Reitan & Wolfson, 1993), arose directly from the parent field of "mental abilities testing," and flourished largely because of its formidable psychometric strengths. Among the most important of these was criterion-oriented validity; the HRNB has been shown in many studies to have proven utility in detecting the presence, lateralization, and localization of brain dysfunction as defined by neurologic criteria such as clinical examination and neuroradiological findings (Boll, 1981; Filskov & Goldstein, 1974; Kløve, 1974; Parsons, 1986). The focus on statistical prediction gave rise to a general reliance on a broad, fixed battery of tests as the fundamental basis of neuropsychological assessment. A broad, *comprehensive* battery was favored because of its perceived sensitivity and because of its ability to evaluate patients for general indications of brain dysfunction (Goldstein, 1986; Kane, 1991; Russell, 1986), and a *fixed* battery was favored because it encouraged rapid proliferation of a database necessary for establishing stable normative comparison standards.

Although psychometric approaches have focused on statistical prediction of brain damage from psychological tests, the neurologic approach has emphasized the examination of brain–behavior relationships through analysis of behavioral syndromes and pathognomic signs at the single-case level (cf. Rourke & Brown, 1986). This intensive "case-analytic" method has been particularly favored in settings in which neuropsychological assessment is conducted for purposes of qualifying, rather than identifying, the behavioral effects of brain damage. With recent advances in clinical and radiologic diagnosis in neurology (cf. Mazziotta & Gilman, 1992), neuropsychologists are consulted less frequently to detect or localize brain impairment. Instead, they are now more likely to be asked to evaluate the nature or underlying cause of a neuropsychological complaint (e.g., whether a memory problem is primarily rooted in encoding or storage operations), or to attempt to elicit behavioral signs that might help differentiate between two behaviorally similar disorders (e.g., organic dementia vs. dementia syndrome of depression; cf. Caine, 1986; LaRue et al., 1986; Richards & Ruff, 1989). Because of this, it is increasingly important to discover the specific character of the observed defect and the causes or factors responsible for its appearance. This is what Luria (1980), Vygotsky, and others have called "qualification of the symptom."

Recognition of the fundamental importance of this latter goal has led to the use of flexible batteries designed to be more specifically responsive to the deficits with which the individual patient presents. In describing the rationale underlying such flexibility, Luria (1980) wrote:

> The neuropsychologist who has the task of diagnosing a patient's condition does not know which process or which aspect of the patient's mental activity should be the focal point for subsequent investigation. He must first make preliminary studies of the patient's mental processes, and from these preliminary results he must single out the crucial changes and then subject them to further scrutiny. (p. 388)

Luria's flexible approach is based on the idea that the neuropsychological examination should be constructed so as to result in a qualitative, structural analysis of the patient's symptoms, rather than in binary statements regarding whether an ability is "spared" or "impaired."

Reliance on Quantitative Versus Qualitative Data

Although the psychometric tradition has been primarily concerned with the quantification and measurement of mental abilities, neurology has been more concerned with (a) eliciting characteristic signs and symptoms of brain disease, and (b) linking behavioral syndromes to regional brain function through a process of clinical-anatomic correlation. This distinction reflects a relative reliance on quantitative versus qualitative data, and some have argued that fixed battery clinicians rely more heavily on quantitative criteria, whereas flexible battery clinicians are more interested in qualitative data. Although this is generally true, it is important to note that adopting a flexible battery approach does not in any way require the clinician to neglect or deemphasize quantitative data, nor is it necessarily the case that fixed battery proponents are unconcerned with qualitative aspects of performance. As Incagnoli (1986) indicated, the quantitative/qualitative distinction refers more directly to the manner in which neuropsychological test data are evaluated rather than to the method of administration by which the data are obtained.

One of the most important contributions of psychometrics to neuropsychological assessment has been the introduction of a variety of neuropsychological tests that are comprised of a series of relatively homogeneous items, that involve at least interval-level measurement, and that meet appropriate standards of reliability and validity (Rourke & Brown, 1986). Such tests yield numerical scores (e.g., number of items passed), which can be evaluated by comparing the subject's performance to appropriate normative standards. Scores on individual tests are often combined in complex (multivariate) ways to form the basis for interpreting the results of the battery (cf. discussion of pattern analysis in the next chapter). For example, decades of research with the HRNB have yielded quantitative criteria for inferring presence or absence of brain impairment, laterality, lesion size/type (e.g., diffuse vs. focal; acute vs. chronic), and intrahemispheric locus of damage (Boll, 1981; Reitan & Wolfson, 1993; Russell, 1986; Russell, Neuringer, & Goldstein, 1970). It is important to recognize that strong reliance on quantitative indicators almost always implies a fixed battery approach because such indicators depend on rectangular data sets.

In contrast to a quantitative performance analysis, a qualitative analysis is primarily intended to reveal the factors responsible for failure or success on neuropsychological tests, rather than to indicate nominal success or failure. Concern with the reasons for impairment rather than the presence of impairment often requires adjustive testing procedures, because most neuropsychological tests can be failed (or passed) in a number of different ways. Thus, attempts to elicit qualitative signs of brain impairment have tended to involve a flexible battery approach. In the literature, the term *qualitative* has been used to describe analyses based either on the patient's approach to a cognitively complex task (the distinction between *process* and *achievement;* cf. Kaplan, 1983) or to refer to an analytic method designed to isolate the functional basis of a neuropsychological deficit in information-processing terms (Luria, 1980; McCarthy & Warrington, 1990). These two meanings of the term are discussed more fully in the next section.

Although I have aligned *fixed* with *quantitative* and *flexible* with *qualitative,* it is not accurate to say that fixed battery proponents are unconcerned with qualitative data or that flexible battery practitioners neglect quantitative criteria. Evidence to the contrary can be found in the writings of "fixed" (Reitan & Wolfson, 1993) and "flexible" (McKenna & Warrington, 1986) proponents alike, and the recent "process" modification of the WAIS–R (WAIS–R–NI; Kaplan et al., 1991) is a practical tour de force in how "qualitative" performance features can be measured and analyzed in quantitative terms. Lezak (1995) stated the majority opinion when she wrote,

> The integrated use of qualitative and quantitative examination data treats these two different kinds of information as different parts of the whole data base. Test scores that have been interpreted without reference to the context of the examination in which they were obtained may be objective but meaningless in their individual applications. Clinical observations unsupported by standardized and quantifiable testing, although full of import for the individual, lack the comparability necessary for many diagnostic and planning decisions. Descriptive observations flesh out the skeletal structure of numerical test scores. Each is incomplete without the other. (p. 151)

The main difference between fixed and flexible battery proponents appears to be in the relative weight given to quantitative and qualitative test data.

Rourke and Brown (1986) provided a convincing argument that quantitative and qualitative data are more closely related than they may seem at first glance. In fact, many "qualitative" performance dimensions have been quantified in meaningful ways (e.g., Goldberg & Costa, 1986; Kaplan et al., 1991). For example, Kaplan et al. (1991) advocated the use of a *scatter score*, which characterizes performance variability within several of the WAIS–R subtests. Each time the patient passes one item and fails the next (or vice versa), a scatter score of 1 is recorded (otherwise, a 0 is registered). Because items within each of these tests are difficulty graded, it is frequently the case that a patient will pass earlier items and will then reach a threshold beyond which failure will occur relatively consistently. Such a pattern will result in a relatively low scatter score. Large scatter results from the situation in which there is inconsistent responding from item to item, and may reflect variable effort, attentional fluctuations, or some other "state" variable. Quantitative evidence of such problems, derived from what is essentially a qualitative variable, may be important in the differential diagnosis of a variety of conditions, including epilepsy, attention deficit disorder, closed-head injury, major depressive disorder, or other forms of serious psychopathology.

AN INTERMEDIATE APPROACH: MULTIPLE FIXED BATTERIES

In many settings, the referral base is sufficiently varied, and the ability of the neuropsychologist sufficiently sophisticated, to result in the implementation of distinct protocols for different diagnoses, referral questions, or referral sources. Here, the clinician makes an a priori decision to tailor the assessment approach to the individual case by subjecting each homogeneous patient group to a different subset of available tests. Such decisions may be based on predictive validity considerations (e.g., what best predicts outcome or clinical status in a given population), or on a more informal assessment of what is meaningful and useful for a given question or referral source. This approach represents an intermediate position between fixed and flexible batteries in that it combines a priori test selection with a recognition that the neuropsychological test protocol should directly target the unique problems presented by different patient groups.

Three types of multiple fixed batteries can be distinguished: the general *screening* battery, the *population-specific* battery, and the *domain-specific* battery. General screening batteries contain a wide variety of maximally sensitive items designed to elicit clinically relevant abnormalities worthy of more detailed, follow-up testing. Population-specific batteries provide more extensive guidelines for the evaluation of individual patient populations or disease entities (e.g., dementia, epilepsy, HIV seropositive status, neurotoxic exposure, multiple sclerosis, etc.), and are in wide use in clinical research settings where the goal is to provide a selective but standardized evaluation of cognitive domains judged to be most relevant to diagnosis or treatment outcome. The domain-specific batteries contain procedures designed to provide a detailed assessment of a particular cognitive domain (e.g., language, memory, visuospatial/perceptual skill). Examples of each of these types of batteries are provided in Table 13.1.

The multiple fixed battery approach is, like the flexible battery, designed to be problem-specific. The specific cognitive skills that are sampled in such problem-specific batteries are based on empirical as well as clinical considerations. Available clinical and research literature serves as the basis for determining which clinical procedures (a) most likely differentiate target patients from those without the target deficit, and (b) yield information most relevant to clinical decision making. Such an approach requires a clinician who is experienced in dealing with the target population, and who is attuned to the diagnostic and prescriptive contributions that neuropsychological evaluation can make to patient care.

Although the decision to adopt a multiple fixed battery approach is often theory driven, such an approach may emerge for purely practical reasons. For example, the clinician may become aware that an individual referral source (an agency, a physician, a school system, a managed-care organization) makes use of a specific set of assessment instruments, so a decision is made to administer these instruments to any individual, regardless of specific diagnosis, referred from that source. For example, tests of intellectual ability and academic achievement might be included in any learning disability referral from the local school system, regardless of their apparent relevance for each individual case. The decision to employ such tests might be based primarily on statutory definitions of learning disability (e.g., a significant IQ–achievement split) and only secondarily on a theoretical model of learning disability. Similarly, a multiple fixed battery approach might informally evolve as a way of handling different referral questions. For example, a specific set of tests (including learning capacity, interpersonal adaptation and motivation, and vigilance) might be employed in a battery designed to assess rehabilitation potential, whereas a different set of tests might be employed in the evaluation of effects of epilepsy surgery. Decisions about which tests to include in the protocol should, of course, be based on a measured evaluation of the kinds of information needed to make important diagnostic or treatment decisions in the clinical environment.

Multiple fixed batteries can also be used in the form of a "tiered" approach to neuropsychological assessment. Here, increasingly stringent or restricted criteria are placed on neuropsychological test performances such that patients who meet certain criteria are subjected to further testing. Such an approach has been described as a *step battery* (Tarter & Edwards, 1986), and has been characterized as a method of "successive hurdles" (Rourke & Brown, 1986). Here, an initial screening battery is given to all patients, followed by specific tests designed to pursue potentially significant findings. Based on results of the initial screening

TABLE 13.1

Examples of Screening, Population-Specific, and Domain-Specific Batteries

Battery Name	Reference	Domains Assessed
Screening batteries		
Dementia Rating Scale (DRS)	Mattis (1988)	Attention, initiation, perseveration, memory, construction, language
Pittsburgh Initial Neuropsychological Test System (PINTS)	Goldstein, Tarter, Shelly, and Hegedus (1983)	Intelligence, memory, motor and constructional skill
Neurobehavioral Cognitive Status Examination (NCSE)	Kiernan et al. (1987); Mysiw, Beegan, and Gatens (1989)	Consciousness, orientation, attention, language (comprehension, naming), construction, memory, calculation, reasoning (similarities, judgement)
Population-specific batteries		
NIMH AIDS Battery	Butters et al. (1990)	Attention, speed of processing, memory, abstraction, language, visual perception, construction, motor functions, psychiatric symptoms
WHO Neurotoxicology Battery	WHO & Nordic Council (1985)	Visuomotor skill, reaction time, visual memory, mental tracking, mood
Epilepsy Battery	Dodrill (1978)	Intelligence, verbal and nonverbal memory, language screening, visuomotor skill, abstraction, attention, motor speed, sensory/perceptual
Multiple Sclerosis Battery	Peyser, Rao, LaRocca, and Kaplan (1990)	Global dementia screening, fund of information, attention–concentration, memory, language, visuospatial skills, abstract reasoning, concept formation
Consortium to Establish a Registry for Alzheimer's Disease (CERAD) Battery	Morris et al. (1989)	Verbal fluency, naming (Boston Naming Test), Mini-Mental State word list memory (three learning trials, one delayed recall trial, one recognition trial), constructional praxis

Continued

TABLE 13.1 *(continued)*

Battery Name	Reference	Domains Assessed
Domain-specific batteries		
Birmingham Object Recognition Battery	Riddoch and Humphreys (1993)	Object naming, object and semantic matching, decision tasks; visual screening; some tasks require direct matching, and others require matching across different views
Boston Diagnostic Aphasia Examination Boston Spatial-Quantitative Battery (BDAE and "Parietal Lobe Battery")	Goodglass and Kaplan (1972)	34 Subtests in 9 defined areas of language (fluency, auditory comprehension, naming, oral reading, repetition, paraphasia, automatic speech, reading comprehension, writing); 2 tests of musical competence; 7 subtests in the spatial-quantitative battery (drawing to command, stick memory, 3-D blocks, finger agnosia, right–left orientation, map orientation, arithmetic, clock setting)
Florida Affect Battery	Bowers, Blonder, and Heilman (1993)	Tests of facial affect processing, including naming, discrimination, and pointing; facial identity discrimination; vocal prosody discrimination and comprehension
Memory Assessment Clinics Memory Battery	Crook, Salama, and Gobert (1986); Crook & Larrabee (1988)	Facial recognition, paired-associate memory, facial memory (delayed nonmatch to sample), memory for object location, digit memory (telephone dialing), recall of TV news broadcast, reaction time in simulated automobile driving task; attempts to make memory testing more "ecologically valid"; computer-assisted
Multilingual Aphasia Examination	Benton and Hamsher (1989)	Visual naming, oral word productivity, auditory comprehension, repetition (MAE; memory span for words), spelling, reading comprehension, ratings of articulation and writing praxis
Western Aphasia Battery (WAB)	Kertesz (1979)	Similar in content to Boston Diagnostic Aphasia Examination

battery, a decision is made to expose the patient to one of several available sub-batteries designed to evaluate specific domains of neuropsychological performance. The decision to admit the patient for further testing is made on the basis of quantitative criteria (i.e., whether tests within the screening battery were passed or failed; Tarter & Edwards, 1986).

The screening tier usually addresses a broad range of neuropsychological functions (e.g., intellectual performance, attention, memory, language, visuoperceptual, and psychomotor processes). It is designed to be maximally sensitive and minimally specific to conditions producing neuropsychological impairment. Depending on the results obtained, a more restricted and in-depth battery of tests follows. For example, a more specific battery of memory tests would be given to a patient who, on the basis of the screening examination, has an apparent memory disorder. Similar domain-specific batteries could be created to evaluate patients with apparent disorders of language, attention, problem solving, and so forth. Several such domain-specific batteries might be employed by the clinician who wants to implement a more exhaustive evaluation of a neuropsychological deficit. The domain-specific batteries are populated by tests capable of yielding increasingly specific information about the patient's pattern of strengths and weaknesses within the target domain.

Tarter and Edwards (1986) provided a clear three-stage example of this approach. The first stage involves a screening battery that measures a broad variety of skills, including intellect, memory, language, perceptual skill, problem solving, and attention. Because of the nature of the screening battery, only a limited number of maximally sensitive tests is included. If the patient does well on the screening battery, assessment is terminated. If the patient fails a particular area, he or she is admitted to the second stage, which involves either intensive assessment of specific modalities (e.g., vision) or a specialized set of tests designed to provide a more in-depth evaluation of one or more of the major categories of neuropsychological skill (e.g., memory, language, or executive skill). Based on the results of this stage, assessment is either terminated or the patient is admitted for what Tarter and Edwards called *idiographic testing*. This phase of the evaluation is appropriate when specific aspects of the case call for more specialized assessment than would normally be afforded by the fixed battery. Tarter and Edwards cautioned against a formalized decision tree in this phase, suggesting that, "at this stage of the assessment, clinician judgement and experience are crucial for selecting the most appropriate measures and for obtaining maximal information . . . from the client" (p. 146).

THREE FLEXIBLE APPROACHES

Having described the basic features of the flexible battery approach, we now turn to a brief review of the basic conceptual models that most flexible battery clinicians employ in clinical practice. In addition to the distinguishing features I described in a previous section, flexible batteries are different from fixed batteries in that they typically are conducted from the point of view of a theoretical model of brain function. Because of this, most flexible battery clinicians construct their assessments in a way that will conform to theoretical assumptions about the manner in which specific kinds of brain damage will affect cognitive abilities. These models guide clinicians in understanding and conceptualizing the ways in which cognitive abilities are affected by neurological disease, and provide a basis for test selection.

One of the distinctive characteristics of the flexible battery approach to neuropsychological assessment is its hypothesis-testing orientation. The specific hypotheses that are tested in a given patient are largely dependent on the clinician's theoretical preferences. Three conceptual frameworks that commonly drive hypothesis formulation in the flexible battery framework include the neuropsychological investigative program of Luria (1973), the cognitive neuropsychology approach (Ellis & Young, 1986; McKenna & Warrington, 1986; McCarthy & Warrington, 1990) and the Boston "process" approach to neuropsychological assessment (Milberg et al., 1986; Kaplan, 1983, 1990; Kaplan et al., 1991). Each of these frameworks is briefly described next.

Luria's Neuropsychological Investigation

Luria's (1980) neuropsychological investigation is most widely known in the United States through Christensen's (1979) compilation of his qualitative techniques into a coherent battery. Luria's assessment approach is based on an integrated theory of brain function, and his neuropsychological assessment techniques flow directly from specific aspects of his theory. The key relevance of Luria's views for neuropsychological assessment lies in his belief that the fundamental purpose of neuropsychological assessment is to describe the functional nature of neuropsychological symptoms, rather than their presence or absence in a given case. Luria's approach is thus essentially qualitative, and is designed to describe the conditions under which a patient's problem becomes "clinically significant."

One of Luria's most important contributions was the introduction and formalization of the notion of a *functional system* in the brain. In Luria's terms, a functional system in the brain consists of a collection of brain regions and their interconnections that operates in an integrated, dynamic way to form the substrate for a complex psychological function. In the normal brain, for example, complex skills such a memory or perceptual ability are not discretely localized; instead, such processes depend on the integrated activity of diverse, hierarchically organized brain areas. Taking memory as an example, several decades of research have implicated mesial temporal, diencephalic, and basal forebrain structures as the neural substrate for different forms of memory and learning

(Bauer, Tobias, & Valenstein, 1995; Squire, 1987). It makes sense to speak of this distributed anatomic substrate as a functional system because such diverse regions appear to function in an integrated fashion to support complex memory skills. For our purposes, the most important aspect of the functional systems view is the idea that the nature of the patient's cognitive deficit (i.e., the specific symptoms the patient exhibits) will differ depending on the specific location of the damage within the functional system, and on the response of the other (undamaged) system components to the loss. As indicated earlier, Luria believed that the neuropsychological investigation should be patient and problem centered, and was particularly strong in his point of view that the examiner *could not know* what tests to give without first conducting preliminary evaluation of the patient's symptoms. Based on this preliminary analysis, specialized procedures designed to systematically explore the role of specific cognitive demands and input–ouput factors are then conducted. For Luria, the properly constructed examination included tests of simple, complex, and integrative skill. Examination increasingly focuses on the manner in which problems are solved, rather than on whether they are solved.

Luria (1980) specifically rejected the use of a fixed battery, which he saw as useful only in providing general indications of brain impairment. He wrote:

> In order to gain a better understanding of the nature of the defects interfering with the performance of a particular task and to identify as precisely as possible the factor(s) responsible for the difficulties, it is not enough to merely carry out a particular experiment in the standard manner. The experiment must be suitably modified so that the conditions . . . making the performance of the test more difficult, as well as those enabling compensation to take place, can be taken into account. (p. 392)

In addition to formalizing the notion of a functional system and describing pioneering assessment methods, Luria's approach is important because it emphasizes the need to understand complex patterns of symptom presentation (the so-called *syndrome analysis* that is central to behavioral neurology) and their clinicopathological correlations with regional brain impairments. Because various brain regions potentially participate in a number of functional systems, localized brain lesions frequently lead to disturbances in a group of functional systems. The result is what Luria called a *symptom-complex* or syndrome, made up of "externally heterogeneous, but, in fact, internally interconnected symptoms" (Luria, 1980, p. 83). Thus, for example, large lesions in the left parieto-temporal-occipital junction may be associated with disturbances of language, praxis, visual object processing, naming, and other cognitive skills. Discovering and analyzing the basis of such symptom co-occurrence was, for Luria, an essential goal of the neuropsychological examination. As shown later, this means that the clinician practicing within this kind of flexible battery framework must have working knowledge of such syndromes if he or she is to appropriately plan and interpret a neuropsychological examination.

Cognitive Neuropsychology

The test-analytic strategy of European cognitive neuropsychology provides another example of the use of flexible-adjustive assessment methods. The cognitive neuropsychology approach is a relatively new approach that represents a hybrid between syndrome analysis in classical behavioral neurology and the information-processing tradition in cognitive psychology (Ellis & Young, 1986; McCarthy & Warrington, 1990). The major goal of cognitive neuropsychology as a discipline is to utilize findings from brain-impaired individuals to inform and constrain available theories of specific cognitive processes. Thus, assessments within this tradition are performed from the viewpoint of a particular *theory or model of normal cognitive functioning* (Coltheart, 1985; Ellis & Young, 1986). It is assumed that neurologic diseases produce orderly patterns of breakdown that reflect the way in which cognitive abilities are normally organized in the brain. Thus, an underlying model of normal function not only informs the clinical evaluation, but also must account for selective neuropsychological disturbances seen in the clinic. In practice, the underlying theory leads to the development of assessment methods, and the results of assessment lead to further modifications in theoretical approach. Thus, the road between the clinic and the laboratory is a two-way street. Excellent examples of this bidirectionality are evident in the manner in which recent cognitive neuropsychological models of object and face recognition (e.g., Bruce & Young, 1986) or reading (e.g., Marshall & Newcombe, 1973) have resulted in the introduction of new, highly specific, neuropsychological tests (see Riddoch & Humphreys, 1993). As Shallice (1988) pointed out, the cognitive neuropsychology approach dates back at least to Wernicke's (1874) description of behavioral subtypes of aphasia, and his introduction of a model of language function that actually predicted the existence of patients who at that point had not yet been clinically discovered.

Flexible assessment procedures are important to the cognitive neuropsychology approach because different patients will suffer impairment at different points in the model. Observing behavioral dissociations (selective impairments in some skills, but not in others) is centrally important in drawing inferences about cognitive structure from neuropsychological test data, because they reveal something about how such skills are normally organized in the brain and help localize the deficit within the overall organizational scheme (McCarthy & Warrington, 1990; Shallice, 1988; Teuber, 1955).

For example, suppose a patient presents to the clinic with a specific inability to decipher the meaning of emotional facial expressions, but is able to recognize facial identity and can extract age, gender, and other information from visual analysis of faces. The selectivity of this deficit serves as preliminary evidence that "emotion recognition" represents a discrete component in the overall organization of face recognition abilities. This possibility will be strengthened if another patient can be found who shows the opposite pattern of performance.

This is what is called a *double dissociation*, and constitutes the strongest evidence of underlying cognitive structure because it rules out the possibility that the first patient's problem arose simply because emotion recognition was more difficult than recognizing age, gender, or identity.

Because the cognitive neuropsychology approach is driven by an underlying theory of information-processing, research within this tradition has resulted in the discovery of new patients and in the creation of new tests of highly specific neuropsychological skill. As indicated earlier, this was a striking characteristic of Wernicke's (1874) model of language disturbances. One good contemporary example comes from British work on visual object recognition (Humphreys & Riddoch, 1987; McCarthy & Warrington, 1990). Impairment in the ability to visually identify objects may result from significant primary visual sensory impairment, from higher order perceptual difficulty, or from a failure in relating normal perception to stored memories of what familiar objects look like. In order to distinguish these possibilities, specific tests have been constructed at each of these three levels. At the first level, it is important to determine whether the patient has sufficient visual field, acuity, and shape discrimination abilities to allow object recognition. At the second level, it is important to determine whether the patient is capable of forming an integrated visual percept of an object, and to ascertain whether the patient is able to perceptually categorize objects as belonging to the same functional or semantic class. Patients have been described, for example, who are capable of identifying the broad category to which a viewed object belongs but who fail to appreciate the object's specific identity (Warrington, 1975). The ability to form an integrated percept might be tested by requiring the subject to match familiar objects across different views (Warrington & James, 1986), whereas tests of perceptual categorization might require the subject to determine whether two objects belong together (McCarthy & Warrington, 1986). It is important to recognize that such tests often are not available on the commercial market, and are usually constructed in the course of evaluating a single patient or a homogeneous group. For this reason, formal clinical application of the cognitive neuropsychology approach has not been widespread, at least in the United States, but this is changing (see Riddoch & Humphreys, 1993, in Table 1).

The Boston Process Approach

A third example of a flexible battery framework is the Boston *process approach* to neuropsychological assessment (Kaplan, 1983, 1990; Milberg et al., 1986). Drawing on the seminal contributions of Werner (1937), the process approach is based on the assumption that observing and reporting the manner in which a patient solves a problem (performance process) is more important in understanding the patient's neuropsychological status than is simply observing and reporting success or failure (task achievement). Qualitative data about the patient's problem-solving approach is thought to be more useful than global summary scores in assisting rehabilitative professionals who work toward remediating a cognitive deficit or who monitor recovery from brain injury.

Practice within the process approach involves increasingly fine-grained analysis of a patient's cognitive deficit by (a) systematically exploring and exploiting the information-processing requirements of otherwise standard tasks by attempting to control the input, processing, and output demands, and (b) requiring the subject to perform increasingly sensitive or "process-pure" measures until the specific nature of a cognitive deficit can be determined. Decisions regarding which tests to employ are made on the basis of early data returns. An emphasis is placed on qualitative performance variables (e.g., how an item is passed or failed) in addition to whether it is passed or failed. In her workshops, Edith Kaplan gives the following example: A patient who gets 8 of 9 blocks correct on the more difficult trials of block design will earn the same 0 score as a patient who eats or throws the blocks. But it is obviously critical to distinguish these two performances, because they might mean something different as far as the underlying neuropsychological basis for the test failure is concerned.

Proponents of the process approach contend that the strategy employed by the patient in attempting to solve problems must be examined if the patient is to be properly understood. Such strategies reflect a complex mix of variables related to preillness status (e.g., educational and occupational history, handedness, specific talents) and to the patient's neurologic disease itself (e.g., lesion laterality, intrahemispheric focus, etiology). Because each patient will be characterized by a unique combination of these variables, the specific approach and testing procedures employed to elucidate the nature of a neuropsychological deficit may differ substantially from patient to patient.

Although the process approach utilizes many of the same clinical tests that are found in common fixed batteries, standardized tests are frequently modified to answer specific questions which arise during initial aspects of testing. The examiner may choose to "test the limits" by allowing the subject more time to complete the problem or by providing specific structure or cueing not present in the standard administration format. Importantly, such modifications are not random attempts to provide more data, but are motivated by a knowledge of the neuropsychological demands imposed by each task and by an understanding of how specific neuropathological processes can affect response strategy. Two specific examples of strategic variables that have received recent attention will illustrate this basic point.

Featural Versus Configurational Processing. Most common neuropsychological tests consist of a series of elements or stimuli arranged together within a spatial, temporal, or conceptual framework (Milberg et al., 1986). Therefore, one important strategic variable is the extent to which the patients differentially respond to low-level detail ("features") versus higher level configural or contextual information. According to proponents of the process approach, the featural versus configural dichotomy becomes particularly important in light of recent evidence that the left and right hemispheres may differ in their reliance on featural (left) versus configurational (right) processing. If this is true, then qualitatively different patterns of performance deficit might be expected to result from unilateral lesions of the right versus left hemisphere. This has been demonstrated in studies of Block Design performance in unilateral stroke patients (cf. Kaplan et al., 1991). Patients with right hemisphere strokes (who suffer a relative impairment in configurational processing) more often break the 2 × 2 or 3 × 3 configuration, whereas patients with left-hemisphere damage (who are relatively impaired in the ability to process features) preserve the overall configuration but have specific difficulty correctly reproducing internal details (Kaplan, 1990; Kaplan et al., 1991). According to Milberg et al. (1986), the featural–configural distinction is not restricted to Block Design, but is a relatively stable variable that can manifest itself in numerous neuropsychological tests.

Hemispatial Priority. The two cerebral hemispheres differ not only in terms of their specific information-processing contributions to complex tasks, but also in their contribution to overall deployment of attention across visual space. Although the attentional capacities of the two hemispheres are probably not equal, it is generally true, given the contralateral organization of sensory and motor skills, that each hemisphere "prefers" to process information and to direct activity in contralateral hemispace. That is, the right hemisphere likely is dominant in mediating activity taking place in the left side of personal space, and vice versa.

These considerations have led Kaplan (1990; Kaplan et al., 1991) to formulate a general rule that can be used to qualitatively evaluate performance on any task that takes place on both sides of the midline. This general rule states that *the patient will prefer to work, or will perform better, in the side of space contralateral to the more intact hemisphere.* Again using a Block Design example, the patient with a unilateral right-hemisphere lesion will be more likely to begin block construction on the right side of the design (contralateral to the more intact left hemisphere) and will construct the design in an unusual right-to-left manner. Because most individuals in Western cultures adopt a left-to-right strategy (because of the bias imposed by reading), perturbations of this dominant approach may have implications for diagnosing lesion laterality. This general principle can be used to qualitatively interpret any test in which stimuli or responses are distributed across both sides of space.

Because of its emphasis on the patient's problem-solving strategy, the process approach focuses on qualitative performance variables in addition to standard quantitative scores. As indicated earlier, however, such variables can be quantified and subjected to the same type of normative process as more traditional "achievement" measures. In fact, this has been accomplished for selected tests and is a major feature of the WAIS–R–NI (WAIS–R as a Neuropsychological Instrument), a process-oriented approach to intellectual testing (Kaplan et al., 1991). In this context, it should be noted that adopting a process approach does not require the examiner to forfeit the usual quantitative scores; where possible, modifications to test administration have been designed in such a way as to allow the usual scores to be calculated. The reader is directed to the WAIS–R–NI manual for further details.

These three approaches share a common belief that the goal of neuropsychological assessment should be to discover the specific nature of the patient's cognitive deficits. Although they emphasize different aspects of the overall picture, all seek to uncover the "structure" of such deficits, and all go beyond provision of quantitative summary scores or indices. One additional feature common to all three approaches is that the clinician practicing the flexible battery must have certain skills and knowledge about brain-behavior relationships in order to implement them effectively. It is to this topic that we now turn.

SKILLS REQUIRED
OF THE FLEXIBLE BATTERY CLINICIAN

One of the primary goals of the flexible battery approach is to provide neuropsychological assessments that are responsive to the specific questions contained within a professional consultation or to the specific problems presented by an individual patient or patient population. In order to be effective in pursuing this goal, the neuropsychologist must be able to integrate various sources of information in formulating a neuropsychological assessment plan that is maximally useful to the patient and other health care professionals. In the medical area, the neuropsychologist must possess basic knowledge of neurology, internal medicine, psychiatry, and other specialties, and in particular must understand neuropsychological implications of those neurologic, systemic, and psychiatric diseases that are likely to present in the neuropsychologist's setting. Because the neuropsychologist functions within an interdisciplinary environment, he or she must also have a basic understanding of major diagnostic tools within clinical medicine that are relevant for functional localization or differential diagnosis of brain disease. The neuropsychologist is likely to frequently encounter information derived from the clinical neurologic exam and from diagnostic procedures such as computed tomography (CT), magnetic resonance imaging (MRI), electroencephalograph (EEG), or functional neuroimaging. Because of this, the neuropsychologist should have at least a basic understanding of the goals, technological basis, and possible outcomes of each of these procedures (see DeMyer, 1974; Mazziotta & Gilman, 1992).

The neuropsychologist practicing within a flexible battery framework normally possesses basic knowledge in the behavioral manifestations of major neurologic syndromes. Thus, basic biomedical, neurologic, neuroradiologic, and behavioral manifestations of the major neurologic syndromes (stroke, dementia, epilepsy, closed-head injury, degenerative disorders, congenital and developmental disorders, neoplastic disorders, substance abuse, and psychopathological states [e.g., depression, schizophrenia]) will guide initial decisions about the tests that are likely to be fruitful in describing the nature of a patient's cognitive deficits.

One of the primary issues facing the clinician who uses a flexible battery concerns the manner in which decisions are made regarding test selection. If such rules are not articulated, or if they are not based on neurobehaviorally sound principles, the resulting approach can, at best, be subjective, difficult to teach, and impossible to replicate. (This problem has, in fact, been a major criticism by advocates of the fixed battery approach, who argue that such decision rules have never been explicitly articulated and that, as a result, practice within a flexible battery approach is more a matter of art than of applied neuropsychological science). Although the experience of the clinician may play an important role in the efficiency and accuracy of decision-tree-oriented approaches to clinical assessment (Kleinmuntz, 1968), this in itself does not convincingly argue for or against a particular approach.

The flexible battery clinician generally selects tests that satisfy certain specific criteria thought to be important either for functional localization or for characterizing the nature of a neuropsychological deficit in information-processing terms. In order to intelligently select tests, the flexible battery clinician needs to be generally familiar with both of these general areas. With regard to functional localization, the past two decades of neuropsychological research, together with advances in neuroanatomic analysis, have revealed numerous orderly relationships between damage to specific neural systems and appearance of specific neuropsychological syndromes and deficits (cf. Tranel, 1992, for an excellent review). Such findings permit unprecedented correlation of specific psychological processes with damage to localized brain regions. Various symptoms and syndromes resulting from damage to frontal, temporal, parietal, and occipital regions are widely known within the behavioral neurology literature, and have been delineated with sufficient specificity to have meaningful impact on neuropsychological test selection. Furthermore, our understanding of the neuroanatomic correlates of specific neurologic diseases (e.g., Alzheimer's disease, closed-head injury, viral infections of the central nervous system [CNS], anoxia, aquired immune deficiency syndrome [AIDS], specific stroke syndromes) has advanced to the point where distinctive patterns of neuropsychological presentation, couched in information-processing terms, are proving useful in differential diagnosis.

One specific example of how advancements in functional localization can help inform neuropsychological test selection concerns the differential diagnosis of dementia vs. depression. It is known, for example, that an early neuropathological signature of Alzheimer's disease involves damage to the medial temporal-hippocampal region (Hyman et al., 1984), and that, as the disease progresses, it likely spreads to include parietal and frontal association cortices. An early behavioral feature of Alzheimer's disease is a marked anterograde memory impairment, and as the disease progresses, the gradual involvement of association cortex is likely responsible for the increasingly severe fallout in premorbidly acquired knowledge and semantic memory, and for the disturbances in language that become so prominent later in the disease. The cognitive symptoms of Alzheimer's disease may be difficult to distinguish from the memory dysfunction and cognitive slowing characteristic of the "dementia syndrome of depression" (Caine, 1986), particularly during early stages of the illness. However, an understanding of the neural substrate underlying depressive illness may yield important clues for differential diagnosis if the neuropsychological examination is planned accordingly.

Recent evidence suggests that subcortical white matter changes and an increased ventricle-to-brain ratio are two neurobehavioral markers that may predispose to depression in geriatric populations (Jeste, Lohr, & Goodwin, 1988; Morris & Rapoport, 1990), but little if any data exists to suggest specific involvement of either the medial temporal/hippocampal system or of association cortex. Thus, neuropsychological tests of new learning and of semantic memory might be useful in distinguishing between depression and dementia. Indeed, there is some evidence that depressives, but not demented individuals, can make use of categorical cueing in list-learning (Weingartner et al., 1982). Independent studies suggest that demented, but not depressed, individuals frequently show language impairment including prominent naming defects (Bayles & Tomoeda, 1983; Cummings & Benson, 1992; Whitworth & Larson, 1989) and an increased category/exemplar ratio (increased production of categorical designations like *furniture, fruit,* and *clothes* relative to specific exemplars like *chair, orange,* and *sweatshirt*) in verbal fluency tasks, suggesting a disruption of semantic memory organization (cf. Rosen, 1980). These data makes it clear that including a detailed, qualitative evaluation of semantic memory, language, and new learning is essential to this specific differential diagnosis. Importantly, different domains of functioning might be more important evaluative foci in other diagnostic contexts, and it is thus important for the flexible battery clinician to be aware of the manner of presentation of the major forms of neurologic disease.

The flexible battery proponent must also be aware of the information-processing characteristics of a large number of neuropsychological tests. It is customary to describe neuropsychological tests in terms of the overall cognitive skill they are intended to measure. Thus, it is common to describe a test as measuring short-term memory, naming, constructional skill, abstract concept formation, and so on. As indicated earlier, however, most commonly used neuropsychological tests are multifactorial, and can be analyzed in terms of the input, processing, and output demands they impose on the patient. Understanding neuropsychological tests at this "microgenetic" level allows the clinician to evaluate resulting patterns of failure and success in light of the possibility that specific aspects of the patient's information-processing capacity have been disturbed.

The flexible battery clinician must be prepared to consider such microgenetic task demands in evaluating patterns of neuropsychological deficit, and must be concerned about whether performances on various tasks that share input, processing, or output demands lead to convergent conclusions about the locus of impairment. Suppose a patient displays significant deficits on a variety of neuropsychological tests including WAIS–R Digit Symbol, WMS–R Visual Reproduction, the Rey–Osterrieth Complex Figure, Grooved Pegboard, Luria Recursive Writing Sequences, and Thurstone (written) Verbal Fluency. Such a pattern of deficits could mean that the patient has diffuse brain disease manifested by defects in psychomotor speed, visual memory, language, and complex motor sequencing. However, this pattern of deficits can be explained more simply by noting that all of these tests require either graphomotor or fine motor output. Understanding such commonalities makes it less likely that a clinician will simply accept the "face valid" explanation of what each test measures (e.g., Digit Symbol measures "psychomotor ability," Visual Reproduction measures "visual memory," etc.), and makes it more likely that the clinician will seek to explain deficit patterns in more parsimonious ways. It should be pointed out that such considerations are firmly rooted in the widely accepted notion (cf. Campbell & Fiske, 1959) that most measures of psychologically meaningful constructs should be evaluated in terms of both *trait variance* (the neuropsychological function[s] tapped by the test) and *method variance* (the manner in which such function[s] are affected by the specific assessment method).

ADVANTAGES AND LIMITATIONS
OF THE FLEXIBLE BATTERY APPROACH

When compared to the more prevalent use of a fixed battery, the flexible battery approach has certain clear advantages and limitations (Kane, 1991). As can be seen from preceding sections, a major advantage in the use of flexible batteries is that a precise description of the patient's deficits from the viewpoint of some specific neuropsychological model is an achievable goal. Because the course of the examination is problem dependent, proponents argue that the flexible battery is more economical and time-efficient (Kane, 1991). Thus, it is argued, a specific, focused referral question might be answered by giving only a few procedures rather than a full battery of tests. Although this is generally true, it is sometimes the case that precise characterization of the nature of a neuropsychological deficit may involve follow-up testing that is actually more time-consuming and exacting than if a standard battery had been used.

The flexible battery is easy to alter based either on the introduction of new tests or advancements in research. Fixed batteries are, by their nature, more difficult to revise, and there is a practical limit as to how many new tests can be added.

A fixed battery that assays a number of cognitive functions is sometimes seen as more clinically sensitive than a highly selective flexible battery, particularly if, in selecting a battery, there has been insufficient sampling of cognitive domains relevant to the patient's problem. The counterargument is that the knowledgeable flexible battery clinician will rarely make such an error because test selection is guided by an understanding of the domains of functioning that are relevant in the individual context. In a related argument, some fixed battery proponents have argued that, by using a standard battery, unsuspected strengths and weaknesses can be evaluated (Kane, 1991).

Proponents of the fixed battery approach have sometimes depicted the flexible battery approach as too "deficit centered," and have suggested that the flexible approach gives short shrift to the patient's cognitive strengths. This argument seems inconsistent with the fact that one of the goals of a flexible approach is to reveal circumstances under which the requirements of a task allow the patient to compensate effectively for the deficit (Luria, 1980).

One clear advantage of the fixed battery approach is that the repeated administration of a standard corpus of tests permits the development of a normative base against which patient performance can be evaluated, whereas the use of a flexible, changeable battery makes the building of a normative database more difficult. However, it should be emphasized that the process of test standardization and norms collection is not the exclusive bailiwick of the fixed battery clinician. For example, most practitioners of the Boston process approach do, in fact, rely on a "core" set of tests that have proven useful in generating the kinds of clinical hypotheses on which the flexible battery depends (Milberg et al., 1986), and recent publication of norms for both quantitative (Borod, Goodglass, & Kaplan, 1980) and qualitative (Kaplan et al., 1991) aspects of this battery will narrow the gap between fixed and flexible batteries on this issue.

Because a fixed battery involves the standard administration of a predetermined series of tests, it can be administered by a trained technician or psychometrician, who can collect and score the data for later interpretation by the neuropsychologist. Thus, the fixed battery approach might be considered more cost-effective because it does not require large amounts of professional administration time. Although this may, in principle, be possible within the flexible battery framework, effective use of a flexible battery often requires the examiner to have more advanced knowledge of neurologic syndromes, functional anatomy, and psychopathology. Also, use of a technician seems somewhat inconsistent with the general view among flexible battery proponents that direct interaction with the patient and observation of microgenetic aspects of behavior are important sources of information in interpreting test results that require a professional level of competence.

A final issue has to do with comparative strengths and weaknesses of these two approaches when it comes to training of clinical neuropsychologists. In my view, students should learn the fundamentals of both fixed and flexible approaches, because such learning almost assuredly requires the student to understand neuropsychological assessment in historical perspective. In practicum training, initial training within a fixed battery approach has certain benefits for the beginning student. The opportunity to master a standard, comprehensive battery may be an effective way to learn how to administer neuropsychological tests, to gain an appropriate understanding of psychometric issues, and to acquire basic skills in test interpretation (e.g., the use of appropriate comparison standards; see Lezak, 1995). After students gain experience with actual clinical application, they can then learn to vary procedures, generate and test idiographic hypotheses, and more precisely examine the compensatory strategies the patient attempts to use in response to their cognitive impairment. Because flexible battery approaches flow directly from underlying models of brain function, they provide a conceptual framework within which advanced students can begin to understand how complex skills are functionally organized in the brain. This conceptual framework provides a rational basis for acquiring skills in neuropsychological interviewing and behavioral observation, and provides the foundation on which test-selection decisions are made. Training within a flexible battery approach more firmly grounds the student in behavioral neuroscience, and seems a particularly effective method for helping students acquire an appreciation of construct validity in neuropsychological assessment, because it focuses centrally on the underlying skills and abilities responsible for success and failure on specific tests.

SUMMARY AND CONCLUSIONS

The flexible battery approach to neuropsychological assessment represents a measured attempt to systematically adopt a decision-tree-oriented approach to clinical evaluation. Proponents of this approach contend that it involves a process of assessment, and yields the kind of results that are most relevant to what Luria and Vygotsky described as "qualification of the symptom." All flexible battery approaches attempt to provide a functional description of the patient's neuropsychological status, and depend on a priori models of brain function and dysfunction as guides to clinical decision making during assessment. Major examples of this approach include Luria's investigative program, the European cognitive neuropsychology tradition, and the Boston process approach to neuropsychological assessment.

Because the flexible battery approach is Markovian in nature, the clinician must possess certain background information so that the decision tree is implemented systematically and so that decisions are based on sound neuroscientific and psychological principles. Such information includes knowledge of etiologic factors in brain disease, knowledge of neurologic signs and symptoms, and an understanding of clinical diagnostic tests employed by other medical and non-medical disciplines. It further includes advanced knowledge about the quantitative and qualitative bases of a formidable array of available neuropsychological tests and about how to creatively apply and modify such tests in response to the needs of the individual patient.

From time to time, proponents of the flexible approach have sparred with fixed battery proponents regarding which approach is more neurobehaviorally sound, relevant to the kinds of referral questions most commonly faced by contemporary neuropsychologists, or more likely to lead to advances in our understanding of brain-behavior relationships. Although such debates are interesting and entertaining, they have shed more heat than light on clinical practice because they have commonly assumed that "which is the better approach?" can be answered by considering the "weight of evidence" in favor of one or the other strategy. As I have argued, the fixed and flexible battery approaches are most strongly distinguished not by the adoption of particular procedures but by the manner in which the resulting data are collected and analyzed. The fixed battery approach most commonly appeals to concepts developed within the psychometric tradition, whereas the flexible battery approach most commonly utilizes neurologic and information-processing constructs. Because of their distinct roots, each approach plays an important role in the professional activity of neuropsychologists and in the training of new scientist-practitioners. These two traditions provide alternative, but not mutually exclusive, frameworks for conceptualizing quantitative and qualitative data, and, as I have indicated, recent attempts have been made to bridge the quantitative–qualitative distinction. Although this chapter has emphasized the virtues of the flexible battery approach, it should be recognized that the most effective clinical practice will be one that recognizes, utilizes, and attempts to further our diverse heritage in psychometrics, neuroscience, and cognitive psychology.

REFERENCES

Bauer, R. M., Tobias, B. A., & Valenstein, E. (1993) Amnesic disorders. In K. M. Heilman & E. Valenstein (Eds.), *Clinical neuropsychology* (3rd ed., pp. 523–602). New York: Oxford University Press.

Bayles, K., & Tomoeda, C. K. (1983). Confrontation naming impairment in dementia. *Brain and Language, 19*, 98–114.

Benton, A. L., & Hamsher, K. de S. (1989). *Multilingual aphasia examination* (2nd ed.). Iowa City, IA: AJA Associates.

Boll, T. J. (1981). The Halstead–Reitan neuropsychology battery. In S. B. Filskov & T. J. Boll (Eds.), *Handbook of clinical neuropsychology* (Vol. 1, pp. 577–608). New York: John Wiley & Sons.

Borod, J. C., Goodglass, H., & Kaplan, E. (1980). Normative data on the Boston Diagnostic Aphasia Examination, Parietal Lobe Battery, and the Boston Naming Test. *Journal of Clinical Neuropsychology, 2*, 209–216.

Bowers, D., Blonder, L. X., & Heilman, K. M. (1993). *Florida Affect Battery.* Gainesville: University of Florida.

Bruce, V., & Young, A. W. (1986). Understanding face recognition. *British Journal of Psychology, 77,* 305–327.

Butters, N., Grant, I., Haxby, J., Judd, L. J., Martin A., McClelland, J., Pequegnat, W., Schacter, D., & Stover, E. (1990). Assessment of AIDS-related cognitive changes: Recommendations of the NIMH Workgroup on neuropsychological assessment approaches. *Journal of Clinical and Experimental Neuropsychology, 12,* 963–978.

Caine, E. D. (1986). The neuropsychology of depression: The pseudodementia syndrome. In I. Grant & K. M. Adams (Eds.), *Neuropsychological assessment of neuropsychiatric disorders* (pp. 221–243). New York: Oxford University Press.

Campbell, D. T., & Fiske, D. W. (1959). Convergent and discriminant validation by the multitrait–multimethod matrix. *Psychological Bulletin, 56,* 81–105.

Christensen, A.-L. (1979). *Luria's neuropsychological investigation. Text* (2nd ed.). Copenhagen: Munksgaard.

Coltheart, M. (1985). Cognitive neuropsychology and the study of reading. In M. I. Posner & O. S. M. Marin (Eds.), *Attention and performance* (Vol. 11, pp. 3–37). Hillsdale, NJ: Lawrence Erlbaum Associates.

Craik, F. I. M., & Lockhart, R. S. (1972). Levels of processing: A framework for memory research. *Journal of Verbal Learning and Verbal Behavior, 11,* 671–684.

Crook, T., Salama, M., & Gobert, J. (1986). A computerized test battery for detecting and assessing memory disorders. In A. Bes, J. Cohn, S. Hoyer, J. P. Marc-Vergenes, & H. M. Wisniewski (Eds.), *Senile dementias: Early detection* (pp. 79–85). London: John Libbey Eurotext.

Crook, T. H., & Larrabee, G. J. (1988). Interrelationships among everyday memory tests: Stability of factor structure with age. *Neuropsychology, 2,* 1–12.

Cummings, J. L., & Benson, D. F. (1992). *Dementia: A clinical approach* (2nd ed.). Boston: Butterworth-Heinemann.

DeMyer, W. (1974). *Technique of the neurologic examination.* New York: McGraw-Hill.

Dodrill, C. B. (1978). A neuropsychological battery for epilepsy. *Epilepsia, 19,* 611–623.

Ellis, A. W., & Young, A. W. (1986). *Human cognitive neuropsychology.* Hillsdale, NJ: Lawrence Erlbaum Associates.

Filskov, S. B., & Goldstein, S. G. (1974). Diagnostic validity of the Halstead–Reitan neuropsychological battery. *Journal of Consulting and Clinical Psychology, 42,* 419–423.

Goldberg, E., & Costa, L. D. (1986). Qualitative indices in neuropsychological assessment: An extension of Luria's approach to executive deficit following prefrontal lesions. In I. Grant & K. M. Adams (Eds.), *Neuropsychological assessment of neuropsychiatric disorders* (pp. 48–64). New York: Oxford University Press.

Goldstein, G. (1986). An overview of similarities and differences between the Halstead–Reitan and Luria–Nebraska neuropsychological batteries. In T. Incagnoli, G. Goldstein, & C. J. Golden (Eds.), *Clinical application of neuropsychological test batteries* (pp. 235–275). New York: Plenum Press.

Goldstein, G., Tarter, R., Shelly, C., & Hegedus, A. (1983). The Pittsburgh Initial Neuropsychological Testing System (PINTS): A neuropsychological screening battery for psychiatric patients. *Journal of Behavioral Assessment, 5,* 227–238.

Goodglass, H. (1986). The flexible battery in neuropsychological assessment. In T. Incagnoli, G. Goldstein, & C. J. Golden (Eds.), *Clinical application of neuropsychological test batteries* (pp. 121–134). New York: Plenum Press.

Goodglass, H., & Kaplan, E. (1972). *Assessment of aphasia and related disorders.* Philadelphia: Lea & Febiger.

Humphreys, G. W., & Riddoch, M. J. (1987). *To see but not to see: A case study of visual agnosia.* Hillsdale, NJ: Lawrence Erlbaum Associates.

Hyman, B. T., Van Hoesen, G. W., Damasio, A. R., & Barnes, C. L. (1984). Alzheimer's disease: Cell-specific pathology isolates the hippocampal formation. *Science, 225,* 1288–1298.

Incagnoli, T. (1986). Current directions and future trends in clinical neuropsychology. In T. Incagnoli, G. Goldstein, & C. J. Golden (Eds.), *Clinical application of neuropsychological test batteries* (pp. 1–44). New York: Plenum Press.

Jacoby, L. L. (1983). Remembering the data: Analyzing interactive processes in reading. *Journal of Verbal Learning and Verbal Behavior, 22,* 485–508.

Jeste, D. V., Lohr, J. B., & Goodwin, F. K. (1988). Neuroanatomical studies of major affective disorders. *British Journal of Psychiatry, 153,* 444–459.

Kane, R. L. (1991). Standardized and flexible batteries in neuropsychology: An assessment update. *Neuropsychology Review, 2,* 281–339.

Kaplan, E. (1983). Process and achievement revisited. In S. Wapner & B. Kaplan (Eds.), *Towards a holistic developmental psychology* (pp. 143–156). Hillsdale, NJ: Lawrence Erlbaum Associates.

Kaplan, E. (1990). The process approach to neuropsychological assessment of psychiatric patients. *Journal of Neuropsychiatry, 2,* 72–87.

Kaplan, E., Fein, D., Morris, R, & Delis, D. C. (1991). *The WAIS–R as a Neuropsychological Instrument. Manual.* San Antonio, TX: Psychological Corporation.

Kertesz, A. (1979). *Aphasia and associated disorders.* New York: Grune & Stratton.

Kiernan, R. J., Mueller, J., Langston, J. W., & Van Dyke, C. (1987). The Neurobehavioral Cognitive Status Examination: A brief but differentiated approach to cognitive assessment. *Annals of Internal Medicine, 107,* 481–485.

Kleinmuntz, B. (1968). Processing of clinical information by man and machine. In B. Kleinmuntz (Ed.), *Formal representation of human judgement.* New York: John Wiley & Sons.

Kløve, H. (1974). Validation studies in adult clinical neuropsychology. In R. M. Reitan & L. A. Davison (Eds.), *Clinical neuropsychology: Current status and applications* (pp. 211–235) New York: Hemisphere Publishing Company.

LaRue, A., De'Elia, L. F., Clark, E. O., Spar, J. E., & Jarvik, L. F. (1986). Clinical tests of memory in dementia, depression, and healthy aging. *Psychology and Aging, 1,* 69–77.

Lezak, M. D. (1995). *Neuropsychological assessment* (3rd ed.). New York: Oxford University Press.

Luria, A. R. (1973). *The working brain: An introduction to neuropsychology* (B. Haigh, Trans.). New York: Basic Books.

Luria, A. R. (1980). *Higher cortical functions in man* (2nd ed.). New York: Basic Books.

Marshall, J. C., & Newcombe, F. (1973). Patterns of paralexia: A psycholinguistic approach. *Journal of Psycholinguistic Research, 2,* 175–199.

Mattis, S. (1988). *Dementia Rating Scale.* Odessa, FL: Psychological Assessment Resources.

Mazziota, J. C., & Gilman, S. (1992). *Clinical brain imaging: Principles and applications.* Philadelphia: F. A. Davis.

McCarthy, R. A., & Warrington, E. K. (1986). Visual associative agnosia: A clinico-anatomical study of a single case. *Journal of Neurology, Neurosurgery, and Psychiatry, 49,* 1233–1240.

McCarthy, R. A., & Warrington, E. K. (1990). *Cognitive neuropsychology: A clinical introduction.* New York: Academic Press.

McKenna, P. & Warrington, E. K. (1986). The analytic approach to neuropsychological assessment. In I. Grant & K. M. Adams (Eds.), *Neuropsychological assessment of neuropsychiatric disorders* (pp. 31–47). New York: Oxford University Press.

Meier, M. (1974). Some challenges for clinical neuropsychology. In R. M. Reitan & L. A. Davison (Eds.), *Clinical neuropsychology: Current status and applications* (pp. 289–323). New York: John Wiley & Sons.

Milberg, W. P., Hebben, N., & Kaplan, E. (1986). The Boston process approach to neuropsychological assessment. In I. Grant & K. M. Adams (Eds.), *Neuropsychological assessment of neuropsychiatric disorders* (pp. 65–86). New York: Oxford University Press.

Morris, J. C., Heyman, A., Mohs, R. C., Hughes, J. P., van Belle, G., Fillenbaum, G., Mellits, E. D.,

Clark, C., & the CERAD investigators. (1989). The Consortium to Establish a Registry for Alzheimer's Disease (CERAD). Part I. Clinical and neuropsychological assessment of Alzheimer's disease. *Neurology, 39*, 1159–1165.

Morris, P., & Rapoport, S. I. (1990). Neuroimaging and affective disorder in late life: A review. *Canadian Journal of Psychiatry, 35*, 347–354.

Mysiw, W. J., Beegan, J. G., & Gatens, P. F. (1989). Prospective cognitive assessment of stroke patients before inpatient rehabilitation: The relationship of the Neurobehavioral Cognitive Status Examination to functional improvement. *American Journal of Physical Medicine and Rehabilitation, 68*, 168–171.

Neisser, U. (1967). *Cognitive psychology.* New York: Appleton-Century-Crofts.

Parsons, O. A. (1986). Overview of the Halstead-Reitan Battery. In T. Incagnoli, G. Goldstein, & C. J. Golden (Eds.), *Clinical application of neuropsychological test batteries* (pp. 155–192). New York: Plenum Press.

Peyser, J. M., Rao, S. M., LaRocca, N. G., & Kaplan, E. F. (1990). Guidelines for neuropsychological research in multiple sclerosis. *Archives of Neurology, 47*, 94–97.

Platt, J. R. (1966). Strong inference. *Science, 146*, 347–353.

Popper, K. R. (1959). *The logic of scientific discovery.* New York: Harper.

Reitan, R. M., & Wolfson, D. (1993). *Halstead–Reitan Neuropsychological Battery: Theory and clinical interpretation.* Tucson, AZ: Neuropsychology Press.

Richards P. M., & Ruff, R. M. (1989). Motivational effects on neuropsychological functioning: Comparison of depressed vs. nondepressed individuals. *Journal of Consulting and Clinical Psychology, 57*, 396–402.

Riddoch, M. J., & Humphreys, G. W. (1993). *Birmingham Object Recognition Battery (BORB).* Hove, UK: Lawrence Erlbaum Associates.

Rosen, W. (1980). Verbal fluency in aging and dementia. *Journal of Clinical Neuropsychology, 2*, 135–146.

Rourke, B. P., & Brown, G. G. (1986). Clinical neuropsychology and behavioral neurology: Similarities and differences. In S. B. Filskov & T. J. Boll (Eds.), *Handbook of clinical neuropsychology* (2nd ed., pp. 3–18). New York: John Wiley & Sons.

Russell, E. W. (1986). The psychometric foundation of clinical neuropsychology. In S. B. Filskov & T. J. Boll (Eds.), *Handbook of clinical neuropsychology* (2nd ed., pp. 45–80). New York: John Wiley & Sons.

Russell, E. W., Neuringer, C., & Goldstein, G. (1970). *Assessment of brain damage: A neuropsychological key approach.* New York: John Wiley & Sons.

Shallice, T. (1988). *From neuropsychology to mental structure.* New York: Cambridge University Press.

Smith, A. (1973). *Symbol Digit Modalities Test. Manual.* Los Angeles, CA: Western Psychological Services.

Squire, L. R. (1987). *Memory and brain.* New York: Oxford University Press.

Tarter, R. E., & Edwards, K. L. (1986). Neuropsychological batteries. In T. Incagnoli, G. Goldstein, & C. J. Golden (Eds.), *Clinical application of neuropsychological test batteries* (pp. 135–153). New York: Plenum Press.

Teuber, H.-L. (1955). Physiological psychology. *Annual Review of Psychology, 6*, 267–296.

Tranel, D. (1992). Functional neuroanatomy: Neuropsychological correlates of cortical and subcortical damage. In S. C. Yudofsky & R. E. Hales (Eds.), *The American Psychiatric Press textbook of neuropsychiatry* (2nd Ed., pp. 57–88). Washington, DC: American Psychiatric Press.

Warrington, E. K. (1975). The selective impairment of semantic memory. *Quarterly Journal of Experimental Psychology, 27*, 187–199.

Warrington, E. K., & James, M. (1986). Visual object recognition in patients with right hemisphere lesions: Axes or features? *Perception, 15*, 355–366.

Weingartner, H., Kaye, W., Smallberg, S., Cohen, R., Ebert, M. H., Gillin, J. C., & Gold, P. (1982). Determinants of memory failures in dementia. In S. Corkin, K. L. Davis, J. H. Growdon, E. Usdin, & R. J. Wurtman (Eds.), *Alzheimer's disease: A report of progress in research* (pp. 171–176). New York: Raven Press.

Werner, H. (1937). Process and achievement: A basic problem of education and developmental psychology. *Harvard Educational Review, 7,* 353–368.

Wernicke, C. (1874). *Der aphasische symptomenkomplex.* Breslau, Poland: M. Cohn & Weigert.

Whitworth, R. H., & Larson, C. M. (1989). Differential diagnosis and staging of Alzheimer's disease with an aphasia battery. *Neuropsychiatry, Neuropsychology, and Behavioral Neurology, 1,* 255–265.

World Health Organization & Nordic Council of Ministers Working Group. (1985). *Environmental health 5: Organic solvents and the central nervous system.* Copenhagen: Author.

CHAPTER FOURTEEN

The Cognitive-Metric,
Fixed Battery Approach
to Neuropsychological Assessment

Elbert W. Russell

Private Practice, Miami, Florida

This chapter presents an approach to neuropsychological assessment that combines cognitive science with traditional psychometrics to form a type of assessment called the cognitive-metric approach. It attempts to apply the scientific rigor found in experimental neuropsychology to neuropsychological assessment.

A secondary related theme is the application of objective scientific methods to test batteries as well as to individual tests. Objective psychometric methods related to individual tests have been well developed in psychology (Anastasi, 1988; Kline, 1986). By contrast, almost no effort in psychology has been devoted to the study of how tests are integrated in a battery. Some beginnings of such a study are presented. As illustrative material, two computerized methods of scoring neuropsychological test batteries are examined.

HISTORY OF NEUROPSYCHOLOGICAL BATTERY
ASSESSMENT METHODS

The cognitive-metric approach has developed out of the advances and controversies in neuropsychology as well as cognitive psychology. From the inception of neuropsychology assessment, the primary controversy has been between the qualitative, now championed by the process approach, and the quantitative or psychometric approach.

The Qualitative Period

In the early part of this century the primary advocates of the qualitative approach were Kirk Goldstein, a neurologist, and Martin Scheerer, a psychologist. Goldstein and Scheerer (1941) developed the first group of tests that were used extensively in neuropsychological assessment. Their concept was that the level of functioning demonstrated by a test did not indicate brain damage, as much as how the particular patient dealt with the test materials. They were concerned with why a patient obtained a score. Goldstein and Scheerer felt that the brain-damaged patient lost the abstract attitude and developed a more concrete approach to solving problems (Walsh, 1978). This was essentially the same concept that Werner (1956) called microgenesis.

In describing the *process approach*, Kaplan (1988) referred to H. Werner (1937, 1956) as an advocate of the process approach. Werner was one of a group of holistic neuropsychologists in the early part of this century who were opposed to psychometric methods. In this regard the process approach has changed little in its method for 50 years. The primary change that has occurred since the 1930s is that the process approach is no longer holistic.

Recently, Kaplan (1988) and her colleagues made attempts to quantify the processes of the process approach. Such tests as the California Verbal Learning Test (CVLT; Delis, Kramer, Kaplan, & Ober, 1987) were developed with elaborate scoring systems and a normative database that allows for a careful quantitative analysis of cognitive subcomponent processes. In so doing, the CVLT has become a carefully constructed psychometric test.

Psychometric Developments

The most commonly used batteries of tests in neuropsychology are the Wechsler intelligence scales. The first of these was the Wechsler–Bellevue Intelligence Scale, introduced in 1939 (Wechsler, 1939). The general form and theory of the Wechsler tests remained the same since the Wechsler–Bellevue until the publication of the WISC–III (Wechsler, 1991) and the WAIS–III (Wechsler, 1997), which introduced some new subtests that clarified the factor structure of the tests. Thus for half a century the major test of cognitive functions did not change in any essential fashion.

The Wechsler subtests were all normed simultaneously. This is coordinated norming, and it permits the comparison of one subtest directly with another. These tests are the only set of tests universally used throughout neuropsychology (Butler, Retzlaff, & Vanderploeg, 1991). The irony is that they were not designed as neuropsychological tests, but measures of normal intellectual ability.

The psychometric approach, which had been developing outside of neuropsychology since the beginning of the century, was introduced into neuropsychology by Halstead and Reitan in the late 1940s and 1950s as the Halstead–Reitan Battery (HRB). This was originally designed as a group of tests by Halstead (1947). Reitan (1955a) added new tests, including the Wechsler–Bellevue, and transformed the original group into a set that was specifically designed to examine neurological conditions (Russell, 1995, 1997, 1998). Although he did not use scale scores, the particular selection of tests was designed to cover all areas of brain functioning. Reitan introduced the idea, adopted from neurology, that tests should be balanced between the right and left hemispheres. In many cases, the same measures, such as the tapping test, could be used to compare the two sides of the body.

The Boston Diagnostic Aphasia Examination (BDAE; Goodglass & Kaplan, 1983) is one of the best designed neuropsychological sets of tests that has yet been developed. As such, it can be used as a model for newer sets of tests. It was designed on the basis of a specific theory of aphasia, the Wernicke–Geschwind theory (Goodglass & Kaplan, 1983). The tests were designed to cover all aspects of aphasia; both brain areas and cognitive functions were represented in the theory. A coordinated norming system was undertaken, such that all of the tests were normed together. The primary difficulty with the battery was that the subtests were not anchored in the normal range, because the subtests were primarily designed for subjects with explicit aphasia. Thus, there is difficulty in using this aphasia battery with subjects that have very mild aphasia or in comparing the aphasic impairment with other types of impairment.

Recent Developments

After the creation of the HRB about 1955, no major developments related to neuropsychological batteries occurred for almost 35 years, other than the BDAE and its counterpart, the Western Aphasia Examination (Kertesz, 1979). Since then the major development has been the creation of several batteries that use coordinated norms, in that all of the tests in the battery were normed simultaneously. All of these batteries in their most recent versions were also designed so that they could be scored by means of a computer.

One of these batteries is the Luria–Nebraska Neuropsychological Battery (LNNB; Golden, Purisch, & Hammeke, 1985). Luria developed a qualitative, flexible approach to assessment based on his theoretical formulations of brain functioning (Luria, 1973, 1980). Christensen (1979, 1984) compiled and described many of these procedures, which Golden and his colleagues subsequently quantified and standardized. Although the LNNB has an overemphasis on verbal functions (Russell, 1980b), it remains the only battery of tests other than those derived from the HRB that has been validated as a whole. Also, at present the scoring for the LNNB can be accomplished through a computer program. Because this chapter is primarily concerned with the HRB, the LNNB is not discussed further.

Recently, three computerized scoring procedures have been developed for the HRB and two derivative batteries (Russell, 1997). The first of these, the Neuropsychological Deficit Scale (NDS), was first published by Reitan in 1987. In this program Reitan captures much of his thinking that is used to determine the existence of brain damage and the lateralization of damage. The program simplifies the scoring of the HRB.

The second computerized scoring system to be published was the Comprehensive Norms for an Expanded Halstead–Reitan Battery (CNEHRB). The CNEHRB was published in 1991 by Psychological Assessment Resources (Heaton, Grant, & Matthews, 1991), primarily as a set of norms. The computer scoring program was a convenience that was added to the battery. This battery is an extended form of the HRB in that it added a number of other tests to the basic HRB.

A third computerized scoring system was published in 1993 under the name of the Halstead Russell Neuropsychological Evaluation System (HRNES; Russell & Starkey, 1993). It was derived from a computerized scoring system copyrighted in 1988 (Russell, Starkey, Fernandez, & Starkey, 1988). Western Psychological Services has further developed this battery. The HRNES has introduced many new applications into neuropsychological testing (Russell, 1997, 1998). It is also an extended version of the HRB, but added several tests that are commonly utilized in neuropsychology. From the beginning, the HRNES was designed as a computer scoring system so that the computer program is more developed than that of the other systems (Russell, 1997).

The NDS, CNEHRB, and HRNES are discussed in more detail in chapter 15 as examples of the application of the cognitive-metric approach to neuropsychological assessment.

FOUNDATIONS OF THE COGNITIVE-METRIC APPROACH

The primary principle of the cognitive-metric approach is the belief that the same scientific rigor found in experimental methodology should characterize neuropsychological assessment. In research this is hypothesis testing and validation of theories. In assessment the scientific approach includes demonstrating the reliability and validity of the instruments. The cognitive-metric approach insists that assessment must be as able to demonstrate the accuracy of its methodological basis. In the cognitive-metric approach to neuropsychological assessment these methodological bases include: (a) adequate instrumentation and measurement methodology, (b) development of tests that adequately represent brain functioning, (c) a set of tests that models all aspects of brain functioning, and (d) an interpretive approach that allows for an understanding of test data and its relationship to brain functioning.

Instrumentation and Measurement

An indispensable aspect of any scientific field is its instrumentation. Science has progressed as much through the development of new instruments as the creation of new theories. Instrumentation includes methods of measurement. In many cases the development of new instruments permits the use of more accurate measurement. In neuropsychology the primary instruments are tests. The test measurement system, embodied in a neuropsychological battery, applies quantitative methods to examination procedures.

Necessity of Tests.   There is a paramount principle of testing that applies to all neuropsychological approaches. The principle is that one cannot determine whether a function is impaired unless that function is evaluated. That is, unless you apply some form of test to a particular function, you cannot determine whether there is a deficit. There are, of course, a few exceptions in regard to gross phenomena, such as frank aphasia or hemiparesis. However, to determine the type of aphasia, the neuropsychologist requests the patient to perform different tasks to test various aspects of language. Many of these methods are represented formally in the Boston Diagnostic Aphasia Examination (Goodglass & Kaplan, 1983). When an expert simply listens to a patient's speech the expert is listening for certain deficits, and these specific observations represent rudimentary testing. Such structured observations are informal qualitative testing.

Established Psychometric Standards.   For over a century, psychology has been developing the methods and standards related to testing. These are established and are set forth in books and in the American Psychological Association (1988) *Standards for Educational and Psychological Testing.* There is no ambiguity in the stance of the cognitive-metric approach. It accepts psychology's standards of validity and reliability. Wherever possible, interpretations are based on tests that meet these standards.

The use of clinical lore and qualitative methods is justified when no tests are available that provide the needed information for an interpretation. Lore and qualitative observations, although often necessary at this point in the development of neuropsychology, do not constitute solid knowledge. Science represents a gradual accumulation of knowledge. The candid position of the cognitive-metric approach is that we do not know everything. An advanced science is aware of what it does not know.

Assessment Versus Research.   Although the cognitive-metric approach applies scientific rigor to assessment, it accepts the condition that assessment follows a different procedure than does scientific research. Although this should be obvious, some of the implications of the difference are not so obvious. Many neuropsychologists transfer research methods uncritically to assessment procedures.

Unfortunately, statistically significant findings that discriminate in the research setting between groups of subjects may be totally ineffective in the clinical setting with individual patients.

The primary difference between research and assessment is that in scientific research one proceeds from data to theory, whereas in an assessment one goes from theory to data. For instance, instead of attempting to determine what functions are related to particular areas (i.e., constructing theory), assessment interpretations are derived from previously constructed theory that specifies which tests are related to different brain regions and cognitive abilities. That is, the examiner interprets a particular patient's behavior on the basis of the examiners knowledge of the entire body of neuropsychology theory and lore.

The Nature of Neuropsychological Tests

A second set of principles in the cognitive-metric approach concerns the theoretical nature of tests. Until there is some understanding of how tests are related to the brain, attempts to design and utilize neuropsychological tests are at best mere groping in the dark. In neuropsychological theory this relationship of brain to tests is now in a preliminary stage.

Representation. Testing is a representational activity. A test is a procedure designed to represent some aspect of brain functioning in a public form. A brain function may be represented by the results of the particular task required by a test, and the ability to perform the task represents the effectiveness of the function.

To the extent that they are represented by test scores, mental processes can be observed and recorded. Through the use of tests, the functioning of the brain becomes manifest as test scores and the contents of the "black box" (i.e., brain functioning) become observable. In fact, functions are discovered and generally named by what they do, the type of task.

As early as 1922, Tolman redefined the "behavioral response" as the *behavioral act* (Kimble, 1985); that is behavior was what the behavior accomplishes in performing a task, not specific movements. This molar behaviorism was accepted by almost all behaviorists (Kimble, 1985). However, in effect, this redefinition of behaviorism nullifies the emphasis on behavior. It attaches the primary emphasis to the results of a task rather than the behavior of the organism. That is, the emphasis is on the effect the person accomplished on an objective task, not on the subject's behavior. The effect is recorded publicly as the test result. This emphasis on the task results, which are external to the person, is especially appropriate for neuropsychology. Except for motor behavior, the specific behavior of the organism is largely irrelevant. To demonstrate that one has an intact calculation function, the behavioral manner in which the answer is presented is largely inconsequential. That is, one can answer the question what is 2 plus 3 by writing 5, or V. One can show five fingers or five toes, one can knock five times on a table or put five objects into a container. There is almost an infinite number of different behaviors that can signify the answer. In cognitive psychology one is testing the use of a symbolic system in the brain, not a behavior. The left parietal aspect of the brain (and probably other areas as well) is being tested, not the motor strip.

Aspects of Cognitive Functions. There are two aspects of a brain function, form and proficiency. *Form* refers to an activity, how the brain accomplishes a task to produce a result. The form of the test, such as linguistic or spatial relations, represents the nature of the brain function. *Proficiency* of brain function refers to how well the function is performed. Proficiency is termed the ability of the person. Form is examined in a qualitative or process study, whereas ability is examined in a quantitative result. Any test of a function will contain both aspects, even though it specifically measures proficiency or ability.

Tests Represent Functions. A function is made manifest through performing a task. A test is a specified task, and tasks must be specific in form. The type of task that is required by the parameters of the test determines the function that is being measured. Thus, there is a specificity between testing and function. This is true of both qualitative and quantitative testing.

The form of a test is derived from the function. Tests must be delineated through experimental procedures that design test characteristics to match the characteristics of the function. Thus, the test is designed to represent a function by building into the test characteristics of the function. The aim of neuropsychological research is to determine both the existence and characteristics of brain functions. When correctly designed, tests will represent the content of a function, what function it is, and the formal aspects of the function, such as gradations in ability.

An "amount" of ability is measured by specific procedures incorporated into the test that are quantified in the results, that is, the test score. Traditionally, ability is measured in two general ways, speed and power. These measure how effective a person is in performing a function.

Modeling Brain Functions

A model is an abstract representational form in which each component has a specified relationship to the entity being modeled. It is standard practice for engineers and scientists to employ physical and mathematical models to represent complex structures and processes. In psychology, mental models have been used to represent aspects of cognition (Pellegrino, 1988).

Just as a single test represents a specific brain function, so an integrated set of tests represents either an area of brain functioning, such as language (aphasia batteries), or the functioning of the entire brain. Most neuropsychology batteries are attempts to represent the functioning of the whole brain; as such they are a brain function model.

The brain acts in a closely integrated manner. Every activity that is directed by the brain is produced by a system of functions (Luria, 1973, 1980). Because the brain acts through systems of functions, a single test can not represent brain functioning. An adequate model of brain functioning will employ multiple measures to represent the multiple functions of the brain. An examination should use a particular combination of tests representing, as much as possible, the functions of the brain. A full neuropsychological examination, using a well-designed, integrated set of tests, would be a "brain function model" that represents the whole functioning of the brain. Thus, the patterns of impairment may be represented by patterns of tests results.

A "Set" of Tests.   Since Halstead's (1947) work and the development of the Wechsler–Bellevue in the late 1930s (Wechsler, 1939), cognitive and neuropsychological tests have generally been given in sets, called batteries. Utilization of groups of tests has become the standard practice in neuropsychology. The scientific criteria and theory related to individual tests have been well developed in psychology (Anastasi, 1988; Kline, 1986). The literature is full of the psychometric requirements for individual tests, such as reliability and validity (Franzen, 1989). However, there has been little psychometric discussion of the requirements for a set of tests composing a battery, fixed or flexible. Nunnally (1978) stated "Ultimately psychometrics is concerned not only with such individual variables, but with the way that they relate to one another" (p. 329). To date, almost no effort has been devoted in neuropsychology to the study of how tests should function in a battery.

A set of tests is an integrated group of tests that is designed to be used as a unit. It is designed to represent quantitatively the complex functioning of the brain. The term *set* emphasizes the integration of a group of tests, rather than a group in which tests are selected in a haphazard manner. A *battery* may be either a set of tests or an unintegrated group of tests. The tests are integrated through systematic coverage and through structural considerations, such as coordinated norming and uniform scoring methods that increase accuracy and provide a complete and constant background. The set of tests may be selected to represent the entire brain, a specific area of the brain, or a system of functions.

Constant Background.   A central concept related to the brain function model is that of a constant background. In a constant background the set of tests remains constant within a battery and from one subject to another. With the background of tests as a constant, any variation that occurs on or between the tests is due to the variation within the subject and not due to differences between tests. An analogy may be made with a mirror. In a sense a set of tests is a mirror of a person's functioning. If the mirror is constant in that the glass does not vary from one point to another and the complete mirror is used each time, the reflected image is true and can be trusted. However, if the different parts of the glass vary in angle so that the surface is uneven, then one does not know whether the shape of the perceived image is due to variations in the object or variations in the medium, the mirror.

In neuropsychology there are two major aspects to a constant background. These are constancy between tests within a battery and constancy from one examination to another. The formal structure of the tests within a battery provides internal constancy, and a consistent set of tests (i.e., a fixed battery) provides an external or content constancy.

Internal Constancy. Internal consistency is produced by the formal structure or characteristics of a set of tests, including the norms, types of scales, and correction factors (e.g., age and education adjustments). The integration of a set battery of tests is primarily obtained by coordinated norming so that all of the tests are, in effect, normed on the same population sample. Consequently, the norming does not vary from one test to another. This enables one to compare the results of one test to another and one subject to another.

A norm is a constant background against which one can compare an individual's behavior or an individual's test score. That is, when an examiner says, "This behavior is abnormal or unusual," the examiner is comparing that behavior against a fixed background of what is normal or usual behavior. In the qualitative approach, the individual compares a patient's performance against an understanding of what is normal. These norms may be experiential or learned or part of clinical lore; nevertheless, they represent a background for comparison. In a qualitative neuropsychological approach, because the background is subjective (clinical experience or lore) it may or may not be constant.

The concept of a constant background is related to that of a control group in research. The control group is used to compare the results of experimental procedures against normal functioning or against a selected criteria. The control group, which remains unchanged, acts as a constant background against which the effects of the treatment can be observed and measured.

In assessment, the individual case results are compared against the scientifically established norms derived from a normal control group. In this case, a constant background is derived from the undamaged or normal group, against which the effects of a particular form of damage can be perceived.

External or Content Constancy. External or content constancy occurs when a fixed battery is employed. The content of the battery remains constant from one testing to another. Thus, a fixed battery of tests forms a constant background against which a person's particular strengths and weaknesses become evident. If the background is not constant, the differences that are found may be due to the differences between the various tests that are used, as well as the various norming methods employed with the various tests. In a flexible battery the results may be due to the particular tests that happen to be selected at a particular time. In a fixed battery, the relationships between tests and the functions that those tests represent can be studied across many different neurological conditions, so that patterns can be discovered and verified.

Advocates of a flexible battery assert that the primary advantage of a flexible battery is that this approach takes the individual patient into consideration, and because patients vary, the tests should vary (Lezak, 1984). There is a problem with this concept. Testing is designed to discover how an individual varies from other persons. Except for obvious things like hemiparesis, how does the examiner know that the subject is varying without some form of a constant background? It is the fixed battery that provides the constant background against which the patient's variation can be observed. A clearer picture of the whole person is obtained if the same background is retained, rather than changing the background each time a different person is tested. A fixed battery permits more accurate observation of a person's individuality than does an individualized battery of tests. This is the reason that most advocates of a flexible battery eventually settle down to administering a fixed core of tests.

Even when individual problems such as hemiparesis do not permit the administration of the entire battery, a large coordinated fixed battery has an advantage in that when necessary tests may be selected from the battery and will retain their coordination. As such the examiner can still compare the tests with each other. If they had been selected from various norming procedures the advantage of coordinated norming would not exist.

Methods of Interpretation

The methods of interpretation in an assessment are related to the question of whether one uses a cognitive-metric or more qualitative flexible approach. In the flexible and qualitative approach to interpretation, a method that is often used has been called *ongoing hypothesis testing*. In addition to hypothesis testing, at least two other methods are known. These are *algorithms* and *pattern analysis*. In an algorithmic approach there is a series of alternative questions. Answering each question leads to another that further elaborates the assessment. Alternatively, in a pattern analysis approach the neuropsychologist examines the data for particular patterns without necessarily any hypothesis or question ahead of time.

Ongoing Hypothesis Testing

In ongoing hypothesis testing, the neuropsychologist has a particular hypothesis about a patient (Luria & Majovski, 1977), and tests are selected to determine whether the hypothesis is true. After confirming or disconfirming the first hypothesis the examiner then selects another hypothesis to disconfirm until the assessment is completed. This method is modeled on the experimental method; however, as was pointed out earlier, assessment is a different procedure than research, and methods that work well in one setting may not be applicable to the other.

To a certain extent all neuropsychologists, regardless of their persuasion, use some hypothesis testing, or at least they answer questions, which is the same procedure. That is, it is merely a matter of terminology whether one calls something hypothesis testing or answering a question. For instance, a question may be, "Does the patient have brain damage?" This is stated in hypothesis testing as "The patient does not have brain damage—Disprove this." The testing method will be the same whichever way the question is framed (Russell, 1997).

In ongoing hypothesis testing, as soon as the examiner disconfirms one hypothesis, this leads to another hypothesis. The difficulty with such ongoing hypothesis testing is that, in its pure form, it is quite limited. The limitation involves obtaining the new hypothesis. For instance, after the patient is assessed to have brain damage, how is the next hypothesis selected? There are hundreds of kinds of brain damage, dozens of locations, and many types and quantity of deficits. To obtain a new hypothesis or question, the neuropsychologist must either look for patterns on the tests that have already been administered, or follow a loose logical progression based on experience and knowledge, that is, an informal algorithm. In doing so, the neuropsychologist has abandoned the pure hypothesis testing approach and moved to other interpretive strategies (Russell, 1997).

In practice, another major problem that may occur with the hypothesis testing approach when using a flexible battery is related to coverage. When one simply selects tests based on a hypothesis, many areas and functions of the brain may not be examined. Rourke and Brown (1986) thoroughly discuss this problem with hypothesis testing. They consider it the most serious flaw in the flexible or hypothesis testing method.

Algorithms

The primary methods of analysis used in the cognitive-metric approach are algorithms and pattern analysis. The algorithm method has been called a decision approach (Tarter & Edwards, 1986). In the algorithm method there are a series of questions that are formed ahead of time. In practice, these are usually not formalized but are implicit, in that the examiner simply knows neurology well enough to be able to ask the appropriate question at each step. Each question will lead to a second group of questions, depending on the answer to the first one. For instance, the first question may be, "Is there brain damage?" If the test results indicate that there is no brain damage, that is the end of the process. However, if there is brain damage, then the next question might be, "Is the damage lateralized to the right or the left hemisphere?" and so forth.

The algorithm method may use either a fixed or a flexible battery. The examination is directed by a series of interlocking questions that have been formed prior to an examination. At each step these questions cull information from the test results to answer the particular question in the algorithm.

To some extent this is the way all neuropsychologists analyze a protocol. That is, they begin the examination with a series of questions derived from their experience and knowledge. The answer to each question leads to another series of questions until the assessment questions (including questions unexpressed by the referral) are answered. In fact, this is what neuropsychologists who claim to use the ongoing hypothesis testing method actually do. They do not begin the examination with a formal hypothesis such as "This patient has no brain damage." Rather they ask, "Does this patient have brain damage?" If the patient does have damage they already have one or several questions in mind to ask next. This is what is meant by the word *ongoing*. The difference between hypothesis testing and an algorithm is that in an algorithm the next set of questions is already preselected, based on a person's knowledge, whereas in pure hypothesis testing it is not.

Pattern Analysis

The third major method used in interpretation is pattern recognition or pattern analysis. An experienced neuropsychologist using a set battery such as the WAIS–R or the HRB will recognize certain patterns of test results in the test matrix. To a large extent the examiner who utilizes pattern identification does the opposite of hypothesis testing. Instead of beginning with a conception of the problem, the hypothesis, the examiner systematically explores the data with minimal preconceptions to discover the patterns in the data. Most of the patterns that have been identified in the literature to date have been related to the Wechsler tests because they are set batteries. Some of these patterns are familiar. Lateralization of brain damage is indicated by the difference between verbal and performance tests (Matarazzo, 1972; Russell, 1984). However, this may be confused with a fluidity pattern that has also been identified (Barron & Russell, 1992; Russell, 1979, 1980a).

Reitan's Four Methods of Pattern Analysis. Reitan (1964; Reitan & Wolfson, 1985, 1986) was one of the first neuropsychologists to propose a theory for methods of assessment. He delineated four methods of interpretive inference: (a) level of performance, (b) differential patterns of ability, (c) comparisons between the two sides of the body, and (d) pathognomonic signs. It is clear that the first three interpretive methods are forms of pattern analysis, whereas the fourth is a form of the qualitative approach.

Level of performance is the beginning of pattern analysis. When an index is used, such as the Halstead Index, it is an average level of performance, which in itself is a type of pattern. The second method is the pattern of performance.

Patterns are simply combinations of levels of performance for several tests. In Reitan's actual practice the patterns appear to be largely confined to the WAIS, at least on the variables presented in the General Neuropsychological Deficit Scale (GNDS; Reitan, 1991). On examination, the third method, comparison of right and left sides of the body, is also a type of pattern analysis. It is the pattern of test results that occurs when the tests that are related to each side of the body are compared to each other. Finally, this leaves pathognomonic signs as the only method that does not involve pattern analysis. The signs themselves are actually qualitative signs that indicate types of brain damage. In practice, as demonstrated by the GNDS, Reitan utilized signs only in regard to the Aphasia Screening Test (Reitan, 1991). Many of the answers on the aphasia examination are written or drawn. Consequently, they can be examined qualitatively without testing the patient oneself. Reitan was able to derive a large amount of data from a small number of items on this test using this sign approach.

In the Russell version of the Halstead tests, the HRNES (Russell & Starkey, 1993), instead of examining signs as related to particular pathologies, the number of items that are failed are counted and therefore quantified. Hence, this sign approach itself has been quantified and the score for the Aphasia Screening Examination becomes part of the patterns used in the total test battery. Of course, one can still use the Aphasia Screening Test qualitatively.

Comparisons. The foundation of pattern analysis is comparison. In fact, almost all of neuropsychological interpretation is based on comparisons. Even in the qualitative approach, the examiner compares a particular abnormal performance against a normal performance. Also the examiner may compare the patient's performance against knowledge of a particular type of abnormal performance in order to assess or diagnose the particular type of problem. Other types of comparisons are right–left comparisons and comparisons with different forms of disease patterns. In order to determine whether a person is improving in rehabilitation, one must compare previous test results with the new results.

In an article advocating a qualitative approach, Luria and Majovski (1977) stated that they do not quantify the results. However, in describing a particular impairment, they stated that the type of impairment is very different from what you would normally expect. In this regard, they are not only making a comparison between what the patient did and a normal performance, but also are making a quantitative nomothetic comparison, abnormal versus normal ability.

In the cognitive-metric approach, comparisons are based on the concept of a constant back ground. There must be equivalence of all test scale scores that are used before reliable comparisons can be made. In isolating a pattern the individual's particular performance is compared against an array of other theoretical patterns in order to determine which form the individual resembles. Such a series of comparisons is only possible when the test scores are equivalent, thus creating a constant background.

Dissociation.   In neuropsychology the basis for reliable comparisons is a modification of the concept that Teuber (1955, 1975) proposed called *double dissociation*. Double dissociation is a dissociation between both two tests and two areas of the brain. It also can be applied to conditions other than areas of the brain. For illustrative purposes, however, we use areas. Teuber's method primarily applies to research, although with the modification called multiple dissociation, it also applies to assessment.

Double Dissociation.   Double dissociation is concerned with research. To understand double dissociation, refer to Table 14.1. At the top of Table 14.1 are three different forms of damage: right hemisphere, left hemisphere, and no damage (control). Along the side are possible methods of research, numbered 1 to 4, for the use of two tests, A and B. Patterns of test findings can be related to particular areas of the brain.

TABLE 14.1
Double and Multiple Dissociation

DOUBLE DISSOCIATION

Brain Damage Type

Methods	Right Hemisphere	Left Hemisphere	Control
1. Test A	Impaired	—	Not impaired
2. Test A	More impaired	Less impaired	Not impaired
3. Test A	More impaired	—	Not impaired
Test B	Less impaired	—	Not impaired
4. Test A	More impaired	Less impaired	Not impaired
Test B	Less impaired	More impaired	Not impaired

MULTIPLE DISSOCIATION[a]

Tests	Right Frontal	Right Parietal	Left Frontal	Left Parietal
Test A	XXX			
Test B		XXX		
Test C			XXX	
Test D				XXX

[a]Tests are related to the area of the brain marked with XXX. For multiple dissociations, possible combinations indicating locations of brain damage are:

1. Tests A, B, C, D not impaired = no damage.
2. Tests A, B, C, D impaired = diffuse.
3. Tests A and B more impaired, Tests C, D less impaired = right hemisphere.
4. Tests C and D more impaired, Tests A, B less impaired = left hemisphere.
5. Tests A and C more impaired, Tests B, D less impaired = bifrontal damage.
6. Tests B and D more impaired, Tests A, C less impaired = biparietal damage.
7. Test A more impaired, Tests B, C, D less impaired = right frontal.
8. Test B more impaired, Tests A, C, D less impaired = right parietal.
9. Test C more impaired, Tests A, B, D less impaired = left frontal.
10. Test D more impaired, Tests A, B, C less impaired = left parietal.

Method 1. Impairment of Test A is thought to indicate impairment in the right hemisphere, because patients with right-hemisphere damage performed more poorly than normals. Obviously, the problem here is that almost any kind of brain damage, not just right-hemisphere damage, could produce impairment on Test A. Amazingly, there are still a few research studies being published in which the procedure is no more complicated or informative than this.

Method 2. Comparing patients with right- and left-hemisphere damage with one test finds that Test A is more impaired with right-hemisphere damage than with left-hemisphere damage. The researcher states that impaired performance on Test A indicates right-hemisphere damage. Although this is a somewhat better procedure, the average amount of damage may be greater for the subjects with right-hemisphere damage than the left in this sample.

Method 3. Two tests, A and B, are used, and A is more impaired for right-hemisphere damage than B. The researcher states that A is more of a right-hemisphere test and so indicates a function in the right hemisphere. However, the problem here is that A may simply be more sensitive to damage in general than B. This has occurred in regard to fluid and crystallized intelligence (Barron & Russell, 1992; Russell, 1979, 1980a). The entire issue of whether alcoholism produces more right-hemisphere damage than left was apparently due to the situation that the WAIS subtests, which were thought to indicate right-hemisphere damage, were also more sensitive to brain damage in general (Barron & Russell, 1992). That is, they were fluid tests, whereas those related to the left hemisphere were crystallized.

Method 4. The procedure that most unequivocally demonstrates lateralization is double dissociation. This is the finding that Test A is more impaired for right-hemisphere damage than Test B, and Test B is more impaired for left-hemisphere damage than Test A. Under these circumstances, one can be fairly confident that A is related to the right hemisphere and B is related to the left hemisphere. It is only this finding that definitely indicates lateralization or localization of damage (Teuber, 1955, 1975). This kind of procedure also applies to types of disease entities and rehabilitation treatments.

Multiple Dissociation.   An extension of the double dissociation method is the basis for assessment. In assessment many tests are used in a process of multiple dissociation. The assessment procedure proceeds from theory, concerning the relation of tests or functions to certain areas of the brain, to interpretation. Individual test results are evaluated in accordance with the accepted theory.

As an example, in Table 14.1, there are four tests, A, B, C, and D. Theory based on previous research has related A to right frontal-lobe functioning. This is indicated by the X's in the table. Test B is related to the right parietal lobe, C to the left frontal lobe, and D to the left parietal lobe. The patterns that can be seen are fairly obvious. They are presented below the table. If none of the tests are impaired, then there is no brain damage. If all of the tests are impaired, then there is diffuse brain damage. If only Test A is impaired, then there is evidence for damage in the right frontal area and nowhere else. If A and B are impaired and C and D are not, then the damage is right-hemisphere damage. If A and C are more impaired, then bilateral frontal damage is indicated.

Consequently, the various possible patterns that occur among these tests indicate where the damage is located. Obviously, the more tests that are in a battery, the more possible combinations exist. This table was limited to frontal and parietal lobes for simplicity. Also, it is desirable to have more than one test of each of the areas or abilities. Redundancy is required in order to verify that a pattern does exist.

This process of multiple dissociation applies to all areas of interpretation, not just to location. It is the method of determining chronicity, type of pathology, and the assets and deficits of the patient related to activities of daily living.

Both double and multiple dissociation presume a constant background. The multiple comparisons used in assessment, especially pattern analysis, require a constant background. The individual is not just being compared one function at a time against a normal background, but all functions are being compared against each other using a total constant background made up of all the tests in the battery.

Formulas and Indices. A *formula* or *index* is a formalized way of quantifying a particular empirical pattern. The formula, if correctly constructed, will select out of all of the tests results those that are particularly important for a certain diagnosis or assessment pattern. Using quantitative methods, a formula determines whether the battery results contain this particular pattern. Formulas have been isolated for Alzheimer's disease (Russell & Polakoff, 1993) and left-hemisphere damage (Dobbins & Russell, 1990; Russell & Russell, 1993).

An index method is equivalent to a complex formula in that it is a formalized way of quantifying particular empirical patterns. Many indices, such as the Halstead Impairment Index (Halstead, 1947) and the Average Impairment Rating (Russell, Neuringer, & Goldstein, 1970), have been developed (Russell, 1995). These have been found to be as accurate as clinical assessment (Heaton, Grant, Anthony, & Lehman, 1981). An index to assess lateralization and diffuse brain damage (Russell, 1984; Russell & Starkey, 1993) also has been developed and found to be quite accurate. Many other indices and programs for determining lateralization have been developed (Adams, Kvale, & Keegan, 1984; Reitan, 1991; Russell, 1995; Swiercinsky, 1978). Obviously many proposed formulas and indices are variable in their accuracy. However, they have a major advantage in that they can be disproved or shown to be accurate in a certain proportion of cases. No such exactness is possible with any other interpretation method (Russell, 1995).

Mixed Method

In the practical situation, most neuropsychologists use a combination of the interpretive methods just described. In regard to the cognitive-metric fixed battery approach, all methods are utilized. The person may initially look for particular tests in order to determine whether there is or is not brain damage following an algorithm. Each step in the algorithm may be conceptualized as a hypothesis, but, based on knowledge, the hypotheses are ordered ahead of time, so that one leads to another. Observation of patterns is something that can be done with a fixed battery. Here, after one or two of the original questions in the algorithms are examined, the examiner may simply look over the test data for certain patterns.

In what is probably one of the most informative descriptions of how neuropsychologists examine test data in the literature, Reitan and Wolfson (1986, pp. 142–144) described their method in some detail. They used the mixed method. In this description the examiner systematically explores the test data looking for patterns while being guided by knowledge of what each test contributes to the picture of the whole person. Certain questions guide the process, such as "What is the course of the lesion?" It is evident that this method begins with minimal preconceptions concerning the patient and only gradually builds a picture of the person. To a great extent this method was derived from Reitan's practice of examining the data blind. In such a situation it is difficult to obtain any hypothesis before seeing the data, and the initial question would not be any more extensive than "Does this person have brain damage?"

REQUIREMENTS FOR A COGNITIVE-METRIC SET OF TESTS

Unless there is accurate representation of brain functions by a set of tests, there is no possibility of an adequate assessment. Accurate representation is obtained through a set of representative tests and a consistent background. Any battery has both a formal structure and content.

Content refers to the particular tests that compose the battery. How thoroughly the functions are represented is referred to as *coverage*. Coverage applies to both areas of the brain and types of functions. The coverage must be complete enough to represent the functioning of the brain. Adequate coverage is a major requirement for an integrated battery.

Formal structural characteristics are general features that all tests have in common. These include characteristics such as gradation, range, and norms. In the present discussion of an integrated battery, the additional structural requirements of accuracy and equivalence are addressed.

Coverage

If the set of tests in a battery is to be an adequate representation of the brain, then coverage is an essential concern. Coverage follows the principle that one cannot tell whether a function is impaired unless that function is tested. As a brain model, a set of tests should be designed to cover all areas of the brain and all cognitive functions, in as much depth as efficiency allows. The exceptions to this are the special purpose batteries such as aphasia batteries. The principles provided here also apply to these special batteries within their domain.

Types of Coverage

There are two types of coverage important in neuropsychological assessment: areas of the brain, and types of cognitive functioning.

Anatomic Area. Neuropsychological test batteries have traditionally attempted to fashion complete coverage by anatomic area. That is, an attempt is made to select tests that cover all of the various areas of the brain. This approach has been utilized from the time when it was realized that different areas of the brain have different functions. A proper selection of tests helps determine the localization of the damage (Reitan, 1964). Also, to some extent, the diagnosis of a pathology is dependent on what areas are impaired.

The most well-recognized division of functions related to area is that of lateralization (Matarazzo, 1972; Russell, 1972, 1974, 1979). Any well-organized test battery today will have tests that are related to both hemispheres of the brain, usually in a balanced or equal amount (Russell, 1980b). Because coverage by area is well known, in that there are large areas of textbooks devoted to it (Kolb & Whishaw, 1985), little more need be said concerning this subject.

Cognitive Functions. In recent years, there has been a tendency for neuropsychologists to downplay coverage by area and emphasize coverage by function. This change in emphasis has occurred since the mid 1970s when the computerized axial tomography (CAT) scan began to localize lesions more exactly than was possible using neuropsychological tests. Some neuropsychologists have argued that the detection of brain damage is passé (Mapou, 1988) and that neuropsychologists should concentrate on assessing cognitive functions. Ironically, studying cognitive functions does not require brain-damaged subjects at all. When neuropsychologists deal only with function, neuropsychology looses its distinctive aspect and it becomes a branch of normal psychometrics or cognitive psychology that have studied intellectual abilities and individual differences for a century. The problem is that neuropsychologists are not as sophisticated in these areas as cognitive and psychometric psychologists or even psychologists in vocational guidance.

Nevertheless, there is a contribution that neuropsychology can make in both the research and applied fields. In research, neuropsychology is in a unique position to study the deferential effects that brain damage produces. In fact, one of the major concerns should be to determine what are the human cognitive functions and to categorize them (Rourke, 1991). In the clinical setting, neuropsychologists understand the effect of specific lesions and brain conditions on human functions. This is important to medical and legal as well as psychological activities.

Principles of Coverage

There are several principles that must be kept in mind when designing a battery of tests that has adequate coverage. Some of these principles are fairly obvious and should be common sense for a knowledgeable practicing neuropsychologist. Nevertheless, they should be expressly stated so that they can be treated in theoretical discussions.

Completeness. The first of these may be called completeness or thoroughness. As much as possible, a battery of tests, except specialized batteries, should contain tests related to all areas of the brain and all known functions. An integrated set battery is designed to have as adequate coverage as possible for both area and function. In regard to area, all areas of the brain should be represented. At present, this subdivision of the brain by area may be refined to the level of lobes and in some cases to parts of a lobe. The same thoroughness is required for functions. All major types of functions such as memory, verbal abilities, and spatial relations should be represented in a battery. This is especially important if the purpose of the battery is to determine the amount of impairment produced by brain damage to a person's total functioning.

It would appear that a huge battery would be required to cover both areas of the brain and cognitive functions. However, this is not as difficult as one might imagine because generally different areas have different functions and the same tests may simultaneously cover both aspects. A set battery should have been designed carefully over a period of time to contain thorough coverage for both area and function. A flexible battery, which is put together for each new patient, may very well have lacunae in different areas of coverage. Thus, problems may be missed that a fixed battery would discover (Rourke & Brown, 1986).

Balance. A second principle is that of balance. Balance simply means that there is an equal number of tests devoted to each area of the brain and to each major type of function. Balance related to area is best understood in terms of right- versus left-hemisphere functions. One of the criticisms of the Luria–Nebraska Neuropsychological Battery is that it lacks balance (Russell, 1980b). As with all of Luria's work, the emphasis was primarily on verbal functions. Consequently, the Luria–Nebraska is very heavily weighted in the verbal area. Alternately, the Halstead–Reitan Battery is quite well balanced in regard to lateralization (Russell, 1980b).

Balance also should apply to the difference between anterior and posterior parts of the brain, as well as to localized areas. Balance can be applied to smaller areas such as lobes or even parts of lobes. The principle is that every area should be represented by tests but not overrepresented. In constructing a battery, it is preferable to add a test related to an uncovered area rather than duplicate tests within areas, even when the duplicated tests are well known.

Balance also concerns different types of functions and "crystallized" versus "fluid" abilities (Barron & Russell, 1992; Horn, 1976; Russell, 1979, 1980a). For instance, one should not overload a battery with verbal as opposed to spatial relations tests (Russell, 1980b). Our lack of understanding of the function of areas and the difficulty in finding tests related to various areas often has meant not only that balance is lacking, but that we may not even know it is lacking. For instance, most neuropsychological batteries lack tests of social intelligence or what Guilford (1967) called *behavioral abilities*.

Redundancy.   A third principle related to coverage, and one that is somewhat less known, is redundancy (Russell, 1984). One of the characteristics of any cognitive test is that the scores for the same person are somewhat variable over time. That is, there is normal variability. This variability can lead to false identification of the existence of brain damage or descriptions of impaired functions simply because a subject was not paying attention or because something else interfered with the subject's functioning on a particular test. The seasoned neuropsychologist does not trust a single incidence of a particular phenomena. *Redundancy* means that the same functions or areas are covered by more than one test. It is important to add redundancy to a battery in order to "cross-check" the results that are obtained from any test. When one has several tests that are all impaired related to the same area or function, then one has more confidence that there is indeed an impairment in that area.

The more basic the decision, such as separation of brain damage from normality, the greater should be the redundancy. This overlapping often occurs in the Halstead–Reitan battery. Many of the tests in this battery are highly sensitive to brain damage; consequently, one can compare these sensitive tests to each other to insure that there is damage. The utilization of an index rather than a single score to determine brain damage is in large part based on the concept of redundancy.

Efficiency.   An additional principle is that of efficiency. In some ways, this is the opposite of coverage as well as redundancy. It is obvious that a test battery cannot be infinitely long. At the present time, there are so many tests available that one could presumably test a person for 100 hr without running out of tests. Consequently, the number of tests must be limited at some point. To some extent efficiency may be retained even though there is redundancy. This is accomplished by using overlapping tests. *Efficiency* means that within the limits imposed by both thoroughness of coverage and redundancy, the length of the battery must be as short as possible. This subject is discussed at greater length under the heading of practical considerations.

Known Tests. The final principle in determining the nature of a fixed battery is that known tests are preferable to unknown tests. Known tests have known reliability, validity, and information concerning their actions. One's understanding of the effects of damage on known tests is greater than unknown tests. It is only when there is an obvious lack in a particular area of coverage and no known tests are adequate that a new test should be added to an otherwise well-designed battery.

Another reason for using known tests is that information can be more readily transmitted to other clinicians. When one reads a report based on a set of unknown tests, the clinician will not be able to determine how well the testing has been done or how well it has been interpreted. In fact, the clinician may not be able to follow the interpretation to any great extent.

Accuracy

Accuracy, as the second general requirement for a set of tests, constitutes part of the formal structure of an integrated battery. *Accuracy* signifies how closely a test corresponds to the characteristics of the function that it represents. Unless the individual tests are accurate, a constant background is not possible. That is, the accuracy of the constant background is dependent on the accuracy of the individual tests. The more accurate the scales are, the more ability they have for assessment and diagnosis.

Standard Requirements

All of the standard traditional requirements for individual test construction apply to tests in an integrated battery. These requirements include item analysis, reliability and validity (Kline, 1986; Nunnally, 1978). Although there is not room in this chapter to discuss these requirements, there are differences between validating individual tests and validating an entire battery. As in many things, Nunnally (1978, pp. 327–497) appeared to be ahead of his time in being aware of the problems related to sets of tests. In the past a battery of tests has not usually been validated as a whole, but rather each individual test has been validated separately. When a set of tests such as the WAIS or WMS has been validated, typically it has been treated as a single test with a single result, such as an IQ score. It is this summary score that is usually validated against a criterion such as academic ability.

Neuropsychology batteries, such as the HRB, have begun to be validated as a set of tests (Russell, 1995). They have been validated in at least two ways. First, piecemeal studies demonstrate that the tests in battery will predict many individual conditions. This has been the most common procedure. Second, patterns derived from the battery may be validated. Neuropsychologists such as Reitan have demonstrated that using the HRB as a whole they can predict many different conditions such as damage in different areas of the brain (Reitan, 1964).

More formalized methods such as computer programs can demonstrate the ability of a battery to also assess different conditions (Goldstein & Shelly, 1982; Russell, 1995; Russell et al., 1970; Wedding, 1983a, 1983b). Finally, a battery is validated when formulas utilizing different groups of tests in the battery are found to identify different conditions, such as Alzheimer's disease (Russell & Polakoff, 1993) or left temporal-lobe damage (Dobbins & Russell, 1990; Russell & Russell, 1993). If patterns using different tests work for many conditions, the battery becomes increasing valid in terms of construct validity.

Scale Development

In this chapter the primary problems concerning accuracy that are addressed are the requirements of scales. There are several questions related to scales that become critical when tests are used in a set. These questions are dealt with through examining the solutions that the HRNES and CNEHRB have utilized. The problem of scale direction is particularly critical in neuropsychology.

Scale Direction. In neuropsychology some scales are impairment scales, such as the Category test, and some are attainment, such as the Finger Tapping Test. When neuropsychologists intuitively deal with scales, particularly raw score scales, they are able to make mental corrections for the different directions in which scales run so that it is possible to mix attainment and impairment scales in a battery. However, this becomes a problem when one applies statistics to the test scores. For example, in a factor analytic study, if a factor is primarily dominated by impairment scales so that impairment scales are positive, the attainment scales will be negative. Ultimately, in order to understand the factor structure the psychologist must decide which direction the tests in a factor proceed and then reverse the signs for all of the tests that go in the other direction. The same problem occurs when an examiner is exploring patterns among a great many scale scores. Thus, to improve the ease of dealing with large sets of tests, scales should run in the same direction. The direction may be either impairment or attainment.

Although it is clear that scales should all run in the same direction in a battery, the question is whether the scales should be impairment or attainment scales. Neuropsychological scales are basically cognitive ability measures, and in the psychology, ability scales almost always run in the attainment direction. It seems appropriate for larger numbers to indicate better performance. By mathematical convention, scales increase on going to the right and up. In neuropsychology, it appears that the direction has been decided, because both the CNEHRB and the HRNES have chosen to use attainment scales. This convention is accepted by both batteries and will undoubtedly become standard for neuropsychology as it has for other ability tests.

Type of Scale. A number of different types of scales exist in neuropsychology and in psychology in general (Anastasi, 1988; Lezak, 1995). There are two major groupings of scales: percentiles and standard score scales. Percentiles are utilized fairly commonly for educational tests, but have the psychometric disadvantage that the size of the interval varies depending on the distance the scores are from the group mean. Percentile scales are difficult to interpret or to use psychometrically. Consequently, percentile scales are primarily used for descriptive purposes.

Standard score scales are derived from z-scores in which the mean is zero and the standard deviation is one. In a z-score scale the numbers below the mean are negative. This is a difficult situation for scaling, and consequently there is general agreement that z-scores themselves are not utilized as a scale in tests. Over the years there have been a number of methods of transforming z-scores into different types of standard scores (Lezak, 1995).

The Wechsler intelligence tests utilized an approach where for intelligence the mean is 100 and the standard deviation is 15. However, for the subtests making up the Wechsler measures the mean is 10 and the standard deviation is 3. This makes it difficult to mentally transform subtest scaled scores into IQ score equivalents or vice versus, a process that is essential for comparative purposes. In addition, other neuropsychological measures do not tend to use this standard score method. Interpretation of a large set of tests requires the ability to easily compare level of performance across all measures.

An alternative standard score to z-scores or the Wechsler scores are T-scores. T-scores utilize 10 as a standard deviation, and 50 to indicate the mean. Apparently, 50 was originally used as the mean in order to prevent the scale scores from having more than three digits in them. That is, it was thought that the scales would never run above 100. However, as we see in the MMPI, scales do run above 100, and so there is no advantage to setting the mean at 50. Additionally, 50 is mathematically more awkward than 100 if you want to combine scales.

An alternative method is to use decimal scales. This type of scale has been utilized throughout science in almost all areas except the human sciences. In a decimal scale, the intervals are set at 10. Applying this to psychology, one would set the mean at 10 and have a standard deviation of 1. There are two advantages to this. One is that it is easy to compare scales with each other or to index scales. The average for any group of scales is approximately the same as the score for any individual scale in the index. Exact combinations require minimal mathematical manipulation (Russell & Starkey, 1993). Second, the scale can be subdivided into an infinite number of subdivisions. For instance, in regard to measure of length, a meter can be divided into centimeters or expanded into kilometers. There is nothing equivalent to this in psychology.

Decimal scales, in which the mean is 10 and the standard deviation is 1, could be applied to psychological measurement. If one needs to increase the finesse of the scale, decimal points can be used. Also, the scales could be increased and decimals removed by multiplying by 10. This would create scales that may be called C-scores (centile-scores). Then the mean becomes 100 and the SD 10. The scale is then quite flexible, without requiring complex calculations or conversions.

Equivalence

The third general characteristic and requirement for an integrated set of tests is equivalence of scales. In regard to the formal structure of an integrated battery, the most important requirement of a set of tests is that the scores of all the tests are equivalent. In order to make multiple comparisons the set must contain a constant background. An internal constant background is created when all of the scales are equivalent so that the same scores indicate the same amount of ability or impairment. Equivalency requires that all of the scales either be normed on the same sample of subjects or that samples are equated by some statistical method.

Norming Problems

There are some critical problems concerned with norming that are related to a set of tests. A primary problem is obtaining enough subjects. However, how representative a sample is of the normal population is less dependent on the size of the sample than how typical it is. For instance, a sample of 500 subjects gathered from 12 locations may not be representative of the country as a whole, if the locations are all college campuses. Although the sample could be large and conform to all the requirements of a normal curve, it would not represent the normal population.

Normal adult subjects are difficult to obtain especially when the battery is long. One solution is to utilize subjects from what is called a negative neurological sample or medical sample (Russell, 1997). These are subjects that were sent to a neuropsychological laboratory to be tested because they were suspected of having brain damage and then a neurological examination found that they did not have an organic condition. This type of sample has been criticized. The critics assert that because brain damage was suspected the subjects must have had something wrong and consequently they are not representative of a normal sample. The irony here is that although the standard criterion for the existence of brain damage is the neurological diagnosis obtained using methods such as computed tomography (CT) or magnetic resonance imaging (MRI), this same criterion is rejected as the criterion for the absence of brain damage.

Russell (1990; Russell & Starkey, 1993) examined the type of problems that a negative neurological sample contained and found that it was largely composed of subjects with a diagnosis of mild depression or some form of neurosis accompanied by memory or somatic complaints, and mild personality disorders. Research has not found that these types of patients have depressed scores on neuropsychological tests (Gass & Russell, 1986; Reitan & Wolfson, 1997).

The nonmedical samples that have been obtained to date are also faulted. These "normal" subjects, which have been obtained "off of the street," have not had a neurological examination and so they may be abnormal. In fact, these "normal" samples have not been normal in the sense of being an unbiased random sample of the total population of a country (Russell, 1995). First, they are volunteers and in many cases they were paid. An example of such a volunteer sample is the Fromm-Auch and Yeudall sample (1983). The mean WAIS Full Scale IQ (FSIQ) of this sample was 119 with a mean age of 25.4 years. Thus, the sample was both young and considerably above average in regard to intellectual ability.

In all of the major studies (Fromm-Auch & Yeudall, 1983; Pauker, 1977), subjects have answered a "structured interview" in which they denied the existence of various types of organic problems. When the interview criteria were quite strict, so as to eliminate any condition that indicated possible organic damage, neurosis, psychosis, and mental retardation, then the sample appeared to be "supernormal" (Fromm-Auch & Yeudall, 1983; Heaton et al., 1991; Pauker, 1977). Obviously, a random sample of a normal population will have some subjects with emotional or organic problems.

Another aspect of the situation with normals is that a fairly high proportion of people above 50 will have some undiagnosed neurological problems that reduce their mental ability, such as cerebral arteriosclerosis (Russell, 1990). In a normative study of older people for Russell's version of the WMS, Haaland, Linn, Hunt, and Goodwin (1983) found lower ability than would be expected from direct extrapolation of the decrease in ability at the earlier ages. Thus a screened voluntary sample may be too "normal" at the younger range and too impaired due to undiagnosed cerebral arteriosclerosis at the older age range (Russell, 1995).

Equalization of Scores

Another major problem concerning the equalization of scales is the use of different populations for norming. When different populations are utilized, the means and standard deviations will vary from population to population. Consequently, the performance represented by a scaled score may vary from scale to scale. There is no constant background. This can be observed in a review of various studies using the Halstead–Reitan Battery (e.g., Fromm-Auch & Yeudall, 1983). Comparison of these studies demonstrates that the means and standard deviations vary greatly from one population to another. Consequently, if the norms for different tests had been derived from these different samples a discrepancy in scores might only reflect a difference in norms (Russell, 1998). It should be noted that any comparison of tests in a flexible battery assumes that the means and the standard deviations of the tests are equivalent, whereas in reality, they are usually different.

Coordinated Norming. A solution to the norming problem, utilized by all developed sets of tests, is that of coordinated norming (Russell, 1997, 1998). Coordinated norming means that all of the subtests in a battery were normed on the same population. Consequently, any difference between scale scores represents a difference within the subject and not between population norms. The first popular test that used coordinated norming was the Wechsler–Bellevue (Wechsler, 1939), in which the subtests were all normed on the same sample. Consequently, one could accurately and legitimately compare the scores from one subtest to another. Both the CNEHRB and the HRNES utilize coordinated norming (Russell, 1997).

Age and Education Correction

For over 30 years, it has been known that both age (Reitan, 1955b) and IQ affect performance on neuropsychological tests (Heaton, Grant, & Matthews, 1986; Pauker, 1977). People are better at doing tests when they are in their 20s than when they are in their 60s or 70s, and for many tests they do better when their intelligence is higher (Gade & Mortensen, 1984; Gade, Mortensen, Udesen, & Jonsson, 1985; Heaton et al., 1986; Pauker, 1977; Reitan, 1955b). Because of this, neuropsychological tests should be corrected for age and IQ level. Age is obviously not affected by brain damage, but IQ is affected, so that some other indication of premorbid ability is needed. Education level is the simplest indication of premorbid ability.

The increased accuracy produced by age and education corrections was recently demonstrated in a study by Heaton, Matthews, Grant, and Avitable (1996). This demonstrated that, as expected, correction increases accuracy in separating brain damaged subjects from normals at the more extreme ends of the education and age range. This increased accuracy was especially evident for the older subjects.

Distribution Problems

A problem that has only recently become obvious with neuropsychological testing (Russell, 1987, 1991), but was previously recognized with regard to the Minnesota Multiphasic Personality Inventory (MMPI; Graham, 1990), is that different tests have different performance distributions. Brain-damaged subjects' tests in almost all cases do not have a normal distribution. They are skewed, and in some cases, severely skewed. For instance, in one study (Russell, 1987, 1991), the Aphasia Test with brain-damaged subjects had a skew in which the tests stretch out for 16 standard deviations from the mean in the impaired direction, whereas the mean for the test was within 1 standard deviation of the top of the distribution.

Not only are brain-damaged subjects' distributions abnormal, but the distributions vary widely from test to test. As long as one is measuring abilities near the normal mean, this difference in distribution does not affect the test results to any great extent. However, when measuring fairly severe brain damage, the difference in distributions may produce a pattern that looks as if a particular type of damage exists, whereas it actually reflects a difference in distributions (Russell, 1987, 1991).

Practical Considerations in Set Design

Although the major structural problems in designing an integrated set of tests have been discussed, there are some other issues that are related to practical aspects of a battery. These include efficiency, good design, adaptability, use of technicians, and crafting a battery for research purposes.

Efficiency. The primary practical problem in designing a test battery is the efficiency of the battery. It is obvious that a battery cannot be too long. There is a paradox in regard to efficiency (Russell, 1986); that is, a test battery cannot simultaneously have adequate coverage, accuracy, and brevity. In a short or brief battery the number of tests is reduced, but adequate coverage, of course, requires many tests. The more tests, the longer the battery is. An alternative to brevity is to reduce the length of the individual tests. However, when one reduces the length of the tests, the accuracy of each individual test is reduced. Consequently, it is not possible to have all three of these attributes simultaneously.

Although a compromise must be made at some point there are some methods of increasing efficiency. A method that requires establishing basal and ceiling scores reduces the administrative length of a long test such as the PPVT–R (Dunn & Dunn, 1981) or Boston Naming Test (Kaplan, Goodglass, & Weintraub, 1983). The reliability is not reduced.

A test should be as short as possible, while retaining its accuracy (Russell, 1986). Statistical studies have demonstrated that as tests grow longer they become more accurate, but that the increase in accuracy decreases with the length of the test. Consequently, there is a point at which you obtain the maximum accuracy with the least length. It has been advised (Nunnally, 1978) that with tests for normals that have with a normal distribution of scores, tests should be at least 20 items long. Obviously, there are many tests in neuropsychology that are either too short or too long. The Digit Span, even in the revised WAIS–R, is too short, whereas the Category Test is too long. It is relatively easy for a test that is too long to be reduced to a useful length. This has been done with the Category Test a number of times (Russell & Levy, 1987). Interestingly, in this regard, the first reduction in the length of the Category Test was accomplished by Reitan (Reitan & Wolfson, 1993).

Another method of increasing efficiency concerns scoring. The more complex the scoring procedures, such as obtaining age and education corrections, the longer is the time and the greater is the possibility of making errors. At least in this area there is a definite solution—that is, to use computer scoring programs. Both the CNEHRB and the HRNES use computer scoring programs.

Good Design. Another attribute of a good test battery is what might be called good design. It is difficult to state the nature of good design, because it is related to such things as ease of administration, whether the patient and examiner like a particular test, and certain aesthetic qualities. It is possible that a test that a subject may enjoy is one that an examiner does not. However, in most cases, if the patient finds a test difficult or unenjoyable it is also unpleasant for the examiner, who, to a certain extent, empathizes with the patient. One of the problems with very long tests, such as the original Category Test, is that they may be unpleasant to take. *Interest* is important in a good design. A test that is designed well will maintain the interest of the subject. An advantage of the Wechsler intelligence tests is that they tend to maintain the interest of the subject.

In some cases a test may be retained that is somewhat unpleasant if it produces a great deal of information. The TPT may be an example of a test that is sometimes found to be disagreeable for the subject but that is worth giving because it produces much information. Interestingly, the TPT is often more disagreeable to the examiner than the subject because it is difficult to watch a patient struggling with the test, but when blindfolded and taking the test for the first time one is less aware of the time.

Research.   The fixed battery has a great advantage over a flexible battery in regard to research; in fact, research almost requires a fixed battery except for single case studies. If the neuropsychologist customarily uses a fixed battery, data can be gathered while the battery is being administered for clinical purposes. If you need to do a study on a new test or combination of new tests, you simply add those tests to the battery and in a year or two you have collected enough data for analysis and publication. Because most psychologists will "try out" new tests, this adding of tests only systematizes an existing process so that it becomes a research study.

The amount of research that has been done on fixed batteries is far greater than on flexible batteries. It is no accident that almost all validity studies of batteries and neuropsychological factor analytic studies have utilized the Halstead–Reitan Battery or the Luria–Nebraska Neuropsychological Battery (Casey, 1991; Russell, 1995). These are the primary fixed batteries. In a fixed battery the same tests are administered across many types of subjects during clinical practice. This creates a pool of subjects from which specific types of subjects can be selected. Large batteries require a huge amount of time to collect a sufficient number of cases for such studies. Only clinical practice can provide such numbers of subjects. From the point of view of research methodology, selecting subjects from a clinical pool to test a hypothesis is no different than selecting them individually from hospital wards and administering the same battery to each. Because an active clinician can also be a researcher, a large proportion of research studies is done with fixed clinical batteries.

CHAPTER SUMMARY AND CONCLUSIONS

In this chapter, the outlines of a theory of cognitive-metric neuropsychology and of test sets or an integrated battery has been explicated. This led to a discussion of instrumentation, the brain function model, multiple dissociation, and a constant background. The nature and requirements for an integrated set of tests were proposed.

Overall, the great advantage of a metric approach to neuropsychology is that psychometric measurement makes possible assessment methods that are public, objective and accurate. This permits research that will continually improve assessment methodology, not just the knowledge base for assessment. As a scientific approach to neuropsychological assessment, one would expect a progressive development of cognitive-metric procedures. Thus, an unlimited methodological development exists for a neuropsychology that adheres to the cognitive-metric approach.

There are especially two major areas where methodological progress may be expected: set theory and computer processing. In regard to the development of test set theory, a better understanding of the nature of representation is being acquired. Theoretical and experimental studies may soon examine the relationship of brain functioning to test construction in greater detail. Certainly, emphasis will be placed on increasing the validity and accuracy of test batteries.

In regard to the concept of a test battery as a brain function model, greater efforts will be made to obtain a constant background for assessment through coverage and methods of equivalence. Coverage is already one of the guiding principles in neuropsychology. Methods designed to obtain equivalence were used to create both the CNEHRB and the HRNES. Future studies will certainly increase both the development and use of methods to obtain equivalence.

Progress in assessment will undoubtedly continue to move from a qualitative, intuitive approach that makes great use of clinical lore to the use of more formally reliable and validated methods. Here, computer processing is clearly the wave of the future. Although computer processing does not guarantee any of the requirements for valid scientific assessment, except perhaps consistency, it does provide programs that are open to correction with further research. Various methods of administration can be examined and the best method for a particular test can be selected. Scoring procedures that increase accuracy but are costly in time and expertise can be computerized and made almost as rapid as the use of raw scores. The use of computer scoring in neuropsychology already includes the Wechsler intelligence and memory tests, the NDS, CNEHRB, HRNES, and LNNB, some children's tests, and some individual tests such as the CVLT (Delis et al., 1987).

Finally, computer interpretation will soon become part of mainstream neuropsychology as it is in other areas of psychology. The computer is capable of almost any cognitive processing in assessment that humans can accomplish (Kleinmuntz, 1968, 1987). The slower development of computer administration (Kane & Kay, 1992), scoring, and interpretation in neuropsychology than in other areas of psychology (Russell, 1995) will certainly be overcome as neuropsychologists accept a more objective approach to assessment.

REFERENCES

Adams, K. M., Kvale, V. I., & Keegan, J. F. (1984). Relative accuracy of three automated systems for neuropsychological interpretation. *Journal of Clinical Neuropsychological, 6,* 413–431.

American Psychological Association. (1988). *Standards for educational and psychological testing.* Washington, DC: APA Press.

Anastasi, A. (1988). *Psychological testing* (6th ed.). New York: Macmillan.

Barron, J. H., & Russell, E. W. (1992). Fluidity theory and the neuropsychological impairment in alcoholism. *Archives of Clinical Neuropsychology, 7,* 175–188.

Butler, M., Retzlaff, P., & Vanderploeg, R. (1991). Neuropsychological test usage. *Professional Psychology: Research and Practice, 22,* 510–512.

Casey, C. J. (1991). *A factor analysis of the Halstead–Reitan neuropsychological battery to investigate the generalized and lateralized effects of brain damage.* Unpublished doctoral dissertation, University of Miami.

Christensen, A. L. (1979). *Luria's neuropsychological investigation* (2nd ed.). Copenhagen: Munksgaard.

Christensen, A. L. (1984). The Luria method of examination of the brain-impaired patient. In P. E. Logue & J. M. Shear (Eds.), *Clinical neuropsychology: A multidisciplinary approach* (pp. 5–28). Springfield, IL: Charles C. Thomas.

Delis, D. C., Kramer, J. H., Kaplan, E., & Ober, B. (1987). *CVLT: California Verbal Learning Test–Research edition.* New York: Psychological Corporation.

Dobbins, C., & Russell, E. W. (1990). Left temporal lobe damage pattern on the Wechsler Adult Intelligence Scale. *Journal of Clinical Psychology, 46,* 863–868.

Dunn, L. M., & Dunn L. M. (1981). *Peabody, Picture Vocabulary Test–Revised, manual.* Circle Pines, MN: American Guidance Service.

Franzen, M. D. (1989). *Reliability and validity in neuropsychological assessment.* New York: Plenum Press.

Fromm-Auch, D., & Yeudall, L. T. (1983). Normative data for the Halstead–Reitan neuropsychological tests. *Journal of Clinical Neuropsychology, 5,* 221–238.

Gade, A., & Mortensen, E. L. (1984, December). *The influence of age, education, and intelligence on neuropsychological test performance.* Paper presented at the 3rd Nordic Conference in Behavioral Toxicology, Arhus, Denmark.

Gade, A., Mortensen, E. L., Udesen, H., & Jonsson, A. (1985, June). *Predictors of cognitive performance: age, education, and intelligence.* Paper presented at the 8th INS European Conference, Copenhagen, Denmark.

Gass, C. S., & Russell, E. W. (1986). Differential impact of brain damage and depression on memory test performance. *Journal of Consulting and Clinical Psychology, 54,* 261–263.

Golden, C. J., Purisch, A. D., & Hammeke, T. A. (1985). *Manual for the Luria–Nebraska Neuropsychological Battery: Forms I and II.* Los Angeles: Western Psychological Services.

Goldstein, K., & Scheerer, M. (1941). Abstract and concrete behavior, An experimental study with special tests. *Psychological Monographs, 53*(2), whole no. 239.

Goldstein, G., & Shelly, C. (1982). A further attempt to cross-validate the Russell, Neuringer, and Goldstein Neuropsychological Keys. *Journal of Consulting and Clinical Psychology, 50,* 721–726.

Goodglass, H., & Kaplan, E. (1983). *The assessment of aphasia and related disorders* (rev. ed.). Philadelphia: Lea & Febiger.

Graham, J. R. (1990). *MMPI–2: Assessing personality and psychopathology.* New York: Oxford.

Guilford, J. P. (1967). *The nature of human intelligence.* New York: McGraw-Hill.

Haaland, K. Y., Linn, R. T., Hunt, W. C., & Goodwin, J. S. (1983). A normative study of Russell's variant of the Wechsler Memory Scale in a healthy elderly population. *Journal of Consulting and Clinical Psychology, 51,* 878–881.

Halstead, W. C. (1947). *Brain and intelligence.* Chicago: University of Chicago Press.

Heaton, R. K., Grant, I., Anthony, W. Z., & Lehman, A. W. (1981). A comparison of clinical and automated interpretation of the Halstead–Reitan Battery. *Journal of Clinical Neuropsychology, 3,* 121–141.

Heaton, R. K., Grant, I., & Matthews, C. G. (1986). Differences in neuropsychological test performance associated with age, education and sex. In I. Grant & K. M. Adams (Eds.), *Neuropsychological assessment of neuropsychiatric disorders* (pp. 100–120). New York: Oxford.

Heaton, R. K., Grant, I., & Matthews, C. B. (1991). *Comprehensive norms for an expanded Halstead–Reitan Battery.* Odessa, FL: Psychological Assessment Resources.

Heaton, R. K., Matthews, C. G., Grant, I., & Avitable, N. (1996). Demographic corrections with comprehensive norms: An overzealous attempt or a good start. *Journal of Clinical and Experimental Neuropsychology 18,* 121–141.

Horn, J. L. (1976). Human abilities: A review of research and theory in the early 1970's. In M. Rosenzweig & L. Porter (Eds.), *Annual review of psychology* (Vol 27, pp. 437–485). Palo Alto, CA: Annual Reviews.

Kane, R. L., & Kay, G.G. (1992). Computerized assessment in neuropsychology: A review of tests and test batteries. *Neuropsychology Review, 3,* 1–117.

Kaplan, E. (1988). A process approach to neuropsychological assessment. In T. Boll & B. K. Bryant (Eds.), *Clinical neuropsychology and brain function: Research, measurement, and practice* (pp. 129–167). Washington, DC: American Psychological Association.

Kaplan, E., Goodglass H., & Weintraub, S. (1983). *Boston Naming Test.* Philadelphia: Lea & Febiger.

Kertesz, A. (1979). *Aphasia and associated disorders: Taxonomy, localization, and recovery.* New York: Grune & Stratton.

Kimble, G. A. (1985). Conditioning and learning. In S. Koch & D. E. Leary (Eds.), *A century of psychology as science* (pp. 284–335). New York: McGraw-Hill.

Kleinmuntz, B. (Ed.). (1968). *Formal representation of human judgement.* New York: John Wiley & Sons.

Kleinmuntz, B. (1987). Automated interpretation of neuropsychological test data: Comments on Adams and Heaton. *Journal of Consulting and Clinical Psychology, 55,* 266–267.

Kline, P. (1986). *A handbook of test construction.* New York: Methuen.

Kolb, B., & Whishaw, I. Q. (1985). *Fundamentals of human neuropsychology* (2nd ed.). New York: W. H. Freeman.

Lezak, M. D. (1984). An individualized approach to neuropsychological assessment. In P. E. Logue & J. M. Shear (Eds.), *Clinical neuropsychology: A multidisciplinary approach* (pp. 29–49). Springfield, IL: Charles C. Thomas.

Lezak, M. D. (1995). *Neuropsychological assessment* (3rd ed.). New York: Oxford University Press.

Luria, A. R. (1973). *The working brain.* New York: Basic Books.

Luria, A. R. (1980). *Higher cortical functions in man* (rev. ed.). New York: Basic Books.

Luria, A. R., & Majovski, L. V. (1977). Basic approaches used in American and Soviet clinical neuropsychology. *American Psychologist, 32,* 959–968.

Mapou, R. L. (1988). Testing to detect brain damage: An alternative to what may on longer be useful. *Journal of Clinical and Experimental Neurology, 10,* 271–278.

Matarazzo, J. D. (1972). *Measurement and appraisal of adult intelligence* (5th ed.). Baltimore, MD: Williams & Wilkins.

Nunnally, J. C. (1978). *Psychometric theory* (2nd ed.). New York: McGraw-Hill.

Pauker, J. D. (1977, February). *Adult norms for the Halstead–Reitan neuropsychological test battery: Preliminary data.* Paper presented at the Annual Meeting of the International Neuropsychological Society, Santa Fe, NM.

Pellegrino, J. W. (1988). Mental models and mental tests. In H. Wainer & H. I. Braun (Eds.), *Test validity* (pp. 49–59). Hillsdale, NJ: Lawrence Erlbaum Associates.

Reitan, R. M. (1955a). An investigation of the validity of Halstead's measures of biological intelligence. *Archives of Neurology and Psychiatry, 73,* 28–35.

Reitan, R. M. (1955b). The distribution according to age of a psychologic measure dependent upon organic brain functions. *Journal of Gerontology, 10,* 338–340.

Reitan, R. M. (1964). Psychological deficits resulting from cerebral lesions in men. In J. M. Warren & K. Akert (Eds.), *The frontal granular cortex and behavior* (pp. 295–312). New York: McGraw-Hill.

Reitan, R. M. (1991). *The Neuropsychological Deficit Scale for Adults computer program. Users manual.* Tucson, AZ: Neuropsychology Press.

Reitan, R. M., & Wolfson, D. (1985). *The Halstead–Reitan Neuropsychological Test Battery: Theory and clinical interpretation.* Tucson, AZ: Neuropsychology Press.

Reitan, R. M., & Wolfson, D. (1986). The Halstead–Reitan Neuropsychological Test Battery. In D. Wedding, A. M. Horton, & J. Webster (Eds.), *The Neuropsychology Handbook* (pp. 134–160). New York: Springer.

Reitan, R. M., & Wolfson, D. (1993). *The Halstead–Reitan Neuropsychological Test Battery; Theory and clinical interpretation* (2nd ed). Tucson, AZ: Neuropsychology Press.

Reitan, R. M., & Wolfson, D. (1997). Emotional disturbances and their interaction with neuropsychological deficits. *Neuropsychological Review, 7,* 3–19.

Rourke, B. P. (1991). Human neuropsychology in the 1990's. *Archives of Clinical Neuropsychology, 6,* 1–14.

Rourke, B. P., & Brown G. G. (1986). Clinical neuropsychology and behavioral neurology: Similarities and differences. In S. B. Filskov & T. J. Boll (Eds.), *Handbook of clinical neuropsychology* (Vol. 2, pp. 3–18). New York: Wiley.

Russell, E. W. (1972, August). The effect of acute lateralized brain damage on a factor analysis of the Wechsler–Bellevue Intelligence Test. *Proceedings, 80th Annual Convention of the American Psychological Association,* Honolulu, HI.

Russell, E. W. (1974). The effect of acute lateralized brain damage on Halstead's Biological Intelligence Factors. *Journal of General Psychology, 90,* 101–107.

Russell, E. W. (1979). Three patterns of brain damage on the WAIS. *Journal of Clinical Psychology, 37,* 246–253.

Russell, E. W. (1980a). Fluid and crystallized intelligence: Effects of diffuse brain damage on the WAIS. *Perceptual and Motor Skills, 51,* 121–122.

Russell, E. W. (1980b, August). *Theoretical bases of the Luria–Nebraska and the Halstead–Reitan Battery.* Paper presented at the 88th Annual Convention of the American Psychological Association, Montreal, Canada.

Russell, E. W. (1984). Theory and developments of pattern analysis methods related to the Halstead–Reitan battery. In P. E. Logue & J. M. Shear (Eds.), *Clinical neuropsychology: A multidisciplinary approach* (pp. 50–98). Springfield, IL: Charles C. Thomas.

Russell, E. W. (1986). The psychometric foundation of clinical neuropsychology. In S. B. Filskov & T. J. Boll (Eds.), *Handbook of clinical neuropsychology* (Vol. 2, pp. 45–80). New York: Wiley.

Russell, E. W. (1987). A reference scale method for constructing neuropsychological test batteries. *Journal of Clinical and Experimental Neuropsychology, 9,* 376–392.

Russell, E. W. (1990, August). *Three validity studies for negative neurological criterion norming.* Paper presented at the 98th Annual Convention of the American Psychological Association, Boston.

Russell, E. W. (1991). A reference scale method for constructing neuropsychological test batteries. In B. P. Rourke, L. Costa, D. V. Cicchetti, K. M., Adams, & J. Plasterk (Eds.), *Methodological and biostatistical foundations of clinical neuropsychology* (pp. 399–415). Berwyn, PA: Swets & Zeitlinger.

Russell, E. W. (1995). The accuracy of automated and clinical detection of brain damage and lateralization in neuropsychology. *Neuropsychology Review. 5*(1), 1–68.

Russell, E. W. (1997). Developments in the psychometric foundations of neuropsychological assessment. In G. Goldstein & T. M. Incagnoli (Eds.), *Contemporary approaches to neuropsychological assessment.* (pp. 15–65). New York: Plenum Press.

Russell, E. W. (1998). In defense of the Halstead Reitan Battery. *Archives of Clinical Neuropsychology, 13,* 365–381.

Russell, E. W., & Levy, M. (1987). A revision of the Halstead Category Test. *Journal of Consulting and Clinical Psychology, 55*, 898–901.

Russell, E. W., Neuringer, C., & Goldstein, G. (1970). *Assessment of brain damage: A neuropsychological approach.* New York: Wiley Company.

Russell, E. W., & Polakoff, D. (1993). Neuropsychological test patterns in men for Alzheimer's and multi-infarct dementia. *Archives of Clinical Neuropsychology, 8*, 327–343.

Russell, E. W., & Russell, S. L. K. (1993). Left temporal lobe damage pattern on the Wechsler Adult Intelligence Scale: An addendum. *Journal of Clinical Psychology, 49*, 241–244.

Russell, E. W., & Starkey, R. I. (1993). *Halstead, Russell Neuropsychological Evaluation System* [Manual and computer program]. Los Angeles: Western Psychological Services.

Russell, E. W., Starkey, R. I., Fernandez, C. D., & Starkey, T. W. (1988). *Halstead, Rennick, Russell Battery* [Manual and computer program]. Miami, FL: Scientific Psychology.

Swiercinsky, D. P. (1978, August). *Computerized SAINT: System for analysis and interpretation of neuropsychological tests.* Presented at the annual meeting of the American Psychological Association, Toronto.

Tarter, R. E., & Edwards, K. L. (1986). Neuropsychological batteries. In T. Incagnoli, G. Goldstein, & C. J. Golden (Eds.), *Clinical application of neuropsychological test batteries* (pp. 135–153). New York: Plenum Press.

Teuber, H. L. (1955). Physiological psychology. *Annual Review of Psychology, 6*, 267–296.

Teuber, H. L. (1975). Recovery of function after brain injury. In *Ciba Foundation Symposium 34, Outcome of severe damage to the central nervous system* (pp. 159–190). Amsterdam: Elsevier.

Walsh, K. W. (1978). *Neuropsychology, A clinical approach.* Hillsdale, NY: Churchill Livingstone.

Wechsler, D. (1939). *The measurement of adult intelligence.* Baltimore, MD: Williams & Wilkins.

Wechsler, D. (1991). *Wechsler Intelligence Scale for Children–Third Edition* (WISC–III), *manual.* San Antonio, TX: Psychological Corporation.

Wechsler, D. (1997). *WAIS–III, Wechsler Adult Intelligence Scale–III, manual.* San Antonio, TX: Psychological Corporation.

Wedding, D. (1983a). Clinical and statistical prediction. *Clinical Neuropsychology, 5*, 49–55.

Wedding, D. (1983b). Comparison of statistical and actuarial models for predicting lateralization of brain damage. *Clinical Neuropsychology, 4*, 15–20.

Werner, H. (1937). Process and achievement: A basic problem of education and developmental psychology. *Harvard Educational Review, 7*, 353–368.

Werner, H. (1956). Microgenesis and aphasia. *Journal of Abnormal and Social Psychology, 52*, 347–353.

CHAPTER FIFTEEN

The Application of Computerized Scoring Programs to Neuropsychological Assessment

Elbert W. Russell

Private Practice, Miami, Florida

Today computers are being utilized in psychology to an ever greater extent (Butcher, 1987). In neuropsychology, computers have been applied to test administration, scoring, and interpretation. Recent advances in the administration of neuropsychological tests by computers have been thoroughly reviewed by Kane and Kay (1992, 1997) and computerized interpretation has been reviewed by Russell (1995, 1997). Consequently, these areas of computer application are not discussed here. Computerized scoring has been utilized in neuropsychology for a number of individual tests and for the Wechsler tests. Computer scoring programs have been available for some of the Wechsler batteries since 1986 (Prifitera, 1986). All current versions of Wechsler tests may be scored by computers. There are computer scoring programs for four adult neuropsychology batteries, one for older children (Reitan, 1992), and one for younger children (Reitan & Wolfson, 1986).

Three of the four computer scoring programs for adult neuropsychology batteries are for versions of the Halstead–Reitan Battery (HRB). The other program is for the Luria–Nebraska Neuropsychological Battery (LNNB; Golden, Purisch & Hammeke, 1985). An excellent recent review of the LNNB was completed by Moses and Purisch (1997). Because this present chapter is primarily concerned with the Halstead–Reitan Battery (HRB), the LNNB is not discussed to any great extent. This chapter is limited to adult neuropsychological scoring systems for the Halstead–Reitan Battery.

THE HALSTEAD–REITAN BATTERY, COMPUTER SCORING PROGRAMS

As Lezak (1995) stated, the Halstead–Reitan Battery "has grown by accretion and revision and continues to be modified by many of its users" (p. 709). This is a commendable attribute of this battery because it means that it has gradually been improved over the years. The original HRB tests were selected by Halstead for their ability to separate brain damage (primarily frontal damage) from normal subjects. Subsequently, Reitan transformed the battery into an instrument that could measure various functions, locate impairment, diagnosis various neurological conditions, and separate neurological from affective conditions.

The most recent advance in regard to the HRB has been the availability of computer scoring programs. These programs, in addition to providing an efficient method of scoring, have also introduced new methodological procedures into neuropsychology norming. These innovations include the coordinated or integrated set of tests with age, education, and gender corrections. The most adequate norms for the HRB are those related to these computerized scoring systems. Norms have been incorporated into the computer programs in order to make the rather extensive calculations involved in these tests more efficient and accurate. In this regard the cognitivemetric approach to neuropsychology, as discussed in chapter 14, is particularly adapted to the use of computers.

Neuropsychological Deficit Scale

The Neuropsychological Deficit Scale for Adults (NDS; Reitan, 1991b) was designed by Reitan to capture much of his thinking concerning adults in assessing the existence and lateralization of brain damage. Reitan's computer program (Reitan, 1991b) calculates three indices derived from the same data, the General Neuropsychological Deficit Scale (G-NDS), the Left Neuropsychological Deficit Scale (L-NDS), and the Right Neuropsychological Deficit Scale (R-NDS). The G-NDS is an index of brain damage designed to take the place of the Halstead Impairment Index (HII). The L-NDS and R-NDS are scales designed to determine the presence of lateralized brain damage. These Neuropsychological Deficit Scales are based on the original Halstead–Reitan Battery. Although HRB raw scores are transformed into scale scores having four levels of functioning, the program is primarily designed as an interpretation aid, not a quantitative scoring and scaling program. It utilizes all of the HRB tests and some of the WAIS subtest scores. All scores need to be entered for the program to work. (In an emergency one can substitute "missing data" scores.) Normative scaling is apparently based on Reitan's experience, but the four levels of scaled scores generally correspond to norms derived from other studies in the middle adult age range.

There have been at least seven validating studies of the G-NDS (Hom, Walker,

& Nici, 1990; Horton & Sobelman, 1997; Oestreicher & O'Donnell, 1995; Reitan, 1991b; Rojas & Bennett, 1995; Sherer & Adams, 1993; Wolfson & Reitan, 1995). The results indicate that the G-NDS may be the most sensitive index of brain damage in existence, at least in the age range to about 60 years (Heaton, Grant, & Matthews, 1996).

Comprehensive Norms
for an Expanded Halstead–Reitan Battery

The second computerized HRB scoring system is the Comprehensive Norms for an Expanded Halstead–Reitan Battery (CNEHRB). The CNEHRB was published in 1991 by Psychological Assessment Resources (Heaton, Grant, & Matthews, 1991). Originally the CNEHRB was intended to be an extensive set of norms for the HRB and some additional tests. Later, a computer scoring and norming program was added for convenience. The CNEHRB norms and program utilize the HRB as the core group of tests but add nine tests to this core in order to better cover cognitive functions and brain areas. The CNEHRB uses either the WAIS or WAIS–R. Scores are corrected for age, education, and gender. Any selection of tests can be scored separately.

To this point, the CNEHRB has been reviewed by Fuerst (1993), by Fastenau and Adams (1996), and by Russell (1997). The review by Fuerst (1993), although pointing out some problems with the computer portion of the program, did not review the underlying norming procedure used by the program (Russell, 1997). The review by Fastenau and Adams (1996) was inappropriate, impractical, and did not compare the program to the alternative of scoring the battery by hand. In their rejoinder, Heaton, Matthews, Grant, and Avitable (1996) pointed out that the primary criticisms of Fastenau and Adams (1996) were based on statistical concepts that are theoretical speculations. This chapter considers that the statistical methods used for norming the CNEHRB were quite adequate and derived from well-accepted statistical methods.

Halstead–Russell Neuropsychological Evaluation System

The third computerized adult scoring system for the HRB was published by Western Psychological Services in 1993 under the name of the Halstead–Russell Neuropsychological Evaluation System (HRNES; Russell & Starkey, 1993). It was derived from an earlier computerized scoring system (Russell, Starkey, Fernandez, & Starkey, 1988). The HRNES is also an extended HRB. Most of the added tests are commonly used neuropsychology tests. The battery includes the HRB, WAIS–R (Wechsler, 1981), Wechsler Memory Scale (WMS; Wechsler, 1974), Wide Range Achievement Test (WRAT) Reading subtest (Jastak & Jastak, 1965), Peabody Picture Vocabulary Test (PPVT; Dunn & Dunn 1981), Boston Naming Test (BNT; Kaplan, Goodglass, & Weintraub, 1983), and Grooved Pegboard. It also includes several tests that were specifically constructed for the battery.

From its inception the HRNES was designed to extend both the HRB and the assessment and interpretation methods pioneered by Reitan, in order to create a new system of assessment. The HRNES was designed for pattern analysis (Russell & Starkey, 1993). Finally, to aid interpretation, the HRNES provides several methods that assist in pattern analysis.

The HRNES has been reviewed five times at this point. The review by Lezak (1995) was highly critical, but the review was almost entirely incorrect in its understanding of and statements regarding the HRNES (Russell, 1998). The other three reviews were quite favorable (Lynch, 1995; Mahurin, 1995; Retzlaff, 1995). Lynch reviewed all three programs briefly. The reviews by Mahurin (1995) and Retzlaff (1995), which are in *The Twelfth Mental Measurements Yearbook* (1995), were thorough and fair. Both were favorably impressed by the battery. Mahurin (1995) state, "the HRNES and kindred programs represent the future of neuropsychological scoring procedures" (p. 451). Retzlaff (1995) concluded, "The HRNES is a major improvement over the use of differing norm sets across all tests used by neuropsychologists" (p. 452). These latter three reviewers all recommended the HRNES for clinical usage. Russell (1997) reviewed and compared the CNEHRB and the HRNES. The results, although given in more detail, are substantially the same as those described in this chapter.

ADVANTAGES OF COMPUTERIZED SCORING

These computer programs improve the efficiency, accuracy, and validity of neuropsychological assessment and provide some aids for interpretation. Validity is discussed at a later point in this chapter.

Efficiency

A primary reason for using a computer scoring program is to improve efficiency. The amount of time and effort required of an examiner to use normative tables for comprehensive batteries, with corrections for age, education, and gender, is almost prohibitive. In the developmental stage of the HRNES (Russell, Starkey, Fernandez, & Starkey, 1988), scoring was compared between the computer and the examiner or technician. It took at least 2 hr for a psychologist, who was familiar with the program, to score all 60 measures. In the computerized form the scoring can be completed as rapidly as the technician can enter the data into the computer, usually in about 15 to 20 min.

Accuracy

Another way that a computer scoring program can improve neuropsychological examination is through improved accuracy. As scoring procedures become more complex, the probability of making errors increases. The HRNES computes over 150 calculations related to 60 test scores. A program does not make errors if the raw scores have been correctly entered. In evaluating the early form of the HRNES (Russell, Starkey, Fernandez, & Starkey, 1988), it was found that examiners made approximately three errors per protocol.

Time Saving Through the Use of Technicians

Computerized scoring is almost designed to utilize the services of a technician (Russell, 1984). Much of the testing and scoring done in neuropsychology is routine and, with a correctly designed battery, can be completed quite well by a trained, bright technician (DeLuca, 1989; Division 40 Task Force on Education, 1991). The use of a technician saves a great deal of time for neuropsychologists.

Flexible Usage of Fixed Batteries

Although both the CNEHRB and HRNES are essentially fixed batteries, they and their computer scoring programs can be used in a flexible manner. After entering in the computer some basic demographic information needed to score all the tests, test selection is not directed. Even if only a few test are used, scoring is faster and more accurate than if done by hand. Both computer programs score each test individually using the same coordinated norms and age / education corrections for each test, so the tests can be used in a completely flexible manner while retaining the norm coordination and correction.

Multiple Comparisons

Because all three adult HRB computer scoring programs are so easy to utilize and all employ approximately the same scoring system, a neuropsychologist can run the same raw data on all three programs and compare the findings. (Some minor adjustments may need to be made to the raw score to fit different programs.)

This may be helpful in a clinical situation or in forensic cases. The neuropsychologist can rescore the other neuropsychologists work using the programs. Because some neuropsychologists modify the procedures used for administering tests, such as administering the Tapping Test only twice with each hand, techniques may need to be used to make the tests compatible.

COMPARING THE COMPUTER PROGRAMS' FEATURES AND INTERFACE

The three HRB adult computer scoring programs have many aspects in common (Russell, 1997). All three programs are IBM compatible programs. The

NDS and CNEHRB are DOS programs, whereas the HRNES is a Windows program. The examiner inputs raw or calculated raw scores, from which the programs calculate scale scores based on actual or experiential norms.

Input

In all three programs the patient's raw scores are entered into the computer guided by the program. The scoring and even test administration procedures may vary somewhat across these three methods. The NDS strictly follows Reitan's methods of administration and scoring. For the most part the CNEHRB also follows Reitan's methods. HRNES scoring occasionally varies slightly from Reitan's methods, so the administration section in the manual should be followed. The HRNES manual provides scoring aids, such as models for scoring TPT Location and the Aphasia Screening Test. The scoring for the Boston Naming Test also has been somewhat modified. Wechsler tests are used in all three programs. It may be more efficient to score the WAIS–R or WAIS by means of their own computer programs and then use those scale scores in the various neuropsychology programs. The HRNES uses WAIS–R age-corrected scale scores, not the general scale scores. Data entry is straightforward, although the CNEHRB and NDS require a moderate amount of small computations for some tests and indices prior to data entry.

Processing

Transformation of raw scores to scale scores differs across the three programs. In the CNEHRB and HRNES the scale scores are corrected for age and education. This processing is derived from the way in which the scoring programs were constructed, so it is discussed in detail under that heading.

Output

All three programs permit scores to be printed and stored. The printouts are fairly extensive with the HRNES and CNEHRB; both provide profiles of the test results so that results can be viewed graphically. The CNEHRB prints the summary results in a condensed form on two pages. This enables the neuropsychologist to easily append these results to a written report.

The HRNES printout has three sections: a score section, a graph section, and an input section. The score section prints the raw score, a corrected raw score (corrected for age, gender, and education), and a scale score for each test. (For WAIS–R Digit Span and the Corsi Board the raw score is not the inputted score, instead the input variable is the traditional span; i.e., the number of items correctly recalled.) The graph section allows one to visualize the amount of impairment for each test. This section is organized by function. For example, all

tests of executive functions are placed together. In some cases a multideter-
mined test may appear in more than one functional area. Because this area is by
functions, it can serve as a guide to neuropsychologists during interpretation
and report writing. The final section of the HRNES printout is a record of exactly what the examiner entered into the computer as a check on the accuracy of
the input.

With both the CNEHRB and HRNES, raw scores and scale scores can also
be printed to the screen. This allows one to view test results without printing
them. One drawback with the CNEHRB program is that in printing to the
screen the program rapidly scrolls through the entire results section unless it is
stopped by pressing the space bar or break button. The HRNES procedure to
print to the screen is somewhat circuitous. It requires one to use "Print," then select "Text File," assign a name, and then press "Enter." At that point the entire
HRNES output file will be printed on the screen. The other programs provide
the choice directly under "print."

In all programs the test results are stored in case they need to be recalled later.
Both the HRNES and CNEHRB have a method for transporting the scores into
a data file using a text format for research purposes.

PSYCHOMETRIC FEATURES
OF THE COMPUTER SCORING PROGRAMS

Each of the three programs developed a different way of establishing a standard
metric relationship for their systems. This relationship is established through
performing several operations that extend from the patients test response to the
final scale score.

In an initial step for both the NDS and CNEHRB, some scores may need to
be calculated from the patients responses to obtain the calculated raw score. For
example, minutes and seconds may need to be transformed into seconds, or
the scores from several parts of a test such as the Category test may need to
be summed. This process can be complex, especially with the TPT Time score,
for which minutes, seconds, and number of blocks placed must be transformed
into minutes. The HRNES computes almost all of these calculated scores for the
examiner. Both the NDS and the CNEHRB programs require the examiner to
calculate these raw scores. In addition the CNEHRB does not calculate the HII
or the Average Impairment Rating (AIR) that it uses. The NDS calculates its own
index, the G-NDS.

Neuropsychological Deficit Scale

The NDS is primarily an interpretation program that uses scale scores as part of
the interpretative process. Raw scores are categorized into a four point impair-

ment scale: 0 = normal, 1 = borderline normal, 2 = mild to moderate impairment, and 3 = severe impairment. Attainment raw scores, such as finger tapping, are reversed so that all scales reflect level of impairment. Raw score categorization into these four levels was based on Reitan's experience, verified by comparing them to control patients (Reitan, 1991a, p. 81). The levels of performance generally correspond to other normative data, at least until the older age ranges. Age, education, and gender corrections are not made. Neuropsychologists must allow for these influences in making their interpretations.

Three summary scores are generated: General Neuropsychological Deficit Scale (G-NDS), Right Neuropsychological Deficit Scale (R-NDS), and Left Neuropsychological Deficit Scale (L-NDS). To calculate these summary scores, the program analyzes the data following four interpretative strategies (Reitan, 1991b, p. 78): level of performance, pathognomonic signs, patterns of performance, and right–left differences. The Level of Performance subprogram assigns scale scores according to severity of impairment. The Pathognomonic Signs program uses indications of brain damage from items on the Aphasia Screening Test that are indicative of brain damage, such as dysnomia. Scores represent severity of the pathological sign. The two Patterns of Performance scores are derived from WAIS and HRB subtest patterns. The Right–Left Differences score is obtained by comparing various tests that involve the two sides of the body, such as finger tapping. The greater the difference is, the higher the impairment score. The program combines all of these scores and obtains total scores. If the total score is greater than 25, the patient is considered to have brain damage.

CNEHRB and HRNES

Although the CNEHRB uses Reitan's scoring method exactly, the HRNES scoring for a few tests varies somewhat from Reitan's procedure in ways that do not change the nature of Reitan's method. When research demonstrated a more efficient method, such as shortening the Category test to form the RCAT (Russell & Levy, 1987), the HRNES utilized the new method. However, if need be, modified test scores easily can be recalculated into original scores with slight adjustments.

Scaling Procedure. The scaling procedure constitutes the operations in which calculated raw scores are transformed into scale scores utilizing a set of norms. The method of transforming raw scores into scale score units is different for the CNEHRB and HRNES. Both the HRNES and CNEHRB use attainment scales based on z-scores. However, the CNEHRB uses T-scores as the final scale score. The HRNES chose a different form of z-score, the decimal scale or C-score (Russell, 1997; Russell & Starkey, 1993). This scale has a mean of 100 and standard deviation of 10.

The first step in the CNEHRB's scaling procedure transforms calculated raw scores into a normalized Scale Score Equivalent (mean of 10 and a standard deviation of 3) based on the norms for the entire sample. The use of 3 points per standard deviation sets the limit on the precision of every scale. These scale scores are subsequently transformed to age; education; and gender-adjusted T-scores. However, it should be noted that no matter how many points are in the T-scores, the initial transformation limits the precision of the scale scores to 3 points per standard deviation (Russell, 1997).

The HRNES uses three steps to transform the scores that are entered into the computer into demographically corrected scale scores. First, calculated raw scores are determined. Second, age; education; and gender-corrected raw scores are calculated. Third, the corrected raw scores are transformed into scale scores using normative tables. Impairment scores are reversed in this process. The lowest possible score for a test is assigned to the test when a CND (Could Not Do) is indicated. Further details for scaling are found in the manual (Russell & Starkey, 1993).

A reference norming procedure was used to create the norming tables for the HRNES (Russell, 1987; Russell & Starkey, 1993, pp. 33–34). This was similar to the approach used in developing the T-scores on the MMPI–2. In this approach scores for each test were predicted from an impairment index, similar to the Average Impairment Score (AIS), derived from the norming sample of normal subjects. As such, the distribution was relatively normal. Because brain-damaged subjects' scores vary greatly in the form of the distribution (Russell, 1987), this method of predicting to the AIS results in similar levels of impairment for comparable C-scores across tests. When new tests were added to the HRNES battery, their scale scores were statistically converted, using this reference scale norming, so that they were coordinated with the rest of the battery.

Corrections for Age, Education, and Gender. Both the CNEHRB and the HRNES adjust or correct for age, education, and gender. The CNEHRB corrects for age, education, and gender in one procedure. The program uses multiple linear regression to convert the scale score equivalent to age; education; and gender-adjusted T-scores. On the basis of an unpublished study showing little performance variation between the ages of 20 and 35 years, the age correction was set to 34 across these younger ages.

The HRNES scale score corrections were applied to the raw score data prior to transformation to scale scores. For the age correction the normal or comparison sample was used to obtain a regression formula for each test. This liner regression was used to predict the midpoint in every age decade for each measure. These predicted scores form the tables that are used in the computer program.

The HRNES does not directly correct for education level as does the CNEHRB. Rather, the HRNES corrects for IQ directly and for education level indirectly. An unpublished study[1] completed by the author found that significant

---

[1] In constructing the HRNES the author kept the test data used to norm the battery available in the research computer memory data bank along with the related demographic and diagnostic categories. Consequently, he was able to easily run far more brief exploratory studies than could be published in research papers. These provided an extensive understanding of how the various tests in the battery were related.

changes in IQ occurred in steps at each graduation level. For example, there is no major difference in IQ between 12 years of education and 15 years of education, but there is after graduation from college. Consequently, the HRNES used four levels of correction: less than a high school graduation (<12 years), high school graduation (12–15 years), college graduation (16–19 years), and an advanced graduate degree (≥20 years). Rather than using education directly, this correction was based on the average WAIS–R Full Scale IQ (FSIQ), which was obtained for each of the four education levels (WAIS FSIQ: <HS = 95, HS = 101, BA = 113, PhD and MD = 123). Corrections are calculated from a linear regression prediction of the HRNES test scores equivalent to the mean WAIS–R FSIQ level for each of the four education levels. For instance, the person with 12 years of education has a correction on all HRNES scores equivalent to a WAIS–R FSIQ of 101, the mean FSIQ for subjects with a high school degree. No corrections are made for educational levels below the 10th grade, because factors other than ability can prevent individuals from attaining a high school education. The computer program contains correction for these four levels. The mean IQ for the entire sample is the high school level, so that if the person has a high school education no correction is made. If the person has a college degree then the difference between college and high school IQs are subtracted from the person's test scores. This corrects the test score so that it is equivalent to the mean high school FSIQ level. The same type of correction is made for people having a graduate degree.

The HRNES correction for gender consists of subtracting the mean difference between male and female scores from the male scores to obtain the female scores. The gender correction was restricted to two measures, Grip Strength and Finger Tapping. Research has shown that for the HRB only these tests were significantly different for the two sexes (Dodrill, 1979; Heaton et al., 1986).

The increased accuracy produced by age and education corrections was recently demonstrated in a study by Heaton et al. (1996). Demographic corrections increased accuracy of differentiating brain-damaged subjects from normals, particularly at the more extreme ends of the education and age ranges.

CNEHRB and HRNES Normative Samples

Negative Neurologicals. In neuropsychology there has been an ongoing debate as to whether medical or negative neurological subjects should be included in normative samples. Theoretical aspects of this problem were discussed in chapter 14. Both the CNEHRB and the HRNES evidently included medical patients with negative neurological findings in their normative samples. Russell (1990; Russell & Starkey, 1993) examined the clinical problems present within a negative neurological sample and found primarily diagnoses of mild depression or some form of neurosis accompanied by memory or somatic complaints, and mild personality disorders. Research has not found that these types of patients have depressed scores on neuropsychological tests (Gass & Russell, 1986; Reitan & Wolfson, 1997).

All of the HRNES subjects had been referred to the neuropsychological laboratory to determine whether the patients had brain damage. In most cases an independent neurological evaluation found that the patients did not have a neurological condition. These formed the normal comparison group for the HRNES.

For the CNEHRB, "All subjects completed structured interviews in which they denied any history of learning disability, neurological disease, other illnesses which affect brain functioning, significant head trauma, serious psychiatric disorder, (e.g. schizophrenia) or alcoholism, drug abuse" (Heaton et al., 1991, p. 5). Because the authors of the CNEHRB did not disclaim the inclusion of negative neurological medical patients, one may presume that they were included. However, the proportion of such patients can not be determined from the CNEHRB manual.

CNEHRB. The CNEHRB is composed of the HRB, along with nine other tests and the WAIS (Heaton et al., 1991). Norms for the WAIS–R, which were not derived from this sample, were introduced later (Heaton, 1992). The normative sample was composed of 378 subjects, and another 108 were used to validate the norms but did not contribute to the norming. Sample sizes for the tests that were added to the HRB varied (Heaton et al., 1991, p. 5, Table 2). The average age of the normative sample was 42.0 years; 34.4% were women. Minority composition of the CNEHRB normative sample was not reported.

Normative subjects for the CNEHRB were collected from 11 sites; however, the sample sizes from the various sites is not provided. Based on examination of the database for a previous study, it is apparent that most subjects came from three sites (Heaton et al., 1986). The great majority of normal subjects were paid "control" subjects from three medical centers in university communities in the northern, midwestern, and western parts of the United States. The intellectual ability of such subjects may not be representative of the United States at large. Rather, such a sample likely would be above the average for the nation as a whole.

The average education level of the CNEHRB sample was 13.6 years. The average WAIS FSIQ was 113.8. Because the WAIS–R FSIQ is 6.9 points higher than the WAIS (Russell, 1992), the WAIS–R equivalent would be 106.9. This is about a half standard deviation above average for the nation. In addition, the manual states that these norms are equivalent to those in the Fromm-Auch and Yeudall study (1983), which had a mean WAIS FSIQ of 119 and a mean age of 25.4 years. This was definitely above average.

HRNES. The HRNES is composed of the HRB, along with 14 other tests. Either the WAIS or WAIS–R can be used. The normative sample was composed of 200 subjects, and another 576 were used in the procedure to construct the scale scores. The sample sizes for the additional tests varied (Russell & Starkey, 1993, pp. 28–29, Table 1). The HRNES sample was collected at two VA Medical Centers. The demographic representativeness of the HRNES sample is provided in the manual, which lists age education, sex, and ethnicity for the various tests (pp. 28–31). The average age of the normative sample was 44.6 years; 12% of the sample were women and 6% were Black. The mean WAIS–R FSIQ for the HRNES normative sample was 102 and their educational level was 12.7 years.

The HRNES normative sample was from the Miami and Cincinnati VA Medical Centers. Because most of the military personal were originally drafted, and essentially a random sample especially during World War II, these subjects should represent a random cross section of the country. Although there were only two locations, these sites, and especially Miami, were highly cosmopolitan. The veterans came from all parts of the country. Except for psychiatric patients, the patients at a VA Medical Center are equivalent to those of any general hospital. By the time most patients entered the VA Medical Centers for this study, war injuries had healed, stabilized, or the patient had died, so combat injuries constituted a very small portion of the physical problems that VA patients exhibited.

The mean WAIS–R FSIQ for the HRNES normal group was 102.1 and their mean educational level was 12.7 years (Russell & Starkey, 1993, pp. 28, 39). This is as representative of the national average for the entire age range of adults as has been obtained. In comparing the HRNES and CNEHRB norms, the HRNES norms are in almost every case somewhat lower than those of the CNEHRB (Russell, 1997) and more representative of the national average.

Although the HRNES norms are more representative of the population at large, this does not mean that the HRNES is more accurate than the CNEHRB in assessing the existence of brain damage. The cutting points indicating brain damage were set differently for the two programs. The cutting point for the HRNES is set at approximately ½ SD below the mean while that for the CNEHRB is set at 1 SD below the mean. Because this is approximately the amount that the CNEHRB scores differ from the HRNES, their accuracy should be almost equal (Russell, 1997).

Supportive Studies.   Kay, Morris, and Starbuck (1993) conducted a study of airline pilots. They found that both the CNEHRB and HRNES age- and education-corrected norm scores were generally equivalent to those obtained by the pilots in the same age and education categories. A second study (Tombaugh & Hubley, 1998) developed excellent norms for the 60-Item Boston Naming Test. The Boston Naming Test is one of the tests that had been added to the HRNES. Examination of the Tombaugh and Hubley (1998) norms found them to be almost identical to HRNES norms in regard to both the age- and education-corrected scores.

Validity Studies

CNEHRB.   There have been at least two validity studies for the CNEHRB. The manual presents the first study (Heaton et al., 1991, pp. 14–19), in which the normative sample (*N* = 486) is compared to a brain-damaged group (*N* = 329) to select a cutting point and to demonstrate the ability of the AIR score of the CNEHRB to distinguish brain-damaged from normal subjects. Age; education; and gender-corrected AIR *T*-scores were used. The most adequate cutting point was a *T*-score of 40. This had correctly classified 88% of normals and 80% of the brain-damaged subjects.

Heaton et al. (1996) subsequently demonstrated that the age- and education-adjusted scores greatly improve the accuracy of a battery over nonadjusted scores, and when applied to the AIR accurately separated brain-damaged subjects from normals across three age levels, <40, 40–59, and 60+ years. The overall hit rate ranged from 76.9% to 84.9% correct.

HRNES.   The HRNES manual presents three studies, concerning all of the major tests in the battery including the two indices, the AIS and the Percent Impaired Index (Russell & Starkey, 1993). In the first study the cutoff points for the indices and the index tests are presented. These points generally fall at one-half *SD* below the mean. The average accuracy for distinguishing brain-damaged from normal (comparison) subjects was 86% for the AIS and 83% for the Percent Impaired score. In the second studies, analyses of variance (ANOVAs) comparing normal and brain-damaged groups were significant for the two indices and all of the tests in the battery. The third study used an ANOVA across right, left, and diffusely brain-damaged subjects and found that the indices for the existence of brain damage were unaffected by lateralized damage.

INDICES OF BRAIN DAMAGE

Early studies by Reitan (1955) and Spreen and Benton (1965) indicated that batteries, but particularly summary measures such as the Halstead Impairment Index (HII), were more accurate than single tests for brain damage. Studies have continued to support the greater accuracy of a group of tests in distinguishing brain damage from nonbrain damage (Russell & Starkey, 1993). Since the development of the HII for brain damage (Halstead, 1947), a number of other indices have been developed. The NDS, the CNEHRB, and the HRNES all utilize indices in their programs. For clarity these are described in Table 15.1.

In this table the Source is the battery or computer program for which the indices were created. The Neuropsychological Key (Russell, Neuringer, & Goldstein, 1970) was fairly widely used but is now out of date. The other three programs are described in this chapter.

Although the calculation procedures are so variable and complex that they

TABLE 15.1
HRB Neuropsychological Indices
of Drain Damage and Lateralization That Are in Use

Source	Index	Type	Date
HRB	HII	Existence of BD	1947
Neuropsychological Key	AIR	Average impairment	1970
	Rennick Index	Existence of BD	
	The Key	Lateralization	
NDS	G-NDS	Existence of BD	1988
	R-NDS	Lateralization	
	L-NDS	Lateralization	
HRNES	AIS	Average impairment	1993
	% Impaired	Existence of BD	
	Lateralization Index	Lateralization	
CNEHRB^a Uses	HII	Existence of BD	1991
	AIR	Average impairment	
	Margin symbols		

Note. A full discussion of these indices including a description of the unused indices and keys is provided in Russell (1995). *Abbreviations:* AIR = Average Impairment Rating, AIS = Average Impairment Score, BD = Brain Damage, CNEHRB = Comprehensive Norms for an Extended Halstead–Reitan Battery, G-NDS = General–Neuropsychological Deficit Scale, L-NDS = Left Neuropsychological Deficit Scale, HRB = Halstead–Reitan Battery, HRNES = Halstead–Russell Neuropsychological Evaluation System, HII = Halstead Impairment Index, NDS = Neuropsychological Deficit Scale, R-NDS = Right Neuropsychological Deficit Scale.
^{a}The HII and AIR are derived from other sources and the Margin Symbols specifies when a single test indicates either severe impairment or lateralized impairment.

cannot be put in a table, the general types of indices are provided. At present there are indices for two kinds of neurological conditions, *existence* of and *lateralization* of brain damage. There are two general types of indices for the existence of brain damage, presence and average impairment. Indices for the presence of brain damage, such as the HII, set a cutting point for each test that indicates brain damage. When a certain number of the tests in the index are in the brain damaged range the index designates the existence of brain damage. The average impairment type of index averages the test scores for the index. A certain score indicates brain damage and the index score also indicates the severity of impairment. The dates at which the various sources were published are also provided.

Halstead Impairment Index (HII)

In its current form the Halstead Impairment Index (HII; Halstead, 1947) is the proportion of seven HRB index tests that fall within the brain damaged range.

These are the Category Test, TPT Total Time, TPT Memory score, TPT Location score, Speech-sounds Perception Test, Rhythm Test, and dominant-hand Finger Tapping. When half of the tests are in the brain-damage range, the index would be .5, indicating the presence of brain damage (Reitan & Wolfson, 1985). The HII has been thoroughly studied and validated (Kane, 1991; Russell, 1995, 1998). It is more accurate than any single test and as accurate as the other indices except for the G-NDS. The accuracy of the HII has varied from 58% to 92% depending on the conditions, but overall accuracy was about 80% correct.

Average Impairment Rating (AIR)

The AIR (Russell, Neuringer, & Goldstein, 1970) is the average of the scale scores of the 12 component subtests that constitute the index. The tests are the 7 tests in the HII, plus the Trail Making Test B, Digit Symbol (WAIS), Aphasia Screening Test, Spatial Relations Test (The Aphasia Test–Cross), and the Perceptual Disorders Test (Russell et al., 1970). Scale scores are required as the basis for the measure. The AIR is as accurate as the HII in determining the existence of brain damage (Anthony, Heaton, & Lehman, 1980; Russell, 1984) and has the advantage of quantifying the amount of impairment, as well as providing a cutting point for damage. The corrected AIR used with the CNEHRB has been found to be considerably more accurate than the uncorrected AIR for older age ranges and for higher levels of education (Heaton et al., 1996).

Neuropsychological Deficit Scale

The NDS includes three indices, one for the presence of brain damage (G-NDS), and two for lateralization (R-NDS and L-NDS).

General-Neuropsychological Deficit Scale (G-NDS). The G-NDS is calculated from the four subprograms in Reitan's Neuropsychological Deficit Scale computer program (Reitan, 1991a). It is very complicated and difficult to calculate the index without the computer program. Each of the four methods used in Reitan's analysis of the HRB are scored separately. The items in each one of these scoring methods are assigned numbers and then summed. This sum is the total score for the G-NDS. G-NDS scores less than 25 are in the brain-damaged range. The G-NDS has been validated in at least seven studies (Hom et al., 1990; Horton & Sobelman, 1997; Oestreicher & O'Donnell, 1995; Reitan, 1991b; Rojas & Bennett, 1995; Sherer & Adams, 1993; Wolfson & Reitan, 1995). These studies have found the G-NDS to be more accurate in separating normals from brain-injured patients than the HII. At least in the middle age range the G-NDS is a somewhat more accurate indicator of brain damage than the indices used by the CNEHRB and HRNES. Consequently, it appears to be the most sensitive index of brain damage in existence, at least in the age range up to about 60 years. However, scores considered to be normal for older people by the CNEHRB and HRNES will fall in the impaired range for the G-NDS (Russell, 1997).

Probably the major reason that the G-NDS is somewhat more sensitive to brain damage than other indices is that it combines the lateralization and severity of impairment into a single score. A brain-damaged subject with an impairment score just within the normal range but with lateralized impairment will be scored as brain-damaged with the G-NDS but not with other methods.

Right and Left Neuropsychological Deficit Scales (R-NDS and L-NDS). The NDS computer program also calculates two scales for lateralized impairment, the R-NDS and L-NDS (Reitan, 1991b). They are scored separately in part because they measure impairment in each hemisphere as well as lateralization. There have been two validation studies of these indices (Reitan, 1991b; Sherer & Adams, 1993). Reitan (1991b) examined the results for a cerebral vascular damage (CVD) group, a group with clear-cut lateralization. Eighty-seven percent of both right- and left-hemisphere lesions were correctly classified, and there were no errors in the opposite direction. This is the highest lateralization hit rate reported in the literature (Russell, 1995). Thirteen percent of both groups were classified diffuse. Correct lateralization classification for head trauma and other categories that do not have clear-cut lateralization were lower. Because the other groups undoubtedly have some damage in both hemispheres, the lateralization score with CVD probably represents the actual accuracy of the R-NDS / L-NDS Index.

The only cross-validation study completed at this time was done by Sherer and Adams (1993). It found the accuracy of the L-NDS and R-NDS to be somewhat less than in the original study, 54.8% correct across all three categories and 88.9% correct for the right and left categories alone.

CNEHRB

The CNEHRB uses two indices, the HII and AIR, and some margin symbols. The HII and AIR must be calculated by the examiner and then entered into the computer program, where they are given age; education; and gender-adjusted T-scores. The CNEHRB program also prints symbols indicating possible brain damage or lateralization of damage. One symbol, the pounds sign (#), indicates when a particular score is below 1 *SD* and consequently is in the brain-damaged range. Findings of possible lateralization significance on a test are marked on the printout by the symbols #L for left-hemisphere impairment and #R for right-hemisphere impairment. These indicate that a certain score, such as left-hand Finger Tapping, is sufficiently different from the equivalent test for the opposite side of the body to indicate a lateralized condition.

HRNES

The HRNES contains two indices of brain damage, the Average Index Score (AIS) and the Percent Impaired Index. It also has an index of lateralization (Lateralization Index). The brain-damage indices, which are calculated by the program, require that at least 7 of the 10 index tests be administered.

Average Index Score. The AIS is the average of the scale scores of the 10 component tests that constitute this index. These tests are the Category Test, Trail Making Test B, Finger Tapping Test, Digit Symbol (WAIS–R), TPT Total Time, TPT Memory Test, Speech Perception Test, Block Design (WAIS–R), Aphasia Screening Test, and the Perceptual Disorders Total score (Russell & Starkey, 1993, Manual) Three of the tests included in the HII were eliminated. These were the Cross Drawing (Spatial Relations) from the Aphasia Screening Test, Seashore Rhythm Test, and TPT Location. Unpublished norming studies indicated that they were not as accurate as the other tests in the index (Russell, 1995; Russell & Starkey, 1993). The WAIS–R Block Design and Digit Symbol were added to the AIS, because they are among the tests most sensitive to brain damage that are used in the total HRB. Although the Aphasia and the Perceptual Disorders tests are not highly accurate for determining brain damage, they extend the range of the AIS. Many of the other tests in the index have a restricted floor. The 10 test scale scores that compose the average of the AIS are age and education adjusted.

Percent Impaired Index. The Percent Impaired Index is the percent of the 10 component tests that constitute this index that fall within the brain-damage range. The Percent Impaired Index uses the same tests as does the AIS. This index is as accurate as the AIS. As with the AIS, the 10 test scale scores that compose the Percent Impaired Index are age and education adjusted.

HRNES Lateralization Index. Details of the Lateralization Index are given in Russell's 1995 paper (p. 53). The Lateralization Index uses HRNES age- and education-corrected scale scores to calculate the index score. This should make the index more accurate, especially in the young and older age ranges. For instance, the difference between the left- and right-hand performance on the TPT that changes with age (Goldstein & Braun, 1974) becomes part of the Lateralization Index (Russell, 1997). The Lateralization Index is distinct from the two HRNES general brain damage indices, AIS and the Percent Impaired Index. Consequently, even if the AIS indicates that the person's total score is in the normal range, the Lateralization Index could indicate lateralized impairment. It is suggested that one seriously consider the possibility of brain damage when either the AIS and/or the Percent Impaired Index is in the impaired range, or the Lateralization Index strongly indicates the existence of a lateralized condition.

The HRNES Lateralization Index requires the following 10 tests: Aphasia Screening Test, Cross Drawing Test, Index Finger Tapping Test, Tactual Performance Test, Grip Strength Test, Suppression, Fingertip Number Writing Test, Finger Agnosia Test, WAIS–R VIQ and PIQ scores, and Visual Field Score.

An earlier form of this index was applied to 151 subjects that had been definitively diagnosed by medical university staff neurologists (Russell, 1984). The subjects included right, left, and diffuse cases. Overall the index was 78.1% accurate, and no errors were made regarding the right versus left discrimination. To date this Lateralization Index has not been cross-validated.

There are several other tests in the HRNES with lateralization significance. These are Speech-sounds Perception, Vocabulary, Block Design, and possibly others as indicated in the HRNES manual, Table 8 (Russell & Starkey, 1993, pp. 40–41). In using the HRNES, neuropsychologists are encouraged to consider these measures in interpretation of lateralization, because they are not part of the Lateralization Index.

SPECIAL FEATURES
OF THE THREE COMPUTER PROGRAMS

Interpretation

The NDS is largely designed to be an interpretative aid. Neither the CNEHRB nor the HRNES was designed as an interpretative program, but both have features that may aid interpretation. The manual for CNEHRB has an excellent section on the interpretation of the program (pp. 35–38) that should be read thoroughly. The manual for the HRNES provides the most extensive information available concerning the parameters of the different subtests. This includes an extensive analyses of the lateralization and diagnostic ability of the various neuropsychological tests included in the HRNES.

Missing Scores

While the indices in the HRNES require certain tests and Reitan's program requires the entire HRB, missing scores may be replaced if necessary. The examiner can substitute an estimated "missing data" number for a missing score. Such substitution of missing data should be used only when there are just one or two missing scores and when the added score will not change the total results. For this purpose the normative mean raw score for the test should usually be used. This is a conservative score, which in forensic cases would not bias any calculated indices toward indicating brain damage.

There is an alternative method that may be used on the WAIS–R when the computer program will not provide an IQ because there is more than one missing score for a section. First, calculate the scale scores for the scores that are available. Second, calculate the average of these scale scores. Third, from tables in the manual determine the raw score for the missing scores that is equivalent to the average scale score calculated in step two. Fourth, use these raw scores to replace the missing scores. Finally, calculate the IQs with this estimated data, with or without using the computer program. Such scores should always be labeled "estimated."

Score Averaging

The HRNES has a scoring feature that allows one to mathematically compare the scale scores of any single score or group of tests to another score or group of tests. A formula is computed by the program that corrects for the difference in standard deviations so that the comparison is mathematically exact. If the examiner wished to compare immediate memory tests to long-term memory tests, they could be selected and the combined scores of each group would be calculated. This provides a mathematical method of looking at patterns. The WISC–III (Wechsler, 1991) has a similar method to compare the WISC–III subtests with the Wechsler Individual Achievement Test (WIAT) subtests (Wechsler, 1992).

Correction for Premorbid IQ

Another feature that the HRNES program contains is a method of entering an IQ to replace the education level. The computer program allows a psychologist to enter an FSIQ in the client menu. This takes precedence over the education correction. For instance, a patient who only completed high school education previously may have taken an IQ test that resulted in an FSIQ of 110. The FSIQ of 110 can be entered into the program and it will take precedence over the high school education level (IQ adjustment of 102) that would have provided an underestimation of his actual premorbid ability. Similarly, an IQ estimate from any of various formulas for estimating premorbid IQ can be entered in the HRNES program as the person's IQ/education level. This method will correct all HRNES scores.

COVERAGE OF ABILITY DOMAINS

A comprehensive neuropsychological evaluation requires examination of the whole brain (Reitan, 1991a, pp. 98, 100; 1991b). The principles of coverage require complete and balanced coverage of all major brain functions in as efficient manner as possible. The three HRB-based computer scoring program that are being discussed recognize this need for coverage. In the following discussion, the emphasis is on coverage of functions rather than brain anatomical locations, although clearly these are related. The particular tests that were added to each battery are discussed in detail in the manuals for the batteries (Heaton et al., 1991; Russell, 1994; Russell & Starkey, 1993).

A comparison of the coverage by these batteries is provided in Table 15.2.

TABLE 15.2
Comparison of Coverage for the NDS, HRNES, and CNEHRB

Functions	HRNES	CNEHRB
Executive functions		
Attention	*Digit Span*	*Digit Span*
	Speech Perception	*Speech Perception*
	Rhythm Test	*Rhythm Test*
		Digit Vigilance
Mental flexibility	*Trails B*	*Trails B*
	Category Test	*Category Test*
		Wisconsin Card Sort
Problem solving	*Category Test*	*Category Test*
	Block Design	*Block Design*
		Wisconsin Card Sort
Fluency	H-Words	Thurstone Word Fluency
	Design Fluency	
Mental processing speed and efficiency	*Digit Symbol*	*Digit Symbol*
	Trails Speed	
Verbal Cognitive Abilities		
Verbal reasoning	*Similarities*	*Similarities*
	Comprehension	*Comprehension*
	Arithmetic	*Arithmetic*
	Analogies Test	Complex Ideational Test
Non-Verbal Cognitive Abilities		
Spatial relations	*Block Design*	*Block Design*
	Object Assembly	*Object Assembly*
Visual reasoning	*Picture Completion*	*Picture Completion*
Social intelligence	*Picture Arrangement*	*Picture Arrangement*
Language		
Aphasia	*Aphasia Screening Test*	*Aphasia Screening Test*
Verbal naming	Boston Naming Test	Boston Naming Test
Verbal recognition	*Vocabulary*	*Vocabulary*
	Information	*Information*
	PPVT–R	
Academic Abilities	WRAT–R Reading	PAIT Reading Recognition
		PAIT Reading Comprehension
		PAIT Spelling
	Arithmetic	*Arithmetic*
Memory		
Immediate	*Digit Span*	*Digit Span*
		Tonal Memory Test
	Corsi Board	
	MSLT Immediate Recall.	
Recent Memory	WMS Logical Memory	Story Memory Test
	WMS Visual Reproduction	Figure Memory Test

Continued

TABLE 15.2 *(continued)*

Functions	HRNES	CNEHRB
Learning	MSLT LTM	
	MSLT ½ hour	
		Story Memory Test
		Figure Memory Test
	TPT Memory	*TPT Memory*
	TPT Location	*TPT Location*
Recognition	MSLT Recognition	
Motor abilities		
Pure motor	*Grip Strength*	*Grip Strength*
	Finger Tapping	*Finger Tapping*
	Grooved Pegboard	Grooved Pegboard
Psychomotor Speed	*Digit Symbol*	*Digit Symbol*
	Trails Speed	
Perceptual Abilities		
Sensory	*Perceptual Disorders*	*Perceptual Disorders*
Perceptual	Gestalt Id. Words	
	Gestalt Id. Objects	
		Tonal Memory Test
Body schema	*TPT Time*	*TPT Time*

Note. Italicized tests are part of the HRB and so are part of the NDS. Some tests are listed more than once in the table because they measure functions in more than one area. MSLT = Miami Selective Learning Test, LTM = Long Term Memory, PAIT = Peabody Individual Achievement Test, PPVT–R = Peabody Picture Vocabulary Test–Revised, Gestalt Id = Gestalt Identification Test, WRAT–R = Wide Range Achievement Test–Revised.

This table presents the various tests of the three batteries in terms of the coverage of functions. The assignment of various tests to types of functions is this author's conception. There undoubtedly will be disagreement as to the relation of a test to a function. Nevertheless, there is considerable agreement, and the present assignments, following the HRNES organization, will generally be those that are accepted by most neuropsychologists (Retzlaff, 1995).

Executive Functions

Study and measurement of executive functions is a major and growing area of neuropsychological assessment. These are usually frontal functions. The tests of executive functions have not been well developed due to the difficulty in differentiating and measuring subcomponents of executive abilities. However, batteries that these computer programs score contain a number of measures that appear to represent executive functions.

Attention.   Attention is probably the most familiar executive function. The CNEHRB contains a test that is specifically designed to measure visual attention, Digit Vigilance (Lewis & Rennick, 1979). In addition, it has the Digit Span, Speech-sounds Perception, and Seashore Rhythm tests, all of which measure aspects of attention as well as other functions. The NDS and HRNES include Digit Span, Speech-sounds Perception, and Seashore Rhythm as measures of attention.

Mental Flexibility.   A second type of executive function is mental flexibility. Impairment to this function often results in perseverative behavior. The CNEHRB includes the Wisconsin Card Sorting Test (WCST; Heaton, Chelune, Talley, Kay, & Curtiss, 1993), a purported measure of mental flexibility. The WCST has been considered to be a frontal test; however, some recent research tends to cast doubt on this conception (Anderson, Damasio, Jones, & Tranel, 1991). The Trail Making Tests, particularly Trails B, and the Category Test also assess mental flexibility. The NDS, HRNES, and CNEHRB all contain Trails B and the Category Test.

Problem Solving.   This form of thinking requires the ability to compare possible alternatives to solve a problem. The subject must test a possibility that appears to be correct while abandoning one that is not correct. The major tests for this type of thinking are the Category Test and the WCST. These require an individual to conceive of a method to classify or organize various stimuli and then to verify that strategy. Only the CNEHRB includes the WCST, whereas all three batteries include the Category Test.

The Category Test appears to be primarily a nonverbal right-hemisphere test (Reitan, 1964; Russell & Starkey, 1993, p. 40). In addition, a study of a patient who was almost completely aphasic from left-hemisphere damage found that he could complete the Category Test in an almost normal manner (Russell, 1976). The Category Test is one of the most utilized and modified tests in the HRB. A number of abbreviated forms of the Category Test have been developed. Of these the existing research appears to slightly favor the abbreviation by Russell, which is the Revised Category Test (RCAT; Russell & Levy, 1987; Taylor, Hunt, & Glaser, 1990). The HRNES permits one to utilize any one of three forms of the Category Test: Reitan's original Category Test, the RCAT, and the Short Category Test Booklet Format (Wetzel & Boll, 1987). The HRNES provides the raw score equivalent to the full Category score as uncorrected score for the RCAT. The CNEHRB scores the original long form.

Fluency.   Another executive function is fluency. This is the ability to rapidly produce new or novel ideas. In this regard, the CNEHRB has the Thurstone Word Fluency Test (Pendleton, Heaton, Lehman, & Hulihan, 1982). The HRNES has the H-Words (Russell et al., 1970) and the Design Fluency Test (Russell &

Starkey, 1993). In the HRNES, fluency tests are balanced with H-Words as a verbal left-hemisphere measure versus Design Fluency as a nonverbal right-hemisphere measure. The NDS has no measures of fluency.

Mental Processing Speed and Efficiency.   Mental speed and efficiency are also viewed as executive functions. Mental speed is the same as the ability that the WAIS–III is calling Processing Speed. This is measured by Digit Symbol on the WAIS–R and by this and Symbol Search on the WAIS–III. Digit Symbol is included in all three programs. In addition, the HRNES has a Trails Speed Test (Russell & Starkey, 1993), which is similar to Trails A except that the person knows ahead of time how to proceed to all of the positions. Thus, Trails Speed eliminates the element of visual scanning or search that is present in Trails A. Consequently, it is a fairly pure measure of psychomotor speed.

Verbal Cognitive Abilities

Verbal Reasoning.   Several of the Wechsler intelligence measures included in all three batteries assess verbal reasoning. These include Arithmetic, Comprehension, and Similarities. Although they involve reasoning to some extent, these verbal measures are almost entirely measures of crystallized ability (Russell, 1979, 1980a). That means that previously learned material, rather than novel reasoning, can be utilized to answer most of the items. In order to compensate for this problem, the HRNES added an Analogies Test (Russell & Starkey, 1993), which is a fluid verbal reasoning test (Horn, 1976). Tests of verbal analogies have been the benchmark of reasoning tests for many years and have been found to be accurate in assessing certain forms of brain damage (Willner, et al., 1973).

The CNEHRB added the Complex Ideational Test as a verbal reasoning test (Heaton et al., 1991). This was originally designed for the Boston Diagnostic Aphasia Examination as a test of the ability to express an understanding of written material without the need to produce complex sentences (Goodglass & Kaplan, 1983. p.35). It involves speech comprehension as much as reasoning. It is quite easy and has a low ceiling for individuals of average intelligence.

Nonverbal Cognitive Abilities

Spatial Relations.   Nonverbal abilities are less well understood than verbal abilities. Of these, spatial relations is probably one of the best understood (Kolb & Whishaw, 1985, pp. 642–676; McCarthy & Warrington, 1990, pp. 73–97). Block Design and Object Assembly measure this function and are included in all three batteries. Block Design is also quite sensitive to right-hemisphere damage (Russell, 1972; Russell & Starkey, 1993). Picture Completion appears to measure some aspects of visual reasoning. These three measures are included in all three batteries.

Social Intelligence.   Another function that is as important as other forms of intelligence is social intelligence. Guilford (1967; Guilford & Hoepfner, 1971) called this a *Behavioral Ability.* This ability enables us to understand and interact with other people. In Guilford's tests there were two forms of social intelligence: the ability to perceive nonverbal communication, and the ability to understand social situations. In most neuropsychological batteries including the NDS, CNEHRB, and HRNES, only the Picture Arrangement measures this function. However, it is not a fully adequate measure of this construct.

Language

Almost all neuropsychological test batteries measure basic language ability in some form. Various forms of aphasia examinations are examples. The Boston Diagnostic Aphasia Examination (Goodglass & Kaplan, 1983) is the most complete of the aphasia examinations, but none of the HRB programs use this test even in an abbreviated form.

Aphasia.   All three of the adult computer programs for the HRB utilize the Reitan–Indiana Aphasia Screening Test. Normal people make few errors on this test, so it is not a good test for determining the mere existence of brain damage. Nevertheless, it is valuable as a screening test for subjects that have language problems. It also has such an extended range that it provides an indication of the severity of damage for severely damaged patients.

Verbal Naming.   Both the CNEHRB and the HRNES added a test of word naming, the Boston Naming Test. Naming was previously assessed in the HRB by only a few items in the Aphasia Examination. The CNEHRB used an experimental form of the Boston Naming Test (Kaplan et al., 1983), whereas the HRNES used the commercial version. The scoring of the HRNES version of the Boston Naming Test is somewhat modified to determine whether the patient knew the object that he or she was asked to name. A ratio between the number of words named and the number known is calculated by the computer. An unpublished study found the ratio to be equally as accurate an indicator of anomia as the initial naming in the Boston Naming Test.

Verbal Recognition.   All three batteries include some version of the Wechsler Adult Intelligence Test that includes Vocabulary and Information as measures of crystallized verbal abilities. The HRNES added the Peabody Picture Vocabulary Test–Revised (Dunn & Dunn, 1981) in order to be able to measure receptive speech or recognition vocabulary. This test does not require the type of verbalization as does the WAIS–R Vocabulary. It is also a very crystallized ability. An unpublished research study by this author indicated that there is practically no decrease in ability with age until late adulthood, over 80 years old. Consequently, it may be a better "hold" test than WRAT–R Reading.

Academic Abilities.   For various purposes it is important to be able to measure academic achievement abilities. The assessment of various learning disabilities requires a comparison between achievement and intelligence test subtests. In regard to academic achievement, the CNEHRB has added the Reading Recognition, Reading Comprehension, and Spelling subtests of the Peabody Individual Achievement Test (Dunn & Dunn, 1981). These tests will assess both reading comprehension and word recognition abilities.

The HRNES included the WRAT–R Reading test. This test is both a crystallized test of verbal ability and a screening measure of dyslexia. The WAIS–R (Wechsler, 1981) Arithmetic test is also included in both batteries, and assesses both verbal reasoning and arithmetic calculation functions.

Memory

Probably in no other area of neuropsychology has so much work been done as in the area of memory (Russell, 1980b; Squire, 1987). In this regard, it is quite evident that the original Halstead–Reitan Battery lacked the usual type of memory tests. The only specific memory tests that it contained were the Memory and Location portions of the Tactual Performance Test (TPT). Even today, these memory tests have not been well studied and their relationship to various other kinds of memory is not clearly understood. Consequently, both the CNEHRB and the HRNES added other measures of memory.

Immediate or Working Memory.   Digit Span has been the primary test for immediate memory, and Digits Forward presents a fairly pure measure of verbal immediate memory; Digits Backward does not. Both the HRNES and CNEHRB utilize Digit Span. The HRNES, but not the CNEHRB, provides separate scoring for the WAIS–R Digits Forward and Digits Backward, thus avoiding the contamination that is caused by combining the two tests.

The CNEHRB also includes the Seashore Tonal Memory test (Seashore, Lewis, & Saetveit, 1960). Digit Span is a left-hemisphere verbal test, whereas the Tonal Memory test seems to be a right-hemisphere test (Heaton et al., 1991). It is probably a better test of right-hemisphere musical memory than the Rhythm Test (Karzmark, Heaton, Lehman, & Crouch, 1985).

In addition to Digit Span, the HRNES includes the Corsi Board (Russell & Starkey, 1993) and the initial memory score for the Miami Selective Memory Test (MSLT). The Corsi Board is a visual spatial analogue to the Digit Span. It should be noted that the HRNES provides the raw scores for both the Digit Span and Corsi Board in the same form as in the traditional digit span rather than summing the two trials. Finally, the MSLT requires the subject to learn a list of words. Because the first trial involves only immediate memory, it provides another measure of immediate memory. Thus, the HRNES has two tests of immediate verbal and one test of immediate nonverbal memory.

Recent Memory.   In regard to recent memory—that is, the ability to put new information into memory store—the CNEHRB has two learning tests, the Story Memory test and the Figure Memory Test (Heaton et al., 1991). In each of these the material—a story or designs—is repeated until the person learns the material to a criterion. Then the subjects are tested for recall of the material after 4 hr. In addition the CNEHRB retains the TPT Memory and Location tests.

The HRNES covers recent memory in both the verbal and nonverbal areas. Over 20 years ago a halfhour recall for the Logical Memory and Visual Reproduction was added to the original Wechsler Memory Scale (Russell, 1975, 1988) as a measure of recent memory. These are included in the HRNES. The HRNES will score Logical Memory and Visual Reproduction from either the WMS or the WMS–R. The first presentation of Logical Memory and Visual Reproductions from the WMS combines both immediate and recent memory; only the half-hour recall provides a pure measure of recent memory. In addition, it should be noted that the Logical Memory stories are semantic memory—that is, they represent memory for meaningful material.

Verbal Learning.   Neither the HRB nor the CNEHRB includes a measure of verbal learning. The HRNES considered several verbal learning tests, one of which was the California Verbal Learning Test (CVLT; Delis, Kramer, Kaplan, & Ober, 1987). However, in the CVLT the long-term delay memory score is contaminated by having an intervening interference memory list. The greater the interference, the less accurate would be the long-term delay memory score, because in real life such intense interference seldom occurs.

Of the several forms for memory tests available, Buschke's Selective Reminding Test (Buschke, 1973) appeared to be the best measure of learning. An unpublished study found that Long Term Storage was the most highly correlated subtest with the new half-hour measure. This appeared to support Buschke's concept of selective reminding. Consequently, using Buschke's Selective Reminding Test as a model, the Miami Selective Learning Test was designed and added to the HRNES (Russell & Starkey, 1993, pp. 13–14). This test is relatively short compared to the original Buschke test. In addition, a halfhour memory and a recognition measure were added.

Incidental Memory.   Both the CNEHRB and the HRNES contain the TPT Memory and Location tests, which provide measures of verbal and figural incidental memory. The TPT Memory test, although mixed, is more verbal, whereas Location is a figural memory test. The TPT Location was found to be a good indicator of normality in that a score above 5 indicated no brain damage. However, an unpublished study found that many normal people obtained low scores on this test so that a low score was nondiscriminatory.

The TPT Memory test has been found to be one possible indicator of malingering in that the patient is not told that it is a memory test and it is not obviously a test of memory. Many malingering patients that appear to have almost no memory on the WMS obtain a normal score on the TPT Memory.

Motor Abilities

In the 1950s Reitan realized that a complete examination of brain functioning required that both sensory and motor functions be examined, in addition to cognitive functions. Reitan created several motor and perceptual tests. These, in essence, quantified several neurological tests by providing a scoring system.

All three computerized scoring batteries include Digit Symbol from the WAIS, as well as the Grip Strength and Finger Tapping tests from the HRB. The CNEHRB and HRNES both added the Grooved Pegboard Test as a measure of complex movement. Although the Finger Tapping test is only moderately sensitive to brain damage in general, it is the most sensitive test to lateralization in the HRB, as well as being sensitive to a number of other conditions like Cerebrovascular Disease (Russell & Polakoff, 1993). In addition, the HRNES added Trails Speed, a relatively pure measure of psychomotor speed.

Perception

All three computerized scoring batteries contain the HRB Sensory-perceptual Examination. The CNEHRB has added an auditory test, Tonal Memory, which was discussed previously. On the other hand, the HRNES added a Visual Gestalt Identification Test (Russell & Starkey, 1993). This is a test of the occipital area of the brain outside of the visual reception area. It has both a verbal and a visual form; thus, it should be able to cover lesions that occur in either the right or left occipital areas of the brain (Russell, Hendrickson, & VanEaton, 1988). Clinical experience indicates that it is a fairly crystallized ability, and as such it is not sensitive to brain damage in general, but it is sensitive to focal lesions. The Word section of the Gestalt Identification Test may well be related to problems in dyslexia. As such, it has been useful in examining patients with a learning disability.

Body Schema. The cognitive functions related to the TPT have never been fully elucidated. The TPT Total Time measure is probably the most sensitive single test for brain damage (Goldstein & Shelly, 1972; Rojas & Bennett, 1995; Russell & Starkey, 1993). It is evident that the TPT involves stereognosis and some motor abilities, but it obviously involves other cognitive skills as well. Clinical observation suggests that the TPT is related to body schema. This function is not well understood (Kolb & Whishaw, 1985), but right parietal damage impairs the TPT for both hands (Russell, 1974) and this impairment appears to accompany neglect, which is related to body schema. Although the TPT time score for each hand lateralizes fairly strongly, reduced Total Time is more related to impairment to the right hemisphere in right-handed persons (Russell,

1974; Russell & Starkey, 1993). If it is true that the TPT measures body schema, then it provides a measure of a brain function that is not adequately covered by any other test. Because factor analyses have often found it to load on a separate factor (Thompson & Parsons, 1985), it appears to be measuring an aspect of brain functioning that other tests do not measure.

A problem with using the TPT Adult form with brain damaged subjects is that it has a rather high basal. Moderately to severely brain damaged subjects can not deal with its complexities. Consequently, Russell (1985) designed a scale for coordinating the Children's TPT 6-hole form board with the adult 10-hole version (Tactile Performance Test–6; Russell, 1985; Russell & Starkey, 1993). This enables severely impaired patients to obtain a valid score that is equivalent to a TPT 10-hole board score. If the patient is severely impaired, then the TPT–6 can be used. Equivalent scores for the TPT Memory and Location were also obtained. These findings were later supported by another study (Campbell & Klonoff, 1988).

RESEARCH

These three computer programs, as fixed batteries, have a great advantage over a flexible battery in regard to research. The CNEHRB and HRNES were designed so that data could be easily gathered from patients who were tested for clinical purposes. Both methods save their data and have methods to export that data into a spread sheet. Both the HRNES and CNEHRB use a text format in transporting the scores into a data file in another research program. As such, the data derived from testing does not need to be reentered by hand into a statistical program but can be sent directly into a research program's statistical data files or spread sheet. Thus, these programs can greatly reduce the tedious entry work of research.

CONCLUSION

Today there are four neuropsychological computerized scoring programs available for scoring test data. The three that were related to the HRB were examined in some detail in order to enable the neuropsychologist to understand and utilize these programs. The CNEHRB and the HRNES utilize sets of norms that are the most accurate in the field. Coordinated norms mean that any test score can be directly compared to another test score for interpretative purposes. Age, education, and gender corrections have been incorporated into the scoring, which increases the accuracy of the scale scores. The coverage of the CNEHRB and HRNES has been expanded from the HRB to include functions and even areas of the brain that are not adequately covered by the HRB. For both validation and interpretative purposes, several interpretative methods have been formalized as indices. These indices have been found to be very accurate.

The advantages of systems in which a computer scales test scores, demographically adjusts raw scores, and makes a few basic interpretative analyses are clear. First, many more measures can be scored in the same amount of time than using hand scoring methods. Second, these systems are more accurate than examiner scoring. Third, these methods will aid research in that data can be collected with much less effort. Finally, these programs have more reliability and demonstrated validity than other methods. Computer systems, including the interpretative aspects, are completely reliable in that the program does not vary from one testing to another. These computer programs have all been validated, whereas the validity of flexible batteries is both unknown and varies with each person and each administration. Interpretation of the scores derived from these computer programs, however, still requires the neuropsychologist's skills and the clinician's expertise.

REFERENCES

Anderson, S. W., Damasio, H., Jones, R. D., & Tranel, D. (1991). Wisconsin Card Sorting Test performance as a measure of frontal lobe damage. *Journal of Clinical and Experimental Neuropsychology. 13*, 909–922.

Anthony, W. Z., Heaton, R. K., & Lehman, R. A. W. (1980). An attempt to cross-validate two actuarial systems for neuropsychological test interpretation. *Journal of Consulting and Clinical Psychology, 48*, 317–326.

Buschke, H. (1973). Selective reminding for analysis of memory and learning. *Journal of Verbal Learning Behavior, 12*, 543–550.

Butcher, J. N. (Ed.). (1987). *Computerized psychological assessment.* New York: Basic Books.

Campbell, C., & Klonoff, H. (1988). Reliability and construct validity of the six block Tactual Performance Test in an adult sample. *Journal of Clinical and Experimental Neuropsychology. 10*, 175–184.

Delis, D. C., Kramer, J. H., Kaplan, E., & Ober, B. (1987). *California Verbal Learning Test–Research edition.* New York: Psychological Corporation.

DeLuca, J. W. (1989). Neuropsychology technicians in clinical practice: Precedents, rationale, and current deployment. *The Clinical Neuropsychologist, 3*, 3–21.

Division 40 Task Force on Education. (1991). Report of the Division 40 Task Force on Education, Accreditation and Credentialing, Recommendations for education and training of nondoctoral personnel in clinical neuropsychology. *The Clinical Neuropsychologist, 5*, 20–23.

Dodrill, C. B. (1979). Sex differences on the Halstead–Reitan Neuropsychological Battery and on other neuropsychological measures. *Journal of Clinical Psychology, 35*, 236–241.

Dunn, L. M., & Dunn L. M. (1981). *Peabody, Picture Vocabulary Test–Revised, manual.* Circle Pines, MN: American Guidance Service.

Fastenau, P. S., & Adams, K. M. (1996). Heaton, Grant, and Matthew's comprehensive norms: An overzealous attempt. *Journal of Clinical and Experimental Neuropsychology, 18*, 444–448.

Fromm-Auch, D., & Yeudall, L. T. (1983). Normative data for the Halstead–Reitan neuropsychological tests. *Journal of Clinical Neuropsychology, 5*, 221–238.

Fuerst, D. R. (1993). A review of the Halstead–Reitan neuropsychological battery norms program. *The Clinical Neuropsychologist, 7*, 96–103.

Gass, C. S., & Russell, E. W. (1986). Differential impact of brain damage and depression on memory test performance. *Journal of Consulting and Clinical Psychology, 54,* 261–263.

Golden, C. J., Purisch, A. D., & Hammeke, T. A. (1985). *Manual for the Luria–Nebraska Neuropsychological Battery.* Los Angeles: Western Psychological Services.

Goldstein, G., & Shelly, C. H. (1972). Statistical and normative studies of the Halstead Neuropsychological Test Battery relevant to a neuropsychiatric setting. *Perceptual and Motor Skills. 34,* 603–620.

Goldstein, S. G., & Braun, L. S.(1974). Reversal of expected transfer as a function of increased age. *Perceptual and Motor Skills. 38,* 1139–1145.

Goodglass, H., & Kaplan E. (1983). *The assessment of aphasia and related disorders* (rev. ed.). Philadelphia: Lea & Febiger.

Guilford, J. P. (1967). *The nature of human intelligence.* New York: McGraw-Hill.

Guilford, J. P., & Hoepfner, R. (1971). *The analysis of intelligence.* New York: McGraw-Hill.

Halstead, W. C. (1947). *Brain and intelligence.* Chicago: University of Chicago Press.

Heaton, R. K. (1992). *Comprehensive norms for an expanded Halstead–Reitan Battery: A supplement for the Wechsler Adult Intelligence Scale–Revised* [Norms manual and computer program]. Odessa, FL: Psychological Assessment Resources.

Heaton, R. K., Chelune, G. J., Talley, J. L., Kay, G. G., & Curtiss, G. (1993). *Wisconsin Card Sorting Test Manual: Revised and expanded.* Odessa, FL: Psychological Assessment Resources.

Heaton, R. K., Grant, I., & Matthews, C. G. (1986). Differences in neuropsychological test performance associated with age, education and sex. In I. Grant & K. M. Adams (Eds.), *Neuropsychological assessment of neuropsychiatric disorders* (pp. 100–120.) New York: Oxford.

Heaton, R. K., Grant, I., & Matthews, C. G. (1991). *Comprehensive norms for an expanded Halstead–Reitan Battery.* Odessa, FL: Psychological Assessment Resources

Heaton, R. K., Matthews, C. G., Grant, I., & Avitable, N. (1996). Demographic corrections with comprehensive norms: An overzealous attempt or a good start. *Journal of Clinical and Experimental Neuropsychology 18,* 121–141.

Hom, J., Walker, C. R., & Nici, J. (1990, August). *A clinical index of neuropsychological performance in Alzheimer's Disease.* Paper presented at the American Psychological Association annual conference, Boston.

Horn, J. L. (1976). Human abilities: A review of research and theory in the early 1970's. In M. Rosenzweig & L. Porter (Eds.), *Annual review of psychology* (Vol. 27, pp. 437–485). Palo Alto, CA: Annual Reviews, 1976.

Horton, A., & Sobelman, S. A. (1997). The General Neuropsychological Deficit Scale and the Halstead Impairment Index. *Perceptual and Motor Skills, 78,* 888–890.

Jastak, J. F., & Jastak, S. R. (1965). *WRAT, The Wide Range Achievement Test, manual.* Wilmington, DE: Guidance Associates.

Kane, R. L. (1991). Standardized and flexible batteries in Neuropsychology: An assessment update. *Neuropsychology Review, 2,* 281–339.

Kane, R. L., & Kay, G. G. (1992). Computerized assessment in neuropsychology: A review of tests and test batteries. *Neuropsychology Review, 3,* 1–117.

Kane, R. L., & Kay, G. G. (1997). Computer applications in neuropsychological assessment. In G. Goldstein & T. M. Incagnoli (Eds.), *Contemporary approaches to neuropsychological assessment* (pp. 359–392). New York: Plenum.

Kaplan, E., Goodglass H., & Weintraub, S. (1983). *Boston Naming Test.* Philadelphia: Lea & Febiger.

Karzmark, P., Heaton, R. K., Lehman, R. A., & Crouch, J. (1985). Utility of the Seashore Tonal Memory Test in neuropsychological assessment. *Journal of Clinical and Experimental Neuropsychology, 7,* 367–374.

Kay, G. G., Morris, S., & Starbuck, V. (1993, October). *Age and education based norms control for the effects of occupation on pilot test performance.* Paper presented at the Annual Meeting of the National Academy of Neuropsychology, Phoenix, AZ.

Kolb, B., & Whishaw, I. Q. (1985). *Fundamentals of human neuropsychology* (2nd ed.). New York: W. H. Freeman.

Lewis, R. F., & Rennick, P. M. (1979). *Manual for the Repeatable Cognitive-Motor Battery.* Grosse Pointe Park, MI: Axon.

Lezak, M. D. (1995). *Neuropsychological assessment* (3rd ed.). New York: Oxford.

Lynch, W. J. (1995). Microcomputer-assisted neuropsychological test analysis. *Journal of Head Trauma Rehabilitation, 10,* 97–100.

Mahurin, R. K. (1995). Review of the Halstead Russell Neuropsychological Evaluation System. In J. C. Conoley & J. C. Impara (Eds.), *The twelfth Mental Measurements yearbook* (pp. 448–451). Lincoln, NB: University of Nebraska Press.

McCarthy, R. A., & Warrington, E. K. (1990). *Cognitive neuropsychology.* San Diego, CA: Academic Press.

Moses, J. A., & Purisch, A. D. (1997). The evolution of the Luria–Nebraska Neuropsychological Battery. In G. Goldstein & T. M. Incagnoli (Eds.), *Contemporary approaches to neuropsychological assessment* (pp. 131–170). New York: Plenum.

Oestreicher, J. M., & O'Donnell, J. P. (1995). Validation of the General Neuropsychological Deficit Scale with nondisabled, learning-disabled, and head-injured young adults. *Archives of Clinical Neuropsychology, 10,* 185–191.

Pendleton, M. G., Heaton, R. K., Lehman, R. W., & Hulihan, D. (1982). The diagnostic utility of the Thurstone Word Fluency Test in neuropsychological evaluations. *Journal of Clinical Neuropsychology, 4,* 307–317.

Prifitera, A. (1986). *WAIS–R microcomputer-assisted interpretive report.* San Antonio, TX: Psychological Corporation.

Reitan, R. M. (1955). An investigation of the validity of Halstead's measures of biological intelligence. *Archives of Neurology and Psychiatry, 73,* 28–35.

Reitan, R. M. (1964). Psychological deficits resulting from cerebral lesions in men. In J. M. Warren & K. Akert (Eds.), *The frontal granular cortex and behavior* (pp. 295–312). New York: McGraw-Hill.

Reitan, R. M. (1991a). *Traumatic brain injury Vol. II: Recovery and rehabilitation.* Tucson, AZ: Neuropsychology Press.

Reitan, R. M., (1991b). *The Neuropsychological Deficit Scale for adults computer program* [Manual from *Traumatic Brain Injury Vol. II: Recovery and Rehabilitation,* first published in 1988]. Tucson, AZ: Neuropsychology Press.

Reitan, R. M. (1992). *The Neuropsychological Deficit Scale for Older Children: Computer program.* Tucson, AZ: Neuropsychology Press.

Reitan, R. M., & Wolfson, D. (1985). *The Halstead–Reitan Neuropsychological Test Battery; Theory and clinical interpretation.* Tucson, AZ; Neuropsychology Press.

Reitan, R. M., & Wolfson, D. (1986). *The Neuropsychological Deficit Scale for Younger Children: Computer program.* Tucson, AZ: Neuropsychology Press.

Reitan, R. M., & Wolfson, D. (1997). Emotional disturbances and their interaction with neuropsychological deficits. *Neuropsychological Review, 7,* 3–19.

Retzlaff, P. D. (1995). Review of the Halstead–Russell Neuropsychological Evaluation System. In J. C. Conoley & J. C. Impara (Eds.), *The twelfth Mental Measurements yearbook* (pp. 451–453). Lincoln, NB: University of Nebraska Press.

Rojas, D. C., & Bennett, T. L. (1995). Single versus composite score discriminative validity with the Halstead–Reitan Battery and the Stroop test in mild brain injury. *Archives of Clinical Neuropsychology, 10,* 101–110.

Russell, E. W. (1972, August). The effect of acute lateralized brain damage on a factor analysis of the Wechsler–Bellevue Intelligence Test. *Proceedings, 80th Annual Convention of the American Psychological Association,* Honolulu, HI.

Russell, E. W. (1974). The effect of acute lateralized brain damage on Halstead's Biological Intelligence Factors. *Journal of General Psychology, 90,* 101–107.

Russell, E. W. (1975). A multiple scoring method for the assessment of complex memory functions. *Journal of Consulting and Clinical Psychology 43*, 800–809.

Russell, E. W. (1976). The Bender–Gestalt and the Halstead–Reitan Battery: A case study. *Journal of Clinical Psychology, 32*, 355–361.

Russell, E. W. (1979). Three patterns of brain damage on the WAIS. *Journal of Clinical Psychology, 37*, 246–253.

Russell, E. W. (1980a) Fluid and crystallized intelligence: Effects of diffuse brain damage on the WAIS. *Perceptual and Motor Skills, 51*, 121–122.

Russell, E. W. (1980b). The pathology of memory. In S. B. Filskov & T. J. Boll (Eds.), *Handbook of clinical neuropsychology* (pp. 287–319). New York: Wiley.

Russell, E. W. (1984). Theory and developments of pattern analysis methods related to the Halstead–Reitan battery. In P. E. Logue & J. M. Shear (Eds.), *Clinical neuropsychology: A multidisciplinary approach* (pp. 50–98). Springfield, IL: Charles C. Thomas.

Russell, E. W. (1985). Comparison of the TPT 10 and the TPT 6 hole form board. *Journal of Clinical Psychology, 41*, 68–81.

Russell, E. W. (1987). A reference scale method for constructing neuropsychological test batteries. *Journal of Clinical and Experimental Neuropsychology, 9*, 376–392.

Russell E. W. (1988). Renorming Russell's version of the Wechsler Memory Scale. *Journal of Clinical and Experimental Neuropsychology. 10*, 235–249.

Russell, E. W. (1990, August). *Three validity studies for negative neurological criterion norming.* Paper presented at the 98th Annual Convention of the American Psychological Association, Boston.

Russell, E. W. (1992). Comparison of two methods for converting the WAIS to the WAIS–R. *Journal of Clinical Psychology, 48*, 355–359.

Russell, E. W. (1994). The cognitive-metric, fixed battery approach to neuropsychological assessment. In R. D. Vanderploeg (Ed.), *Clinician's guide to neuropsychological assessment* (pp. 211–258). Hillsdale, NJ: Lawrence Erlbaum Associates.

Russell, E. W. (1995). The accuracy of automated and clinical detection of brain damage and lateralization in neuropsychology. *Neuropsychology Review. 5*(1), 1–68.

Russell, E. W. (1997). Developments in the psychometric foundations of neuropsychological assessment. In G. Goldstein & T. M. Incagnoli (Eds.), *Contemporary approaches to neuropsychological assessment* (pp. 15–65). New York: Plenum.

Russell, E. W. (1998). In defense of the Halstead–Reitan Battery: A critique of Lezak's review. *Archives of Clinical Neuropsychology, 13*, 365–381.

Russell, E. W., Hendrickson, M. E., & VanEaton, E. (1988). Verbal and figural Gestalt Completion Tests with lateralized occipital area brain damage. *Journal of Clinical Psychology, 44*, 217–225.

Russell, E. W., & Levy, M. (1987). A revision of the Halstead Category Test. *Journal of Consulting and Clinical Psychology, 55*, 898–901.

Russell, E. W., Neuringer, C., & Goldstein, G. (1970). *Assessment of brain damage: A neuropsychological approach.* New York: Wiley.

Russell, E. W., & Polakoff, D. (1993). Neuropsychological test patterns in men for Alzheimer's and multi-infarct dementia. *Archives of Clinical Neuropsychology, 8*, 327–343.

Russell, E. W., & Starkey, R. I. (1993). *Halstead, Russell Neuropsychological Evaluation System* [Manual and computer program]. Los Angeles: Western Psychological Services.

Russell, E. W., Starkey, R. I., Fernandez, C. D., & Starkey, T. W. (1988). *Halstead, Rennick, Russell Battery* [Manual and computer program]. Miami, FL: Scientific Psychology.

Seashore, C. B., Lewis, C., & Saetveit, J. G. (1960). *Seashore measure of musical talent: Manual.* New York: Psychological Corporation.

Sherer, M., & Adams, R. L. (1993). Cross-Validation of Reitan and Wolfson's Neuropsychological Deficit Scales. *Archives of Clinical Neuropsychology, 8*, 429–435.

Spreen, O., & Benton, A. L. (1965). Comparative studies of some psychological tests for cerebral damage. *Journal of Nervous and Mental Disease, 140*, 323–333.

Squire, L. R. (1987). *Memory and the brain*. New York: Oxford University Press.

Taylor, D. J., Hunt, C., & Glaser, B. (1990). A cross validation of the Revised Category Test. *Psychological Assessment, 2*, 486–488.

Thompson, L. L., & Parsons, O. (1985). Contribution of the TPT to adult neuropsychological assessment. *Journal of Clinical and Experimental Neuropsychology, 7*, 430–444.

Tombaugh. T. N., & Hubley, A. M. (1998). The 60-Item Boston Naming Test: Norms for cognitively intact adults aged 25 to 88 years. *Journal of Clinical and Experimental Neuropsychology, 19*, 922–932.

Wechsler, D. (1974). *Wechsler Memory Scale*. San Antonio, TX: Psychological Corporation.

Wechsler, D. (1981). *WAIS–R, Wechsler Adult Intelligence Scale–Revised, manual*. San Antonio, TX: Psychological Corporation.

Wechsler, D. (1991). *Wechsler Intelligence Scale for Children–Third edition (WISC–III), manual*. San Antonio, TX: Psychological Corporation.

Wechsler, D. (1992). *Wechsler Individual Achievement Test (WIAT), manual*. San Antonio, TX: Psychological Corporation.

Wetzel, L., & Boll, T. J. (1987). *Short Category Test, Booklet Format*. Los Angeles: Western Psychological Services.

Willner, A. E., Rabiner, C. J., Wisoff, G., Hartstein, M., Kolker, P., & Stuve, F. A. (1973). An analogy test that predicts postoperative outcome in patients scheduled for open-heart surgery. *Proceedings, 81th Annual Convention of the American Psychological Association, 8*, 371–372.

Wolfson, D., & Reitan, R. M. (1995). Cross-validation of the General Neuropsychological Deficit Scale (GNDS). *Archives of Clinical Neuropsychology, 10*, 125–131.

Author Index

Subject Index

Contributors

Bradley N. Axelrod, Ph.D.
Department of Veterans Affairs
Psychology Service (116B)
4646 John R. Street
Detroit, MI 48201

Russell M. Bauer, Ph.D.
Professor, Department of Clinical and Health Psychology
Box 100165, Health Science Center
University of Florida
Gainesville, FL 32610-0165

Cynthia R. Cimino, Ph.D.
Associate Professor, Department of Psychology, BEH-339
University of South Florida
4202 Fowler Ave.
Tampa, FL 33620

Bruce Crosson, Ph.D.
Professor, Department of Clinical and Health Psychology
Box 100165, Health Science Center
University of Florida
Gainesville FL 32610-0165

Eileen B. Fennell, Ph.D.
Professor, Department of Clinical and Health Psychology
Box 100165, Health Science Center
University of Florida
Gainesville, FL 32610-0165

Carlton S. Gass, Ph.D.
Director, Neuropsychology Section
Department of Veterans Affairs Medical Center
1201 N. W. 16th Street
Miami, FL 33125

Michael Gibertini, Ph.D.
Organon, Inc.
375 Mt. Pleasant Avenue
West Orange, NJ 07052

Deborah C. Koltai, Ph.D.
Bryan Alzheimer's Disease Research Center
Duke University Medical Center
2200 West Main Street
Suite A230
Durham, NC 27705

Glenn J. Larrabee, Ph.D.
Independent Practice
630 S. Orange Avenue, Suite 202
Sarasota, FL 34236

Michael McCue, Ph.D.
Center for Applied Neuropsychology
First and Market Building
100 First Street; Suite 900A
Pittsburgh, PA 15222

Michael Pramuka, Ph.D.
Defense and Veterans Head Injury Program
Physical Medicine and Rehabilitation Service (117)
James A. Haley Veterans' Hospital
Tampa, FL 33612

Paul D. Retzlaff, Ph.D.
Professor, Department of Psychology
University of Northern Colorado
College of Arts and Sciences
Greeley, CO 80639

Elbert W. Russell, Ph.D.
6262 Sunset Dr.
Penthouse 210
Miami, FL 33143

John A. Schinka, Ph.D.
Psychology Service (116B)
James A. Haley Veterans' Hospital
Associate Professor, Department of Psychiatry
University of South Florida
Tampa, FL 33612

Rodney D. Vanderploeg, Ph.D.
Psychology Service (116B)
James A. Haley Veterans' Hospital
Associate Professor, Departments of Psychology and Neurology
University of South Florida
Tampa, FL 33612

Kathleen A. Welsh-Bohmer, Ph.D.
Joseph and Kathleen Bryan Alzheimer's Disease Research Center
Departments of Psychiatry and Medicine
Duke University Medical Center
2200 West Main Street
Suite A230
Durham, NC 27705